D1241511

PREFACE

This book has been written in the endeavor to present a straightforward and impartial account of the history of Europe from the beginning of the chancellorship of Bismarck in Prussia to the outbreak of the Great War.

Emphasis has been laid throughout the entire book upon those events which have affected international relations. The narrative of the domestic politics of the separate states has been curtailed, except where such politics had a distinct bearing upon the part which a state played in international affairs. The alliances and the conflict of interests which have brought about the present Great War have been discussed in detail. The characters and methods of those statesmen who have had the greatest influence in international issues have been developed at length. It has been our plan thus to give the reader a conception of a true history of Europe rather than to present an aggregation of histories of the separate European states.

In order to afford a more adequate understanding of the period, we have endeavored to coördinate events in time. By this means the reader is enabled to gain a knowledge of the general political, economic, and social status in the chief states of Europe at any given range of years.

The campaigns of the important wars of this period have been treated, not with a mass of technical detail, but with sufficient fullness to enable the reader to understand the chief strategical movements and the reasons for their success or failure.

In the division of the work of preparing this volume, the Professor of English and History has undertaken the political, diplomatic, and economic history of the period; the Assistant Professor of History the military campaigns, comprising the Danish (1864), the Austro-Prussian (1866), the Franco-German (1870-1871), the Russo-Turkish (1877-1878), and the entire chapter on the Russo-Japanese War.

It is a pleasure to acknowledge the assistance rendered by instructors in the Department of History, especially by Captain Philip Hayes and Captain Sidney V. Bingham. Acknowledgment is also due to Mr. W. L. Ostrander, Assistant Librarian, who has prepared the Index. A number of the maps, namely, Europe 1871, Germany 1871–1914, Austria-Hungary 1914, Balkan States 1856–1912, Ottoman Empire and the Balkan States 1914, Asia 1914, and Africa 1914, have been reprinted from volume II of A Political and Social History of Modern Europe with the kind permission of its author, Professor Carlton J. H. Hayes.

L. H. H.
A. W. C.

West Point, N. Y.
November, 1917.

TABLE OF CONTENTS

CHAPTER V

CHAPTER VI

CHAPTER VII

PART II

CHAPTER I

CHAPTER II

CHAPTER III

CHAPTER IV

PART III

CHAPTER I

CHAPTER II

CHAPTER III

CHAPTER IV

CHAPTER V

CHAPTER VI

CHAPTER VII

CHAPTER VIII

PART IV

CHAPTER I

CHAPTER II

CHAPTER III

CHAPTER IV

LIST OF MAPS

THE HISTORY OF EUROPE

FROM 1862 TO 1914

FOREWORD

The chief interest in international affairs in Europe during the half century preceding the outbreak of the Great War revolves about the political ambitions and methods of the Prusso-German state. At the beginning of this period Prussia, the least of the five Great Powers in Europe, was inhabited by a capable, energetic, industrious, and on the whole contented people, apparently satisfied with their international status and intensely desirous of pursuing their natural course of development along peaceful lines: at the close of this period Germany, the greatest military power the world has ever known, was under the guidance of an unscrupulous and aggressive minority who, dissatisfied with any position in European politics or world politics less than that of dictator, were willing to embroil Germany in war to gain their ends. The German people at large remained the same, capable, energetic, industrious, and peaceful, but German diplomacy had acquired a new character. The abnormally rapid development of its territory, population, commerce, and resources, its easy and overwhelming victories in war, and its sensational successes in international politics led the government of Germany into the belief that Germany was a super-nation, directly endowed with rights and privileges which all other nations must recognize and accept, and that they (the government) were the persons intrusted with the duty of establishing and maintaining these superior German rights. They were aided in their purposes by the fact that the German people, although not materially changed in character, had become accustomed through long generations of obedience to state authority to accept unquestioningly the decisions and dictation of their government. The successes of the unscrupulous diplomacy of Bismarck in the years between 1862 and 1890 gave a warrant for the arbitrary authority exercised by the government in foreign affairs after 1890. The people of Germany, having seen the power, prestige, and prosperity which resulted from Bismarck's autocratic régime, were inclined to trust blindly the supposedly superior wisdom of their governors. And these governors, intrenched in their positions by an outworn autocratic system (albeit with democratic forms), rode down ruthlessly all criticism and opposition and proffered the gage of battle for supremacy in European and world politics.

The events accompanying the change in the aims and methods of German diplomacy are divisible into four stages: — 1, the coalescence of the German states, with Prussia at their head, into an empire so powerful as to be able to dictate European policy; 2, the maintenance by constructive measures of internal policy and by acute diplomacy of Germany's hegemony in European politics; 3, the recognition by the other great powers outside of German influence of the dangers of continued German leadership, and the consequent formation of a defensive coalition; and 4, the challenge of Germany and her allies to this coalition, resulting in the Great War.

The first period, extending from the beginning of Bismarck's chancellorship in 1862 through the formation of the German Empire and the first years of its prosperity (1875), is in many ways the most important. The dominating personality of Bismarck in Prussia, accompanied by the extraordinary success of his diplomacy, established the ideals of the government of Germany for the subsequent periods. For five years at the beginning of this period

(1862–1867), Bismarck governed Prussia with little regard for that constitution which was supposed to guard the people's liberties; during this period he deliberately brought about three wars — the Danish (1864), the Austrian (1866), and the French (1870) — to increase the power and prestige of Prussia; in the pursuit of his aims for his country, he destroyed the dictatorship which the Austrian Hapsburgs had so long been accustomed to exercise over the German states, and he toppled the French Emperor from his throne; and at the last he was the chief instrument in binding the states of Germany into the most powerful empire in Europe, and in putting the imperial crown upon the head of the King of Prussia. The policy of blood and iron justified itself by these results. Bismarck became the idol of the Prusso-German people. His diplomatic methods, dishonest and unscrupulous as they often were according to his own accounts, were accepted on the authority of his success as necessary and proper, and became the study and standards of German diplomats of a later period.

During the second stage, extending from 1875 to Bismarck's enforced retirement from active political life in 1890, the German chancellor continued to be the dominating figure. His task, however, was different. He had gained in the momentous events of 1862 to 1875 the position of supremacy which he desired for the Prusso-German state: it was his aim now to consolidate its resources and to maintain its prestige. Such a disturbance in the European family of nations as had been caused by his policy in the first stage was certain to cause suspicions and jealousies of Germany's ambitions — he had to allay these and steer for the new nation a peaceful course while it became accustomed to its conditions. His statesmanship during the great constructive period of fifteen years was not less notable than that of the previous thirteen, but it was entirely different and much more admirable. His efforts in this stage, too, were crowned with astounding success. In domestic affairs, he furthered industrial and social measures which had much to do with the marvelous advance of Germany in material prosperity and unity of sentiment. In foreign affairs, he succeeded in retaining the friendship of Russia, even during the trying years following the Congress of Berlin, and in keeping France isolated and helpless. When he laid down his authority in 1890, Germany was still the supreme power on the continent of Europe; — the maintenance of this supremacy for nineteen years is a convincing evidence of his genius.

The third phase began with Bismarck's enforced retirement from political life in 1890 and lasted until 1911. The new Emperor of Germany, William II, proposed to be ruler in fact as well as in name, and to keep a firm control of the imperial policy. His inexperience, however, was fatal to Bismarck's plans. Within a few years Russia and France had concluded a hard and fast offensive and defensive treaty; a decade later Great Britain and France ended a century of discord and misunderstanding by concluding an entente; and in 1907 Russia and Great Britain completed the triangle by coming to an agreement upon the most menacing of the issues that existed between them. Thus German diplomacy had allowed a hostile Triple Entente to be formed against the central empire. Though avowedly defensive in nature, this Entente was capable of being converted into an offensive alliance at an instant's notice. Germany's recourse, when her diplomacy failed, was to her armaments. Her government, looking back to the diplomacy of Bismarck in the years when he established Prusso-German hegemony in Europe, prepared to revert to this policy of blood and iron to maintain its hegemony in the face of a hostile coalition. Its ambitions now transcended the bounds of German territory in Europe and extended to distant overseas colonies. Germany was to be, not only dominant in European politics, but dominant in world politics as well. With such purposes the government took measures to strengthen enormously the German army and to put upon the ocean a navy second only to that of England.

The final stage, from 1911 to 1914, is the shortest of the four. As the aims and ambitions of the German government became more clearly distinguishable, the determined opposition of Great Britain, France, and Russia became more inevitable. The atmosphere of mutual suspicion between members of the two opposing groups of powers became thicker. The Entente nations interpreted each move of Germany as a step in a deep-laid intrigue to weaken their power, whether such move consisted in a link of the Bagdad railroad, a loan to Turkey, or a concession in China; and similarly, the German government viewed every move of the Entente powers as an effort to thwart Germany's legitimate aspirations to a "place under the sun" appropriate to her size and power, whether such move consisted in an Anglo-Russian sphere of influence in Persia, or a French protectorate in Morocco. Under such conditions the conflict could not long be delayed. In the summer of 1914 a relatively insignificant quarrel between Austria-Hungary and Serbia was accepted by the German leaders as an opportunity to assert German dictatorial rights in Europe. No doubt both Germany and Austria-Hungary hoped that no war would result, and that Russia — the nation whose vital interests were most immediately affected — would retire from her position, but the Central Powers ran consciously the risk of war. With startling rapidity the situation developed until on August 1 the Great War began.

Such, briefly stated, are the four stages of the period of European history extending from 1862 to 1914. In our account of the details of these stages, we have at the beginning laid all emphasis upon the history of Prussia, subordinating the account of events in the other states of Europe except as those events were directly affected by Prussia. Later in our account we have attempted to treat more fully the course of development in the other states, still limiting our story, however, to those facts which bore especially upon the international political situation. In the final chapters, the developments in Germany, while still prominent, are not stressed more than those in the other great states. We have thus consciously tried to represent by space and emphasis the relative importance of the individual states in the international history of Europe.

PART I

THE ATTAINMENT OF GERMAN HEGEMONY IN EUROPE

CHAPTER I

PRUSSIA AND BISMARCK

As we look back over the history of the last half century in Europe and strive to arrange events in their just perspective, the part taken by Prussia, and by one man in particular in Prussia, emerges inevitably as the main theme of our narrative. Bismarck deserves the emphasis of space and position. He not only molded the course of events in his own country, but shaped the history of European international relations for a generation. His was the career of the super-diplomat. Often not admirable in his means, purposes, or methods, he has been judged by posterity according to his success in raising the prestige, and securing the position, of his own country. He stamped his character upon his time. It is fitting, therefore, that a consideration of contemporary history should begin with Prussia and Bismarck.

A. ACCESSION OF WILLIAM I: POLITICAL CRISIS

In 1857 the weak and vacillating King of Prussia, Frederick William IV, who had during his reign disappointed the hopes of all loyal Prussians by his policies, became afflicted with mental disease. Since he had no children, his brother, William, became Regent. A year later the King's disease was pronounced incurable, so that the Regency became equivalent to the actual reign. In 1861 the King died and the Regent ascended the throne as William I of

Prussia. With his accession began the greatest period of Prussian history.

Prussia in 1860 was just emerging into a happier condition from a period of ill government. The revolution of 1848 and 1849 had left the country with a constitution, but the provisions of that document were far from satisfactory to the liberal elements among thinking people. It gave Prussia a parliament, the lower house of which was elected by the votes of all men over twenty-five in the kingdom, but by a unique and ingenious method of indirect election the power was placed safely in the hands of the wealthy classes. According to this system, popularly known as the Prussian three-class system, the voters in each district were divided into three classes according to the amount of taxes they paid, and each class was given an equal representation in the convention which elected the member of parliament for the district. Since the wealthy persons dominated the two upper classes of the electorate, they were able consistently to dictate the appointment of one of their own political opinion to the parliament. Furthermore, the upper house, or House of Lords (*Herrenhaus*), was packed by hidebound conservatives, determined to exert every effort to retain their age-long feudal privileges in spite of any attacks by the liberals. These conservatives, "Junkers" as they were called, had the tacit support of the weak King Frederick William IV. Vexatious steps were constantly taken to suppress liberal propaganda. The provisions of the constitution were skillfully "interpreted" by the agents of the King to suit their own reactionary ends; liberal meetings were checked and liberal publications suppressed; the mails were rifled in the search for treasonable statements; an elaborate system of espionage was kept up; arbitrary arrest and imprisonment were not infrequently reverted to; and known liberals were persecuted.

And yet during these years — "the most shameful in

the history of Prussia," as one who lived at the time called them — some very encouraging features were noticeable. Prussia did retain her constitution, even though it was misinterpreted and in cases ignored, and was thus a grade more liberal than her rival, Austria. Furthermore, Prussia had definitely put herself at the head of the German states by her success in organizing and maintaining the customs union (*Zollverein*), which had benefited enormously the economic development throughout Germany. And most important of all, even under the reactionary political régime, Prussia, in common with other German states, had prospered amazingly. During the decade from 1850 to 1860 were laid the solid foundations for the phenomenal economic growth which later made Germany the marvel of modern times. In a comparatively brief period Prussia changed from an agricultural country to a country whose chief wealth was in its industrial enterprises. New capital flowed in for development purposes; business expanded; the mineral wealth was prospected and its mining actively begun; railways were actively extended; and foundries and factories sprung up in all favorable locations.

After the reactionary political policies of Frederick William IV, all classes of people hailed the inauguration of a new king with delight. William I was a tall, stately, handsome man, of military bearing and habits. He had indeed been a soldier all his life, serving at the age of seventeen against Napoleon in 1814, and remaining closely connected with the army through all the succeeding years. He was now [1860] sixty-three years old, a man slow of thought but clear and thorough, deeply religious, able with unprejudiced mind to estimate the abilities of his advisers, and gifted with a rare trust in and loyalty to his subordinates. Although not quick to initiate a policy, when once convinced of its wisdom and justice he was tenacious of his convictions, unqualifiedly brave in action, and steadfast in his endurance of opposition. In political principle he was a monarch of the *ancien régime*, with all the convictions of the divine origin of kings that inspired a Louis XIV or a Frederick the Great. Yet a high sense of honor forbade him to infringe consciously upon the elements of the constitution which had been granted to Prussia. He carefully explained his position at the coronation ceremonies in Königsberg: "The Kings of Prussia receive their crowns from God. I shall therefore take my crown to-morrow from the Lord's table and place it on my head"; and again on the succeeding day when he took the crown: "I am the first King to mount the throne since it was surrounded with modern institutions; but not forgetting that the crown comes only from God, I have shown . . . that I have received it from His hands." He sought to establish in Prussia royal government, and not parliamentary government; to strengthen monarchical tendencies rather than popular tendencies.

The heart of the new King was with his army. It was on the issue of army reform that he began a conflict with his parliament, during which he called to his aid the great chancellor, Bismarck, whose name is always linked with his in history. No sooner was William certain of his position than he instituted measures for military reform. Although throughout his long reign he customarily yielded to his experienced ministers in the realms of diplomacy and internal administration, in military affairs he had every reason to consider himself an expert. No one understood the deficiencies of the existing practices and the causes better than he. No one appreciated more keenly than he the fact that the unpreparedness of the nation was responsible for the humiliation of Prussia before Austria during the previous decade. He realized that the Prussian standing army of 200,000 supported by 400,000 reserves was insufficient to enable her to play the great part he believed she should take in European affairs.

The Prussian military system was still nominally on the

basis established by the genius, Scharnhorst, during the bitter years following Napoleon's victory at Jena. But no changes had been made to adjust the working of the scheme to the growth of the nation in wealth and population. Hence, although nominally service was universal and compulsory, actually a large proportion of the youths who came of age for service were refused annually, so that the size of the standing army had long remained practically stationary. The nation which in 1860 had a population of 18,000,000 was defended by the same size annual levies as those raised in 1814 from a population of about 11,000,000. Of the more than 150,000 youths who annually came of age for military service, only 40,000 were drafted.

With the idea of furthering reform, William during his regency appointed von Moltke head of the Prussian general staff and von Roon, a great organizing genius, minister of war. They assisted him in the preliminary plans for military reform. William wished to take all the youths physically qualified—amounting to about 65,000 annually—form new regiments from them, and increase the period of enlistment. He would thus impose the greater part of the burden of military service upon the young men of the country rather than upon the older men in the reserve force, and, by lengthening the term of service, would materially increase the number of effectives under arms. Prussia under his system would soon have an active army of 400,000 and would, in case of hostilities, not be forced to call upon the middle-aged men of the reserve. For the equipment and maintenance of the new regiments to be formed, and for the right to increase the term of service, the King, under the provisions of the constitution, had to go to his parliament. The liberal majority therein did not look with favor either upon the increase of the army or the lengthening of the term of service. Although grudgingly, and for only a year at a time, it approved the expenditures for the first few years, it held over him the possibility of rejecting the system and refusing the budget. In 1862 the crisis of the issue was reached and its full political significance revealed. With his assumption of the crown the preceding year, William I felt more strongly than before the necessity of carrying his point for good and all. The recent elections, however, had increased the number of the Progressives who constituted the backbone of the opposition to the government. The chamber had, immediately after convening, disapproved the plan for military reorganization. William I had then dissolved the chamber and ordered new elections. Although his agents strained every nerve to increase the body of government supporters in the chamber, the people stood loyally by their representatives and elected an overwhelming number of the Progressives. The issue was rapidly shaping itself into a contest between the royal prerogative and the will of parliament. The new chamber showed its temper immediately after it met. It decided by the enormous majority of 308 to 10 (March 23, 1862) to strike out of the budget the sum which had been appropriated the preceding year for the maintenance of the new regiments, and which, according to custom, had been incorporated in the budget for the coming year. Since these regiments were already in existence, the refusal of funds would mean the disbanding of the organizations and the definite defeat of all that the King believed most essential for the welfare of the state. The military issue was seen clearly now to involve a greater political issue. The question was: in a matter of fundamental importance to the state, shall the King or shall the Parliament have the decision? "King or Parliament," it was put in short.

At this juncture the King could see no honorable outlet. He was prepared to abdicate, had indeed already drawn up the formal paper, when some of his advisers urged him to call to the ministry as a last resort Count Otto von Bismarck. Although Bismarck had never previously been in the Prussian ministry, he was experienced in political and diplomatic life, and had gained a rare reputation for unqualified loyalty to his monarch and for audacity and daring in trying situations. Bismarck has given us in his own words the scene when he was called upon to assume the post of head of the ministry.

"As a matter of fact, however, the idea of the King's abdication was fresh to me when I was received at Babelsberg on September 22, and the situation only became clear to me when his majesty defined it in some such words as these: 'I will not reign if I cannot do it in such a fashion as I can be answerable for to God, my conscience, and my subjects. But I cannot do that if I am to rule according to the will of the present majority in parliament, and I can no longer find any ministers prepared to conduct my government without subjecting themselves and me to the parliamentary majority. I have therefore resolved to lay down my crown, and have already sketched out the proclamation of my abdication, based on the motives to which I have referred.' The King showed me the document in his own handwriting lying on the table, whether already signed or not I do not know.

"I replied that his majesty had been acquainted ever since May with my readiness to enter the ministry; I was certain that Roon would remain with me on his side, and I did not doubt that we should succeed in completing the cabinet, supposing other members should feel themselves compelled to resign on account of my admission. After a good deal of consideration and discussion, the King asked me whether I was prepared as minister to advocate the reorganization of the army, and when I assented, he asked me further whether I would do so in opposition to the majority in parliament and its resolutions. When I asserted my willingness, he finally declared, 'Then it is my duty, with your help, to attempt to continue the battle, and I shall not abdicate.'"

B. BISMARCK

The appointment of no man in Prussia could have more sharply emphasized the King's decision to uphold his royal prerogative against the will of the lower chamber. For Bismarck was a nobleman born and bred, stamped by speech and act with the stamp of a royalist adherent.

Otto von Bismarck first made himself conspicuous for his adherence to the royalist cause in the *Estates General* summoned by King Frederick William IV in 1847. Bismarck was at that time a young man of thirty-two; he had received a university training at Göttingen; had tried the taste of diplomatic life and had soon rebelled against its routine and drudgery; had retired to the management of his family's estate and by occasional wild pranks gained the reputation in his district of being the "mad Bismarck"; and finally, when he showed signs of settling down, had accepted one of the many local political offices. He was the type of the rough and masterful country squire, inspired with a fanatical loyalty to the person of the King and to the institution of Kingship. Nobleman though he was, he was not unpopular among the country folk. He was a young man of abnormal size, strength, and agility; he had received a medal for bravery for plunging into a river on one occasion at the risk of his life to save a drowning groom; he had read widely; if occasionally he was one of a crowd of roisterers, it was considered but a sign of the healthy animal energy and spirits of the man.

Although the Estates General which Bismarck attended in 1847 as the representative for his district was summoned by the King merely to legalize by its approval a loan for the introduction of railways in Prussia, when once convened it extended its discussion to the current political problems. Bismarck listened, at first in silence and with some dismay, to the debates. The liberals had no idea of coöperating with the King. Just as the Estates General when convened in France in 1789 had immediately assumed the right to discuss matters foreign to the immediate issue (*i.e.* the raising of money), so the Estates General in Prussia seemed headed toward revolution by the same general course. Ever a man of indomitable courage, Bismarck, even though a Junker without experience or reputation beyond the limits of his own district, could not continue silent in the presence of such tendencies. He was roused, first by the continued reference to English institutions, to protest that the analogy between England and Prussia did not hold:

"Parallels with foreign countries have always something disagreeable. . . . At the Revolution (*i.e.* 1688), the English people were in a very different condition from that of Prussia to-day; after a century of revolution and civil war, it was in a position to be able to give away a crown and add conditions which William of Orange accepted. On the other hand, we are in possession of a crown whose rights were actually unlimited, a crown held by the grace not of the people but of God, and which of its own free-will has given away to the people a portion of its rights — an example rare in history."

And again, speaking in another debate:

"For me, the words 'by the Grace of God,' which Christian rulers add to their name, are no empty phrase; I see in them a confession that the Princes desire to wield the scepter which God has given them according to the will of God on earth."

He was in the minority, a decided minority, so that words like these reaffirming the ancient principle of the divine right of kings called for a high moral courage at the time. He became a marked man among the liberals and the hope of the unyielding royalists. His friends were ready to applaud, whereas his opponents held him up to scorn as a reactionary, an exponent of medievalism in government. The King himself, though forced by the exigencies of the situation to disregard him at the time, later showed in a marked way his personal pleasure at the language of his new champion.

In the very next year, 1848, the revolution which had begun in Paris spread to Berlin. The King became virtually a prisoner in his palace, forced to grant to Prussia a constitution. These startling events again aroused Bismarck. The monarchy which as an institution he honored was disgraced, and the King whom as a person he loyally loved was humiliated. With patriotic fervor he wrote and sent to the King a letter filled with expressions of fealty and devotion, and then hurried to Berlin to offer his sword for his monarch's defense. He was ready to raise the peasants in his own district and summon them to him at the capital, but in Berlin he found that the King had already nullified the efforts of loyalists by his own desertion of their cause. Berlin was terrorized. The analogy of the French revolution was in everybody's mind. Bismarck himself was in danger of his life. "Being known, since the days of the United Diet" (*i.e.* the Estates General), "to many people by sight," he writes, "I considered it advisable to shave my beard and put on a broad-brimmed hat with a colored cockade." Yet his personal danger did not influence him to betray his principles in the slightest. As he sat in the new Estates General convened to make arrangements for the elections under the recently granted constitution, and as an address was proposed thanking the King for his concessions, Bismarck was one of the two members who voted against the address, saying:

> "I have not changed my opinion in the last six months; the past is buried, and I regret more bitterly than any of you that no human power can reawaken it, now that the Crown itself has cast the earth on its coffin."

During the summer he and a devoted group of royalists, still irreconcilable, founded the *New Prussian Gazette* or, as it is usually called, the *Kreuz Zeitung*, that they might have an organ for the full and free expression of their opinions. They became the center of the conservative opposition, and their paper its official mouthpiece. In the autumn the King, to the delight of the royalists, gained the courage to use the army to put an end to the anarchical conditions in Berlin. The assembly was dissolved, the King replaced the constitution which he had been forced to grant with one of his own choice, and convened a new assembly to ratify it. Bismarck was mentioned to the King at this time for the ministry, but the King returned the memorandum with the significant note: "Red reactionary; smells of blood; will be useful later."

Bismarck sat in the successive assemblies from 1849 to 1851, taking a most active part in the debates. He persisted in his aggressive royalism, criticizing unendingly all liberal measures. His one ideal was to maintain the individuality and position of Prussia foremost among the German states. His horizon was rapidly widening, however, in his parliamentary experience, for he became involved in debates on questions affecting Prussia's policies outside of Prussia proper, affecting Prussia's position in the German Confederation. And in these debates as in debates upon domestic policy he evinced an unwavering faith in the ultimate destiny of his country, whatever loss of prestige it might temporarily suffer.

These characteristics became especially prominent in the debates of the Prussian assembly during the years 1849 and 1850. The constitutional assembly of delegates from all the German states had convened in Frankfort in 1848, and, after great difficulties, had evolved a German constitution binding into one empire the German states outside of Austria, and had, in April of 1849, offered the imperial crown to King Frederick William IV. The King hesitated. Acceptance meant war with Austria, for Austria would never consent peaceably to a rival German empire which should be equal or greater than herself in numbers and power. Frederick William finally declined, giving as his reason his repugnance to universal suffrage which was a provision of the constitution, and his unwillingness to accept a title and authority bestowed and bestowable by a popular assembly. This decision of the King was debated in the Prussian assembly, where Bismarck had his seat, and an address was moved to declare the Frankfort constitution in force and to request the King to accept the crown. Bismarck passionately defended the King. In a notable speech he said:

> "The Frankfort constitution bore upon its brow the broad impress of popular sovereignty, and incited the King to hold his free crown as a mere fief from the people, which simply meant the extinction of his power. The Frankfort crown might be very brilliant, but the gold which gave it genuineness must first be got by melting down the Prussian crown."

The liberals felt the most intense anger at this speech. They caused to be printed and distributed ten thousand copies of it, in order that the people might appreciate the principles of the reactionary element in Prussia.

Again after the humiliation of Olmütz, Bismarck championed the King's cause. At Olmütz, the Prussian King yielded his own plans for the regeneration of Germany before the threats of Austria. All liberals in Germany were bitterly disappointed. In the Prussian chamber the liberals moved that the King be requested to dismiss the ministers responsible for the Olmütz surrender. Bismarck felt the humiliation as keenly as his colleagues, but believed that Prussia was not ready for the decisive struggle with Austria. In a speech he said:

> "If Prussia had gone to war for her union idea, — that mongrel product of timid rulers and tame revolution, which would have the effect of mediatizing her under the chambers of the petty states, — she would only have resembled the Englishman who fought a victorious combat with a sentinel in order to be able to hang himself in the sentry-box, a right he claimed for himself and every free Briton."

So Bismarck kept his gaze focused on the greatness of Prussia, Prussia before all else. "Prussians we are, and Prussians we will remain," he said in one of his speeches. "I know that in these words I but express the creed of the Prussian army and of the majority of my countrymen; and I hope to God that we shall also remain Prussians long after this bit of paper (referring to the German constitution) has moldered away like a withered autumn leaf."

In July of 1851 Bismarck was for the first time admitted

into the inner circles of governmental affairs. He was appointed Prussian envoy to the Federal Diet at Frankfort. The American, John Lothrop Motley, fellow student at Göttingen and lifelong friend, thus writes of Bismarck's own account of his appointment:

"In summer of 1851 he told me that the minister, Manteuffel, asked him one day abruptly, if he would accept the post of Ambassador at Frankfort, to which (although the proposition was as unexpected a one to him as if I should hear by the next mail that I had been chosen Governor of Massachusetts) he answered, after a moment's deliberation, 'Yes,' without another word. The King, the same day sent for him, and asked him if he would accept the place, to which he made the same brief answer, 'Ja.' His majesty expressed a little surprise that he made no inquiries or conditions. When Bismarck replied that anything which the King felt strong enough to propose to him, he felt strong enough to accept. I only write these details, that you may have an idea of the man. Strict integrity and courage of character, a high sense of honor, a firm religious belief, united with remarkable talents, make up necessarily a combination which cannot be found any day in any Court; and I have no doubt that he is destined to be Prime Minister, unless his obstinate truthfulness, which is apt to be a stumbling-block for politicians, stands in his way."

His appointment to the Frankfort diet marked a most significant change in his career. During the eight years he served therein, he was involved in international diplomacy rather than in local Prussian questions; he was rubbing elbows with some of the most acute politicians of his generation and learning to "play the game" according to their rules; and he was fastening upon a few fundamental policies for the guidance of Prussia. His political horizon widened still further.

The Frankfort Diet was a body composed of delegates from the sovereigns of the states in the German confederation. Its function was to act as a congress for the consideration of issues rising between the states in the confederation and of interests affecting the confederation as a whole.

In its character and organization it was a revival of the Diet of the Confederation, which had been established at the Congress of Vienna and suspended during the troubles of 1848.

If Bismarck set out for Frankfort with any preconceived notions of the value of the Diet in the affairs of Germany, he was soon disillusioned. In a letter to his wife written soon after his arrival, he says:

"Our intercourse here is nothing but mutual distrust and espionage; and then if there was only anything to spy out and conceal! Nothing but miserable trifles do these people concern themselves about; and the diplomatists here strike me as being infinitely more ridiculous with their important ponderosity concerning gathered rags of gossip than even a member of the Second Chamber in the full consciousness of his dignity. . . . I am making giant strides at the art of saying nothing in a great many words. I write reports pages long, as rounded and polished as leading articles; and if Manteuffel, after he has read them, can say what is in them, he can do more than I can. We all play at believing that each of us is crammed full of ideas and plans if he would only speak, and we are every one of us perfectly well aware that all of us together are not a hair better as to knowledge of what will become of Germany than Gossamer Summer. No one, not even the most malicious democrat, can form a conception of the charlatanism and self-importance of our assembled diplomacy."

Yet once established, he enjoyed his life there. Motley writes of the Bismarck household: "It is one of those houses where every one does what one likes. The show apartments where they receive formal company are on the front of the house. Their living-rooms, however, are a *salon* and dining room at the back, opening upon the garden. Here there are young and old, grandparents and children and dogs all at once; eating, drinking, smoking, piano-playing, and pistol-firing (in the garden), all going on at the same time. It is one of those establishments where every earthly thing that can be eaten or drunk is offered you; porter, soda-water, small beer, champagne, burgundy, or claret are about all the time, and everybody is smoking the best Havana cigars every minute." Bismarck was able to get away for short trips to interesting regions in that part of Europe, thus varying the monotony of Frankfort existence and official reports. Another extract from one of his letters to his wife reveals a vein of romanticism and nature-love which in the busy years before him was, it seems, gradually choked:

"Saturday afternoon I drove out with Rochow and Lynar to Rüdesheim; there I took a boat, rowed out upon the Rhine, and swam in the moonlight, with nothing but nose and eyes out of the water, as far as the Rat Tower near Bingen, where the bad bishop came to his end. It gives one a peculiar dreamy sensation to float thus on a quiet warm night in the water, gently carried down by the current, looking above on the heavens studded with the moon and stars, and on each side the banks and wooded hill-tops and the battlements of the old castles bathed in moonlight, whilst nothing falls on one's ear but the gentle splashing of one's own movements. I should like to swim like this every evening."

The diet itself was a hotbed of intrigue. Bismarck had gone there inspired with a feeling of friendship for Austria, because he realized that no nation in Europe had so persistently maintained the struggle against the rising hosts of liberalism, and had so consistently held by the sacred rights of the sovereigns. He had uttered pro-Austrian sentiments in speeches in the assembly, as: "Prussia should join Austria to crush the common foe, the Revolution"; and again: "I consider Austria the representative and heir of a traditional German power which has often gloriously wielded the German sword." He soon found, however, that Austria was using the machinery of the Confederation to increase continually her own prestige and to humiliate the other German states, including Prussia. Sometimes this attempt at humiliation was shown in trivial ways, as in the assumption by the Austrian delegate of the privilege of smoking at the council board where — before Bismarck arrived — no one else dared do so; or in the Austrian's studied insolence in being in negligé costume when he received, in more or less formal audience, a delegate from another of the German states. At other times, Austria attempted to dictate arrogantly the policy of the confederation, treating all the other German states, including Prussia, as inferior.

The Prussian King could not have sent to the Frankfort diet a man of a temper better calculated to oppose the Austrian presumption. When Thun, the Austrian President of the Diet, began to smoke at the sittings of one of the commissions, Bismarck, with characteristic audacity, asked him for a light; when Thun received in his shirt sleeves, Bismarck said, "You are quite right, it is very hot," and removed his own coat. Poor Count Thun, after a dispute with Bismarck, used to retire exhausted at five in the afternoon; and another of the Austrian delegates, when leaving Frankfort to take a post at Constantinople, remarked that "it would be like an Eastern dream of the blessed to converse with the wise Ali instead of Bismarck." Naturally, the Austrians hated Bismarck, and attempted to discredit him in every way possible. Insults were frequent. On one occasion, an archduke asked him whether certain medals he was wearing were won in the presence of the enemy. "Yes," answered Bismarck quickly, "all won before the enemy, all won right here in Frankfort."

The trouble he caused the Austrian delegate did not, however, decrease his influence at the Prussian court. Through these years, when little rumor of his activities filtered through the Prussian nation as a whole, his reputation and influence with his sovereign steadily rose. His long reports were models of their kind. He gradually became the chief adviser to the Prussian government on German affairs, and was used again and again upon delicate negotiations with other courts, thus gaining an invaluable knowledge of men, methods, and affairs. His advice on Prussian policy more than once determined the action of his government during these years. For example, in the diplomacy leading up to the Crimean War, the question of Prussia's attitude became of supreme importance to the powers of Europe. Great Britain and France in 1854 determined on war, sent their fleets to the Black Sea and invited the coöperation of Austria. Austria, though the Russian troops on her border were a constant menace to her, dared not join the western powers without the aid of Prussia and the German states, so she appealed to the Diet at Frankfort. The issue depended wholly upon Prussia. The smaller German states, though they had no interest in sending their soldiers to the Crimea, could not have resisted the combined pressure of Austria and Prussia. Should Prussia side with Austria, or with Russia? At this crisis Bismarck was summoned from Frankfort to confer with the Prussian government. He found the palace filled with intriguers, and the vacillating King in a fever of indecision. Bismarck's own arguments were for armed neutrality, and he carried the day. "What has Austria done for us," he asked, "that we should do police service gratis for her?" And again:

> "Although a war with that empire (Russia) would be a serious matter for us, I should not attempt to say anything against it if it held out the prospect of yielding us a prize worthy of us. But the very notion appalls me that we may plunge into a sea of trouble and danger on behalf of Austria, for whose sins the King displays as much tolerance as I only hope God in Heaven will one day show toward mine. . . . The interest of Prussia is my only rule of action, and had there even been any prospect of our promoting this interest by taking part in the war, I should certainly never have been one of its opponents."

Bismarck learned through these years to foresee with absolute certainty a war with Austria. Soon after the Peace of Paris which closed the Crimean War, he wrote a long report to his home government on his conception of what should be the Prussian foreign policy, the central idea of which lay in the sentence: "It is my conviction that at no distant time we shall have to fight with Austria for our very existence, and that it is not in our power to obviate this." He was ready to shape all the policy of the government to this clearly discernible end. "My attitude towards Foreign Governments springs not from any antipathy," he wrote, "but from the good or evil they may do to Prussia." And he went so far as to advocate at one time an alliance with Napoleon III (whom all Prussian leaders looked upon as their natural enemy) in order to be sure to overawe Austria, urging upon his home government "freedom from prejudice, that our decisions should be independent of all impressions of dislike or affection for Foreign States and their government."

January 29, 1859, Bismarck received news that he was appointed ambassador to St. Petersburg. Frederick William IV had in the previous year been pronounced incurably insane and his brother, William, had assumed the regency. It was impolitic to start the regency with the continuance of Bismarck at Frankfort, for Bismarck was persistently opposed to Austria, and William desired the good will of that country.

Bismarck jestingly referred to his transference by saying that he had been *kaltgestellt* (placed in ice), a phrase applied to the cooling of champagne. His stay in the Russian capital was not pleasant. He was out of the current of German and Prussian affairs. Watching from a distance, he felt that his country's policy was drifting "more and more into the Austrian wake." He was oppressed by severe illness during the greater part of his service, an illness which seems to have left him with a nervous irritability, far different from the robust good nature which had characterized his earlier years. And yet, even here, his service was of great advantage to him. He widened his knowledge of contemporary statesmen and diplomatists, and gained the warm personal regard of the Czar.

In the conflict which developed between the regent and his parliament, Bismarck's advice was again sought. He was the one strong man of the King's adherents. He was summoned back from St. Petersburg for consultation. The King, still hesitating to appoint him minister, dispatched him to Paris early in 1862, where he renewed his previous acquaintance with the leaders in the French nation. He had been there but a few months when he was summoned post-haste back to Berlin, where he found the King on the point of abdicating, as we have already described. On September 22, 1862, he was appointed minister.

Such was the political career of the man whom the King had chosen at the crisis to guide the Prussian ministry. At the news of his appointment, the Liberals were raised to the highest pitch of anger. To them, Bismarck was the Bismarck of 1847–1851, the "red radical" who was too royalist for Frederick William IV. His career since 1851, it must be remembered, had been in the field of governmental diplomacy outside of Prussia, so that even if there had been any change in his convictions it would not have been known by the home politicians. His appointment was believed to be a defiance to them.

C. THE POLITICAL SITUATION

The most immediate problem which confronted Bismarck was, of course, that due to the opposition of the majority of the lower chamber of the Prussian parliament. He did not underestimate the dangers in this crisis. He was pledged in the words with which he had accepted office to uphold the royal prerogative and to carry through the royal program of military increase and reorganization. Such a program could only be carried through by the expenditure of large sums of money. Such expenditure could, under the constitution, be authorized only by the parliament. The parliament was unalterably opposed to the program, and had made its attitude unmistakably evident in the debates on the money bill. A dissolution had been ordered, and the succeeding elections had served to strengthen the liberal opposition to the government. The country had given its representatives the evidence of its approval of their course. Government was at a deadlock at the moment.

The issue, however, was greater than that contained in the mere appropriation of funds for army increase and reorganization. It had become a question of royal government versus parliamentary government. Political thinkers felt that Prussia was then at the parting of the ways. If the King were forced to modify or withdraw his measures, the fatal step which would give a precedent for parliamentary supremacy would be irrevocably taken. Henceforth, parliament would always hold the control of governmental policies and action. On the other hand, if the King were able to carry out his policies despite the opposition of parliament, a step would be taken which would in large measure nullify those provisions in the constitution that had been thought to guarantee popular liberties. Royal government would take a new lease of life in Prussia: the popular government which the people had thought they obtained in Frederick William IV's constitution would be proven an illusion. The awakening of the people might mean another revolution.

Though the domestic political problem was important and dangerous in nature, the question of Prussia's foreign relations was no less so. Prussia's position in Europe was perilous. She could be certain of the bitter hostility of Austria just so long as German affairs continued under the confederation, for Austria would never endure Prussian leadership among the German states. Bismarck felt that Prussia was too great and proud a nation to be in Austrian leading-strings. Yet Prussia had no friends in Europe at the time Bismarck took office. If Austria should league with France or with Russia, Prussia might be overwhelmed.

Foreseeing clearly as he did the inevitable conflict with Austria, Bismarck was confronted with the problem of finding friends for Prussia among the European nations, or at least of assuring himself of the neutrality of the great nations when the conflict should come.

CHAPTER II

THE EUROPEAN STATES IN 1860

WE may well at this point turn from our consideration of conditions in Prussia to outline briefly the state of affairs in the neighboring countries of continental Europe. We shall thus be able to gain a general idea of the forces which Bismarck encountered in the field of his foreign diplomacy. His accurate knowledge of the strength and weakness, of the ambitions and fears, of the rulers and the diplomats in contemporary states was what enabled him at critical moments in Prussian international relations to gain his most brilliant successes.

A. GERMANY

The conflicting influences in the Congress of Vienna after the overthrow of Napoleon had prevented any satisfactory solution of the problem involved in the creation of a government for the collection of states in what was known as Germany. Napoleon's conquests had destroyed forever the Holy Roman Empire, and had resulted in reducing the number of separate states from some hundreds to thirty-nine; but even under the inspiration of a common opposition to the French conqueror these thirty-nine states had not been able to achieve a political unity. Those who, in the Congress of Vienna, advocated the creation of a powerful and unified German state out of the separate German units found themselves thwarted by the effort of Austria, whose chancellor, Prince Metternich, believed that Austrian influence could be more securely maintained, and Austrian

THE GERMANIES
1815 – 1866
SCALE OF MILES
0 25 50 75 100
NORTH SEA
BALTIC SEA
SWEDEN
RUSSIA
DENMARK
JUTLAND
DUCHY OF SCHLESWIG
DUCHY OF HOLSTEIN
MECKLENB'G-SCHWERIN
KINGDOM OF HANOVER
POMERANIA
BRANDENBURG
PRUSSIA
POLAND
SILESIA
SAXONY
WESTPHALIA
NETHERLANDS
ELECT. OF HESSE
OLDENB'G
Gottland
Bornholm
Rugen
Jasmund
Falster
Laaland
Fehmarn
Seeland
Funen
Alsen
Sylt
Helgoland
(Br.)
Zuyder Zee
Helsingor
Copenhagen
Malmö
Veile
Fredericia
Kolding
Flensbg
Idstedt
Schleswig
Friedrichstadt
Kiel
Rendsburg
Itzehoe
Lubeck
Stade
Bremerhaven 1827
Heppens 1854 PRUSS.
Wilhelmshaven
Altona
Ratzeburg
Hamburg
Bremen
Luneburg
Schwerin
N. Strelitz
Rostock
Stralsund
Stettin
Colberg
Danzig
Marienburg
Konigsberg
Memel
Tilsit
Thorn
Bromberg
Gnesen
Posen
Rogalin
Warsaw
Minsk
Kalisch
Koschmin
Frankfort
Berlin
Potsdam
Brandenburg
Magdeburg
Dessau
Torgau
Halle
Leipzig
Bautzen
Gorlitz
Zittau
Liegnitz
Breslau
Ols
Landeshut
Hanover
Brunswick
Minden
Osnabruck
Pyrmont
Detmold
Munster
Gottingen
Cassel
Langensalza
Gotha
Weimar
Gera
Wartburg
Dusseldf.
Cologne
Aix la Chapelle
Leeuwarden
Amsterdam
Utrecht
R. Vistula
Narew R.
Bug R.
Vistula
Memel R.
Warta R.
R. Oder
Prosna
Spree
Elbe R.
Havel
Weser
Ems
Eider
Maas

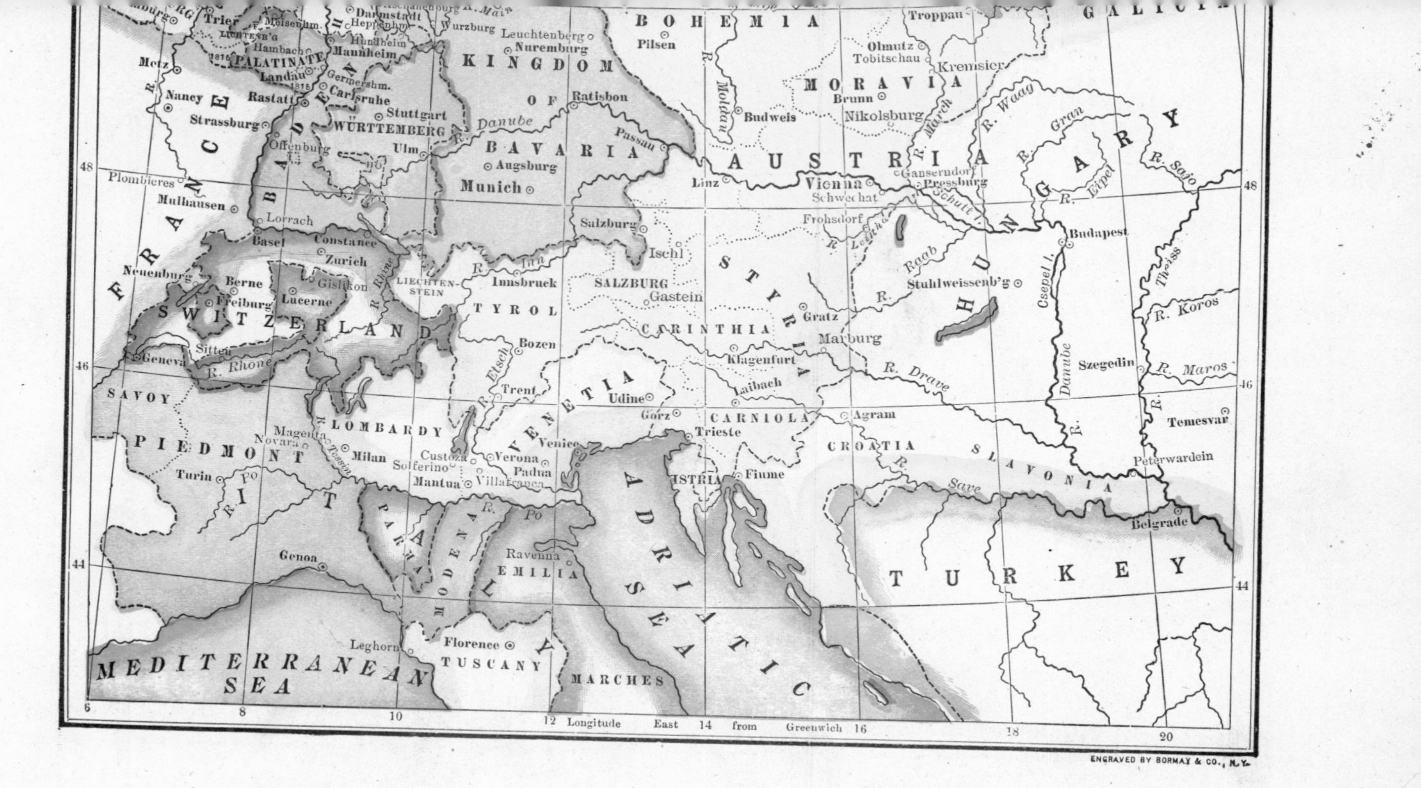

BOHEMIA
Pilsen
R. Moldau
Budweis
MORAVIA
Olmutz
Tobitschau
Brunn
Nikolsburg
Kremsier
Troppau
R. March
GALICIA
AUSTRIA
HUNGARY
R. Waag
R. Gran
R. Eipel
R. Sajo
R. Theiss
R. Koros
R. Maros
Vienna
Schwechat
Gansserndorf
Pressburg
Schutt I.
Linz
Frohsdorf
R. Leitha
R. Raab
Stuhlweissenb'g
Budapest
Csepel I.
Danube
R. Danube
Szegedin
Temesvar
Peterwardein
Belgrade
KINGDOM OF BAVARIA
Leuchtenberg
Nuremburg
Wurzburg
Ratisbon
Danube
Passau
Augsburg
Munich
Darmstadt
Heppenhm.
Hundheim
Mannheim
Trier
Meisenhm.
Hambach
PALATINATE
Landau
Germersh.
Carlsruhe
Rastatt
Stuttgart
WÜRTTEMBERG
Ulm
BADEN
Offenburg
Lorrach
Metz
Nancy
Strassburg
FRANCE
Plombieres
Mulhausen
Basel
Constance
Zurich
Gislikon
Neuenburg
Berne
Freiburg
Lucerne
SWITZERLAND
R. Rhine
Sitten
Geneva
R. Rhone
LIECHTENSTEIN
Salzburg
Ischl
SALZBURG
Gastein
R. Inn
Innsbruck
TYROL
Bozen
R. Etsch
Trent
STYRIA
Gratz
Marburg
CARINTHIA
Klagenfurt
Laibach
CARNIOLA
R. Drave
Agram
CROATIA
SLAVONIA
R. Save
VENETIA
Udine
Gorz
Trieste
Fiume
ISTRIA
Venice
Verona
Padua
Villafranca
Mantua
Custoza
Solferino
LOMBARDY
Magenta
Novara
Milan
R. Tessin
SAVOY
PIEDMONT
Turin
R. Po
ITALY
PARMA
MODENA
R. Po
Ravenna
EMILIA
Genoa
Leghorn
Florence
TUSCANY
MARCHES
ADRIATIC SEA
MEDITERRANEAN SEA
TURKEY
48
46
44
6
8
10
12 Longitude East 14 from Greenwich 16
18
20
ENGRAVED BY BORMAY & CO., N.Y.

territory possibly expanded, if these units were bound loosely together in a confederation. So in the final treaty of Vienna provision was made for a German Confederation, whose thirty-nine independent states sent delegates to a common Diet at Frankfort-on-the-Main.

Unsatisfactory as this Confederation was to those who hoped to see a Germany, united and strong, playing its part in European affairs, it is a fact that for the next generation the German states enjoyed a measure of peace and prosperity they had not known for a century. During these years they recovered from the successive ravages of the Thirty Years' War and the Napoleonic Wars. Population increased rapidly; the standard of living rose with the general comfort and intelligence of the people; business expanded as the rewards of energy and application again seemed secure; and the material wealth of the separate states grew greatly.

This rise in general prosperity and intelligence among the people of the German states had two important political effects: first, it strengthened the ranks of those who demanded more liberal government in the separate states; and second, it increased the number of those who realized the benefits which would result from the creation of a unified Germany.

The Treaty of Vienna had stipulated that the States of Germany should be given constitutions. Most of the sovereigns had lived up to this provision, beginning with the Duke of Saxe-Weimar in 1816. During the ascendancy of Prince Metternich, however, Austria and Prussia, the most powerful of the German states, withheld their constitutions, and the governments of the smaller states were inclined too often to rule autocractically in spite of the constitutional guarantees. The continuance of peace and spread of prosperity increased the numbers of those in the well-to-do middle classes who desired a share in the government. They had the time to think on political problems;

they had the education and ability to understand the nature of the institutions under which they lived; and they desired the power to insure their continued enjoyment of their constitutional privileges, and to secure the extension of those privileges.

The second result of this period of prosperity was the growth of sentiment among the people of these states for German political unity. As education became more widespread, the bonds of the common race, language, and literature were more appreciated. The masses of people in one state became better acquainted with the characteristics and ideals of those in neighboring states. The community of interests of all Germans was more clearly manifest to thinking people. The opportunities of a united Germany to take its place among the great nations of the world were evident, whereas the weakness of the existing loose and inefficient confederation prevented any advantage being taken of such opportunities. The strength and scope of the sentiment for national unity increased enormously during the period between 1815 and 1848.

The wind that fanned into flame the sparks of liberalism in the German states came from France. February 24, 1848, the people of Paris rose in revolt, swept Louis Philippe from the throne, and proclaimed a democratic republic. Four days later the revolutionary movement communicated itself to the first of the German states. With a speed that bore witness to the thorough unanimity of popular sentiment it spread from state to state.

"Its course was everywhere the same. Mighty assemblies of the people proclaimed the demands of the times: the concession of all those assumed privileges of freedom, the summoning of a German Parliament, the providing of every citizen with arms, and, above all, the transference of the ministerial offices to champions of the Liberal party. In violent petitions, accompanied sometimes by boisterous tumults in the streets and with terrible threats in the event of a refusal, these claims were laid before the ruling Princes. Nowhere did it come to acts of bloody outrage; for in view of the imposing unanimity of the whole population, not a single government dared to make any resistance, and very soon the leaders of the Opposition everywhere occupied ministerial seats." (VON SYBEL, I. 147–148.)

On March 13, 1848, the revolution spread to Vienna, and the German world was astounded by the news of the resignation of Prince Metternich, the bulwark of the autocratic régime. March 18, Frederick William IV of Prussia, after an insurrectionary outbreak in the streets of Berlin, convoked the United Provincial Diet of Prussia for consultation on the framing of a Prussian constitution.

In the meanwhile, self-constituted leaders arranged for a national popularly elected assembly to meet at Frankfort in order to draw up a scheme for a united Germany. This assembly met May 18, 1848. The difficulties in the way of its success were great. One strong and vociferous party demanded the establishment of a republic: the opposition advocated an empire. One group proposed the exclusion of both Austria and Prussia on the ground that their interests were irreconcilable and that no political unit could be created which would hold both: a second proposed the admission of Prussia and of the German part of Austria, thus excluding Hungary and keeping the new state homogeneous: a third proposed the exclusion of Austria and the inclusion of Prussia with the crown of empire bestowed upon the King of Prussia. Such issues, and the many involved questions connected with the draft of a constitution, caused long debates. All through the year 1848 the assembly was in session. In the spring of 1849, it came to the most vital of the questions to be decided — the question of the monarch for the new Germany. March 28 the vote was taken. Two hundred and ninety members voted for Frederick William, King of Prussia: the remainder did not vote at all. A deputation of thirty-two members was appointed to wait upon Frederick William and gain his acceptance of the election.

During the long period of the assembly's discussions, however, the reactionary elements had reëstablished their authority throughout the various states of Germany. The Austrian army had quelled the rebellion in the Italian provinces and was preparing to overcome Hungary; King Frederick William had granted his people the coveted constitution and was now revising it to suit more his autocratic powers; several of the smaller states had succeeded in suppressing the insurrections, often with the help of troops from the larger states. The reëstablishment of the autocratic governments in their authority undermined the power of the German assembly. This assembly had never been officially convened by the German governments; its power from the beginning had been due solely to what support it could command among the people at large. As soon as the evidence of this support was removed, its power waned. With the complete success of reaction, its power disappeared.

King Frederick William of Prussia earnestly desired German union, and equally earnestly desired to occupy the foremost place in such union. The offer which was brought to him from the assembly, however, was from an unrecognized and unauthorized source, and had been made, he knew, by only a small majority of the delegates in the assembly. Its acceptance would mean war with Austria and possibly with many other states of the old confederation. Further, its acceptance would put him in the position of respecting the will of the representatives of the people in the German states rather than respecting the will of the sovereigns of those states. After careful consideration Frederick William gave to the deputation a non-committal answer which it interpreted as a refusal. April 3, 1849, the deputation wended its way back to Frankfort.

The rejection of the imperial honor by Frederick William ruined all the work of the assembly. Immediately after his decision was made known, the futility of further deliberations was evident. Gradually one delegation after another was withdrawn until the mere remnant was dispersed at Stuttgart, whither it had removed itself, June 18, 1849. Though its work seemed to have been valueless, the future showed that it had accomplished something. It had for a time centered the ambitions of all Germans upon a common political end, and had struck upon the only way in which this end could ultimately be secured. Its failure was not due to its own incompetence, but to the rival ambitions of Austria and Prussia — in its failure it indicated what the difficulty was which must finally be overcome.

The ferment created by the assembly did not at once die away. Frederick William of Prussia, though he had been unwilling to accept the imperial crown from what he considered an unauthorized body, sincerely desired German unity. He therefore undertook to frame a union on his own lines, namely, a voluntary union of German sovereigns, with himself at its head. Gaining the consent of Hanover and Saxony, he called a convention of the German princes at Erfurt in March, 1850, to form a new constitution for Germany. He found himself at once opposed by Austria, whose chancellor, von Schwarzenberg, made it a cardinal feature of his policy to increase Austrian influence among the German states and to humiliate Prussia. Schwarzenberg set up a counter proposal, namely, the reëstablishment of the old Federal Diet, which in the revolutionary movements of 1848 had been necessarily suspended. He rallied German states into a league of his own. The feeling on both sides grew intensely bitter. War seemed imminent; orders of mobilization were issued; and Prussians were enthusiastic over the prospect of establishing their authority once for all in Germany.

With war apparently a matter of only a few days, Frederick William and his advisers were forced to weigh carefully the prospect. France was hostile, and had her armies of observation ranged along Prussia's western border. Russia was on terms of intimate friendship with Austria and threatened Prussia from the east. Frederick William felt that Prussia would have to give way. He sent Manteuffel, then his chancellor, to Olmütz to confer with Schwarzenberg. In the conference Manteuffel was completely outwitted by the bold and skillful Austrian diplomat. In all essential principles Prussia was made to yield. Provision was made for the relinquishment of Frederick William's scheme for German unity, and it was agreed that the old Federal Diet should be restored. This "Humiliation of Olmütz," as it was long known among loyal Prussians, aroused the most intense indignation in Prussia. It was felt that Prussia, when her armies were ready and the opportunity was offered, had surrendered without a battle all that she could possibly have lost with a battle. The results enhanced Austria's position among the German states, and correspondingly reduced the prestige of Prussia.

These events we have outlined took place a decade before our history opens. An understanding of them is necessary, however, to appreciate the conditions in the German states following 1851. Everywhere the practice of governments slipped back into the familiar autocratic grooves. The liberals had apparently spent themselves in their one outbreak of 1848: they accepted sullenly the reëstablishment of autocracy. The muzzle of suppression again forced a silence. Freedom of speech and freedom of the press were restricted. Arbitrary arrest and imprisonment were common. The elaborate system of espionage instituted in the larger states was imitated in the smaller. The net results of the revolutionary movements of 1848 in Germany were apparently nothing. The Germany of 1860 was but little removed from the Germany of the era of Metternich.

B. AUSTRIA

As we looked back a decade to gain an idea of causes of conditions in the German states just previous to the opening of our history, so likewise in our consideration of Austria we must go back to the events of 1848–1851. For by the events of these years, and the final success of the autocracy in reëstablishing its power, were determined political conditions in Austria up to 1860.

The resignation and flight of Metternich at the first breath of the revolutionary storm of March, 1848, were signals for the disruption of the whole Metternich system in the Austrian dominions. From every side, from Hungary, Bohemia, the Italian Provinces, and the provinces of Austria proper, came news of rioting and of liberal demands. The liberalism that had been so effectively bottled up during Metternich's long régime now burst forth with new life and vigor.

The most dangerous and bloody of the revolts occurred in the Lombardo-Venetian provinces. The hatred of Austrian domination there had long been intense: the news of the success of the French revolutionists, and of the fall of Metternich, combined to rouse the people to a frenzy. Radetzky, the Austrian commander, had less than 20,000 troops scattered through the provinces. The uprising, beginning with bloody street fighting in Milan, March 18, came upon him before he could get reënforcements. He was compelled to withdraw his troops to the famous Quadrilateral formed by the fortresses on the Adige and Mincio rivers. Venice revolted in his rear, and Charles Albert, King of Piedmont, rushed 25,000 troops to the aid of the rebels in Lombardy. All of the Italian provinces seemed at the moment to be lost.

While this Italian situation was at its worst, the demands from other parts of the empire poured in upon the Emperor. The Hungarian Diet, under the inspiring radical leadership of Kossuth, had passed on March 15th and following days a series of reform laws (The March Laws) by which Hungary was to be practically an independent nation, united with Austria only by the person of the sovereign. A delegation of Hungarians proceeded to Vienna and, on March 31, received the hard-pressed Emperor's acceptance of the reforms. The Czechs of Bohemia acted at the same time and, on March 19, dispatched their deputation to demand from the Emperor political equality between Czechs and Germans in Bohemia, freedom of thought, speech, and the press, and local autonomy. Their demands, too, were at once granted. And the people in the provinces of Austria proper took advantage of the situation to put forth their demands for a constitution, guarantees of civil liberty, and rights of local self-government. Again the Emperor was forced to yield without reserve, promulgating the constitution April 25, 1848. Thus at all points in the empire the forces of revolution had been astonishingly successful: autocracy had yielded all demands.

Radetzky, however, persuaded his Emperor that, could the Italian rebellion be quelled, the revolutionary movements in other parts of the empire could afterwards be suppressed without undue difficulty. Reënforcements were sent to him in Lombardy, and he undertook a campaign against the rebels and the Piedmontese. In the bloody battle of Custozza, July 24, 1848, and again the following spring in the great battle of Novara, March 23, 1849, Radetzky won decisive victories, and could, indeed, have invaded Piedmont but for the hostility of France and England. The Italian rebels dispersed: Radetzky soon restored the Austrian system in northern Italy.

Inspired by Radetzky's success in Italy, the government now turned to the problem offered by conditions in other parts of the empire. The embarrassment caused by the fact that the Emperor Ferdinand had granted the demands of Austrians, Czechs, and Hungarians was removed by the abdication of Ferdinand and the elevation of his nephew

Francis Joseph, a boy of eighteen, to the throne. Francis Joseph, on the advice of his councilors, refused to recognize or accept the concessions made by his predecessor. Troops quickly put down the rebels in the Austrian provinces and overawed them in Bohemia. Hungary, however, was recognized as the most difficult problem of all.

After winning their coveted liberal laws from the Emperor, the Hungarians had fallen to quarreling among themselves. The Magyar element, desiring to dominate the government, quickly alienated the other races in the country by oppressive political restrictions. The Croatians, who felt especially aggrieved, rose in revolt. Austria took full advantage of the situation. The young Emperor requested the aid of Nicholas I of Russia to quell the Hungarian rebellion; Austrian armies invaded Hungary from the west; Russian troops poured in from the north and east; and the unhappy Magyars received no aid from the people of the races they had antagonized. They had declared their independence April 14, 1849, but they were unable to maintain it against the combined armies sent against them. The last important body of Magyar troops surrendered at Vilagos August 13, 1849. The revenge taken by the Austrian government was immediate and severe. Kossuth and his companions fled into exile; hundreds of Magyar leaders and generals who were implicated in the war were summarily executed; and Hungary was reduced to the position of a mere Austrian province, losing all the political rights she had possessed before the rebellion.

The leaders of the Austrian government put into practice during the next ten years the lessons they deduced from the revolt. In effect, they believed that the revolt had proved the necessity of wholly eliminating racial, linguistic, and political distinctions within the boundaries of the empire, and of creating an overwhelmingly strong central government. Acting under this belief, they reëstablished the Metternich system with an unusual severity intended to

Germanize the entire population. Inasmuch as Hungary had proved the most stubborn opponent to autocracy, the system, known as Bach's system from the name of the Austrian minister of the interior from 1849 to 1859, was applied to it with special thoroughness. No part of the ancient Hungarian constitution was recognized. No concessions were made to local racial or linguistic differences. All of the former elected local officials were replaced by Germans directly appointed by the crown. Hungary was split up into five administrative districts in the effort to destroy the sentiment of unity. German was officially designated as the only state and official language. The Austrian taxation system, including some taxes never before levied in Hungary, was applied without change or adjustment to that country. Thus by a policy of racial, linguistic, and economic coercion the Austrian government endeavored to force a political unity.

This policy might have been continued indefinitely had not events abroad forced its abandonment. Austria by her policy during the Crimean war had forfeited the friendship of Russia. When that war broke out in 1854, Russia expected that Austria, in gratitude for Russian assistance in conquering Hungary in 1849, would favor Russian interests. But Austria's own vital concern in this direction was with the free navigation of the Danube, and the Austrian government feared that Russian possession of the provinces of Moldavia and Wallachia would imperil such freedom. The Austrian influence, therefore, was cast against Russia: indeed, Austria would have entered the war on the side of the allies had it not been that Frederick William of Prussia, largely at Bismarck's instigation, refused Prussian assistance, and the Austrian diplomats feared that Prussia would take advantage of Austria's war to assert Prussian influence among the German states. The loss of Russia's friendship meant that Austria must increase her own strength. And further, the Italian war of 1859 had a direct bearing upon the internal situation in Austria. Cavour, the brilliant minister of Victor Emmanuel of Piedmont, had enlisted the sympathy of Napoleon III of France in Italian liberation from Austria. Early in 1859 the Piedmontese began to mobilize for war. Austria, naturally alarmed by these preparations, finally sent an ultimatum April 23, 1859, demanding demobilization within three days. A week later the Austrian troops crossed the Ticino river to invade Piedmont. France at once declared war, and sent a large and well-trained army to Piedmont's assistance. In the short war that followed, the Austrian troops were defeated, notably in the battles of Magenta (June 4, 1859) and Solferino (June 24, 1859), and were driven back to the defenses of the Quadrilateral. At this point Napoleon III arranged an armistice preparatory to peace. The final treaty provided for the cession of Lombardy to Piedmont, but left Venice in the hands of the Austrians.

The failures of Austrian diplomacy and of the Austrian armies, and the loss of Lombardy, aroused again unrest in Austria. The Hungarians had never been Germanized; the Bohemians were ready to demand once more their political rights; and the Austrian provinces desired a constitution. The ambitious centralization policy of the government, instead of strengthening the empire, had actually weakened it. Disaffection was rife. In the near future loomed the prospect of a decisive struggle with Prussia for leadership in Germany. The Bach system, proved a failure, collapsed after the disastrous Italian campaign; Bach himself resigned; and the government began to experiment with liberalism in the endeavor to win by concessions the support of the dissatisfied elements in the empire. In a manifesto issued after the dismissal of Bach, the Emperor promised his people to end the "inherited abuses" in the empire.

In 1860 the first attempt was made to placate the people. An enlarged imperial council met and drafted a constitution for the whole empire. This constitution, published

October 20, 1860, and known as the October Charter, restored to the provinces their pre-revolutionary parliaments and institutions, and provided for an imperial uni-cameral diet of one hundred members chosen from the provincial parliaments and having deliberative powers. The vital question with this constitution, as indeed with all the emperor's attempts, was: Will Hungary be satisfied?

The answer was soon evident. Hungary had passed beyond the time when she would be satisfied with her pre-revolutionary status: her statesmen, led by the patriot Deák, demanded the March Laws of 1848, which had been accepted by the former Emperor in the days of the revolution.

Francis Joseph and his councilors were not ready to accept these March Laws, inasmuch as the maintenance of the essential unity of the Empire was considered of greatest importance, so they made another attempt to conciliate Hungary. February 26, 1861, a new imperial constitution was promulgated, differing from the October Charter chiefly in the creation of a Diet of two chambers having broad and fundamental financial and legislative powers. The members of the Diet were to be chosen by the parliaments of the provinces. The pre-revolutionary political rights insured to the provinces by the October Charter were not disturbed. The constitution of February 26, 1861, was the surrender of autocracy: Would Hungary accept?

Excitement among the Hungarians was during these months at a fever heat. They realized the concessions the government had made, but they were inspired to hope for the further concessions which would give them what they demanded. They therefore refused to accept the constitution, decided not to send members to the newly created Diet, and demanded again the restoration of the March Laws of 1848. When the new Diet met, May 1, 1861, the Emperor, Francis Joseph, opened it in person: no representatives from Hungary or the Slav provinces were on the benches.

Such was the situation at the time our history opens. The Austrian government had definitely taken the turn leading to liberal constitutional government, not because of any innate desire for liberalism, but because in view of the situation in Germany and abroad it desired to rally to its loyal support all classes in the empire. Its concessions had been rejected by its largest and most important province, Hungary, and the Hungarians, sullen and resentful, were kept from open rebellion only by the constant threat of force. The Austrian national finances reflected the result of the disorders: the national debt had more than doubled in the decade. The normal economic life had been interrupted. The power and influence of Austria had been weakened. No man outside of the inner circle of the Austrian government understood better the disaffection and unrest in Austria than Bismarck, who during the greater part of this period had been the Prussian representative in the German Diet at Frankfort. He made daring use of his knowledge when he became chancellor.

C. ITALY

The history of Italy during the period just previous to 1862 is the narrative of the successful diplomacy of one man, Count Camillo di Cavour, prime minister of Piedmont (or Sardinia) from 1852 until his death in 1861 (with the exception of a few months in 1859). Cavour was a devoted patriot, firmly attached to the principles of Italian unity and independence, and in his position proved himself a master of statecraft.

After the decisive defeat of the Italian troops in the campaigns of 1848 and 1849, Charles Albert, King of Piedmont, abdicated in favor of his son, Victor Emmanuel. Italy seemed to fall back into the shameful conditions of the pre-revolutionary days: — Austria resumed her control over the Lombardo-Venetian territories; autocratic government was reëstablished in the several Italian states of central and southern Italy; and the Pope returned to Rome. But Charles Albert's efforts had not been wholly in vain. He had fought and lost, it was true, but he had focused the attention of patriotic Italians throughout the whole peninsula upon Piedmont, and had fixed Piedmont as the leader of those who desired Italian independence from Austria. Victor Emmanuel, receiving the throne from his father, gained the further gratitude of the Italian liberals by resisting Austrian inducements to abolish the Piedmontese constitution and to reëstablish autocracy in his kingdom. Piedmont stood out as the one liberal state in the peninsula.

It was this liberalism of the government which first gained the enthusiastic support of Cavour. As a young man he had studied the parliamentary institutions in England, and had become, nobleman though he was, a firm believer in liberalism. He was elected a member of the first parliament in Piedmont, entered the Piedmontese ministry in 1850, and became prime minister in 1852.

As prime minister, Cavour inaugurated an ambitious and progressive internal policy at the same time that he was engaged in the international field. Piedmont had greatly increased her debt by the expenses of Charles Albert's campaigns. Her finances were disorganized. She seemed on the verge of bankruptcy. Two plans were possible: the obvious one of retrenchment; or the audacious one of costly stimulation of industry and commerce until the people could without effort endure the increased financial burdens. Cavour chose the second plan. He raised large sums by loans for public improvements; he built railroads, introduced more modern methods of agriculture, and entered into favorable commercial relations with neighboring states, thus encouraging industry and trade. Piedmont forged ahead in material prosperity and soon all danger of national bankruptcy disappeared.

His most sensational successes, however, were gained in the field of international politics. He realized that Piedmont alone could never hope to wrest the Italian territories from powerful Austria. He conceived it his duty, therefore, to gain an ally who would be willing to aid Piedmont in war against Austria. His first step in this direction was to join in the Crimean war of 1854 and 1855 by the side of England and France. Severely criticized though he was for involving Piedmont in a war in which she had no apparent material interest, Cavour dispatched an Italian army of 15,000 to the Crimea. He gained his reward at the end of the war by being admitted to the Congress of Paris, and being permitted before the representatives of the European powers to plead the cause of Italian independence from Austrian rule. The material advantage for Piedmont from his participation in the Crimean war and the Congress of Paris was nothing: the moral advantage was incalculable — Piedmont had again placed herself before the world as the leader of those Italians who hoped to throw off the Austrian yoke, and had pleaded the cause of Italy publicly before the European powers.

The ally from whom Cavour now hoped for material aid was Napoleon III of France. Napoleon had at one time lived in Italy; had been a member of one of those secret societies working for Italian independence; and had been impressed favorably by Italian aid in the Crimean war and by Cavour's presence at the Congress of Paris. In 1858 he invited Cavour to meet him at Plombières, a health resort in the Vosges mountains. In their secret meeting at the end of July, 1858, the two intriguers agreed verbally upon an alliance against Austria, France to come to Piedmont's aid in order to expel the Austrians from the Lombardo-Venetian territories, and Napoleon to receive as his reward when the task was accomplished the provinces of Savoy and Nice. In December, 1858, these agreements were put in writing.

Cavour directed his diplomacy now to causing Austria to attack Piedmont. By constant irritation, and by a threatening concentration of troops on the Lombard border, he finally drew from Austria an ultimatum demanding demobilization. This was his opportunity. The presentation of the ultimatum put the initiative upon Austria. When Austria crossed the Ticino river a week later for the invasion of Piedmont, Napoleon led his armies to Victor Emmanuel's assistance.

The allied French and Piedmontese armies won consistently over the poorly led Austrians. In the great battles of Magenta (June 4, 1859) and Solferino (June 24, 1859), the allies succeeded in driving the Austrians back to the Quadrilateral. All northern Italy was freed: it remained only to force the Austrians from their defenses and Venice and the Trentino might be gained. Before this final step was taken, however, Napoleon III, without consultation with his ally, offered an armistice, and soon after entered upon negotiations for peace.

The disappointment of Victor Emmanuel and Cavour was intense. They had seemed on the threshold of complete attainment of their aims, and now without warning their ally refused to take the final steps for victory. Cavour, beside himself with anger, urged desperate measures; and when overruled by the king, resigned and went into retirement. Victor Emmanuel accepted the gains the allies had made, and looked forward to their completion under more favorable auspices. In the provisions of the treaty of peace, the Treaty of Zurich (November 10, 1859), Lombardy was ceded to Piedmont, but Venice remained under Austrian domination. Napoleon did not claim the cession of Savoy and Nice, inasmuch as he recognized that he had not carried out to the full his part of the compact.

Events moved rapidly after this time. Piedmont's success, combined with her liberal constitution and her previous championship of freedom from Austria, drew to her as to a magnet the other Italian states. The people in central Italy, in Parma, Modena, and Tuscany, had overthrown their autocratic governments during the war, and their leaders now demanded union with Piedmont. Napoleon III was unwilling to see this further enlargement of Piedmont, though he could not consistently use force to oppose it. Cavour, who had again become prime minister in January, 1860, could not afford at this critical point to lose the friendship of his powerful ally, and yet the addition of the territory in central Italy was most desirable. After careful negotiations, Cavour bargained to cede to France the provinces of Savoy and Nice, and in return to gain Napoleon's consent to the union of the states of central Italy with Piedmont. Plebiscites were held in these states in March, 1860, to assure the world of the overwhelming sentiment in favor of the union with Piedmont; Victor Emmanuel accepted the sovereignty; and the first parliament of the enlarged state met at Turin, April 2, 1860.

Thus in the spring of 1860, Italy was divided into four main parts: Venice and the Trentino, under Austrian domination; Piedmont, a liberal constitutional kingdom extending across northern and down into central Italy; the Papal territories, including Rome, Umbria, and the Marches; and the kingdom of Naples, an autocracy under Francis II, comprising all of the lower half of the peninsula, and Sicily. All of Italy was, of course, in a ferment as a result of the momentous changes of the preceding year.

In May, 1860, the next step in the unification of Italy was begun. Garibaldi, a soldier of fortune with a long picturesque career of intrigue and fighting against Austrian power, set sail from Genoa with a thousand volunteers to assist revolutionists in Sicily. He had no official recognition from Victor Emmanuel, but undoubtedly the Piedmontese government was aware of, and secretly approved, the expedition. At the attack of Garibaldi, the kingdom of Naples collapsed. Sicily was conquered and held by Garibaldi in the name of Victor Emmanuel; and the people of the mainland welcomed the Garibaldeans with open arms. In less than five months Garibaldi had conquered Naples. Emboldened by his successes, he started to move against Rome.

At this point Cavour intervened. Napoleon III was interested in behalf of the French Catholics in the maintenance of the Pope's authority intact in Rome. Garibaldi might, by an attack upon the Pope, endanger all the gains he had already made. Victor Emmanuel's army moved south through Umbria and the Marches, defeated the remnants of Francis II's army at Gaeta, and met Garibaldi at Naples. Garibaldi surrendered his power wholly to the King. In October and November, the people of Naples, Umbria, and the Marches were invited to register their votes in a plebiscite on the question of whether they desired union with Piedmont in a united Italy. Overwhelming majorities voted in favor (Naples approximately 1,700,000 Yes, 10,500 No; Umbria 97,000 Yes, 400 No; the Marches 130,000 Yes, 1000 No). On March 17, 1861, the Kingdom of Italy was proclaimed, and Victor Emmanuel II became its first king.

The events of these crowded years had created a united Italy of more than 22,000,000 inhabitants, worthy by its size to take its place among the great powers of Europe. Its national aspirations, however, had not been completely attained. Venice and the Trentino were still under Austrian rule, and Rome, the ancient capital of Italy, was in the hands of the Pope. No patriotic Italian could be satisfied with such gaps in complete unity. Italian policy in the new kingdom was guided by the desire to add these territories to Italy.

A few months after the completion of the great events we have outlined above, the one man who had been primarily responsible for them, and whose genius was acutely needed in the difficult work of political organization and economic reconstruction in the new kingdom, died. Cavour's death was in the prime of life, June 6, 1861, when he was but fifty-one years old. He had risen by sheer ability to a most commanding position in European politics: he was sorely missed in Italy in the years that followed.

D. RUSSIA

Czar Nicholas I of Russia died March 2, 1855, in the midst of the reverses of the Russian armies in the Crimean war. His successor, Alexander II, then in his thirty-eighth year, assumed the reins of government when Russian fortunes were at their lowest ebb. The shameless corruption of high-born officials had disgraced the government and had resulted in untold sufferings among the soldiers; the Russian diplomacy, beginning the war with the expectation of easily gaining Constantinople, had so far failed that a great European coalition had formed against Russia, and Russia stood without an ally; and the Russian armies, which at first had advanced to the Danube, had been forced back, and the great fortified naval base at Sebastopol was under siege by the allies. From a popular war, the war had become unpopular. The blame for the scandal of official corruption was laid, as always, to the government. Public opinion among the masses of the people was aroused as it seldom had been before in this autocratic country.

The fall of Sebastopol in early September, 1855, gave the allies the sense of victory, and offered an interim for peace negotiations. The Russian finances were exhausted, and the banks were refusing to accept the paper money offered by the government; the Turks were inciting revolt in distant provinces; Poland showed signs that she was preparing to take advantage of Russia's difficulties to strike for freedom; and Finland was in danger of tearing loose to join again with Sweden. In this situation, Alexander accepted Austrian offers of mediation. February 1, 1856, the preliminaries of peace were signed. From February 25 to the end of March a European Congress sat in Paris considering the terms of the final treaty. And the Treaty of Paris was signed March 30, 1856. The astute diplomacy of the Russian minister Gortchakoff had saved Russia from any serious or disgraceful losses. As a net result of the war she gave up the right of protection of Christians of her faith in the Turkish dominions, accepted the principle of the neutrality of the Black Sea, and bound herself together with Turkey to maintain no naval forces therein, and surrendered a little territory.

The disgrace of the Crimean war was the signal for the inauguration of a policy of social and economic reform in Russia. The basis of this policy lay in the emancipation of the serfs. The war had revealed to Russian statesmen that so long as a majority of the Russian agricultural workers were in a condition of serfage, Russia could not hope to rival the material and economic progress upon which the wealth and success of the nations of western Europe were founded. Once the freedom of the press and of speech was allowed — as it was to an unusual degree shortly after the signing of the Treaty of Paris — expression of opinion from all parties in Russia was heard that the abolition of serfage would be the beginning of a new unity of sentiment and of a new industrial and economic progress in the country. All other reforms were dependent upon this basic reform — the emancipation of the serfs.

The serfs in Russia numbered at this period (1856) approximately 47,000,000. Of these, 25,000,000 were held on lands owned by, or under the direct control of, the crown. The lot of these crown serfs was not hard. They enjoyed certain privileges not given to the serfs of private proprietors — a right to a measure of local government, courts in which they were judged by judges elected by their own body, and a community organization having an elected council. Except for restrictions upon their freedom of movement from place to place, upon their right to acquire property or to dispose of property, and upon their choice of occupation, these crown serfs were freemen already in all but name. The lot of the serfs belonging to individual proprietors was less favorable, differing, however, in accordance with the character of the proprietor. Although protected by law from the extremes of tyranny — corporal punishment had to stop short of maiming or death; not more than three days a week could be exacted for labor on the proprietor's land; and no serf could be compelled to marry against his will — the serfs were in person and property alike wholly under the control of their masters. Aside from the evil moral and social effects of such a system, the economic results were exceedingly poor. Forced labor was inefficient and wasteful. Lack of the incentive provided by the personal ownership of property prevented the serfs from exerting themselves in the cultivation of the land or in any industry. Ignorance and superstition abounded.

It was not difficult for the government to take the necessary steps to make freemen of the crown serfs. Inasmuch as they were under the control of the Czar himself, he held it within his power at any time to remove from them the remaining restrictions and to declare them freemen. Pursuant to his policy, he emancipated these serfs by a series of imperial decrees beginning in July, 1858.

The problem of providing for the emancipation of the 22,000,000 serfs of private owners, however, was beset with difficulties. It was essential, in order that the serfs in their new freedom might be given the wherewithal to support themselves, that they be allotted land; yet such land had to be taken from the proprietors. The adjustment of the relations between freedmen and proprietors, and of the prices to be paid for land allotments, called for the most careful negotiations. A committee appointed at the end of 1856 to consider these questions was in session the greater part of three years without making substantial headway. In 1859 the Czar intervened to hasten their decisions. And finally, February 19, 1861, the manifesto of emancipation was completed.

The emancipation provided by this decree was immediate and complete. The former serfs became landed proprietors, a certain proportion of their former masters' land being distributed among them, and the remainder left to the proprietors. The peasants were required to pay the government for the land they received in installments extending over fifty years: the proprietors received in national bonds the value of the land which was diverted from them. The model of communal government, as it had existed previously in the crown lands, was used for the political organization of the communities of the newly freed serfs. To settle the many involved questions arising from the edict of emancipation, the office of "Arbiter of the Peace" was created, and men of position and character appointed as such in districts all over Russia.

Russia was in the midst of the readjustments accompanying the execution of the edict of emancipation at the time our history opens. Disorders prevailed in many parts of the empire. The peasants, far from feeling grateful for their new privileges, believed that the land should have been handed over to them without their being called upon to assume any financial burden. It was unjust, they thought, to have to purchase the very land on which their little huts stood, and the fields which they had so long been cultivating for themselves. Only gradually, and sometimes by the use of force, could matters be settled. Great credit during this trying period is due to the patience and tact with which the appointed "Arbiters of the Peace" dealt with the situation, and to the sacrifices which the former proprietors showed themselves willing to make for the common good.

E. FRANCE

The revolution of 1848 in France forced the abdication of Louis Philippe and resulted in the establishment of a republic. The first President, Louis Napoleon, was elected December 10, 1848, and took the oath of office ten days later. Ample evidence exists that, from the beginning of his presidency, he intrigued for the downfall of the republic and the reëstablishment of the old empire with himself at its head. In 1851, after long disagreement with his parliament, he and his agents carried through a *coup d'état* by which he assumed the dictatorship and promulgated a new constitution. A year later a carefully organized plebiscite declared in favor of the restoration of the empire. December 2, 1852, Louis Napoleon became Napoleon III, Emperor of France.

This Napoleon who had undertaken to carry on the imperial succession was the nephew of the great Napoleon and the head of the Napoleonic line. He had retained from his early manhood a supreme faith in his destiny and an unconquerable determination to govern France. In 1836 he had gathered a few adventurers about him at Strasburg, raised the imperial eagle, and endeavored to stampede the troops of the garrison to his cause. His attempt ended in failure, and he himself was arrested and exiled. Four years later (1840), he landed at Boulogne in the effort to arouse the people, but was quickly caught, tried, and sentenced to imprisonment for life in the great fortress of Ham. Six years later he escaped from the fortress in disguise and fled to England. The overthrow of Louis Philippe and the establishment of a republic gave him his opportunity to enter openly into political life in France. He was elected to the new assembly, and soon after posed as the candidate of the people for the presidency. The Napoleonic tradition gave him an importance not warranted by any ability he had shown up to that time. The masses of France had forgotten the sufferings of the nation under the Napoleonic régime and remembered only its power and splendor. In the belief that this representative of the Napoleonic line might unify France and restore the country to its former prestige in Europe, the people gave him their votes for President, and approved his elevation to the imperial dignity in 1852.

Napoleon was at this time (1852) a man of forty-four, rather pale and phlegmatic in appearance, with a character deeply affected by the trials and disappointments of his past life. He had been perforce an intriguer to gain the throne: he continued to be an intriguer all his life. He could conciliate men by a cordiality and graciousness of manner, but he expected all his associates to subordinate their own interests to his own cause. He could — and did at times — adopt policies which could have been dictated only by reckless impulse: on the other hand, he could at other times follow with iron determination a policy he deemed wise in spite of the most formidable opposition. He was an enigma to the people of his own time, and has not emerged clearly even yet. Bismarck, who had abundant opportunity to know him, and whose judgment with regard to character was rarely at fault, said:

"It is my impression that the Emperor Napoleon is a discreet and amiable man, but that he is not so clever as the world esteems him. The world places to his account everything that happens, and if it rains in eastern Asia at an unseasonable moment, chooses to attribute it to some malevolent machination of the Emperor. Here especially we have become accustomed to regard him as a kind of génie du mal who is for ever only meditating how to do mischief in the world. I believe he is happy when he is able to enjoy anything good at his ease; his understanding is overrated at the expense of his heart; he is at bottom good-natured, and has an unusual measure of gratitude for every service rendered him."

The accession of Napoleon to absolute power in the restored French empire was, naturally, of the most vital concern to the other great powers of Europe. In all the chancelleries, the name of Napoleon was associated with memories of unbounded ambition, of a career of military conquest, and of French territorial aggrandizement. In England, especially, the fears of a resumption of the policies of the first Napoleon led to a campaign of vituperation against Napoleon the Little, as he was dubbed, which lasted during his entire reign — even when England and France were allies in the Crimean War — and followed him to the grave. All his acts and declarations were scrutinized to discover the first intimation of offensive purpose.

Napoleon's reign may be divided in general survey into two parts: the first, from its beginning in 1852 until the Italian War in 1859, a period of conspicuous success; the second, from 1859 to the débacle in 1870, a period of gradual deterioration. In this chapter we shall indicate the features of its success and point out the turning point, thus bringing our outline of the situation down to the opening of our history.

The organization of government effected by the new Emperor was admirably adapted to maintain the supreme authority in his own hands. He was Commander-in-Chief of the armed forces, both military and naval; he had the right to declare war and to make peace; he had the right to conclude treaties of commerce or of alliance; he had unlimited power of pardon; he had the initiative in legislation as well as the power to promulgate the laws and to issue the ordinances necessary for their execution; he determined the apportionment of the budget among the administrative departments, and could contract loans; he had absolute control over the appointment and dismissal of his ministers; and he could convene, adjourn, or dissolve the legislative bodies. The power of appointment of subordinate officials gave to his highly centralized government a firm hold on the political situation throughout the nation, for he selected the prefects in the departments and the mayors and deputy mayors in the communes. He achieved at a single stroke, under the above organization, as secure a hold on the government as had Napoleon I at the height of his power. The legislative bodies — Council of State, Senate, and Chamber — sank to be mere agencies of Napoleon III's supreme will.

The Emperor realized, however, that a government resting on force alone was unstable. He undertook, therefore, from the beginning of his reign to carry through measures and projects which should satisfy the important classes in France. The Catholic party, headed by the clergy, had been on his side at his elevation to the throne: he showed it signal favors in the years following, as by concessions in the matter of education, by munificent grants to churches and charitable organizations, and by official representation at the church ceremonies. The sound business and financial interests of the country were conciliated by governmental encouragement of enterprise, extension of railroad lines, organization of the Postal and Telegraphic services, and a favorable attitude toward commercial and manufacturing activities. The masses of the people were to be satisfied by the assurance of "good times," plenty of work, and a fair wage. To bring about these conditions, the government inaugurated a policy of public improvements on a vast scale, giving employment to thousands and beautifying the cities and increasing the harbor facilities throughout France. Haussmann planned and built the broad boulevards which are so conspicuous a feature of the center of Paris to-day. The huge docks at Marseilles were rapidly pushed to completion. The harbor of Havre was enlarged. Lyons and Lille were beautified. The Emperor himself established a luxurious and resplendent court, reputed the finest in Europe. In 1855 he opened an enormous international exposition in Paris, bringing to that capital a host of visitors and giving an impressive spectacle of the mechanical and scientific progress of the time. However one might criticize the means by which Napoleon had gained the throne, no one could criticize the wisdom with which he had stimulated economic life, and no one could at this time doubt the strength of the support he had in the nation.

The Emperor had promised his people peace when he had assumed the crown. Ultimately, the breaking of that promise was the cause of his downfall. The first war in which he engaged, however, the Crimean War of 1854 to 1855, added to his prestige. His troops distinguished themselves beside their English and Piedmontese allies, and the Congress for the settlement of the terms of peace was held in Paris. The French people were proud of the valor of their armies, and their vanity was touched by the selection of their capital as the meeting place of the Congress.

The second war, however, the Italian War of 1859, although successful, brought down upon the government a storm of criticism, and created a strong opposition party in the country. Napoleon was sincerely interested in the cause of Italian liberty. As a young man, he had been a member of the Carbonari, one of the secret societies conspiring for Italian independence. He had been instrumental in securing the acceptance of Piedmont's aid in the Crimean War; and he had gained a hearing for Cavour in the Congress of Paris in 1856. He showed the inclination after hearing Cavour in this Congress to commit France to Piedmont's aid in expelling Austria from the Italian peninsula. As soon as his inclination became known, the influence of the Catholic church was exerted to restrain him. The clergy felt — with justification, as events proved — that any popular liberal movement centering around Piedmont would later affect the territories or position of the Pope. After attempting to allay the fears of the Catholics in France, Napoleon met Cavour in secret conference at Plombières and arranged the terms by which France would aid Piedmont. Broadly stated, these were that France would assist in sweeping the Austrians from the entire peninsula and that Piedmont in return would cede to France the provinces of Nice and Savoy. As soon as Cavour was certain of Napoleon's assistance, he endeavored to bring about the war. Hostilities began in April of 1859. The French and Piedmontese troops met with complete success, but Napoleon offered an armistice before the Austrians had been completely cleared out of Italy. In the peace which followed, Lombardy was added to Piedmont, but Venice was left under Austrian domination. Napoleon himself, realizing that he had not fulfilled his entire contract, did not press at the moment for the cession of Nice and Savoy.

The motives for Napoleon's sudden measures for an armistice have never been satisfactorily explained. Whether he was appalled by the loss of life in the great battle of Solferino, or whether he doubted the possibility of driving the Austrians from their strong defensive positions in the Quadrilateral, or whether he did not desire the establishment of too strong a kingdom on his southeastern border, we do not know. His action, however, took away much of the glory of his military enterprise. He lost the gratitude of Victor Emmanuel, and he declined in prestige at home.

In the events of the following year he showed an indecision which still further increased the opposition to his policy. Parma, Modena, and Tuscany were added to the already enlarged Piedmont, Naples was conquered, and two important districts of the Papal territories — Umbria and the Marches — were admitted to the new kingdom of Italy. And while this new kingdom was forming, Napoleon took no effective steps to check it. Not even the acquisition of Nice and Savoy could compensate French statesmen for French impotence at a time when such important changes were taking place. And the Catholic adherents were enraged that the Emperor had permitted the spoliation of the Pope. Napoleon's reputation as a wise ruler and a skillful diplomat suffered its deathblow from his Italian policy.

At the same time (1860), Napoleon alienated another important class of his supporters by negotiating a commercial treaty with England whereby import duties were materially reduced. Although the treaty did not commit France to the policy of Free Trade, it was a definite step in that direction. When the news of this treaty was divulged, the great manufacturing interests of the country took instant alarm. Meetings of protest were held and great indignation expressed. The Emperor had lost irrevocably the support of the manufacturers and protectionists throughout France.

At this juncture, Napoleon turned to the Liberals for political aid. In decrees promulgated in November, 1860, he increased the powers of the Senate and Legislative Assembly by permitting them to move and discuss freely each year an address in reply to the speech from the throne. At the same time he authorized the publication of full reports of parliamentary debates. These decrees were the first step in the liberalization of the empire — and in the undermining of the Emperor's power. The parliament could use the "address in reply" as an opportunity to criticize the Emperor's policies; and the country at large could read the eloquent appeals addressed to the legislative chambers. The first steps toward liberalism once taken, the Emperor found himself importuned insistently by the Liberals to grant greater concessions in the same direction.

Such was the condition of affairs at the time our history opens. Napoleon had turned two of the most powerful bodies of his supporters, the Catholic interests and the manufacturing interests, into the ranks of the opposition. His personal popularity was waning; his prestige had been shaken. He was treading the first steps in the path of the liberalism which was fatally undermining his government.

CHAPTER III

BISMARCK'S POLICIES, 1862–1864

Having now outlined briefly the conditions in the neighboring states of Europe, we may return to the critical and confused situation in Prussia. There the newly appointed chancellor was confronting a majority in the parliament hostile to the policy he had promised at his accession to carry out. Successive elections in 1861 and 1862 had shown how strongly and consistently this "Progressive" majority was supported by the country at large. To combat it, Bismarck had his own genius and daring and the support of the Emperor: nothing more.

A. INTERNAL POLITICS

In the conflict with his parliament, Bismarck went frankly and directly to the point immediately after he assumed office. In his first conference with the Budget committee of the lower chamber he made his position clear. He warned the committee not to exaggerate the powers of its chamber, for a budget was not decided by the lower chamber alone, but by joint action of the lower chamber, the upper chamber, and the crown. Then, after dwelling somewhat on the attitude of the parliament toward the constitution and on the new liberalism throughout the country, he sounded in a famous phrase what later came to be regarded as the keynote of all his policy: "Not by speeches and majority votes are the great questions of the time decided — that was the great blunder of 1848 and 1849 — but by blood and iron."

Bismarck's attitude produced a very bad impression. His words seemed reckless. He was considered a bully, a *Junker* of the type so unpleasantly familiar to Prussia in the absolutist days of Frederick William IV. His arrogant self-confidence before the committee, his cynicism and occasional sarcastic hits, offended his hearers. What was he, a new and untried minister whose lease of office might extend but a few days or at most a month, to warn a legislative committee not to exaggerate its powers! And what right had he, an open and avowed reactionary, to criticize the events of 1848 and 1849 whereby the liberals had gained from the reluctant King Frederick William IV their prized constitution! And above all, what did these references to blood and iron mean? That arms were to be used and blood shed?

The dismay which had been aroused in the parliament communicated itself to the King, who at the moment was in Baden-Baden. Bismarck's position was indeed precarious. His enemies were busy intriguing to undermine his influence with the King, and the King was, in the situation, absolutely his only support. We have from Bismarck's own pen a graphic account of how he retained the King's support after the convulsion caused by the "blood and iron" speech:

"In the beginning of October I went as far as Jüterbogk to meet the King, who had been at Baden-Baden for September 30, his wife's birthday, and waited for him in the still unfinished railway station, filled with third-class travellers and workmen, seated in the dark on an overturned wheelbarrow. My object in taking this opportunity for an interview was to set his Majesty at rest about a speech made by me in the Budget Commission on September 30, which had aroused some excitement, and which, though not taken down in shorthand, had still been reproduced with tolerable accuracy in the newspapers. . . .

"I had some difficulty in discovering from the curt answers of the officials the carriage in the ordinary train, in which the King was seated by himself in an ordinary first-class carriage. The after-effect of his association with his wife was an obvious depression, and when I begged for permission to narrate the events which had occurred during his absence, he interrupted me with the words: 'I can perfectly well see where all this will end. Over there, in front of the Opera House, under my windows, they will cut off your head, and mine a little while afterwards.'

"I guessed, and it was afterwards confirmed by witnesses, that during his week's stay at Baden his mind had been worked upon with variations on the theme of Polignac, Strafford, and Louis XVI. When he was silent, I answered with the short remark, '*Et après, Sire.*' '*Après*, indeed; we shall be dead,' answered the King. 'Yes,' I continued, 'then we shall be dead; but we must all die sooner or later, and can we perish more honourably? I, fighting for my King's cause, and your Majesty sealing with your own blood your rights as King by the grace of God; whether on the scaffold or the battlefield, makes no difference to the glory of sacrificing life and limb for the rights assigned to you by the grace of God. Your Majesty must not think of Louis XVI; he lived and died in a condition of mental weakness, and does not present a heroic figure in history. Charles I, on the other hand, will always remain a noble historical character, for after drawing his sword for his rights and losing the battle, he did not hesitate to confirm his royal intent with his blood. Your Majesty is bound to fight, you cannot capitulate; you must, even at the risk of bodily danger, go forth to meet any attempt at coercion.'

"As I continued to speak in this sense, the King grew more and more animated, and began to assume the part of an officer fighting for kingdom and fatherland. In presence of external and personal danger he possessed a rare and absolutely natural fearlessness, whether on the field of battle or in the face of attempts on his life; his attitude in any external danger was elevating and inspiring. The ideal type of the Prussian officer who goes to meet certain death in the service with the simple words, 'At your orders,' but who, if he has to act on his own responsibility, dreads the criticism of his superior officer or of the world more than death, even to the extent of allowing his energy and correct judgment to be impaired by the fear of blame and reproof — this type was developed in him to the highest degree. Hitherto, on his journey, he had only asked himself whether, under the superior criticism of his wife and public opinion in Prussia, he would be able to keep steadfast on the road on which he was entering with me. The influence of our conversation in the dark railway compartment counteracted this sufficiently to make him regard the part which the situation forced upon him more from the standpoint of the officer. He felt as though he had been touched in his military honour, and was in the position of an officer who has orders to hold a certain position to the death, no matter whether he perishes in the task or not. This set him on a course of thought which was quite familiar to him; and in a few minutes he was restored to the confidence which he had lost at Baden, and even recovered his cheerfulness. To give up his life for King and fatherland was the duty of an officer; still more that of a King, as the first officer in the land. As soon as he regarded his position from the point of view of military honour, it had no more terror for him than the command to defend what might prove a desperate position would have for any ordinary Prussian officer. This raised him above the anxiety about the criticism which public opinion, history, and his wife might pass on his political tactics. He fully entered into the part of the first officer in the Prussian monarchy, for whom death in the service would be an honourable conclusion to the task assigned him. The correctness of my judgment was confirmed by the fact that the King, whom I had found at Jüterbogk weary, depressed, and discouraged, had, even before we arrived at Berlin, developed a cheerful, I might almost say joyous and combative disposition, which was plainly evident to the ministers and officials who received him on his arrival."

The committee of parliament stood by its convictions and recommended to its chamber a resolution requiring the government to introduce the budget for 1863, and declaring that expenditure of funds definitely refused by the chamber was unconstitutional. The house adopted its committee's report. The budget was passed without provision for the army reorganization and increase, and, when presented to the upper chamber, was amended to conform to Bismarck's wishes and returned to the lower chamber. This action suited Bismarck well, for the responsibility for conflict was now to a certain extent shared by him with the upper house. There existed a legislative deadlock, the lower house refusing to incorporate into the budget the money for army reorganization and increase, the upper house refusing to pass a budget without such provisions.

Each house persisted in its attitude. In the midst of the struggle the parliament was prorogued and the session of 1862 closed.

In this condition of affairs Bismarck took advantage of the failure of the constitution to make a definite statement of what should be done in case of legislative deadlock. No budget at all had been passed. The lower chamber had acted within its rights under the constitution in amending the government's budget, the upper house had likewise acted within its rights in rejecting the budget as amended by the lower house; yet the result was that after each house had acted within its constitutional rights, no budget had passed, no measure for paying the legitimate expenses of the government for 1863 had become law when the year 1863 began. The government, however, could not cease to function. It could not be expected to discharge even that army which it had, to dismiss its ambassadors, to shut up and vacate government offices. Bismarck therefore interpreted the lack of definite constitutional provision against parliamentary deadlock as allowing him to continue for the year the financial provisions of the preceding year. This interpretation suited his purpose admirably, for in the preceding year (1862) the parliament had grudgingly provided for the increased army. By his interpretation, therefore, he gained his end exactly as though definite financial provision had been made for the governmental policies.

Bismarck continued thus to interpret the constitution for the benefit of the government so long as the period of conflict continued. When parliament met at the beginning of 1863, the lower house moved and carried an address to the sovereign accusing the ministers of having violated the constitution and demanding their dismissal. The King refused to receive the committee appointed to deliver the address, and criticized the stubbornness and presumption of the chamber. As the session continued, von Bismarck and von Roon in their tilts with the chamber became so offensive that the President attempted to check them, whereat they refused to attend the sessions altogether until they should be allowed free speech. Again the chamber appealed to the King for the dismissal of his ministers, and again the King refused and strongly criticized the attitude of the assembly. At the end of May the parliament was again prorogued, and a few days later an edict was promulgated for the suppression of freedom of the press. The conditions as thus briefly outlined continued with increased bitterness of feeling until after the Austro-Prussian war.

In a country thoroughly accustomed to parliamentary government, or more thoroughly accustomed to the privileges and rights conferred by a constitution, such arbitrary actions would have resulted in revolution. In Prussia, however, the people had as yet scarcely realized the meaning and value of their new constitution. Although it had been in force for more than a dozen years, it had, as we have stated, been so "interpreted" during most of those years by Frederick William IV and his advisers that its provisions had been almost nullified. The aggressive determination of the government to carry through its policy was in line with the nature of all government in Prussia up to the accession of William I, and, though protested vigorously by liberals in parliament, was accepted by the country at large without sign of actual rebellion. The people continued to pay their taxes to the government, thus furnishing it with the necessary revenue to maintain its policy. Undoubtedly economic prosperity favored Bismarck. During these years of political conflict and bitter animosity between government and parliament, the country grew rapidly in material wealth. The government's taxes were easily met, and popular discontent was difficult to arouse when the people were able to enjoy a higher standard of living than they had known for a generation past. Thus, aided by conditions within Prussia — the habit of obedience to authority ingrained through long custom in the people, and unusual economic prosperity — Bismarck was able to keep the pledge that he made to the King when he took office, namely, that he would carry through the reorganization of the army even in opposition to the majority in parliament and its resolution.

B. FOREIGN DIPLOMACY

Before he accepted the post of head of the ministry, Bismarck's unerring judgment had told him that the final justification for his high-handed action in domestic politics would lie with the success or failure of his foreign policy. At the same time that he accepted the leadership in the ministry, he took the post of minister of foreign affairs in order that he himself might handle the many difficult problems involved in international diplomacy. In this field he was to prove himself supreme. All his experience at Frankfort, in Russia, and France, and in the many delicate missions he had been called upon to undertake in the years following 1851, and all the knowledge he had gained of the characters of the leading contemporary statesmen, were called into play during the next few years. As we look back from this distance we can see how he towered above the men of his time. The statesmen in England, France, Austria, and Russia failed entirely to fathom his designs or to cope with his intrigues. In international diplomacy Bismarck was a genius moving among men of little minds.

i. *Bismarck and Russia*

Bismarck had himself been in Russia at the time of the great changes accompanying the emancipation of the serfs. He knew the Czar Alexander and was well aware of his desire for reform. He realized, further, how completely Austria had alienated Russia by her attitude during the Crimean War. He sought, therefore, for an opportunity to render to Russia some signal service which would bind this powerful state to Prussia by ties of gratitude. His chance came with the Polish rebellion of 1863, which in turn arose out of the false hopes excited by Alexander's reforms.

Once the Russian Czar had entered upon the path of reform, he found new demands being constantly made upon him. Even in the midst of the turmoil of readjustments due to the emancipation of the serfs, the liberals in the empire pressed for radical measures of further reform. The reorganization of the army and navy, shown to be necessary by the experiences of the Crimean War, was begun in 1862; a Commission set at work in the same year upon a thorough reconstruction of the judiciary and legal procedure; another commission struggled with the problem of creating representative political bodies for local government; and the Czar's ministers were adopting various measures to stimulate the growth of commerce and industry in all parts of the country.

The benevolent reforms of Alexander had been extended to Poland, but, instead of placating the Poles, had resulted in inciting them to impossible demands and ambitions. In March of 1861 the Czar by an imperial decree endeavored to conciliate Poland by granting it a separate Ministry of Instruction and Public Worship, and by establishing in all the districts and provinces elective boards with authority to present a statement of the local wishes and necessities to a Council of State at Warsaw, the capital. A year later (1862), still further concessions were granted, one being the reopening of the University of Warsaw which had been closed in 1832, and another the adoption of Polish as the official language. That summer Alexander appointed his brother Viceroy at Warsaw, and replaced by Poles all the Russian governors of Polish provinces. But the Poles wanted, not reforms, but independence, with their ancient territorial boundaries. The Polish magnates, the nobility, were wealthy and powerful, and believed that they faced an opportunity to reëstablish Poland in its ancient grandeur. Early in 1863, a revolution broke out.

All Europe sympathized with the Poles. The governments of Great Britain, France, and Austria united in presenting proposals for Polish autonomy and in remonstrating against the severity of the measures being prepared for the suppression of the rebellion. Popular feeling in Great Britain, France, and Austria supported the governments. The glories of ancient Poland were rehearsed, the bitter injustice of the eighteenth century partitions of Poland was recalled, the long struggle of the Poles for liberty and the feats of individual Poles in aiding other peoples to gain their freedom were emphasized. Western Europe was inspired with a sincere enthusiasm for the Polish cause. And even in Prussia and throughout Germany, popular sentiment was united in favor of the Poles. The liberal party, true to its principles, looked upon the Poles as fighting the fight of progress against reaction, of liberalism against autocracy.

Bismarck, however, in politics and diplomacy was not to be swayed by emotion, but by expediency. He did not ask whether the Polish rebellion were just, but whether its success would be a good or a bad thing for Prussia. In this question as in all, he decided and acted with an eye to what he conceived to be Prussian interests. And in his opinion, the success of the Polish rebellion would have weakened Prussia, for, in the first place, the Polish nobles would seek to incorporate in the regenerated Poland the provinces which in the eighteenth century partitions had fallen to Prussia's share, and in the second place, the success of a liberal rebellion in Poland would encourage the forces of liberal rebellion in Prussia. He had been disgusted with the German sympathy with the Poles in 1848; and now, in 1863, he despised what he believed to be the hasty and ill-considered sympathy of the mass of people for the revolutionists.

Believing as he did, Bismarck had two courses open to him: to remain passive, or to aid Russia actively. The Prussian people wished and expected him to join England, France, and Austria in their joint representations and remonstrances, so that even passive neutrality would have disappointed them. Their bitter anger can be imagined when it became known that the King (of course by advice of Bismarck) had written an autograph letter to the Czar proposing that the two governments should take steps in mutual accord to cope with the common danger. A convention was agreed upon whereby the rebels might be pursued across the border by either government. Two Prussian army corps were mobilized and stationed along the Polish frontier.

The results of Bismarck's policy, so far as the success of the Polish rebellion was concerned, were immediate and decisive. Aided by the cordon of troops on the Prussian side, the Russians had, by the Spring of 1864, pitilessly exterminated the rebels. In the readjustment of political relations, Poland lost all of the peculiar rights she had previously possessed, and was reduced to a mere province of Russia. The peasants were freed and made proprietors of the land they occupied. The Russian government undertook a campaign to Russianize Poland, to suppress the Polish language, religion, and customs in favor of the Russians.

The results, so far as internal affairs in Prussia were concerned, were to increase the hatred of the liberals for Bismarck. On the floor of the lower chamber the liberal leaders in carefully prepared attacks assailed the government's position. With a freedom of speech not exceeded in the most democratic state they protested that Bismarck's action had isolated Prussia among the civilized states of Europe and had endangered her very existence.

The results, so far as external political relations were concerned, were at first dangerous, and later, as Bismarck had foreseen, very favorable for Prussia. Bismarck's act aroused the most intense feeling among the nations which had protested to the Czar. There was actual danger that they would unite and wage war on Prussia: indeed, Napoleon III did propose that Great Britain, France, and Austria should in identical notes remonstrate with and threaten Prussia. Great Britain, however, holding fast to her previous policy of non-interference, refused to consent to this joint action. France and Austria alone dared not attack united Russia and Prussia. In the meanwhile, Prussia had gained the warm gratitude and friendship of Russia. Bismarck by his act had assured Russian supremacy in Poland; he had foiled active intervention by Great Britain, France, and Austria; he had been willing to risk war in support of the Russian Czar's authority. The impulsive gratitude of the Czar and of the Russian people, and their hatred of Austria, assured Bismarck that in Prussia's inevitable struggle with Austria he could count upon Russian friendly neutrality. Prussia was no longer politically isolated.

ii. *Bismarck and Austria*

Both the domestic policy and the Russian policy were, however, subordinate to the policy of Prussia toward Austria. Bismarck believed that he was guiding Prussia through trials that meant life or death for her. The supreme one of these trials would be the struggle with Austria for supremacy in German affairs. The perspective through which we now see events of that period shows that Bismarck was right. The great states of Europe had latent ambitions which, if fulfilled, would have meant the partial dismemberment of Prussia and her definite relegation to the place of a second-rate power. For example, France desired the territory to the left of the Rhine for the acquirement of what she believed to be her "natural boundaries"; the King of Saxony still hoped for the restoration of the Saxon boundaries of 1814; and Austria had never ceased to lament the loss of Silesia, wrested from her by Frederick the Great. Bismarck had a clearer conception of these perils than those legislators who refused to appropriate funds for the increase and reorganization of the army, that sole safeguard against foreign aggression. Furthermore, Bismarck believed that he saw in the success against Austria the means for elevating Prussia above the worst of these perils. History now acknowledges the sincere patriotism which actuated him, and the Prussian nation pays him its homage as its one wise man in a crucial period.

Austria was at the moment in the throes of the severe internal crisis caused by Hungarian disaffection. The Hungarian Diet, led by the patriot Deák, resolutely refused to accept the constitution promulgated by Francis Joseph in 1861, denied the legality of laws not approved by itself, and sent no delegates to the newly created Imperial Council (Reichsrath). Finally the Emperor, resorting again to force, established military rule throughout all of Hungary, though he was careful to declare that such military rule was to last only until the constitution could be put into operation. The Imperial Council, which was practically a parliament of the whole empire, met in May of 1861 and continued in session until December of 1862, but of course without the Hungarian delegates.

The Imperial Council (Reichsrath) in the years following failed dismally to solve the problems underlying the discontent in the empire. The persistent opposition of Hungary, and the withdrawal of the Czech delegates of Bohemia, after finding themselves insulted, oppressed, and without hope of procuring the revision of their own unjust constitutional laws, practically nullified all of the Reichsrath's work. The progress of the nation toward insolvency continued with alarming deficits of about fifty million florins a year. The members of the Reichsrath themselves recognized the failure of the government and were from 1864 onwards, opposed to the imperial cabinet. The last session ended in July, 1865.

Francis Joseph himself was at last convinced of the failure of the system established by his "Diploma" of October, 1860, and was ready to welcome any practicable suggestions for information. Deák, who, so long as the Vienna government had refused to be conciliatory, had inspired the obstinate opposition of the Hungarian patriots, now in 1865 formulated in two declarations a program of constitutional changes which would satisfy Hungary. The Emperor, Francis Joseph, received these declarations with unfeigned satisfaction, especially Deák's statement: "We are always prepared to take any legal measures to modify our laws so as to secure the safety and solidarity of the monarchy." In September of 1865 Francis Joseph suspended the "February Patent," thus repudiating the whole scheme. The Magyar leaders in Hungary, the Czech leaders in Bohemia, and the Slavs and Poles in their respective provinces joyfully formulated their demands and presented them to the Emperor. And just at this critical moment, the war-clouds lowered and broke.

Yet at this period the internal conflict was by no means the only serious problem confronting Austria. Her position in the German Confederation was, in the ideals of her Emperor and his ministers, one of her chief interests. Francis Joseph's emphasis upon Austrian primacy among the German states can be better understood when it is realized that he was the inheritor of a tradition extending back to the first Hapsburg Holy Roman Emperor, Rudolph, who was elected in 1273. Thus Austria and the Austrian Emperor, head of the Hapsburg House, had been the leader in German affairs for six centuries. Even though after the middle of the sixteenth century the Holy Roman Empire had but a shadow of its former prestige, and even though in 1806 it officially ceased to exist, yet in German affairs the Hapsburg House retained the prestige of six hundred years of leadership. No monarch in Europe fell heir to a prouder tradition.

It was in her attempt to maintain her position in the German Confederation that Austria's ambitions came into conflict with Bismarck's conception of Prussia's rights. In Austrian eyes, Prussia was an upstart nation: in Bismarck's opinion, Austria was bent upon humiliating Prussia, and relegating her to second place, an indignity to which no country of Prussia's wealth and power should submit. Prussia did not have the long tradition of leadership in the Holy Roman Empire behind her, it was true, but the history of the House of Brandenburg had been honorable and successful. Bismarck counted present strength more than past glory. Absolutely unemotional in diplomacy and statecraft, and unscrupulous in method, he was not overawed by Austrian traditions or delicate about the means by which he planned to overthrow Austrian power.

Bismarck's first check to Austrian policies in the German Confederation was delivered a few months after he accepted the post at the head of the ministry. In July of 1863 Francis Joseph attempted to settle decisively the German question. He invited all the German princes to a meeting at Frankfort, whereat he expected to gain their approval of a "reform" in the Confederation which would give the central authority permanently to Austria and her friends. Francis Joseph in person tried to persuade William I to attend this conference, but Bismarck, believing that a conference under Austrian auspices would increase Austrian prestige among the German states, used every effort, even to a threat of resignation, to induce his royal master to refuse. Bismarck has left us an account of the difficulty he had in carrying his point:

"It was not an easy task to decide the King to stay away from Frankfort. I exerted myself for that purpose during our drive from Wildbad to Baden, when, on account of the servants on the box, we discussed the German question in the small open carriage in French. By the time we reached Baden I thought I had convinced my master. But there we found the King of Saxony, who was commissioned by all the princes to renew the invitation to Frankfort (August 19). My master did not find it easy to resist that move. He repeated over and over again: 'Thirty reigning princes and a King to take their messages!' Moreover he loved and honored the King of Saxony, who of all the princes had personally most vocation for such a mission. Not until midnight did I succeed in obtaining the King's signature to a refusal to the King of Saxony. When I left my master, both he and I were ill and exhausted by the nervous tension of the situation."

Bismarck's success in keeping the King of Prussia from the Frankfort convention nullified all efforts of the Austrian Emperor to accomplish the results he desired, or indeed, any results at all. The smaller states knew too well that any decision by a convention which did not include Prussian representatives would be subject to protest; and a protest by a state of the size and strength of Prussia meant a threat of war. Above all things the smaller states desired to prevent war, whose issue would probably mean their own extinction within the boundaries of the successful belligerent. Thus Francis Joseph's plans came to naught because Bismarck succeeded in persuading William I not to join the other princes at Frankfort.

iii. *The Schleswig-Holstein Issue*

Bismarck made his attitude toward Austria sufficiently clear in the Frankfort convention matter, but the next issue which rose between the two nations called for all of his adroitness and diplomatic skill. His methods are open to the charges of double dealing and unscrupulous perversion of motives, but in passing judgment we must remember two material facts: 1, that he was fencing with experts in diplomatic intrigue, men who for an apparent advantage would stoop to any means; and 2, that he was sincerely and single-mindedly serving the interests of Prussia as he conceived them.

The issue arose concerning the disposition of the two duchies of Schleswig and Holstein, located at the base of the Danish peninsula. At this period (1863) Holstein had over 500,000 inhabitants, practically all Germans. Schleswig, the more northern duchy adjoining Denmark, had approximately 400,000 inhabitants, of whom the majority, something over 250,000, were Germans. Politically the two duchies were united with Denmark, but the union was a personal union due to the fact that the King of Denmark was also Duke of Schleswig and Holstein. The duchies were not incorporated into the Danish kingdom. Holstein was a member of the German Confederation, giving to its Duke (the King of Denmark) a representation in the German Diet. Schleswig was unattached.

The issue was forced over the position of Schleswig. For a full generation this question had been an acute issue in European international politics. In a conference at London in 1852 the diplomats had attempted to settle it by agreement upon a *London Protocol* providing that the same individual might be King of Denmark and the Duke of Schleswig, but further providing that the duchy should not be incorporated into the Danish kingdom. Under the provisions of this Protocol the duchy had existed, with more or less friction between the German and Danish elements in its population, until Denmark itself precipitated a crisis in 1863. The Danish parliament then adopted, and the King proclaimed, a new constitution incorporating Schleswig into Denmark. As it chanced, the Danish King, Frederick VII, died within a few days after the proclamation of the new constitution; but the situation was not changed, for his successor, Christian IX, confirmed his action three days after accession to the throne.

At once popular feeling throughout Germany was aroused. Sympathy was wholly with the German majority in the Duchy who desired Schleswig admitted into the German Confederation as a new member. The act of Denmark was clearly a breach of the London Protocol. The Diet of the Confederation protested vigorously and, after a short delay, authorized the sending of an army into the duchies to prevent the consummation of Denmark's plans. All Germany supported this move.

At this point Bismarck's manipulation of the situation began. He had declared in the very year in which he became chancellor that the Danish question could be settled only by war. He had no desire to see a new state in the German Confederation, especially a state which might lean toward the support of Austria's prestige. He had no sympathy with the German sentiment which anticipated the existence of a new German state just because it added one more state to the confederation. He did not care to consider the rights and wrongs of the rival claimants to the dukedom after the death of the Danish King (1863). He thought he saw a chance so to manage the question as to incorporate ultimately the two duchies into Prussia.

He proceeded cautiously at first. He declined to assent to the Diet's proposal to send an army of the confederation into the duchy on the ground that the cause of the trouble was primarily a breach of the Protocol of 1852 and did not concern the confederation. He then entered into negotiations with the Austrian government, representing that the movement for the independence of Schleswig and Holstein and their admission into the German confederation was the result of radical and revolutionary propaganda, and that the two governments should act in concert to prevent the settlement of the question by such doubtful means. The widespread agitation and the inflammatory addresses throughout Germany gave some color to his representations. By thus working on Austrian fears of radicalism, he persuaded her to agree to join Prussia in military action against Denmark on the avowed ground that it was the duty of Austria and Prussia, as signatories of the Protocol of 1852, to enforce the provisions of that document upon Denmark. This formal agreement between these two powers, signed on January 16, 1864, provided for: (1) a demand upon Denmark for the withdrawal of the November Constitution within 48 hours; (2) independent joint action by Prussia and Austria if the Confederate Diet refused to join proposed measures; (3) the preparation of the necessary military forces; (4) the suppression of possible hostile demonstrations in case of the occupation of Schleswig; (5) the acceptance of a conference of powers only after the withdrawal of the November Constitution; and (6) further consultation in case of interference by either power. While this agreement between Austria and Prussia was under consideration, the Confederate Diet also discussed the questions involved and protested against the measures proposed. Whereupon the lesser states were informed that Austria and Prussia would not be bound by the decisions of the Diet, but would proceed to act as two great powers. Bismarck thereupon dispatched to Denmark, on the sixteenth of January, the very day the agreement was signed, the joint Austro-Prussian ultimatum demanding the immediate repeal of the constitution and giving the impossibly short time of forty-eight hours for compliance. The triumph of Bismarck's diplomacy in winning over Austria to a policy of joint action may be better appreciated when it is remembered that but a few months before Prussia had ruined Austria's plans for a reform of the confederation by refusing to join the Congress of the Princes at Frankfort.

Bismarck's purpose was not at the moment clearly understood in Prussia or in Germany, and of course not in Austria. Bismarck afterwards said: "From the very beginning I kept annexation before my eyes, without losing sight of the other gradations." At the moment, however, Austria, the people of Prussia, and Germany believed that the impending Danish war was to be fought in defense of the London Protocol of 1852, and they looked forward at the conclusion of the war to the admission of Schleswig to the

German Confederation. Popular sentiment favored this course. Even such a close friend of Bismarck as von Roon, the minister of war, favored it. Above all, the King himself, to whom Bismarck gradually unfolded his real ambitions, favored this course. Bismarck stood alone in Prussia and in Germany. His most difficult task was to persuade the King to support his policy. "Without having investigated the complicated legal questions of the succession," wrote Bismarck in later years with respect to the King's attitude, "he stuck to his motto: 'I have no right to Holstein.'" Bismarck resorted, as he had previously done in the matter of the Frankfort convention, to a threat of resignation before he could win over the reluctant King to his policy.

In Denmark, the ultimatum could not be accepted. Even had the new King of Denmark been disposed to recede from his position and withdraw the constitution, he had to have the consent of his parliament; and the time given for answer, two days, was insufficient for the necessary procedure. The King felt, however, that he had his people united in his support and more than reasonable expectation of foreign intervention in his favor, so he adopted a firm attitude. On January 31, 1864, in preparation for the advance into Schleswig, Prussia and Austria announced that the integrity of Denmark would be respected, and that they were willing to take part in a European conference; but that if Denmark opened hostilities, all treaty stipulations were annulled and foreign interference would make the fate of Denmark all the more severe.

iv. *The Danish War*

When King William of Prussia gave the word which started the combined armies of Austria and Prussia, he set in motion for the first time that splendid military machine for which Bismarck had contended so vigorously in the Landtag. Three corps moved forward: the two Prussian corps under

Prince Frederick Charles, and General von der Mülbe, and the Austrian corps under Field Marshal von Gablenz. From Great Britain came vague threats and a demand for a conference of the signers of the London Protocol from Lord Palmerston; from nearer home came protests from the smaller German states who saw danger for themselves in these aggressive moves of Prussia. Hanover remonstrated with Bismarck against the march through her territory; Hamburg, Lübeck, and Eutin likewise raised their voices in formal protest against the entrance of the Prussian troops. But in vain. Bismarck's only concession was to bring the Austrian troops north by way of Silesia to avoid their crossing Saxony or Bavaria. By the end of January, 1864, the allied armies were at the Eider River.

Field Marshal von Wrangel, who had been given command of the allied armies, was past eighty years of age. He had gained a splendid reputation as an officer, but as a commander-in-chief he was lacking in several essential qualities — sound and sure judgment, firmness of decision, a broad view of strategical matters, and equability of temper. He commanded an army, however, in which the invigorating influence of von Moltke was already beginning to be felt. Men and officers alike were well trained and well disciplined, and the organization was equal to that of any army in Europe. Moreover, the Prussians possessed a great advantage over their northern enemy in that they were armed with the needle-gun, a breech-loading, bolt-action rifle which was the forerunner of the modern military rifle. In the light of present-day knowledge of small arms, the needle-gun, with its slender firing pin so easily broken, with its device for checking the gas escape at the breech so crude as to make firing from the shoulder impossible after the first few shots, with its tendency to rapid fouling, — the needle-gun seems but an imperfect weapon with which to go to war. But it could be fired at least three times as rapidly as any other gun then in existence, and to the Danes, armed as they were with the muzzle-loading rifle, the needle-gun must have seemed a very formidable weapon.

The condition of the Danish army presented a complete antithesis to that of the allied powers. In General de Meza, their commander-in-chief, the Danes possessed an able, prudent, and energetic officer. But he was so hampered by two things as to be helpless — a vacillating war department and an untrained army. Denmark did not spend the money on her army that Prussia spent on hers. Though universal service was required, the training of the individual soldier lasted but ten months. The officers, insufficient in number, were underpaid and imperfectly educated to their duties. When the war broke out, the army was suddenly increased to four times its standing strength, and necessary officers were created from whatever material was at hand. Denmark opposed to the allied army of 57,000 splendid soldiers an organization of but 44,000 untrained, undisciplined, poorly officered troops. Of these, the Schleswig contingent was known to be favorable to the Germans.

Denmark possessed one advantage, however, in that her navy, though small, was superior to the Prussian navy, and commanded the Baltic. By its means she hoped to transport her troops, destroy the Prussian ships, and blockade and harass the German seaport towns. To contend successfully against it, the allies made plans to bring Austrian ships from the Mediterranean.

A second advantage for Denmark was the Dannevirke. This was the ancient frontier line of defense between Danes and Germans, extending west from Schleswig city, on that arm of the Baltic known as the Schlei, to the headwaters of the Rheide River, a distance of 10½ miles. It was first built in the ninth century, and since then had been many times taken and retaken. After its last defense in 1848, it had been rebuilt and fortified until in 1864 it was considered well-nigh impregnable. Napoleon III said that the Germans would halt two years before it. To the eastward on the Schlei, the position was still further strengthened by fortifications at Missunde, a crossing point of the Schlei. The western flank of the Dannevirke was protected by the rivers Rheide and Treene, and by the low swamps and bogs along their banks. On a total front of forty-three miles, from the Treene River to the Baltic proper, the Danes extended their army of 44,000, with the bulk of it — some 29,000 — at the Dannevirke itself. Here, behind their fortifications, they awaited the attack of the Prussians.

To von Moltke making his preparations, the Danish plan was plain. He did not purpose to wear out his army in assaults upon a strongly fortified position. Nor did he mean to waste time in besieging the fortified towns of Düppel and Fredericia. To him the success of the Danes lay in one army: his own success lay in defeating that army in Jutland before it could withdraw from island to island in the archipelago and draw out the war interminably. His plan, therefore, was as follows: to cross the Schlei at some weakly defended point east of Missunde, meanwhile making demonstrations in front of the Dannevirke; to fall upon the Danes' left flank; prevent their retreat to Düppel; to drive them to the west, and there annihilate them. Then when his armies had overrun Jutland and the islands of Fünen and Alsen, he felt that Prussia could make what terms she would.

The plan as outlined was without flaw. Unfortunately, though, in transmitting it to von Wrangel, the King did not see the necessity for insisting upon details. Accordingly, he instructed his commander-in-chief upon two points only of von Moltke's plan, viz.: the Danes must not be allowed to reach a point of embarkation, and their retreat to Düppel must be cut off. The remaining details were left to von Wrangel. The commander at once proceeded to depart very markedly from von Moltke's plan in that he determined that the flanking party to the east should attack at Missunde and cross there, instead of nearer the sea where the Schlei was unfortified and only feebly defended. Prince Frederick Charles was to undertake this attempt on Missunde while the Austrians attacked Schleswig, and the other Prussian corps advanced against the western wing of the Danes. This was the first departure from the plan of the Chief of Staff. If the Prince should be successful in his assault, he was to cross the Schlei and move at once on Düppel without attacking the Danes in flank. Here was the second deviation from von Moltke's plan.

On the morning of the first of February, 1864, Prussians and Austrians crossed the Eider and marched on the Dannevirke. The Danes resisted them in minor engagements only, so that by noon of the second the Prussians were before Missunde, and by the third the Austrians confronted the advanced posts before the Dannevirke. Prince Frederick Charles began the storming of the forts immediately. For three hours Missunde withstood the fire of sixty-four Prussian cannon, whereupon the Prince, seeing that the loss was almost entirely with his own army, determined to give up the attack and cross elsewhere. He desisted from the attempt, obtained permission from von Wrangel to force a passage farther to the east, and on the morning of the sixth, effected a crossing without opposition.

Meanwhile the Austrians had been completely successful. The Danes fell back behind the Dannevirke, and the Austrians planted their cannon before the fortifications. The third corps (Prussian), which was advancing against the western wing of the Danish army, now discovered that the severe cold had frozen the swamps and marshes which the allies had expected to be a serious obstacle. Without opposition this corps arrived at the fortifications. General de Meza knew of this weakening of his defenses by the weather, saw the futility of resistance, and determined upon an immediate evacuation of the Dannevirke. There were two alternatives, — to make an attack upon the allies in front of his fortifications, or to retreat upon Düppel.

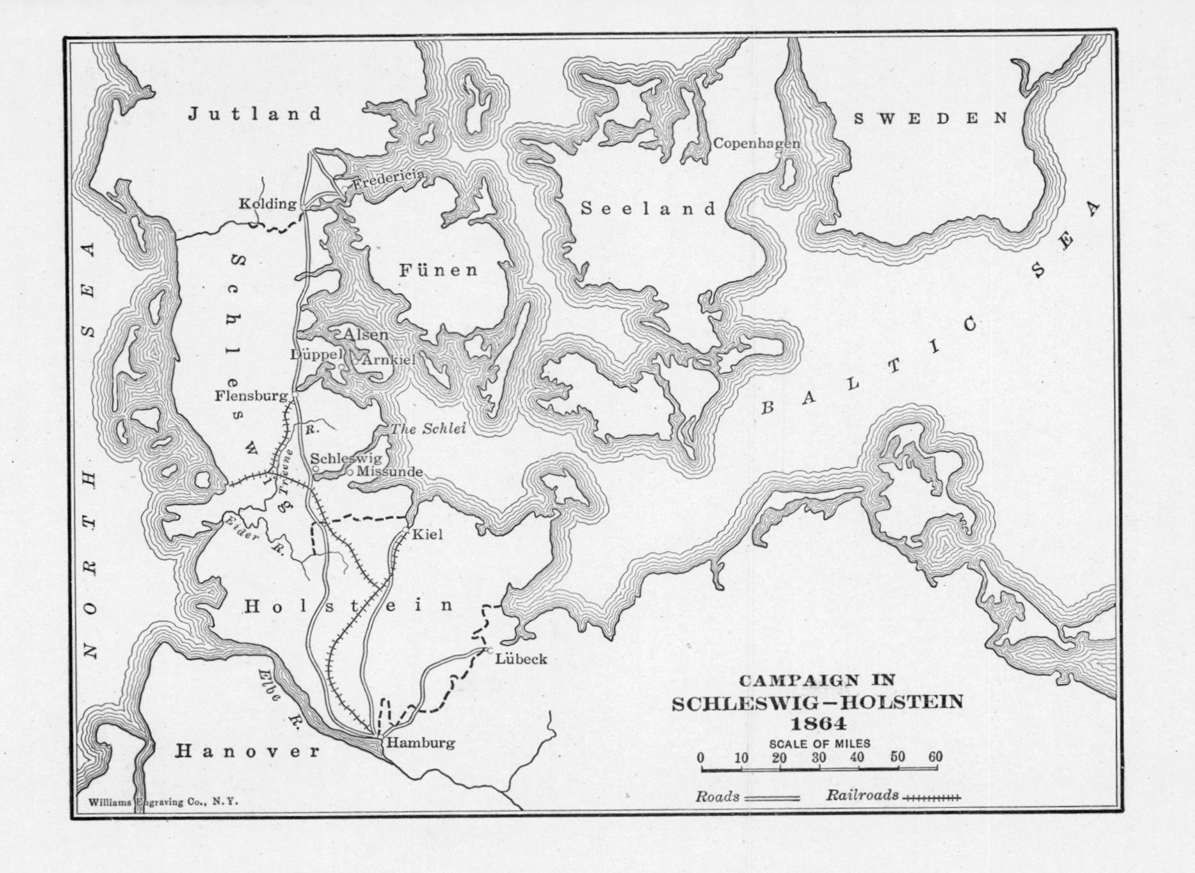
Jutland
SWEDEN
Copenhagen
Seeland
Fredericia
Kolding
Fünen
BALTIC SEA
NORTH SEA
Schleswig
Alsen
Düppel
Arnkiel
Flensburg
The Schlei
Treene R.
Schleswig
Missunde
Eider R.
Kiel
Holstein
Lübeck
Elbe R.
Hamburg
Hanover
CAMPAIGN IN
SCHLESWIG-HOLSTEIN
1864
SCALE OF MILES
0 10 20 30 40 50 60
Roads
Railroads
Williams Engraving Co., N.Y.

Knowing as he did the condition of his army, he could arrive at but one decision, so on the evening of the fifth, he wisely began his retreat to Flensburg. He arrived there safely, sent two brigades of his infantry and all of his cavalry to the north, and transferred the remainder of his army across the gulf of Flensburg to the works at Düppel. When, after crossing the Schlei, Frederick Charles got in touch with the Austrians, the Dannevirke was abandoned and the Danish army was well on its way to Flensburg. Von Moltke's plan was ruined.

The first corps under the Prince was left before Düppel, while the remainder of the allied army pursued the Danes through north Schleswig. There was practically no resistance to the advance northward, and on the eighteenth of February the Prussians crossed the frontier of Jutland and occupied Kolding. This progress was quite to the liking of von Moltke and Bismarck, but unhappily for Prussian aspirations, the whole campaign was halted at this point by the reluctance of Austria. The Emperor Francis Joseph feared the other German states, he feared France, and he feared that a break with Great Britain would mean a coalition of France and Great Britain against the allies. Moreover, the imperial finances were in a hopeless condition, Hungary was on the point of revolt, and there was the usual unrest in Venetia and Galicia. The Emperor's reason as given to Bismarck, however, was a purely military one. He was afraid to advance into Jutland, he said, while Düppel and Fredericia remained in Danish hands. What argument could there be for invading Jutland? Bismarck replied in a very convincing telegram: "The reasons are threefold: reprisals for the capture of German ships, the scattering of the Danish forces, and the breaking down of the Danish resistance to an armistice and conference." These reasons were sufficient to remove the Emperor's objections. The plan as now modified was to lay siege to Düppel but at the same time to continue the occupation of Jutland to prevent attacks from Fredericia. The new agreement between the allies was signed on the fifth of March, and the military orders were issued at once. While the new agreement was under discussion, von Wrangel had developed an opposition to the plan of attacking Düppel, and had failed in several instances to coöperate with the war department. When activities were renewed, the command was given to Crown Prince Frederick — not actually, but virtually, since von Wrangel was to make no dispositions without first consulting the Prince.

While Jutland was being occupied, the siege of Düppel was begun. The fortifications consisted of a curved line of ten redoubts with both flanks resting on Alsen Sound. Within this line a second line of trenches with lunettes was constructed behind the front attacked, and finally, a réduit was built to cover the bridge to Alsen. The Germans began the siege in earnest on the fifteenth of March. Six redoubts were attacked. Heavy guns — twenty-four and thirty pounders — were brought for the siege, until by the time of the assault, a hundred and eighteen were in position. Under fire of these cannon, the parallels were constructed — the first on the thirty-first of March, the second on the eighth of April, and a third, only six hundred feet from the Danish works, on the tenth of April. Prince Frederick Charles had hoped to cut off any possible retreat of the Danes to Alsen by crossing the sound and capturing the bridgehead on the Alsen shore. He made his plans with great secrecy and on the night of April second attempted to cross. The coming of a sudden storm compelled him to abandon this feature of the plan and to rely solely on the mainland attack. He therefore constructed a fourth parallel but four hundred feet in front of the Danish redoubts to make his assault doubly certain. All day of the seventeenth the Prussian batteries kept up a constant fire. At 2 A.M. of the eighteenth they opened again and shelled the works until 10 A.M., when six columns rushed forward to the assault. The result was never for a moment in question, and within half an hour the Prussians were in possession of the redoubts. They were unable, however, to prevent the Danes from withdrawing behind the réduit and thence retreating to Alsen, destroying the bridge behind them. The cost of the success to the allies was the loss of about a thousand men. To an equal Danish loss in killed and wounded was added a loss of thirty-five hundred prisoners, one hundred and fifteen cannon, and four thousand rifles.

The occupation of Jutland was marked by dissension. Von Wrangel wished to attack Fredericia: von Moltke would not hear of it. The Danish troops elsewhere resisted feebly, and soon all Jutland south of Lijm Fjord was in the hands of the Germans. When Düppel fell, the Danes gave up the idea of holding Fredericia. On the twenty-eighth of April, the garrison was transported to Fünen, and the Austrians entered the works. Von Moltke wished to attack Fünen at once, but the Austrian Marshal von Gablenz would not agree, and the plan was dropped.

The war now came to a standstill. Bismarck had acceded to Great Britain's demands for a conference, and the delegates had met in London on April 25. On May 12, a truce of one month was arranged — a truce which was later extended to June 25. In London, by insisting upon incorporating Schleswig with Denmark, the Danish delegates so alienated the neutral powers, that after long debates and extended sessions, the conference came to nothing. The truce was marked in a military way by the succession of Prince Frederick Charles to von Wrangel as commander-in-chief, nominally as well as actually, and by preparations for a descent upon the islands of Alsen and Fünen.

When the truce ended, Prince Frederick Charles again took up the aggressive and arranged for an immediate secret crossing to Alsen. On the night of the twenty-ninth of June, General Herwarth, who had succeeded the Prince as corps commander, assembled his troops on the shore of the sound opposite Arnkiel. He had previously collected here sufficient boats and pontoons to hold twenty-five hundred men, and he had chosen a crossing point of not more than a thousand feet in width. The attempt was successful. Though Herwarth's men were discovered in crossing, the Danes had not sufficient force at hand to resist them. The boats brought reinforcements regularly to the allies, and their troops pressed relentlessly southward. The Danes gave up all hope of resistance, and hastened an embarkation from the southernmost point of the island. By the first of July, except for twenty-five hundred prisoners in the hands of the Prussians, there was not a Dane on Alsen.

This victory marks the ending of official resistance by Denmark. The government asked itself: If Alsen could be taken, why not Fünen? Why not Copenhagen itself? The German armies completed without difficulty the occupation of Jutland, and by July 20 reached the northernmost point of the peninsula. A naval victory for the allies during this same period completed the despondency of the Danes, and they concluded an armistice willingly.

On August 1 a preliminary peace was signed, by which Denmark yielded up all rights in the duchies of Schleswig, Holstein, and Lauenburg, this last named being a very small duchy to the south of the other two. After some further negotiations to determine the exact boundaries and to apportion the duchies' share of the Danish debt, the final treaty of peace was signed at Vienna October 27, 1864.

Bismarck had succeeded in the first stage of his policy. He had forever separated the duchies from Denmark. He had managed to have them handed over to the joint possession of Austria and Prussia. Further, throughout the whole proceedings, he succeeded in having Prussia appear diplomatically in the right and his opponent diplomatically in the wrong, thus giving neither to France nor to England a legitimate excuse for intervention on the side of Denmark.

And still further, in this first step toward the realization of his ambitions, he had been able to enlist Austria on his side, thus forestalling a possible attack upon the Prussian rear while the army was fighting in Denmark. He had every reason to congratulate himself upon the success of his policy. And yet, before the annexation upon which he had set his heart was completed, he had serious problems to solve.

CHAPTER IV

BISMARCK, PRUSSIA, AND EUROPEAN POLITICS, 1864–1866

A. THE SCHLESWIG-HOLSTEIN ADJUSTMENT

THE successful termination of the Danish War by no means solved the Schleswig-Holstein question. The duchies had, it is true, been permanently separated from Denmark, but their ultimate status had not been determined in the treaty of peace, had not indeed been agreed upon by the two countries in their preliminary negotiations before the war. Provisionally, they were jointly administered by the two powers. Such arrangement was temporary, however, and particularly unsatisfactory to Austria, for under any joint administration Prussia would have a distinct advantage over Austria because of her proximity to the duchies. Austria, therefore, desired that the question of succession should be at once determined. She favored the candidacy of Prince Frederick of Augustenburg, under whom it was to be expected that the duchies would be admitted to the confederation. The same desire was held by Germans throughout the confederation and by Prussians. Bismarck, however, was persuading the King to support him in a policy directed toward a different end, namely, the ultimate incorporation of the duchies into Prussia. It was necessary in pursuance of this policy to prevent the Prince of Augustenburg from obtaining the throne. The Prussian chancellor could not give an absolute and unqualified refusal to Austria, for such action would have put Prussia in the wrong before Germany and the rest of Europe, and also might have revealed too clearly his real intentions. So Bismarck delayed the decision by questioning the validity of Augustenburg's claim to the duchies and by proposing an investigation into the merits of all the claims which had been presented. On its face this proposal seemed fair and just, for no one could deny that Augustenburg's claim was legally doubtful, since his father had definitely renounced his right to the duchies in favor of the King of Denmark, and no one could deny that the rights of other claimants should be investigated. Bismarck's hope was that before such investigation should be completed he might so intrigue as to be able to invite war with Austria and thus cast the final disposition of the duchies (and of the larger question concerning Prussian primacy in Germany) to the decision of force. When Austria showed herself disposed to urge still further the Prince's cause, Bismarck assented on the condition that Prussia, in order to prevent Danish aggression, should be allowed to have control of the army and finances in the duchies. Naturally, as Bismarck had expected, both Austria and the Prince rejected these terms, so the question remained open for further parley. Thus, through the remainder of 1864 and the first half of 1865, the Schleswig-Holstein issue was the cause of an almost continuous series of notes and "conversations" between Austria and Prussia. The problem was actually more difficult now that the Danish War was finished.

If Austria had been in good condition internally and externally she would have cut these negotiations short. She would have arbitrarily asserted her will and, by a sufficient show of force, carried her will into execution. But Austria faced civil war within, and strong hostile nations without, her boundaries. Prussia was by no means her only enemy: the Schleswig-Holstein problem was not so serious as the problem presented by her internal affairs.

Hence Austria was forced to accept for the time being an unsatisfactory status for the two duchies. In the convention of Gastein (August 14, 1865), the two great states patched up an agreement whereby Austria undertook to administer Holstein and Prussia Schleswig. Further, Austria, in consideration of a sum of money paid to her by Prussia, yielded up all her claims upon the small duchy of Lauenburg and allowed that territory to be incorporated into Prussia.

The Convention of Gastein was regarded by Bismarck as a mere stop-gap. "We have," said he, "papered over the cracks." It was of no importance in settling the real issue at stake. One element in the convention, the acquisition of Lauenburg by Prussia, was important as it affected the King. Bismarck remarks: "After the Gastein Convention and the occupation of Lauenburg, the first addition made to the kingdom under King William, his frame of mind, so far as I could observe, underwent a psychological change; he developed a taste for conquest." Bismarck himself, realizing that the inevitable conflict with Austria was drawing near, utilized the temporary respite in the endeavor so to arrange the relations of Prussia with other states of Europe that Austria would find no allies in the struggle.

B. THE OTHER POWERS OF EUROPE AND THEIR RELATION TO A POSSIBLE AUSTRO-PRUSSIAN CONFLICT

i. *Russia*

Of Russia's friendly neutrality he felt certain. No change in the relations between Russia and Prussia had occurred to diminish the gratitude Alexander felt for Prussian aid at the time of the Polish rebellion in 1863. Indignation against Austria was still hot in the Czar's empire.

ii. *Great Britain*

Great Britain was during these years gradually transferring her chief interests from European politics to her world commerce. The position of Great Britain in continental affairs just after Waterloo, as contrasted with her position during the years just after 1860, reveals a great decrease in prestige accompanied by a notable increase in material prosperity.

Albert, the Prince Consort, died December 14, 1861, and left Queen Victoria to bear the burden of government alone. The Liberals, led by Palmerston and Russell, with Gladstone as chancellor of the exchequer, had a comfortable working majority in the House of Commons. In spite of the severe distress in the Lancashire mill districts resulting from the Civil War in the United States and the stoppage of cotton supplies, the country was on the whole prospering amazingly. The exports which in 1852 had been £75,000,000 had risen by 1866 to £188,000,000; and the total foreign trade, which was £375,000,000 in 1860, increased to £534,000,000 in the six years. The Liberals claimed for themselves the credit for this abounding prosperity. Gladstone, in his position at the exchequer, had in particular laid the foundations of a reputation which was soon to make him the logical prime minister. Domestic politics were uniformly calm. The most serious issues were to be found in the discussions accompanying the annual budgets.

But this quiet in domestic politics and this increase in material prosperity were accompanied by a great decrease in prestige in foreign affairs. Dreading to interrupt by war or by threat of war the stream of prosperity, the Liberal ministers revealed a weakness which the continental statesmen were quick to realize. Great Britain's doctrine of "splendid isolation" and "non-interference" prevented her from playing an important part in European politics during this period when such momentous changes were taking place. For example, Palmerston, Russell, Gladstone, and all the Liberal leaders sympathized deeply with the Poles in their rebellion of 1863; they wished to lend their moral support to "oppressed nationalities," but they were unwilling to back up their protests by a show or threat of force. They wrote a note to the Czar, and the Czar, supported by Prussia, returned a reply politely telling them to attend to their own affairs. And the matter stopped at that point. Furthermore, British statesmen, as well as the other statesmen of Europe, failed to appreciate the character and ambitions of Bismarck. Bismarck, of course, knew of the British note to Russia and of the Russian reply. He gauged the British spirit by this correspondence. Hence, a year later, when Lord Russell declared that Great Britain "could not see with indifference a military occupation of Holstein, which is only to cease upon terms injuriously affecting the constitution of the whole Danish monarchy," Bismarck paid little attention to the statement, and, with Austria, entered upon the Danish War in full confidence that Great Britain would not support Denmark with force. Hence, too, in 1865 and 1866, Bismarck felt that he could disregard Great Britain and the prospects of British interference in an Austro-Prussian war.

iii. *France*

In France, Napoleon had, as we have seen, passed the time of his greatest popularity. His Italian policy had alienated the strong Catholic party, and his free trade tendencies as illustrated by his commercial agreement with England in 1860 had lost him the support of the powerful manufacturing interests. He had been forced to grant some significant concessions to the liberals in order to gain needed political support in his parliament.

Napoleon was too shrewd not to be aware of the change in sentiment toward him among the people. It was certain that, were the opportunity offered to make a brilliant stroke to recoup his lost prestige, he would eagerly grasp it. Indeed, he had tried to dazzle the French by the prospects of a great Mexican empire under French protection and had wasted precious French lives in that far-off country from 1862 to 1866, only to be thwarted finally by the threatened armed intervention of the United States. It would more than make up for his past failures, however, if he could, during the progress of an Austro-Prussian war, acquire the long-coveted Rhine provinces. Bismarck, knowing Napoleon and fully informed of the political and popular conditions in France, realized that before any decisive steps could be taken against Austria he must come to some understanding with the French Emperor. For this purpose he arranged for a secret meeting with Napoleon.

In October, 1865, Bismarck, ostensibly for the sake of his health, went to take the sea baths at Biarritz in southwestern France. Napoleon and the imperial family chanced also at the same time to be "taking the baths" at Biarritz. For a fortnight Bismarck remained there in close and constant association with the Emperor, exerting himself to be agreeable. "A really great man," writes M. Mérimée, who met him at this time, "free from feeling and full of *esprit.*" Just what understanding Bismarck reached with Napoleon during these days has never been disclosed. He had forcible arguments to use in gaining the good will of the Emperor. He knew that Napoleon favored the principle of nationalities and would thus be inclined to look with satisfaction upon the incorporation of the German-inhabited provinces of Schleswig and Holstein into the Prusso-German state. And he knew that Napoleon was intensely interested in the success of Italy, and would therefore be pleased with a Prussian suggestion of a Prusso-Italian alliance. Undoubtedly Bismarck influenced Napoleon by the use of such baits. The German chancellor's success appeared later. From subsequent events we can be certain that Napoleon agreed to remain neutral in the event of war between Austria and Prussia and to further a Prussian alliance with Italy, and that Bismarck dangled before the Emperor's eyes the hope of territorial compensation for France in the

Rhine region. The two parted on good terms. Napoleon anticipated an Austro-Prussian war wherein both states would weaken themselves and thus leave France the sole arbiter of western Europe, free to reimburse herself along the Rhine for her magnanimity in not taking sides against Prussia. Bismarck trusted for the moment in French neutrality and expected after the war to be able to trick Napoleon out of his expected reward.

iv. *Italy*

Bismarck's next step was to approach Italy (in accordance with his understanding with Napoleon) in an endeavor to form an offensive alliance whereby Italy would attack Austria from the southeast at the same moment Prussia attacked her from the north. Italy was the natural enemy of Austria. Although the grip which Austria had so long had upon the Italian peninsula had been broken by French aid in 1859, the Italians could not forget that Venice was still under Austrian control. It was Bismarck's idea, therefore, to promise that, in the event of Prussia receiving Italian aid, Prussia in the treaty of peace would demand the province of Venetia for Italy.

Italy, since her unity and freedom, had found difficult problems and was struggling hard to solve them. After Cavour's death in 1861, his power fell into weaker and less experienced hands. No one man had the force of character and the grasp of affairs that had enabled Cavour in the critical days of the formation of the kingdom to gain his success for his King. These later leaders debated at one moment the necessity of constructing good roads and railroads, of encouraging industry and commerce, of organizing a strong police force to cope with the bandits who infested all the middle and southern parts of the country; and at the next moment they secretly connived at some wild scheme, like that of Garibaldi to arouse the Italian people and march in a body to seize Rome. Neither domestic nor foreign policy was marked by wise persistence and careful foresight. The leaders feared Austria, well knowing that she held in Venetia a gateway by which at will she might pour a disciplined army into the peninsula to win back all that she had lost. They realized also that, should Napoleon's policy change or his power weaken, the new Italy could not long endure. Thus Italy in the years following Cavour's death, impoverished, misgoverned, endangered by foes within and without the peninsula, with the greatest difficulty maintained her national existence. Yet, in the midst of all complexities of domestic and foreign politics, all Italian statesmen held to the cardinal principle that united Italy must include Venice and have Rome as its capital.

The negotiations between Bismarck and the Italian diplomats were very delicate and involved, for neither party completely trusted the other. The Italians feared that Prussia would involve them in war with Austria, and then, for some advantage yielded by Austria, would leave them to their fate. Bismarck on his part feared that Austria, seeing the possibility of attack from both sides, would cede Venetia to Italy, and that thereupon Italy, her end gained, would not assist Prussia by waging war. A wholesome fear and distrust of Napoleon entered into Bismarck's problem, too, for Napoleon's official word could not be implicitly trusted, and an alliance between Austria and France would checkmate all of Bismarck's moves and give France her coveted provinces along the Rhine.

The negotiations, which began in 1865, when the Schleswig-Holstein controversy seemed to be reaching a climax, were broken off at the time of the Gastein convention, and were renewed again in the spring of 1866. They finally culminated in a definite treaty in April. By the provisions of this treaty it was agreed that, if Prussia went to war with Austria within three months upon an issue involving reforms in the German confederation, Italy would at once also declare war; that neither country would make a separate peace; and that Prussia would continue the fighting until the province of Venetia was given up by Austria. It was thus Bismarck's task to provoke an Austro-Prussian war within three months. "I have at last succeeded in determining a King of Prussia to break the intimate relations of his house with that of Austria," he said to one of his confidants, "to conclude a treaty of alliance with Italy, to accept arrangements with imperial France; I am proud of the result."

C. DIPLOMACY LEADING TO THE WAR

As might be expected, events moved with accelerated speed once the Italian alliance was sure. It was Bismarck's intention, however, to place the blame for war upon Austria. He was assisted in this by Austria's military preparations. It had not been possible to keep entirely secret from Austria the Prussian-Italian negotiations. As these negotiations had progressed to a favorable conclusion, Austria disposed her troops along the frontiers from which she might expect attack. The situation became critical. Bismarck injected the issue of reform, according to the treaty stipulations with Italy, by proposing to the diet a scheme, the most important feature of which was the election of a German national parliament by universal suffrage. Austria sought in the German confederation for friends to offset the alliance formed against her and succeeded in pledging to her aid the largest and most important states, including Bavaria, Würtemberg, Saxony, and Hanover. As the tension continued and the purpose of Prussia became more unmistakable, Austria offered to Italy, through Napoleon III, the province of Venetia, provided France and Italy would not prevent Austria from acquiring Silesia from Prussia. Italy was under strong temptation to accept this offer whereby without a war she might gain all that a war could possibly yield her, but her minister, General La Marmora, had too strong a sense of honor, and refused. Shortly afterwards, when relations were strained to the breaking-point, the Austrian ambassador asked Bismarck pointblank if he intended to violate the Gastein Convention, to which the cynical chancellor replied: "No; but you don't think I should tell you if I did."

The anxiety of these days for Bismarck, and the daring of his diplomacy, can with difficulty be imagined. Austria stood with the traditions of centuries of greatness behind her, with the heritage of leadership among the German peoples, and with all the great south-German states of the confederation linked to her in alliance. Prussia was the upstart state seeking to transform itself into one of the great powers, to push its way and obtrude itself to the first place in the councils of Europe. And Bismarck was almost alone in Prussia in his wish for the test of force. During the anxious months before the outbreak of war, the King received petition after petition beseeching him to dismiss Bismarck and keep peace with Austria. Bismarck's life was in danger from fanatics who believed they would be performing a patriotic service by removing him from the scene before he provoked what was often described as a fratricidal war. Bismarck was daring all on the outcome. Had the war ended, as the greater part of Europe believed it would, in favor of Austria, or had the war been long and doubtful and Napoleon taken advantage of Prussia's struggle to claim and seize land along the Rhine, all Prussia would have risen to condemn Bismarck as the cause of the national ruin. Both the minister and his royal master would have been plunged into lasting ignominy.

By the beginning of June all Europe realized that war was but a matter of a few days. Austria had mobilized her armies, and in her financial condition could not long endure the abnormal expense without a decision. She finally gave Prussia the necessary pretext for action by proposing that the final disposition of Schleswig and Holstein be referred to the Diet of the Confederation for report. Upon this proposal, Bismarck was quick to move. He asserted that it was a breach of the Convention of Gastein, and Prussia poured troops into Holstein. On June 11 Austria declared Prussia's act an act of hostility, and, in the Diet of the Confederation, moved the mobilization of the federal forces to punish Prussia. On June 14, the Austrian motion in a slightly modified form was carried, after the Prussian chancellor had declared that Prussia would regard every member who voted for it as her enemy. Aligned with Austria in the vote was all of Germany except a few of the small northern states. Prussia's representative thereupon formally withdrew from the Diet and war began.

D. THE AUSTRO-PRUSSIAN WAR

If Prussia's diplomatic success in the Seven Weeks (or Austro-Prussian) War was the work of a single great man — von Bismarck — her strategic success was equally the work of another great man — von Moltke.

Helmuth Carl von Moltke was born at Parchim in Mecklenburg on the 26th of October, 1800. His first military service was with the armies of Denmark, whither his father had moved when the boy was five years old. He obtained his commission as Second Lieutenant when he was eighteen, but he seems to have foreseen the possibilities of service with the Prussian army so clearly that at twenty-one, he resigned from the service of Frederick VI, and sought that of Frederick William III. As a second lieutenant he attended the general war school where he made such a reputation that upon his promotion to First Lieutenant in 1833, he was detailed to a minor position on the General Staff. In 1835 he became military adviser to the Sultan of Turkey, in whose service he remained two years, and whom he assisted in that unfortunate campaign against the usurping Mehemet Ali of Egypt. After the disastrous battle of Nezib (where he commanded the Turkish artillery), von Moltke returned to Prussia and took up his regular military work there. His superior officers recognized his worth as a staff officer, and appointed him to increasingly important positions, until he was given that of Chief of Staff of the 4th Army Corps, where he served directly under the Crown Prince William.

In 1857, within a week from the time when he became regent for his brother, Prince William appointed von Moltke — now a Major-General — Chief-of-Staff of the entire army. From that day dates the modern conception of waging war. Immediately von Moltke began a reorganization of the Staff Corps which resulted in the brilliant victories of 1866 and 1870. At once he began adapting the tactical and strategical methods to the new systems of communication and transportation; he started the training of his staffs in the army in accordance with those methods; he worked out schemes for the mobilization of his armies under all conditions; and, lastly, he made a careful study of European politics in connection with the possibilities of military activities. Thus, his Danish campaign (though sadly bungled by von Wrangel) was admirably conceived and worked out long before the breach of diplomatic relations occurred. Von Moltke's personality dominated the military policy of Germany until his retirement from the Staff in 1888, but his methods are still employed the world over. By his death in 1891, Germany lost the greatest strategist of the last hundred years, but she had profited to the utmost from his talents. His great success lay in that he always tried to get at the meaning of war, and never thought of it as a combination of set rules and fixed moves. He was bold, but cautious, and when his operations exposed his armies to great dangers, it could always be said that no one saw those dangers more clearly, nor guarded against them more carefully than von Moltke. It is related of Wellington that he once proudly remarked, "Many men can march troops. I can feed them." Von Moltke could do both.

Because of the alliances of both states, Austria and Prussia were forced to wage war over a wide area. The combined states of Hanover, Bavaria, Baden, and Hesse threatened Prussia to the west and north, Austria and Saxony to the south. The Italian alliance balanced this disadvantage by forcing Austria to keep troops in Venetia. A few words are sufficient to account for the minor operations. The Northern army, or Army of the Main, was everywhere successful, occupied almost the whole of the hostile territory to the west, and was soon in a position to dictate the terms of peace. In Venetia, the Italians and Austrians met in a single engagement at Custozza where the latter were victorious. The campaign is worthy of notice principally because it kept three Austrian corps from participation in the Bohemian operations.

Bohemia, where the approaching struggle was destined to center, has many times been the fighting ground of German armies. In the Thirty Years' War, in the War of the Austrian Succession, and in the Seven Years' War, many a battle was fought within Bohemia's boundaries. If an east and west line were to be drawn through Prague, the capital of Bohemia, it could be used as the base of a triangle whose sides, formed by the Metal Mountains on the northwest, and by the Giant Mountains on the northeast, meet in an obtuse angle some sixty miles to the north. The territory included within this triangle formed the theater of operations of the principal activities. Beyond the left side of the triangle lies Saxony, with a connecting pass where the river Elbe has forced its way through the Metal Mountains. Beyond the right side lies Prussian Silesia, with communicating passes through the Giant Mountains at Parschnitz, Branau, and Nachod. Within the angle of the two mountain ranges, the Elbe and the Iser form two other barriers to troops coming from Saxony

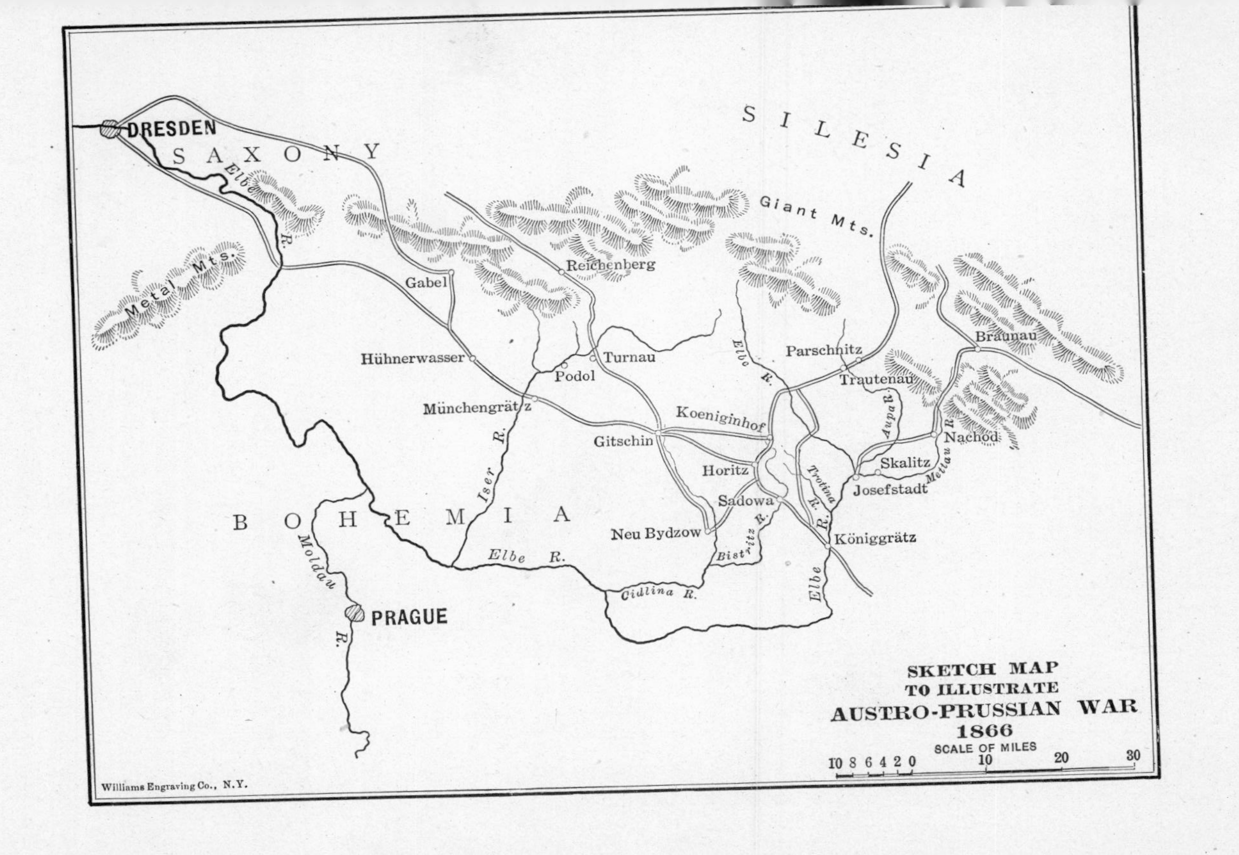
SKETCH MAP
TO ILLUSTRATE
AUSTRO-PRUSSIAN WAR
1866
SCALE OF MILES
10 8 6 4 2 0 10 20 30
DRESDEN
SAXONY
SILESIA
BOHEMIA
Giant Mts.
Metal Mts.
Elbe R.
Moldau R.
Iser R.
Cidlina R.
Bistritz R.
Trotina R.
Aupa R.
Mettau R.
PRAGUE
Gabel
Reichenberg
Hühnerwasser
Turnau
Podol
Münchengrätz
Gitschin
Koeniginhof
Horitz
Sadowa
Neu Bydzow
Parschnitz
Trautenau
Braunau
Nachod
Skalitz
Josefstadt
Königgrätz
Williams Engraving Co., N.Y.

and Silesia — barriers which must be crossed by separate Prussian armies seeking to unite on Austrian territory. The terrain varies from steep mountainous country at the foot of the ranges to open rolling country in the valley of the Elbe, where the decisive battle was fought.

The army which von Moltke was preparing to send into Austria had its beginnings in the labors of General Scharnhorst. When, after the defeat of Jena in 1806, the humiliating treaty of Tilsit provided that the Prussian army should not number more than 43,000 men, Scharnhorst evolved the idea of replacing the professional army by a national one, in which it should be the duty of every physically fit male citizen to serve. He fixed upon three years as the period of training, and proceeded to pass thousands of men through the army, retaining them after their active service in one of the various classes of reserves. Thus, while the letter of the treaty was observed, the spirit was evaded, and forty thousand men were added yearly to the effective forces of Prussia. Upon the accession to the throne of William I (1861), the standing, or active, army was increased to 63,000, so that by the time the Austrian difficulty came to a head, Prussia's forces, reserves and actives, numbered some 660,000 men. Not all these were organized, however. The effective army was composed of eight regular army corps and the Guard Corps — the last, a corps chosen from all over Prussia, whereas the other corps were enlisted each from a province or district. Each corps was composed of two divisions, and the divisions in turn were composed of two brigades of infantry, a regiment of cavalry, and an *Abteilung* (24 guns) of artillery. The brigade was made up of two regiments of three battalions each, the battalion numbering, when mobilized, about 1000 men. These divisions, with the additional corps troops, brought the strength of the invading army up to 278,600 men. The troops were divided into three armies as follows: Half of the 7th Corps, the 8th Corps with reserve cavalry and artillery, under General Herwath von Bittenfeld, constituted the Army of the Elbe; the 2d, 3d, and 4th Corps, under Prince Frederick Charles, of Schleswig-Holstein fame, made up the 1st Army; and the 1st, 5th, 6th, and Guard Corps, and a cavalry division, under Crown Prince Frederick of Prussia, formed the 2d Army. The Army of the Elbe was to assemble in Prussian Saxony, the 1st Army in Lausitz, and the 2d Army in Prussian Silesia.

The Prussian infantry employed the needle-gun which had been used with such effect in the Danish War, and which despite its defects was still the most effective military arm on the continent. It could be fired more rapidly than any other and it could be loaded while the soldier was in a prone position. The artillery — 1000 guns in all — was armed with 4-, 6-, and 12-pounder bronze guns, of which about 40 per cent were rifled. The effective range of the best of them was not more than 1400 yards. In the matter of training, the infantry was the superior arm, and throughout the war was better handled tactically than either the cavalry or the artillery.

To oppose this Prussian force, Austria could draw upon 600,000 men. Her military system, based on that of France, was that of conscription — a method which implies that the individual chosen by lot for service had the liberty of purchasing a substitute from among those who had escaped being drawn for enlistment in the recruit lottery. It is a system which does not produce so high a standard in the army as that of universal service, nor does it supply so many reserves. Austria from a population of 35 millions could muster 600,000 men: Prussia from 18 millions could depend upon 660,000 men A total of ten Austrian Army corps of four brigades each (there was no regular divisional organization) was formed into two armies: the Army of the North, consisting of the 1st, 2d, 4th, 6th, 8th, 9th, and 10th Corps with reserve cavalry and artillery, under Field Marshal von Benedek; the Army of the South, composed of the 5th, 7th, and 9th Corps, under the Archduke Albrecht. The former was to mobilize in Moravia, the latter in Venetia.

As to arms, their infantry weapon, the muzzle-loading rifle, had a longer range than the Prussian needle-gun, but was inferior in every other respect. Their guns, numbering 800, were of the same sizes as those of their adversary, but were all rifled and had a longer range — about 1700 or 1800 yards. The artillery gained a reputation for good shooting during the war: the infantry one for bad. As compared with the Prussian forces tactically, Austria's artillery was perhaps better trained than was her enemy's; her infantry was neither as well trained nor as well commanded.

In the matter of mobilization, Austria had the advantage. Prussia was confronted with the problem of concentrating her armies to meet any Austrian attack without invading Saxon territory — a situation forced upon her by King William's anxiety to avoid the appearance of aggression. And because Saxony juts northward into Prussian territory the military leaders feared that the Southern allies might concentrate at a single point from which they could strike either at Breslau or Berlin. So von Moltke was forced to the expedient of detaining his troops at the five termini of the railroads to the Prussian frontier, and then bringing the different portions of his army together by a flank march along the Saxon boundary. In the face of an active aggressive enemy such a movement would have been perilous, but the Prussian Chief of Staff knew his opponent and felt safe in issuing his orders as he did.

Austria, like her enemy, wished to give the appearance in the eyes of Europe of being more sinned against than sinning, but whereas Prussia was prepared to maintain this hypocritical policy only in the field of diplomacy, Austria was prepared to carry it into the theater of military operations as well. Such a resolve necessarily hampered the Austrian commander-in-chief in his choice of a plan of action, and threw upon him the impossible problem of attempting to select his field of battle after having surrendered the initiative without a contest. A concentration with the idea of invading Prussia behind it, might have been made in Moravia, in Bohemia, or in Saxony. Any one of these plans would have caused the northern adversary much uneasiness. Instead, a purely defensive scheme was designed whereby the Austrian army of the north, concentrated near the fortress of Olmütz, should await the advance of the Prussian army upon Vienna.

The news of this concentration provoked a blunder on the part of the Prussians. Austria's massing of forces at Olmütz apparently meant an attack upon Breslau. The Crown Prince (in all probability against the direct wish of von Moltke), was accordingly ordered to move his army eastward to meet such an attempt. By this movement, the front of the Prussian army, which had been reduced from 275 to 155 miles by the hazardous flank march described above, was again extended dangerously, and the gap of some thirty miles which had existed between the right of the 2d Army and the left of the 1st Army was widened by about fifty miles. Von Benedek, the Austrian commander, failed to take advantage of the opportunity offered, and the day which followed the declaration of war (night of June 15–16, 1866) found him still awaiting for an overt act from his enemy.

Not so von Moltke. Within a few hours of the declaration, the Army of the Elbe crossed the Saxon frontier, and commenced a triumphant march upon Dresden. The Saxon troops, following the plan of their allies, abandoned their own territory and fell back to join the Austrians. This advance of the Prussians determined von Benedek to move into Bohemia and take up a position near Josefstadt between the two advancing Prussian armies. Even von Moltke admits that this move was wise if von Benedek were constrained to act upon the defensive, but most strategists are agreed that the Crown Prince's army in Silesia offered a more favorable objective, and that von Benedek lost his greatest chance of success when he failed to grasp the opportunity to defeat his enemy in detail. Such a move would have necessitated an assumption of the aggressive, and von Benedek was already committed to the defensive. His position was not, however, without merit. By placing his armies near Josefstadt, he brought into play on his side the natural obstacles of the terrain outlined above. The divided Prussian armies were separated by the Giant Mountains and the Metal Mountains, by the Elbe and the Iser. To have held the passes of the mountains, at Parschnitz, Nachod, and Braunau in the Giant Range and those at Getschen and Reichenberg in the Metal Range, meanwhile keeping the bulk of his army ready to strike in any direction against either of his advancing foes, would have made the chances of success largely in von Benedek's favor. But he chose the other course and prepared for a passive defense.

The campaign now moved with great rapidity. On June 16 von Bittenfeld crossed the Saxon frontier. In less than three weeks the opposing armies met at Königgrätz in a battle which was the deciding point of the war.

On the 18th of June the Army of the Elbe and the 1st Army were united under Prince Frederick Charles, and plans were laid for the invasion of Bohemia. Prince Frederick Charles and the Crown Prince were to advance into Bohemia, one from the northwest, the other from the northeast, and endeavor to concentrate near Gitschin. A concentration might have been made by moving either army to join the other behind the cover of the mountain ranges, but such a movement would have given the Austrians ten or twelve days' time in which they could have reached Josefstadt without hindrance. No; the concentration must be made by marching toward the center of the circle. The danger was great, but the advantage to be gained was decisive, and von Moltke, although he realized the peril, deliberately accepted it for the sake of ultimate success. The union of the two armies took place on the field of Königgrätz. Let us follow the movements of each army separately.

Having failed to close the passes of the Metal Mountains, von Benedek now sought to take advantage of the River Iser, the second natural obstacle in the way of the advancing army of Prince Frederick Charles. Accordingly, on the 26th of June he issued orders to the Crown Prince of Saxony, commanding the Saxon and Austrian troops on the Iser, to hold the crossings of the river at all costs. The orders came too late, for on the 25th, in the minor engagements at Hühnerwasser and Turnau, the Prussians had secured the crossings of the Iser — an advantage they followed up by defeating the Saxon Crown Prince's troops at Podol on the 26th. These actions, though of not great compass, compelled the Saxons to withdraw toward Gitschin. Their retreat was covered by an unsuccessful rear guard action at Münschengrätz on the 28th of June, and their defeat at that point enabled the Prussians to confront them again on the 30th at Gitschin. Here ensued an all day's battle with the chance of success always on the side of the Prussians. The final entry into the village found the allied forces in the greatest confusion, their trains hopelessly entangled in the streets, and their troops in panic. Though the Saxons managed to retire in something like order, the Austrians retreated in a disorder which was not reduced until the 2d of July. On the same day (June 30) communication was established between the Prussian armies. July 2, the eve of Königgrätz, found the army of Prince Frederick Charles in the neighborhood of Horitz and Milowitz prepared to advance upon the Austrian army.

Meanwhile the Crown Prince of Prussia was leading the 2d Army through a similar series of victories to the east. His was a more difficult task then that of the 1st Army, for the scarcity of roads through the Giant Mountains necessitated the division of his army into three parts in order that it might take advantage of the passes of Parschnitz, Braunau, and Nachod. The first encounter was at Trautenau on the 27th of June, and here for the only time during the war were the Austrians victorious. The Prussian attempt to cross the Aupa at Trautenau was defeated after several hours of heavy fighting, and the first corps was pushed back across the frontier. The victory was not of any great value to the Austrians, for not only did they fail to inflict a decisive defeat, but they lost nearly five times as heavily as their discomfited enemy. At Soor on the following day they lost more than they had gained at Trautenau, for by their defeat they failed to prevent a union of the various parts of the Crown Prince's army. To the southward, the same day that witnessed Trautenau (June 27) saw an ineffectual attempt on the part of the Austrians to stop the Prussian advance through the pass at Nachod. A Prussian success at Skalitz on the following day left no obstacle in the way of the reunion of the units of the 1st Army. One more brush with the Austrians at Schweinschädel on the 29th of June brought the now exultant 2d Army to the line of the Elbe, where on the 30th they established a connection with the army of Prince Frederick Charles.

The continued successes of the advancing Prussians made it evident to von Benedek that he could never reach Josefstadt, for though the lack of skill in the handling of the Prussian cavalry had permitted the defeated Austrians after each of these battles to withdraw with morale unshaken, the reverses at Gitschin, with the disorderly rout which followed, pointed plainly to an inevitable disaster. Either he must take up a stand farther to the south, or he must change his plan entirely and retreat. The general force of circumstances compelled the former, and by the evening of July 2 he had taken up a position between the

Bistritz and the Elbe and was prepared for battle. His line was a rough semicircle, the main portions on the ridge between the Bistritz and the Elbe reaching from Charbusitz on the south nearly to Horenowes on the north, with advanced detachments thrown out to the front to cover the crossings of the Bistritz. Both flanks were refused almost to the Elbe, and his cavalry divisions were placed centrally within the defensive ring. His dispositions were not the best. His cavalry was completely deprived of its mobility, his semicircular line was ill suited to meet the obvious enveloping attack, and his main line of communications, the road from Sadowa to Königgrätz, was within easy grasp of the enemy once he broke through the defense. Finally, the unfordable Elbe river was behind him, a menace to a retreating army almost as formidable as the pursuing foe. And yet the position which he had chosen had some points in its favor. The ridge upon which his main line was posted effectively concealed the movements of troops in its rear, the field of fire was everywhere good, and his right flank was protected by the Trotina river, a sluggish marshy stream as it approaches the Elbe, and at this time greatly swollen by heavy rains.

Von Moltke did not expect to find the Austrians behind the Bistritz. He had given von Benedek credit for selecting the best battle ground available and was therefore prepared to learn that his adversary had taken up a position behind the Elbe where his left front would rest upon the fortress of Königgrätz, and his right would be covered by the Aupa and Mettau rivers. This would have been a strong position from which von Moltke would be forced to dislodge the opposing army by an enveloping attack on the right flank, or should that fail, by outmaneuvering von Benedek with a flank march to the south to threaten the Austrian line of communications. Again the inability to make the most of the cavalry was demonstrated, for after the two Prussian armies established communication on June 30, contact with

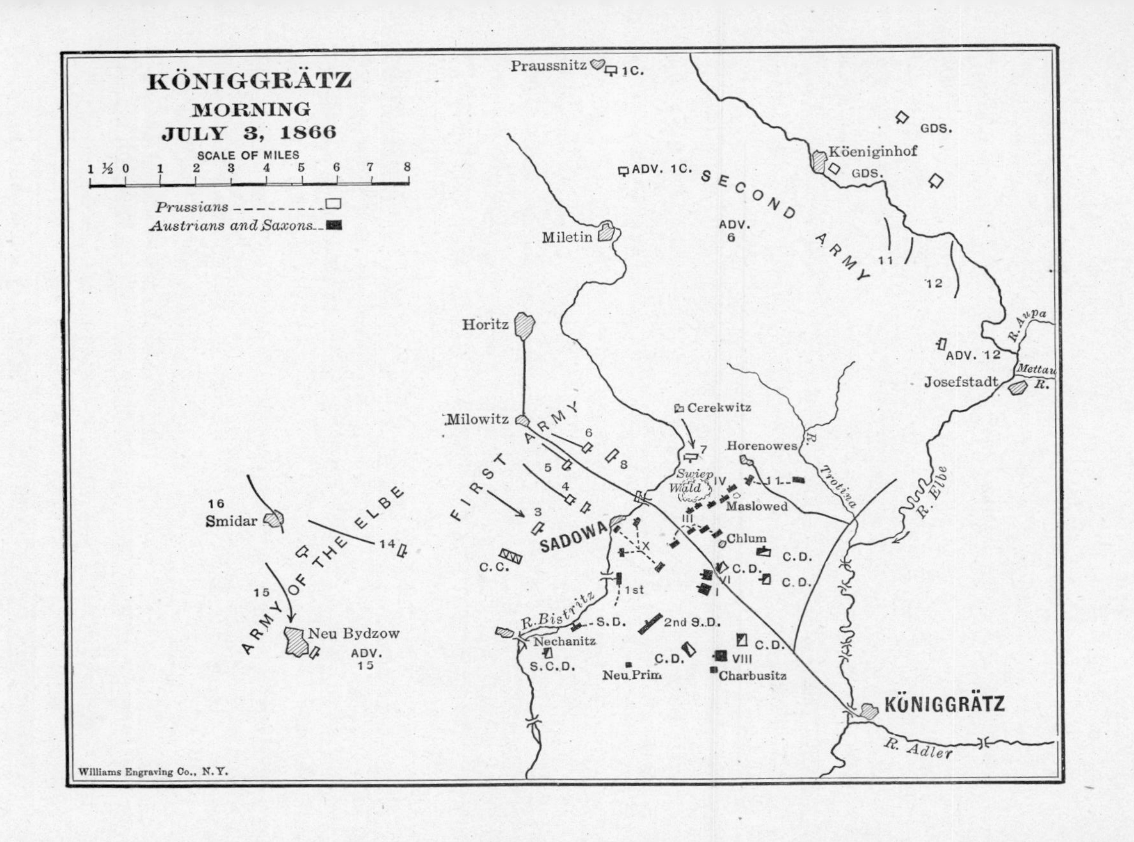
KÖNIGGRÄTZ
MORNING
JULY 3, 1866
SCALE OF MILES
1 ½ 0 1 2 3 4 5 6 7 8
Prussians
Austrians and Saxons
Praussnitz
1C.
ADV. 1C.
SECOND ARMY
Köeniginhof
GDS.
GDS.
ADV. 6
11
12
Miletin
Horitz
R. Aupa
ADV. 12
Mettau R.
Josefstadt
Cerekwitz
7
Milowitz
FIRST ARMY
6
8
5
4
3
Horenowes
R. Trotina
R. Elbe
Swiep Wald
IV
11
Maslowed
III
Chlum
X
SADOWA
C.C.
C.D.
C.D.
C.D.
VI
I
1st
16
Smidar
14
ARMY OF THE ELBE
15
Neu Bydzow
ADV. 15
R. Bistritz
S.D.
2nd S.D.
Nechanitz
S.C.D.
C.D.
C.D.
VIII
Neu Prim
Charbusitz
KÖNIGGRÄTZ
R. Adler
Williams Engraving Co., N.Y.

the enemy was lost, and when it was again established on July 2 with the two armies only four and a half miles apart, the Austrians were found to be occupying not the line behind the Elbe which von Moltke expected, but that behind the Bistritz already indicated. This discovery necessitated new plans on von Moltke's part. The Prussian Chief of Staff, who with King William was now at Gitschin, determined upon that hardest of tactical maneuvers, — the combined frontal and flank attack delivered by converging armies coming from widely separated initial points and moving on separate lines of communication.

The plan of battle, however, was not outlined by von Moltke but by Prince Frederick Charles, commanding the combined 1st Army and the Army of the Elbe. Acting under general instructions to attack should the enemy be encountered west of the Elbe, the Prince, as soon as he learned of von Benedek's position behind the Bistritz, issued orders for an attack to begin on the morning of the 3d of July. His plan contemplated a frontal attack on the Austrians by the 1st Army, combined with an attack on von Benedek's left flank by the Army of the Elbe. The 2d Army was asked to detach one corps to protect the left of the attacking 1st Army. Such a plan made no use of the 2d Army, but gave all the danger and glory of the attack to Prince Frederick Charles, and would undoubtedly have met with defeat but for the timely intervention of von Moltke. When the courier reached him with Prince Frederick Charles' attack order, he refrained from changing the rôle outlined for the 1st Army and the Army of the Elbe, but modified the function of the 2d Army very materially. He saw that the 2d Army must attack simultaneously with the other two if success were to be obtained, and accordingly he sent to the Crown Prince the following message: "Your Royal Highness will be good enough to take the necessary steps to march to the assistance of the 1st Army with all your forces, moving against the right flank of the enemy, who will probably be discovered on the march, and immediately attack him."

Because of a misunderstanding at the Crown Prince's headquarters, the attack order for the 2d Army was not issued until about 5 A.M. on the morning of the 3d — two hours after the 1st Army was to be in position. Prince Frederick Charles, therefore, advanced to the attack knowing that the 2d Army could not reach the battle field before noon, and that for six hours at least he must resist the entire Austrian Army. For this reason he had determined to force the crossings of the Bistritz but delay a general attack until he could be assured of the support of the Crown Prince. Under cover of mist and driving rain, his first battalions moved forward to open the attack on Sadowa, the crossing point for the Eighth Division. To the north, General Fransecky, commanding the 7th Division, had been given orders to advance when the attack became general. A heavy artillery duel which followed the forcing of the Sadowa bridge was taken by the General as a signal to advance, and accordingly he hurled his troops into action in the Swiep Wald or Maslowed Wood. This was a strong point in the Austrian line, and within two hours twelve Prussian battalions and three batteries (12 guns) found themselves opposed to forty battalions and a hundred guns. The Eighth Division was rushed forward to succor the Seventh, and troops in rear were hurried in turn to aid the Eighth, but still the Austrians maintained a superiority. Fortunately for the Prussians, the thick mist prevented their foes from making the best use of their longer range weapons, and the needle-gun was able to demonstrate its superiority at the shorter range. Nevertheless, from eleven in the morning until two in the afternoon, the Prussian battalions were in a most dangerous situation.

Then suddenly the Austrian attack lessened, and word flew about that the Crown Prince had arrived. It was true. From the north came the unbroken battalions of the 2d

Army across the muddy fields, driving straight toward the church tower in Chlum. The fighting in the Swiep Wald relaxed and Chlum became the center of action. Here, too, the Prussian arms triumphed, though only after bitter fighting, and the Austrians were routed. Though von Benedek directed a counter-attack which resulted in the retaking of Roseberitz, the Prussian success was assured. King William ordered up the remaining divisions of the 1st Army, and by 4:30 P.M. the Austrians were in full retreat. Their artillery, however, kept up a determined fire which effectually covered their withdrawal. Meanwhile, the Army of the Elbe and the 2d Army had met across the front of the 1st Army and the victorious forces were thrown into a confusion which made the pursuit of their vanquished enemy impossible. The retreating troops maintained order until they found that the fortress of Königgrätz, at which point they had hoped to cross the Elbe, had closed its gates to them, whereupon the orderly retreat broke, each man looked to himself for orders, and the army became a crowded mass of fugitives, seeking safety in flight.

Partly because of the existing confusion, partly because of political conditions, the Prussian movements which followed the battle of Königgrätz were leisurely. The Crown Prince's army was directed against the Austrian forces at Olmütz, while the 1st and Elbe Armies were marched toward Vienna. From a strategical viewpoint, von Benedek's army should have been the objective of all the Prussian forces, but politics dictated a march upon the Austrian capital. The Archduke Albrecht, who had been recalled from Italy to succeed von Benedek, began at once to withdraw his forces to the Danube. Four corps had been transported from Olmütz by train when the Prussian cavalry destroyed rail communications. The remaining three corps then started to march to Vienna, and though they encountered the 2d Prussian Army at Tobitschau with unhappy results, they were able to join the archduke on the Danube near Pressburg. Here at the little town of Blumenau occurred the final action of the war. An armistice which had been arranged to take place on the 22d of July broke off the battle sharply at noon of that day. This was the last encounter in a campaign which by a series of lightning-like strokes had reduced the army of Austria to a mere cipher. "Von Moltke," says Lord Acton, "in one pitched battle, succeeded where Gustavus, Turenne, Frederick, and even Napoleon had failed."

E. THE TREATY OF PEACE

The war had resulted contrary to the expectations of the most interested observer, Napoleon III. Austria had not been victorious, and the war had been incredibly short. All of the French Emperor's plans were upset by the outcome. The very day after the battle of Königgrätz, the Emperor of Austria telegraphed to Napoleon requesting him to use his good offices in intervention, and confirming the cession of Venice to Napoleon for ultimate transfer to Italy. Napoleon, acceding to Francis Joseph's request, called upon the belligerents to stop hostilities and began negotiations for peace.

These negotiations, so far as Austria was concerned, passed rapidly through the various stages. Although the Prussian King and a strong group of his advisers were anxious to demand territorial compensation from Austria and to restore German unity under Prussian auspices, Bismarck's schemes carried the day. He argued against any territorial compensation from Austria on the ground that such cession would be an indignity which Austria could not forgive, whereas, now that the rivalry between the two powers in Germany was removed, they ought to be natural friends, ready to stand together in close alliance against the possibly hostile powers of Russia and France. Further, he argued against any effort at the moment to consolidate all the German states of the old confederation, because he realized that such an attempt would at once involve the interests of France, and perhaps induce an Austro-French alliance which would lose for Prussia all that she had gained in the war. Curiously enough, he had in his arguments the support of the Crown Prince, who up to this time had been his determined opponent. Bismarck has in his own words given the circumstances:

"The resistance which I was obliged, in accordance with my convictions, to offer to the King's views with regard to following up the military successes, and to his inclination to continue the victorious advance, excited him to such a degree that a prolongation of the discussion became impossible; and, under the impression that my opinion was rejected, I left the room with the idea of begging the King to allow me, in my capacity of officer, to join my regiment. On returning to my room I was in the mood that the thought occurred to me whether it would not be better to fall out of the open window, which was four storeys high; and I did not look round when I heard the door open, although I suspected that the person entering was the Crown Prince, whose room in the same corridor I had just passed. I felt his hand on my shoulder, whilst he said: 'You know that I was against this war. You considered it necessary, and the responsibility for it lies on you. If you are now persuaded that our end is attained, and peace must now be concluded, I am ready to support you and defend your opinion with my father.' He then repaired to the King, and came back after a short half hour, in the same calm, friendly mood, but with the words: 'It has been very difficult business, but my father has consented.' This consent found expression in a note written with lead pencil on the margin of one of my last memoranda, something to this effect: 'Inasmuch as my Minister-President has left me in the lurch in the face of the enemy, and here I am not in a position to supply his place, I have discussed the question with my son; and as he has associated himself with the Minister-President's opinion, I find myself reluctantly compelled, after such brilliant victories on the part of the army, to bite the sour apple and accept so disgraceful a peace.' I do not think I am mistaken as to the exact words, although the document is not accessible to me at present. In any case I have given the sense of it; and, despite its bitterness of expression, it was to me a joyful release from a tension that was becoming unbearable. I gladly accepted the Royal assent to what I regarded as politically necessary without taking offence at its ungracious form. At this time military impressions were dominant in the King's mind; and the strong need he felt of pursuing the hitherto dazzling course of victory perhaps influenced him more than political and diplomatic consideration.

"The only residuum that the above note of the King's, which the Crown Prince brought me, left in my mind was the recollection that I was obliged to vex a master whom personally I loved as I did him."

Bismarck's own aim was to gain Napoleon's acquiescence in a very considerable extension of Prussian territory to be acquired by the incorporation into Prussia of certain of the smaller German states which she had conquered in the war. That acquiescence once gained, late in July, Bismarck hurried the negotiations with all possible speed. An armistice was arranged on the 22d of July and four days later the preliminaries of peace were signed at Nikolsburg. Two days after the preliminaries were signed, these were ratified. Although Bismarck could delay negotiations when he chose, he well knew the necessity at the present moment of rushing through all these arrangements before their full import could be understood by Europe at large.

The definite Treaty of Peace based upon these preliminary provisions was signed at Prague on the 23d of August. By the terms of this treaty, Austria agreed: (1) to the union of Venetia with the Kingdom of Italy; (2) to the recognition of the dissolution of the German Confederation; (3) to the establishment of a new confederation north of the river Main in which Austria should have no part; (4) to the acquisition by Prussia of all of Schleswig and Holstein and of any other territories in North Germany; and (5) to a payment to Prussia of 40,000,000 thalers indemnity.

The war against those German states which had been allies of Austria dragged on for a time after the preliminaries of peace with Austria had been signed. Although certain representatives of these states had appeared at Nikolsburg and wished to be included in the negotiations for peace, Bismarck, preferring to deal with them separately, had denied their request. Early in August, however, their forces had been defeated and an armistice for the discussion of terms arranged. Bismarck had no intention of making the proposals onerous for them any more than he had for Austria. He was looking forward to the future when all Germany might have to stand together against a non-German enemy, and he did not desire to create at this time a legacy of bitterness which should prevent such alliance. Some little territory was taken from Bavaria and Hesse-Darmstadt in order to rectify the Prussian frontier, and relatively small indemnities were required. By October, peace terms had been arranged and signed with all of the states.

Outside of the main end for which she had striven, that is, the removal of Austria from the affairs of Germany and the establishment of Prussia as the primary power in that area, Prussia had made material gains of enormous importance. She annexed to Prussian territory the two provinces of Schleswig and Holstein, the kingdom of Hanover and the duchies of Hesse-Cassel and Nassau, and the Free City of Frankfort. In all, she thus increased her population by about four and one half million.

It is interesting to notice in concluding this chapter how complete was Bismarck's vindication in the eyes of the Prussian people by the result of the war. On September 20, King William and his victorious army made its triumphal entry into Berlin. In the pageant, just in front of the King, rode von Bismarck with von Moltke and von Roon. The wild enthusiasm of the Prussian people at the sight of Bismarck could hardly be restrained. In the joy and pride of victory, and in their realization of all which that victory meant for Prussia, they forgot the weary years of conflict, the unconstitutional measures by which their army had been maintained against the wishes of their own representatives. The next elections showed unmistakably the trend of public feeling. The adherents of the government were greatly increased in numbers and, joining with seceders from other groups, gradually built up a National Liberal party which was the bulwark of the ministry in succeeding parliaments. When Bismarck, yielding to the constitutional principles at a time when he had become so popular that the budget controversy might have been closed in his favor without debate, requested from the parliament an indemnity for having carried on the government for four years without a budget, the chamber granted the request by a huge majority. His great personal triumph came a few weeks later when, he having retired to the country for a much-needed rest, the parliament included him among the victorious generals to whom a donation was given, and, for his distinguished services to his country, voted him a large sum of money. With this sum the statesman bought himself a country château at Varzin, to which he became more and more devoted as the years went by.

CHAPTER V

BISMARCK *VERSUS* NAPOLEON III

A. NAPOLEON III'S ATTEMPTS TO GET COMPENSATION

BISMARCK'S haste in completing the peace negotiations with Austria was largely due to the fact that Napoleon had already begun to press for payment for French neutrality during the war according to his understanding of the Biarritz conversations. At the very time that Bismarck was concluding peace with the states of the old confederation, Napoleon was demanding the cession of the Bavarian Palatinate, and of the Hessian districts west of the Rhine, to France. When this demand was peremptorily refused, and the French ambassador was shown that insistence upon any such claims would mean a conflict with united Germany, Napoleon was compelled to withdraw from his position, thus admitting his inability to enforce his wishes by war. A few weeks later the French Emperor returned to the quest with a demand that Prussia compensate France by aiding him to acquire Luxemburg and invade Belgium. The crafty Bismarck allowed him to formulate his demands openly and to put them into writing, and then declined to proceed further with these negotiations. Again Napoleon changed his ground, reducing his demands to include merely the occupation of Luxemburg. German patriotism, however, was inflamed at the prospect of transferring a territory with German subjects to French control, so that in March of 1867 this project was blocked. Prussia yielded only so far as to agree to a convention under the terms of which Prussian troops were to be withdrawn from Luxemburg, the fortifications were to be dismantled, and its perpetual neutrality was to be guaranteed. Thus in his desire for "compensation" for his neutrality during the war of 1866, and in his expectations that France would emerge after that war as the arbiter of the fortunes of western Europe, Napoleon had been deceived and cruelly disappointed.

B. NAPOLEON'S LOSS OF INFLUENCE IN FRANCE

Political conditions within France were, during this period, rapidly imperiling the prestige which the Emperor had gained through the earlier years of material prosperity. His absolutism had resulted in creating a strong Liberal opposition; his magnificent schemes for public works and for beautifying Paris and other great cities of France had so drawn upon the public treasury that able financiers were alarmed for the continued solvency of the country; his alliance with the Italian patriots had excited the vehement and fearless opposition of the Catholics, who saw the temporal domains of the Pope threatened.

The sensational failure of his grandiose plans for a Mexican empire also played an important part in weakening his power and influence at this critical time. In 1861, foreseeing the need of continued glory to enhance his success in his own country, he had conceived the idea of establishing in Mexico a new empire with his own nominee, Maximilian of Austria, as Emperor. In 1862 France, England, and Spain had been engaged in an expedition against Mexico to force that country to pay her debts to them, but England and Spain had soon withdrawn, leaving France to her own devices. Maximilian, at Napoleon's instigation, had accepted the proffered throne, had gone to Mexico, and had found the greatest difficulty in maintaining any semblance of power against the Mexican patriots under Juarez in the north and under Diaz in the south. His expedition was maintained by French troops wholly and by French funds.

Just during the period of the Austro-Prussian war and the subsequent negotiations this Mexican expedition was costing France fifteen million francs a month and was keeping forty thousand of the pick of the French army across the sea. A new difficulty arose when the United States, freed from the burden of the Civil War, protested against the French expedition in terms which required its withdrawal or war. By the end of 1866 Napoleon had come to realize that his cause was hopeless. After urging the Emperor Maximilian to withdraw, he ordered the return of the French troops, the last contingent leaving February 5, 1867. Four months afterwards (June, 1867) the unfortunate Maximilian, who had proudly refused to withdraw from his empire and the few supporters he had won, was treacherously delivered over to Juarez and immediately shot.

The momentous events in central Europe, also, had injured the prestige of the Emperor. The *amour propre* of the French people had been outraged. They began to appreciate the significance of what had taken place during the eventful year 1866. An hereditary enemy had been allowed by diplomacy and by war to increase her territories and to strengthen her position enormously while France submitted ineffectual demands and accepted rude rebuffs. "It was not Austria, but France, who was defeated at Sadowa," was a common saying throughout the country, a saying justified by the fact that the Prussia which had emerged from that battle now threatened the traditional importance of France in European politics. In 1867, when Bismarck was attending the famous Industrial Exposition at Paris, he called upon General Vaillant, Chief of the French General Staff. During conversation the Frenchman said: "I admire and love Prussia, and I admire and love you; but we shall have to cross bayonets for all that." And when Bismarck, with feigned surprise, asked why, Vaillant answered: "We are both of us cocks, and cannot allow others to crow better than ourselves." Through all circles the feeling grew that a war to the finish between France and Prussia was inevitable. A distinct war party sought *revanche* for Sadowa.

The Emperor, aging and rapidly failing in health, had a better understanding of the real international situation than his advisers or his people. He appreciated the strength of Prussia, as shown by the overwhelming defeat of Austria in a single battle; he knew the military weakness of France; he anticipated the united German opposition which a French attack would call into being. Knowing these elements in the situation, he sought to achieve by political and diplomatic means the successes which his people demanded. Hence arose his repeated demands of Bismarck for territorial compensation, his repeated efforts to gain land, first on the west bank of the Rhine, then Luxemburg and Belgium, and finally Luxemburg alone. When he was thwarted in all these attempts, he turned to international politics to seek allies who would strengthen his position. He courted the favor of the Russian Czar, invited him to Paris during the exposition of 1867 and entertained him magnificently. Unfortunately for his purposes, in the midst of the festivities a Pole attempted to assassinate the Czar, and, when tried before a French jury, received a verdict of "extenuating circumstances." During the same year Napoleon attempted to come to an understanding with Francis Joseph of Austria: he visited Francis at Salzburg, arousing bitter comment among the south Germans; he received Francis at Paris; but, in spite of some significant hints of a possible alliance, no definite terms could be agreed upon.

Napoleon's position became more and more precarious. He attempted, indeed he was forced, to recoup some of his prestige by concessions in domestic politics. His opponents had become bolder with the successive failures of his foreign policies and more outspoken in their demands for reforms. In the spring of 1868 he allowed legislation extending freedom of the press and of public meeting. The politicians took advantage of the new privileges to publish dozens of republican papers to carry on an active propaganda against the government; and the Socialists used the privileges to meet for discussions of economic questions, discussions which soon degenerated into debates on the imperial institutions, religion, rights of property, and the like. In the spring of 1869 the elections resulted in a marked increase of the opposition. On June 28 the Liberal party brought forward a demand for "the creation of a responsible ministry, and the recognition of the right of the Legislative Body to regulate the essential conditions of its own activity." The Liberals obtained a majority, and the Emperor had to yield his autocratic powers. On December 28 Émile Ollivier was made prime minister and authorized to form "a homogeneous cabinet, representative of the majority of the Legislative Body"; on January 2, 1870, the new ministry was formed and faced the serious political dissensions and general unrest throughout the country.

C. INTERNAL AFFAIRS IN GERMANY

In the meanwhile Bismarck had been busy consolidating the profits of the Austro-Prussian war. In addition to the territory annexed to Prussia, he had achieved two ends by the war: 1, the complete suppression of Austrian prestige in the German states; and 2, the right to form a confederation of the North German states.

The South German states were left unattached as a result of the war: it was Bismarck's policy to bind them as closely as possible to Prussia. Bismarck would have liked to have included them in the new confederation, but was wise enough to recognize that at the moment this result could not be accomplished. He saw that it was advisable to wait for the inevitable union of the two parts of Germany until on the one hand the foreign powers were in no position to enforce their objections, and on the other the South German

States heartily desired to join the newly formed Confederation. At the moment Austria and France would both have objected, and might have found in their objections to any such union a bond of alliance against Prussia. Furthermore, the governments of Bavaria and Würtemburg had no desire to restrict their sovereignty by entering the confederation; and among the people many elements lamented the exclusion of the German element in Austria from future participation in German affairs. Yet, in spite of these influences against union at the moment, all these South German states realized that an understanding with Prussia and the new North German Confederation was their best safeguard against the encroachments of Napoleon. Under these circumstances Bismarck was able to conclude with his late South German foes a secret military defensive and offensive alliance. This alliance, when made known in 1867, excited the utmost chagrin in Vienna. Count Beust, at this period Austrian Chancellor, wrote in his memoirs:

> "To call things by their true names, these treaties were a masterpiece of treachery. It has frequently happened that treaties were not kept, but that a treaty should be broken in anticipation was a novelty reserved for the genius of Count Bismarck. To sign treaties with the South German States, reducing them to a permanent condition of dependence on Prussia, and then to conclude a few days later a treaty with Austria (Peace of Prague) stipulating for these states an independent international existence, — this was indeed the *ne plus ultra* of Machiavellism."

Although this alliance was, of course, for military purposes only, it served to emphasize the fundamental unity of interests existing between the North and the South German States. A few months later a revision of the provisions of the Customs Union (*the Zollverein*) resulted in the South German States expressing their willingness to rest the control and direction of economic matters for all the German states in the legislature of the North German Confederation. The South German States sent their delegates to Berlin for deliberation on the economic problems. Even though such deliberations were not political, it impressed the Germans as a striking fact that representatives of all Germany were on these occasions seated in a single assembly. The political drift of such impressions is obvious. With military and economic union, political union seemed a near possibility. Bismarck himself was changing rapidly: he was losing the narrow Prussianism, the Junker spirit, which had characterized him in his earlier years of diplomatic life, and was becoming Pan-German.

The new confederation for the North German States — the North German Confederation — was formed with incredible speed. When the Prussian delegate withdrew from the Diet of Frankfort in June of 1866, and thus signalized the outbreak of war, Bismarck had issued an invitation to the North German States to form a new confederation. Immediately after the agreement upon terms of peace he renewed his invitation, extending it to the German states north of the river Main. All accepted within a few weeks. Their delegates assembled in Berlin in December.

Bismarck had a draft of a constitution ready for them. His general principle was to guarantee the independence of each state, to safeguard its territories against external aggression, and to permit local self-government within the component states under their accustomed forms. He believed that the strength and endurance of the new confederation would depend wholly upon the goodwill of the various members. For legislative purposes his draft provided for a *Reichstag*, or lower chamber, whose members were elected by manhood suffrage, and a *Bundesrath*, or upper chamber, whose members were delegates from the sovereigns of the separate states. The King of Prussia became head of the new confederation, and his chancellor presided in the Bundesrath. The military system throughout all of the states was to be modeled upon the Prussian system, and Prussia was to have the chief command in peace or in war. Bismarck encouraged speed in the deliberations of the delegates: "Gentlemen," he said, "let us work quickly, let us put Germany in the saddle; it will soon learn to ride." On the 2d of February, 1867, the delegates accepted, after considerable wrangling but with little material alterations, Bismarck's draft. Bismarck felt, he said, like Hotspur when, "breathless and faint" after battle he was "pestered with a popinjay" of a too fastidious lord. Ten days later a constituent Reichstag was elected to deliberate upon the constitution. On April 16, 1867, this Reichstag passed the constitution by a vote of 230 to 53. Within a few months the Diets in each of the several states formally adopted it. On July 1 it definitely went into effect. Thus in six months from the time the delegates first assembled, the constitution was actually in force.

It is significant of Bismarck's temper and foresight that immediately after the North German Confederation came into being he exerted every effort to bring the military systems in the different states up to the level of the Prussian system. Additional levies were quickly recruited, Prussian drill methods used, and the general level of efficiency in the armies raised. These efforts were redoubled after 1868, for Bismarck, always an adept at reading the political horoscope, became convinced that Napoleon would sooner or later be forced into a war with Prussia in his attempt to regain his prestige. Shortly afterwards, foreseeing the tremendous impetus that would be given thereby to the unification of Germany, he began to welcome the thought of such a war. Of his recollections of that period he wrote:

"I took it as assured that war with France would necessarily have to be waged on the road to our further national development, for our development at home as well as the extension beyond the Main, and that we must keep this eventuality in sight in all our domestic as well as in our foreign relations. . . . I did not doubt that a Franco-German war must take place before the construction of a United Germany could be realized. I was at that time preoccupied with the idea of delaying the outbreak of this war until our fighting strength should be increased by the application of the Prussian military legislation not only to Hanover, Hesse, and Holstein, but as I could hope even at that time from the observation I had made, to the South Germans."

D. BISMARCK'S DIPLOMATIC PREPARATIONS FOR THE FRANCO-GERMAN WAR

i. *Austria*

The situation required, as it did before the Austro-Prussian war, a careful estimate of conditions throughout Europe, a reckoning of possible friends and foes.

Naturally, Austria would seem at first thought a possible ally of France. She had been Prussia's recent enemy; and the young Austrian Emperor when on a visit to Napoleon in 1867 had significantly hinted at the possibility of an Austro-French alliance. Austrian domestic troubles had been partially settled in the years following the Austro-Prussian war. At the outbreak of that war, it will be remembered, Francis Joseph, having suspended the previous system of government, was receiving the programs formulated by Magyars, Czechs, Slavs, and Poles for their respective areas. Of these programs the only one that needed immediate serious attention was that of the Hungarians (Magyars), since the greatest part of the unrest in the country and the failure of the government could be traced to the opposition of the Hungarians. During the war, of course, all domestic issues had been laid aside: after the war, the Emperor Francis Joseph showed the most conciliatory spirit. In a message sent to the diets throughout the empire February 18, 1867, he said:

"During a long course of years the constitutional organization of the monarchy has suffered from hitherto inseparable contradictions between the older rights of the Hungarian constitution and the liberal institutions which the Emperor has made it the aim of his life to establish throughout the monarchy. During the continuance of this conflict the restoration of the greatness of the Empire and of the historical position it has so long occupied among the other states of Europe is not to be hoped for, and, owing to the relations which have arisen out of the recent calamities, every new delay that occurs in the settlement of pending questions is fraught with the most decided disadvantages."

He then summoned Deák secretly to Vienna and asked him to formulate Hungary's demands. Fortunately, Deák was able to assure the Emperor that Hungary demanded "only what she demanded before Sadowa." As Austria was at this time in no position to resist, Francis Joseph appreciated the moderation of the Magyar leaders in not using Austria's dire need to increase their demands. Negotiations proceeded rapidly. By the close of the year 1867 the famous Compromise (*Ausgleich*) was completed. By its provisions a dual monarchy, the Austro-Hungarian monarchy, was created, consisting of two powers of equal rank having the same reigning dynasty. Each power was to have its own parliament, its own ministry, and its own administrative system; each was to be entirely independent of the other in all internal affairs. Yet in external affairs and in certain joint activities, it was necessary to have the machinery for common action: it was therefore provided that there should be a ministry of three departments — Foreign affairs, War, and Finance — which should act for both countries as one. Questions of tariff and currency were to be regulated by ten-year agreements between the two countries — a most unsatisfactory arrangement, for each renewal period has brought a struggle between the two powers over the details of the compact. For Hungary, this Ausgleich was a great triumph: she gained the independence for which she had struggled so long and so bitterly.

But the solution of the Hungarian problem immediately raised a problem of the same nature in a different part of the empire. The Czechs of Bohemia, inspired by Hungary's success, issued a declaration that Bohemia had the same traditional rights as Hungary and that her relations with the monarchy should be adjusted by special agreement between Francis Joseph and a Bohemian Diet chosen by a just and equal suffrage. They then proceeded to adopt the tactics which, as they thought, had gained the victory for Hungary: they withdrew from the Bohemian Diet; they refused to appear in the Reichsrath; they organized a passive resistance to all acts of Austria and showed themselves proud and hostile toward Austrian efforts at conciliation. Such was the situation in 1870.

To summarize briefly the domestic situation as it affected Austrian policy during the impending Franco-Prussian war: (1) by the terms of the Compromise, Hungary had been acknowledged as an equal independent sovereign power acting jointly with Austria in foreign affairs and in defence, and Hungarian influence was cast decisively against alliance with France and against participation in the war; (2) Bohemia was carrying through a passive revolution against Austrian authority, on which successive Austrian ministries broke and fell, and Austria feared that if she warred with France against Prussia the discontented Bohemians might yield up the Austrian frontiers to her enemies; and (3) Austrian finances were not yet satisfactory and Austrian military reorganization not yet completed.

Not only did the domestic situation influence Austria to be neutral, but certain features in the foreign situation also played a part. Austria understood that she had forfeited, by her protest against Russia's suppression of the Polish rebellion in 1863, the favor of Russia. Her diplomats were shrewd enough to see that Bismarck had cherished the friendship he had established between Russia and Prussia at that time. There was real danger, therefore, that, should Austria ally herself with France, Russia would attack her from the east, and, perhaps, wrest away her Polish provinces. Furthermore, Italy on the southwest had appreciated

Prussia's aid in gaining Venice and was now casting covetous eyes on *Italia irredenta* (Italy unreclaimed) in the Trentino and Trieste. Should Austria enter the war, Italy might well ally herself again with Prussia and pour troops against Austria from the new Venetian strongholds.

We may be sure that Bismarck, the shrewdest and best-informed statesman at that time in Europe, appreciated to the full the Austrian situation. Though he was not, of course, in a position to make much of the domestic difficulties of Austria, he managed to emphasize to the utmost the Russian menace and the friendship between Prussia and Italy.

ii. *Great Britain*

Although the entrance of Great Britain into the war would have tipped the balance decisively, both powers felt that England was too much concerned with her domestic policies to interfere in a continental war. Lord Palmerston died in the autumn of 1865 and Earl Russell (the Lord John Russell who had in March, 1831, introduced the first reform bill) succeeded him as the prime minister. Earl Russell, with a good Liberal majority in the Parliament, immediately pressed for an extension of the electoral franchise, and Gladstone, leader of the party in the House of Commons, seconded his efforts with the utmost enthusiasm. In 1866 Gladstone introduced the new Reform Bill into the Commons. The measure was bitterly attacked, the ministry defeated and forced to resign, and the Conservatives placed in power under the leadership of Lord Derby, with Benjamin Disraeli as the Conservative head on the floor of the House of Commons. Two years later (February, 1868), Lord Derby was forced on account of ill health to resign, and Disraeli was summoned by the queen to the head of the ministry.

The next fifteen years of British history revolve about the rival careers of Disraeli and Gladstone. At this time

Disraeli, the conservative leader, was a man of sixty-three, his rival was five years younger. The two men were wholly dissimilar. Benjamin Disraeli was the descendant of an expatriated Portuguese Jew. His father renounced Judaism when Benjamin Disraeli was a child, but the physical features and the name of both father and son marked them through life as beings apart from the ordinary Englishman. Of regular education Disraeli had little: he browsed in his father's library and sought to educate himself along his own ideas. At seventeen he entered a solicitor's office as clerk, at twenty he began his preparations for the bar, at twenty-one he had by his writings brought himself to the attention of Murray, the great publisher, and at twenty-two he published a novel, "Vivian Grey," which took the contemporary reading world by storm. Benjamin Disraeli became one of the literary lions of the day and focused attention on himself by the most daring eccentricities of dress, manners, and expression. One who knows Disraeli's career always thinks at once of the original fopperies which characterized his early appearance in society — perfumery, lace, jeweled satin shirt-front, a profusion of expensive rings outside his gloves, a turn for epigram and irony, cool effrontery under trying circumstances. "He wore green velvet trousers," writes Sir Henry Bulwer of Disraeli's appearance at one dinner party, "a canary-coloured waistcoat, low shoes, silver buckles, lace at his wrists, and his hair in ringlets. . . . Yet if on leaving the table we had been severally taken aside and asked which was the cleverest of the party, we should have been obliged to say 'The man in the green velvet trousers.'" He first entered Parliament in 1837, but did not in his early appearance make a success. In 1839 he married an heiress fifteen years older than he, with whom he lived in the most ideal harmony and sympathy until her death. His parliamentary opportunity came with his attack on Peel in the years following 1845. He distinguished himself by the brilliancy of his speeches and marked himself as the Conservative leader. He overcame all the racial and social prejudices of his Conservative contemporaries by the sheer supremacy of his intellect. He was attacked as a Jew adventurer and accused of posing as a man of mystery; his peculiarities of dress and manner were ridiculed; every effort was made by the hidebound Conservatives to shake him off and get rid of him, but in their need they had to resort each time to his brilliancy to save them. In the three years after 1848 he was the Conservative leader on the floor of the House of Commons and did much to reconstruct his party. In 1852 his first notable political reward came in the shape of the chancellorship of the exchequer in Lord Derby's Cabinet. In 1858 he was again finance minister under Derby, and in 1866 he was naturally in the same position in Lord Derby's third ministry, to succeed in 1868 to the premiership when his chief was forced by ill health to retire.

William Ewart Gladstone was the son of John Gladstone, a grain merchant of Liverpool, and descended from Scotch ancestry. He had a regular academic training — Eton and Oxford — and topped it off with six months of foreign travel. He was elected for one of the Rotten Boroughs in 1832, and made an immediate success in his speeches. He became one of the faithful workers in the Parliament, conspicuous not by his brilliancy or by his oddity, but by the thoroughness and care with which he mastered the details of any problem set for him to solve. His first tilt with Disraeli came when the latter was chancellor of the exchequer in 1852–1853. Disraeli was defending his budget. With characteristic audacity he attacked his opponents with all his wonderful powers of irony, taunts, and cutting epigram. Gladstone in wrath rose to reply: he called the chancellor of the exchequer to book for his unbridled language, his lack of respect for decency and propriety, and pitilessly dissected the budget and showed its impracticability. As the two men faced each other in that first encounter the contrast in their characters was evident: the one brilliant, imaginative, clever and unscrupulous in debate, unconventional in language and appearance; the other a typical Englishman, a fine speechmaker but no master of satire and epigram, a sound thinker but not gifted with wide imaginative vision, careful and logical in debate, and strictly conventional in language and appearance. The duel that began at this time lasted as long as Disraeli lived. On this special occasion Disraeli was beaten, Lord Derby resigned, and Gladstone became chancellor of the exchequer in the new cabinet. In this office he built up a reputation as England's greatest finance minister; he made himself indispensable. During all but a few months of the time from 1853 to 1865 Gladstone remained at this office, becoming finally, upon the retirement of Lord Russell from active politics in 1867 acknowledged head of the Liberal party.

The Conservative party took warning from the popular demonstrations in 1866 attending the defeat of the reform bill and hastily submitted in 1867 a bill of their own. In its final form this bill created practically a "household franchise," *i.e.* gave the vote to every householder. The Conservatives recoiled from their own work: Thomas Carlyle said that the passage of the Bill was equivalent to "shooting Niagara"; and the prime minister, Lord Derby, confessed that "he was taking a leap in the dark."

After Lord Derby's retirement, Disraeli was unable to keep the ministry in power. Over questions arising in connection with Ireland he faced the prospect of defeat by the aggressive Liberals under Gladstone's leadership. Parliament was therefore dissolved in 1868 and the country called upon to decide the nature of the government by its votes. In this election (1868) the Liberals received an enormous majority. Disraeli resigned and Gladstone became prime minister.

During these years both Disraeli and Gladstone had been too engrossed in domestic politics to pay much attention to the course of events on the continent of Europe. The victory of Prussia at Sadowa, the consolidation of the states of North Germany into a confederation, the growing dissatisfaction of the French with the settlement of territory after Sadowa — these things made comparatively little impression in Great Britain. The whole nation was becoming self-centered and introspective: few had the vision to see how these central European changes could ever affect Great Britain.

Both Bismarck and Napoleon understood Great Britain's non-intervention policy and did not expect her to interfere. Bismarck, however, at the outbreak of the war, took a decisive step to prevent any last possibility of her intervention on the side of France. He recognized that in British eyes the neutrality of Belgium was most desirable. He had retained in his possession, since the negotiations following the Austro-Prussian war, Napoleon's proposals that Prussia should help France acquire Belgium in return for France's benevolent neutrality. These proposals Bismarck caused to be published in the *London Times*. The greatest excitement was aroused in Great Britain: any danger of English intervention upon the side of France was at a stroke removed. The English negotiated with each of the belligerent nations a treaty by the provisions of which each was bound with Great Britain's help to oppose any violation of Belgian neutrality.

iii. *Italy*

To one other country Napoleon might look for support — Italy. As a result of her joint action with Prussia during the Austro-Prussian war of 1866, Italy had gained Venice, but her army had been overwhelmingly defeated at Custozza and her navy at Lissa, so that the war had yielded her no glory. A period of moral depression followed. The government was deeply in debt and saw no way for relief; the pillaging and marauding in central Italy continued; Rome was still in possession of the Pope; and no leader arose who had the ability to deliver the unhappy country from its difficulties. Napoleon, however, although realizing that Italy could be of little real value to him as an ally, did approach her with the object of forming an alliance. King Victor Emmanuel felt the impulse of generosity toward his ally of 1859, who had helped him gain the first decision against Austria, but the letters and negotiations between the two monarchs were couched in vague and general terms. As a preliminary to any discussion, the Italian government demanded the withdrawal of French troops from Rome, but Napoleon was forced by the Catholic influences in France to withhold his consent to this demand. Then, just as the crisis became perceptibly acute, Napoleon alienated irrevocably Italian sympathies by forcibly defending the Pope in his possession of Rome. With French troops opposing by force of arms the patriots' advance upon Rome, all possibility of an Italian-French alliance vanished.

iv. *Other States in Europe*

Throughout the rest of Europe Bismarck believed that France might search in vain for allies. Denmark, though having fought Prussia in 1864 and though hungering for Schleswig and Holstein, realized that a mistake at this moment might easily mean her ruin and incorporation into Prussia, so that she was unwilling to commit herself to the French cause. Russia so openly sympathized with Prussia because of Prussia's aid in the Polish rebellion of 1863 that Bismarck could actually count on her to threaten Austria, if Austria showed any signs of intervention. Sweden and Spain had sunk back into second-rate powers and were outside of the circle of interested nations.

E. THE OUTBREAK OF WAR

Although the statesmen in both nations perceived the dangerous drift of popular sentiment, the actual outbreak of war came with dramatic suddenness. Bismarck manipulated events in 1870 with consummate skill and audacity to put France in the wrong before all Germany and thus unite popular opinion in both North German and the South German states against the enemy. The issue was over a relatively trifling matter. The throne of Spain, which was at the time vacant, was offered to Prince Leopold of the Hohenzollern family with the consent of the Prussian King. France was notified officially of Leopold's candidacy July 2. Four days later the French ministry, fearing for Prussian influence in Spain and at the same time seeking a great diplomatic victory, framed an arrogant note demanding Leopold's withdrawal as a candidate. To Bismarck this demand was Prussia's opportunity, but the King did not seek war and, realizing the state of popular feeling in France, caused Leopold's name to be withdrawn on July 10. Bismarck was intensely disappointed; he even considered handing in his resignation. In later years he wrote of his feelings at the time:

"My first idea was to retire from the service, because, after all the insolent challenges which had gone before, I perceived in this extorted submission a humiliation of Germany for which I did not desire to be responsible. This impression of a wound to our sense of national honor by the compulsory withdrawal so dominated me that I had already decided to announce my retirement at Ems. I considered this humiliation before France and her swaggering demonstrations as worse than that of Olmütz, for which the previous history on both sides, and our want of preparation for war at the time, will always be a valid excuse. . . . In the same sense I conversed with the minister of war, von Roon: we had got the slap in the face from France, and had been reduced, by our complaisance, to look like seekers of a quarrel if we entered upon war, the only way in which we could wipe away the stain."

Then the French government, under the inspiration of the court leaders and the war party, committed the fatal error on July 12 of making an additional demand that Leopold's candidacy should never in the future be renewed. Such a demand was in itself of the nature of an insult.. The King, who was then at the village of Ems, rejected it and sent a telegram to Bismarck, stating what he had done and authorizing Bismarck to make the news public. This telegram reached Bismarck as he was dining with von Roon and von Moltke in Berlin. Bismarck himself has described the scene and his action:

"Having decided to resign, in spite of the remonstrances which Roon made against it, I invited him and Moltke to dine with me alone on the 13th, and communicated to them at table my views and projects for doing so. Both were greatly depressed, and reproached me indirectly with selfishly availing myself of my greater facility for withdrawing from service. I maintained the position that I could not offer up my sense of honor to politics, that both of them, being professional soldiers and consequently without freedom of choice, need not take the same point of view as a responsible Foreign Minister. During the conversation I was informed that a telegram from Ems, in cipher, if I recollect rightly, of about 200 'groups,' was being deciphered. When the copy was handed to me it showed that Abeken had drawn up and signed the telegram at his Majesty's command, and I read it out to my guests, whose dejection was so great that they turned away from food and drink. On a repeated examination of the document I lingered upon the authorization of his Majesty, which included a command, immediately to communicate Benedetti's fresh demand and its rejection both to our ambassadors and to the press. I put a few questions to Moltke as to the extent of his confidence in the state of our preparations, especially as to the time they would still require in order to meet this sudden risk of war. He answered that if there was to be a war he expected no advantage to us by deferring its outbreak; and even if we should not be strong enough at first to protect all the territories on the left bank of the Rhine against French invasion, our preparations would nevertheless soon overtake those of the French, while at a later pěriod this advantage would be diminished; he regarded a rapid outbreak as, on the whole, more favorable to us than delay. . . .

"Under this conviction I made use of the royal authorization communicated to me through Abeken, to publish the contents of the telegram; and in the presence of my two guests I reduced the telegram by striking out words, but without adding or altering, to the following form.[1] 'After the news of the renunciation of the hereditary Prince of Hohenzollern had been officially communicated to the imperial government of France by the royal government of Spain, the French ambassador at Ems made the further demand to his Majesty the King that he would authorize him to telegraph to Paris that his Majesty the King bound himself for all future time never again to give his consent if the Hohenzollerns should renew their candidature. His Majesty the King thereupon decided not to receive the French ambassador again, and sent to tell him through the aide-de-camp on duty that his Majesty had nothing further to communicate to the ambassador.' The difference in the effect of the abbreviated text of the Ems telegram as compared with that produced by the original was not the result of stronger words but of the form, which made this announcement appear decisive, while Abeken's version would only have been regarded as a fragment of a negotiation still pending, and to be continued at Berlin.

"After I had read out the concentrated edition to my two guests, Moltke remarked: 'Now it has a different ring: it sounded before like a parley; now it is like a flourish in answer to a challenge.' I went on to explain: 'If in execution of his Majesty's order I at once communicate this text, which contains no alteration in or addition to the telegram, not only to the newspapers, but also by telegraph, to all our embassies, it will be known in Paris before midnight, and not only on account of its contents, but also on account of the manner of its distribution, will have the effect of a red rag upon the Gallic bull. Fight we must if we do not want to act the part of the vanquished without a battle. Success, however, essentially depends upon the impression which the origination of

[1] The original telegram as sent by Abeken was in substance as follows:

"His Majesty writes to me: 'Count Benedetti spoke to me on the promenade, in order to demand from me, finally in a very importunate manner, that I should authorize him to telegraph at once that I bound myself for all future time never again to give my consent if the Hohenzollerns should renew their candidature. I refused at last somewhat sternly, as it is neither right nor possible to undertake engagements of this kind *à tout jamais*. Naturally I told him that I had as yet received no news, and as he was earlier informed about Paris and Madrid than myself, he could clearly see that my government once more had no hand in the matter.' His Majesty has since received a letter from the Prince. His Majesty having told Count Benedetti that he was awaiting news from the Prince, has decided, with reference to the above demand, upon the representation of Count Eulenburg and myself, not to receive Count Benedetti again, but only to let him be informed through an aide-de-camp: That His Majesty had now received from the Prince confirmation of the news which Benedetti had already received from Paris, and had nothing further to say to the ambassador. His Majesty leaves it to your Excellency whether Benedetti's fresh demand and its rejection should not be at once communicated to our ambassadors and to the press."

the war makes upon us and others; it is important that we should be the party attacked, and this Gallic overweening and touchiness will make us if we announce in the face of Europe, so far as we can without the speaking-tube of the Reichstag, that we fearlessly meet the public threats of France.'

"This explanation brought about in the two generals a revulsion to a more joyous mood, the liveliness of which surprised me. They had suddenly recovered their pleasure in eating and drinking and spoke in a more cheerful vein. Roon said: 'Our God of old lives still and will not let us perish in disgrace.' Moltke so far relinquished his passive equanimity that, glancing up joyously towards the ceiling and abandoning his usual punctiliousness of speech, he smote his hand upon his breast and said: 'If I may but live to lead our armies in such a war, then the devil may come directly afterwards and fetch away the "old carcass."' He was less robust at that time than afterwards, and doubted whether he would survive the hardships of the campaign."

This alteration in the phrasing had given to the French nation the impression that their ambassador had been distinctly snubbed. Popular feeling in France could not then be controlled. On the evening of July 14, Napoleon III with his council of state decided upon war. On the 15th mobilization orders were issued to the French forces and on the evening of the same day to the Prussian army. The formal declaration of war was received in Berlin July 19.

The North German Confederation rose to a man to the support of Prussia. The Reichstag voted a large loan for mobilization. In the South German states the pan-German sentiment was aroused by the insolence of the French demands. Even the dullest statesman saw that these states would lose their coveted independence if France were allowed to subdue Prussia. The decision was quickly taken. In Bavaria, Würtemberg, and Baden the necessary appropriations were voted immediately. Napoleon confronted a united Germany at the very outbreak of the war.

CHAPTER VI

THE FRANCO-GERMAN WAR

Out of each succeeding struggle of the nations, with the disaster and humiliation which overtake one or the other, with the economic crippling and the frightful loss of life, comes at least one new lesson for the world to learn in the grave business of maintaining states. The Franco-German war pointed out for all who would take the pains to notice that war had ceased to be the work of paid adventurers or professional soldiers who fought in the pay of a king or government, but had become instead a stern duty of all the citizens of the country involved, a duty not to be delegated to hirelings but performed in the spirit of self-sacrifice for the sake of the nation. One by one the states of the world have made a tardy recognition of the lesson. That Prussia had already known this truth and had profited by it in the organization of her armies was the most weighty reason for her speedy success over the armies of France in 1870. There was no lack of patriotism amongst the French; there was no decay in the physical or moral fiber of the individual Frenchmen; but they were not lessoned in the grim business which they accepted as Napoleon's premier phrased it "with a light heart." Instead, there was the disastrous necessity of learning in the face of the rifles of men who had been long schooled in this essential duty to their country.

The German army evolved by Scharnhorst has already been described, but a few details might well be added. At the time of the Franco-German war, from the young men arriving at the age of twenty, there were chosen every year 100,000 to form the standing army, where they served for three years. This number formed but a small part of citizens reaching military age, but the essential feature of the system was that service was compulsory and that any one might be chosen. Following the service in the standing army came a second period of four years in the Reserve and a third of five years in the Landwehr — in all twelve years, during some part of which the individual received military training. In addition to these men so trained, the government reserved the right to call to the colors in time of war any able-bodied man from the age of seventeen to that of forty-two. A careful registration was made to account for every man who had seen service, equipment and clothing were kept ready for his use, and orders were issued informing him in detail of his duty when the call for mobilization was issued. The same painstaking care had arranged in time of peace for the mustering of animals, the collecting of food and other supplies, the formation of trains — all to such effect that within a fortnight after the formal declaration of hostilities, the North German Confederation mobilized an army of over a million men and concentrated a full half of them on the Rhine frontier. It was a feat unique in military history.

Across the Rhine a system of conscription prevailed. Alarmed by the Prussian success of 1866, the French, in 1868, had passed a new recruiting law whereby members of the standing armies enlisted for five years and later formed a Reserve for four years. Military service in France was at first avoidable by payment, and in later years by substitution. But this law had not had time to prove its value. Trained reserves were few and a complete organization had not been worked out for them. The depots which furnished the arms and equipment were large and few in number, so that crowding and confusion in a time of hurry were unavoidable. There were many cases where members of the reserves had to travel completely across France to draw their equipment only to return over the same route to join their regiments perhaps only a few miles from their homes. In the standing army, organization into the higher tactical units was rare, and maneuvers were infrequent, so that neither general nor staff officers had had that training which is so essential to the proper performance of their functions. Against Germany's well-trained million, France could put into the field only 567,000. From these must be subtracted the Algerian troops, and those at depots and garrisons. The remainder was 330,000 men.

A comparison of the armament of the two nations shows that whereas France's infantry carried the superior weapon, Germany's artillery was equipped with a more effective field piece. The needle-gun which had performed service for Prussia in two previous wars was markedly inferior to the Chassepôt of the French in range, in rapidity of fire, and in striking power. The former was sighted to 600 meters, the latter to 1200. To offset this French advantage, the German artillery was armed with steel breech-loading guns firing percussion shells of nine and twelve pounds. The French arm was composed of guns of equal caliber, but of the old muzzle-loading type. In addition, the French army placed great confidence in the forerunner of the modern machine gun, the mitrailleuse, which, though upon occasion it did great execution, generally failed to meet the expectations of the French, particularly when it was arrayed against the German field guns.

As we look back at the swift disaster which overtook France, it is hard to believe that no idea of their military inferiority ever entered the minds of her people. Her officers of high rank must have had reports from Germany which told them plainly that in everything which pertains to war they were hopelessly behind their enemy, and her Emperor certainly knew enough of the political situation to be sure that the south German states would join the Northern

Confederation against France, yet neither the one party nor the other gave any intimation of the true state of affairs to the population of the country at large. On the contrary, the generals gave out that the army was in a state of complete readiness, and the Emperor himself outlined an invasion of Germany which involved the neutrality, or rather the inactivity, of Bavaria, Würtemburg, and Baden. No doubt existed in Paris that the war would have a speedy ending. Everywhere was heard the cry "On to Berlin!"

To satisfy the popular demand, activities were begun at once. Seven army corps, totaling 210,000 men, were rushed to the frontier before the mobilization was complete. Staffs had to be formed and skeleton organizations filled in after the troops had reached their station. Indeed, the French army may be said to have mobilized on the frontier. In marked contrast was the German procedure. Each corps was mobilized in its own district and sent to the frontier as a unit, complete in men, animals, and equipment.

The French Army was divided into two wings: the left, composed of the 2d, 3d, 4th, 5th, Guard, and 6th (in reserve) Corps, numbering 163,000 men, was commanded by the Emperor in person; the right, consisting of the 1st and 7th Corps, numbering 47,000 men, was commanded by Marshal MacMahon. These two armies were later added to until in the early days of August they totaled 270,000 men. Their artillery numbered 925 guns. The Emperor's headquarters was at St. Avold in Lorraine, MacMahon's across the Vosges Mountains at Hagenau, in Alsace. The whole army was dispersed irregularly along the frontier from Thionville to Strassburg. Within a few days the impossibility of an aggressive movement became patent to those in command, and the idea of an invasion of Germany was replaced by that of moving the armies along the border in the hope of finding an ideal defensive position. It was the same error which the Austrians committed before Königgrätz — the error of supposing that they could surrender the initiative without an effort and yet hope to choose the place of the deciding contest.

In response to the restless feeling in Paris, a reconnaissance in force was ordered toward Saarbrück, where the French, greatly superior in numbers, were successful. They were able to take the town, but the victory was of no value to them because in the face of the German armies they could not cross the Saar. Von Moltke in commenting on the action says: "France was waiting for a victory; something had to be done to appease public impatience, so, in order to do something, the enemy resolved (as is usual under such circumstances) on a hostile reconnaissance, and it may be added, with the usual result." The French had struck in the air without accomplishing any result. They had, indeed, launched their only strictly aggressive move of the war. Thereafter the French were concerned not with attacking the enemy's country but with defending their own.

Meanwhile, the Germans mobilized and concentrated on the frontier with but little fear of the French invasion. They knew that should the Emperor lead his troops across the Rhine into South Germany, they would be on his flank and in a position to strike a dangerous blow at his armies. They did fear a vigorous aggressive against their own armies, but it was a feeling that soon passed when they learned of the haphazard way in which France was mobilizing. The Germans were organized into three armies: the First, under General von Steinmetz, consisting of the 1st, 7th, and 8th Corps, numbering 85,000 men; the Second, under Prince Frederick Charles, composed of the 2d, 3d, 4th, 9th, 10th, Guard, and 12th Corps, numbering 210,000 men; and the Third, under the Crown Prince Frederick of Prussia, constituted of the 5th, 6th, and 11th Corps, the 1st and 2d Bavarian Corps, and the Würtemburg and Baden divisions, numbering 180,000 men. Thus against France's 270,000 men and 925 guns were arrayed the German armies of

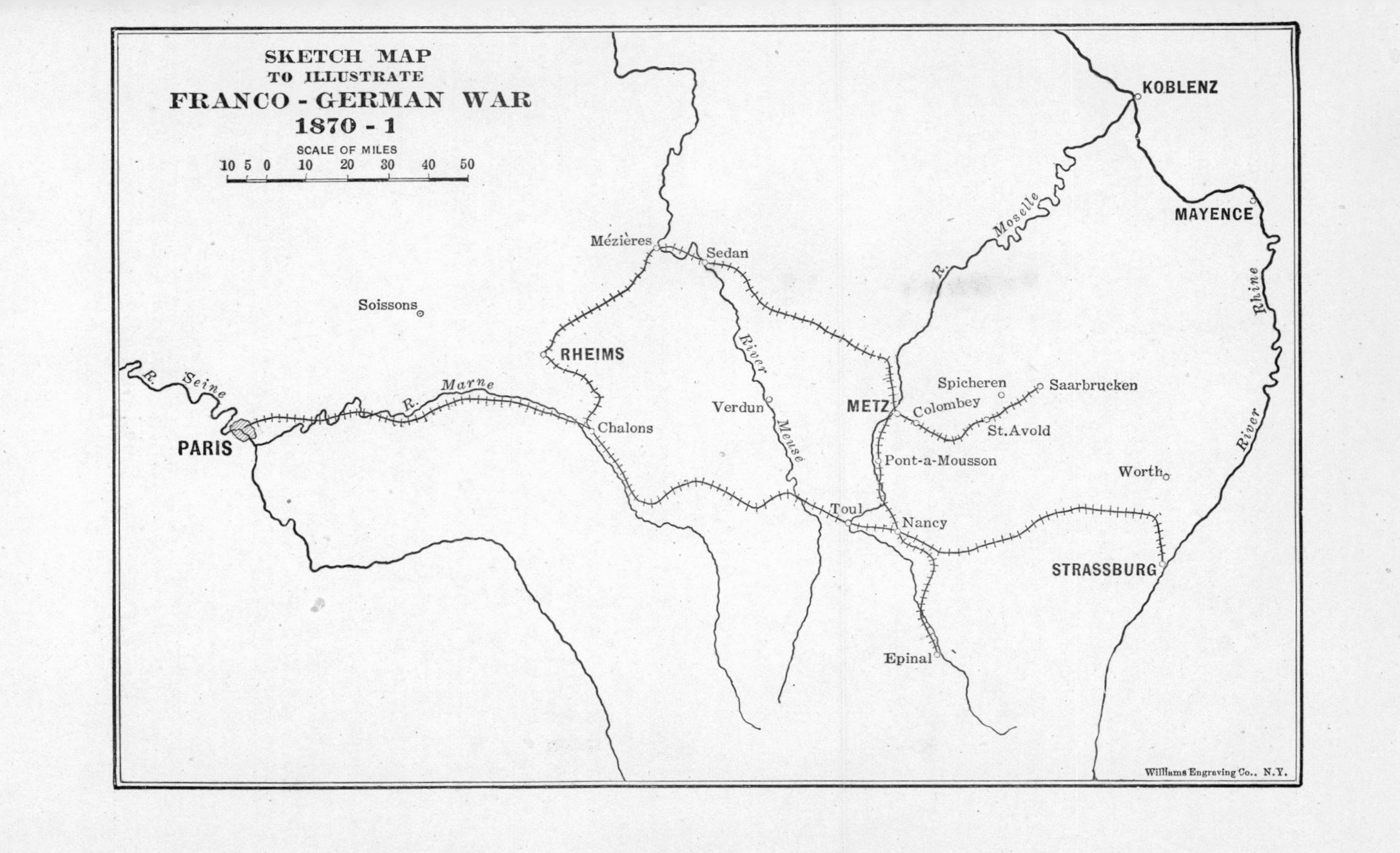
SKETCH MAP
TO ILLUSTRATE
FRANCO - GERMAN WAR
1870 - 1
SCALE OF MILES
10 5 0 10 20 30 40 50
KOBLENZ
MAYENCE
R. Moselle
Rhine
River
Mézieres
Sedan
Soissons
RHEIMS
R. Seine
Marne
R.
PARIS
Chalons
River
Verdun
Meuse
METZ
Spicheren
Saarbrucken
Colombey
St. Avold
Pont-a-Mousson
Worth
Toul
Nancy
STRASSBURG
Epinal
Williams Engraving Co., N.Y.

475,000 and 1584 guns. The First army concentrated on the German right with the Second on its left: they were to invade Lorraine. The Third army was on the left of the line: it was to invade Alsace.

The German plan contemplated as its general objective the city of Paris, but because two French armies lay between him and the French capital, von Moltke did not look beyond his first meeting with those armies. He knew that the capture of Paris, while it would give him an immense moral victory, would not affect the outcome of the war. France's real strength was in her armies. To crush those armies was to paralyze France's resistance and leave the way open to Paris. Von Moltke's special objective, therefore, was the army of the Emperor. He knew of the division into two commands, one in Lorraine, the other in Alsace, and arranged his own forces accordingly. The First army on the right, and the Second on its immediate left, were to oppose Napoleon in Lorraine; the Third army was to operate against MacMahon across the Vosges in Alsace. The orders to all were the same: first defeat the army in front of you, then march on Paris. Viewed thus without the details of the campaign, the plan seems simple. It was simple, but it was successful. The Third army defeated MacMahon at Wörth; the First and Second defeated Napoleon's armies about Metz; portions of all three united to crush MacMahon at Sedan; and the victors of Sedan marched on Paris.

Because the Third army's task of passing through the Vosges Mountains would retard it, and because its route to Paris was the longest, it was put in motion first, on the 4th of August, 1870. Two days later it encountered MacMahon's forces in the first of the great battles of the war, that of Wörth. The French First Corps under MacMahon occupied the heights on the right bank of the Sauer River. Against it before the day was ended was hurled practically all of the 3d German Army. MacMahon attempted to reënforce by ordering divisions from the 5th and 7th Corps, but only one division arrived in time to assist in the battle. At nightfall the defeated French retired in confusion upon Lunéville, leaving the passes of the Vosges Mountains unguarded, and, except for the fortified towns, abandoning the province of Alsace to the enemy.

On the same day the advancing 1st and 2d German armies encountered the 2d French Corps at Spicheren and in a prolonged action defeated it, although it was later supported by the 3d, 4th, and 5th Corps. The battle was unexpected by the Germans, but the brigade and division commanders hurried their troops to the sound of firing to such good effect that they were able greatly to outnumber the French. This constant arrival of new organizations operated to change the commander of the battle three times during the day, but such was the German organization that no confusion resulted therefrom.

Thus, by night of August 7, the French had been defeated at both ends of their line, their flanks had been pushed back, and their commanders had been thrown into consternation by the double defeat. No plan of resisting the invader seemed possible now other than abandoning the frontier and withdrawing to the line of the Moselle River. The 2d, 3d, 4th, and Guard Corps retreated to Metz where they were joined by the 6th, and the army of MacMahon with the 5th Corps withdrew as far as Châlons, where a new corps, the 12th, was added. Marshal Bazaine replaced the Emperor in executive command of the army of the Rhine.

As soon as von Moltke had reëstablished communications between his armies he gave orders for a general advance on the Moselle, directing the 2d Army (less the 3d Corps) to march on Pont-à-Mousson, and the 1st Army to follow to the right and rear of the 2d. The 3d Corps was to follow the St. Avold-Metz road and maintain touch with the French. On the 10th of August this corps encountered the French army under Bazaine. Von Moltke, knowing that one corps could not resist an entire army, halted the right of his line and started the remainder on a great wheel toward Metz in the hope of meeting his enemy in a decisive battle. Before these orders could be effected, a sudden retreat of the French caused their revocation, and again the Germans started their march to the Moselle. On August 13, Bazaine once more changed his mind and determined to make a stand in front of Metz. For the second time von Moltke gave the order for the wheeling movement to bring all his troops into action. At Colombey, about four miles east of Metz, contact was established, the French turned to fight, and all day a battle continued in which the Germans barely held their ground. At its conclusion the French withdrew to the cover of the Metz forts.

The battle of Colombey, though really indecisive, left an impression of victory with the Germans. They conceived of their vanquished foe as retreating with all speed upon Verdun, and they pressed forward anxiously to overtake and destroy him. Arrived at the Moselle, on the 15th of August, Prince Frederick Charles ordered General von Alvensleben to march with the 3d Corps on Mars-la-Tour. Here, on the 16th, the unsuspecting corps commander came full on the French army. Hoping to conceal his weakness he made up his mind to attack. All day he forced the issue, and pushed his corps forward. In the afternoon he was supported by portions of the 9th and 10th Corps, but he was still hopelessly outnumbered, and should have been overwhelmed. This was the battle of Vionville-Mars-la-Tour.

In the morning, von Alvensleben's exhausted troops saw the French skirmishers advancing and prepared for what seemed a hopeless resistance. But the French demonstration was only to cover their army's withdrawal. Meanwhile, Prince Frederick Charles, von Moltke, and the King had arrived on the field of battle. Reinforcements were ordered, and the Germans prepared to redeem their strategical blunder. By the afternoon of the 17th of August, von Moltke was certain that Bazaine had drawn up for battle on the line of St. Privat-Gravelotte, his left flank resting on the fortress of Metz. Had the German chief been opposed by a commander as active and vigorous as himself, he would have been in grave danger. For Bazaine was on the German flank and might have made a swift march to the southeast where, by throwing out flank and rear guards to hold the 1st German army, he might have destroyed von Moltke's lines of communication. This maneuver, successfully carried out, though it might not have affected the result of the campaign, would at least have severely hampered the invader. Bazaine, however, knew that his staff was incapable of this brilliant but difficult feat, and prepared merely for a defensive in front of Metz. And von Moltke, too, knew the French staff so well that he gave no thought to his communications but prepared at once to destroy Bazaine's army.

The marshal had taken up a strong position along a ridge running almost due north from the Moselle. Along the southern half runs the Mance River in a deep wooded ravine. Beyond the source of the Mance the ridge slopes away, open and rolling, toward the Orne. At intervals along the ridge are the villages of Gravelotte, Armanvillers, St. Privat, and Roncourt. The 2d, 3d, 4th, and 6th Corps in order from left to right held the ridge, while the Guard Corps was held in reserve behind the left of the line. This disposition was the weakness of Bazaine's position. His left was naturally strong, but because of small engagements on that flank on the afternoon of the 17th, he feared for that portion of his line, and in consequence left the right in the air. Had he placed his cavalry there in support, or had the 6th corps been furnished with tools wherewith to entrench, the outcome of the battle would unquestionably have been different. Von Moltke himself recognized this fact when he spoke of the position as being "almost impreg-

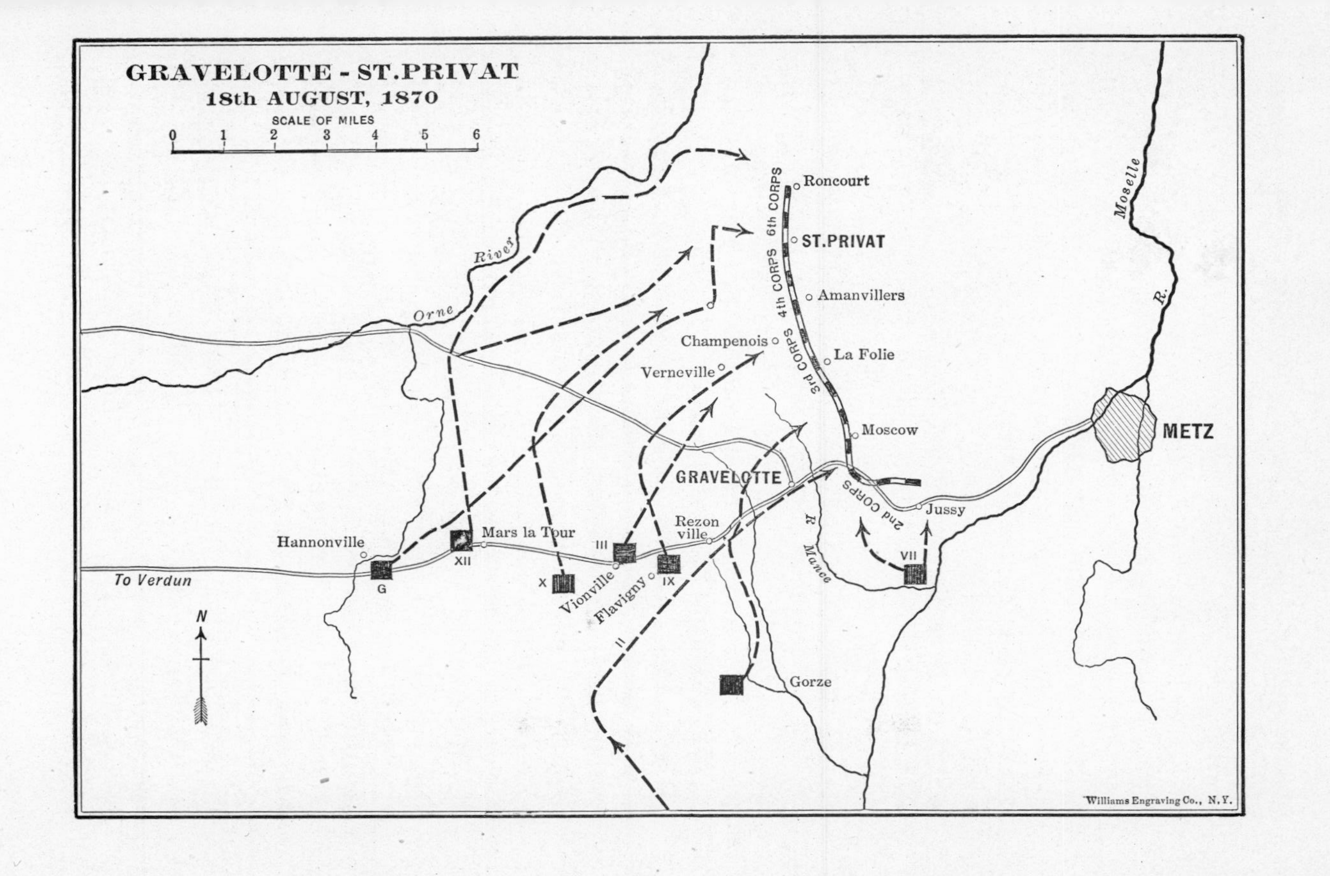
GRAVELOTTE - ST. PRIVAT
18th AUGUST, 1870
SCALE OF MILES
0 1 2 3 4 5 6
Moselle
R.
METZ
Orne
River
Roncourt
ST. PRIVAT
Amanvillers
La Folie
Moscow
Jussy
6th CORPS
4th CORPS
3rd CORPS
2nd CORPS
Champenois
Verneville
GRAVELOTTE
R
Mance
Gorze
Rezon ville
Hannonville
Mars la Tour
Vionville
Flavigny
To Verdun
G
XII
X
III
IX
II
VII
N
Williams Engraving Co., N.Y.

nable," and he saw too that this weakness on the right made success possible, for he says, "the French left wing could not be shaken even by the most devoted bravery and the greatest sacrifices." But even with success for Bazaine in the battle, unless it was followed by the utter rout of the Germans — an improbable contingency — the strategic victory was von Moltke's, for he had maneuvered the French into a position where he stood between them and their capital, and from which retreat was impossible, once they had accepted the challenge to fight.

At noon on the 18th of August, the 9th German Corps opened the battle by an attack on the French line at Verneville. Von Moltke's cavalry reconnaissance had not determined the extent of the hostile line and it was believed that the right of Bazaine's army was at Armanvillers. The error was soon discovered, the 10th and Guard corps were deployed on the left of the 9th, while the 12th Corps was given the task of trying to turn the French right. It was not until four in the afternoon that the Germans learned that Roncourt was the extreme flank, whereupon the 12th corps had to be sent still farther north. At five o'clock, the commander of the German Guard Corps, fearing that darkness would leave the battle undecided, began an attack on the 6th French Corps at St. Privat. At first he was repulsed with a loss of 6000 men in ten minutes, but almost immediately the artillery of the 9th and 10th Corps centered on St. Privat, and, timing his advance with that of the attack on Roncourt by the 12th Corps, the guard commander made a second attempt on St. Privat, and this time pushed home his assault. The successful capture of St. Privat and Roncourt crumpled the 6th French Corps, which fell back into disarray, leaving the flank of the 4th Corps unprotected. Though firing kept up on the left of the French line, where the French had easily held their positions, the collapse of the 6th Corps meant the ending of the battle.

Under cover of the night Bazaine withdrew his forces

within the walls of the fortress at Metz, and when morning broke, though his troops were safe for the time being, they had ceased to exist as a mobile army. Von Moltke at once formed the Guard, 4th and 12th Corps and two cavalry divisions (in all 90,000 men) into the 4th Army or Army of the Meuse, with which he immediately set out in pursuit of Marshal MacMahon. The remaining seven corps were left under Prince Frederick Charles to invest the fortress of Metz.

Meanwhile, MacMahon had assembled his army of four corps at Châlons. Here in a conference with the Emperor (who had left Bazaine before Gravelotte-St. Privat) it was decided to march the army to Paris and prepare for the defense of the capital. Immediately after Bazaine's disaster there came a peremptory demand from Paris in the name of the Empress that an advance be made toward Metz for the purpose of relieving Bazaine's army. There were many things to influence Marshal MacMahon's decision. He knew that the Crown Prince's army was advancing on Paris. If he should meet and defeat it, his success would only check the Germans temporarily, and he ran the great danger of being himself annihilated. If he should retreat on Paris, he would then have the best opportunities for a successful encounter with the enemy, but such a course would mean the abandoning of Bazaine's army to its fate, and it would ensure the overthrow of the Napoleon dynasty by the now infuriated Parisians. Politics rather than military necessity carried the day, and MacMahon started toward Metz.

His route of march was determined by a communication from Bazaine to the effect that he hoped to break through the hostile investing lines around Metz, and make his way to Paris by way of Montmédy. The Germans were not certain of MacMahon's exact position, but they knew that he had abandoned Châlons for Rheims and accordingly the latter town was selected as their objective. On the afternoon of August 25 they received definite information that he was moving eastward, apparently to succor Bazaine, and accordingly von Moltke issued orders which changed the front of the advancing 3d and 4th armies from west to north. A decisive battle was imminent and von Moltke meant to have all the troops available to insure a victory. Steadily MacMahon continued his march, urged on by insistent demands from Paris. Wrong though he was in heeding them, one must not use them to account for all his mistakes. A great factor in his defeat was that he employed only one cavalry division for reconnaissance and that on his northern flank, when he and every private in his army knew that the enemy was on the southern flank. Efficient cavalry employed on the right could have foretold his ultimate defeat.

The two armies came together on August 29 in a minor engagement at Nouart, and on the following day the 5th French Corps at Beaumont was surprised and badly beaten by the Army of the Meuse. MacMahon, learning at last that his continued march to Metz was impossible, began a hasty retreat down the Meuse, the Germans close behind him. His route lay toward Sedan, a fortress town only seven miles from the Belgian frontier. With a neutral country to the north and the German armies to the south-east, south, and southwest, there was only one avenue of escape from Sedan, the northwestern route by way of Mezières. There was desultory fighting all day of August 31, and nightfall found MacMahon's troops clustered around Sedan, anxiously awaiting the action of the morrow which was destined to be the last.

Von Moltke laid his nets with his customary skill. The 3d Army was ordered to move to the westward to prevent the withdrawal by way of Mezières. The Army of the Meuse was given the task of the direct attack. Specifically, the corps orders were as follows: for the 3d Army, the 11th Corps to move on Vrigne and later to deploy on the line

St. Menges-Fleigneux; 5th Corps to follow and join the 11th; 1st Bavarian Corps to cross the Meuse and take up a position before Bazeilles; 2d Bavarian Corps to occupy the heights of Wadelincourt and Frenois, and shell the enemy from the rear: for the Army of the Meuse, 4th Corps to take up a position in front of La Moncelle; 12th Corps to prolong its line north past Daigny; Guard Corps to move toward Givonne, and connect with the 11th or 5th Corps (3d army) as soon as possible.

The battle field in shape is a rough triangle with the Meuse river for its base, and the ravines of Illy and Givonne Creeks for sides. Along the banks of these creeks were the defensive positions which the French took up on the night of August 31, the 12th Corps from Bazeilles to Daigny, the 1st on its left as far as Givonne, the 7th on the Illy between the village of that name and Floing. The 5th Corps was held in reserve close to the fortress. Opposite all of these positions there is high ground suitable for attacking artillery, and the approaches to them give plenty of cover. Both of the French lines were in strong natural positions, with good cover for reserves, but without sufficient depth—a slight reversal crowded them back upon the fortress of Sedan.

At half-past four on the morning of September 1, the 1st Bavarian Corps began the attack on Bazeilles, and shortly thereafter the 4th Corps took up the attack in front of Moncelle and Daigny. Marshal MacMahon was seriously wounded in the attack on Moncelle, and upon leaving the field turned over the command to General Ducrot. The new commanding officer scented defeat and at once ordered a withdrawal of the 1st and 12th Corps. As this movement was being undertaken, the command again changed hands, passing this time to General Wimpffen, who immediately countermanded the order and directed a renewal of the fight. The struggle for Bazeilles was continued, but before noon the French were obliged to abandon it and withdraw on Balan. At the same time the Prussian

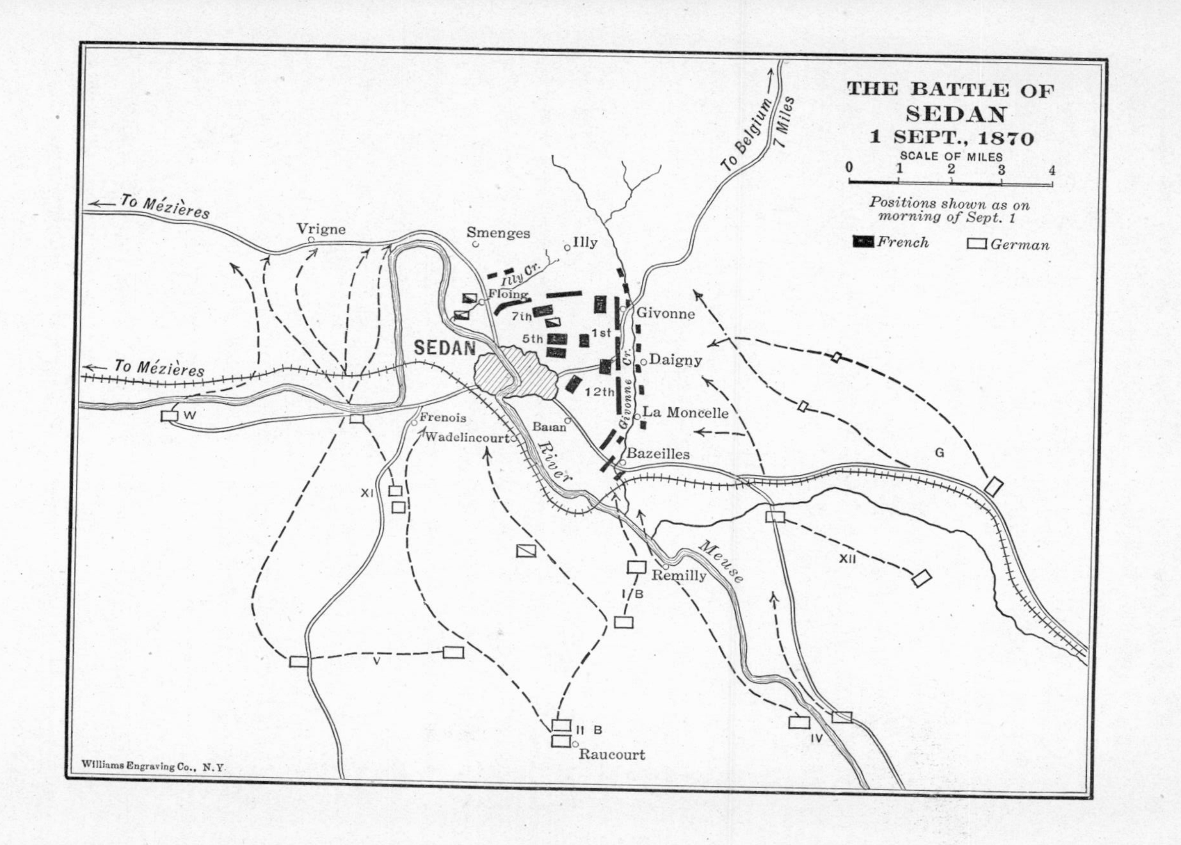
THE BATTLE OF
SEDAN
1 SEPT., 1870
SCALE OF MILES
0 1 2 3 4
Positions shown as on morning of Sept. 1
French
German
To Belgium 7 Miles
To Mézières
To Mézières
Vrigne
Smenges
Illy
Illy Cr.
Floing
7th
5th
1st
12th
SEDAN
Givonne
Daigny
Givonne Cr.
La Moncelle
Bazeilles
Baian
Frenois
Wadelincourt
River
Meuse
Remilly
I/B
II B
Raucourt
W
XI
V
XII
IV
G
Williams Engraving Co., N.Y.

Guard Corps joined hands with the 5th German Corps to the north of Sedan, whereupon the attack upon the Illy, which had been steadily growing hotter, became overpowering, and little by little the 7th French Corps was forced back toward Sedan.

The German ring about the French army was now complete. Hope of retreating by way of Mezières had long been given up and as the afternoon wore away the approaching disaster became more and more apparent. By three o'clock the Emperor was in favor of surrendering in order that lives might be saved, for he knew now that the struggle was hopeless. General Wimpffen, however, representing the hot- and empty-headed war ministry in Paris, would not hear of such a course, and, gathering what men he could, tried to force a way through the German lines to the southeast. The attempt was brave, but suicidal. It met, as it could meet, only with failure, and the French hoisted the white flag in token of complete surrender. The following day they signed the capitulation which gave to the Germans 80,000 prisoners. Among them was the Emperor of France.

The battle of Sedan broke the backbone of French resistance. Wörth, Spicheren, Gravelotte, Sedan coming in quick succession had paralyzed one army and destroyed the other. Bazaine, surrounded by the enemy in Metz, could be depended upon for no further assistance. His opportunity of breaking out had long gone by, if indeed it had ever existed. In Strassburg, in Toul, in Belfort, other French forces were held immobile by the troops of King William. In various parts of France frenzied efforts were being made to raise and equip armies wherewith to continue resistance, but the attempt was a tardy one. Catastrophe had already overtaken France. Von Moltke had accomplished the first part of his plan, the destruction of the opposing armies, and was now ready to undertake the second part. Sedan had cleared the road to Paris.

The German armies now advanced on the capital, encountering only one check in the shape of Vinoy's corps which had reached Sedan too late to take part. The city was reached on September 19. The defeat of General Ducrot's forces near Versailles left the Germans free to invest Paris, and within two days they had arranged their troops for the approaching siege. The capitulation within a few days of Toul and Strassburg, the former an essential point on the line of communications, left the roads clear from Paris to Berlin, and at once von Moltke began moving material for the siege. Late in October the surrender of Metz, with all the armies and supplies contained in it, assured the safety of the armies before Paris, and left von Moltke free to give his attention to the besieged city.

There is not space here to give the details of the siege. General Trochu, who commanded the defenders, had 400,000 men in his forces, but they were mostly raw undisciplined recruits of a revolutionary type; several times they were on the edge of revolt. Over such as these the trained German troops had an immense superiority which they maintained throughout the siege. Despite the many gallant sorties and the heroic work of her defenders, Paris was unable to rid herself of her enemy, and on January 27, 1871, agreed on an armistice, which ended in capitulation.

Outside in several quarters of France was being waged the "People's War" directed by the indefatigable Gambetta. But these armies, too, were "pushed raw to the battle," and one by one came to melancholy ends. Never was a braver resistance than was made by these citizen armies of France, but never was a more hopeless one. When Paris fell, hope for France died, and reluctantly the people gave up the struggle and turned their attention to bearing the burden imposed upon defeated France.

Bismarck's politics can receive no clearer illustration than by comparing the actions of the victorious armies in Vienna in 1866 and in Paris in 1870. Austria, whom he desired as an ally, was spared the humiliation of having a conquering army march through her capital. But the French, whom he designed to humiliate as deeply as possible, were forced to see the triumphant battalions marched through the streets of Paris, and to feel as Jugurtha must have felt when, to grace a triumph, he was forced to parade in chains through the streets of Rome. Every effort was made to sooth Austria: every effort was made to irritate France. The success was complete, for within a few years Austria was joined in close alliance to her former enemy, and in France there was apparent that growing hatred which at last culminated in the horror of 1914.

CHAPTER VII

EUROPEAN READJUSTMENT, 1871–1875

A. BISMARCK DURING THE FRANCO-GERMAN WAR

DURING the active campaign, of course, the European interests centered about the military duel between France and Prussia, but once that campaign had passed its crisis and victory for Prussia was certain, political and diplomatic affairs resumed their customary importance. Von Roon and von Moltke had for a season displaced Bismarck in the public eye because of the immediate importance of success in war. Bismarck himself complains bitterly of the neglect which he, the civil authority and diplomatic arm of the government, suffered during the campaign at the hands of the military men. Immediately after the ultimate military success became assured, however, Bismarck in the ensuing negotiations became again the chief personage before the public.

Shortly after war was declared, Bismarck packed up and, with his corps of scribes and aides, prepared to accompany the army. A member of that corps (Busch) thus describes the ordinary procedure of Bismarck and his staff:

"Throughout the whole war the Chancellor wore uniform. It was generally the well-known undress of the yellow regiment of heavy Landwehr cavalry. During the early months of the campaign he, as a rule, only wore the Commander's Cross of the Order of the Red Eagle, to which he afterwards added the Iron Cross. I only saw him a couple of times in a dressing gown. That was at Versailles, when he was unwell, the only time, as far as I know, that anything ailed him throughout the whole war. When travelling he was usually accompanied in the carriage by Herr Abeken, but on some occasions he took me with him for several days in succession. He was very easy to please in the matter of his quarters and was willing to put up with the most modest shelter when better was not to be had. Indeed, it once happened that there was no bedstead and that his bed had to be made upon the floor.

"Our carriages usually followed immediately after those of the King's suite. We started generally about 10 o'clock in the morning, and sometimes covered as much as sixty kilometres in the day. On reaching our quarters for the night our first duty was to set about preparing an office, in which there was seldom any lack of work, especially when we had the Field Telegraph at our disposal. When communications were thus established, the Chancellor again became what, with short intervals, he had been throughout this entire period: namely, the central figure of the whole civilized European world. Even in those places where we only stayed for one night he, incessantly active himself, kept his assistants almost continuously engaged until a late hour. Messengers were constantly going and coming with telegrams and letters. Councillors were drawing up notes, orders, and directions under instructions from their chief, and these were being copied, registered, ciphered, and deciphered in the Chancellerie. Reports, questions, newspaper articles, etc., streamed in from every direction, most of them requiring instant attention.

"Never, perhaps, was the well-nigh superhuman power of work shown by the Chancellor, his creative, receptive, and critical activity, his ability to deal with the most difficult problems, always finding the right and the only solution, more strikingly evident than during this period. The inexhaustible nature of his powers was all the more astounding, as he took but little sleep. Except when a battle was expected and he rose at daybreak to join the King and the army, the Chancellor rose rather late, as had been his custom at home, usually about 10 o'clock. On the other hand, he spent the night at work, and only fell asleep as daylight began to appear. He was often hardly out of bed and dressed before he commenced work again, reading despatches and making notes upon them, looking through newspapers, giving instructions to his Councillors and others, and setting them their various tasks or even writing or dictating. Later on there were visits to be received, audiences to be granted, explanations to be given to the King. Then followed a further study of despatches and maps, the correction of articles, drafts hurriedly prepared with his well-known big pencil, letters to be written, information to be telegraphed, or published in the newspapers, and in the midst of it all the reception of visitors who could not be refused a hearing yet must occasionally have been unwelcome. It was only after 2, or even 3 o'clock, in places where we made a longer stay, that the Chancellor allowed himself a little recreation by taking a ride in the neighborhood. On his return he set to work again, continuing until dinner time, between 5.30 and 6 P.M. In an hour and a half at latest he went back to his writing-desk, where he frequently remained till midnight."

Bismarck was with his King when the white flag was raised over Sedan and when the French General under a flag of truce brought the famous note from the French Emperor to the Prussian King:

"Monsieur mon Frère — N'ayant pu mourir au milieu de mes troupes, il ne me reste qu'à remettre mon épée entre les mains de Votre Majesté. — Je suis Votre Majesté le bon Frère
Sedan, le 1er Septembre, 1870. —Napoléon."

Early the following morning Bismarck was routed out of bed to meet the French Emperor in person at the little village of Donchéry. "A short, thick-set man, in a red cap braided with gold lace, and wearing red trousers and a hooded cape lined with red, steps from behind the house and speaks at first to the French Officers, some of whom are sitting along the hedge by the potato field," writes Dr. Busch, describing the scene. "He has white kid gloves, and smokes a cigarette. It is the Emperor. At the short distance which I stand from him I can clearly distinguish his features. There is something soft and dreamy in the look of his light gray eyes, which resembled those of people who have lived fast. His cap is set a little to the right, in which direction his head is also bent. The short legs do not seem in proportion with the long upper part of the body. His whole appearance has something unmilitary about it." Possibly Napoleon's appearance at the time reflected the despondency of his feelings, for he was upon a mission to arrange with the Germans for the surrender of his army. At his meeting with Bismarck he endeavored to arrange a personal interview with the Prussian King in the hope that by working upon the royal sympathies he might gain easier terms of surrender. Bismarck, however, insisted upon unconditional surrender before he would grant the Emperor access to King William. After but a short delay Napoleon, realizing that his army was surrounded and helpless and that further resistance meant useless slaughter, accepted the terms.

With the fall of Sedan, the career of Napoleon III closed. Two days later, September 4, the Empire fell as a result of a spontaneous Paris revolution. Napoleon himself went to Cassel in Germany where he remained a prisoner until the end of the war. In 1871 he retired to England with his wife, the Empress Eugénie, and his son. In his career he had wheeled the full circle. From an exile, teaching mathematics in a Swiss college or serving as special constable in a London riot, he had risen to be Emperor of one of the greatest states of the world and now became again an outcast, living in seclusion in England. During the two remaining years of his life, he vainly sought to justify his course in the critical moments of 1870 and 1871, and to assure to his son a chance for ultimate succession to the throne of France. On January 9, 1873, he died. His son, the Prince Eugène, after having been educated in the English military school at Woolwich, served with a British expedition against the Zulus in 1879, and was killed. With his death this Napoleonic line ended.

After playing his part in the negotiations following the fall of Sedan, Bismarck pushed on towards Paris. He was during this whole period a very busy man. The government of Prussia, of which he was the Chancellor, was being carried on from a point far within the boundaries of France: the practical difficulties of administration were thereby immensely increased. During these critical months it was essential that public opinion in Prussia should be directed in certain channels by semi-official publications and that the policies of the government should be presented in the most favorable light: all this work fell to the lot of Bismarck. It was well known that M. Thiers had been sent by the new provisional government in France on a mission to the neutral states in Europe to solicit assistance: it was Bismarck's duty to counteract by every means possible the effect of Thiers' solicitations. The French press was spreading abroad untrue and unsubstantiated charges of inhuman atrocities on the part of the invading troops: Bismarck undertook with success to refute these accusations. From the time the Germans began to plant their cannons before the forts of Paris, the representative of the provisional government, M. Jules Favre, entered into negotiations with the Germans for an armistice or a peace; the negotiations on the part of Prussia, Bismarck had to conduct. And most important of all for the future, conferences were proceeding with representatives of the South German States for the creation, constitution, and organization of a united German Empire: and these conferences, requiring the utmost tact and diplomacy, were conducted on the part of Prussia wholly by Bismarck. This brief summary of the magnitude and variety of the duties that fell to the share of Bismarck during these months may give an idea of how completely his time was occupied. From October 6, when he and his staff established themselves comfortably at Versailles to await the fall of Paris and the close of the war, he was constantly engaged in the most important and arduous negotiations.

B. EVENTS IN EUROPE DURING THE FRANCO-GERMAN WAR

During these months some events of great moment were taking place in Europe. Since these events were all closely dependent upon, or affected by, the existing war, it is well to consider them at this point.

i. *France*

Within the French capital the fall of Sedan had resulted, as has been mentioned, in the immediate fall of the imperial government. On Saturday, September 3, the Emperor sent to Paris his telegram, "The army has been defeated and is captive, I myself am prisoner." The next day, Sunday, the Parisian mob, shouting "Down with the Empire! Long live the Republic!" invaded the hall where the legislative assembly was in anxious session. The leaders in the assembly without delay proclaimed a Republic and hastily organized a Government of National Defense. Empress Eugénie, after a futile attempt to rally support for Napoleon, fled from the city. During the remainder of the war the Government of National Defense constituted the only real government of France.

As the German armies approached Paris, this new government attempted to come to terms of peace. Its representatives were willing to lay all the blame for the war upon the captured Emperor; they argued that, since Napoleon was captured and his government overthrown, the Germans had no further cause for war and should at once come to terms of peace and withdraw from French territory. They were unwilling to recognize the hopelessness of their situation at the moment. They refused to consider terms which would involve any loss of territory; they must have peace with honor; they would never submit, to paraphrase Favre's grandiloquent language to Bismarck, "To the cession of an inch of their soil or a stone of their fortresses." This insistence upon the national honor of France had no effect upon the logical cold-blooded Bismarck. He argued that French honor was no different from the honor of other nations in Europe, that France had certainly intended in the event of her victory to annex German territory, that Prussia had as much right to force the annexation of French territory and intended so to do. When the results of the negotiations became known, the French nation was spurred to heroic efforts. The Paris garrison made repeated sorties, but all in vain. A representative of the government, Gambetta, ascended from the city in a balloon, was wafted beyond the German besieging lines, and traveled through central and southern France, rousing the people to expel the German invaders. He recruited large levies, but these hastily organized and insufficiently drilled troops were no match for the veteran Germans. In October of 1870 the great fortress of Metz surrendered, thereby releasing a huge German army to block whatever efforts Gambetta's troops might make. The Parisians were gradually starved into submission. After one final desperate sortie on January 19, Favre opened negotiations for capitulation. On Saturday, January 28, these negotiations were finished and an armistice declared. Dr. Busch gives an account of the final moments:

"Saturday, January 28th, — At 11 o'clock the French negotiators again arrived — Favre, Durbach, and two others, who are understood to be also leading railway officials; and two officers, another general, and an aide-de-camp, both men with a good presence. They take lunch with us. Then follows a lengthy negotiation at Moltke's lodgings. The Chief afterwards dictates to the Secretaries Willisch and Saint Blanquart the treaties of capitulation and armistice, which are drawn up in duplicate. They are afterwards signed and sealed by Bismarck and Favre, at twenty minutes past seven, in the green room next to the Minister's study upstairs.

"The French dined with us. The general (Valden is his name) ate little and hardly spoke at all. Favre was also dejected and taciturn. The aide-de-camp, M. D'Herrisson, did not appear to be so much affected, and the railway officials, after their long privations, devoted themselves with considerable gusto to the pleasures of the table. According to what I can gather from the latter they have, as a matter of fact, been on very short commons in Paris for some time past, and the death rate last week amounted to above five thousand. The mortality was especially heavy amongst children up to two years of age, and coffins for these tiny French citizens were to be seen in all directions. Delbrück afterward said that "Favre and the General looked like two condemned prisoners who were going to the gallows next morning. I pitied them."

ii. *Italy*

Outside of its immediate theater of operations, the war played a decisive part in events in Europe. In Italy the war gave the government its chance to make Rome the capital. French soldiers, it will be remembered, were maintained in Rome by the Emperor Napoleon to prevent the Italian government from assaulting and capturing the city; but with the first Prussian success it became evident that the French would have to withdraw these troops to aid in their home defense. In August of 1870, after the war had been going on but a month, the last French soldiers left Rome. A month later the fall of Sedan and the end of the Empire absolved Italy from all her obligations to Napoleon with respect to Rome. King Victor Emmanuel invited the Pope, Pius IX, to consent to the occupation of Rome by the government troops. The Pope refused. Without delay a well-trained army of more than thirty thousand troops was ordered to the attack. The Papal forces resisted, but were hopelessly outnumbered. The Italian cannon soon made a breach in the wall, and the troops entered the city September 20, 1870. On October 2, after a plebiscite in which 133,681 voted for, and only 1507 against, unity with Italy, Rome was formally joined with the rest of the peninsula under the royal government.

iii. *Russia*

In Russia, too, war had provided an opportunity for achieving one of its national ambitions. Certain articles of the treaty of Paris (1856) had forbidden Russia to maintain naval forces in, or naval arsenals on, the shores of the Black Sea. Both military and economic reasons caused Russia to chafe under these restrictions. The Black Sea was Russia's only all-the-year-round ice-free body of water: consequently, the prohibition of naval forces on the Black Sea practically resulted in preventing Russia from having any naval forces at all. Furthermore, the Black Sea was the great outlet for the immense harvests of grain exported from the fertile plains of central and southern Russia. This outlet, however, could at any moment be absolutely closed at the whim of a foreign power controlling the Bosphorus and the Dardanelles. If Russia were not allowed to have naval forces on the Black Sea, she had no prospect of being able in time of trouble to force open a channel for her huge harvests of grain. The two nations who in the negotiations following the Crimean War had been instrumental in forcing these restrictions upon Russian freedom in the Black Sea, were France and Great Britain. Their desire had been to prevent Russia from becoming as threatening as a naval power as she always was as a military power. In 1870, however, the successive disasters to the French armies made it certain that Russia might safely change these conditions with regard to the Black Sea; for France could offer no effective opposition, and Great Britain alone would scarcely dare to wage war against Russia, especially at so troubled a period in continental affairs. Consequently, in a note dated October 31, 1870, after the fall of Sedan and of Metz, the Russian Chancellor denounced and repudiated the so-called Black Sea clauses of the Treaty of Paris. Although Great Britain immediately protested, her statesmen recognized the impracticability of waging war over the issue under the existing conditions. Her protest was effective only so far as to obtain a concession that the whole matter should be laid before a conference of the powers. At this conference, which was held in London early in 1871, it was agreed that both Russia and Turkey might maintain unlimited naval armaments in the Black Sea, and that Turkey had the right to close the Bosphorus and the Dardanelles to naval vessels.

iv. *Formation of German Empire*

For the future history of Europe, however, the most important events during these months from October, 1870, to January of 1871 were being directed by the adroit diplomacy of Bismarck in his dealings with the South German governments. At the very beginning of the war, the idea of complete German unity had been uppermost in the minds of statesmen of both North German and South German states. And yet so proud and independent were certain of the monarchs of the larger South German states that the task of persuading them to enter into any union in which they would play a more or less subordinate part to Prussia seemed next to impossible. Some men, headed by the Crown Prince, were inclined to threaten the South German states and to force them into a union. "There is no danger," the Crown Prince is reported to have said to the Prussian Chancellor, "let us take a firm and commanding attitude. You will see I was right in maintaining that you are not sufficiently conscious of your own power." Bismarck, however, saw the problem from a different angle. It was his desire to create a unity in which no component unit should be dissatisfied with its conditions of membership. He was willing to make concessions, some material concessions, in order that this satisfaction might be assured. He was willing to treat with each of the South German states separately, and to meet demands even further than the Prussians might generally approve for the sake of this essential harmony. Toward the last of the negotiations, the success of German unity hinged upon the arrangement with Bavaria. The concessions which Bismarck was willing to grant to this great and powerful State will illustrate the lengths to which he was willing to go in order to obtain the desired good will of the members in the new union: — Bavaria's King was to maintain his command over his army in times of peace; Bavaria was to have a special influence in the decisions of the Empire on foreign affairs; Bavaria was to have its own postal and telegraph system; and Bavaria was to retain its own laws with respect to marriage and citizenship.

Dr. Busch describes the scene as Bismarck entered the dining room the evening of the signing of the Bavarian treaty:

> "Well, the Bavarian Treaty is made and signed. German unity is secure, and the German Emperor too." We were all silent for a moment. I then begged to be allowed to bring away the pen with which he had signed it. "In God's name, bring all three," he said; "but the gold one is not amongst them." I went and took the three pens that lay near the document. Two of them were still wet. Two empty champagne bottles stood close by. "Bring us another bottle," said the Chief to the servant. "It is an event." Then, after reflecting for a while, he observed: "The newspapers will not be satisfied, and he who writes history in the usual way may criticize our agreement. He may possibly say, 'The stupid fellow should have asked for more; he would have got it, as they would have been compelled to yield.' And he may be right so far as the 'compelled' is concerned. But what I attached more importance to was that they should be thoroughly pleased with the thing. What are treaties when people are compelled to enter into them! And I know that they went away pleased. . . . I did not want to squeeze them or to make capital out of the situation. The Treaty has its deficiencies, but it is for that the more durable. The future can supply those deficiencies."

Bismarck's remarks are important as showing that he fully appreciated the criticism to which the treaty would be subjected, and as revealing the considerations which led him to make such important concessions.

The finishing touch that was necessary for the completion of the work of creating the German Empire was the installation of a German Emperor. Bismarck had felt from the beginning of the negotiations that "the assumption of the Imperial title by the King of Prussia upon the extension of the North German Confederation was a political necessity, since, by its reminder of days when it meant theoretically more but practically less than now, it constituted an element making for unity and centralization." This finishing touch Bismarck at this time prepared to take, but he had more difficulty than he had expected in persuading the direct and simple-minded old King to assume the imperial dignity. For William feared that his elevation to this position would cause a departure from the traditional plain ways of the Prussian court to the luxury and outward magnificence of an Imperial court. "At the first mention of it," writes Bismarck, "he said, 'What have I to do with fancy-ball Major?'" His compunctions could be overcome only by evidence that his elevation in rank was desired by all Germany; and such evidence could be shown only by the united requests of the German princes, accompanied by a declaration from the Prussian parliament. It was Bismarck's success in gaining these documents which broke down the King's objections. On December 17, 1870, the King of Bavaria (at the instigation of Bismarck) undertook, on behalf of all the German governments, the duty of proposing to the Prussian King that he should assume the title of Emperor. At about the same time the Prussian parliament submitted to its ruler a memorial of similar import. William then consented. The coronation ceremonies were held January 18, 1871, in the Hall of Mirrors in the Palace of Versailles, while the German cannon were pounding Paris. Around the dais on which the Prussian king was crowned were grouped the representatives of the reigning families in Germany and the military and diplomatic leaders of Prussia. The Grand Duke of Baden in person led the cheers after the ceremony for the Emperor William, cheers which were taken up by the German armies for miles around. The following day the Parisian troops made their last desperate sortie; on the 23d negotiations for the surrender of Paris began.

C. THE CONCLUSION OF THE FRANCO-GERMAN WAR

With the capture of the French capital, the Franco-Prussian war was practically completed. Although military operations continued, it is true, in central and southern France, these operations had no effect upon the final outcome of the negotiations for peace. The leaders of the French people were willing to treat with the successful Germans, and Bismarck for the Germans was willing to name terms. This final phase, the aftermath of the war when peace was being arranged, lasted for four long months.

At the beginning of the negotiations, Bismarck refused to recognize the credentials of the existing government in Paris. That government, formed by and out of the National Assembly in Paris after the fall of the Empire, had never received the approval of the nation. Bismarck argued that the nation at large might repudiate any terms which this self-constituted French government might accept. Upon his suggestion, therefore, an armistice (the Armistice of Versailles) was concluded at the end of January to allow the French to elect men distinctly empowered to represent them in the peace parleys with the German victors.

In these elections, hastily held, the royalists and conservatives counseled peace, whereas the Republicans and radicals, instigated by the fiery eloquence of Gambetta, desired to continue the war still further. The country at large, especially the peasantry, was heartily weary of the war. Hence, though the people were republican at heart, they voted for royalist and conservative deputies in order to be assured of immediate peace. Thus the elections resulted in a National Assembly of more than 700 members, practically pledged to make peace.

This assembly meeting at Bordeaux and immediately taking over the power from the Provisional Government of National Defense, authorized Thiers to conduct the negotiations with Bismarck. Thiers' position was difficult. He fully realized that Germany held the upper hand and that France would have to submit to her terms. Thiers expected that these terms would include the surrender of Alsace and Lorraine and a huge money indemnity, perhaps as high as five billions of francs. After he had met Bismarck, he learned that Bismarck's terms in actual fact closely corresponded to his expectations, except that the money indemnity was a thousand million francs greater. Thiers' patriotic duty was to endeavor, by all means possible, to reduce these terms. He argued; pleaded; even threatened further resistance, though in his heart he well knew that further resistance was not possible. Bismarck was obdurate. The utmost concessions he would make were to reduce the indemnity to five thousand million francs and to yield from Alsace the city of Belfort: but in return for these concessions the French had to agree to a formal German entry into Paris. When these preliminary terms were finally understood, Thiers retired to present them to the Assembly for its consideration.

i. *The Commune*

In the meanwhile, the National Assembly had fallen out with the civil authorities in Paris: in other words, the Assembly which had been chosen to represent the people of all France was at odds with the governing elements in the French capital.

The reasons for the trouble were both economic and political. Paris had been sorely stricken by the siege. The stoppage of all normal business and industrial life had thrown tens of thousands of men out of employment. During the siege, these men had been drafted into the National Guard, and the pittance they received as pay therein had kept them and their families from actual starvation. When the siege was raised, the wealthier men left Paris: the poorer and more miserable were forced to remain. As business could not at once recover from the shock of the siege, these men in Paris were still without employment and wholly dependent upon the pay they received as members of the Guard. The National Assembly, apparently not understanding the situation, ill-advisedly passed a measure disbanding the Guard, except for certain persons holding regular certificates of poverty, and thus, before any other source of income was open to the workingmen, deprived them of their National Guard pay.

Again, during the progress of the siege, a general moratorium had been in force, protecting people from the attempts of creditors to collect debts. When the siege was raised, business was so slow in recovering that the people requested an extension of this moratorium. The Assembly refused this request, rendering thousands of men liable to prosecution for failure to meet their obligations.

Added to these economic troubles was the Parisian distrust of the political purposes of the Assembly. Paris was overwhelmingly republican in sympathy. Its people had no wish to see another monarchy enthroned in France, or the way opened for another *coup d'état* such as that whereby Louis Napoleon had become emperor. The monarchist complexion of the National Assembly was well known and caused it to be " suspect." Further ground for suspicion was given to the excitable masses in the city by the decision of the Assembly (March, 1871) to meet, not in Paris, the natural place, but in Versailles, with its traditions of monarchy.

Among a people thus rendered discontented, wretched, and suspicious, the anarchists, socialists, and radical republicans were able to enlist many thousands of followers. When the Guard had been disbanded, the discharged men had retained their arms. The means for forcible insurrection were at hand. The old National Guard organization provided an organization through which the leaders could act. A committee chosen from the Guard prepared to defend Paris against any attack by the forces of the Assembly. Cannon were mounted at strategical points in the city, and attempts by the Assembly to seize them were resisted (March 18, 1871). The committee issued a proclamation calling upon the other cities of France to constitute themselves likewise free communes, and suggesting the formation of a central government of France constituted by the delegates of all communes.

In the eyes of Thiers and his colleagues, the Parisians had been guilty of the basest treachery in thus beginning civil war at a time when the government was negotiating to rid the country of the foreign invader, and when the German army was still in possession, under the terms of the armistice, of the forts on two sides of the capital city. The national forces moved to the siege of Paris. From the beginning of April until the end of May, civil war was waged, a war far exceeding in ferocity any part of the Franco-German struggle. On the 28th of May, the last of the rebels were shot down in the cemetery of Père-Lachaise. In the days following, the government took a terrible revenge, imprisoning, banishing, and summarily executing thousands. The terrible days of The Commune left a legacy of bitterness and hatred between the Parisians and their national government which lasted for a generation.

ii. *The Treaty of Frankfort*

The representatives of the French government did not allow the Paris rebellion to interrupt their negotiations for peace. They met the German commissioners at Frankfort in May and signed the final terms. The National Assembly, which in the meanwhile had moved its place of meeting to Versailles, ratified the action of the French commissioners on May 18 by the overwhelming vote of 433 to 98. The final phase of the war was finished. By the provisions of the Treaty of Frankfort, Germany was to be paid within the space of three years a war indemnity of five thousand million francs in specie; German forces were to be quartered in French cities and maintained at French cost until this indemnity should be paid; Germany was to have favorable commercial treatment from France; and Germany was to receive Alsace (except Belfort) and a large part of Lorraine.

D. EUROPEAN READJUSTMENT FOLLOWING THE WAR

A period of readjustment followed the war. Internal development in France, Italy, and Germany had been sharply and rudely interrupted at the outbreak of the war. International relations throughout all Europe had been radically altered by the war's result. The individual states turned again to the normal pursuits of times of peace, and attempted to resume the current of their economic and industrial life. By artificial stimulation in many lines they tried to regain the ground they had lost during the conflict.

i. *France*

No state confronted so serious a situation after the war as France. A great portion of the most valuable part of her territory was under military occupation by the Germans; a civil war had just cost thousands of lives in her capital and had left a legacy of the bitterest class hatred; an enormous indemnity was to be raised and paid to the victorious German state; the actual cession of two of her eastern provinces was to be carried out; and at the moment the country possessed no authorized government.

For the next few years following this war, the National Assembly retained the governing power. Its authority, however, was questionable, for it had been elected solely for the purpose of negotiating peace with Germany, and, when that peace had been signed, might legitimately have been expected to dissolve. This Assembly did France a service by remaining in existence and carrying her through the trying days of reconstruction. It elected Thiers "Chief of the Executive Power" and depended upon him for guidance. Thiers, indeed, was the man of the hour in France, the one strong man who held the confidence of the people. He labored self-sacrificingly in the interest of his country. In June of 1871, confident of the support of his nation, he appealed to the country for a huge loan, 2,250,000,000 francs. Subscriptions poured in for more than double the sum requested. The next month half of the German indemnity was paid, and the German troops were withdrawn from Normandy. A year later Thiers appealed to the country again for a loan, this time for three billion francs, and again the country rose to his appeal and oversubscribed the amount more than seven times. In March of 1873, the last installment of the German indemnity was paid. In autumn the last German soldier was withdrawn from French soil. These labors won for Thiers the title of *Liberator of the Territory*.

During these years the Assembly had supported Thiers in all his measures and had to a considerable extent shared his popularity. As the country became more settled, however, and the irritation due to foreign occupation was ended, it was necessary to solve the problem of a permanent form of government for France. Thiers had been a stanch royalist at the time he became "Chief of the Executive Power," and he had the support of a clear majority of royalists and conservatives in the assembly. In his two years of difficult experience at the head of the government, however, Thiers had become convinced that the country was in no mood to accept another monarchy. Members of the majority in the assembly endeavored to change his opinions and to force a vote or to initiate a *coup d'état* for the establishment of a monarchy. At first Thiers merely asked for a delay, but finally he declared outright his belief that the safety and security of France demanded the establishment of a republican form. As soon thereafter as the royalists felt they could do without him, they voted him down on a question of fundamental policy and forced his resignation (May 24, 1873). His successor, Marshal MacMahon, elected by the royalist votes, held office pending further action on the form and nature of the government.

With Thiers' resignation, the idea of a republic seemed doomed. At this crisis, however, the royalists' plans were thwarted by the character of the chief royalist claimant, the Comte de Chambord. This nobleman, proudly adhering to the divine right theories of his Bourbon ancestors, refused absolutely to consider any concessions to the people of France, or to give up the white flag so long associated with his House. He would not accept the tri-colored emblem, and from this fact men argued that he would not accept the constitutional limitations they proposed to put upon him. The royalist movement was wrecked against the fixed determination of the Comte de Chambord. After a few years, the character of the Assembly was changed by subsequent elections, and the royalist majority cut down. Early in 1875 the committee, which two years before had been appointed to draw up a constitution for France, brought in its report. In the debates which followed, the republicans urged an amendment to include in the proposed constitutional laws the word "Republic." In a memorable moment, January 30, 1875, the Assembly accepted the amendment by a majority of one vote. The step once taken, the Assembly rapidly passed a series of "Organic Laws," by them patching up a constitution which provided for a President of the Republic, a Senate, and a Chamber of Deputies. Not even the most optimistic expected the hastily formed constitution to endure. The Royalists accepted it as a mere stop-gap until the fulfillment of their aspirations: the thoroughgoing Republicans regarded it as a compromise soon to be set aside for a more liberal and radical instrument.

Four turbulent years of political strife followed. The president of the Republic, MacMahon, owed his election to the monarchists: he therefore was ready to use every means to advance the monarchist cause. His lower legislative house, the Chamber of Deputies, was Republican by a large majority (approximately 360 to 170); his upper house, the Senate, was Monarchist (Conservative) by a very small majority. He chose for his chief minister the Duc de Broglie, a monarchist of extreme conservative policies. After two years of strife, MacMahon, on the advice of his monarchist friends, dissolved the chamber and ordered new elections in October of 1877. The campaign preceding these elections was recognized by both parties as decisive for the fortunes of France. The Republicans united upon a common platform and chose a committee for control of the appeal to the electorate. Gambetta, on the Republican side, made some of the most brilliant speeches of his career, coining the famous phrases, "our foe is clericalism," and "when the country shall have spoken, he (MacMahon) must either submit or resign." The Monarchists (Conservatives) had the powerful support of the president. Republican journals were prosecuted or suppressed; changes in the adminstrative personnel were made to build up a kind of political "machine" whose interest would lie in maintaining the existing government; presidential manifestoes in support of the Conservatives were published to the people; and the presidential indorsement given to conservative candidates. In spite of the prestige of the government and the strenuous electioneering of the Conservatives, the people stood loyal to the Republicans. The Chamber of Deputies was Republican by a large majority; the Senate in the following year (1878), at the elections for the renewal of one-third of its members in accordance with the constitution, became Republican by a safe margin (approx. 178 to 126). MacMahon, unable longer to struggle against a hostile legislative body, resigned and Jules Grévy, a Republican, became president in 1879. His election signalized the complete success of the Republican form of government in France. Since 1879 the Republicans have retained firm control of all three organs of political power. The Third Republic has lasted now for forty years, a longer term than any form of government has lived in France since the outbreak of the French Revolution.

While this political struggle was going on in the French Assembly, the people at large were redeeming the losses incurred by the war and taking up again their regular economic life. France with marvelous quickness entered into the spirit of the period — the period when railroads were being built, new commercial opportunities opened, new countries explored and new colonies gained. The millions of francs raised by the huge loans over and above the war indemnity payments were wisely invested in the furtherance of railroad and industrial development; the national finances — which, it was said, were carried away in a hat by the finance minister appointed in February of 1871 — were refunded on a sound basis; the colonies and colonial expansion were again subjects of keen interest and enterprise; the military system was wholly reorganized on a basis of five years of compulsory service, and the fortifications on the borders of the country were remodeled and strengthened at enormous cost in order that France might live and work within her boundaries in security. The world was astounded at the dynamic energy with which France labored to redeem her losses. During these years the French nation gave an example of soundness and financial strength which allowed it speedily to assume its former position as one of the world's leaders.

ii. *Germany*

To the east of France the German Empire was during these years following the war adjusting itself rapidly to

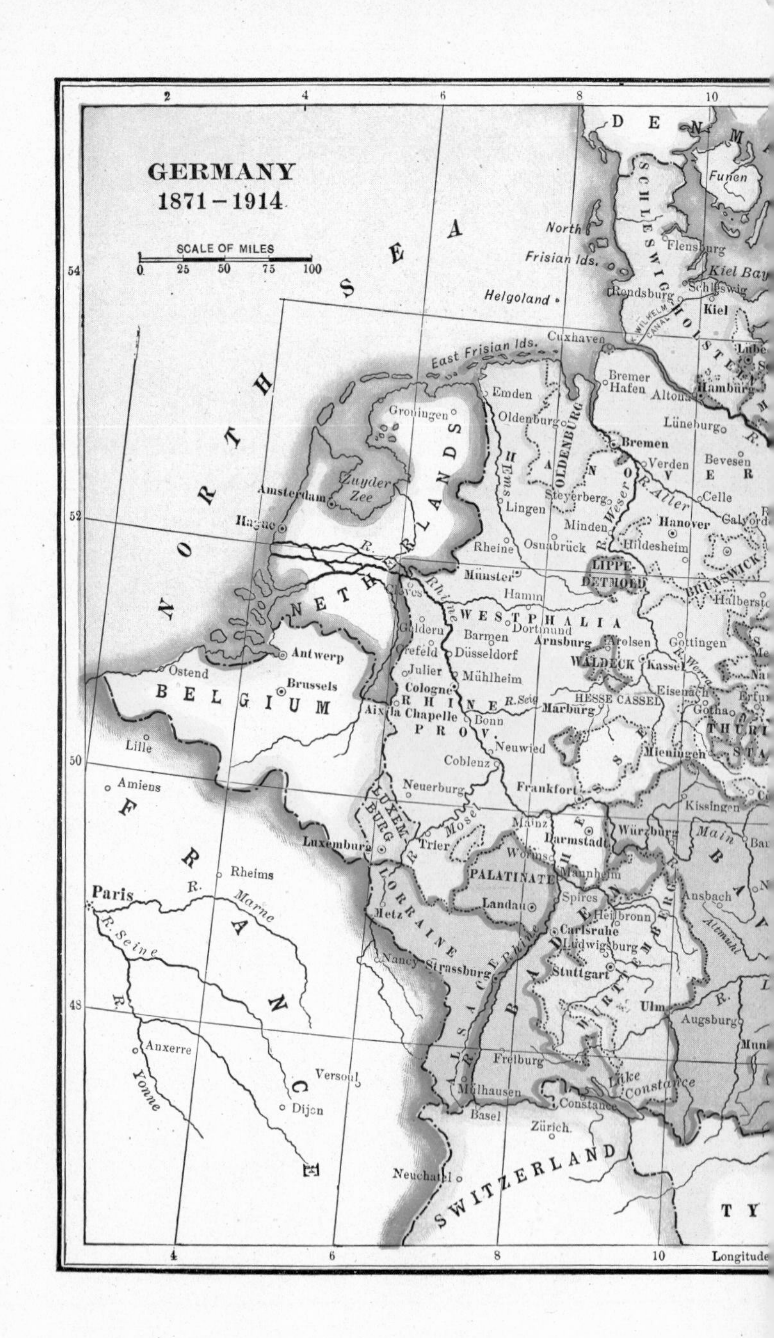
GERMANY
1871 – 1914
SCALE OF MILES
0 25 50 75 100
NORTH SEA
North Frisian Ids.
Helgoland
East Frisian Ids.
DENMARK
Funen
SCHLESWIG HOLSTEIN
Flensburg
Kiel Bay
Schleswig
Rendsburg
Kiel
WILHELM CANAL
Cuxhaven
Bremer Hafen
Altona
Hamburg
Emden
Oldenburg
OLDENBURG
Lüneburg
Bremen
Verden
Bevesen
Celle
Hanover
Hildesheim
Groningen
Zuyder Zee
Amsterdam
Hague
NETHERLANDS
Lingen
Steyerberg
Minden
Rheine
Osnabrück
Münster
LIPPE-DETMOLD
BRUNSWICK
Halberstadt
Cleves
Hamm
WESTPHALIA
Dortmund
Barmen
Arnsburg
Arolsen
Göttingen
WALDECK
Kassel
Geldern
Crefeld
Düsseldorf
Antwerp
Ostend
Brussels
BELGIUM
Julier
Mühlheim
Cologne
RHINE PROV.
R. Sieg
Bonn
Aix la Chapelle
Marburg
HESSE CASSEL
Eisenach
Gotha
Meiningen
Lille
Neuwied
Coblenz
Frankfort
Amiens
FRANCE
Neuerburg
LUXEMBURG
Luxemburg
Trier
Mosel
Mainz
Darmstadt
Würzburg
Kissingen
Main
Worms
Mannheim
PALATINATE
Landau
Spires
Heilbronn
Carlsruhe
Ludwigsburg
Stuttgart
Ansbach
Altmühl
BAVARIA
Rheims
R. Marne
Paris
R. Seine
Metz
LORRAINE
Nancy
Strassburg
ALSACE
BADEN
WÜRTTEMBERG
Ulm
Augsburg
R. Yonne
Auxerre
Freiburg
Mülhausen
Basel
Lake Constance
Constance
Zürich
Vesoul
Dijon
Neuchatel
SWITZERLAND
R. Rhine
R. Weser
R. Aller
R. Werra
Longitude

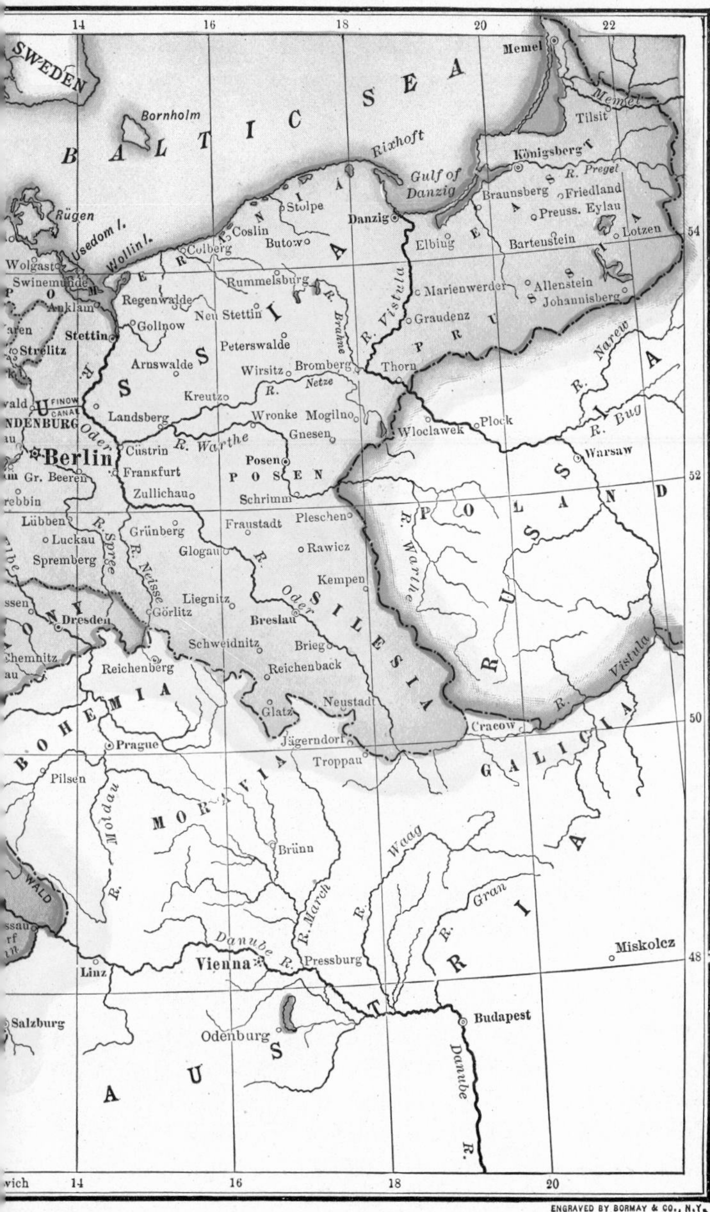

ENGRAVED BY BORMAY & CO., N.Y.

its new unified life. The name Germany no longer stood for a region cut up into a number of semi-independent political entities, but for a strong unified German state. Yet the new state was not without its problems in internal affairs. In the first place, the population was not wholly homogeneous: Germany neither contained all the Germans nor did it contain nothing but Germans. Furthermore, among the non-German elements of the population were some, as the Poles and the people of Alsace and Lorraine, who had been incorporated into the German empire against their will. In the second place, the admission of the South German States into the alliance which formed the Empire had resulted in an enormous increase of the Roman Catholic element of the population and had sown the seeds of religious dissension. And lastly, in the decade from 1860 to 1870, the lower and middle classes of society, not only in Prussia but in all the German states, had received a great impulse toward political development, and with the privileges they possessed under the constitution of the new empire were in a position to make their votes count heavily.

In the new German Empire Bismarck was easily the most commanding and influential figure. He was appointed Chancellor of the Empire, and by virtue of this office directed both the domestic and foreign policies of Germany; he was President of the Council and Minister of Foreign Affairs in Prussia, and thus directed both domestic and foreign policies of the most important unit of the imperial federation; and he was, for the twenty years between 1870 and 1890, the Prussian Minister of Commerce, and thus shared in the promotion and development of the tremendous industrial growth of the Prussian State in Germany.

Of the problems in domestic affairs which confronted the new empire, the one which pressed first for solution was the conflict induced by the religious dissensions. This conflict, commonly called the *Kulturkampf*, began immediately after the promulgation of the Doctrine of the Infallibility of the Pope. Bismarck and the government were drawn into the religious controversy by the fact that a considerable body of Germans protested against and repudiated the new doctrine. Since this doctrine in Bismarck's mind implied a distinct claim of the supremacy of the Catholic church over the civil authorities, his sympathies were wholly with the protesting Germans. With his customary energy he carried the fight to extremes. He persecuted the Roman Catholics by a series of stringent laws, such as those requiring university education and state examinations for theological students, those allowing appeal from ecclesiastical decisions to a public court of laymen, and those authorizing the state to stop payments to the bishops and priests of the church and to suppress or banish religious orders from the country. It is hard for us to-day to realize how bitter the struggle was in Germany. By fines and imprisonment, by stoppage of salaries and by banishment, Bismarck emptied hundreds of parishes of the priests and closed the churches. Of the twelve bishoprics in Germany, eight were vacant. And in the end it was evident that the Chancellor's persecution, like other persecutions, was actually strengthening the cause of the people persecuted. Catholics indignantly protested against the infamous attacks of the Chancellor. Protestants looked upon the conflict with disfavor. Bismarck was forced to recognize the futility of his measures. After 1875, he gradually relaxed the severity of the application of the laws and prepared to recede from his position.

In the routine affairs attending the organization and material progress of the Empire, Bismarck showed his genius as he had previously done in diplomatic affairs. Discerning with keen eye the importance of commercial and industrial development in his age, he diverted a part of the enormous indemnity received from the French war into business channels and caused a great "boom" throughout his country. He foresaw the growth of the transportation systems in the coming economic period and was responsible for the creation of "An Imperial Bureau of Railroads," which played a very important part in the railroad development of Germany. In 1875 he established a single gold standard of currency (the *mark*) for the entire Empire. In the same year he extended imperial jurisdiction over the whole range of civil law, over legal procedure in both civil and criminal cases, and over the organization of justice. Furthermore, in that year the Reichsbank (Imperial Bank) was instituted under his direction to become the central institution in Germany for exchange, finance, and the issue of bank notes. Each of these measures played its part in fostering a new national sentiment throughout the Empire. The breaking down of barriers which had formerly existed between the separate states, the centralization of the legal and financial systems, the impulse to railroad and industrial development imparted from a central source, — all these coöperated subtly to influence the people to identify themselves with the fortunes of the new State and to forget the local interests with which they had formerly been occupied. As time passed, and new generations came into being who were more completely under the spell of the imperial influences, the feeling of unity grew constantly stronger. Bismarck was fully conscious of this development. Whatever criticism may be directed against Bismarck's character, methods, or policies, it is certain that a genuine enthusiasm for Germany underlay all that he did.

iii. *Italy*

The other country in Europe on which the Franco-German War had had the most notable influence in internal development was Italy. The acquisition of Rome had, it is true, completed Italian unity by bringing the entire peninsula under the rule of Victor Emmanuel; but it had brought in its train a number of most serious problems.

In the first place, the Pope would listen to no arguments for reconciliation, would agree to no concessions. He excommunicated the King of Italy, publicly declared him a robber King, and proclaimed abroad that the head of the Roman Catholic church was living as a prisoner in the Palace of the Vatican. In the second place, it was certain that the influence of foreign Catholic states might be enlisted to take Rome from Italy and restore it to the Pope. It was well known that papal emissaries were busy in Austria and France, endeavoring to gain strength to accomplish such restoration. And lastly, it had to be remembered that the mass of Italians were themselves devoted Catholics, even though they approved incorporation of Rome into the Italian kingdom. No measures could be taken by the Italian government which might be interpreted as in any way persecuting or oppressing the Pope. The problem was one beset with difficulties.

The measure adopted to solve this problem was, on the whole, one of the wisest acts of statesmanship in the annals of the new Italy. On May 13, 1871, the Law of Papal Guarantees was duly passed, defining on the part of the Italian government the status of the Pope and the relations between the Papacy and the civil authority. By the provisions of this law the Pope's claim to royal honors and prerogatives was recognized and the inviolability of the Pope's person proclaimed; the use of the Vatican and Lateran palaces and of the Villa Gandolfo was assigned to him, and the payment of an annual pension amounting to $650,000 was guaranteed to him. The Pope proved obdurate even in the face of these guarantees, for he looked upon them, not as concessions from the Italian government, but as conditions imposed by one conquering power upon its defeated enemy. He refused to acknowledge the loss of Rome; refused to leave the Vatican, inasmuch as he would then have to cross territory claimed by a foreign power; and refused to accept a pension, inasmuch as he might thereby acknowledge the justice of the Italian claims. The important end accomplished by the Law of Papal Guarantees, however, was the satisfaction of Italian Catholics, and, to a considerable extent, of foreign Catholic nations. The Italian government had attempted by this law to show its respect for the Pope and for papal institutions, and to reveal its intentions to reimburse the Pope for his losses. The success of their measure is proved by the fact that since that date no serious attempt has been made to take Rome away from Italy and restore it to the papacy.

The question of relations with the Pope was, however, by no means the only difficult problem confronting the Italian government. The kingdom had begun its career with a crushing burden of debt, and as the years passed the various governments which succeeded one another were unable to devise satisfactory means for lightening the weight. The taxes levied were uniformly very unpopular. The Grist Tax, commonly called the "Tax on Hunger," and the extension of the tobacco monopoly throughout Sicily, roused especially bitter feeling among the lower classes of the population. Not only was the country financially impoverished, but the economic and industrial situation was bad. Italy had been for generations so ravaged by wars and plundered by unscrupulous rulers that the country had never taken its proper place industrially among the states of Europe; and now that it was at last united under a liberal government it was so far behind in the competition that its struggles seemed to give it no headway. Again, a third problem was presented by the social conditions. The population was not homogeneous. The northern Italians had in education, wealth, and standards of living so far outstripped the southern that they looked upon the latter as a different and inferior race. Although populous cities flourished in the north — Venice, Milan, Florence, Turin, Genoa, and Rome — the south was given over to a wretched ignorant peasantry. And while the finances of the country were disorganized, the economic resources undeveloped, the social conditions unsettled, the statesmen of the country were fighting in the legislature for temporary political advantages. No leader emerged with a genius sufficient to direct the course of the struggling nation toward prosperity. Italy was, during the five years following the capture of Rome, poverty-stricken, debt-ridden, and, on the whole, miserably unhappy.

iv. *Other States*

Of all the various states of Europe, the three upon whose domestic affairs we have dwelt — France, Germany, and Italy — were those whose internal development was most notably affected by the results of the Franco-Prussian War. The other states of Europe, although naturally influenced by the radical change in the grouping of the powers in Europe, were not materially influenced in their internal development. Russia continued with ponderous slowness her attempts at reformation in her vast Empire; Austria-Hungary during these years was adjusting herself to the provisions of the Ausgleich and was gradually overcoming the opposition of Bohemia and other provinces; Great Britain continued under the ministry of Gladstone until 1874, piling up huge commercial balances year by year and paying strict attention to her home affairs.

E. INTERNATIONAL RELATIONS FOLLOWING THE FRANCO-GERMAN WAR

In international relations in Europe, the Franco-Prussian War made changes more notable than any to which attention has been drawn in individual states. A new great and powerful state had been created in central Europe. It had shouldered its way into the group of the great powers and, at the moment, stood among the strongest of all. It may be said, of course, that Prussia was before the time of

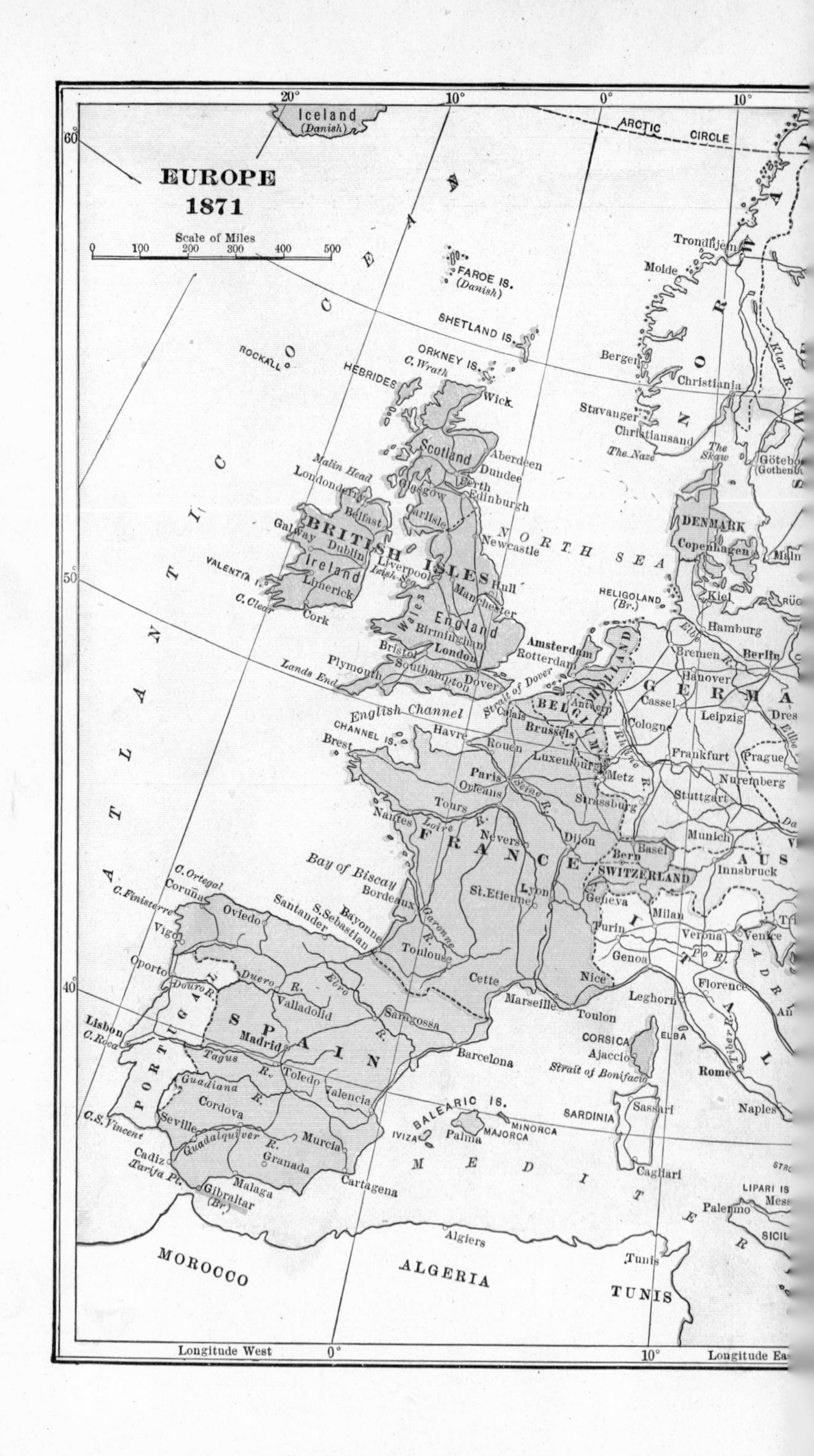

EUROPE
1871
Scale of Miles
0 100 200 300 400 500
Iceland
(Danish)
ARCTIC CIRCLE
FAROE IS.
(Danish)
SHETLAND IS.
ORKNEY IS.
C. Wrath
ROCKALL
HEBRIDES
Wick
ATLANTIC OCEAN
Scotland
Aberdeen
Dundee
Perth
Edinburgh
Glasgow
Malin Head
Londonderry
Belfast
Carlisle
BRITISH ISLES
Galway
Dublin
Newcastle
Ireland
Liverpool
Irish Sea
Hull
VALENTIA I.
Limerick
Manchester
C. Clear
Cork
Wales
England
Birmingham
Bristol
London
Plymouth
Southampton
Dover
Lands End
NORTH SEA
Trondhjem
Molde
Bergen
Christiania
Stavanger
Christiansand
The Naze
The Skaw
Klar R.
DENMARK
Copenhagen
HELIGOLAND
(Br.)
Kiel
Hamburg
Elbe R.
Bremen
Berlin
Amsterdam
Rotterdam
HOLLAND
Hanover
GERMA
Strait of Dover
English Channel
BELGIUM
Antwerp
Calais
Brussels
Cassel
Leipzig
Cologne
Rhine R.
CHANNEL IS.
Havre
Brest
Rouen
Luxemburg
Frankfurt
Prague
Paris
Metz
Orleans
Seine R.
Nuremberg
Stuttgart
Tours
Strassburg
Nantes
Loire R.
Nevers
Munich
FRANCE
Dijon
Basel
Bern
SWITZERLAND
Innsbruck
Bay of Biscay
Bordeaux
St. Etienne
Lyon
Geneva
Milan
C. Ortegal
Coruña
C. Finisterre
Oviedo
Santander
S. Sebastian
Bayonne
Garonne R.
Turin
Verona
Venice
Vigo
Toulouse
Genoa
Po R.
Oporto
Duero R.
Ebro R.
Cette
Nice
Florence
Douro R.
Valladolid
Saragossa
Marseille
Leghorn
Toulon
SPAIN
Lisbon
C. Roca
Madrid
PORTUGAL
Tagus R.
Barcelona
CORSICA
ELBA
Ajaccio
Strait of Bonifacio
Tiber R.
Rome
Toledo
Guadiana R.
Valencia
Cordova
BALEARIC IS.
MINORCA
SARDINIA
Sassari
Naples
C.S. Vincent
Seville
IVIZA
Palma
MAJORCA
Murcia
Guadalquiver R.
Cadiz
Granada
Tarifa Pt.
Malaga
Gibraltar
(Br.)
Cartagena
Cagliari
MEDITERR
LIPARI IS.
Palermo
SICIL
Algiers
Tunis
MOROCCO
ALGERIA
TUNIS
Longitude West
Longitude Ea
60°
50°
40°
20°
10°
0°

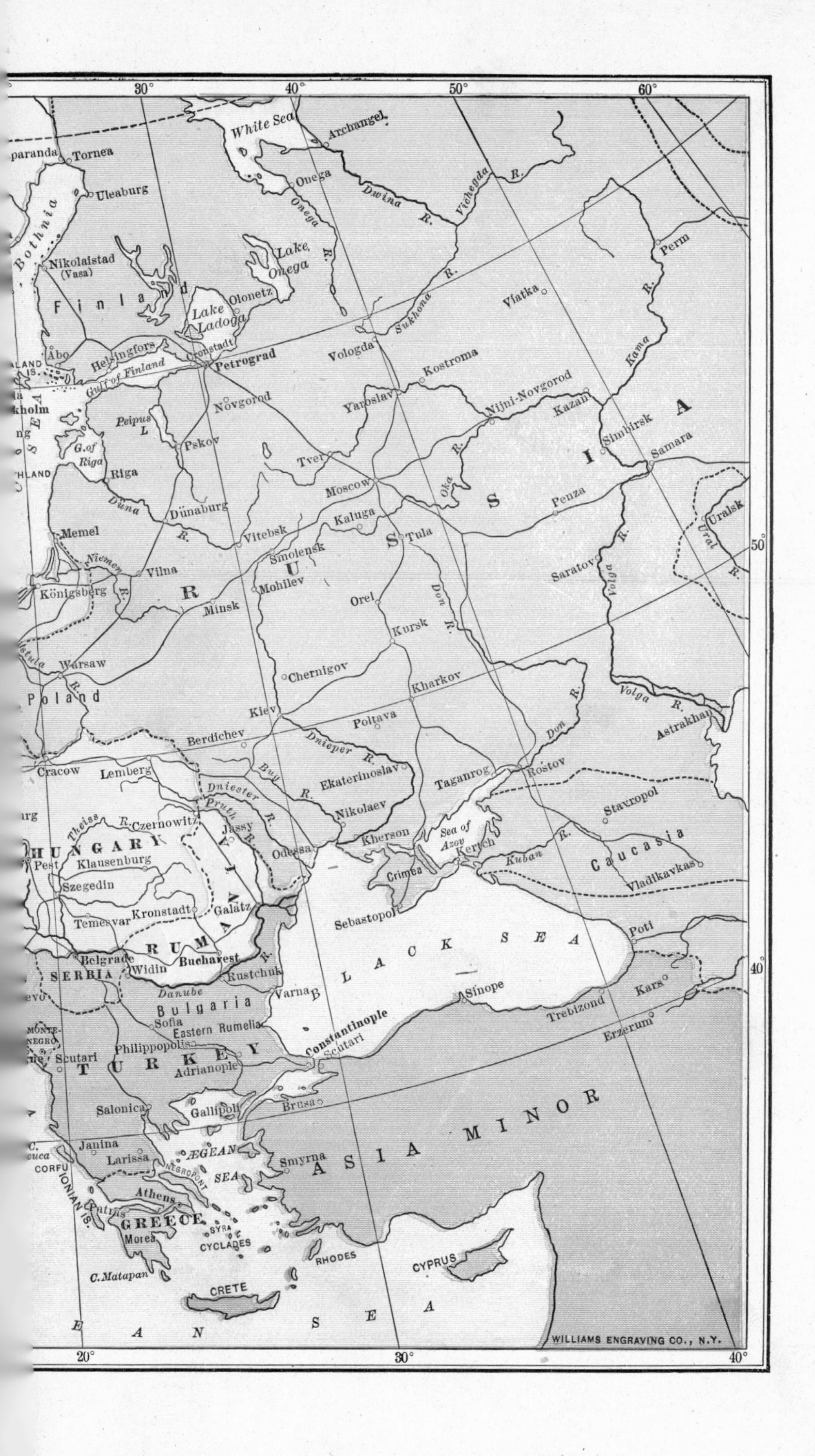

White Sea
Archangel
Tornea
Uleaburg
Bothnia
Onega
Dwina R.
Vichegda R.
Onega R.
Nikolaistad (Vasa)
Lake Onega
Perm
Finland
Olonetz
Lake Ladoga
Sukhona R.
Viatka
Åbo
Helsingfors
Cronstadt
Petrograd
Vologda
Gulf of Finland
Kostroma
Kama R.
Novgorod
Yaroslav
Nijni-Novgorod
Kazan
Peipus L.
Pskov
Simbirsk
G. of Riga
Riga
Tver
Samara
Moscow
Oka R.
Düna
Dünaburg
Penza
Kaluga
Uralsk
Memel
Vitebsk
Tula
Ural R.
Smolensk
Niemen R.
Vilna
Saratov
Volga R.
Königsberg
Mohilev
Orel
Don R.
Minsk
Kursk
Warsaw
Chernigov
Kharkov
Poland
Volga R.
Kiev
Poltava
Astrakhan
Berdichev
Dnieper R.
Don R.
Cracow
Lemberg
Buy R.
Ekaterinoslav
Taganrog
Rostov
Dniester R.
Stavropol
Pruth R.
Czernowitz
Theiss R.
Nikolaev
Jassy
Kherson
Sea of Azov
Kuban R.
Caucasia
HUNGARY
Pest
Klausenburg
Odessa
Kerch
Crimea
Vladikavkas
Szegedin
Kronstadt
Galatz
Sebastopol
Temesvar
RUMANIA
BLACK SEA
Poti
Belgrade
Bucharest
SERBIA
Widin
Rustchuk
Danube
Varna
Sinope
Kars
Bulgaria
Trebizond
Sofia
Eastern Rumelia
Constantinople
Erzerum
MONTE-NEGRO
Philippopolis
Scutari
Scutari
TURKEY
Adrianople
Salonica
Gallipoli
Brusa
ASIA MINOR
Janina
Larissa
ÆGEAN SEA
Smyrna
CORFU
NEGROPONT
IONIAN IS.
Athens
Patras
GREECE
SYRA
Morea
CYCLADES
RHODES
CYPRUS
C. Matapan
CRETE
SEA
WILLIAMS ENGRAVING CO., N.Y.
30°
40°
50°
60°
50°
40°
20°
30°
40°

Bismarck one of the great powers of Europe, but the Prussia of 1861 was the least of the powers, whereas the Germany of 1871 was among the first. The Prussia of 1861 was a nation of 19,000,000, supporting with difficulty the armaments necessary to maintain a recognized place in the councils of Europe: the Germany of 1871 was a compact nation of 41,000,000, with the prestige of an overwhelmingly successful war against France and with financial conditions insuring prosperity. No statesman in Europe in any of his diplomatic considerations could henceforth afford to leave out of account the German Empire.

In the years immediately following the Franco-Prussian War the chief issue around which international questions in Europe revolved was the probability of a war of revenge waged by France against Germany. At first thought, it might seem foolhardy for France to consider a war with a power by which she had been so thoroughly defeated, but we must consider that she hoped to insure success by preliminary diplomacy. Could France ally herself with strong military states, she might hope to attack Germany and regain Alsace and Lorraine. The prospects for French success seemed good. The new German state lay in the center of Europe, sandwiched between three great states, with two of which she had recently been at war. A coalition formed between France and Austria might hope to crush the upstart power; or, if Russia could be weaned from her friendship with Germany, a coalition between Russia and France would accomplish her purpose.

Bismarck was not slow to appreciate the danger. Even while the French and German plenipotentiaries were in Frankfort signing the final articles of peace, the German chancellor was planning to circumvent all French attempts to form a coalition against his state. He himself sought to form an alliance between Russia, Austria, and Germany, and thus to isolate France from the great states of the continent. By great tact and careful diplomacy, he contrived to bring together at Berlin in September of 1872, ostensibly for the formal and ceremonious recognition of the new German Imperial dignity, the Emperors Alexander of Russia, Francis Joseph of Austria, and William of Germany. The cordial understanding which was achieved by the three Emperors at this time gave rise to the belief that there was between them a definite alliance, and repeated references were made in political circles to the Dreikaiserbund (League of the Three Kaisers). We know now that no definite alliance was formed at this time, that there never was an actual Dreikaiserbund; but the "cordial understanding" was sufficient to check French diplomacy. So long as it continued, France could look in vain throughout Europe for an ally against Germany. A year later (1873) King Victor Emmanuel of Italy visited Berlin. Rumor had it that he, fearing a union of Catholic powers to wrest Rome from Italy and restore it to the Pope, was seeking aid from Bismarck.

Thus by 1875 France was the only radically discontented state in Europe. No French politician who did not make the recovery of Alsace and Lorraine the keystone of his policy could hope for popular acclaim. Any mention of a war of revenge was certain to arouse intense enthusiasm throughout France. Bismarck was fully aware of this situation and on his guard against it. Upon one occasion in 1875, when Marshal MacMahon invited the French assembly to proceed with the plan of reorganization of the French army, the German press blazed forth again with the war spirit and was hotly answered in kind by the press of France. Evidence exists that Bismarck allowed, and even encouraged the German press in the effort to intimidate France. So bitter became the mutual recriminations that to the outside observers war seemed a matter of but a few days. Then British and Russian representations at Berlin were made to calm the storm. Queen Victoria wrote a personal letter to William I, and Alexander II of

Russia went to Berlin to urge the necessity for peace. German provocation quickly ceased, and the fear of war passed. There is doubt, however, whether Bismarck really expected or desired war at this time. It is more probable that he was merely brandishing the sword as a threat. Indeed, he had no reason to wish war. He had gained for Germany all that he could legitimately desire: another war would only imperil the existing situation.

Outside of France, there seemed at the moment (1875) no reason to expect trouble. Austria-Hungary, Italy, and Germany were upon the most friendly terms. Great Britain had at the time shown no indication of a departure from her long-standing policy of non-interference in continental affairs. Bismarck might well feel that his work was accomplished.

F. SUMMARY: BISMARCK AND PRUSSIA, 1862-1875

From this year (1875) we can take a quick look back and see how completely Bismarck had dominated European politics since his accession to the chancellorship in Prussia. He had so manipulated the Schleswig-Holstein affair as to bring on a war between Denmark on the one side and Prussia and Austria on the other. At the same time, he had so represented affairs at outside courts that no nation intervened to save Denmark. Two years later he plunged Prussia into war with Austria, but again he so skillfully handled the threads of international diplomacy that his opponent fought without an ally. Once more, only four years later, he threw down the gauntlet to France; in the face of all Europe he contrived to beat France to her knees and at the same time to unite the majority of German-speaking peoples into a compact empire. In less than eight years he had guided Prussia through three wars to become the keystone of one of the greatest empires in the world. In accomplishing these results, Bismarck was actually opposing the natural course of events in Europe. Prussia was in the process of becoming a liberal monarchy in which the parliament should be superior in authority to the King: Bismarck stemmed the tide of liberalism and strengthened autocracy. Schleswig and Holstein might have become German states, members of the loose German confederation: Bismarck incorporated them into Prussia. Prussia might have remained the least of the great powers in Europe: Bismarck made her an essential unit in one of the first. No country in Europe failed to be influenced in its history by the momentous events of these years. As the years following the French Revolution may be called the Era of Napoleon, and the years following the overthrow of Napoleon the Era of Metternich (up to 1848), so the generation beginning with 1862 may fitly be called the Era of Bismarck.

PART II

THE MAINTENANCE OF GERMAN HEGEMONY IN EUROPE

CHAPTER I

THE RUSSO-TURKISH WAR

THE next international issue in which Bismarck played a prominent part was that created by the delicate negotiations following the Russo-Turkish war. The German chancellor, having framed the German empire according to his own designs, desired the continuance of peace throughout Europe. He could not, however, exert an influence over affairs in the Balkan peninsula, where Germany at that time had no direct interest, so he was unable to check the outbreak of war. As soon as the conflict had finished, however, and the territorial settlement became a general European question, Bismarck believed that the prestige of Germany demanded that he take a part in the international deliberations. He was, therefore, forced by what he believed to be political expediency to represent his country in the final congress (the Congress of Berlin), and to make the importance of his appearance and votes therein correspond to his conception of the place of Germany in continental European affairs.

A. THE NEAR EASTERN PROBLEM

The Russo-Turkish war arose out of the unsatisfactory conditions in the Balkan peninsula. The problem presented by these conditions was by no means a new one. The Eastern Question, as the problem was called, had perplexed European statesmen ever since the first intrusion of the Turks into Europe. Briefly stated, the Eastern Question consists of the issue raised by attempts to readjust relations between Mohammedan Turks and their Christian subjects and their neighboring states. It will be remembered that the warlike Turks, after capturing Constantinople in 1453, extended their power up to the very walls of Vienna. Repulsed there by the Austrians aided by the Poles under Sobieski in the memorable battle of Vienna (Sept. 12, 1683), the Turks were in the following decades gradually forced back, yielding up fertile Hungary, Transylvania, the Crimea, and retiring behind the Dniester River, the Carpathians, and the Transylvanian Alps. Behind these boundaries they held the entire southeastern point of Europe, not to speak of enormous territories in Asia Minor, for more than a hundred years.

At the beginning of the nineteenth century, however, signs of disintegration of the empire became evident. From the beginning of the Turkish occupation differences of race and differences of religion had created the bitterest animosity between the conquerors and their subject people. Roumanians and Greeks were Caucasian, Serbs and Bulgars were Slav, and all four peoples were Christian. The ignorant and fanatical Turks had made no effort to adjust their government to these perplexing racial and religious differences, but had persisted in maintaining their attitude of a superior race toward inferior races. The Christians were to the Turks but low-born people, fit only to bear burdens and to pay taxes. Before Moslem judges in Moslem courts, the Christian subjects of the Sultan had no hope for justice; under Moslem police they had to submit to continual extortion; under Moslem tax-gatherers, who had bought their position and whose profits depended on the amounts they could screw out of the people, Christians could expect no mercy or fair distribution of the burden. The government was a continual tragedy of purposeless cruelty and oppression.

The natural result of such continued misrule on the part of a sovereign power would have been formidable rebellion on the part of the subjects, but the distinctions in race and national aspirations among the various Christian peoples prevented them from uniting to throw off the Turkish yoke. Roumanian hated Bulgar, Bulgar hated Serb, Serb hated Greek, and Greek hated Albanian, each with as intense hatred as he bore toward the Turk. Unity of action was impossible under these conditions. It was not until a general weakening of the Turkish power at the beginning of the nineteenth century that individual peoples dared to revolt. With the first prospect of success, one Christian people after another fought for its freedom. The hardy mountaineers of Montenegro had never been fully subjugated; they again rebelled with success. Between 1804 and 1817 Serbia fought, in the end winning practical autonomy. In 1829 Greece, after a long and barbarous conflict, received foreign aid and gained complete independence. In the same year Russia defeated Turkey and forced her to yield rights of self-government to the important provinces of Moldavia and Wallachia (Rumania). In 1861, shortly after the Crimean war (1854–1856), these two provinces united into the principality of Rumania and emerged with only nominal allegiance to the Sultan. From this time forward the only large and important body of Christians remaining under the hated Turkish dominion in Europe was the Bulgar. It was inevitable that the Bulgars, seeing the happier condition of their fellow Christians in neighboring regions who had successfully revolted against the Turk, should make the great effort.

B. THE BULGARIAN ATROCITIES

European attention was focused upon the Eastern Question in 1875 and 1876. In 1875 the peasantry in Herzegovina, harassed by the extortions of the tax-gatherers in the year following a particularly bad harvest, revolted. During the following months the revolt spread through the larger and more populous neighboring province of

Bosnia and deeply excited the Bulgars. Early in 1876 an insignificant uprising at Tartar Bazardjik in the Maritza valley resulted in the death of a few Turkish officials. The revenge taken by the Turks was terrible. Since the Bulgarian region was near the Turkish capital it bore the brunt of the punishment. The Sultan poured some 15,000 regular troops and hordes of irregulars known as Bashi-Bazouks into the Maritza valley. The atrocities committed by these troops, especially by the Bashi-Bazouks, made foreign intervention inevitable. Of the eighty villages in the fertile valley they wiped out sixty-five, murdering, burning, and pillaging with a free hand. The scenes in Batak became famous. The correspondent of the London Times sent to his paper so graphic an account of the Turkish procedure in that town that a Parliamentary commission was dispatched to the spot to ascertain the truth. The report of the commission confirmed the correspondent's account. The commander of the Bashi-Bazouks had given his word of honor that if the people at Batak would yield, not a hair of their heads would be harmed; but when they did yield, they were butchered like sheep. Some fled to the little wooden schoolhouse; the house was fired and the victims burned alive. Some fled to the stone church; the roof was torn off and burning wood and oil-soaked rags hurled down among the people. The official report estimated that in Batak alone five thousand persons were massacred.

"I visited this valley of the shadow of death on the 31st of July, more than two months and a half after the massacre," the report read, "but still the stench was so overpowering that one could hardly force one's way into the church. In the streets at every step lay remains rotting and sweltering in the summer sun. Just outside the village I counted more than sixty skulls in a little hollow."

The Sultan excused the atrocities on the ground that his troops were suppressing rebellion, and rewarded his commander at Batak with a medal for bravery.

All Europe was aroused by the Bulgarian atrocities. The Balkan people who had in recent generations suffered the Turkish misrule, — the Serbians, Montenegrins, Roumanians, and Greeks, — realized more keenly than any other people the extent of cruelty of which the Turkish mind was capable. Serbia and Montenegro at once declared war against Turkey (July 1 and 2, 1876). The Russians became inflamed at the accounts of the sufferings of the people of the same race and the same religion. Thousands of Russians in the near-by districts went to Serbia to enlist in the Serbian army for the war against the infidel oppressors. In Great Britain, the shock afforded by the startling details of the massacres aroused the people from a kind of lethargy in which they lived so far as affairs in Turkey were concerned. Turkey had in the Crimean war been Great Britain's ally, so that there existed a tradition of friendship between British and Moslems. Herzegovina, Bosnia, and Bulgaria awakened no such interest as the name of Greece had in the 1820's. After the story of the massacre became known, the feeling in Great Britain sharply changed. Gladstone, who had in 1874 resigned and retired to private life, issued from his retirement with a pamphlet on the Bulgarian Horrors, and the Question of the East, in which he insisted that the government

> "shall apply all its vigour to concur with the states of Europe in obtaining the extinction of the Turkish executive power in Bulgaria. Let the Turks now carry away their abuses in the only possible manner, namely, by carrying off themselves. This thorough riddance, this most blessed deliverance, is the only reparation we can make to the memory of those heaps and heaps of dead; to the violated purity alike of matron, of maiden, of child; to the civilization that has been affronted and shamed; to the laws of God, or, if you like, of Allah; to the moral sense of mankind at large."

C. ATTITUDE OF GREAT BRITAIN AND RUSSIA TOWARD TURKEY

Could Great Britain and Russia have combined with the small Balkan states, the expulsion of the "unspeakable Turk" from Europe might have been accomplished, but even while the bodies of the Bulgarian Christians lay rotting in the sun grave questions of international policy were agitating the powers and keeping them from taking active measures.

i. *Great Britain*

In Great Britain, Benjamin Disraeli became prime minister in 1874, the head of a safe Conservative majority in both houses of Parliament. His advent signalized a decided change in governmental policies. Whereas Gladstone in the preceding years had occupied himself with domestic problems, internal reforms, and the material prosperity of the Kingdom, Disraeli attempted to kindle the imaginations of Englishmen by the idea of imperialism, by a picture of the British colonies consolidated with the mother country into the farthest flung and mightiest empire the world has ever seen. Great Britain's destiny was far more magnificent than the mere material prosperity of the British Isles: Englishmen should look abroad, around the world. Himself gifted with the vivid imagination of the east, Disraeli attempted to impress his dreams upon the narrow and somewhat conventional British mind.

In 1875, when he had been minister but a single year, an opportunity was offered him to make a sensational move in this new imperial policy. The Suez canal, built by a French company and formally opened in November of 1869, had been an immediate success and had changed radically the conditions of commerce with the Far East. Chinese, Australian, and Indian commerce, which formerly had gone the long voyage around the Cape of Good Hope, now sailed direct through the canal. Inasmuch as Great Britain had become the world's great sea-carrying nation, practically seventy-five per cent of the tonnage by this route was British. Above all, the canal was the direct route to Great Britain's richest colony, India. Of the 400,000 shares of the canal company, 176,602 were owned by the inefficient and bankrupt Khedive of Egypt. In 1875 it came to Disraeli's knowledge that the Khedive was contemplating the sale of these shares, that indeed he was preparing to enter into negotiations with France on the matter. With the utmost haste and secrecy, Disraeli got into communication with the Khedive by telegraph and bought the shares for the British government for about four million pounds. The announcement of the purchase surprised and delighted the people. It was the first startling awakening in recent years to an interest in a world of affairs outside those of their own narrow islands. A year later, 1876, Disraeli proposed and put through Parliament a measure designed still further to impress upon Great Britain the imperial idea — namely, a measure creating the British Queen the Empress of India. Victoria, pleased at what she considered an addition to her titles, assumed the imperial dignity January 1, 1877.

Disraeli's elevation to the premiership in Great Britain, his control of the Suez canal, and his emphasis on imperial policies combined with the traditional British misunderstanding and distrust of Russia to influence Great Britain's attitude in the Balkan situation in 1876. It had been a cardinal principle of British colonial policy to check all Russian expansion, especially Russian expansion toward Constantinople. Great Britain with the allies had fought the Crimean war in 1854–1856 in pursuance of this policy. Now that Great Britain controlled the Suez canal, it was even more essential than before that no strong power with opposing interests should be allowed to establish itself at the Bosphorus, in easy striking distance of the British direct line of communication with her richest colony. After an analysis of the situation as cynical and cold-blooded as any ascribed to Bismarck, Disraeli could look dispassionately on the sacrifice of the Bulgarian Christians without advocating any attack on the assassins. In his mind, the imperial interests of Great Britain, which demanded that Great Britain should support Turkey against Russia, outweighed the sufferings of the Christians in Turkey. When he had to parry criticism of his policy in Parliament, he emphasized the honorable qualities of the Circassian Turks, claimed the reports of the massacres were grossly exaggerated, or by his supreme power of ridicule and irony attempted to put his critics at a disadvantage. Even when popular opinion in Great Britain seemed turned against him, and some members of his cabinet resigned in disapproval of his policies, he maintained steadily the same principles.

ii. *Russia*

In Russia the suspicions of Great Britain were fully appreciated, but public feeling had been deeply touched by the misfortunes of the Slav Christians under the Turkish yoke. The daring of Serbia and Montenegro in declaring war against so formidable a foe as Turkey called forth from all Russia the greatest admiration; their successive defeats by the Turkish forces aroused a fiery sympathy. When in October of 1876 all of lower Serbia was in Turkish hands and the road was open to Belgrade, the Czar was forced to act. He stopped the Turkish advance by compelling the Turks to grant the Serbians an armistice, and then again appealed to Great Britain to agree with him upon some means of settling the situation. Affairs in Turkey were intolerable, he informed the British ambassador, and if the great powers of Europe were not prepared to act with energy and firmness, he would be obliged to act alone. Great Britain could agree to no action which would weaken

Turkey. In pursuance of his fixed policy, Beaconsfield went so far as to order the fleet at this critical stage in negotiations to Besika Bay near the entrance to the Dardanelles. There is reason to believe that Disraeli personally favored war against Russia, but was outvoted in his cabinet. A few months were passed in further negotiations. Turkey, relying upon the possibility of British assistance, would yield nothing. Great Britain, although not daring to offend public opinion at home by active intervention in Turkey's favor, would take no measures against Turkish interests. Russia alone was anxious for war. The Czar disclaimed all desire for conquest, specifically pledged his word that "he had not the smallest wish or intention to be possessed of Constantinople," and declared himself actuated solely by humane motives. He declared war against Turkey April 24, 1877.

D. THE RUSSO-TURKISH WAR

At first glance the war between Turkey and Russia suggests an encounter between a giant and a pygmy. Russia, with her broad fields, her inexhaustible supplies, drawing her army from a population of ninety millions seemed to have all the requisites of success when compared with the mountainous land where the Turk recruited his army from amongst the seventeen million Mohammedans who were eligible for service. Circumstances, however, combined to balance the scales. The Crimean war, only twenty years before, had crippled Russia, and the treaty which followed had prohibited her a fleet on the Black Sea. This latter disability had been removed with the tacit consent of Bismarck in 1870, but money was needed to rebuild the new ships. Moreover, she needed to reorganize and equip a modern army, to build railroads, and to develop resources, if she were to carry on a brilliant war after the fashion of the Germans. For all these things the money was lacking, and the bankers of Europe were Great Britain and France who had imposed the terms of the Treaty of Paris. On the other hand, Turkey had in Great Britain a ready source of supply for whatever gold was needed, and though the political corruption in Turkey diverted much of this from its proper uses, nevertheless enough money was used honestly to arm her forces with modern weapons and to build a number of first-class ships for the navy. By reason of these, command of the Black Sea was Turkey's during the war.

In organization and commanders, the Russians had their opponents at a disadvantage. In 1874 the Czar had issued an imperial ukase which provided for universal service whereby 150,000 men entered the standing army yearly. Service of six years with the colors was followed by nine years in the reserve, and five in the militia. All who were not chosen for active service were trained in the militia. The Czar's officers of the better class had made a study of the methods of von Moltke, and had a fair understanding of strategy as outlined by him, but were deficient in a knowledge of tactics. The men in the ranks were the impassive, ignorant peasants, devoted to the Czar; good soldiers when well led, but stupid and lacking in initiative.

The army which was organized to carry on the war consisted of nine corps, each of two infantry divisions and one cavalry division. To each corps was added artillery organizations with a total armament of 108 guns — four- and nine-pounder bronze guns of an obsolete model. The infantry was armed in part with the Berdan rifle, an up-to-date small-bore weapon, and in part with the Krenk rifle, a converted breech-loader, much inferior to the former. In the cavalry, the Lancer and Hussar regiments carried sabre, lance, and Berdan carbine; the Cossacks, sabre, lance, and Berdan rifle; the Dragoons, sabre and Krenk rifle. In addition to the above were siege guns, pontoon trains, and other necessary equipment, which brought Russia to a strength of 200,000 men, 850 field pieces, and 400 siege guns.

As for Turkey, the army was in a wretched condition. Her forces were acquired by a system of compulsory service, limited to the Mohammedan portion of her population. Service in the standing army, the Nizam, was of four years' duration, and was followed by a service of twenty years in three classes of reserves. Exemptions from the Nizam were easily obtained, and the training in the reserves was fragmentary. The government had taken some steps to prepare the army for the war, but the defects were of a nature that could not be removed by a few weeks of frenzied preparation. It has been said that there were no books on the art of war in the Turkish language. However that may have been, it is certain that the army officers received no regular training for their positions, and possessed no knowledge of strategy, tactics, or organization. The rank and file were good marchers and good fighters, who needed only leadership to produce a splendid army.

Theoretically, this army of Turkey was organized with the corps as the unit, but such was the confusion that frequently battalions of different corps fought in the same brigade. For fighting purposes the unit was the battalion and the higher forms were organized as occasion demanded. Three quarters of the infantry was armed with the Peabody-Martini rifle; the remainder with the Snider. The Martini was as good a rifle as was in existence at the time; the Snider was inferior but was an excellent weapon. The former was sighted to 1800 yards, the latter to 1300. The cavalry was badly mounted and had little or no training. Its arm was the Winchester rifle and revolver, the former being replaced in some squadrons by the lance. The artillery was armed with Krupp breech-loaders, four- and six-pounders. These were greatly superior to the Russian field pieces, but the advantage in weapons was more than counterbalanced by the lack of training in the personnel. To oppose her enemy, Turkey had in Europe 265,000 men and 450 guns, but both men and guns were scattered here and there about her territory and only casual efforts were made to collect them. The large Turkish armies are accounted for by the fact that Turkey had just engaged in a war with Serbia the previous year, and fully 95,000 of these troops were in Bosnia, Montenegro, and Herzegovina.

The principal battle ground of the war was that strip of what is now Bulgaria which lies between the Danube River and the Balkan Mountains. The Turkish frontier in 1877 was along the Danube River. At Rassova, the Danube turns northward, and here between the river and the sea is that territory known as the Dobrudja. Through this barren swampy country lies the most direct road from Russia to the Dardanelles, and along it the victorious armies of 1828 marched to Constantinople. But at that time, Russia commanded the Black Sea and was able to bring supplies from the sea for her advancing columns. In 1877 Turkey was supreme on the sea, and could not only prevent the supply of such an advancing army, but could land troops to attack its flank. Moreover, at Silistria, Varna, Shumla, and Rustchuk, in the so-called Quadrilateral, were strong forts which must either be reduced by the invader, or masked by strong detachments of his forces.

To the west along the Danube were the fortified towns of Sistova, Nikopol, Rahova, and Vidin. The Russians had information that Osman Pasha was at Vidin with 30,000 men, that some 10,000 men were at the other three Danubian cities, that Abdul Kerim Pasha, the Turkish commander-in-chief, was in command of the Quadrilateral with 85,000 men, and that Ali Pasha was in the Southern Dobrudja with 18,000 men.

Knowing these dispositions, General Nepokoitschitzki, the Russian chief of staff, formed the following plan: One Russian corps would enter the Dobrudja to protect the Russian flank from Turkish troops coming from east of the Danube; the remainder would force a crossing of the Danube between Rustchuk and Nikopol, leave detachments

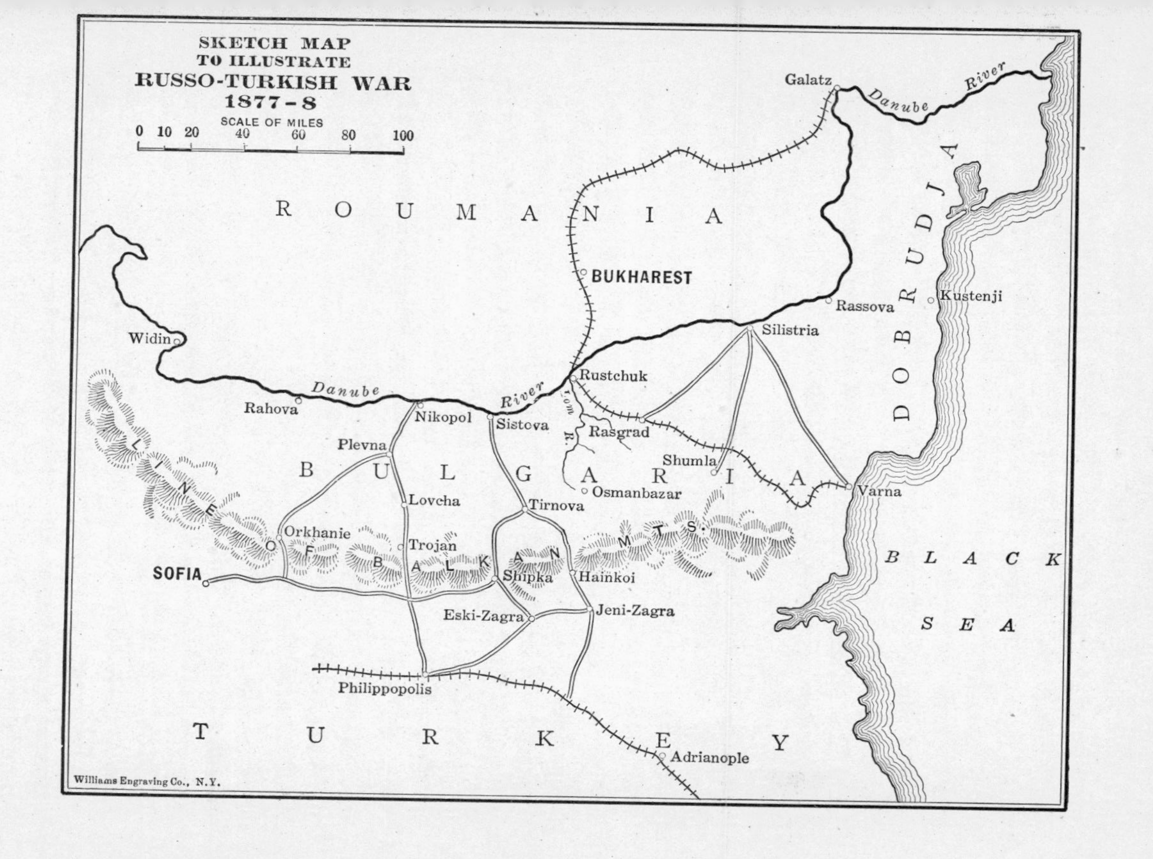
SKETCH MAP
TO ILLUSTRATE
RUSSO-TURKISH WAR
1877-8
SCALE OF MILES
0 10 20 40 60 80 100
ROUMANIA
BULGARIA
DOBRUDJA
TURKEY
BLACK SEA
Danube River
Lom R.
LINE OF BALKAN MTS.
Galatz
BUKHAREST
Rassova
Kustenji
Silistria
Widin
Rustchuk
Rahova
Nikopol
Sistova
Rasgrad
Plevna
Shumla
Varna
Osmanbazar
Lovcha
Tirnova
Orkhanie
Trojan
SOFIA
Shipka
Hainkoi
Jeni-Zagra
Eski-Zagra
Philippopolis
Adrianople
Williams Engraving Co., N.Y.

to mask the forts of the Quadrilateral and the army at Vidin, and march over the Balkan to capture Adrianople. There would then be nothing between the Russian army and the Golden Horn. The plan was faulty in that it proposed that one army should leave detachments strong enough to deal with two opposing armies, each almost equal in strength to itself, and yet march on rashly into the hostile country. Nepokoitschitzki overlooked the fact that so long as Turkey controlled the sea she could bring troops from her provinces to meet this small invading force, and he did not recognize the fact that geographical points are not necessarily strategic points. In his study of von Moltke, he had not grasped the principle which should have guided him in this war, viz.: that while the capture of Adrianople and Constantinople was important, the real strength of Turkey as of every other country, lay in her armies, and against them his blows should have been struck.

The crossing of the Danube was apt to prove a difficult task, for the Turkish gunboats were in control of the river, and the Turkish forts commanded all the good crossing points. But the Russians had completed an understanding with Rumania whereby the Czar's armies were to be allowed to cross Rumanian territory, so that the Grand Duke Michael was able to march his troops at once to Bucharest. In spite of this great help, though hostilities were commenced on the 24th of April, 1877, it was the 24th of June before the Russians had cleared the Danube of the Turkish craft from Nikopol to Rustchuk, and had prepared the rafts and pontoons for the crossing. On the 22d day of June, the XIV Corps crossed at Galatz and pushed south into the Dobrudja to carry out the first part of the Russian plan. Two days later a feint of crossing was made just before Nikopol, and on June 26, the Turkish commander being entirely at sea as to the Russian intention, the real crossing was effected by the VIII Corps at Sistova. Only a half-hearted attempt was made to oppose it, so that the Russian commander established his bridge successfully and started pushing his troops across as rapidly as possible. Abdul Kerim remained inactive, and offered no further opposition to the crossing. By leaving garrisons to hold the fortresses and marching with his main body toward the probable crossing point, an active Turkish commander could have made the passage of the Danube a costly undertaking for the Russians. Abdul Kerim, however, not only took no such steps, but remained ignorant of the Russian concentration at Bucharest, and refused to believe that the affair at Sistova was anything more than a "demonstration."

Once across the Danube, the Russians lost no time in beginning their southward march. General Gurko was placed in command of a special advance guard of 10 battalions of infantry, 31 squadrons, and 32 guns, which was to push rapidly to the south, secure a pass over the Balkans, damage Turkish lines of communication as much as possible, and endeavor to stir up a revolt in Bulgaria. On the 3d of July, Gurko crossed the Russian bridge at Sistova, and hurried to Tirnova, where, after defeating a small force of Turks, he gained information of the mountain passes to the southward. Shipka Pass, the main thoroughfare through the Eastern Balkans, was held by a detachment of 3000 Turks, but none of the minor passes was held in force. Gurko waited in Tirnova until the arrival of the VIII Corps, and then after arranging with that Corps' commander for a simultaneous attack of both ends of Shipka Pass, he pushed on to the southeast and crossed the Balkans by the Hainkoi Pass. His march was so delayed by small hostile bands, that he was unable to coöperate with the VIII Corps when that body attacked the Pass on July 17. As a consequence the attack from the north was repulsed, but the Turkish commander felt unable to hold the situation, and accordingly, on the night of July 18–19, abandoned the Pass. The Russians occupied it and held it until the end of the war.

The authorities at the Turkish capital were frightened by the vigor of Gurko's advance, and realizing that Abdul Kerim was doing nothing to ward off the approaching danger, they selected Mehemet Ali to supersede him as commander-in-chief of the Turkish forces in the field. The new commander assumed his duties on July 19 and at once began concentrating at Rasgrad. Meanwhile the Russians continued pouring troops across the bridge at Sistova. The VIII Corps crossed as we have seen on June 26. The XII and XIII Corps crossed from July 3 to July 8; the IX was across by the 10th; the XI Corps followed; and the IV corps effected it's crossing during the last days of July. The VII Corps remained at Odessa, and the X in Crimea.

A new danger now became apparent to the Russians — Osman Pasha, who had been isolated at Vidin, received orders to move with his 30,000 men toward the Russian armies. His plan was to unite with the Turkish force at Nikopol and attack the Russian flank between Biela and Tirnova; but before he could put it into operation, a successful attack on Nikopol by the IX Russian Corps on July 16 caused him to move to Plevna and take up a defensive position there. Within two days the Russians advanced on Plevna, and after an artillery bombardment of about an hour attacked at four separate points. The assault was so badly managed that the Turks gained an easy victory, whereas the Russians were forced to retire after having lost about 3000 men. This is known as the first battle of Plevna.

Plevna now became the real vortex of Russian activities. The Russians dared not ignore the presence of thirty thousand of the enemy on their flank. An advance to the south was impossible. The immediate defeat of Osman Pasha and the occupation of Plevna became imperative. Detachments of the IV and XII Corps were joined to the IX, and on July 30, 1877, General Krüdener advanced to the second attack. Osman Pasha had in the meantime received reinforcements of fourteen battalions and had strengthened his position by entrenchments. The Russians attacked after a six-hour artillery action, but not with the same assurance which marked the first battle of Plevna. General Krüdener had thoroughly reconnoitred the position and realized the uncertainty of success, but his orders from the Russian headquarters left him no alternative. The assault was easily repulsed, and the Russians retired with a loss of 7300 men. The defeat was so decided that for the moment all other activities ceased, and the full attention of the invaders was turned upon Plevna. Two new infantry divisions were mobilized, 175,000 militia were called to the colors, and the Rumanian troops which had been offered to Russia were accepted.

The end of July saw the Russian army divided into four parts: one corps in the Dobrudja; two corps opposed to Osman Pasha at Plevna; three corps facing Mehemet Ali on the Lom river (near Rasgrad); and Gurko's detachment south of the Balkans where Suleiman Pasha had an army of 30,000 which had come from Montenegro. The Turks were in a position to make a splendid strategic move. Had Suleiman avoided Gurko and joined either Mehemet or Osman, his force would have been able to win a decisive victory for either one. No such step was made, however, and in addition, no offensive was made by Osman after his two successes at Plevna. With Oriental inactivity the Turks seemed to wait calmly while their enemy increased his army until it should be able to outnumber their own. One further stupidity marked the handling of Suleiman's army. Gurko, who was unaware of the arrival of Suleiman's army, on July 29 attacked what he thought was the small command of Reouf Pasha but what was really the two forces combined. The defeat which ensued forced him to withdraw over the Balkans, leaving a small garrison on the Hainkoi Pass. Instead of following up his victory,

Suleiman waited at Yeni Zagra until August 17, when he attempted to retake the Shipka Pass. In the desperate fighting of the next few days, Suleiman lost 12,000 of his men without result, for the Russians could not be driven out. In September he repeated the attack with the same result — no gain and a frightful loss of men. Thus the army which might have turned the tide for either Mehemet or Osman north of the Balkans was dashed to pieces on the Shipka Pass.

The August attack on the Pass was followed by activities on the Lom river. Mehemet Ali planned to advance by way of Osman Bazar, effect a junction with Suleiman, and then, having driven the Russians out of Tirnova, advance to the relief of Osman at Plevna. During late August and early September he gained some success against the Czarevitch, who was commanding the opposing line, but on September 21 he met a decisive reverse at Cerkovna and was forced to give up his plan without having effected anything. In justice to Mehemet, it should be said that his plan was good, but its effectiveness was destroyed by the lack of coöperation on the part of Suleiman, who had gained the ear of the ministers at Constantinople. On October 2 the supreme command passed from Mehemet to Suleiman.

But these movements and the fighting on the Shipka were of lesser importance. The perplexing difficulty was Plevna. Reinforcements in great numbers had been brought by the Russians and by September they were vastly superior in strength to Osman Pasha's army. In early September they attacked and captured Lovcha, which was an important point on Osman's line of communications with Sofia. Encouraged by this, the Russian commander now decided upon a third attack of Plevna. His plan was similar to the other two — a long artillery bombardment followed by a simultaneous attack from three sides. Four days of incessant but ineffective artillery fire were followed by an infantry attack of savage intensity. For two days intermittent assaults were kept up, at the end of which time the baffled Russians withdrew, having taken and held only one redoubt. The attempt had cost them 20,000 men, whereas the Turks had lost but a quarter as many. The same error characterized all three attacks on Plevna — the dispersion of troops so that the final assault was made on too large a front.

A detailed account of the ensuing operations at Plevna belongs, not to such a brief sketch as this, but to a study of fortification. An investment of the town became necessary, and General Todleben, the hero of Sebastopol, was given the task. His preparations consumed the month September 25 - October 25, 1877, during which time Osman Pasha revictualed his army and raised his force to a fighting strength of 48,000. The siege now began in earnest. Suleiman on the Lom made spasmodic attempts, all of which were futile, against the forces confronting him, probably with the idea of marching to the assistance of Osman. On the Shipka Pass, Vessil Pasha continued to hold the Russians, but, except for small demonstrations, remained inactive. The only definite attempt made for the relief of Osman was when an army under Mehemet Ali was concentrated at Sofia and Orkhanie. Russian detachments, however, drove the Turks from the latter town, and held them fixed in the passes of the Balkans. In the early days of the siege, Osman had begged to be allowed to attempt to join Mehemet, but the authorities had refused him permission. Now in the early days of December, they saw that the fall of Plevna was inevitable and they gave a tardy consent to his plan.

The attempt was doomed to failure, but circumstances necessitated its being made. Osman's supplies were almost exhausted and fully a quarter of his troops were ineffective from disease. On the night of December 9 he massed his troops on the west of Plevna, hoping to force his way through the encircling enemy. In the darkness of a winter dawn he made his attempt and deployed his troops on the left bank of the Vid preparatory to a final attack. But the watchful Russians had discovered his plan and had massed troops at the sortie point. In addition, the forts to the east, depleted of men because of the contemplated evacuation, were captured by the Rumanians and Russians, and their guns turned against the Turks. Osman's wagon-trains were fired into on the bridges by the Russian artillery, and a hopeless confusion resulted. The Turks kept up the despairing struggle for a full five hours, at the end of which Osman surrendered unconditionally.

With the fall of Plevna, the fear of an attack on the Russian flank was removed, and though it was now the dead of winter, the Grand Duke determined to continue his advance toward Adrianople. The Czarevitch's army on the Lom was left north of the Balkans to guard the communications. The remaining troops moved southward in three columns: one under General Gurko by way of the Curiak pass near Orkhanie; one under General Kartzoff through the Trojan Pass; and a third under General Radetzky over the Shipka Pass. Gurko captured Sofia and advanced on Adrianople, pursuing the army of Mehemet Ali. Radetzky fell upon the army of Vessil Pasha at Shenovo on January 9, 1878, and captured it to a man. Suleiman had named Tatar Bazardjik as his point of concentration, where he was joined by Mehemet Ali. The rapid advance of General Radetzky after his success at Shenovo assured Suleiman that he could never reach Adrianople, so after a few spiritless skirmishes around Philippopolis, he set out for the Aegean on January 19, and finally arrived at Enos on the 28th. From here his army went by sea to Constantinople. The remaining Turkish troops under Mehemet Ali, were pushed rapidly back toward the Dardanelles, and when the armistice was declared, on January 31, the remnants of the Turkish armies were facing the Russians from behind the Buyuk-Tchemedji lines, less than thirty miles from Constantinople.

The fall of Plevna had been the turning point in the war. Without its capture, the Grand Duke could not have advanced south of the Balkans. But even with Plevna taken, the Turkish hope was not lost. Had Suleiman been possessed of any knowledge of strategy, he might yet have averted the ultimate catastrophe. A rapid concentration at some central point such as Adrianople would have enabled him to meet separately the three advancing Russian columns through the Curiak, Trojan, and Shipka Passes, and deal a crushing blow to one or more of them. Instead, he delayed his concentration and left Vessil Pasha to be annihilated at the Shipka where his army was useless. It is true that the war ministers at Constantinople were constantly interfering with and hindering the generals, but they could not have prevented the following up of victories had the commanding officers been minded to take advantage of them. The Turkish soldier had fought well, and in any engagement where numbers were anything like equal had proved himself the superior of the Russian. The blame for the defeat must fall where it belongs — on the officers commanding the Turkish armies in the field.

The fact must not be overlooked that while this campaign was being carried on in the Balkans, another was being directed in Asia Minor. In the neighborhood of Erzerum and Kars fierce fighting was carried on by numbers out of all proportion to the benefit either side expected to gain from the campaign.

The fall of Adrianople on January 20, 1878, marked the last effective resistance of the Turkish army. The line to Constantinople was open, the morale of the Turkish troops had been broken by a series of defeats, hope of British intervention on the side of the Porte was gone. As the Russian army began to move out of Adrianople toward the Turkish capital, the Sultan sued for peace.

CHAPTER II

THE CONGRESS OF BERLIN AND THE TRIPLE ALLIANCE

A. EUROPEAN INTERVENTION IN THE NEAR EASTERN QUESTION

WITH Russia's decisive victory and the prospect of peace between the two warring states, the settlement of the issues at stake again passed into the larger sphere of general European interests. The near Eastern Question — *i.e.* Turkey, her territory, and her relations with her subject Christian peoples and her neighbor Christian nations — was not one which could be settled by two nations with consideration of their own interests alone. It was a question, an issue, in which all the great powers of Europe were vitally concerned. Great Britain and Austria-Hungary especially were actively interested in the trend of events. On December 13, 1877, the British government reminded Russia of its pledge not to acquire Constantinople, and expressed the hope that the city would not be occupied, even temporarily, as a military measure. Three days later Russia replied that under the circumstances it must have full liberty of action. The fall of Adrianople and the advance of the Russian armies beyond that point toward the Turkish capital increased the tension between Great Britain and Russia. Popular feeling in Great Britain, which had been aroused by Gladstone's flaming pamphlet to sympathize with Russia and condemn the Turks, now underwent a complete "about face," for Russia seemed to have lost the character of a state championing oppressed Christians and to have unmasked her real character as ambitious and grasping. Russia on her part, resenting the suspicion of her bad faith, consented to an armistice (January 31, 1878) preliminary to the discussion of terms of peace, and moved forward to occupy the Tchataldja lines. At this forward movement the British fleet cleared for action, loaded its guns, and sailed into the sea of Marmora. The Russians on their part sowed the near-by waters with mines and awaited attack. For weeks the two forces confronted one another in a situation where the slightest incautious move would have precipitated war — a war, which, as Bismarck wittily remarked, would have been a fight between an elephant and a whale. Diplomacy finally triumphed, however, and the respective forces were withdrawn to safe distances.

Austria-Hungary was equally aroused at this time. The Emperor had in the beginning looked with complacency upon the Russian successes, for he had signed a treaty with the Czar agreeing to maintain neutrality providing that in the final settlement no territorial arrangement inimical to Austrian interests should be made, and providing that Austria-Hungary should receive the Turkish provinces of Bosnia and Herzegovina. As the war progressed, however, Russia stood forth as the champion of the Slavs, so that Austria-Hungary feared her rival had no intention of handing over the provinces inhabited by Slavs to Austrian control. Furthermore, the new Bulgarian state was planned (according to credible rumors) to extend to the Adriatic sea. Such extension of a state certain to be under Russian influence was an encroachment upon territory which Austria had already marked out for herself. Ever since the Italian lands had been lost, Austria-Hungary had looked forward to territorial expansion and political influence along the Albanian coast. Inspired by these considerations, Austria-Hungary, as well as Great Britain, let it be known that no settlement by Russia and Turkey alone would be satisfactory to her. As early as February 5, 1878, the imperial chancellor sent a circular note to the powers of Europe suggesting a general congress to establish "the agreement of Europe on the modifications which it may be necessary to introduce" into the treaties affecting Balkan conditions.

In the meanwhile, the negotiations between Russia and Turkey for peace proceeded rapidly. The Treaty signed at San Stefano, a little village on the shores of the sea of Marmora, formally terminated the war March 3, 1878. Its chief provisions had to do with the creation of the new state, Bulgaria, whose boundaries were made very broad, reaching from the Danube to Thessaly and including most of Albania, Macedonia, and Thrace. This Bulgarian state was given autonomy, but was still tributary to the Turkish Sultan. In addition to the creation of an autonomous Bulgaria, the Turks were obliged to recognize the complete independence of Russia's small allies, Serbia, Montenegro, and Rumania, and to make substantial territorial concessions to Serbia and Montenegro. Rumania was compelled to deliver up Bessarabia to Russia and to take in exchange the district near the mouth of the Danube known as the Dobrudja. And Turkey was pledged to pay a war indemnity amounting in our money to $700,000,000, for part payment of which Russia took considerable territory in Asia Minor (the districts of Ardahan, Kars, Batum, and Bayazid). Since only a narrow strip across the peninsula, from Constantinople to the Adriatic Sea, was left to Turkey, Gladstone's expressed desire for the expulsion of the Turks from Europe had been nearly accomplished by the terms of this treaty.

Knowledge of these terms awakened keen dissatisfaction in international political circles. Apparently the only states satisfied were Russia and the newly created Bulgaria. It was a treaty between two states made with only Slav interests in view, on issues which affected other races and other states. Each of the smaller Balkan states saw certain of its ambitions thwarted by some of the provisions.

The Serbians, dreaming of a greater Serbia that should include all speaking the Serbian language, wished for expansion to the south and west; but by the treaty all territory to the south had been incorporated into the new Bulgaria. Greece looked forward to the day when modern Greece should include all the territory of ancient Greece; but she saw her hopes checked by the inclusion of the northern coast of the Ægean Sea and all of central Macedonia in the new Bulgaria. The Rumanians were especially outspoken in their opposition to the treaty, for in their eyes Russia had shown base ingratitude for their services at the siege of Plevna in forcing Rumania to give up to Russia the large fertile Bessarabian district in exchange for the low and marshy Dobrudja. Had the small states in the Balkan region been the only objectors, however, their protests might have gone unheeded, for Russia's strength had no fear of their weakness; but the interests of other great and powerful nations were also involved. It was a fundamental feature of Austro-Hungarian policy to prevent Russian influence in the Balkan region. If the terms of the treaty of San Stefano were to be carried out, Austrian expansion to the southeast would be definitely checked and Russian influence would in all probability be predominant throughout the peninsula. And Great Britain, foreseeing in Turkey's weakness Russia's opportunity to expand in the future toward the Mediterranean Sea, was also unwilling to see Turkey so reduced in territory and power. Furthermore, Great Britain believed that Bulgaria, with its large and populous territory, would be practically a vassal of Russia, thereby adding to the power of that hereditary enemy.

Austria-Hungary in her circular note of February 5, 1878, had taken the lead in expressing the dissatisfaction of Europe with the terms of the treaty. The British government at once assented to the principle of a congress, and to support her position, voted several million pounds for armament and recalled troops from India to be ready for possible trouble. Confronted by these demands and military preparations, and weakened by a year of war, Russia reluctantly consented to submit the Treaty of San Stefano to the proposed Congress of powers. The place of meeting was to be Berlin. Bismarck had made a notable speech in the Reichstag, February 19, disclaiming any German territorial interests in the Balkan region and offering to serve as "honest broker" between the parties most concerned. On June 3, 1878, the German government issued the invitations: on June 13, the Congress met for its first session.

Certain essential principles with respect to the changes in the provisions of the Treaty of San Stefano had been agreed upon between Russia and Great Britain before the actual meeting of the Congress. Count Schuvaloff (Russian Ambassador to Great Britain) spent the month of April in London trying to discover with what concessions Beaconsfield's government would be content. From his conferences he learned that Great Britain would insist upon a reduction of the area of Bulgaria, an extension of the boundaries of Turkey, and an acknowledgment of the interests of other European powers in the Balkan affairs. On May 7 Schuvaloff left London for the Russian capital to lay the British proposals before the Czar. On the result of his mission hinged the issue of peace or war. If the Czar should refuse to concede the changes demanded by Great Britain, the British fleet stood ready to take the offensive in behalf of Turkey. After a fortnight of deliberation, the Czar decided not to risk the gains which he had already made in another war. Schuvaloff returned to London and, on May 30, negotiated an agreement with Great Britain on the chief points at issue. From that time the Congress of Berlin was assured, but its business was restricted to a determination of particular boundaries rather than of general principles.

B. THE CONGRESS OF BERLIN

The importance of this Congress and of the Treaty signed thereat cannot be overestimated in the consideration of the course of history from 1880 to the present day. The governments sent their keenest diplomats to the German capital. Disraeli (Earl of Beaconsfield) represented Great Britain, assisted by Lord Salisbury and Lord Odo Russell, the British Ambassador to Berlin; Count Andrássy, Chancellor of Austria, was present in person; Prince Gortchakoff of Russia, Alexander II's chief Minister, was accompanied by Count Schuvaloff, Russian Ambassador to England, and d'Oubril, Russian Ambassador to Germany; Bismarck, with Baron von Bülow and Prince Hohenlohe-Schillingsfürst, took charge of affairs affecting Prussian or German interests. Although no rulers were present in person, as had been the case in some previous European Congresses, no Congress had ever assembled a more notable group of European diplomats.

The Congress met for its first session at 2 P.M., June 13, 1878. Prince Hohenlohe in his Memoirs gives the following description of the first meeting:

"At half-past one I drove to Bismarck's palace, formerly that of Radziwill. In the large room I found only Radowitz, who was busied with the arrangement of the necessary papers. In what was formerly the great ball-room a green table, shaped like a horseshoe, had been placed.

"In the middle the president's seat; on either side France, left, Austria, right; then England next to Austria, Italy to France; further down, Russia on the right, Turkey on the left. Opposite Bismarck sits Radowitz as recorder; I on the left, Bülow on the right.

"The Secretary of State soon came, and then the Imperial Chancellor. We went to the buffet, which was spread in an adjoining room, and drank port and ate biscuits. The plenipotentiaries gradually arrived. Count Corti, a small, ugly man, who looked like a Japanese, with Launay; then the Turk, an insignificant young man; Count Schuvaloff; then old Gortchakoff, very shaky; and, lastly, the Englishmen and the Frenchmen, Waddington in laced uniform. The first meeting between Lord Beaconsfield and Gortchakoff was interesting as a historic event. A move was then made into the room where the sittings were held. Bismarck made an introductory speech, and proposed to elect the officials. Andrássy, after previous consultation with the other plenipotentiaries, rose and proposed the election of Bismarck as president. He then made proposals as regards the secretary and recorder, which were accepted. I then introduced the personnel."

Of the details of the deliberations within the Congress, we know little. Interesting hints leaked out with regard to the rivalry between Beaconsfield and Gortchakoff. It was credibly reported that in the midst of debate Gortchakoff on one occasion indignantly gathered his maps together, folded them up, and prepared to leave the Congress; and on another occasion, Beaconsfield dramatically ordered a special train to be in readiness to take him and his staff to Calais. At such moments the peace of Europe trembled in the balance. The task of the president of the Congress, Bismarck, was not easy, but all parties paid tribute to the supreme tact with which he managed to settle the disputes that arose.

Just one month to a day from the beginning of the Congress, its deliberations were finished and a treaty signed. One notable remarked that no one was satisfied with the result, which fact was excellent evidence of the fairness and justice with which the decisions had been made. Beaconsfield on his return to London declared that he had gained "Peace with Honor," and Great Britain as a whole applauded what was popularly considered as a decided rebuff to Russia.

C. THE TREATY OF BERLIN

The Treaty of Berlin, which was completed and signed July 13, was a long document of sixty-four articles revising completely the arrangements concluded in the Treaty of San Stefano. A statement of the principal political and territorial provisions of the Treaty of Berlin will show how materially the San Stefano Treaty was modified. (1) The territory, which in the San Stefano Treaty constituted the new Bulgaria, was divided into three parts, (*a*) Macedonia, thrust back under the direct dominion of the Sultan, (*b*) Eastern Roumelia, given autonomy but subject to the Sultan, and (*c*) Bulgaria, given autonomy and the right freely to choose its own sovereign prince, but still to be considered a part of the Turkish realm, and to be tributary to the Sultan. (2) The complete independence of Serbia, Montenegro, and Rumania was recognized. (3) Austria-Hungary obtained the right to occupy and administer the two Turkish provinces of Bosnia and Herzegovina, and to maintain a military force in the Sanjak of Novi-Bazar. (4) Russia was confirmed in her possession of Bessarabia, in return for which Rumania received the Dobrudja. (5) Russia added to her territories a considerable tract in Asia Minor, including the Armenian districts of Ardahan, Kars, and Batum.

A brief consideration of these provisions will show that they were not dictated by any sincere desire to arrive at a lasting and satisfactory settlement of the Balkan troubles. Each nation in the congress was intent upon securing for itself every possible advantage irrespective of the rights, wishes, or welfare of the Balkan people. Great Britain, Russia, and Austria-Hungary were all equally at fault. Great Britain, in fact, nine days before the congress met, concluded a treaty with Turkey whereby in return for the permission to occupy the Turkish island of Cyprus, she pledged herself to maintain, by the use of force if necessary, the integrity of the Sultan's remaining possessions in Asia. Furthermore, Great Britain was a party to the crime of thrusting the Macedonian Christians back under the Turkish yoke, because she believed her own interests demanded a Turkey at the Dardanelles strong enough to repulse

THE BALKAN STATES
1856-1912
Scale of Miles
0 50 100 150 200
Boundaries, 1856-1878
Proposed Boundaries (Treaty of San Stefano, 3 March, 1878)
Boundaries (Treaty of Berlin, 13 July, 1878), 1878-1912
Longitude East from Greenwich
HUNGARY
RUMANIA
Moldavia
Wallachia
BOSNIA
Herzegovina
Croatia
SERBIA
MONTENEGRO
BULGARIA
EASTERN RUMELIA
TURKEY
Albania
THESSALY
Epirus
GREECE
RUSSIA
Bessarabia
Dobrudja
Crimea
BLACK SEA
ASIA MINOR
ADRIATIC SEA
IONIAN SEA
ÆGEAN SEA
Sea of Marmora
ITALY
Buda Pest
Szegedin
Agram
Temesvar
Belgrade
Grosswardein
Klausenburg
Hermannstadt
Kronstadt
Carpathian Mts.
Transylvanian Alps
Balkan Mts.
Chotin
Jassy
Kishinev
Piatra
Dakau
Galatz
Ismail
Kilia Mouth
St. George Mouth
Nikolaiev
Rimnik
Ploesti
Bucharest
Krajova
Slatina
Magurelli
Tchernavoda
Kustendji
Mangalia
Silistria
Rustchuk
Shumla
Varna
Nicopolis
Sistova
Plevna
Beila
Tirnova
Sofia
Salatitza
Shipka Pass
Kazanlik
Slivno
Hainkoi
Karabunar
Burgas
Agathopoli
Midia
Philippopolis
Kostendil
Vranja
Nish
Novibazar
Alexinatz
Krashevatz
Semendria
Jagodina
Negotin
Banialuka
Zoornik
Sarajevo
Mostar
Spalatro
Zara
Niksics
Cetigne
Cattaro
Antivari
Dulcigno
Scutari
Scutari L.
Ipek
Uskub
Istib
Divra
Monastir
Goritza
Shatista
Salonica
Nevrekop
Kavala
Mastanly
Adrianople
Dedeagatch
Enos
Constantinople
Bosphorus
Gallipoli
Dardanelles
Broussa
Troja
Smyrna
Konitza
Janina
Larissa
Arta
Durazzo
Trieste
Fiume
Istria
Venice
Ancona
Pescara
Rome
Campobasso
Naples
Salerno
Potenza
Barletta
Bari
Brindisi
Taranto
Gulf of Taranto
Policastro
Cosenza
Catanzara
Reggio
LIPARI IS.
CORFU
THASOS
IMBROS
LIMNOS
MITYLENE
CHIOS
EUBŒA
VEGLIA
CHERSO
LUNGA
BRAZZA
CURZOLA
Danube
Theiss R.
Szamos
Maros R.
Drave R.
Save R.
Drina
Lim R.
Drin R.
Vardar R.
Struma R.
Maritza R.
Aluta R.
Arjish R.
Jalomitza R.
Sereth R.
Pruth R.
Dniester R.
Bug R.
Sakaria R.
WILLIAMS ENG. CO., N.Y.

the encroachments of Russia. Austria-Hungary's motives in occupying Bosnia and Herzegovina were wholly selfish. These two districts, which were inhabited mainly by Serbians, had been looked upon by Serbia as the legitimate field for future annexation whereby Serbia might expand to the sea. Austrian occupation and administration, definitely intended to prevent Serbian expansion in this direction, forced Serbia to be a wholly inland nation, condemned to send its products to the great highway of commerce across a foreign territory. Russia, in spite of her protestations of humane motives at the beginning of the war, showed every inclination to profit by the result. Russia forced Rumania to give up the rich province of Bessarabia in exchange for the much less desirable Dobrudja; and annexed large and populous districts in Turkish Armenia, including the excellent port of Batum on the Black Sea. And lastly, all the states assembled, disregarding utterly the common desire of Bulgarians north of the Balkans and of those south to be united into one state, separated them into two. The short-sightedness and selfishness of the diplomats at Berlin bore fruit in the continuous unrest of later years in the Balkan region — a condition which ultimately precipitated the most terrible of European wars.

D. DIPLOMATIC RESULTS OF THE CONGRESS OF BERLIN

One very important result of the proceedings of the Congress of Berlin was the rupture of the friendly relations which had since 1863 existed between Russia and Prussia (now become the chief state in Germany). Russia left the Congress feeling cheated and humiliated. After waging a war at great cost of men and money, she had been forced to give up the rightful rewards of her victory. Gortchakoff, the brilliant Russian Chancellor, had previously conceived an intense personal distaste for Bismarck, inspired, according to Bismarck's idea, by jealousy of the German Chancellor's great reputation: he now declared that the Berlin Congress was the "darkest episode of his career" and ascribed his diplomatic defeat wholly to Bismarck's attitude. He argued that if the German representatives had supported him in his arrangements, he would have been able to carry them through triumphantly. Russians recalled how in 1866 their country had neglected to profit during Prussia's war against Austria, and how in 1870 she had actually threatened Austria to prevent Austria from going to the help of France. They now accused Prussia of base ingratitude. The Russian press heaped odium upon Bismarck; Russian royalty who chanced to pass through Berlin refused to meet him; the Czar protested to the German Emperor against Bismarck's policy; the Russian armies on the German frontier were strengthened. Although war was not actually threatened, the relations between the two countries were no longer those of the preceding period of "cordial understanding."

The excuse commonly given for Bismarck in his attitude toward the Russian position in the Congress is that he, being wholly neutral in the matter, had acted in accordance with his conception of the rights and wrongs of the question at issue. Bismarck in his recollections indignantly denies that Russia had any reason to expect more than benevolent neutrality; more than that he should act, as he had promised, in the rôle of "honest broker." "They sought with success to lay the guilt of the unsuccessful issue of the war on the German policy," Bismarck writes, "on the 'disloyalty' of the German friend. It was a dishonest fiction. We had never let them expect anything but a benevolent neutrality." The German Chancellor had, indeed, on one occasion professed entire indifference to the whole Eastern Question, saying that "it was not worth the bones of a Pomeranian grenadier."

Knowing the politic and unemotional quality of Bismarck's diplomacy, however, we may fairly question whether his attitude in the Congress was as disinterested as he wished people to believe. He must have realized that the conflicting interests of Austria-Hungary and Russia were such that any permanent friendship between them was out of the question: it followed that he had to decide at the moment whether to link the fortunes of Germany for the future with the one or the other. It was impossible to steer a middle path.

Several elements favored an alliance with Russia: — the traditional friendship that had existed between Prussia-Germany and Russia, the gratitude which Bismarck owed Russia for Russia's benevolent neutrality in 1866 and 1870–1871, the tremendous actual and potential military power of the great Slav state. Bismarck himself stated in his reminiscences that the Russian alliance was offered to him:

"Even before the Congress Count Shuvaloff touched on the question of a Russo-German offensive and defensive alliance, and put it to me directly. I discussed openly with him the difficulties and prospects that the question of the alliance offered us, and especially the choice between Austria and Russia if the triple alliance of the Eastern Powers were not maintained."

On the other hand, weighty considerations pointed to the greater desirability of opening a way for a close alliance with Austria-Hungary by supporting her cause in the Congress. To support Austria-Hungary was to align Germany, not only with that state, but with all the other chief powers of Europe, for Russia stood alone in the Congress in her attempt to uphold the Treaty of San Stefano: whereas to support Russia would be to alienate, not only Austria-Hungary, but Great Britain and France as well. Bismarck reports that he told Shuvaloff:

"that if we sacrificed our relations with all the other Powers to the firmness of our alliance with Russia, we should find ourselves, with our exposed geographical situation, in a dangerous dependence on Russia in the event of an acute manifestation of French or Austrian desire of revenge."

And he spoke again of his distrust of the permanence of the Russian alliance in case of trouble:

"I expressed a fear that if the German policy confined its possibilities to the Russian alliance, and, in accordance with the wishes of Russia, refused all other states, Germany would with regard to Russia be in an unequal position, because the geographical situation and the autocratic constitution of Russia made it easier for her to give up the alliance than it would be for us, and because the maintenance of the old traditions of the Russo-Prussian alliance after all rests on a single pair of eyes — that is, it depends on the moods of the reigning emperor of Russia."

Furthermore, the general international situation at that time showed that the chief danger to Germany's position lay in the possibilities of an alliance between Austria-Hungary and France. Austria-Hungary had been defeated in 1866, and France in 1870–1871: what could be more natural than that they should unite to defeat and humiliate their common conqueror? Could Bismarck win the favor of Austria-Hungary by his support in the Congress and pave the way for an alliance, he would postpone indefinitely the formation of a menacing Austro-French coalition. In favor of an alliance with Austria-Hungary, too, was the fact that the reigning houses in the two countries were of the same blood. Could Austria-Hungary be induced to forget the war of 1866, the two Germanic empires could be leagued together in bonds not woven alone of political expediency, but of ties of a common race and language. It was a more natural alliance than that between German and Slav. The long close relations of the days of the Holy Roman Empire might be revived, with the difference that Germany and Austria-Hungary would stand side by side, equal in rights and privileges, with a united front against all foes.

Some such considerations as these we have noted weighed with Bismarck in determining his attitude in the Congress. He undoubtedly hoped, however, that by adroit manipulation he could favor Austria-Hungary, and at the same time retain the friendship with Russia. The suspicious and exacting jealousy of the Russian Chancellor, Gortchakoff, balked him. He was quickly made to feel that he had forfeited for Germany the friendship of Russia.

i. *The Dual Alliance*

The keen resentment aroused in official circles in Russia by Gortchakoff's recital of Bismarck's attitude in the Congress aroused Bismarck to the necessity of pressing forward the negotiations for the alliance with Austria-Hungary. It was possible that Russia would attack before he could form this alliance; in such an event, his position was very dangerous, for Russia could approach either Austria-Hungary or France with excellent chance for assistance in an attack against Germany. Fortunately for Bismarck's plans he found Andrássy, the new premier in Austria-Hungary, willing to accept his advances. After relatively brief negotiations, the two states concluded the treaty of the Dual Alliance, October 7, 1879. The pertinent provisions, published to the world in 1888, were as follows:

"1. Should, contrary to the hope and against the sincere wish of the two High Contracting Parties, one of the two Empires be attacked by Russia, the High Contracting Parties are bound to stand by each other with the whole of the armed forces of the Empires and, in consequence thereof, only to conclude peace jointly and in agreement.

"2. Should one of the High Contracting Parties be attacked by another Power, the other High Contracting Party hereby binds itself, not only not to stand by the aggressor of its High Ally, but to observe at least an attitude of benevolent neutrality towards its High Co-contractor.

"If, however, in such a case the attacking Power should be supported by Russia, either in the form of active coöperation or by military measures menacing to the party attacked, the obligation defined in Clause I of reciprocal help with the entire armed strength comes immediately into force in this case also, and the war will then also be waged jointly by the two High Contracting Parties until the joint conclusion of peace."

By the provisions of this alliance, Bismarck believed that he had again won for Germany a security in foreign affairs.

Should the irritation in Russia increase to the point of war, Germany was certain of an ally; should France yield to her desire for revenge and attack Germany, Austro-Hungarian neutrality was assured; should France in a war against Germany be aided by Russia, Austro-Hungarian assistance was pledged.

ii. *The Triple Alliance*

To make assurance doubly sure, Bismarck desired a third power in the alliance. Since Russia was at the time definitely alienated, and France bitterly hostile, he turned toward Italy. In that country the traditional friendship with France had been broken by the persistence of the French government under Napoleon in supporting the claims of the Papacy to temporal power, and the seeds of good relations with Germany sown by the alliance during the war of 1866 against Austria. Bismarck's machinations to kill all remaining friendship in Italy for France and to draw Italy into the German-Austrian alliance illustrate the devious ways by means of which great statesmen sometimes work to accomplish their ends.

Italy desired colonial development on the Mediterranean coast of Africa, especially in Tunis and Tripoli. Tunis, particularly, was desirable, for it approached Italian territory (Sicily) at the narrowest point of the Mediterranean and would in the hands of a hostile power be a continual menace. Under the circumstances it might be thought that the simplest way to gain Italy's friendship and adherence would be to assist her in gaining Tunis. Bismarck, however, did not offer this assistance. He well knew that France, which already possessed the neighboring country of Algeria, coveted Tunis and was making representations to certain of the great powers to allow the extension of her power over that country. Bismarck is said to have volunteered secretly his cordial consent to France's plans, believing that such consent might do a little toward helping

France to forget the war of 1870, and feeling certain that Italy, which could know nothing of his consent, would be thrown by the result into the German-Austrian alliance. All proceeded according to his plan. Taking advantage of the many pretexts for intervention in Tunis, France sent an expedition there in 1881 and quickly established a French protectorate. Feeling rose high in Italy: the traditional hostility toward Austria was forgotten in the new rage against France. While Italian statesmen were in this mood, Bismarck found it easy to persuade them that their best interests lay in an alliance with the central Germanic powers. A year later, 1882, Italy yielded to his arguments. The famous Triple Alliance was formed.

Although the provisions of this alliance have never been made public, their tenor is undoubtedly the same as that of the original alliance between Germany and Austria. The Triple Alliance at once became the chief factor in international politics in Europe. Of this Triple Alliance Germany was acknowledgedly the most powerful member, and in Germany Bismarck was in absolute control of the country's policies. The alliance included territory through the center of Europe from the Baltic to the Mediterranean, supporting more than 100,000,000 people in states maintaining a constantly mobilized military power of 2,000,000. Bismarck in the formation of the alliance had carried his dependence upon the value of "blood and iron" to its logical conclusion. It was certain that, in any international issues, Germany's decision, backed by 2,000,000 well-trained and well-equipped soldiers, would weigh heavily in the final reckoning. Bismarck, by virtue of his position at the head of the most powerful member of this great alliance, exercised a supreme control over the diplomacy of Europe.

Although Bismarck's policy, at this critical period succeeded in establishing Germany as the most powerful state in Europe, it had a baneful influence upon the course of subsequent international relations. Since the fall of Napoleon the powers of Europe had gradually become accustomed to decide conflicting interests by formal deliberations in Congresses rather than by hasty appeal to war. As a result of these Congresses and of the treaties concluded therein, a large and important mass of decisions of a judicial nature had been accumulated whereby it might be hoped to avoid war in the future. The effect of Bismarck's Triple Alliance was to inject into international issues mere military force as a deciding element. Other powers would inevitably be led to fear that in future Congresses issues would be settled, not according to the justice of the respective claims or according to the provisions of the treaties in force, but according to the selfish wishes of the members of the Triple Alliance. The rule of force would take precedence over the rule of law and justice; military strength would replace treaty agreements and European Congresses as the court of final appeal.

Again, the formation of the Triple Alliance was in itself a challenge to the other nations not included therein, to form an opposing alliance. The other states in Europe were certain to feel that, in order to resist probable "bullying" by Germany and the Triple Alliance, it was necessary for them to combine in an alliance with equal or greater military resources. Russia, France, and Great Britain, who stood alone at this time, could not fail ultimately to be impressed with the advantages that would accrue to each of them by reconciling their differences and pooling their interests. We shall see that, a decade later, an alliance was actually formed between two of these great powers and the way was made easy for the coöperation of the third.

And finally, with the existence of two great opposing alliances in Europe, followed inevitably a rivalry in armaments. Each group would strain every nerve to equip itself so thoroughly that, should war arise out of any of the conflicting interests, it would be able by force to gain a decision in its favor. The mighty military preparations of the twenty years preceding the great war that broke out in 1914 sprang directly from the existence of the two hostile alliances in Europe. Although each alliance was nominally formed for defense alone, the statesmen at the head of each could not allow its military forces to fall behind those of its opponent. The period of great armaments, with their appalling expense to the world, dates from the formation of the two powerful opposing alliances in Europe.

CHAPTER III

EUROPEAN DEVELOPMENT, 1880–1890

I. GREAT BRITAIN, FRANCE, RUSSIA, AND THE NEAR EAST

THE next decade of European history, from 1880 to 1890, was not marked by any significant outward changes in international relations.[1] Although there was one small war between two of the Balkan states, and although at times intense ill-will was excited among the great powers — as between Great Britain and France over British activities in Egypt, between Russia and Austria-Hungary over the Balkan situation, and between Germany and France at the time of the Boulanger madness — the decade was peaceful. The outstanding feature in international politics continued to be the Triple Alliance. This alliance, of course, insured Germany's position so long as conditions on the continent remained the same. Bismarck, however, realizing the dangers of the formation of an opposing alliance, used every resource of diplomacy to keep Russia and France apart. He connived at Jules Ferry's ambitious colonial enterprises, for he hoped that France might in these colonial undertakings forget Alsace and Lorraine, and that the great expense and complications resulting from the acquisition of colonies would so embarrass France that she would be unable to threaten his own country. In the case of Russia, he ordered the German press to flatter that nation at every opportunity; he intimated to Alexander III that monar-

[1] The entrance of Italy into alliance with Germany and Austria-Hungary (1882), forming the Triple Alliance, has already been mentioned.

chical Germany would be a more suitable and powerful ally than republican France; he expelled from Berlin persons suspected of hostility to the Czar; he arranged for mutual visits between the royal families; and in 1884 he brought together the sovereigns of Austria-Hungary, Germany, and Russia in an attempt to renew the cordial understanding of the period previous to the Turkish war.

It is curious to note how, just as soon as Bismarck desired peace in Europe, peace followed. After he had been instrumental in bringing on three wars — the Danish of 1864, the Austro-Prussian of 1866, and the Franco-Prussian of 1870 — and had thus established the German Empire in the foremost place on the continent, his interest in promoting war promptly ceased. Subsequent to 1870, Germany became, so long as Bismarck remained chancellor and minister of foreign affairs, the strongest factor in the maintenance of peace in Europe. Although he could not prevent the Russo-Turkish war in 1877-1878 — which, indeed, was waged on issues that lay beyond the sphere of German interests at the time — he was instrumental at the Congress of Berlin in preventing its results from involving other of the great powers in Europe. As his policy of "blood and iron" was the chief cause of the wars from his accession to power in 1862 to the establishment of the Empire, so his policy of peace was largely responsible for peace among the great powers from 1871 to 1890.

During this decade of peace, then, we may trace the course of internal developments in certain of the more important States and indicate, where necessary, the bearing of such developments upon the general European political situation. We shall see that, though outwardly international relations did not alter, certain changes in domestic conditions in individual states paved the way for the momentous events of the decades following.

A. Great Britain

With Disraeli as premier, the Conservative party had made a creditable record in the years of its power following 1874. Disraeli had proposed as the platform of his party "the Constitution, the Empire, and Social Reform": he and his associates had tried to live up to this platform. In domestic legislation, the Conservatives carried through sound measures improving agricultural conditions, codified various acts and regulations on labor in the notable Factory and Workshops Act of 1878, attacked the problem of properly housing the poor in the Artisans' Dwellings Acts of 1875, and introduced new standards of safety for ships and sailors by the Merchant Shipping Act of 1876. The most conspicuous achievement of the ministry, however, was its success in furthering the imperial idea and in reëstablishing Great Britain's prestige in continental politics. The purchase of the Suez Canal shares in 1875, and the assumption of the title Empress of India by the Queen in the following year were features of this imperialism. The diplomacy of Beaconsfield (Disraeli was elevated to the peerage in 1876) in the troubled period preceding and during the Russo-Turkish war, and his influence in the Congress of Berlin, signalized the new attitude of Great Britain in international affairs. All Britons thrilled at the supposed triumph of British diplomacy expressed in Beaconsfield's report that he had brought back "Peace with Honor."

In the years immediately following the Congress of Berlin, however, Beaconsfield's prestige and that of his party were severely undermined. In distant India, Great Britain had become involved in a war against the Afghans over the right to force the Amir of Afghanistan to harbor a British representative. Even though the British were finally successful, the triviality of the cause of the war, the reverses suffered at its outset, and its great expense, weakened public confidence in the Conservative policy. And again, in 1879, the British government determined to crush the Zulus, who were troubling the recently annexed Transvaal region in South Africa. The very beginning of this campaign was marked by the massacre of a British force at Isandhlwana (January 22, 1879), for which of course the government was held responsible. Add to these foreign mishaps a disastrous harvest in 1879, a temporary industrial and commercial depression throughout the British Isles, and a campaign of scathing denunciation undertaken by Gladstone in a series of notable speeches, and it can be seen that the government stood little chance of winning the elections of April, 1880. In those elections the Liberals were returned to power with a majority of 41; Beaconsfield resigned; and Gladstone again became prime minister.

With one brief interval Gladstone remained in power for six years, from 1880 to 1886. His premiership marked an about face in the foreign policies of Great Britain. Whereas Disraeli had emphasized the imperial position of Great Britain, and had insisted upon the importance of British interests in world politics being appreciated and respected by the continental states, Gladstone desired to concentrate all his attention upon domestic problems. He believed that the national welfare would best be fostered by a policy of peace and non-interference abroad and reforms at home. Hence, this great power, which had been so efficiently represented at Berlin by the picturesque Beaconsfield, now apparently desired nothing better than to withdraw wholly from international politics so far as it was possible to do so.

In Gladstone's achievements only three points of special political significance need to be noted: — first, the passage of a reform bill extending the suffrage; second, the emergence of Irish Home Rule as an issue of first importance in British politics in recent times; and third, his policy with relation to Egypt.

i. Parliamentary Reform Bill

Although the previous reform bills in Great Britain (1832 and 1867) had extended the franchise liberally to members of the middle classes and to householders in the boroughs (*i.e.* incorporated cities and towns), they had done little for those who lived in the counties. Hence the people in the counties, mainly those living in small villages or on farms, were at a disadvantage compared with persons of a similar station in the boroughs. Gladstone's bill, introduced and passed in 1884, was intended to remedy the injustice of these conditions. It extended the chief provisions of the borough franchise to apply to conditions in the counties, with the result that it doubled the number of county voters and increased the total electorate about two millions. Accompanying the reform bill was an act, passed the following year (1885), redistributing the seats in the House of Commons. The general principle was laid down that the number of borough and county representatives depended upon the population — one member for constituencies between 15,000 and 50,000; two members for those between 50,000 and 165,000; three members for those having 165,000, and one more member for each additional 50,000 inhabitants. The total membership of the House was increased from 652 to 670.

ii. Irish Home Rule

Another issue of importance in Gladstone's ministry from 1880 to 1886 was the Irish question. This was not by any means a new problem, for the government of Ireland had been a continual trouble to the British parliament since the first attempts at conquest in the twelfth century. Conditions in British politics at this period, however, for the first time in modern years gave Irish patriots a chance to advance their Home Rule arguments with a chance of success.

English treatment of Ireland is a long tragedy of misunderstanding and oppression. Great Britain, endowed with colonies stretching around the world, boastful of her success in colonial government, has failed dismally in the affairs of the island at her doors. By the cruel oppression of six centuries of revolts, by alienating the land from the Irish and handing it over to the English and Scotch, by hostility to the religion of the mass of the people, and by colonizing an important section of the country (Ulster province) with Scotch Presbyterians, the English have sown the seeds of an ineradicable hatred in the hearts of the Irish. At the beginning of the nineteenth century, the English by flagrant bribery forced the Irish parliament to approve an Act of Union (1801), whereby thereafter the Irish parliament was abolished and only one hundred Irish members admitted to the British parliament. In that parliament, of course, the few Irishmen were swallowed up and lost. Their protests were unheeded and their votes carried no weight. The one body through which Irish grievances might have been expressed was swept away by the Act of Union. Ireland relapsed into sullen wretchedness.

The Irish patriots had to wait long for an opportunity to retrieve their fortunes. The successive reform bills and redistribution of seats in parliament, however, held out the prospect of a time in the future when their group might hold the balance of power and exact concessions. In 1880, when the Liberals overthrew Beaconsfield and Gladstone became prime minister, the Irish party had a solid body of sixty-one patriots in the House of Commons, led by one of the most adroit Irishmen of modern times, Parnell, and determined to use every opportunity afforded by parliamentary procedure to gain an advantage for Ireland.

We may believe in justice to Gladstone that at this juncture it was not only political expediency, but a sense of right that led him to take steps to allay the unrest in Ireland. One manifest injustice was the condition of land tenure. After the rebellions of previous centuries, large parts of Ireland had been confiscated and given out of hand in great estates to Englishmen. These English landlords, who seldom visited their estates yet drew large incomes from the rentals, were looked upon by the Irish as usurpers, and their bailiffs or agents as tyrants. Yet the Irishman's sole livelihood was gained from the land, so that he was at the mercy of these landlords and their bailiffs. He had to take the land on whatever terms, however unjust or exorbitant, the bailiffs might impose. To remedy the injustice of this condition, Gladstone introduced a Land Act in 1881 outlining a policy of "Three F's," as it was known:—Free Sale, Fixity of Tenure, and Fair Rent. By the Free Sale clause, tenants were authorized to sell their occupation interests; by Fixity of Tenure, the tenants were secured from eviction except for nonpayment of rent; by Fair Rent, tenants were enabled to have their rental fixed by a newly created Land Commission Court.

It was a noble effort to alleviate conditions in Ireland, but was wholly unsatisfactory to Parnell and his followers. They sought, not partial remedies, but a complete change in system; they demanded national self-government and an unconditional liberation of the land for the people — in other words, Home Rule and the restoration of confiscated land. They used every effort to gain their ends. In Parliament, they resorted to methods of obstruction, such as dilatory motions, demands for roll calls, and endless speeches; in Ireland, their followers resorted to violence to emphasize their dissatisfaction. In the Parliament which met in 1886, the Irish nationalist members increased to eighty-six, and held the balance of power.

On April 8, 1886, Gladstone introduced a Home Rule Bill, providing for an Irish Parliament with an Irish ministry empowered to manage Irish affairs, but without power on questions affecting the Crown, the army and navy, foreign policy, colonial affairs, or the endowment or establishment of any religion. The Bill sought to satisfy the Irish demands without infringing upon British sovereignty over affairs of the national government and without endangering the position of the Protestants in Ireland.

This Bill split Gladstone's party in Parliament. A strong group terming itself Liberal-Unionist — *i.e.* liberal in politics, but determined to maintain the union between England and Ireland — seceded and prepared to vote with the opposition. After long and bitter debate the Bill was defeated on its second reading, June 8, by a vote of 343 to 313. Gladstone dissolved Parliament and appealed to the country. His party was defeated, the elections returning 316 Conservatives and 78 Liberal-Unionists against 191 Liberals and 85 Home Rulers. Gladstone immediately resigned and was succeeded as prime minister by Lord Salisbury.

iii. Egyptian Policy

Combined with the failure of his Irish Home Rule policy in defeating Gladstone in 1886 was the disgrace which attended his policy in Egyptian affairs. Nothing illustrates more vividly his narrowness of vision than his incapacity to appreciate the importance of Egypt to the British Empire and to deal effectually with the issues raised there during his ministry.

Disraeli's purchase of the Suez Canal shares had given Great Britain a new and special interest in Egypt. Hence, when the Egyptian public debt began to increase at an alarming rate, and the payment of interest to the British bondholders was jeopardized — the debt increased from $16,000,000 in 1863 to $470,000,000 in 1876 — special commissioners were sent out to Egypt to examine into the finances of the country and to submit a report thereon. As a result of their report, describing the country as suffering "from the ignorance, dishonesty, waste, and extravagance of the East . . . and at the same time from the vast expense caused by hasty and inconsiderate endeavors to adopt the civilization of the West," the British and French governments formed a joint Commission (May 2, 1876) with functions which were later expanded to include the administration of all the finances of the country. Captain Evelyn Baring (raised to the peerage as Earl Cromer in 1901) became the British member. In 1879 the extravagances of Khedive Ismail had become so unbearable that the Powers forced the Sultan, whose subject he was, to depose him and to appoint as his successor his son Tewfik.

The difficulty of the Egyptian problem was increased by the disaffection throughout the country, especially within the army. Rebellion broke out in 1881. In June the rebels attacked the European population at Alexandria and massacred fifty persons. Thousands of Christian foreigners fled from the country. The necessity for military intervention was manifest.

Great Britain invited France to join with her in joint intervention, but France, apparently suspicious of her motives and desiring to take advantage of Egyptian anarchy to extend her own boundaries in Egypt, refused. Great Britain thereupon acted alone. In a few months the well-trained British troops (including a contingent of natives from India) dispersed the Egyptian rebels in northern Egypt, and reëstablished the authority of the Khedive. So far the British government had acted with promptitude and decision.

The problem actually became more involved, however, after the suppression of the rebellion. If British troops were removed, no security existed for the Khedive against a new rebellion; yet to leave British troops there was certain to lead other Powers to suspect Great Britain's motives in the country. After long delay the policy of the government was announced by a member of the ministry in a speech to the House of Lords, December, 1882:

"We shall not keep our troops in Egypt any longer than is necessary; but it would be an act of treachery to ourselves, to Egypt, and to Europe if we withdrew them without having a certainty — or until there is reasonable expectation — of a stable, a permanent, and a beneficial government being established in Egypt."

A few months later a new revolt broke out in the vast district of southern Egypt known as the Egyptian Soudan. Egyptian troops commanded by British officers were sent south (September, 1883) against the rebels, and were defeated and cut to pieces (November, 1883). Two months later the British government sent out General Charles Gordon, formerly governor-general of the Soudan, to Khartum to report on the situation. When he arrived in Egypt, the Khedive appointed him again governor-general of the Soudan, the British cabinet approved the appointment, and he went into the disaffected district in that official capacity.

Gordon reached Khartum in safety, but within a few weeks was closely besieged there by the forces of the rebels. His peril was evident, but Gladstone, involved in problems of parliamentary reform and projects for allaying or suppressing the unrest in Ireland, delayed the sending of assistance. March 25, 1884, Queen Victoria telegraphed to Lord Hartington, a member of the ministry:

> "It is alarming; General Gordon is in danger; you are bound to try and save him. Surely Indian troops might go from Aden and could bear climate though British cannot. You have incurred fearful responsibility."

Still weeks and months passed without a decision. Gordon maintained himself with the utmost difficulty against the hordes of Arabs who surrounded the town. At last, moved by the threat of members of his ministry to resign unless something were done at once, Gladstone in August asked for a small appropriation ($1,500,000) "to undertake operations for the relief of General Gordon should they become necessary." But the expedition which then set out to fight its way to Khartum arrived too late. January 26, 1885, the Arabs successfully stormed the town and put to the sword its inhabitants, among them the brave General Gordon.

The grief and anger of the country over the tragedy of Gordon's death were intense. Victoria sent a passionate telegram to the prime minister — "it was too fearful to consider that the fall of Khartum might have been prevented and many precious lives saved by earlier action." The House of Lords passed a vote of censure of the government by 189 to 68.

The hesitating and vacillating policy of Gladstone continued even after Gordon's death. With the country aroused, it would have been possible to send a strong force at once against the rebels, but after many delays Gladstone decided to withdraw the British troops which had penetrated to a point near Khartum. By the middle of the summer these troops had left for northern Egypt, and the Soudan was left for a dozen years in the hands of the rebels.

The pitiful spectacle of an English governor-general being abandoned to his fate among hordes of rebel infidels played no small part in Gladstone's defeat at the polls in 1886.

iv. The Salisbury Ministry

The Irish Question was perforce the chief issue before the Salisbury ministry when it took office in 1886.[1] When Lord Salisbury had been in the opposition in parliament, he had advocated coercion in Ireland: he was now in a position to put this policy into effect. Stringent measures were at once adopted. Irish nationalists were imprisoned; troops effectually quelled outbreaks. Ireland was pacified, but not conciliated.

[1] Lord Salisbury had been prime minister for a few months in 1885, following the resignation of Gladstone, but could not command a majority in the Commons and resigned. Gladstone again took the premiership over the elections.

At the same time Lord Salisbury introduced some constructive measures in the endeavor to improve the Irish conditions. In 1891 the parliament passed a Bill by which the government obligated itself to purchase land from the landowners for the peasant, advancing the whole cost and receiving payment therefor from the peasant in annual installments extending over a period of fifty years. Under this Bill, the tenant would actually pay in his installments less than he had previously paid as rent, and would at the end of fifty years be absolute owner of his property. Within the next five years, some 35,000 tenants took advantage of the provisions of this Bill to acquire their land.

Another feature of Lord Salisbury's premiership was his establishment of the principle of a two-power naval standard. In 1889 he gained from the parliament the approval of, and funds for, an enormous increase in the British navy. An average of ten capital ships a year was to be added to the navy during the next seven years, at an estimated total expense of more than $100,000,000, and the navy was henceforth to be maintained the equal of any other two navies in the world united. The importance of this naval policy in view of later international developments was very great.

v. Death of Disraeli

Before passing from British affairs of this decade we should note the death of Disraeli, Earl of Beaconsfield, on April 19, 1881. He had been in retirement since his defeat at the elections the preceding year. At his death the full measure of public esteem was for the first time revealed. This "charlatan," "mystery man," "Jew adventurer," as his opponents contemptuously termed him, had captured the hearts of the English people. Queen Victoria herself placed a wreath upon his coffin and caused to be erected in the church where he was buried a tablet bearing the following inscription written by herself:

"To the dear and honored memory of Benjamin, Earl of Beaconsfield, this memorial is placed by his grateful Sovereign and friend Victoria R. I. 'Kings love him that speaketh right.'"

Since his death his reputation has steadily grown. He, and he alone, is credited with the regeneration of the imperial idea in Great Britain. He was a man with a vision reaching far beyond the narrow limits of his home islands and with an imagination grasping the possibilities of the future. He left as an heritage to Great Britain the conception of a world policy which, however neglected during the years immediately following, gradually became the leading principle of later statesmen.

vi. Effect of Great Britain's Policy of Splendid Isolation upon the International Situation

The absorption of English interests in domestic concerns during this decade, and the resumption of the former policy of "splendid isolation," had indirectly an effect upon the general continental situation. In the Congress of Berlin, Beaconsfield had signalized dramatically Great Britain's entrance into the field of European politics, and had indicated that henceforth Great Britain would be a factor to be considered in any political or territorial readjustments. Had British diplomacy continued in this course, the diplomats of the continental states would have been forced to revise their plans and to weigh carefully the effect of each of their policies upon British opinion. Especially would Great Britain's participation in European affairs have affected Bismarck, for he would have had to reckon with another possible ally of France and enemy of Germany. The practical withdrawal of Great Britain from the international arena made Bismarck's task easier. British power and British opinion — though carefully watched, of course, for signs of change — could to all intents and purposes be disregarded.

Bismarck once remarked that had he served his country

as ill as Gladstone had served Great Britain, he would be ashamed to look his fellows in the face. His thought probably was that Gladstone, with an opportunity to raise Great Britain to a pinnacle of unassailable international supremacy, had frittered away his strength in domestic problems of relatively little importance. If Bismarck could take — as he did — the second-rate Prussia and elevate it to the central position in the most powerful state of the greatest alliance in Europe, what might he have done had fate assigned him to the premiership of Great Britain, with its position already established and its empire reaching around the world?

B. France

In France, the decade between 1880 and 1890, following the decisive victory of the republicans at the polls in 1879 and the election of the republican Grévy as president, was marked by the disturbed conditions which would naturally result from the readjustment of political groups. Grévy conducted himself in what he believed to be the proper manner for the president of a parliamentary republic. Whereas MacMahon had declared strong personal policies and had attempted to influence the decisions of the parliament, Grévy abstained from all such exercise of authority. He neither proclaimed his policy nor attempted to interfere in the conduct of affairs. He left all such activities to his ministers. The presidency thus soon lost suggestion of monarchical power. Grévy's example was followed by his successors.

i. Domestic Politics

The abstention of the President of the Republic from interference in party politics in France threw the conduct of the government into the hands of the ministers, who were wholly dependent upon the legislative body for their support. France thus had a purely parliamentary government. The difficulties of carrying through a consistent policy over any considerable length of time under this system quickly became evident. The legislative body was exceedingly suspicious of any of its ministers who gave the appearance of assuming undue authority, and deposed them from office by the simple expedient of refusing legislative support. For example, when Gambetta, long one of the most prominent and popular republicans in France, headed a ministry in November of 1881, surrounded himself in office with his personal devotees, arranged a triumphal entry into his native town, and theatrically addressed the chamber in a kind of "speech from the throne," he quickly lost all his popularity and the support of the legislative, and had to resign three months later (January, 1882). The longest-lived ministry, that of Jules Ferry, endured only a little over two years (February, 1883 to May, 1885). Between 1880 and 1887, ten different ministers rose and fell. Conditions fostered the activities of politicians rather than the development of statesmen, and few important constructive legislative measures were passed. In 1887 Grévy, his power weakened by a scandal in which his son-in-law was implicated, resigned, and Carnot, likewise a republican, was elected president.

The next few years were marked by the climax of the Boulangist movement. General Boulanger was a dashing figure, usually pictured on horseback, and was well qualified to draw the attention of the people. He became the hero of the self-styled "patriots," who believed that all governmental policies and activities should be directed to the sole end of success in war and of revenge against Germany. Boulanger was made Minister of War in January of 1886, and at once made himself notorious by his outspoken sympathy with the army, especially with the common soldier, and by his insinuations that under his leadership Alsace and Lorraine might be recaptured. He controlled a number of newspapers in France, through which he was able to keep himself and his policies before the people. He rapidly gained adherents from various disaffected political elements. His constructive program was vague: he announced it in three phrases — Dissolution, Revision, Constituent Assembly — implying the dissolution of the existing legislature and the election of an assembly which should so revise the constitution as to provide for a single legislative chamber and an executive independent of that chamber. His party, calling itself the *Revisionist* or *National* party, conducted a vigorous and novel campaign to keep him before the people. Wherever in all France a vacancy in the existing chambers was to be filled, General Boulanger was nominated; posters and portraits of the candidate were spread broadcast through the district; biographies were distributed to all the electors; and hired claques applauded each reference to him in the campaign oratory. In five months of 1888 he was elected deputy for six different constituencies; and in January of 1889, when he stood for the Paris seat, he triumphed by a majority of 240,000 to 165,000.

In the face of this agitation and these remarkable successes, the government finally took strong measures, for his successes not only threatened the overthrow of the existing government, but were responsible for a serious crisis in the relations of France with Germany. The ministry, therefore, introduced and succeeded in passing a law making it illegal for any person to offer himself as a candidate for the national legislature in more than one district. In February, 1889, the Assembly summoned the General to appear before the Senate to answer to the charge of conspiracy against the safety of the state. If Boulanger had possessed at the moment the energy and courage to attempt a *coup* for the control of the government, he might have succeeded; but he failed to meet the situation. Alarmed by the summons, he fled to Belgium. In his absence he was condemned by the court. Two years later, 1891, he committed suicide.

The republican government emerged from the crisis in a much stronger position than before. The Boulangist movement, with the flight of "the man on horseback," collapsed. The republicans of all shades of opinion, uniting in the general elections of 1889 to oppose the enemies of the parliamentary system, carried 366 seats against 210. Their victory in these elections proved the strength of the Republic and served to discredit thoroughly its opponents. Their victory further had a marked effect in impressing upon foreign powers the stability of the existing government.

It might be thought that, with ministry succeeding ministry in quick succession, — fourteen ministries in the decade from 1880 to 1890 — no continuity in policy would be possible. The evil effects of the continual changes of ministry have in France been offset, however, by two facts: first, that the successive ministries have often contained leading persons of previous ministries; and second, that a change in ministry has not resulted in a change in the political principles of the ministry. Thus all the ministries of the decade were republican ministries, pledged to uphold and maintain the existing form of government. And thus, certain of the leading ministers, as Ferry, Fallières, Tirard, and Cochéry, retained their portfolios, or were given other portfolios, in successive ministries. Louis Cochéry was Minister of Posts and Telegraphs in all the successive ministries from 1881 to 1886; Charles Tirard was Minister of Commerce and Agriculture in the ministries of 1881 and 1882, and Minister of Finance in the ministries from 1883 to 1885. The fall of a ministry was more often determined by the personal rivalries of leaders than, as for example in parliamentary government in England, by the overthrow of one party by another with different policies and totally different personnel. Whereas the fall of a ministry in Great Britain meant a complete change in all the portfolios and usually a complete change in policy, in France it meant simply the change in the person of the premier and in a few of the portfolios without necessarily any change in general policy.

ii. Foreign Policy: Colonial Expansion

The most important acts in foreign policy consisted in the acquisition, under the leadership of Jules Ferry, of a great colonial empire. This policy was encouraged by Bismarck, for he foresaw that France would thus be diverted from the obsession of a war of revenge; that the enormous cost of taking and developing colonies would weaken France financially; and that France would thus inevitably be brought into conflict with other powers having colonial ambitions. Ferry, on his part, had visions of the broadening of national interest: he realized the importance of new markets for French goods; he saw that in the rivalry of the great states France must gain her share of colonial territory. Thus under his influence France established a protectorate over Tunis, and gained a foothold in Tonkin, Madagascar, and the French Congo. Although his policy entailed enormous expenses, threw Italy temporarily into the alliance with Austria and Germany (the Triple Alliance), aroused the suspicions of England, and created strong political opposition in France, it may be defended in the light of history by the fact that it raised France to a favorable position as a colonial power during the important negotiations of the following decade. Between 1890 and 1900 the most important colonial treaties were made: France, wholly as a result of Ferry's policy, was an indispensable signatory to every treaty. By virtue of her colonies, as well as by virtue of her size, power, and material resources, she took her place among the greatest nations of the modern world.

C. Russia

In Russia the results of the Congress of Berlin were heralded by the malcontents as the crowning humiliation in a long chain of mistaken policies. The Edict of Emancipation had favored the landowners and nobility, so that the burden of expense of the peasant under the new dispensation was actually in many cases worse than under the old. The Czar, not a strong character, had naturally succumbed to the reactionary influences of the court circles, so that espionage, suppression of liberty of thought and speech, and arbitrary arrest and imprisonment were common features of the despotic government. Education was made difficult, and real enlightenment, as by the study of comparative government, modern scientific theories, the latest developments in philosophy, rendered almost impossible by the rigid exclusion of foreign books on such subjects. Hence, in a country where education was the first requisite for advancement in official or professional life, the means of education were denied to all but a favored few. As a climax to these mistakes in domestic policy, Russia drifted into a war with Turkey, a war marked by inefficiency and peculation among the higher officials and contractors, and by almost superhuman bravery among the common soldiers. At the end of the war, Russian diplomacy broke down utterly: her chief gain, Bessarabia, made an enemy of her previously devoted ally, Rumania; her plans for a greater Bulgaria under Russian protection were completely frustrated; even her intention so to diminish Turkish territory in Europe as to render the Turk harmless in the future ended in failure. Every element in the domestic, social, and political situation, and in foreign relations, stirred the malcontents in Russia.

In a state where police rule was the supreme rule, open expression of opinion was, of course, impossible, so that the disaffected element had to resort to secret intrigue and conspiracy. This element was mainly composed of young men and women with more or less education, sincerely stirred in the beginning by a patriotic indignation at the terrible abuses in their country, and aroused later by unjust police persecution to take active measures against the government and its officials. From this element originated the group popularly known as Nihilists (from Latin Nihil — nothing), so called because of its attitude of disapproval of all Russian institutions. The famous novelist, Turgenieff, defined a Nihilist as "a man who submits to no authority, who accepts not a single principle upon faith merely, however high such a principle may stand in the eyes of men." Between 1870 and 1880, the Nihilists, preaching the political gospel of socialism, adopted the policy of educating the peasants. They mingled with the ignorant classes and attempted to enlighten them. Although they did not counsel revolutionary action, their unsparing criticisms of the government, their application of the rule of reason to all Russian institutions, and their denunciation of such institutions as did not measure up to their ideal standards, soon brought them into trouble with the authorities. The usual course of procedure followed — arbitrary imprisonment, sentence without trial, and exile. Hundreds of them fled from Russia.

The police persecution finally drove a small body among the Nihilists, influenced, perhaps, by anarchistic doctrines, into a policy of Terrorism. Since they could not apparently advance liberal measures by peaceful propaganda, since they could not even remain in Russia and have the rights of free thought and free speech, these Terrorists determined systematically to assassinate those men whom they held responsible for their wrongs until the government should be intimidated into reform. More remarkable conditions have seldom existed in any state. The Terrorists were well though secretly organized; they hunted down their prey systematically; and after an assassination they published and spread broadcast their justification of their act. In spite of an elaborate system of espionage and thousands of imprisonments and exiles, the organization continued, its members becoming more and more desperate. Finally, its leaders determined to strike at the fountainhead of Russian misrule by an attempt to assassinate the Czar. In April of 1879 a Terrorist schoolmaster fired five shots at the sovereign, but missed. In December of the same year the train on which the Czar was supposed to be traveling was blown up, but he had secretly taken a different train. In February of 1880 a mine was exploded in the Winter Palace, killing and wounding more than sixty persons, but the Czar again escaped.

These successive attempts, expressing the determination of the conspirators, naturally produced a great effect in St. Petersburg. The Czar called to his aid General Boris-Melikóff, a hero of the Turkish war and an administrator of proved ability. Melikoff was given dictatorial powers to suppress the rebellion. Instead of force, however, he chose a policy of clemency. By his advice the Czar allowed liberty to the zemstvos and to the public press, pardoned many political prisoners, and dismissed some of the most notorious agents of the government. Melikoff's supreme act, however, was to submit to the Czar proposals leading to the formation and promulgation of a constitution. After long hesitation, the Czar, on March 13, 1881, returned the draft to Melikoff with his approval and ordered it read to the Council of Ministers in a fortnight.

On that same afternoon, March 13, 1881, the Terrorist group launched another attempt, this time successful, against Alexander's life. As the Czar was riding in the streets of St. Petersburg, a bomb was thrown at his carriage. He escaped, as by a miracle, but a number of his escort were killed and wounded; he dismounted to assist the wounded, and another bomb exploded near him, tearing him to pieces. The tragedy of his assassination at the very moment he was planning to give the country its long-desired constitution was not, of course, known until after his death.

Alexander III, son of Alexander II, succeeded to the

throne and reigned until his death in 1894. He was a man of thirty-six, of great physical size and strength. He was stubborn and strong-willed, subject to violent exhibitions of anger at persistent opposition. Although his mental abilities were not above the average, he was straightforward, courageous, and honest. His education and training were those of the ordinary Russian Grand Duke.

If the Terrorists had expected a change for the better with the change in sovereigns, they were disappointed. Alexander III's entire reign was reactionary. At its beginning he sounded the keynote by a proclamation indicating his own steadfast resolve to maintain the autocratic power:

"Dedicating ourselves to our high functions, we call upon our faithful subjects to serve us and the realm with truth and fidelity; and to strive for the extirpation of the heinous agitation which has disgraced the land, the maintenance of religion and morality, the extinction of greed and falsehood, and the reëstablishment of harmonious working in the institutions given to Russia by her great benefactor (Alexander II)."

The Terrorists were pitilessly hunted down until their organization was finally broken up and the separate individuals hanged, imprisoned, exiled, or forced to flee from the country. The powers of the zemstvos were again restricted. The limited freedom allowed the press was withdrawn. The persecution of the Jews, countenanced, or at least not suppressed, by the government, drove tens of thousands out of the country. The secret police were augmented in number and power. Freedom of speech was unknown. Those who hoped for more liberal government were overawed by the ruthlessness and efficiency of the government's police agents and were forced to wait in silence for more opportune times.

Yet the reign of Alexander III, though hard upon the liberal element in Russia, was not without progressive features. The new monarch showed himself especially interested in the well-being of the peasant class which formed so large a part of the population of his empire. In January, 1884, by a ukase he abolished the hated poll tax, the last remaining relic of serfdom; he readjusted for the benefit of the peasantry the arrangements in the Edict of Emancipation providing for payment by the peasants for their land; he tempted the peasants for their own good from the too thickly populated districts to the thinly populated districts by offers of land and governmental assistance; he established a system of Peasants' Banks which advanced money at a low rate of interest to the peasantry for the purchase of land; and he attempted to improve social conditions by lessening the number of dram shops. By such measures as these he gained the title of the "Peasants' Czar," by which he is still remembered in Russia.

D. The Near East

The years immediately following the Congress of Berlin were troubled in the Balkan regions by the problem of territorial changes dictated by that Congress, especially by the difficulties of establishing exact boundary lines where the Congress had specified vague directions. A commission from the great powers was appointed to carry out the provisions of the treaty.

i. The Execution of the Terms of the Treaty of Berlin

In the northeast, Rumania and Bulgaria were at loggerheads over the boundary between Rumania's new territory, the Dobrudja, and Bulgaria. Not until June of 1880 was the question settled by giving the fortress of Silistria to Bulgaria, but drawing the Rumanian line so close that some of the outpost defenses were actually put under Rumanian control.

In the northwest, Austro-Hungarian troops acted promptly sixteen days after the signing of the treaty of

Berlin in sending troops into Bosnia to take possession of the administration of that province. They were met by immediate resistance on the part of the native Mohammedans and were forced into a short but severe struggle to establish their authority. Not until the end of October, 1879, was the revolt quelled and effective occupation assured. The two districts, Bosnia and Herzegovina, were both troublesome and rebellious, however, for two years more.

In 1882 the Austro-Hungarian government appointed Baron von Kállay the administrator of the occupied territory. He had formerly been consul-general at Belgrade, Serbia, had written a history of Serbia, and was *persona grata* to the Serbian population. Under his wise and tactful administration, great constructive work was undertaken and the districts gradually became more reconciled to the Austro-Hungarian government.

In the west, Montenegro, to which had been assigned by the Treaty of Berlin the two Albanian districts of Gusinje and Plava, found extreme difficulty in taking over her new possessions. The Mohammedan Albanians, naturally great fighters, having little regard for the decisions of the Congress of Berlin, objected to being transferred without their consent from one government to another. They foresaw that their lawlessness, which was with them a time-honored privilege under the loose and inefficient Turkish régime, might be effectually curbed by the Montenegrin government. The Sultan, though he openly dispatched envoys to the Albanians to persuade them to yield, was not ill-pleased by their resistance. So fierce was the fighting during 1879, and so obvious the impossibility of little Montenegro establishing her control, that the powers intervened and suggested a modification of the provisions of the treaty. By this change, Montenegro was given the seaport of Dulcigno and a strip of seaboard as far as the mouth of the river Bojana. By a display of force and by threats the powers induced Turkey to agree to these terms, and Montenegro was established in her new possessions at the end of 1880.

In the south the readjustment of the new boundaries between Greece and Turkey as provided by the Treaty of Berlin took three years. The Turkish government pursued its customary dilatory policy, feeling certain that the jealousies of the great powers would prevent their intervention on behalf of Greece. Successive Greco-Turkish commissions failed to agree. In 1880 Greece, obtaining no assistance from the powers, began to mobilize her troops to gain the desired territory by war. The threat of war brought speedy intervention, and, May 24, 1881, a convention was at last signed giving Greece the large part of Thessaly and a portion of Epirus, a gain altogether of some 8750 square miles.

ii. Bulgaria

In allowing the modifications of the Montenegrin territories and the readjustment of the Greco-Turkish boundaries, the great powers had given convincing testimony that they were not prepared to support by force the terms of the Treaty of Berlin. This fact undoubtedly had some effect in inducing the Bulgarians and Eastern Rumelians to rearrange according to their own desires the provisions of that treaty in so far as it affected them.

It will be remembered that the Treaty of Berlin bisected the Bulgarian territory as arranged by Russia (Treaty of San Stefano) into two parts, Bulgaria and Eastern Rumelia, of which Bulgaria was constituted an autonomous principality and Eastern Rumelia was thrust back under the sovereignty of Turkey. This arrangement was intensely unpopular. The people of Eastern Rumelia, Bulgarians by blood, speech, and religion, desired political amalgamation with Bulgaria. During the years following the Treaty, they were restive and dissatisfied under Turkish rule.

In the meanwhile, the new Bulgarian state had organized

under Russian auspices, adopted its constitution, and chosen (April 29, 1879) as its first ruler Prince Alexander of Battenburg, a nephew of the Czar. The Bulgarian people and their new ruler both felt, naturally, under the strongest obligations at the beginning to Russia, by whom their national existence had been secured. Within a few years, however, they began to resent the Russian attitude toward their country. The Russian commissioners, who were placed in high and controlling positions in the government, treated Bulgaria as if it were a Russian province. Prince Alexander finally, in 1883, adopted an attitude of independence, restored the constitution which had been suspended at Russian instigation in 1881, and showed a disposition to govern Bulgaria for Bulgaria's sake and not for Russia's. The Russian emissaries withdrew at once from Bulgaria, and the authorities began to intrigue against the too independent prince.

In Eastern Rumelia the Turkish government appointed a governor-general acceptable to the people, gave the district a conservative constitution, and made no effort to molest or persecute the inhabitants. The Bulgar population continued, however, in spite of their peace and prosperity under these privileges, to desire union with Bulgaria. In 1885 the leaders determined to take matters into their own hands. They arrested the governor-general without difficulty, and issued a proclamation declaring the union of the two Bulgarias under Prince Alexander. Alexander hesitated to defy Turkey and the powers by accepting the revolution, but was warned by Stambuloff, then Speaker of the Bulgarian Chamber (Sobranje), that he could not disregard the will of his people:

"Sire, the union is made — the revolt is an accomplished fact past recall, and the time for hesitation has gone. Two roads lie before Your Highness — the one to Philippopolis and as much farther as God may lead; the other to the Danube and Darmstadt. I advise you to take the crown the Bulgarian nation offers you."

Alexander yielded, marched his army to Philippopolis (September 21, 1885), and received the full support of the Sobranje in his course.

This breach of the Treaty of Berlin aroused great excitement, not only in the Balkans but among the diplomats of the great powers. To be sure, it was the accomplishment of what Russia had herself provided in the Treaty of San Stefano, but since then Russia's attitude had changed. The Russian agents had failed to retain their control over, and their influence in, Bulgaria, so that the Czar's government no longer desired an increase of Bulgarian territory. Alexander III of Russia, therefore, professed great indignation at his nephew's act in accepting the throne of united Bulgaria, and sympathized with the protests of Turkey. The Bulgarian independence of Russian influence had gained the friendship of Great Britain, however, so that British diplomats insisted that the will of the people of the country should be respected. Since Turkey was unable because of internal complications to do more than protest, and since Great Britain's influence offset Russian opposition, the *coup* seemed likely to succeed without hostilities.

Among the Balkan states, however, the formation of united Bulgaria had seriously disarranged the balance of power. The new state was overwhelmingly larger and stronger than its neighbors. Greece and Serbia felt that their vital interests were affected, and demanded territorial compensation. After waiting a short time in vain for intervention in their behalf, they began to arm. On November 16, Serbia began hostilities by marching across the Bulgarian frontier with a force of about 14,000 men. November 19, the Serbs met the Bulgarians in equal force near the village of Slivnitza. Alexander of Bulgaria set a wonderful example to his troops and after a three-day battle gained a decisive victory, driving the Serbs in disorder back across the boundary. He started to invade Serbian territory but was checked by the Austro-Hungarian government. November 28, an armistice was signed; and March 3, 1886, the Treaty of Bucharest definitely ended the war.

Greece continued to mobilize for war and a number of skirmishes took place on the frontier. Great Britain intervened at this time, not in favor of Greece as was hoped, but in favor of peace. The demand was made that Grecian troops be restored to a peace footing. When the Greek government continued hostilities, the British navy established a blockade of Greek ports. This coercion was successful. Greece was forced to disarm and to accept the new Bulgarian state. By the middle of June, 1886, the crisis was over.

Alexander of Bulgaria did not long enjoy the fruits of his victory. His defiance of Russia excited continual Russian intrigues against him. Now that Bulgaria was enlarged, it was the more desirable to establish Russian influence therein. Unable to accomplish their ends peaceably and openly, Russian agents resorted to force. At two o'clock on the morning of August 21, 1886, the Russian conspirators broke into the palace, roused Alexander from his bed, and at the point of revolvers forced him to sign a formal paper abdicating the throne. They then kidnaped him and landed him the following day in Russian territory. Before Europe at large knew what had happened, the *coup* was complete.

Stambuloff, speaker of the Sobranje, promptly organized a revolt in Alexander's favor, succeeded in rallying the nation to his side, and invited the former ruler to return. Alexander's spirit was broken, however. He saw no chance to rule successfully so long as he had the opposition of Russia. September 7, 1886, he publicly abdicated and retired to the less exciting life of an officer in the Austro-Hungarian army.

Stambuloff by his energy and determination saved his country at this period. He was the chief prop of the regency appointed by Alexander at the time of his abdication and was instrumental in frustrating the Russian attempts to gain control of the government. It was necessary, however, to choose a new ruler at the earliest possible moment. This task proved difficult, for the opposition of Russia was certain to make government difficult and dangerous. For six months the Bulgarian crown went begging among the scions of noble houses in Europe, one after another refusing the perilous honor. Finally Prince Ferdinand of Saxe-Coburg accepted the throne and was duly elected Prince of Bulgaria by the Sobranje, July 7, 1887. With the aid of his great minister, Stambuloff, often referred to as the Bulgarian Bismarck, he defied Russian hostility. As the years passed, he gained the reputation of being wise as a ruler, astute as a diplomat, and sincerely devoted to the good of his adopted country.

iii. The Effect of the Balkan Changes upon the International Situation

These changes we have mentioned above bore upon the larger European situation insofar as they affected the ambitions of Russia and Austria-Hungary respectively in the Near East. At the close of the Russo-Turkish war, Russian influence was naturally the greatest in the Balkans. Russia had decisively defeated the unspeakable Turk, had won independence for Bulgaria, and had taken a long step forward toward the coveted Constantinople. Even the check administered to Russia in the Congress of Berlin did not weaken her prestige in southeastern Europe. The small states, mostly Slav in blood, religion, and traditions, still looked to the Czar as the greatest protecting power against possible Turkish encroachments.

This favored position Russia lost in great measure during the decade from 1880 to 1890. Austria-Hungary, by gaining the administration (and by tacit consent the final reversion) of Bosnia and Herzegovina, established herself at the gateway of the Balkans. The Austro-Hungarian government won the gratitude of Serbia in 1886 by checking the Bulgarian invasion after the battle of Slivnitza. German princely houses supplied monarchs to Rumania and Bulgaria, and a queen for Greece. And when Bulgaria turned against Russia because of Russian intrigues for power, it was but natural that it should incline toward the powers of the Triple Alliance.

Furthermore, Germany, having allied herself with Austria-Hungary, showed a disposition to associate herself with that country in her Balkan aspirations, and even to expand these aspirations beyond the Balkans into Turkey. As the immense possibilities which lay in the Turkish possessions in Asia Minor were realized, the German enthusiasm increased. An energetic development of this country would bring untold prosperity to a great state. Bismarck began to feel the *Drang nach Osten* as well as Austria-Hungary. His action supporting Austria-Hungary in the Congress of Berlin, and thus assuming the credit, to some extent at least, of saving Turkey from the rapacity of Russia, gave him an entering wedge for the cultivation of good relations with the Porte. Even though Great Britain had long been the protector of Turkey, her influence might be supplanted there by adroit diplomacy. The initial step was taken by lending to the Turkish government German officers for the much-needed reorganization of the army. From 1883 to 1895 one of the most promising of the younger officers of the German army, Colmar von der Goltz, labored successfully with this problem. The results were shown in the overwhelming victory achieved by Turkey in the short Greco-Turkish war of 1897. A second step was taken by diverting German capital into railroad, mining, and development concessions in Asia Minor. Thus the first link of what became known as the Bagdad railroad, the link from Contantinople to Angora, was built in 1888, and work begun on the branch from Eski-Shehir to Konia. From this period on, Germany was as keenly and vitally interested in the pressure toward the east as was her Austro-Hungarian ally.

The influence which the Germanic powers gained in the Balkans and Turkey in this period after the Congress of Berlin has never since been shaken off. When Austria-Hungary accepted Italy as an ally in the Triple Alliance (1882), she practically acknowledged the impossibility of ever recovering her lost Italian provinces. The growth of her influence in the regions to the southeast, however, gave her diplomats the hope that what they had lost in Italy, they might eventually regain from the Balkans. And Germany, becoming more and more inspired by the potential wealth of Asia Minor, invested heavily in concessions in this region, and came to look upon it as definitely within her sphere of influence. The stone which Bismarck had once rejected as not worth the bones of a single grenadier verily became the cornerstone of German policy.

CHAPTER IV

EUROPEAN DEVELOPMENT, 1880–1890

II. THE POWERS OF THE TRIPLE ALLIANCE

A. Italy

ITALY lost her first King, Victor Emmanuel, January 9, 1878. He was idolized by the people, for whose emancipation from the hand of Austria he had striven so long and so successfully. His courage, sincerity, frankness, and honesty, coupled with good common sense, earned him the spontaneous title of *il re galantoumo*, which is inadequately translated by the words 'The King who was an honest man.' Over his tomb was placed the simple inscription: "To the Father of his Country." His son Umberto (Humbert), a man of thirty-four, succeeded to the throne as Umberto I, took the oath to the constitution, January 29, and was loyally accepted by the people.

A month later the Pope, Pius IX, died and was succeeded by Leo XIII, then sixty-eight years of age. The momentary hope that the inauguration of a new King of Italy and a new Pope at practically the same time might favor a more satisfactory adjustment of the relations between the Italian government and the papacy was soon dispelled. The government made no overtures to the pontifical court, and the new Pope quickly proved that he intended to follow the precedent of the deceased Pius IX. He refused to recognize the Kingdom of Italy; he refused to leave the confines of the Vatican; he continued to picture himself as the prisoner of the "Robber King."

i. Internal Developments

The decade 1880–1890 was not a successful one in Italian politics, finance, or economics. In the parliament few great constructive measures were carried through successfully; in the exchequer, the small surpluses of the first few years gave way to increasing deficits; in the industrial life of the peninsula, the mass of the people remained poor, miserable, and discontented. No statesman rose to prominence with a power and a vision equal to the problems of the situation.

One of the fundamental causes of the failure of the government to achieve better results lay in the actual operation of the parliamentary system under Italian conditions. The members of the chamber were not divided, as in Great Britain where the parliamentary system had worked well, into two equal parties, but into a number of small groups of various shades of political opinion. No one group could command a majority of the votes. Each ministry, therefore, was a coalition ministry, dependent in its parliamentary action upon the united support of a number of the political groups; and each legislative measure had to be a compromise bill, so designed that it would not alienate any of the government's supporters. The ministry's position was never secure. It could not afford to refuse any concessions demanded by the deputies or groups of deputies on which its life depended. Its weakness too often resulted in indecision and vacillation. Its members were forced to "play politics" to secure their own position. Great constructive legislation gave way before petty personal rivalries for political advantage.

A grave consequence of these conditions was reflected in the financial conditions of the country. Italy had begun her independent existence under a staggering burden of debt: she was unable to lessen this burden as the years passed. The construction and development of railways, the building of roads, and the enlargement and improvement of harbor facilities were urgently needed to assist industrial progress. When these were undertaken, the government contracts were used as political bribes to satisfy the demands of the government's supporters. The contracts were let at abnormally high prices. One railway line, estimated cost $200,000,000, was actually contracted for at $400,000,000. The deficit of the country was $5,000,000 in the fiscal year 1885-1886; $14,000,000 in 1887-1888; and $47,000,000 in 1888-1889. A great part of the amount of these deficits was due to the excessive cost of government undertakings.

Industrial and social conditions failed to improve. Taxes were heavy, the cost of food high, illiteracy common. The government had provided in 1881 for the gradual removal of the hated "Grist Tax" on cereals, but had substituted therefor heavy grain duties, and excessive duties on sugar and petroleum. The government had passed in 1877 a universal education law, but, since its execution had been left to the communes, it had not been effectively established. With natural inclination to blame the existing government, the people became dissatisfied with the monarchy and swelled the number of the Republican and Radical parties. Serious riots broke out in 1889 in Rome, Milan, Turin, and in the southern district of Apulia, but were suppressed by force.

At this period when unrest was rife throughout Italy, the government passed (1882) an electoral reform bill which had been under discussion in parliament for several years. By this bill, the property qualification for the suffrage was lowered from 40 lire (c. $8.00) to 19 lire 80 centesimi (c. $3.95); and provision made that all men over 21 who had received a primary school education should have the suffrage. The effect of this bill was to increase the electorate from 625,000 to 2,000,000. As disaffection spread in the country at large, the greater part of the increased electorate went to swell the ranks of the Republican and Radical parties, thus increasing the difficulties of the government in maintaining a loyal majority in the chamber.

ii. Foreign Policies

While the government was thus beset with serious domestic problems, it persisted in committing itself to a foreign policy befitting one of the great powers. Italian statesmen favored colonial expansion, a large and costly army and navy, and entrance into foreign alliances at a time when the country was incurring annual deficits of millions of dollars and was quelling hunger riots by force.

The diplomats of Italy at the Congress of Berlin felt that Italy was isolated in Europe. The danger of such isolation lay in the relations between the Papacy and the Italian government. If some foreign power, as France, should uphold the claim of the Papacy to the possession of Rome, Italian statesmen realized that Italy, fighting alone, would be condemned to defeat. They therefore favored entrance into a Triple Alliance with Germany and Austria-Hungary for Italian security. The difficulties of such diplomacy, however, were very great. Austria-Hungary had, before 1866, been the traditional enemy of Italy: it would be hard to reconcile public opinion to a close alliance with the Austrians. Furthermore, should news of the Italian diplomacy leak out before the alliance was consummated, it might bring on the attack by the French which the Italians so feared. And lastly, Germany and Austria-Hungary had given little outward evidence that they desired Italy in the alliance. Indeed, certain popular demonstrations in Italy in favor of acquiring the remaining Italian territories under Austrian dominion (*Italia Irredenta*, consisting of the Trentino and the port of Trieste), had aroused in 1880 and 1881 serious resentment on the part of the Austro-Hungarian government.

While the pros and cons of the benefits of this alliance

were under discussion by Italian statesmen, France took a step which had great influence in their decision. Tunis, in northern Africa, had long been regarded as the natural and desirable ground for Italian colonial enterprise: it was fertile; it was weakly guarded by Turkey; and it was the nearest African territory to Italy. They had no knowledge at the time that at the Congress of Berlin Bismarck had already encouraged France to take the country when convenient, and had actually been instrumental in arranging for the consent of England. The sensational awakening of the Italians came suddenly in the spring of 1881. France sent in an expeditionary force against the will of the Bey of Tunis to punish some marauders. The force acted with great speed: April 26, it occupied the island of Tabarca; May 2, it seized the important town of Biserta; and May 12 it extracted from the Bey the Treaty of Bardo acknowledging a French protectorate. The entire *coup* was begun and carried through before the Italians were aware of its significance.

Italian indignation was intense. Added to the chagrin and disappointment at being deceived was the fear that Italian interests at Tunis were endangered and that Italian shores were laid open to attack from a new quarter. The government, however, was in no condition to take hostile military action; but they welcomed more eagerly the idea of an alliance with the central powers.

At this time conditions favored the Italian wishes. The growing rivalry between Russia and Austria-Hungary in the Balkans made it essential that Austria-Hungary should be insured against attack in the rear in case she had to fight Russia. Bismarck, seeing the Austro-Hungarian danger and realizing that the security of Austria-Hungary strengthened Germany's power (inasmuch as Austria-Hungary was Germany's ally), encouraged the Austrian diplomats to take advantage of Italian resentment against France to bring Italy into the alliance.

With both parties willing, the details of the alliance were quickly arranged. King Humbert and Queen Margherita of Italy paid an official visit to Francis Joseph in Vienna, staying at the Hofburg from the 27th to the 31st of October, 1881. The Austrian emperor and the Austrian people extended to their Italian guests the most cordial reception. The negotiations were completed and the results embodied in a treaty, the Treaty of the Triple Alliance, May 20, 1882. For nearly a year afterwards, the existence of the treaty was kept secret. When its existence was finally revealed, the most influential of the Italian political groups were enthusiastic in its favor. Italy had secured herself against the loss of Rome, and looked forward to gaining some compensation in the distant future for Tunis.

Entrance into the Triple Alliance entailed an increase in Italy's military and naval program, however, which the Italian treasury was little able to bear. We know how Bismarck laid all emphasis upon force in international politics: we can be reasonably certain that in the Treaty of the Triple Alliance specifications were made as to the strength which Italy should be prepared to add to that of her allies. It has been reported that Italy engaged to act with two armies on her northwestern border against the French *armée des Alpes* (war strength, 250,000), and to provide a third army to go into Germany and fight against either France or Russia as might be expedient. At any rate, on May 11, 1882, a week before the treaty was signed, the Italian parliament passed a new Army Bill, including a special credit of 120,000,000 lire for the creation of two new army corps to bring the regular army to a strength of 850,000 effectives. And thereafter, even with her impoverished treasury, Italy's budget contained annual estimates of between $40,000,000 and $50,000,000 for armament.

B. *Austria-Hungary*

i. The Dual Empire

In 1880 the Dual Empire had lived for thirteen years under the provisions of the so-called *Ausgleich*, or Compromise, of 1867. The Emperor-King — Emperor of Austria and King in Hungary — received the hearty allegiance of both parts of his country. One of the most serious dangers he had formerly to face, the danger of a Hungarian revolution, was permanently removed.

One feature of the constitution of the Dual Empire gave trouble. It was provided in the Ausgleich that the mutual economic and financial relations between the component states of the Dual Monarchy should be revised at ten-year intervals. The initial agreement was made in 1867: revisions were due, therefore, in 1877 and in 1887. Each recurring period of revision caused a long dispute, often resulting in a serious political crisis. The questions to be settled — the quota of the national revenue which each should provide, the rate of duty upon certain imports (as coffee, sugar, and petroleum), the management of the central financial institution — were all ones over which national interests and jealousies might easily be aroused. The settlement had to be agreed upon first by the ministers of Austria and of Hungary; then it had to be submitted to the respective parliaments in the two countries, where it was discussed by special committees; finally it had to be debated and passed in each of the parliaments as a whole. The first revision, that in 1877, took two years from the time discussion began in the spring of 1876 to the final passage of the bill in June of 1878. The second revision, that in 1887, took a little less time, because Count Taafe, the Austrian premier, was able to command a solid majority in his parliament.

The foreign policy of the Dual Empire was profoundly affected by the conclusion of the Dual Alliance with Germany in 1879 and the Triple Alliance with Germany and Italy in 1882. The support of Germany gave Austro-Hungarian diplomats an assurance of safety in their endeavors to advance their interests in the Balkan regions, and the adhesion of Italy to the alliance in 1882 removed the danger of an attack from the rear in case of trouble with Russia. Austria-Hungary definitely abandoned her expectations of retrieving the position she had lost in the Italian peninsula, and set herself to acquiring a dominating influence, that might lead later to territorial expansion, in the western Balkans.

ii. Austria

In Austria Francis Joseph had as his chief minister from 1879 to 1893 Count Taafe. Count Taafe had in his boyhood been chosen to be one of the playmates of the young Francis Joseph, so that a close personal friendship existed between the minister and his sovereign. Beneath a cynical manner and pleasure-loving habits, Count Taafe had an unswerving loyalty to his Emperor, a patriotic love of his country, and an exceptional ability in handling men.

In politics, Taafe adopted every practical method to increase the power and prestige of the Emperor. The German element in the state had, during the years immediately preceding Taafe's appointment, persistently blocked the Emperor's measures, because it feared these might increase Slav power in the state. Taafe turned directly to the Slav elements, the Czechs (in Bohemia) and the Poles (in Galicia), for political support. To each of these elements he granted substantial concessions. The Czechs secured control in the Bohemian Diet and in the Bohemian delegation to the Reichsrath; they were given their own university by a division of the University of Prague into two universities, one German and the other Czechish; and the Czechish language was established on a status in Bohemia equal to the German. The Poles were allowed to obtain control of the Diet in Galicia and were given a liberal hand in administration of

AUSTRIA HUNGARY
1914
Scale of Miles
0 50 100 150 200
Germans
Czechs
Slovaks
Ruthenians
Poles
Magyars
Slovenes
Serbo-Croats
Italians and Ladins
Rumans
GERMANY
SAXONY
POLAND
RUSSIA
BOHEMIA
MORAVIA
SILESIA
GALICIA
BUKOWINA
LOWER AUSTRIA
UPPER AUSTRIA
SALZBURG
STYRIA
TYROL
CARINTHIA
CARNIOLA
KÜSTENLAND
HUNGARY
TRANSYLVANIA
CROATIA
SLAVONIA
BOSNIA
HERZEGOVINA
DALMATIA
SERBIA
RUMANIA
BULGARIA
MONTENEGRO
ALBANIA
BAVARIA
SWITZERLAND
ITALY
VENETIA
ADRIATIC SEA
BLACK SEA
Carpathian Mts.
Transylvanian Alps
Balkan Mts
Alps
Vienna
Buda-Pest
Prague
Lemberg
Cracow
Trieste
Belgrade
Rome
Bern
Longitude East from Greenwich
WILLIAMS ENG. CO.

the province. Naturally, Taafe's policies were distasteful to the strong German element which desired to maintain its ascendancy in the state. The policies succeeded, however, in holding together the diverse nationalities in the state throughout an exceedingly critical period in Austrian history.

iii. Hungary

In Hungary Count Kálman Tisza, leader of the Liberal Party, was head of the government from 1876 to 1890. Deák, who had done so much for Hungarian independence, died January 29, 1876. His mantle descended to Tisza. Count Tisza was an exceedingly forceful man, who devoted his entire energies to the unification of his country and to its material prosperity. He was practically dictator in Hungary during his long ministry, so all the political development during this period can be ascribed to him.

Hungary was confronted with a difficult and complicated problem resulting from the confusion of peoples and languages within the Kingdom. The Magyars, the politically dominant race, composed approximately one-half the population: Germans, Slovaks, Rumanians, Ruthenians, Croatians, and Serbians made up the other half. Tisza aimed to convert the Kingdom into a unified and homogeneous Magyar state. He endeavored to force the Magyarization of the subject races. To accomplish his purpose, he established Magyar as the only official language, and required Magyar to be the tongue used and taught in the schools. The subject races, each clinging to its own language, customs, and traditions, felt that they were being persecuted by being compelled to use and study Magyar. Tisza sternly repressed all outbreaks against his policy of Magyarization, and proceeded in the belief that within a few generations the country would be successfully unified.

With this policy of Magyarization, Tisza combined an effort to further the economic development of his country. When he first accepted the premiership, Hungary was in a poor financial condition, unable to raise loans except at an extortionate rate of interest; it was without a railroad system adapted to the commercial and industrial needs of the people; it lacked any considerable oversea trade. When he left the cabinet, Hungary's finances were in excellent condition; it had a large and scientifically developed railway system; the foreign commerce naturally continued to go in large measure to Austria and to adjacent countries, but Fiume, its only seaport of consequence, had become the clearing point for a gradually increasing export business.

Count Tisza raised a host of enemies during his ministry by his arbitrary system. It is undoubtedly true that he maintained his parliamentary support by questionable methods in the elections, and that, for the sake of pursuing his policy of Magyarization, he abused the liberal principles he was supposed to represent. He was aiming toward a great end, however, and his measure of success in the material progress of Hungary, and in the increased prestige which Hungary gained in the affairs of the Dual Empire, is used as argument by his adherents to justify his statesmanship. The opposition to him reached a climax in the years 1889 and 1890, when open threats of revolution were made on the floor of the Hungarian parliament. In the spring of the latter year (March 13) he placed his resignation in the hands of his King.

C. Germany

In Germany, Bismarck maintained his ascendancy in domestic and foreign policies. He was now, 1880, a man of sixty-five and had for eighteen years (1862–1880) been the foremost statesman in Germany. His character and attainments were recognized and appreciated by the German people, however much they might disagree at times with his policies. On the occasion of his seventieth birthday, in 1885, the nation joined in a remarkable demonstration of esteem, raising by popular subscription more than two million marks for him. He retained the affection and confidence of his Emperor. The famous "Never" of William I in answer to Bismarck's request in 1877 to be allowed to resign indicated the reliance his aged master placed upon him. Contemporary statesmen in other European countries honored and feared him. The true magnitude of his achievements in international statecraft had at last been understood by them.

i. Bismarck's Domestic Policies

To Bismarck, this decade of peace was welcome for the opportunity to concentrate attention upon pressing domestic problems. The Kulturkampf, which had so disturbed Germany in the first years after its unity had been achieved, was abandoned by Bismarck before a greater menace in the growth of radicalism, and especially of Socialism. In Germany, the growth of the empire and the concessions which had during the critical years been made to the people, had immensely stimulated the radical forces. At the time when he had needed the enthusiastic support of the whole people, the chancellor had recognized the folly of inciting civil discord by attempting to suppress the radicals. One offspring of the radical movement, Socialism, gained an enormous number of adherents. It mustered half a million voters in the elections of 1870, and later won a dozen seats in the Reichstag. The aged Emperor, more conservative at eighty than when he first ascended the throne, stanchly opposed radicalism, and especially the theories and policies of the Socialists. It fell to Bismarck's part to strengthen again the forces of authority in the state as opposed to the wishes of a considerable mass of the people.

His first attempts to check radicalism were by suppression. Two attempts upon the aged Emperor's life in 1878 gave him the excuse for introducing and passing in the Reichstag in October of that year a drastic bill aimed against the Social

Democratic party. A recital of a few of the provisions of that bill, the Socialists' Act (*Socialistengesetz*), will indicate its severity.

> "Associations which aim, by social-democratic, socialistic, or communistic agitation, at the destruction of the existing order in State or society are forbidden.
>
> "Meetings in which social-democratic, socialistic, or communistic tendencies, directed to the destruction of the existing order in State or society, make their appearance are to be dissolved.
>
> "All printed matter, in which appear social-democratic, socialistic, or communistic tendencies, directed to the destruction of the existing order of State or society in a manner dangerous to the peace and, in particular, to the harmony between different classes of the population, is to be forbidden.
>
> "The collection of contributions for the furthering of social-democratic, socialistic, or communistic endeavors, directed toward the destruction of the existing order of the State or society, as also the public instigation to the furnishing of such contributions, are to be forbidden."

Although the Socialists themselves, aiming to overthrow the government and professing to be hostile to all existing institutions, could have no legitimate complaint against the efforts of the government to crush them, the bill itself was a mistake. It gave the Socialists at once the character of martyrs beneath a system as choking and autocratic as that maintained by Metternich. Although the execution of the bill, resulting in hundreds of prosecutions and punishments, thoroughly demoralized the outward organization of the Social-democratic party and forced the Socialists to work secretly, it aroused the keenest resentment among great masses of the people and actually converted many to the oppressed party.

Bismarck's attempt to suppress the Social-democratic movement among the radicals in Germany was supported a few years later by a series of great constructive measures of world-wide significance. His theory was that the forces of Socialism were recruited from the dissatisfied and miserable classes of the people, and that these forces would be permanently weakened by a program of social legislation for the betterment of these classes. Hence, in the message from the Throne, November 17, 1881, was announced a series of measures to promote the well-being of the workers of the Empire, these measures consisting of: (1) accident insurance; (2) sickness insurance; and (3) old-age or incapacity insurance. In the face of terrific opposition in parliament, Bismarck undertook to carry through these measures. In 1883 was passed the sickness insurance bill; in 1884 the accident insurance, and in 1889, by a small majority, the old-age and incapacity insurance. The general principle of these measures was the requirement that every workingman should be insured, and thus be comfortably taken care of in such individual crises as would otherwise result in poverty and misery. In the original bills Bismarck had placed the entire burden of insurance upon the state, but the parliament modified the bills so that (1) in accident insurance the employers should pay the entire premium, (2) in sickness insurance the employers should pay one-third and the employees the two-thirds of the premium, and (3) in old age or incapacity insurance, employer, employee, and state should share in the premium payment.

These three consecutive measures of social legislation form one of the greatest achievements of Bismarck's career. They constitute his attempt to allay social unrest and unhappiness. He was a pioneer in this work. His primary motive, as has been indicated, was to create within the state a contented body of people who would be inclined to support the government and not to promote radicalism and socialism in politics. In defending his program, which was popularly known as State Socialism, before the Reichstag, he once said:

"Give the workingman the right to employment as long as he has strength, assure him care when he is sick, and maintenance when he is old. If you will do that without fearing the sacrifice, or crying out 'State Socialism' as soon as the words 'provision for old age' are uttered . . . then I believe these gentlemen (*i.e* the Socialists) will sound their bird call in vain; and as soon as the workingmen see that the government is deeply interested in their welfare, the flocking to them will cease."

Although these measures did not check the growth of the Socialist party in Germany, they had a pronounced effect upon the attitude of the people toward the government. The younger generation, especially, seeing the interference of the government in so many details of the economic life for the benefit of the living and working conditions of the laboring classes, learned to regard their government as a kindly guardian of their interests. Bismarck strengthened the influences that made for paternal government. His ideas in state insurance have been since this period widely studied and, in more or less modified form, followed in other countries.

In economic legislation as well as in social legislation, Bismarck introduced notable measures during this decade. In 1879 he definitely abandoned the policy of free trade for that of the protective tariff. He had two reasons for changing his policy. In the first place the Imperial budget had, almost from the beginning in 1871, shown an annual deficit, which had to be met by contributions from the separate states of the Empire. Bismarck strongly wished to have the Imperial Treasury in a position to help the states of the Empire rather than to be a solicitor of funds from the states. In this connection, too, he was looking forward to his state insurance schemes which would call for large expenditures from the imperial funds. In a protective tariff he saw the opportunity to fill the Imperial Treasury. In the second place he was honestly convinced that Germany was suffering in her economic conditions from the free trade policy. The iron and steel industry was demoralized by the importation, free of duty, of the products of the English mines and manufactures; the agricultural districts were unable to compete with the grain imported, free of duty, from Russia. In introducing his protective policy to the Reichstag in a speech May 2, 1879, he said:

"We have hitherto, owing to our policy of the open door, been the dumping ground for the over-production of other countries. It is this, in my opinion, that has depressed prices in Germany, that has prevented the growth of our industries, the development of our economic life. Let us but close the door, let us raise the somewhat higher barrier which I am now proposing, and see to it that at least we preserve for German industry the same market that we are now good-naturedly allowing foreigners to exploit. . . . The fact is that our condition is unsatisfactory and, in my opinion, is worse than that of any of our protectionist neighbors. If the dangers of protection are as great as they are painted by enthusiastic free-traders, France would have been a ruined and impoverished country long ago, because of the theories which she has followed ever since the time of Colbert. . . . For the abstract teaching of science in this connection I care not a straw. I base my opinion on experience, the experience of our time. I see that protectionist countries are prospering, that free-trade countries are retrograding, and that great and powerful England, the mighty athlete, who, having hardened her sinews, stepped out into the open market and said: 'Who will fight me? I am ready for any and all,' even she is gradually returning toward protection, and will in a few years adopt it, in order to keep for herself at least the English market."

After a long and bitter political struggle Bismarck won the day for his measures. Germany has ever since remained a protectionist state. The chancellor and his successors have pursued the undeviating policy of encouraging by every means possible the economic and agricultural interests of the Empire. The remarkable stimulation of home industry which began immediately after the protective tariff took effect, seems to have justified, to the German people at least, his initial arguments. A few statistics will show how immediate the effect of the tariff was upon German economic conditions. Naturally, the first result would be a falling off in imports:

Imports 1877, 1878, 1879	Imports 1880, 1881, 1882
1877 — 3,872,400,000 marks	1880 — 2,844,268,000 marks
1878 — 3,715,600,000 marks	1881 — 2,990,248,000 marks
1879 — 3,888,100,000 marks	1882 — 3,134,656,000 marks

The stimulation to one of the chief industries affected by the tariff is seen in the rapid increase in the production of pig iron:

Before the Tariff	After the Tariff
1877 — 1,899,000 tons	1880 — 2,692,000 tons
1878 — 2,119,000 tons	1881 — 2,879,000 tons
1879 — 2,201,000 tons	1882 — 3,344,000 tons

Likewise this stimulation may be seen in the production of coal:

Before the Tariff	After the Tariff
1877 — 37,530,000 tons	1880 — 46,974,000 tons
1878 — 39,590,000 tons	1881 — 48,688,000 tons
1879 — 42,026,000 tons	1882 — 52,119,000 tons

In a further attempt to centralize power in the empire and to increase the revenue of the monarchy, Bismarck advocated the imperial ownership of all the railroad lines, as well as of the postal and telegraph service. He realized that the stragetic and commercial importance of the railroads would increase with the years. His plan was to purchase all the private lines and to join to the imperial system thus begun the railroads belonging to the individual states of the German Federation. His imperial scheme was defeated by the opposition of the separate states to the idea of surrendering their railroads into an imperial system. He did, however, succeed in carrying his plan through the Prussian parliament to apply to the railroads in Prussia. At the time, 14,000 kilometers of the 20,000 kilometers in Prussia were owned by private capital. These private lines were gradually acquired by the state, so that now Prussia owns and operates all of its railroads.

ii. Bismarck and the Foreign Situation

During these years of internal reforms, Bismarck never lost his grasp of the foreign situation. His problem was to keep the peace, to maintain the Triple Alliance, to check the formation of an opposing alliance, and to foster so far as possible friendly relations with his neighbors. The difficult elements in the problem lay in the hostile attitude of powerful factions in Russia, including the Czar himself, in the conflict of interests between Austria-Hungary (Prussia's ally) and Russia, and in the disposition of a determined party in France to bring about a war of revenge.

To Bismarck, the Russian attitude was more threatening than the French. He therefore exerted every endeavor to conciliate the Czar and the Russian people. His greatest success came in 1884 when he brought together in person the sovereigns of Austria-Hungary, Russia, and Germany and renewed the cordial understanding of the period before the Russo-Turkish war. At the same time he concluded with Russia a secret treaty by which each nation pledged itself to friendly neutrality in case the other were attacked. Hence in 1884 and 1885 Bismarck seemed to have established Germany in an unassailable position in international politics. Austria-Hungary and Italy were bound to her by the ties of the Triple Alliance; the Russian Czar had renewed the cordial understanding of previous years, and had guaranteed friendly neutrality in case of an attack upon Germany; France had turned from the European field to waste money and strength in distant colonial enterprises.

The situation, however, as the sequel showed, hung in a very delicate balance. The events of the years from 1885 to 1888 seriously disturbed this balance. The crisis in the Near East, precipitated by the action of Eastern Rumelia in amalgamating with Bulgaria and by the short Serbo-Bulgarian war, revealed how diametrically opposed were the vital interests of Austria-Hungary and Russia. Austria-

Hungary forbade the Bulgarians to pursue the retreating Serbians upon threat of sending troops to defend Belgrade; Alexander III made no secret of the fact, that, had troops been so used, Russia would have marched her armies to the aid of Bulgaria. The cordial understanding which Bismarck had patched up two years before was irretrievably shattered.

This disturbance was followed immediately (1886–1887) by the Boulangist excitement in France. Germany could not fail to be affected by Boulanger's thinly veiled threats of revenge, and by the strength of his political following. When Boulanger, as Minister of War in France, introduced a new law raising the peace strength of the French army to half a million men, Bismarck, as was natural, retaliated by advocating legislation raising the German army to the same number. In his speech before the Reichstag at the introduction of his army increase, the German Chancellor said:

"We have no desire for war; we belong (to use an expression of Prince Metternich's) to the states whose appetite is satisfied; under no circumstances shall we attack France; the stronger we are, the more improbable is war; but if France has any reason to believe that she is more powerful than we, then war is certain."

At this moment (1887–1888), the Czar, duped by some forged papers on the recent Near Eastern crisis into believing that Bismarck had undermined Russian influences in Bulgaria in favor of Austria-Hungary, loosened the anti-German elements in Russia. The Russian press, in virulent attacks upon Bismarck, demanded his resignation or immediate war. The Czar himself, traveling across Germany, ostentatiously avoided meeting the Emperor. Bismarck had hardly exposed the forgery and restored friendly relations with Russia when, in 1888, the publication of the text of the Dual Alliance of 1879 between Austria-Hungary and Germany caused hostility in popular circles in Russia to blaze out anew. The Russian government had been secretly informed of the Treaty of Dual Alliance shortly after it was made, but the Russian people were offended and startled by the revelation of the extent of the military preparations made by Austria-Hungary and Germany against them.

In the face of such international complications, in February of 1888 Bismarck pleaded before the Reichstag for the passage of the army increase bill and for an appropriation of twenty-eight million marks for the purchase of munitions and supplies. Rarely had he been more eloquent. Some striking sentences of his speech sounded like a threat, or at least a defiance of the European powers. He reviewed the events of the past generation, showing that scarcely a year had been free from the menace of a great European war, in which all the powers of Europe would divide into two hostile coalitions; he emphasized the fact that this menace would never cease; he urged that Germany should be prepared:

"We must make greater exertions than other powers on account of our geographical position. We lie in the middle of Europe; we can be attacked on all sides. God has put us in a situation in which our neighbors will not allow us to fall into indolence or apathy. The pike in the European pool prevent us from becoming carp; but we must fulfill the designs of Providence by making ourselves so strong that the pike can do no more than amuse us. . . .

"The fears that have arisen in the course of the present year have been caused by Russia more even than by France, chiefly through an exchange of provocations, threats, insults, and reciprocal investigations, which have occurred during the past summer in the Russian and French press. . . .

"God has given us on our flank the French, who are the most warlike and turbulent nation that exists, and He has permitted the development in Russia of warlike propensities which, until lately, did not manifest themselves to the same extent. . . .

"It is not fear which makes us lovers of peace, but the consciousness of our own strength. By courtesy and kind methods we may be easily — too easily perhaps — influenced, but by means of threats, never. We Germans fear God and nothing else in the world."

These words were uttered in all the intensity of deep conviction. Bismarck unquestionably believed in his ability to maintain the peace in Europe even in the midst of his enemies. A few weeks later, March 9, 1888, the entire situation was changed by the death of the aged Emperor, William I, a few days before his ninety-first birthday.

iii. William II and the Resignation of Bismarck

The year 1888 is known among Germans as the year of the three Emperors. William I, who died in March, was succeeded by his son, Frederick, who at his succession was in the last throes of suffering from cancer of the throat. Frederick died June 15 without having taken any measures of consequence during the few months he had reigned. His death elevated his son, William, to the throne, under the title of William II.

The whole of Europe waited to learn the character of the new Emperor, raised so suddenly and unexpectedly to power in Germany. William II was, in 1888, but twenty-nine years of age. He had, in the few months when his father was Emperor, indicated his intention of following the guidance of Bismarck. At a dinner, April 6, 1888, William proposed a toast to the great chancellor: "The Empire is like an army corps that has lost its commander-in-chief in the field, while the officer who stands next to him in rank lies severely wounded. At this critical moment forty-six million loyal German hearts turn with solicitude and hope toward the standard and the standard bearer, in whom all their expectations are centered. The standard bearer is our illustrious Prince, our great Chancellor. Let him lead us. We will follow him. Long may he live!" And this intention was further emphasized in his address to the Reichstag upon his accession, in which address the following extracts were especially noteworthy:

"I have summoned you, Gentlemen, that I may make my declaration before you to the German people, that I am resolved, as

Emperor and King, to walk in the same path in which my illustrious grandfather won the confidence of his federal allies, the love of the German people, and the good will of other countries. Whether I also shall succeed in this rests with God, but I will earnestly and laboriously endeavor to attain this end. . . .

"In foreign politics I am resolved, so far as in me lies, to maintain peace with all men. My affection for the German army, and the position I hold toward it, will never lead me into the temptation of jeopardizing for my country the benefits of peace, unless war be a necessity forced upon us by an attack upon the empire or its allies. Our army is meant to maintain peace, and to be in a position, if peace is broken, to win it back with honor. That it will be able to do with the help of God, through the strength which your recent unanimous vote has guaranteed to it. To use this strength for wars of aggression is very far from my heart. Germany requires neither added martial glory nor any fresh conquests, now that she has definitely won the right in war to exist as a united and an independent nation. . . .

"With trust in God and in the defensive power of our nation I feel confident that it will be granted to us to defend, and to confirm by peaceful labor, what was won in arms under the leadership of my two predecessors on the throne, now resting in God. . . ."

As the months passed, however, William II showed an increasing impatience at the methods and policies of his chancellor. The Emperor was young, energetic, ambitious, and impulsive. He thoroughly believed in the divine origin of his power, and avowed this belief openly and often. He had an exceptionally keen and well-trained mind, and an enormous capacity for hard work. At his succession, he found Bismarck actually wielding the Emperor's power in Germany. Bismarck himself was Imperial Chancellor, and head of the Bundesrath; he was, also, Imperial Minister of Foreign Affairs, and Minister of Commerce; he was, further, President of the Ministry in Prussia. He had, in addition to the offices, the immense prestige of his successes: he had carried his policies in the past against the will of his colleagues, even at times against the will of the Emperor himself; he had opposed and defeated the Reichstag, and his acts had in the end been approved by that body; he stood forth as the greatest figure in the international diplomacy of Europe. Furthermore, he had so constituted the administrative departments that their heads were men elected by him and responsible to him. His chief assistant in the Foreign Office was his son, Herbert; the Minister of the Interior was a cousin; in critical affairs he depended upon the assistance of his own family or of his own private secretaries. The various ministers were not regarded as equals or as colleagues, but as subordinates. Thus the new Emperor, desirous of taking an active part in his government, found no duties allotted to him but to affix his imperial signature to the acts of his minister. William's suggestions of policy were coldly received or rejected as impracticable. His energetic journeys to and fro in his empire, his frequent trips to foreign lands, and his many speeches were strongly criticized in journals more or less under administration influence. Above all, his natural and legitimate desire to consult openly and informally with any of his ministers on questions of imperial policy led to an open breach with the chancellor. The Emperor himself described the final incidents of this breach to Prince Hohenlohe:

"STRASSBURG, April 26, 1890.

"I drove with the Emperor to the shooting box at Sufflenheim. It was about an hour's drive, and during this time the Emperor related the whole story of his differences with Bismarck without interruption. He said that relations had become strained as early as December. The Emperor then desired that something should be done upon the question of the workingmen. The Chancellor objected. . . .

"This friction had considerably disturbed the relations between Bismarck and the Emperor, and these were further strained by the question of the cabinet regulations of 1852. Bismarck had often advised the Emperor to grant the ministers access to himself, and this was done. But when communication between the Emperor and his ministers became more frequent, Bismarck took offense, became jealous, and revived the cabinet regulations of 1852 in order to interrupt communications between the emperor and his ministers. The Emperor protested and demanded the repeal of the regulation; Bismarck made a show of consent, but nothing was done in the matter. The Emperor therefore demanded that he should either issue an order repealing the regulation, or hand in his resignation. This decision the Emperor communicated to Prince Bismarck through Hahnke. The prince hesitated, but gave in his resignation on March 18."

The final incidents related by persons friendly to Bismarck showed more clearly the quarrel between the two men. When the Emperor insisted that his wishes must be observed, if not by Bismarck, *then by another*, Bismarck asked, speaking in English, "Then I am to understand, your majesty, that I am in your way?" The Emperor answered, "Yes." Bismarck immediately left to draw up his formal resignation. After twenty-eight years of service, however, it is not easy to frame such a document. The Emperor heard that the leader of the parliamentary opposition had visited Bismarck at his home. Fearing some intrigue, he sent an urgent message demanding the resignation at once. Bismarck made no reply. Early the following morning, the Emperor in person drove to Bismarck's house. The Chancellor was summoned from bed. The Emperor demanded to know what had taken place upon the previous afternoon's interview and stated that ministers were not to discuss political questions with parliamentary leaders without the imperial approval. Bismarck refused to allow any supervision over his guests in his own house.

"Not if I command it as your sovereign?" asked William.

"No," replied Bismarck, "the commands of my King cease in my wife's drawing-room."

No reconciliation was possible after this incident. Bismarck hastily prepared and tendered his resignation. The Emperor attempted in his letter of acceptance to make it appear that the resignation was voluntary and friendly. He raised Bismarck to the rank of Field Marshal in the army and created him Duke of Lauenburg.

Strong arguments, supported by some significant evidence, have been advanced to prove that the break between William II and Bismarck resulted from deeper and more important causes than those outlined above. It is said that the two men were irreconcilably opposed with respect to the imperial policy to be adopted toward Russia. Bismarck, it is well known, had gone out of his way to conciliate the great Slav power. Even after the break which occurred as a result of the German attitude in the Congress of Berlin, Bismarck had revived with some success the friendly relations between Germany and Russia, and had even succeeded in 1884 and 1887 in arranging for a Russo-German military convention. In 1890 it was time for a renewal of the agreements between the two states. Russia was in a receptive mood, but Germany withheld her offer and allowed the agreements to lapse. It was just at this time that Bismarck resigned. It is argued that he insisted upon the renewal, and that the Emperor absolutely refused. Some color is given to these arguments by the viciousness with which journals inspired by Bismarck after the breach attacked the Russian policy of the Emperor and criticized the diplomacy which resulted in the formation of the Dual Entente.

Thus passed from the field of active participation in events the most conspicuous figure of the age. No honors could compensate him for the manner of his retirement. He became an embittered critic of the Emperor and of imperial policies. To the pilgrims who visited him in his retirement, to the political gossip-gatherers, and to newspaper reporters, he said many unwise things. He dictated his Reflections and Reminiscences, in them laying bare to an astonished Germany the machinations by which their unity had been achieved. He had never been a man who admitted many to intimate friendship, so that after the death of his wife and brother he suffered from loneliness. In 1895 a peace was patched up between him and the Emperor: the Emperor visited the aged statesman upon his birthday at his country house, and Bismarck returned the call at the Emperor's palace in Berlin. We may well believe, however, that the reconciliation was but superficial. The great chancellor died July 31, 1898. His epitaph, according to his own desire, was: "A faithful servant of Emperor William I."

PART III

THE FORMATION OF A DEFENSE AGAINST GERMAN HEGEMONY IN EUROPE

CHAPTER I

INTERNATIONAL AFFAIRS IN EUROPE, 1890–1905

SINCE 1871, the time of the completion of German Unity, and even more completely since 1879, the time of the formation of the German-Austrian alliance, Bismarck had dominated international politics on the continent of Europe. His downfall in 1890, therefore, sent a thrill through all the European chancelleries. The new German Emperor was at this period an unknown quantity. However much the Iron Chancellor had upon occasions "rattled the sword," his influence in European affairs since 1871 had, it was generally recognized, been instrumental in keeping the peace: his sudden and unexpected displacement might mean the inauguration on the part of the young and inexperienced Emperor of a new policy which would ultimately lead to war. Certain of William II's public acts and utterances were capable of being interpreted as indicative of his reliance upon force in international relations. The sedate statesmen in diplomatic affairs distrusted the sovereign's youth, his impulsive energy, and his assumption of the reins of government over the heads of his ministers. The leaders in each of the great continental powers felt it necessary to take immediate steps for protection in case their worst fears were realized.

A. FORMATION OF THE *DUAL ENTENTE*

The first definite momentous result of Bismarck's fall from power was the establishment of an *understanding*, an

Entente, between Russia and France. This *understanding,* it has been pointed out, was a logical outcome of the formation of the Triple Alliance in 1882; but by Bismarck's unremitting skill and tact it had been delayed during his continuance in office. The old German Chancellor had artfully intimated to the Russian Czar the dangers of an alliance between his autocratic country and a state wherein revolutions and the revolutionary spirit were rife; he had encouraged France in her expensive colonial acquisitions; he had connived at Russia's far-eastern policies; he had striven to maintain the most cordial relations between Germany and France on the one hand and between Germany and Russia on the other, so that no temptation for the creation of an opposing alliance might exist. His diplomacy had met with marked success. Immediately after he lost power, however, the influences keeping France and Russia apart ceased, and the reasons for an understanding between them loomed above all other considerations. France could never forget the humiliating defeats of 1870 and 1871; she could not forgive the loss of Alsace and Lorraine; she thought of the German threats of war in 1875; she feared the increased German army to be provided by the recent army bill of 1889. Russia on her part held Germany responsible for her failure in the Congress of Berlin; she realized more and more keenly the irreconcilable conflict between her interests in the Balkan regions and the interests of Germany's ally, Austria-Hungary; and she, too, feared the threat of an increased German army. Thus on the part of both states national sentiment against Germany combined with the need of national security to favor an alliance.

A material basis for a friendly understanding was established even before Bismarck's fall from power. Russia was always in need of funds for the exploitation of her enormous natural resources and for the development of her industries. Her credit was considered good. For some years previous to 1888, she had obtained these necessary funds from a group of German bankers. In that year, however, after some reluctance on the part of this group to float a further loan, she welcomed a suggestion from France that the loan be offered on the French market for popular subscription. The Russian securities, to the amount of five hundred million francs, were quickly absorbed by the French investors. In the two years following, two more loans, each of a similar amount to the first, were equally well received by the French. More than a hundred thousand people subscribed. So long as the Russian credit was good, the government saw the possibility of obtaining further huge sums for her development from the French. These successful financial transactions created a highly favorable atmosphere for diplomacy.

The retirement of Bismarck gave the French leaders the opportunity to press the negotiations to a conclusion. Within a few weeks after his fall from power the French minister of the interior arrested a group of Russian Terrorists who were in Paris preparing explosives for an attempt upon the Czar's life. In the summer of the same year, the French Minister of War contributed further to the good feeling between the two governments by turning over for Russian uses the huge arms manufactory at Châtellerault. The final act was staged publicly for the benefit of popular opinion. In the summer of 1891 the French fleet anchored in Russian waters off Kronstadt. The Czar made a formal visit to the flagship and stood with bared head while the French bands played the national airs of the two countries. The French officers were fêted by the Russians, and the French sailors fraternized on the most friendly terms with the sailors of the Russian ships in the harbor. This little theatrical display met with considerable success: it was hailed with transports of joy in France and assured popular approval of the pending alliance. A few weeks later, August 22, 1891, a treaty between the representatives of the two countries was signed; in June of the following year a military convention completed the alliance.

The terms of the treaty have never officially been made public. According to unofficial reports, it contains no specific reference to any power of the Triple Alliance, no statement of duration, but is a document of a few provisions declaring that if either nation be attacked, the other will come to its aid with all its powers, and that peace shall only be concluded in concert and by mutual agreement. Thus in its general nature it is exactly similar to the treaty at the base of the Triple Alliance.

B. EFFECT OF THE *DUAL ENTENTE* UPON THE INTERNATIONAL SITUATION

The formation of this alliance, this *Dual Entente*, profoundly altered the international political situation in Europe. It was a step toward an equilibrium of forces, a Balance of Power. In one pan of the scales lay the Triple Alliance; over against it in the other pan lay the *Dual Entente*. The *Entente* was undoubtedly popular in Russia, but the Russians did not have as much to gain from it at the moment, apparently, as the French. It was the French who had taken the initiative in the proceedings leading up to the treaty, and it was the French who gave the most open manifestations of approval afterwards. French statesmen were aware how their country had been isolated in Europe; they had resented the dictatorship of Germany over continental affairs. In their opinion, the *Entente* rescued France from her isolation and broke the German dictatorship. Undoubtedly, too, a large group in France hailed the *Entente* as the first step toward a successful war of revenge. Even though it was common knowledge that the understanding and military convention were upon a defensive basis, these "patriots" looked forward confidently to a war against Germany wherefrom France would emerge with Alsace and Lorraine and the huge indemnity which had been wrested from her after the Franco-Prussian war.

More important than its effect upon the status of popular sentiment in France and Russia, however, was the effect of the Balance of Power upon the general condition of affairs in Europe. The early years of the nineteenth century had seen what was called the Concert of Powers: the change from that condition to the Balance of Power was one that brought a constant peril of a great European war. The term "Concert of Powers" is applied to that unity of policy and action with which the great powers of Europe considered and decided conflicting issues in European politics during the years following the fall of Napoleon I. This unity sprang out of the Quadruple Alliance against Napoleon: it was continued after his downfall under the influence of Prince Metternich of Austria. It acted with greatest harmony and influence from 1818 to 1822; it had great power over continental affairs up to the fall of Metternich in 1848; it continued in existence, though with diminished harmony, in connection with affairs in the Near East until the Congress of Berlin in 1878. Its greatest contribution to European politics was the establishment of the custom of Congresses, in which the diplomats of the great powers met, considered, and decided upon issues between separate states. At the height of its prestige it occupied the place of an international tribunal on all matters affecting Europe at large. Its purpose was primarily and always the maintenance of general European peace throughout all the involved disputes which might arise between individual states. Its general policies were guided by recognition of the fact that each and every great state in Europe had a vital interest in any and all territorial changes, and that any arrangement involving such changes could be more peacefully settled by agreement among the military powers than by separate negotiations between individual countries. Thus, though the system established by the Concert of Powers ultimately broke down, it was throughout its existence a factor in the maintenance of peace.

Contrast with this system the state of affairs brought about by the Balance of Power. No better condition for causing friction, or for magnifying the amount of friction, between European states could have been created. The two alliances were mutually hostile. Even though in the treaties the names of states were not openly mentioned, it was common knowledge that Germany, Austria-Hungary, and Italy were leagued against Russia and France, and vice versa. The alliances were unlike previous alliances in recent European history, for those previous alliances had been formed in the presence of great issues and had been promptly dissolved once the crisis had passed. Thus the continental alliance against France did not survive the Congress of Vienna, and the alliance against Russia fell apart immediately after the Crimean war. The Triple Alliance and the *Dual Entente*, however, were formed at a time when no critical issues of vital importance were pending; they were intended to have a degree of permanence; and they were regarded by each nation as an insurance of its individual rights against the encroachment by any other state. Hence, whereas under the conditions established by the Concert of Powers, a dispute between two states was the signal for a European Congress in which the issue would be discussed and settled peaceably, under the conditions established by the Balance of Power such a dispute became at once the occasion for general war preparations on the part of the two great opposing military alliances. The field of individual disputes was thus greatly widened. The policy of a single state, the policy which was regarded by it as of vital importance, became perforce the policy of all the states of its alliance. France could not raise and settle a dispute with Germany without involving Russia, Austria-Hungary, and Italy; and similarly, Russia could not come into conflict with Austria-Hungary (over the Balkans, for example, which Bismarck had once declared not worth the bones of a single Pomeranian grenadier) without dragging in Germany, Italy, and France.

In addition to these results, the Balance of Power was directly responsible for turning Europe into a collection of armed camps. With two huge opposing alliances, rivalry in military forces and armaments was inevitable. Neither alliance, though formed for defensive purposes, could afford to allow the states of the opposing alliance to be better prepared than were the states of its league. Any improvement in military equipment, any increase in the number of forces, was at once met by corresponding measures in other states. All the resources of science were employed to increase the effectiveness of engines of military use. Each discovery was seized upon, developed, and utilized chiefly for its use in war. New explosives, automobiles, submarines, aëroplanes, the wireless telegraph, all were adopted into the military systems to give some slight handicap in the race. The expenses of the armaments were enormous. The taxes were raised, and the sums spent for other than military purposes cut down. The people through their parliaments consented regularly to the expenditures on the ground that they were necessary for defense. Europe bristled with guns and well-drilled armies, all avowedly for defense, but all ready for instant war. Such a situation in itself constituted an ever-present peril.

C. ATTITUDE OF GERMANY TOWARD THE *DUAL ENTENTE*, 1891-1900

Thus a year after he had dismissed his experienced Chancellor, the young German Emperor faced the difficult foreign situation brought about by the *Dual Entente*. He was in every sense the personal director of the government. Bismarck's successor, Count Caprivi, was recognized both in Germany and abroad as being merely the official mouthpiece of his Emperor, and not in any sense as being himself the molder of German policy.

The purpose of the Emperor's diplomacy was to maintain German leadership in international affairs in Europe in spite of the creation of the *Dual Entente*. The means by which he attempted to accomplish this end were the studied cultivation of cordial relations with both members of the *Entente* and the maintenance of the traditional friendship between Germany (or Prussia, before the formation of the German Empire) and Great Britain. It was, of course, Germany's advantage to have her natural opponents involved in foreign and domestic difficulties, for such troubles would render them less able to dispute Germany. If the relations between Russia and Great Britain were strained, there was less probability of Russia and France being in a position to dictate European policies to Germany.

i. *Internal Affairs in France*

Events in France and Russia for a long time favored William II's diplomacy. In France the revelations disclosed during the successive trials for treason of a certain artillery captain, Alfred Dreyfus, stirred the nation to its depths, and caused factions which for years paralyzed political action. Dreyfus was first tried in 1894, and, upon the evidence of some memoranda supposedly in his handwriting, convicted. The incident seemed to be closed. A few years later, however, suspicion leaked out that the real traitor was being shielded, and that Dreyfus was suffering a terrible and undeserved punishment. Attempts to gain a new trial for the officer were thwarted by high army officials. The public became interested. If Dreyfus were really guilty, why should the army object to proving his guilt beyond the shadow of a doubt? The support of the Catholic Church, which had from the beginning of the republic been hostile to the government, was thrown to the side of the army, thus introducing a religious element into the issue. Since Dreyfus was a Jew, racial and social prejudices were aroused. Zola, the great novelist, interested himself in the case, became certain that Dreyfus had been unjustly convicted, and used all the great power of his pen in arousing the nation. By the summer of 1898 all France was torn by political factions resulting from the case. In August, 1898, a certain Colonel Henry, confessing that he had forged one of the documents by which Dreyfus had been convicted, committed suicide. In June of 1899 a Major Esterhazy, long known to be worthless and unprincipled, fled to England and confessed that he had himself written another of the documents on which Dreyfus had been convicted. Public pressure was so great that Dreyfus was brought from his confinement on Devil's Island for a retrial in August, 1899. The army was determined, in spite of the revelations that had been made, to convict him again for the honor of the service. He did not receive a fair trial. The case against him was shown to be, in the words of the London *Times*, "foul with forgeries, lies, contradictions, and puerilities." He was, however, by the court-martial declared guilty "with extenuating circumstances"—a remarkable verdict in a case of the treason of an army officer. The court had thus attempted to uphold the honor of the army. Although the President of the Republic pardoned Dreyfus, and the parliament passed in 1900 an amnesty bill for all implicated, thus attempting to end the case, Dreyfus and his adherents demanded a full vindication. This was finally obtained by a new trial before the Supreme Court of France (the Court of Cassation) in 1906. Dreyfus was triumphantly acquitted, restored to the army with the rank of major, and invested with the cross of the Legion of Honor.

The political turmoil accompanying the Dreyfus case had torn France for a decade. The conditions in the army had shocked the nation. If the people could not trust the honor of the army, what could they trust? All the elements hostile to liberal republican government in France had flocked to the anti-Dreyfus party. Clericals, monarchists, the remnants of Boulanger's Nationals, — these men, striving to discredit the government, had supported the army. On the other hand, united with those who believed in the innocence of Dreyfus were the liberals who were bent on maintaining the authority of the government over the power of the army, who were anxious to combat race prejudice, and who were devoted to the continuance of the existing form of government. The trial had thus become the focus for a critical internal political struggle for the existence of liberal institutions in France. The final victory of the government was a triumph for liberalism.

ii. *French Colonial Policy*

During this same period, France was committing herself to a colonial policy designed to make real the magnificent dream of Jules Ferry in the early 80's of a French-African empire which should include the entire northern part of Africa. Gabriel Hanotaux, a foreign minister from 1894 to 1898, had imbibed from Ferry the enthusiasm for colonial dominion. Regarding England as a certain enemy to his ideals, he turned to Germany for support. In the German foreign office his approaches were received in a most friendly spirit. The Emperor himself took occasion to express his satisfaction at Germany's relations with France and his hope that the basis for a friendly understanding or alliance might be laid. Hanotaux's policies, however, brought his country to the brink of war against England. In the Egyptian Soudan the territorial claims of the two European countries sharply clashed. The Fashoda incident in 1898 [1] was the culmination of a series of colonial disputes. France was brought to the very brink of war, only drawing back because internal discussions over the Dreyfus case and the

[1] See the following chapter, pp. 336 to 339.

weakness of the army and navy made it evident that she could not win.

Thus by its internal dissensions and by the complications resulting from its colonial enterprises, France was playing into the hands of Germany. William II could feel that German hegemony was secure. His policy was succeeding.

iii. *Russian Colonial Expansion*

Russia, the other member of the Dual Entente, was during this period concentrating her interest upon her expansion in Asia. In central Asia, in Persia, Afghanistan, and Thibet, the activities of Russian agents aroused the suspicions and hostility of the British. In the Far East, where Russia had reached the Pacific Ocean, she was now seeking to push her boundaries to the southward to get a year-round ice-free port. She started the great Trans-Siberian railroad in 1891, intending thus to consolidate her power over her vast empire.

The special opportunity for Germany to show her friendly attitude toward Russia's plans in the East came just after the China-Japanese war in 1894. The provisions of the Treaty of Shimonoseki which ended that war gave Japan the Liao-Tung peninsula with its fine harbor and strong fortress of Port Arthur. The possession of this peninsula by Japan conflicted with Russia's plans. She sought aid to make an effective protest. Germany joined Russia and France in forcing Japan to revise the provisions of the treaty and give up her foothold on the Asiatic continent. It seemed as though Germany, a member of the Triple Alliance, might enter into an understanding with the states of the Dual Entente. When Russia continued to press her influence over the Chinese province of Manchuria, she had Germany's support; when Russia leased Port Arthur and stretched her railroad lines south from Harbin, she acted with the Emperor's knowledge and approval.

Thus in the case of Russia as in that of France, diplomats danced to the German Emperor's music. By recognizing the concentration of Russian interest upon events and opportunities in the Far East, the German Emperor could assure himself that the Czar would not show a disposition to interfere in Europe. Russia, with the bitter hostility of Great Britain along the central Asian boundaries, with absorbing interests in Manchuria and Port Arthur, and with Japan making unmistakable preparations for opposition, was in no position to take a leading part in international politics on the continent.

iv. *German Attitude toward Great Britain*

William II was most successful up to 1900 in preventing his avowals of friendship with France and Russia from affecting in any way the cordial relations which had long existed between Germany and Great Britain. Bismarck had made friendship with Great Britain a cardinal point in his foreign policy during the whole of his long and uninterrupted power; the Emperor adopted the policy as his own upon his accession. The few conflicts in colonial claims were speedily adjusted in agreements between the two governments. The continual friction between the individual members of the *Dual Entente* and Great Britain naturally inclined Great Britain toward Germany. Further, so long as British statesmen clung to their policy of non-interference and "splendid isolation," there was no prospect of a clash between Great Britain and Germany over international European politics. The close friendship between the two countries continued up to the very end of the century. In a speech of 1899, just after the treaty which divided the Samoan islands and secured for Germany the chief one of the group, Lord Salisbury (prime minister) said:

"This morning you have learned of the arrangements concluded between us and one of the continental states with whom more than with others we have for years maintained sympathetic and friendly relations. The arrangement is above all interesting as an indication that our relations with the German nation are all that we could desire."

The German Emperor laid himself open, it is true, to charges of inconsistency, for to the superficial observer he was at one moment pro-French, at another pro-Russian, and again pro-British. His policy succeeded, however, in its main purpose: he kept the peace in Europe, and maintained Germany in her position as the chief figure in European politics. Indeed, when the world saw Germany, France, and Russia uniting in a protest to Japan, and the fleets of France and Russia assembled with the German ships to celebrate the opening of the Kiel canal, it seemed that the two great alliances might lose their mutually hostile character for good and all. The Emperor had effectually neutralized the results of the formation of the Dual Entente.

D. THE FORMATION OF THE *ENTENTE CORDIALE*

An entirely new turn to the international situation was given in the early years of the twentieth century when Great Britain abandoned her traditional policy of "splendid isolation," and approached Germany's enemies in the effort to arrange a peaceful understanding on disputed issues. British diplomats were forced to this new position because of the growing alarm caused by the revelation of the extent and nature of Germany's plans.

i. *Trade Rivalry between Great Britain and Germany*

Even before Lord Salisbury's speech emphasizing the excellent relations between Great Britain and Germany, much ill-feeling had been aroused in sections of Great Britain by the serious inroads which Germany had made upon British commerce. Although British merchants by virtue of Great Britain's commanding position in the commercial world should have gained the lion's share of the huge increase in commerce, statistics showed that they had not. The telltale figures proved that Germany was forging ahead at a rate far in excess of Great Britain's rate. Even though Great Britain's great handicap in the rivalry for the world's market kept her total amount of business above that of Germany, the latter's increases had brought her from an insignificant position in 1871 up to the position of Great Britain's chief competitor in 1900. Germany had outstripped all other rivals.

Comparative statistics indicate more graphically than any general statements can the comparative industrial development in the two countries. To bring forth the full significance of the statistics, we shall give the actual figures covering a single generation, from 1875 to 1905, and the percentage of increase.

Great Britain's population in 1875 was 33,000,000; in 1905 was 43,000,000 — an increase of $30\frac{1}{3}\%$. Germany's population in 1875 was 42,500,000; in 1905 was 60,000,000 — an increase of $41^{+}\%$.

Great Britain's production of coal in 1875 was 132,000,000 tons; in 1905 was 236,000,000 tons — an increase of $78^{+}\%$. Germany's production of coal and lignite in 1875 was 47,800,000 tons; in 1905 was 173,000,000 tons — an increase of $260^{+}\%$.

Great Britain's production of pig iron in 1875 was 6,350,000 tons; in 1905 was 9,600,000 tons — an increase of $51^{+}\%$. Germany's production of pig iron in 1875 was 2,000,000 tons; in 1905 was 10,800,000 — an increase of 440%, and a total of 1,200,000 tons greater than that of England.

Great Britain's merchant marine consisted in 1875 of 21,000 sailing vessels with a net tonnage of 4,000,000 tons and of 4000 steam vessels with a net tonnage of 2,000,000 tons, totaling together 25,000 vessels with a tonnage of 6,000,000 tons; in 1905 it consisted of 10,000 sailing vessels with a net tonnage of 1,600,000 tons, and 10,500 steam vessels with a net tonnage of 9,000,000 tons, totaling together 20,000 vessels with a tonnage of 10,600,000. The increase in tonnage was thus 76+%. Germany's merchant marine consisted in 1875 of 4300 sailing vessels with a net tonnage of 875,000 tons, and of 300 steam vessels with a net tonnage of 200,000 tons, totaling together 4600 vessels with a net tonnage of 1,075,000 tons; in 1905 it consisted of 2300 sailing vessels with a net tonnage of 540,000 tons and of 1600 steam vessels with a net tonnage of 2,900,000 tons, totaling together 3900 vessels with a net tonnage of 3,440,000 tons. The increase in tonnage was thus 220+%.

Great Britain's total import and export business in 1875 was $3,250,000,000; in 1905 was $4,850,000,000 — an increase of 49+%. Germany's total import and export business in 1875 was $1,500,000,000; in 1905 was $3,300,000,000 — an increase of 120%.

These figures indicate a marvelous growth on the part of Germany, when we consider that she entered the competition late, after the best of the markets had long been in the hands of her rivals. It is worth while to emphasize briefly the means by which she forged ahead so rapidly in the struggle. The use of scientific methods in every minute detail of production, transportation, and marketing seems to be the key to the enigma. German *Kultur* has been defined as "the application of a trained intelligence to the practical affairs of life": nowhere has this *Kultur* been more efficient than in the world of business and trade. The German producer has learned how to apply the latest developments of science or machinery to his methods and thus bring forth a product which can be put upon the market at a lower price than that asked by his competitors. Further, the marketing of German products has been intrusted to young men especially trained in technical schools and by foreign travel for the purpose. Thus in the first place, German goods are cheaper; in the second place, by means of coöperation between the expert salesmen and the manufacturer, they are made to fit the peculiar individual needs of the customers. The Germans have shown marvelous adaptability in their commercial methods. Where their British rivals, following traditional customs, offer standard wares in standard forms and demand instant payment through British banking houses, the Germans, after studying the markets, have offered wares made especially to suit the particular needs or peculiar styles of a selected region, and have conformed to the habits of the purchasing section in the matter of payment. The more complete satisfaction of the customer with less expensive and just as serviceable wares, both obtained by the application of scientific methods to each little detail of business, has brought a well-deserved success to German industries and foreign trade.

The Germans have been fully conscious of the significance of this industrial and commercial development. With this consciousness has grown a sense of their own importance in the world. Bismarck once remarked in the early days before he was chancellor: "I don't know how we Germans got the reputation for retiring modesty. There isn't a single man of us who doesn't think that he understands everything, from strategy to picking fleas off a dog, better than professionals who have devoted their lives to it." If the sense of their own importance had remained merely a personal characteristic of the individual Germans, it would not have been important enough to notice in this narrative; but when it became a national characteristic and began to influence the policy of the government, it grew to be a disturbing element in international affairs.

This industrial prosperity reacted upon the political situation in Germany to make her abandon her purely national aspirations and embark upon colonial enterprises.[1]

[1] See following chapter.

The widened horizon thus revealed to German thinkers led them to look forward to the establishment of Germany, not only as the chief power in continental Europe, but as one of the most important powers in world politics as well. As German colonies increased in number, size, and wealth, and as German commerce in German ships penetrated to the farthest seas, the German theorists argued that Germany must prepare herself at once to have a share in the world politics of the future. Her increase in population, her colonial expansion, her far-flung commercial interests demanded, in the opinion of an important body of her people, that she should take her place as an equal with the greatest in all questions of world dominion.

ii. *German Naval Increase*

The study of the situation in the light of their theories disclosed at once a fundamental weakness of Germany — her lack of a powerful navy. Until she could place upon the seas a navy equal ship for ship to that of the greatest naval power, she could not hope to make her wishes of weight in the solution of the great problems of world politics. A small but very earnest and energetic body of thinkers, inspired with this idea, set to work to foster a sentiment throughout Germany for a great increase in naval armaments.

The possibility of building up within a short time a navy equal to that of Great Britain did not at the time (1890) seem unduly difficult. Although in numbers Great Britain's ships were overwhelming, modern inventions had rendered most of them of an obsolete and useless type. The creation of Great Britain's present magnificent and efficient navy dates from the Naval Defense Act of 1889. In that Act, provision was made for the construction of 70 men-of-war, to include 10 battleships, within the next seven years. In his statement advocating this Act before the House of

Commons, Lord Hamilton, the first Lord of the Admiralty in Lord Salisbury's cabinet, announced the policy of the government to be an "establishment on such a scale that it should be at least equal to the naval strength of any two other nations." This two-power standard, as the policy was popularly called, was, however, at that time adopted tacitly against France and Russia, and its disposition was in waters where it would be available against the naval strength of these powers. Hence, had Germany begun an aggressive naval program in 1890, her efforts would actually have been welcomed by Great Britain, and she might have occupied by 1900 a most favorable position upon the seas. The force of the propaganda of the "big navy" advocates in Germany, however, did not bear fruit until the very end of the century.

The foundations of Germany's naval policy were laid by Admiral Tirpitz, appointed Secretary of State for the Navy in 1897. His first naval estimate, presented to the Reichstag in 1898, provided for 19 battleships, 8 coast defense vessels, and 42 cruisers. He had the utmost difficulty in securing the passage of this Act on March 28, 1898. It was evident that, if Germany were to make an effort at great naval strength, the sentiment in the Reichstag must be radically changed. To effect this change, prominent advocates of an aggressive naval building policy founded, April 30, 1898, a month after the passage of the naval act, the famous German Navy League (*Deutsche Flottenverein*). Prince Henry of Prussia, brother of the Emperor, became honorary president, Prince William of Wied the chairman, and the popular Grand Duke of Baden an honorary member. The purpose of the League was to arouse national interest in, and enthusiasm for, a great navy. By the distribution of literature, by lectures, bazaars, motion picture performances, and the like, the people, especially those of the younger generation, in the inland districts were made familiar with naval problems and naval ideals. By the beginning of 1900, less than two years after its foundation, the society had established 286 local branches and had 250,000 contributing members; by 1901, the local branches had increased to 1000 and the membership to 500,000; by 1904, the local branches had increased to 3600 and the membership to 635,000. From its very foundation it bent its main efforts along political lines, to bring such pressure upon the Reichstag that that body would grant the enormous credits asked for naval expansion. In 1900 it had its first notable success. January 25 of that year the most celebrated naval bill was introduced, providing that by 1902 the German fleet should consist of 38 battleships, 14 large and 38 light cruisers, with the necessary small ships of other kinds. The Bill was accompanied by a memorandum with the following striking paragraphs:

> "To protect Germany's sea trade and colonies, in the existing circumstances, there is only one means: Germany must have a battle fleet so strong that even for an adversary with the greatest sea power a war against it would involve such dangers as to imperil his own position in the world.
>
> "For this purpose it is not absolutely necessary that the German battle fleet should be as strong as that of the greatest naval Power, because a great naval Power will not, as a rule, be in a position to concentrate all its striking forces against us. But even if it should succeed in meeting us with considerable superiority of strength, the defeat of a strong German fleet would so substantially weaken the enemy, that in spite of a victory he might have obtained, his own position in the world would no longer be secured by an adequate fleet."

The words and attitude of the sovereign in his speeches during this same period showed how closely connected this movement for a great navy was with the national aspirations for a leading part in world politics. At the farewell dinner of his brother, Prince Henry of Prussia, when the latter was sailing with his squadron in 1897 to assume the German control of Kiauchau, the Emperor said:

"May every European out there, German merchants, and, above all, natives, clearly see that the German Michael has firmly planted his escutcheon with the imperial eagle in the soil in order to give protection to those who desire it. And may our countrymen out there, priests, or merchants, or whatever they may be, rest assured that the protection of the German Empire, in the form of the Emperor's warships, will steadfastly be vouchsafed them. But if anyone should venture to wound or injure us in our good right, then up and at him with your mailed fist."

Again in 1900, at the launching of the battleship *Wittelsbach*, he spoke even more plainly:

"The wave-beat knocks profoundly at our national gates and calls us as a great nation to maintain our place in the world, in other words to follow world policy. The ocean is indispensable for Germany's greatness, but the ocean also reminds us that neither on it nor across it in the distance can any great decision be again consummated without Germany and the German Emperor. It is not my opinion that our German people conquered and bled thirty years ago under the leadership of their princes in order to be pushed on one side when great and momentous foreign decisions are reached. Were that so there would once for all be an end of the world power of the German nation, and I am not going to allow that to happen. To use the fittest and if necessary the most drastic means to prevent this is not only my duty but my noblest privilege."

And upon another occasion during the same year he said:

"I hope that it will be granted to our German fatherland to become in the future as closely united, as powerful, and as authoritative as once the Roman world empire was, and that just as in old times they said, *Civis romanus sum*, one in the future need only to say, *Ich bin ein deutscher Burger*."

iii. *German Colonial Development*

With such encouragement from the head of their government Germans pushed forward their aggressive campaign in distant colonial fields. The occupation of the port of Kiauchau with 60 kilometers of land around it was followed

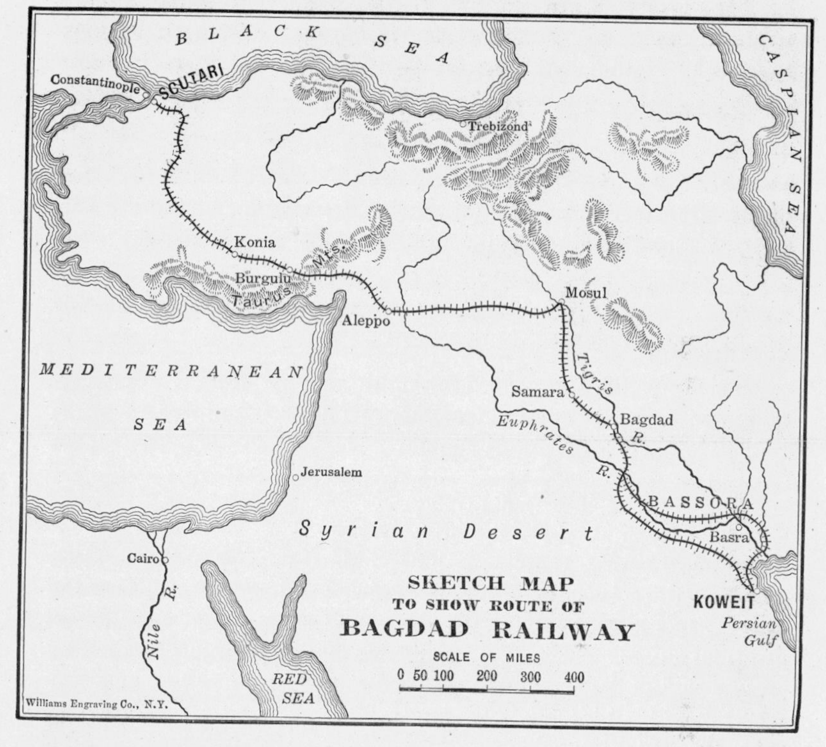

THE BAGDAD RAILWAY

1888. The Anatolian Railway, built from Scutari to Konia (420 miles) by German engineers in 1875 for the Turkish Government, was transferred to a German company.

1899. A concession was granted by Abdul Hamid, Sultan of Turkey, to William II, Emperor of Germany, "my only friend in Europe," for an extension of the Anatolian Railway across Asiatic Turkey to the Persian Gulf. In the same year Great Britain made a treaty with a sheik at the head of the Persian Gulf, by virtue of which she laid claim to Koweit.

1903. Germany made proposals to Great Britain, Russia, and France, for participation in the construction of the proposed line. These offers were declined by the three powers, and the construction was begun by Germany alone.

1904. Track was laid to Burgulu, in the Taurus Mountains (125 miles) and tunneling through the mountains was begun. In October, work was suspended, and was not again taken up until late in 1909.

1911. Great Britain, who had begun to regret her refusal of Germany's offer of 1903, and who had made a number of diplomatic obstructions, agreed to a settlement whereby she would build the proposed line through Bassorah to the Persian Gulf.

1912. Lines were laid eastward from Aleppo to the Euphrates valley, and westward and southward from Mosul.

1914. Line was laid an undetermined distance north from Bagdad. Since 1914 no official reports as to progress have been published. According to newspaper reports the tunnel through the Taurus Mountains has been completed, and all track laid except for a distance of eighty-five miles in the Mosul-Samara section. Below Bagdad, in the Bassorah province, two routes have been proposed, but so far construction has not been begun on either of them. It is certain that the road has played an important strategic rôle in the campaigns in Mesopotamia.

at once by a demand for extensive railroad, mineral, and financial concessions in the great Chinese province of Shantung. The colonial territories were exploited thoroughly, and German financiers began to seek important concessions in Turkish Asia Minor and Mesopotamia, a region practically untouched by European enterprise.

This last move was of the utmost political importance. The first indication of German intentions came in 1899, when a concession for the construction of a railroad from Konia to the Persian Gulf was granted to Germany. German-owned lines had previously been built from the Asia Minor coast opposite Constantinople to Angora (1888) and from Eski-Shehir (a half-way point between Constantinople and Angora) to Konia, so that the proposed line, 1700 miles long, would make a solid German-owned railroad from Constantinople to Bagdad, passing under the Bosphorus by tunnel and throwing out important spur lines to Smyrna, to Alexandretta, and to Aleppo, Damascus, and Mecca. "The network of German railroads," writes Sarolea, "will radiate from Mecca to Constantinople, and from Smyrna to the Persian Gulf. One terminus will be within twelve hours of Egypt, another terminus will be within four days of Bombay." Although access to the prosperous and productive regions of Asia Minor and Mesopotamia with the possibility of a fast overland route for the wares of India was a great triumph for German initiative and enterprise, the railroad concessions were more important in giving Germany a political foothold in Turkey. Asia Minor and Mesopotamia as a German sphere of influence were by far the richest prize that had fallen to Germany's lot. The exultation of Germans was boisterous. They spoke of *unser Bagdad*, and of the BBB (the "Berlin, Byzantium, Bagdad" line). They looked forward confidently to the economic and political domination of this enormously rich region. Some German writers emphasized the strong military advantages such a position would give

Germany in the event of a war against Great Britain, for she might launch a force against Egypt and the Suez Canal with good prospect of success.

In the ensuing years Germany sedulously developed her position in Turkey. German influences penetrated into every branch of Turkish government and administration; German financial assistance laid Turkey under great obligations; German officers reorganized, equipped, and drilled the Turkish army. In every way with painstaking care Germany consolidated and strengthened her advantageous position in Turkey. German interests in that region were, it was realized, of greater importance than German interests anywhere else in the world.

iv. *Effect of German Activities upon Great Britain*

Great Britain could at the beginning of the new century look with equanimity upon the foreign situation. Her vast empire stretched around the world; her great self-governing colonies were bound to her, not by force, but by the ties of patriotic veneration and of self-interest; her merchant marine was the greatest carrier of the world's commerce, yielding steady and enormous profits; her investments were scattered in every land, making her stock exchange the most accurate barometer of the condition of the world's business; and her fleet, showing the result of Salisbury's naval scheme adopted in 1889, was composed of the latest type of warships and was superior in strength to those of any two powers. By her policy of non-interference in the affairs of Europe she had, it is true, receded from her formerly commanding position in continental councils, but in return many of the statesmen felt that by keeping aloof she had actually increased the political value of her attitude upon international issues. That she had followed a policy of "splendid isolation" for a generation was no guarantee to the powers of Europe that she would continue her policy indefinitely, and the strength of her huge fleet might turn the scales in any continental dispute. She seemed to be able at any time to tip the balance of power by her weight one way or another as suited her vital interests.

In domestic affairs the Irish Question had for a time usurped all public interest. Gladstone, aged eighty-two years, became prime minister in 1892 for the fourth time at the head of a victorious coalition of Liberals and Home Rulers. Early in 1893 he introduced the Home Rule bill, essentially the same as the one which had split his party and had been defeated in the parliament seven years before. Again the aged prime minister was the center of a bitter political fight, but this time he triumphed in the Commons by a majority of 34 votes. A week afterwards the bill was thrown out by the House of Lords by the crushing vote of 419 to 41. A year later, after finding various of his attempts at reform balked by the opposition of the conservative House of Lords, he resigned his portfolio into the hands of Lord Rosebery (Liberal). In June, 1895, Lord Rosebery's ministry, defeated in the Commons upon a minor issue, resigned. Lord Salisbury, the conservative leader in the House of Lords, became prime minister and in the ensuing general elections secured an overwhelming conservative majority to support his policies. Salisbury remained prime minister until December of 1905. It was during this decade of his ministry that Great Britain, aroused by the increasing menace of German naval armaments, abandoned her policy of isolation and entered actively into the arena of international diplomacy in Europe to insure her own protection.

Although British merchants had long felt keenly the rivalry of Germany in commerce, it is doubtful whether the inroads upon British commerce alone could have aroused the intense suspicion of Germany which became noticeable shortly after the beginning of the new century. The arguments that successful competition in the world's markets must be due to better methods, and that therefore British merchants should withhold their complaints and improve their methods in order to gain business against German competition, are too obvious an answer to any ill-feeling excited by German success. When, however, to the German success in the world's markets was joined the German attempt to create a great navy, British public opinion at once took alarm.

To understand the immediate and startling effect of Germany's policy upon British feeling, it is necessary to appreciate the nature of Great Britain's attitude towards its fleet. Great Britain's fleet has been her only powerful form of armament. Unlike the continental states, Great Britain has not maintained a large standing army recruited by one or another variety of compulsory service. Her armies, as for example those used in the South African Wars and in distant India, have been raised by voluntary enlistment. Her navy has been, therefore, both her defensive and her offensive arm. Furthermore, her geographical situation is such that this navy has been more necessary for her than any navy for any other power. The population of the British Isles has long outgrown the food production of the land, so that the people are absolutely dependent upon control of the sea lanes to insure them against starvation. It has been said that, were the sea wholly closed to Great Britain for a single week, she would be starved into surrender. From the British side, therefore, the maintenance of a navy of overwhelming power has been regarded as a logical and inevitable result of the situation and necessities of the British Isles. No other country has the same situation and necessities; ergo, no other nation has the moral right to maintain a navy of a power great enough to challenge that of Great Britain. The people, then, at the same time that they insisted upon their logical rights to a great navy, have denied — or at least have been extremely suspicious concerning — the right of any other nation to have an equally great navy.

. Von Tirpitz's remarkable memorandum accompanying the German naval bill of 1900 was the fuel that started the flame. The statements that "*the German battle fleet should be as strong as the greatest naval Power*," and that "*to protect Germany's sea trade and colonies, in the existing circumstances, there is only one means: Germany must have a battle fleet so strong that even for an adversary with the greatest sea power, a war against it would involve such dangers as to imperil his own position in the world*," pointed, of course, *directly* to Great Britain. The Germans — from their side, with reason — felt that their merchant marine and their widely separated colonies would always be held at the sufferance of Great Britain, so long as Great Britain was in a position to take advantage of any issue to declare war, sweep the German commerce from the seas, and isolate the mother country from her colonies. The British, on their side, laid stress upon the purely defensive nature of their armament, and upon their continental diplomacy, and with fast-growing resentment saw ship after ship laid down for the new German navy.

At this critical period came also for the British people a realization of the full significance of German activities in various parts of the world. The world-imperialistic policy of the restless and progressive German Emperor became a feature in the British outlook. Germany's seizure of Kiauchau and her concessions in the Shantung province, her Samoan islands, her recent African empire, and especially her Bagdad railroad, became to the aroused and suspicious British people conclusive evidence of German attempts to found a world empire which should rival and perhaps overthrow that of Great Britain. No man would, of course, maintain aloud that Great Britain was the only nation with a right to a policy of world empire, yet there was undoubtedly a feeling that Great Britain's preëminent success in colonial government qualified her especially for world empire in contrast to the upstart and inexperienced German state. The British have laid their antagonism to German plans to other causes, to be sure, but the fundamental causes lay in the menace of the increasing German navy, in the inroads by German merchants upon British trade, and in the rivalry of a prospective German world-empire to the already established British world-empire.

v. *Diplomatic Situation in Great Britain and France leading up to the Entente Cordiale*

The succession of Edward VII to the throne of England introduced a new element into the situation. Queen Victoria, who ascended the English throne in 1837, died January 22, 1901. She had been throughout her whole reign an ideal constitutional sovereign, yielding her power wholly into the hands of her ministers. Her colorless character did much to establish firmly the supremacy of parliament and of parliamentary ministers in the British system of government. Her son, who succeeded to the throne under the title of Edward VII, was at the time (1901) a man of sixty-one years of age. His mother had jealously and short-sightedly prevented him from participating in affairs of state. His public activities had been confined to sports, as horse-racing and yachting, and to representing his mother upon ceremonial occasions. He had traveled widely in America, India, and upon the European continent, and was especially familiar with and fond of Paris and the French people. Though not until recent years allowed access to state papers, or any share in the policy of the nation he was to rule, he had gained an intimate knowledge of his people and of the people on the continent. He was much broader in his sympathies and more cosmopolitan than the average Englishman.

When Edward VII accepted the pledges of loyalty from

the leaders of his government, he announced that he intended to follow the policy of the late Queen and to govern as a constitutional monarch; but events soon showed that he was not of a character that could entirely obliterate itself before its agents. Edward VII saw opportunities to be of real service to the state even while continuing as a constitutional monarch under the advice of his ministers. As soon as the Boer war ended — and he is credited with having had much to do with its speedy decision and with the very liberal terms of peace granted — Edward VII turned his attention to the possibilities of using his personal influence to strengthen Great Britain's position abroad. The German menace was monthly becoming more alarming. It was essential that Great Britain take immediate steps to fortify herself. Across the channel was one nation which had felt the hand of Germany in the past and still smarted under the humiliation of that defeat. It was to France, then, that Edward VII turned for aid in the threatening foreign situation.

1. Internal Conditions in France

In France the bitter factions into which politicians had divided during the heat of the Dreyfus case had resulted, in 1900, in the formation of a powerful coalition, known as the "Bloc," in the Chamber of Deputies. The "Bloc" was composed of Liberals holding to various shades of Socialist and Radical Republican principles. It had gained control of the government, and its leader, Waldeck-Rousseau, had become prime minister. From that time until the present, the "Bloc" has retained control of the government.

Waldeck-Rousseau sounded the key-note of the "Bloc's" policy in a political speech at Toulouse (October, 1900). The Dreyfus trial had revealed to discerning statesmen that the Catholic Church in France had been the secret and powerful ally of the military party and of the anti-Dreyfusites. Looking back still further, these statesmen recognized that the Catholic Church had been the insidious enemy of the republic since its establishment. For a generation, since 1871, the Catholic Church had thrown all its enormous influence against popular government. Realizing these conditions, Waldeck-Rousseau opened his political fight against the most potent agencies of the Catholic cause, the religious orders or "congregations." He pointed out the enormous increase in membership, wealth, and activity of these congregations. The number of nuns had increased 60,000 between 1877 and 1900; the number of monks in 1900 in France was 200,000; the value of the property held by the orders had grown from $10,000,000 in 1860 to $140,000,000 in 1880 and to $200,000,000 in 1900; the teaching and preaching activities had widened with the increase of the orders in numbers and wealth.

In July of 1901 Waldeck-Rousseau introduced his Law of Associations, intended to be a preliminary step toward checking the Catholic influences in the state. This law provided that all "congregations" must have definite authority for existence or formation from the state; and that no teaching could be carried on except by "congregations" which had been duly authorized. The Catholics fought this law bitterly. In the elections of 1902 the two parties struggled to gain the advantage. The "Bloc" was returned with a comfortable majority. Combes, who succeeded Waldeck-Rousseau as prime minister after the elections, applied the law vigorously throughout the next two years. In 1904 the "Bloc" increased the severity of the government's attitude toward the church by the passage of a law providing that all teaching by religious orders, authorized or unauthorized, should cease within ten years. Other events intensified the bitter feeling between the government and the church. For example, in April of 1904 the President of France, M. Loubet, paid an official visit to the King of Italy to celebrate the reconciliation between France and Italy; the Pope protested vigorously to France and to the other Catholic powers against French recognition of the "usurper" King of Italy; the French people flamed with indignation at what they regarded as an unwarranted interference with their national affairs.

Impelled by the continued opposition of the authorities of the church, and supported by the opinion of the mass of the French people, the government finally took the decisive step of introducing and passing a bill providing for the complete separation of church and state. The relations between the two institutions had, it will be remembered, existed for a century under the provisions of Napoleon's Concordat of 1801, in accordance with which the state and the Papacy coöperated in religious affairs in the following way: (*a*) the state appointed archbishops and bishops with the consent of the Pope; (*b*) the bishop appointed the priests with the consent of the state; (*c*) The state paid the salaries of the clergy, both lower and higher; (*d*) the state, which had since 1789 held possession of all ecclesiastical property, such as churches, parish houses, seminaries, etc., retained ownership, but placed this property at the disposal of the church authorities. The law providing for the separation of church and state was, of course, first of all an abrogation of the Concordat. In general its further significant provisions were as follows: (*a*) the republic ceased to pay the salaries of the clergy, and likewise ceased to have any control over ecclesiastical appointments; (*b*) the republic was willing to establish a system of pensions for the existing priests who had been appointed under the Concordat; (*c*) the government, refusing to recognize the superior rights of any religion, proposed to give the use of its ecclesiastical property to new bodies, formed for the purpose by communicants in each district and known as *associations cultuelles* (Associations of Worship). The law was passed December 9, 1905.

The Pope unqualifiedly condemned this law. Succeeding elections proved that the French people, Catholic though the mass of them were in religion, supported the action of their government. The opposition of the Pope resulted in a new law passed by the French government January 2, 1907, taking away what privileges had been granted to the church by the law of 1905 and providing that the use of ecclesiastical property should be regulated by regular contracts between the priests and the local civil authorities. This law of 1907 permitted the churches to remain open — a most important point — and thus assured to the masses of the French people the opportunity to attend religious service. Inasmuch as the Pope never specifically forbade his priests to make these contracts, this system gradually became accepted as a *modus operandi*. The resulting situation is peculiar: church and state are definitely separated; the Pope has never approved the separation, still maintaining that the French government had no right to annul the Concordat; actual religious services continue to be held in the churches, possession of which is granted by regular civil contract between the individual priests and the local authorities.

2. Foreign Policy of France

While this struggle in domestic politics had been going on, the foreign policy of the government took a new turn. Gabriel Hanotaux had been minister of foreign affairs in France from 1894 until 1898, practically continuously. He had forwarded French colonial expansion, especially in Africa, and had tended to accept in good faith the conciliatory approaches of the German Emperor. He was openly and outspokenly suspicious of and hostile to Great Britain. In the change of ministry in June of 1898, Hanotaux was replaced by Théophile Delcassé. With Delcassé's advent to the foreign office, the spirit of French policy changed radically. Delcassé proceeded to direct the foreign office with a view to securing France's international position against any menace from without, especially from Germany. To accomplish this result, he needed friends in Europe. Confronted almost immediately with the Fashoda issue, he settled this in 1899 by a colonial agreement with Great Britain delimiting the respective spheres of Great Britain and France in northern Africa. He attempted to consolidate the relations between Russia and France by personal visits to St. Petersburg in 1899 and 1901. He made it a cardinal point of his policy to allay the hostility that had so long existed between France and Italy as a result of the French protectorate over Tunis and the French championship of the cause of the Pope when the Italians seized Rome. By notes and verbal assurances during the years 1900, 1901, and 1902 he contrived to reach a satisfactory understanding with the Italian government, the main features of which were: (*a*) that Italy would regard her engagements of the Triple Alliance as purely defensive in nature and would in no case become either the instrument or the auxiliary of aggressive measures against France; (*b*) that France would allow Italy free hand in furthering Italian interests throughout Tripoli; and (*c*) that Italy would take no steps to prevent the accomplishment of French policy in Morocco. This Franco-Italian understanding was a special diplomatic triumph for France because, in the first place, it secured France's safety in the western Mediterranean; in the second place, it removed one possible objector to the development of French influence in Morocco; and in the third place — perhaps most important — it distinctly weakened one important link in the chain of the Triple Alliance forged by Bismarck to curb France.

Having settled the Fashoda issue, strengthened the friendly relations between France and Russia, and established ties of amity and interest with Italy, Delcassé was still anxious to secure France's position on the continent by further international understandings. It is no evidence of a purposeful anti-German policy that Delcassé believed that France had to direct her foreign relations to meet the situation created by the Triple Alliance. It was an open secret that one object of that alliance was to isolate France in Europe: it was the duty of a French foreign minister to do everything possible to rescue France from such intended isolation. Much had been done by putting a new vitality into the relations with Russia and by removing some of the hostility of Italy: success would be complete if Great Britain could be induced to enter continental politics on the side of France. Hence, Delcassé was willing to hold the door open to the British advances.

It is hard for us now to realize the enormous difficulties in the way of such friendship. Not only were there centuries of opposition, jealousy, and suspicion between the two states, but within a half dozen years their peoples had been inflamed to the point of war against each other. Only the peculiar crisis in continental affairs for France and in naval and world-empire policies for Great Britain made it possible to surmount the difficulties. The two countries were drawn into an understanding by their common fear and suspicion of Germany, not by any natural instincts of friendship.

vi. *The Formation of the Entente Cordiale*

Edward VII of Great Britain took the initiative in an attempt to draw the two countries closer together. Although as Prince of Wales he had been a well-known and well-liked figure in France, it took no little audacity and courage to make an official visit to that country in the character of King. In 1903 Edward VII made the visit to President Loubet of France. Among a small part of the people the passions engendered by the Fashoda crisis revived, but the crowds as a whole, at first merely respectful, soon showed noticeable courtesy and sympathy for the familiar figure of the King. Two months later President Loubet returned the visit in London. The basis for peaceful "conversations" was thus established. For eight months negotiations proceeded and finally, April 8, 1904, a definite agreement, commonly called the *Entente Cordiale*, was signed.

This agreement settled permanently all past and outstanding issues that existed between France and Great Britain due to their conflicting colonial claims. France on her part recognized British special interests in Egypt and agreed not to embarrass the British government by demanding that a definite date be set for the evacuation of that country; Great Britain on her part granted France a free hand in developing her policy in Morocco; and both parties promised to support each other diplomatically for the execution of the agreement. Great Britain was thus given a free hand in Egypt, and France in Morocco.

The *Entente Cordiale*, be it noted, was entirely different in kind from the Dual Alliance or the Triple Alliance. Whereas the Alliances were of the nature of defensive military conventions between the contracting powers, the *Entente Cordiale* was merely an understanding between two powers on certain issues which had long been a source of conflict. The *Entente Cordiale* did not provide for military measures, either of defense or of offense, and by its very nature was not specifically directed againt any country, countries, or coalition. It did have, however, a wider importance than that afforded by the mere settlement of territorial claims. It marked the end of Great Britain's policy of isolation and the beginning of a period of active participation in European politics; it freed France from her subservience to Germany and gave her the courage to assume the initiative in Europe and to maintain such initiative even in the face of German opposition. It insured Great Britain against trouble with France during a possible Anglo-German conflict; and conversely, it insured France against trouble with Great Britain during a possible Franco-German conflict.

From the German side, the sudden change in the political field was regarded with great alarm. It was the first definite setback which German diplomacy had received since the establishment of the empire in 1871. William II's policy, so successful up to 1900, had suddenly been checked by the entrance of a new and unexpected factor, Great Britain, in the continental situation. To German diplomats, *Ententes* were the preliminaries to *Alliances*, and they regarded the *Dual Entente* (Russia and France) and the *Entente Cordiale* (Great Britain and France) as the first steps in the formation of a hostile coalition which would threaten and perhaps overthrow the coveted German leadership on the continent. German foreign statesmanship, which had been passive and acquiescent so long as affairs went as it desired, now suddenly became transformed. Germany became aggressive and militant after the formation of the *Entente Cordiale*, suspicious of every move upon the European board.

CHAPTER II

COLONIAL ENTERPRISES

To understand European development during the period we have now reached, we must consider the colonial enterprises entered upon by the individual European nations at the close of the nineteenth and the opening of the twentieth century. The history of Europe in recent years often has hinged upon such remote points as a railroad in Asia Minor, or a protectorate in northern Africa, or a harbor in Korea. The improvement in modern methods of production, transportation, and communication has bound all the world closer together and has resulted in such an expansion of interests that the history of one small section of the world is intimately involved with that of all other sections. Enterprises in different colonial fields have been responsible for most of the crises in European politics since 1900.

A. EUROPEAN ECONOMIC CONDITIONS WHICH FAVORED COLONIAL ENTERPRISES

During the last years of the nineteenth century all Europe participated in an industrial "boom." Although there were single years, of course, when the march of prosperity halted, figures taken at very brief intervals show a continuous increase of economic activities. All the great states enjoyed peace. The development of the means of production, transportation, and communication, which had in recent years been enormously improved over the facilities of past centuries, proceeded at an accelerated pace. The production of coal which had become a most essential element in the driving of modern engines, increased by huge amounts; the mining of iron, which was wrought by modern methods of manufacture in new forms and huge quantities, was carried out on an unprecedented scale; railroad tracks and equipment were extended; steamship lines were led to supply themselves with more and more modern vessels to cope with the growing demand for transportation. The figures of export and import business showed annual increases running into the hundreds of millions of dollars.

By the selection of a few statistics on these fundamental activities in the three most prosperous states in Europe, Great Britain, France, and Germany, we can indicate how remarkable these increases were. The annual production of coal increased in these three countries by 155,000,000 tons in the fifteen years from 1885 to 1900; the quantity of iron mined annually in the same period increased by 9,000,000 tons; the length of the railroads by 15,000 miles and their financial receipts by 500,000,000 of dollars; the tonnage of merchant vessels by 6,200,000 tons; and the gross imports and exports by the stupendous sum of 2,600,000,000 of dollars. No previous period of the same length had been characterized by any such expansion of economic interests. For example, if we consider the period adjacent to that from 1885 to 1900, the statistics from 1870 to 1885 show the following increases: annual coal production, 68,000,000 tons; annual iron mining, 4,500,000 tons; railway construction, 13,000 miles, and railway receipts 250,000,000 of dollars; gross imports and exports, 675,000,000.[1] From the comparison of the figures given with the two periods of similar length it can be seen that the general increase along the economic lines indicated was more than twice as great during the fifteen years from 1885 to 1900 as it was during the fifteen years just previous.

Among the most important of the political effects of this

[1] These figures are approximate. They are based on the statistics collected by the National Monetary Commission. U. S. Senate Document # 578. 1910.

prosperity was the impetus given to colonization. The great states which profited most through economic activities were inspired thereby to reach out and acquire all the unclaimed territory they could discover. The states of Europe participated during these fifteen years in an undignified scramble for colonies, during which bitter antagonisms were at times excited.

The causes which connected the material prosperity of these countries with their desire for colonial expansion were chiefly three in number. In the first place, each state sought new and profitable markets. The modern methods of manufacture enabled a country to produce more than it could use within its own boundaries and among its own people. Its prosperity could be increased largely if it could control a definite market for its surplus products. Each one, therefore, saw in its colonies a present and future possibility for the marketing of its manufactured products. In the second place, the modern method of manufacture demanded more raw material than could be procured within the boundaries of any one state. In some cases, too, raw material of a kind not to be found within the state was largely used in its factories. Hence, European states sought colonies which were rich in natural resources, to be developed for the manufacturing needs of the mother state. And in the third place, certain of the great states sought in colonies an outlet for their surplus population. In those countries where the population outgrew the economic opportunities, the people naturally emigrated where they might live with material comfort. Thus Germany, whose population increased by leaps and bounds after 1870, saw her overflow emigrating to the United States or to South American countries where they fell under the allegiance of alien governments. The strong argument for the acquisition of colonies lay in the fact that a surplus population might be encouraged to settle in such colonies and remain under the allegiance of their home state.

B. THE FIELD FOR COLONIZATION

i. *Africa*

At this period when the definite movement for colonial expansion began, one continent at the very doors of Europe was in great part unclaimed. Africa was commonly called the Dark Continent, not only because of its dark races, but because of the dense ignorance of most Europeans concerning its geography and resources. Although Egypt had been the seat of an ancient civilization and Africa north of the vast Sahara desert had formed part of the Roman Empire, and although during the fifteenth and sixteenth centuries intrepid Portuguese and English navigators sailed along the African coasts trading with the savage tribes, no serious attempts at colonization in Africa had been made previous to the nineteenth century. The African continent seemed to offer no advantages: it had few good harbors; it was drained by few large navigable rivers; its coastal regions were commonly low and (for Europeans) plague-ridden; its inhabitants were black savages, seized and exported by thousands annually in the seventeenth and eighteenth centuries to be sold as slaves. At the beginning of the nineteenth century, after the slave trade was suppressed, interest in Africa died down, for the trade in ivory, gold, and gums had been inconsiderable beside that in slaves. At this time (1815), France had a slender foothold on the coast near the Senegal river; Portugal was established in lower Guinea on the west coast and in a district opposite to the island of Madagascar on the east coast, and laid claim to extensive unknown hinterlands; and Great Britain had taken Cape Colony, at the extreme tip of the continent, from the Dutch during the Napoleonic wars and was holding it as a valuable halfway station on the route to India. All of central Africa was unexplored and, except for Portugal's vague and unrecognized rights, unclaimed. Pictures of the hippopotamus, the elephant, or the black man decorated the early maps to conceal the ignorance of the geographers.

In the third quarter of the nineteenth century a renewed interest in Africa was excited by the accounts of a group of explorers. Livingstone and Stanley in Central Africa, Rohlfs, Schweinfurth, and Nachtigal in Southern Morocco, Sahara, and the Soudan, and Du Chaillu in West Africa published books which stimulated the imagination and awakened the avarice of Europeans. The interior of Africa was revealed, not as a barren desert or as an impenetrable forest, but as a plateau watered by great and navigable rivers and lakes and rich in natural resources. By the year 1875, after the results of the chief explorers had been made known, the chances for profitable colonial acquisitions in Africa had begun to interest European governments. Between that date and the end of the century, so rapidly did those governments act that all of Africa was accurately mapped into colonies, protectorates, or spheres of influence of European states.

ii. *Asia*

Halfway around the world lay another continent which offered to the land-hungering states opportunities to acquire colonies. Asia, however, presented a problem entirely different from that of Africa. Asia had been the original cradle of civilization. Certain of its people had been highly civilized when the Europeans were barbarians. They possessed an immensely rich and well-cultivated country. They were industrious, peaceful, and contented. They had for centuries willfully isolated themselves from the rest of the world, supremely confident of the value and perfection of their own civilization. In their isolation, barred from a knowledge of the progress of the restless enterprising nations in the western world, they had stagnated. They lost the ability to progress. Their civilization revolved in the same circle for generation after generation. They revered the past instead of aspiring for the future.

In relatively modern times the European trader in his search for new markets and for new sources of wealth was attracted to the East. He sought to break through the barriers raised by the Eastern people. By force and intrigue he established trading stations, protectorates, dependencies, and spheres of influence. Throughout the densely populated regions of southern Asia, Portuguese, Dutch, French, and English struggled during the sixteenth and seventeenth centuries for a monopoly of the immensely rich trade with these regions. During the eighteenth century this struggle evolved itself into a duel between France and Great Britain for supremacy in India. This duel France lost. At the beginning of the nineteenth century Great Britain was firmly established in the rich province of Bengal, and in the district around Madras, in a position to extend her acquisitions still further as opportunity offered. To the east of India the Dutch had during this period strengthened their hold in the islands adjoining the Malay Archipelago. After the disastrous period of the Napoleonic wars they retained Java, Sumatra, Celebes, the Molucca (or Spice) islands, and portions of Borneo, comprising altogether an area of more than 700,000 square miles with a native population of approximately 30,000,000. In northern Asia, Russia had crept gradually to the sea over the barren plains of Siberia. Off the southeast coast, Spain held the Philippine islands.

During the first three-quarters of the nineteenth century the Asiatic colonial movements in which we are most interested were those which affected China and Japan. These two empires were typical of the isolation policies of the East. China, firm in her belief in her own superiority, held no intercourse with foreign nations. She had no ambassadors at the European courts: she desired no ambassadors from those courts to her own. Her empire was three times the size of England, France, and Germany combined; the population (although accurate figures are not obtainable) was over 200,000,000; her land produced everything needed for her people. China rejected foreign trade as unnecessary and undesirable. The Japanese Empire consisted of an archipelago off the east coast of Asia, consisting of four large islands and some thousands of small ones. The country was mountainous, much of it volcanic in origin, and ill suited for agriculture. The government was feudal in character. The Emperor was nominally the supreme sovereign; the Shogun, as personal representative of the Emperor, had control of the executive, legislative, and administrative powers. In the sixteenth and seventeenth centuries a few missionaries and traders had reached Japan, but their innovations had been so seriously resented that in 1638 the Shogun adopted a policy of complete isolation. The foreigners were expelled and Japan hermetically sealed from the outside world. Thus she remained for two centuries.

The opening of China and Japan to western influences came at about the same time, but had markedly different results. China had allowed European trade in one port, Canton, under severe irritating restrictions. Through this port the English traders imported enormous quantities of opium. The Chinese government, realizing the baneful effects of the drug upon its people, forbade its importation and in 1837 took active measures to stop the traffic. Their agent destroyed enormous quantities of opium in Canton by force and expelled many of the British merchants who had been employed in the business. Great Britain's interest in maintaining the sale of opium, which was grown in India, led her to take active hostile measures against China. Her fleet fired upon the Chinese fleet, blockaded Canton, and seized the ports of Amoy, Ningpo, Shanghai, and Nanking. In 1842 the Chinese government sued for peace. By the

Treaty of Nanking, China agreed to pay a heavy indemnity, to recognize the official status of British representatives, to cede Hongkong (an island at the mouth of the Canton river) and to open to commerce the ports of Amoy, Foochow, Ningpo, and Shanghai. Other nations now hastened to take advantage of the increased facilities for commerce. France, Belgium, Prussia, the Netherlands, Portugal, and the United States shared in the commercial opportunity. Within a few years, however, the hostility of the Chinese government and people gave rise to fresh dissatisfaction among the Europeans. Great Britain, France, Russia, and the United States jointly requested that a Chinese minister be appointed to negotiate a settlement of the questions at issue. Upon the refusal of the Chinese government, French and British gunboats demolished the forts protecting Tientsin and, in 1858, took that city. Not until two years later were the difficulties adjusted. In 1860 the Chinese Emperor agreed to pay another indemnity, to receive a British ambassador and British consuls at the open ports, and to open Tientsin to foreign commerce. Chinese hostility, inspired from the government, did not wane, however, during the following years. A few more ports were opened to commerce, but China continued to resent the presence of the "foreign devils" in its boundaries. The government made no attempt to adapt itself to the new conditions or to alter its course of civilization.

The opening of Japan to communication with the outside world came at this same period. On behalf of the United States government Commodore Perry in 1853 landed in Japan and demanded that the barbarous and piratical treatment of Americans shipwrecked on Japanese coasts be stopped, and that two ports be opened to American ships for coaling and refitting in case of necessity. Being received by the Shogun, Perry presented these demands to him under the impression that he was the sovereign. Perry accompanied his statement with the threat of war in the event of refusal. The Shogun agreed to the more immediate demands, but asked time to consider the question of opening relations with a foreign state. Perry thereupon sailed away, promising to return a year later. In 1854, upon his return, he negotiated a treaty with the Shogun by which two ports were opened to American ships.

In itself, the opening up of relations with the outside world seems of little importance, but this event precipitated a civil war in Japan. The Mikado had not been consulted by the Shogun on this policy. He and his supporters, with certain of the ancient nobility of Japan, opposed the Shogun and encouraged anti-foreign sentiment. The Shogun, however, impressed with the necessity of admitting foreigners in order to learn the secrets of their guns and ships, continued to open ports to foreign states. Thus Hakodate, Yokohama, Nagasaki, and Kobe were during the next few years opened to commerce. Popular sentiment, encouraged by the Mikado's opposition, broke out in riots in which, in 1862, an Englishman by the name of Richardson was killed. Great Britain took immediate action. Her warships bombarded Kagoshima, one of the most conservative strongholds, and in the year 1864 bombarded Shimonoseki.

The effect produced by British guns was miraculous. The conservative circles veered around immediately to the policy of the Shogun. They realized, as had the Shogun, that in order to secure their own safety thay must place themselves on an equal footing in a military way with the western powers. They must learn the secrets of the foreigners. They had before them the example of China, who by continued hostility to the "foreign devils" and to the introduction of foreign methods had proved an easy prey and had lost by force valuable ports and territory. A distinct change in policy was made more easy by the deaths of the Shogun (1866) and the Mikado (1867) within a year of each other. The new Mikado, Mutsuhito, ascending the throne in 1867, emerged from the retirement in which Mikados had been accustomed to live, selected Yedo (renamed Tokyo) as his capital, forced the new Shogun to resign his office, and prepared to inaugurate an "enlightened rule." The power of the Shogun was broken in a short but severe civil war. The feudal princes patriotically surrendered their traditional powers into the hands of the Mikado. Serfdom was abolished. With his absolute and autocratic powers the Mikado undertook to revolutionize Japanese institutions.

Japanese progress since 1870 has been the marvel of the world. Japanese students penetrated to all parts of the western world, scrutinizing and studying the industrial and commercial methods and the political institutions in the foremost countries. In 1872 an army was organized after German methods and European officers were imported to train it. The foundations of a modern navy were laid and dockyards and arsenals built for its repair and equipment. A university of modern type was founded at Tokyo, foreign professors invited to teach, and the general educational system throughout the country reorganized. A telegraph and postal system was introduced, railway construction begun and speedily developed, and large manufactories built, equipped, and put into operation. Huge industrial towns sprang up. Newspapers and books multiplied rapidly. The legal codes, both civil and criminal, were thoroughly revised in accordance with the best European models. And when, partly as a result of the notable progress along material lines, the people were inspired to petition the Mikado for a constitution, that liberal-minded monarch sent a commission abroad to make an exhaustive study of foreign constitutions and their operation, and in 1889 published the document, drawn up in accordance with the reports of his commission and showing clearly the influences of the United States, Germany, and Great Britain. In 1890 the first Japanese parliament met.

The transformation of Japan profoundly altered the political situation in the Far East. Japan, by virtue of her modern institutions and, it must be confessed, especially by virtue of her army and navy, took her place as an equal in the family of nations. Not only was it no longer conceivable that she should be a prey to the colonizing rapacity of European states, but she herself quickly developed colonial ambitions of her own. Her large population, some 35,000,000, was crowded into a series of narrow islands, only one-sixth of whose soil was fit for cultivation. Her factories began to turn out manufactured products faster than her people could use them. The demand for raw material rapidly increased. Thus the same motives which actuated European states, desire for colonies as a market for products, as a dwelling place for surplus population, and as a source of raw material for her factories, actuated Japan. She became a competitor in the race, with the advantage of proximity to the Asiatic field.

C. STATUS OF THE EUROPEAN NATIONS AT THE BEGINNING OF THE COLONIAL RIVALRY: GREAT BRITAIN, FRANCE, GERMANY, ITALY, RUSSIA.

In the rivalry among the European states for colonial acquisition in Africa and Asia, Great Britain at the beginning had a decided advantage. She had the prestige of having already established the greatest colonial empire the world had ever known. Her colonial governmental system was adaptable and operated with efficiency and little apparent friction. Her navy, more than twice as powerful as that of any other state, insured the safety of her commerce and communications. Her national income, already greater than that of any of her rivals, was increasing yearly by huge amounts. Her surplus population, emigrating to her colonies, built up in distant lands strong communities of English speech and sentiment. In contrast to the British colonial status at the beginning of this period, France had but a single large colony, Algeria. The immense empire over the seas which she had once possessed had been almost entirely lost. Germany entering late into a national unified life, had acquired no colonies. In Germany, Bismarck had been so completely devoted to the creation of a united Germany and the fostering of a national spirit and prosperity that he had up to this period vigorously opposed colonial expansion. In Italy, although the internal difficulties, especially the financial situation, kept the government from embarking on a costly and possibly hazardous colonial policy, her statesmen cast covetous eyes upon the north shore of Africa. Russia had expanded, not by sea as had Great Britain, but by progressive encroachments to the east until she had reached the Pacific.

Such, in brief outline, were the general conditions in the colonial situation at the beginning of 1880. Africa and Asia were considered as legitimate prizes of colonial conquest. Great Britain, France, Germany, and Japan were impelled by recent economic developments to seek colonies. Russia had ever been a land-hungering nation, seeking especially in these modern times a port in a warm climate. Italy coveted the north shore of Africa as a means of protection to herself and of economic opportunity to her people. Russia and Japan confined their colonial ambitions to the continent of Asia; Italy to Africa: the remainder of the states were willing to forward colonial enterprise in either continent.

D. COLONIZATION IN AFRICA

i. *Before 1890*

The awakened interest in the possibilities of colonization in Africa was signalized by a conference, held at the invitation of King Leopold of Belgium, in Brussels, 1876. The avowed purpose of the conference was the foundation of an international society to promote exploration in Africa. This association was not only for scientific, but for philanthropic purposes, since its leaders laid great emphasis upon the part it might play in eradicating the known evils of slave-trade in the interior of Africa. Noted scientists and diplomats from Great Britain, France, Germany, Italy, and Russia attended. With marked enthusiasm, they organized "L'Association Internationale pour l'Exploration de la Civilization de l'Afrique Centrale" (commonly called the "International African Association"). The headquarters of the society were at Brussels: national committees in various states were appointed to forward the cause and to solicit funds.

In 1879 the association secured the services of Stanley, who had just returned the preceding year from a most successful trip in Central Africa. His mission for the association was to explore and map the great Congo River, to enter into treaty relations with native chiefs, and to use every effort to stop the slave trade in interior Africa. He left Europe in August of 1879 and returned five years later (June, 1884), having mapped out an enormous region of 900,000 square miles in the Congo basin, containing 15,000,000 people.

Even before Stanley returned, however, the international and philanthropic character of the association had been lost. The dearth of contributions from other sources forced King Leopold to assume the whole financial burden himself. These expenses averaged about $150,000 a year. To recoup himself for these sums, Leopold began to develop the commercial possibilities of such parts of the Congo basin as were already known. Therefore, in 1882, the International African Association was transformed into the International Association of the Congo; Leopold became president; a distinct flag was adopted; and systematic trade development started.

The alteration of nature and purpose radically changed

the status of Stanley's mission and of the association. Whereas the original African association had received the recognition of Europe by virtue of its international and philanthropic character, the Association of the Congo, which had nothing more than the character of a colonization scheme for commercial advantages, had no such recognition. Portugal had a vague claim upon much of the Congo territory, French explorations had reached parts of this region, and German traders had established many posts along the west coast with which a lively and profitable commerce had sprung up. The possibilities of serious consequences resulting from conflicting claims and injured trade interests led to the first great European Congress on colonial affairs.

This congress met at Berlin, November 15, 1884, with Bismarck as president. Its purpose, as was stated in the invitation, was to discuss "Freedom of commerce in the basin and mouths of the Congo; . . . and a definition of formalities to be observed so that new occupations on the African coasts shall be deemed effective." Representatives from all the European countries and from the United States were present. The last session was held February 26, 1885, at which the diplomats present signed the "General Act of the West African Conference."

This general act, in addition to recognizing the association of the Congo with its vast domain in Africa and providing for complete freedom of commerce within that area, set forth the general rules for the extension of colonial possessions in Africa. Under these rules, all the powers must be notified by any power contemplating the establishment of a new protectorate; actual possession with the maintenance of law and order therein was the only recognized title to colonial territory; and arbitration in case of conflicting claims was compulsory.

The importance of this conference lay in the fact that it constituted a sincere attempt of the states in joint meeting to keep the ambitions of colonial powers in Africa within reasonable bounds. Its provisions, agreed to and made public at the very beginning of the most active period in colonial expansion, established certain fundamental principles, by adherence to which dangerous crises might be avoided. And it set a precedent for future conferences on similar subjects: — it was, indeed, but the first of a series of joint conferences or mutual agreements between two or more states by which colonial issues were amicably settled.

With the way thus cleared, the acquisition of territory in Africa proceeded at an accelerated pace. In Germany a Colonial Society had been founded in 1882. By its lectures, propaganda, and later by its colonial museum at Berlin, it aroused popular interest in the possibilities of German colonial expansion. Bismarck, who had up to this period devoted his entire energies to the development of united Germany, was at last converted. By 1883 German traders established more than sixty stations along the west coast of Africa and were clamoring for the protection of the German flag. One man in particular, Herr Lüderitz from Bremen, had acquired by treaties with the natives a patch of land around the Angra Pequeña, on the west coast, north of the Cape Colony settlement. For this land he demanded German protection. In 1884 Bismarck granted his request and for the first time authorized the raising of the German flag over colonial property in Africa. By huge extensions in the same year and in the two years following, this tiny colony was expanded into the enormous district known as German Southwest Africa. The step once taken, further acquisitions immediately followed. In 1884 by treaties with native chiefs obtained largely through the efforts of the explorer Nachtigal, Germany acquired a foothold in Togoland and the Cameroons, Togoland being on the coast just south of the Sahara desert, and the Cameroons bordering on the Gulf of Guinea. In 1885 German representatives were busy on the east coast, making treaties with the local chieftains covering an enormous tract of land. A protectorate known as German East Africa was officially proclaimed which, by subsequent agreement with Great Britain, who had interests to the north, included roughly 200,000 square miles of territory. Nor did Germany during these years confine herself to Africa. Once the colonial policy was adopted, the country followed it with energy and persistence. While the German traders and explorers were busy in Africa, their brothers in the western hemisphere were inspired with the same ambitions. No foothold on the continent of Asia was at the time possible without provoking a serious crisis either with France or Great Britain, but a number of scattered island territories lay unclaimed and apparently undesired. Germany hastened to raise her flag over these, adding the Bismarck Archipelago, German New Guinea, and the Marshall Islands to her colonies in 1884 and 1885, and the Solomon Islands in 1886. Thus Germany, starting in 1884 with no colonies, had built up before 1890 an empire of 750,000 square miles in Africa, and had secured a number of more or less important footholds in the Pacific.

France had a decided handicap over Germany in the fact that she had retained from previous years some settlements in Africa and Asia. Thus Algeria, Senegal, the Ivory Coast, Guinea, and Gabun in northern and western Africa, and Cochin-China and Cambodia in southeastern Asia might each prove a center from which French territory could be extended. Under the daring leadership of Jules Ferry, prime minister in 1881 and again from 1883 to 1885, France started upon its great modern colonial period. French statesmen began to dream of a vast African empire to reach from the Mediterranean Sea to the Congo. Their explorers, scientists, soldiers, and traders set out to make the dream a reality. In 1881 in pursuance of Ferry's policy, France seized Tunis. Within the next year, France had established herself in control of the upper Senegal and Sahara regions; in 1882 she controlled the Middle Congo. By 1890 she had occupied the territory between the Senegal and the Niger rivers, had located a strong military outpost in the southern Ahmadu region, and connected her Senegal territories with the small colony of French Guinea. In 1885 she sent the earliest of her military expeditions to Madagascar. In the meanwhile she had used Cambodia and Cochin-China as a center from which to push forward her boundaries to the edge of China. In 1883 she consolidated her power by the acquisition of Anam and Tongking. Thus France had, by the pursuit of her vigorous foreign policy, gained over 2,000,000 square miles of territory in the decade ending with 1890.

Her far-flung empire and settlements in every corner of the earth gave Great Britain an overwhelming advantage in any colonial rivalry. Any one of her many dependencies might be made a center from which her power could be extended. The British explorers, scientists, traders, and soldiers were at the front in every part of the earth where there were possibilities of colonization. From small trading stations established by a mercantile company near the mouth of the river Niger, Great Britain extended her power between 1884 and 1886 over an immense rich and thickly inhabited region called (from the river) Nigeria. From the prosperous Cape Colony and Natal settlements established at the Cape of Good Hope in the southernmost extremity of the continent, she pushed her boundaries northward until by 1890 she had added Bechuanaland and Zululand, and had gained a foothold in Rhodesia. In eastern Africa, by an agreement with Germany, she assumed control over the large territory now known as British East Africa. And on the Gulf of Aden, she announced a protectorate over British Somaliland in 1887. During this same period when in western, southern, and eastern Africa she was acquiring these huge territories, she was also expanding in the Far East. Papua became a British protectorate in 1884; North Borneo fell within her sphere of influence in 1881 and was declared a protectorate in 1888; and the adjacent provinces of Brunei and Sarawak were added in the latter year. Thus in western, southern, and eastern Africa, and among the islands of the Malay Archipelago, Great Britain was steadily advancing her colonial interests. Between 1880 and 1890 she added roughly a million square miles to her colonial possessions. Although in actual territory Great Britain fell somewhat short of France, it must be remembered that a large part of French acquisitions comprised the barren and unpopulated Sahara desert, whereas Britain's acquisitions were almost wholly of territory capable of great development.

ii. *After 1890*

We have purposely stopped at the year 1890 in this discussion of colonial enterprise because in that year conflicting claims rendered further negotiations among the powers necessary if a serious conflict were to be avoided. In this year, and in the year immediately following, peace was maintained and colonial boundaries determined, not by a single European Congress, but by a series of important agreements between individual states. The most important of these agreements were the following: (1) An Anglo-German agreement of July 1, 1890; (2) an Anglo-French agreement of August 5, 1890; (3) a Franco-German agreement of March 15, 1894; and (4) an Anglo-French agreement of March 21, 1899. We must take each of these agreements in turn, understand the conditions leading up to it, and appreciate its territorial and political importance.

Of all these agreements the first, the Anglo-German of 1890, was the most comprehensive. German expansion during the five years previous to this date had been contiguous to British expansion in west, southwest, and eastern Africa. Bismarck, once interested in colonial ventures,

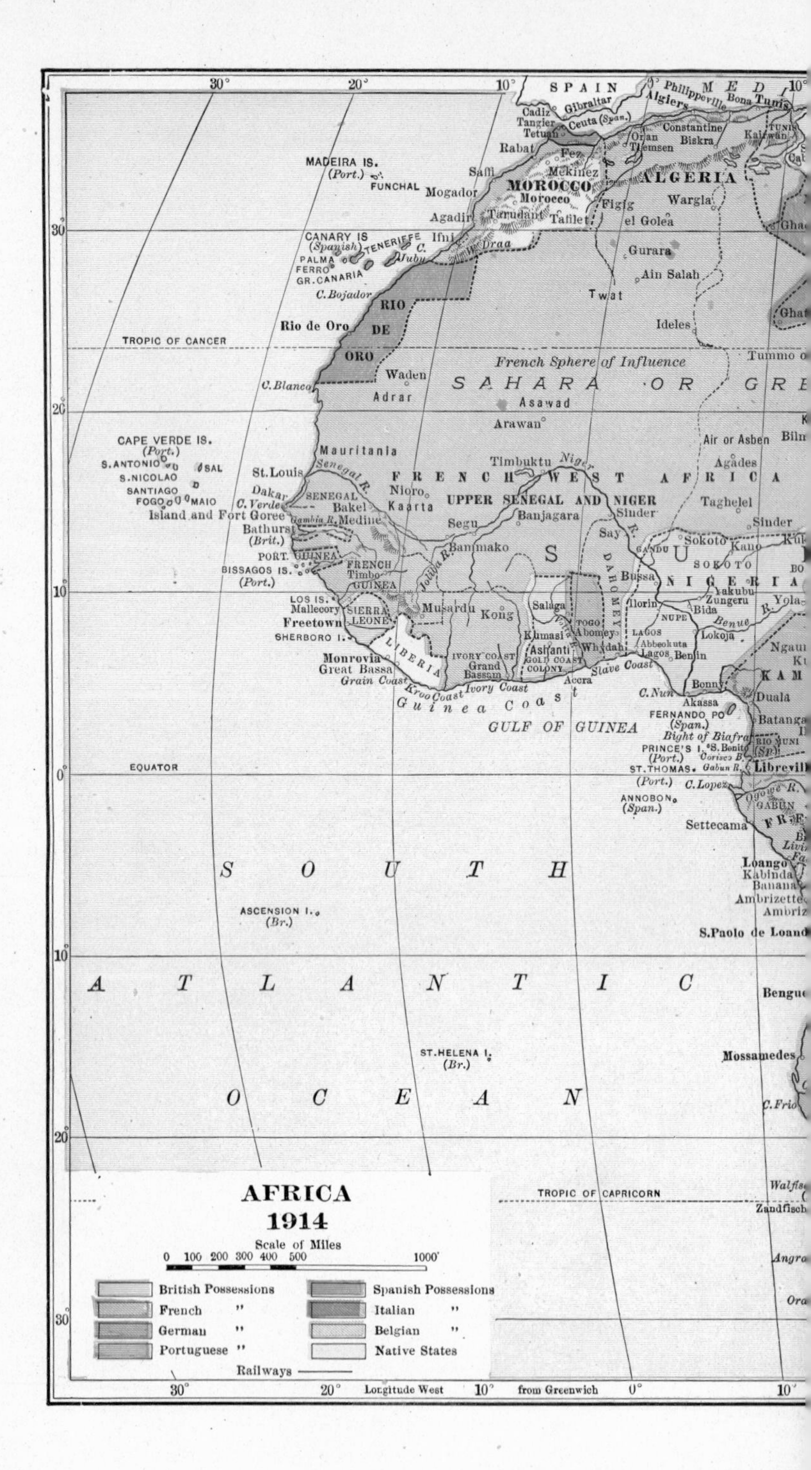
AFRICA
1914
Scale of Miles
0 100 200 300 400 500 1000
British Possessions
French "
German "
Portuguese "
Spanish Possessions
Italian "
Belgian "
Native States
Railways
Longitude West
from Greenwich
SPAIN
Cadiz
Gibraltar
Tangier
Ceuta (Span.)
Tetuan
Algiers
Philippeville
Bona
Tunis
Oran
Tlemsen
Constantine
Biskra
Kairwan
Rabat
Fez
Mekinez
Saffi
MOROCCO
Morocco
ALGERIA
Mogador
Agadir
Tarudant
Tafilet
Figig
el Golea
Wargla
MADEIRA IS.
(Port.)
FUNCHAL
CANARY IS
(Spanish)
TENERIFFE
PALMA
FERRO
GR.CANARIA
C. Juby
Ifni
Draa
C. Bojador
Gurara
Ain Salah
Twat
Ideles
RIO DE ORO
Rio de Oro
TROPIC OF CANCER
French Sphere of Influence
SAHARA OR GR
Tummo
Ghat
C. Blanco
Waden
Adrar
Asawad
Arawan
CAPE VERDE IS.
(Port.)
S. ANTONIO
SAL
S. NICOLAO
SANTIAGO
FOGO
MAIO
Mauritania
Air or Asben
Agades
Timbuktu
Niger
St. Louis
Senegal R.
FRENCH WEST AFRICA
Dakar
SENEGAL
Nioro
Kaarta
C. Verde
Island and Fort Goree
Bakel
Medine
UPPER SENEGAL AND NIGER
Taghelel
Sinder
Bathurst
(Brit.)
Gambia R.
Segu
Banjagara
Say
PORT. GUINEA
Bammako
Sokoto
Kano
SOKOTO
BISSAGOS IS.
(Port.)
FRENCH
Timbo
GUINEA
DAHOMEY
Bussa
NIGERIA
LOS IS.
Mallecory
SIERRA LEONE
Musardu
Kong
Salaga
Ilorin
Yakubu
Zungeru
Bida
Yola
Freetown
SHERBORO I.
LIBERIA
TOGO
Abomey
Kumasi
Ashanti
Whydah
LAGOS
Abbeokuta
Lagos
NUPE
Benue
Lokoja
Benin
Monrovia
Great Bassa
Grain Coast
Kroo Coast
IVORY COAST
Grand Bassam
Ivory Coast
GOLD COAST COLONY
Accra
Slave Coast
Guinea Coast
C. Nun
Akassa
Bonny
Duala
GULF OF GUINEA
FERNANDO PO
(Span.)
Bight of Biafra
Batanga
PRINCE'S I.
(Port.)
ST. THOMAS
(Port.)
RIO MUNI
Libreville
EQUATOR
C. Lopez
Ogowe R.
ANNOBON
(Span.)
Settecama
Loango
Kabinda
Banana
Ambrizette
Ambriz
S. Paolo de Loanda
SOUTH ATLANTIC OCEAN
ASCENSION I.
(Br.)
ST. HELENA I.
(Br.)
Mossamedes
C. Frio
TROPIC OF CAPRICORN
Walfisch
Zandfisch
Angra
30° 20° 10° 0° 10°

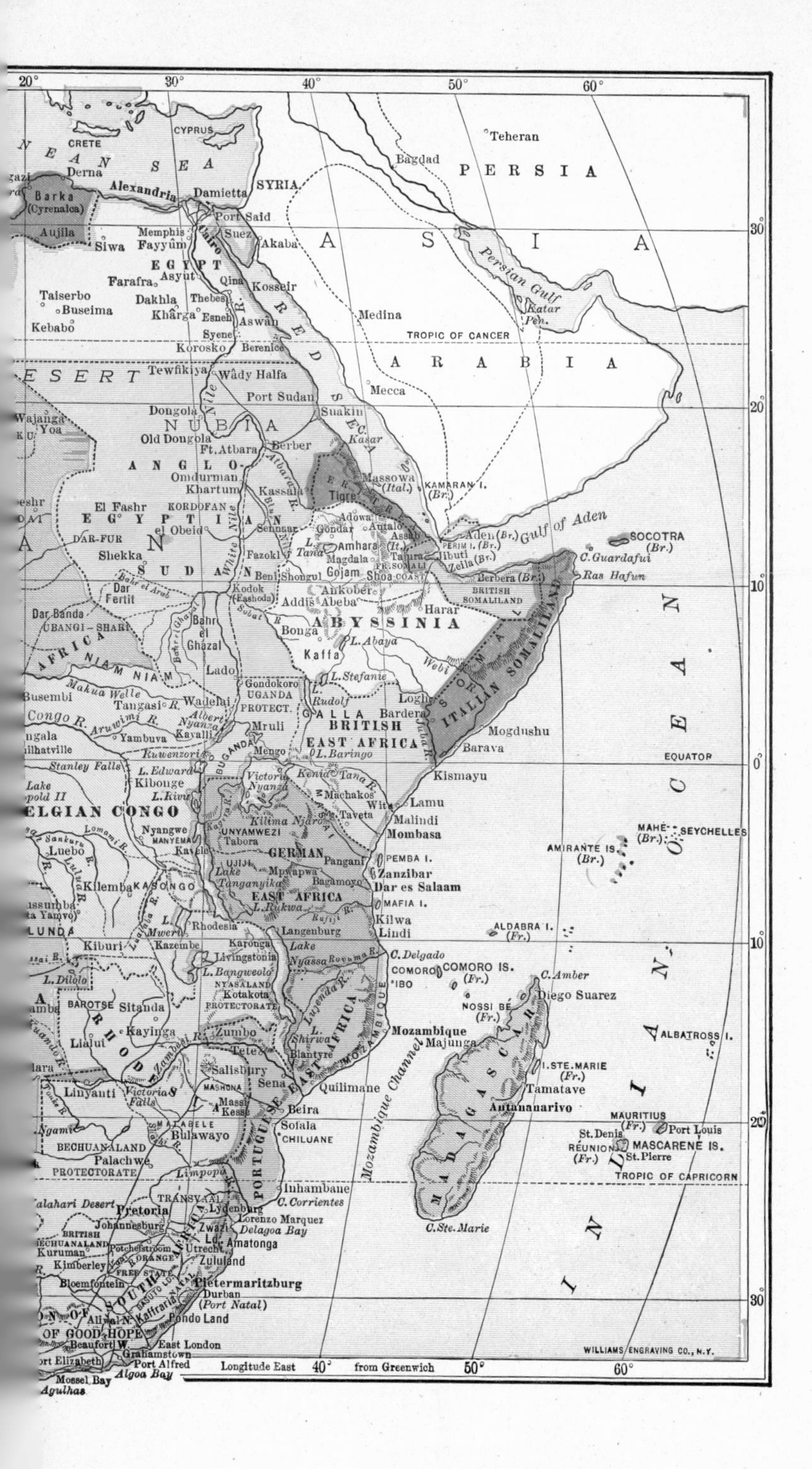
CYPRUS
CRETE
SEA
Alexandria
Damietta
SYRIA
Port Said
Suez
Cairo
Akaba
Barka
(Cyrenaica)
Aujila
Siwa
Memphis
Fayyûm
EGYPT
Asyut
Farafra
Qina
Kosseir
Taiserbo
Buseima
Kebabo
Dakhla
Kharga
Thebes
Esneh
Aswan
Syene
Korosko
Berenice
Tewfikiya
Wâdy Halfa
Port Sudan
Dongola
Old Dongola
NUBIA
Suakin
Ft. Atbara
Berber
ANGLO-EGYPTIAN SUDAN
Omdurman
Khartum
Kassala
El Fashr
KORDOFAN
el Obeid
DAR-FUR
Shekka
Sennaar
Fazokl
Beni Shongul
White Nile
Blue Nile
Kodok
(Fashoda)
Dar Fertit
Dar Banda
UBANGI-SHARI
Bahr el Ghazal
Lado
Gondokoro
UGANDA PROTECT.
Wadelai
Tangasi
Makua Welle
Busembi
Congo R.
Aruwimi R.
Yambuva
Kavalli
Mruli
Stanley Falls
L. Edward
Kibonge
L. Kivu
Ruwenzori
BUGANDA
Mengo
Victoria Nyanza
BELGIAN CONGO
Nyangwe
MANYEMA
Kavels
Luebo
Lulua R.
Kilemba
KASONGO
LUNDA
Kiburi
Kazembe
L. Mweru
L. Dilolo
BAROTSE
Sitanda
Kayinga
Lialui
RHODESIA
Rhodesia
Zambezi R.
Zumbo
Tete
Salisbury
MASHONA
Linyanti
Victoria Falls
Ngami
MATABELE
Bulawayo
BECHUANALAND PROTECTORATE
Palachwe
Limpopo
Kalahari Desert
TRANSVAAL
Pretoria
Johannesburg
Lydenburg
BRITISH BECHUANALAND
Kuruman
Potchefstroom
ORANGE FREE STATE
Kimberley
Bloemfontein
Utrecht
Zululand
Zwazi
Ld. Amatonga
Lorenzo Marquez
Delagoa Bay
Pietermaritzburg
Durban
(Port Natal)
Pondo Land
Kaffraria
SOUTH AFRICA
Aliwal N.
OF GOOD HOPE
Beaufort W.
Grahamstown
East London
Port Elizabeth
Port Alfred
Algoa Bay
Mossel Bay
Agulhas
Teheran
Bagdad
PERSIA
ASIA
Persian Gulf
Katar Pen.
Medina
TROPIC OF CANCER
ARABIA
Mecca
RED SEA
C. Kasar
ERITREA
Massowa
(Ital.)
Tigre
KAMARAN I.
(Br.)
Adowa
Gondar
Amhara
Antalo
Assab
(It.)
L. Tana
Magdala
Tajura
Gojam
Shoa
Ankober
Addis Abeba
Harar
ABYSSINIA
Bonga
Kaffa
L. Abaya
L. Stefanie
L. Rudolf
GALLA
BRITISH EAST AFRICA
L. Baringo
Kenia
Tana R.
Machakos
Kilima Njaro
Taveta
Witu
Lamu
Malindi
Mombasa
UNYAMWEZI
Tabora
GERMAN EAST AFRICA
Pangani
UJIJI
Mpwapwa
Bagamoyo
L. Tanganyika
L. Rukwa
Langenburg
Karonga
Livingstonia
L. Bangweolo
NYASALAND PROTECTORATE
Kotakota
Lake Nyassa
Rovuma R.
Lujenda R.
L. Shirwa
Blantyre
PORTUGUESE EAST AFRICA
MOZAMBIQUE
Sena
Quilimane
Beira
Massi Kessi
Sofala
CHILUANE
Inhambane
C. Corrientes
Aden (Br.)
Gulf of Aden
PERIM I. (Br.)
Jibuti
FR. SOMALI COAST
Zeila (Br.)
Berbera (Br.)
BRITISH SOMALILAND
SOCOTRA
(Br.)
C. Guardafui
Ras Hafun
SOMALILAND
ITALIAN SOMALILAND
Webi
Logh
Bardera
Juba R.
Mogdushu
Barava
Kismayu
EQUATOR
PEMBA I.
Zanzibar
Dar es Salaam
MAFIA I.
Kilwa
Lindi
C. Delgado
COMORO
IBO
COMORO IS.
(Fr.)
NOSSI BÉ
(Fr.)
ALDABRA I.
(Fr.)
AMIRANTE IS.
(Br.)
MAHÉ
(Br.)
SEYCHELLES
C. Amber
Diego Suarez
Mozambique
Majunga
Mozambique Channel
MADAGASCAR
I. STE. MARIE
(Fr.)
Tamatave
Antananarivo
ALBATROSS I.
MAURITIUS
(Fr.)
Port Louis
St. Denis
RÉUNION
(Fr.)
MASCARENE IS.
St. Pierre
TROPIC OF CAPRICORN
C. Ste. Marie
INDIAN OCEAN
WILLIAMS ENGRAVING CO., N.Y.
Longitude East
from Greenwich
20°
30°
40°
50°
60°

had aggressively supported German claims which infringed upon the territory considered by the British within their sphere of influence. As a result, the relations between the two countries became somewhat strained. After the great chancellor's fall in the spring of 1890, however, his successor, Count Caprivi, took immediate steps toward a definite understanding with Great Britain on matters at issue. Lord Salisbury, then prime minister, welcomed these advances, so that a basis of discussion was quickly reached. By the final agreement, signed July 1, 1890, the boundaries of the Cameroons were definitely settled; the German territory in East Africa was extended to the borders of the Belgian Congo; and a long narrow strip of land, called derisively by the chancellor's opponents "Caprivi's finger," was secured reaching from the far upper corner of German Southwest Africa to the Zambesi River. Further than these arrangements, British influence was allowed to be supreme in the island of Zanzibar off the east coast in return for the cession by Great Britain of Heligoland in the North Sea to Germany.

The agreement was bitterly criticized in both countries. In Great Britain the extension of German East Africa to the Belgian Congo, cutting the route of the proposed Cape to Cairo railroad, was particularly blamed. In Germany the relinquishment of the claims to vast territories in Africa and the acceptance of the minute island of Heligoland in return were severely censured by a strong party inspired by the fallen chancellor. It was facetiously said that Germany has exchanged an entire suit of clothes for a trouser button.

A month later in the same year Great Britain and France came to an agreement upon certain conflicting claims in Africa. Great Britain desired particularly that her protectorate over Nigeria, the most promising of her African possessions near the equator, should be fully recognized. France on her part had, since 1883, been actively interested in the huge Island of Madagascar off the east coast, and now desired the recognition of her protectorate therein. France, therefore, in this agreement signed August 5, 1890, accepted the British claims to Nigeria extending to Lake Chad, and in return received British support in her declaration of a protectorate over Madagascar.

The Franco-German convention of 1894 completed the delineation of boundaries in the central Soudan. The French claim to Sahara, the British claim to Nigeria, and the German claim to German West Africa had in previous agreements been recognized, but the exact boundaries where the territories met in the central Soudan had not been definitely determined. As each of the three countries pushed forward its outposts to complete possession of its claim, the necessity for a complete understanding became evident. This understanding was reached in the Franco-German Agreement, signed March 15, 1894. By this agreement Lake Chad was made the neutral boundary at which the territories of the three countries met, and France was enabled to extend her possessions southward from that point to connect with the French Congo.

The last of these important agreements was the aftermath of the sensational Fashoda incident, over which Great Britain and France approached to the very verge of war. The situation arose out of the long-continued incapacity of successive Egyptian sovereigns. As a result of this incapacity, the condition of the people became wretched beyond description and the government, being in a bankrupt state and without credit for further loans, was unable to meet its financial obligations. In 1879, in the protection of their interests, Great Britain and France established through their representatives a system of Dual Control over Egypt, whereby these nations undertook to promote the material and financial welfare of the country. Three years later, in 1882, continued disorders compelled Great Britain to use force. She invited France to join her, but France refused. Then she invited Italy, but Italy also refused. She thereupon undertook the pacification of Egypt alone. The British army quickly defeated the rebels. The Dual Control was abolished and replaced by a British financial adviser, and Egypt entered into the anomalous condition of a supposedly independent state whose sovereign could take no act without the consent of a representative of a foreign state. The immense region of southern Egypt known as the Egyptian Soudan broke out in revolt at this time. The inefficient soldiery and the small British force sent to subdue this revolt were cut to pieces. For a number of years the revolutionists were allowed complete sway in this region, the British financial adviser believing it more important to improve the economic conditions in the main part of Egypt than to spend money and lives in civil war to retake a southern province. In 1896, however, the finances and material prosperity of the country had so much improved that an expedition to reconquer the Egyptian Soudan for the Khedive was encouraged. Sir Herbert Kitchener, at the head of twenty thousand soldiers, undertook the task. His successive defeats of the rebel Dervishes in two years of campaign broke the revolt. He reached Khartum, in which the capital of the revolutionists had been located, in September of 1898.

In the meanwhile France had hoped to take advantage of the situation in the Egyptian Soudan to round out the northeast corner of the French possessions in the Upper Congo and to gain access to the upper Nile. With this intention Major Marchand with eight officers and one hundred and twenty men was sent from the upper Congo district in the summer of 1896 with instructions to traverse the intervening district as far as the Nile. This small expedition accomplished its purpose successfully, reached the town of Fashoda (now called Kodok) in July of 1898, and there raised the French flag and took possession.

Two months after the small French force had established itself at Fashoda, Kitchener's victorious army entered the town and raised the Egyptian flag over a fort not a thousand yards from the French headquarters. In the name of the Khedive of Egypt, Kitchener demanded that Marchand haul down the French flag and leave the territory, asserting that Great Britain in behalf of Egypt would never allow a foreign nation to gain a foothold in the valley of the Nile. Marchand's answer was that he received his orders from the French government and could not leave Fashoda until officially directed to do so.

The issue was thus transferred to the chancelleries of Great Britain and France. While the two armed forces stood at Fashoda, a mud-flat in the midst of a great morass, the British and French ministers negotiated in Europe. France held that Great Britain had no rights in the valley of the Nile which had been acquired by "effective occupation," and that the Khedive of Egypt, having allowed the revolutionists in the Soudan to retain possession of the district for more than a decade, had ceased to have any sovereign rights over that region. Great Britain claimed on her part that her sphere of influence included the entire Nile Valley, and that by Kitchener's successful suppression of the revolt all the sovereign rights of the Khedive were revived. Both sides stubbornly kept to their positions. Popular feeling was so thoroughly aroused over the question that war seemed inevitable.

Had France been in a condition at this time to support her claims by force, war would probably have followed, but certain features of the internal politics handicapped her. Political France was at the height of the bitter factional quarrels excited by the revelations in the trial of Dreyfus for treason. France was most divided over the issue just at the time when Kitchener was facing Marchand at Fashoda. Torn by these discussions at home, and aware of the power of Great Britain, France had to yield. March 21, 1899, France and Great Britain signed an agreement defining the French and British spheres of influence in central

Africa. France gave up all claim to the territory in the Egyptian Soudan, and in return received British recognition of her claims to extensive territory to the east and southeast of Lake Chad. For France, this additional territory rounded out her Sahara dominions south of Tripoli and joined these with those of the upper Congo. For Great Britain, the agreement barred France from access to the upper reaches of the Nile and secured British influence throughout all of Egypt.

Only one other event of consequence need be considered in connection with the expansion of European powers in Africa during this period. The Cape Colony settlement had become one of Great Britain's most extensive possessions on the continent. The original Dutch settlers, commonly called Boers (peasants), had in previous years withdrawn to the north and founded a state (the Orange Free State) in which they could live and enjoy their own institutions free from British sovereignty. By a distinct convention in 1852, known as the Sand River Convention, Great Britain recognized the independence of the Orange Free State and its neighbor the Transvaal Republic. The relations between these countries and Great Britain were complicated, however, by the discovery in 1884 of valuable gold deposits in the Transvaal. British prospectors migrated in huge numbers to the new field. In that country they were, of course, subject to the Boer government. Complaints were soon made by the British settlers that, although they paid a large part of the taxes and in some districts actually outnumbered the Boers, they were allowed no political privileges. The Boers on their part undoubtedly believed that the only way to maintain the government in their own hands was to exclude the British settlers, the Uitlanders, from the suffrage. The feeling grew bitter on both sides. In 1895 a certain Dr. Jameson, at the head of a few hundred cavalrymen, invaded the Transvaal with the obvious object of supporting by force the Uitlanders in their demands. Jameson and his troops were captured and handed over to the British for punishment. The incident of the raid, and the relatively light punishment meted out to the participants by the British, increased the bad feeling among the Boers. In 1897 Great Britain sent a special commissioner into the Transvaal to investigate and report upon conditions. Upon his report in 1899, which emphasized the unfavorable position of the British and the hostility of the Boers, Great Britain demanded that her citizens in the Transvaal should be given political rights. The Boers, believing that compliance with the demand would amount to yielding up control of their country to a foreign element, refused. War began in October of 1899, the Orange Free State joining the Transvaal against Great Britain. After British reverses in the early months, Great Britain raised, equipped, and despatched to South Africa an enormous army to overcome the small forces of the Boers. In the final months of the war (1902) Great Britain had a quarter of a million troops in the field under Kitchener against some fifteen thousand Boers. Peace was made June 1, 1902. The Transvaal and the Orange Free State lost their independence, becoming British colonies.

CHAPTER III

COLONIAL RIVALRY IN ASIA, AND THE RUSSO-JAPANESE WAR

THE *Entente Cordiale* was formed in April, 1904. Two months previously, the other nation in Europe with whom France had an *Entente*, Russia, became involved in a war with Japan brought on by the Russian far-eastern policy. This war in a measure offset the diplomatic advantage which France gained by the *Entente* with England, for it so weakened Russia that for a decade to come she could not be relied upon for effective assistance in case actual war should follow a Franco-German dispute. In this way the Russo-Japanese War and its results played an important part in European politics, so weakening the forces hostile to Germany that they were not able to dispute German dictatorship for a decade longer.

A. Russo-Japanese Rivalry in Asia

i. *Russian Expansion*

The existence of Russia as a disturbing factor in the Far East dates from almost three hundred years ago. Fifty years before the reign of Peter the Great, wandering bands of Russians had crossed the Siberian wastes and reached the Pacific. Russia's hold on this north country was only nominal, however, until the inventions of the nineteenth century made its possession and control from St. Petersburg not only a possibility but a practicability. Perhaps in this direction lay the ice-free port which the crowding nations to the west and southwest had denied her. Through the efforts of Count Muravieff, Russia's great empire builder in the Far East, extensive explorations and settlements were made along the Amur river. Once a Russian population was established there, it became easy to force China to recognize the Russian claim, and in 1857 a treaty was signed whereby the left or north bank of the Amur River was ceded to Russia. This gave the Czar the port of Nikolayevsk at the mouth of the Amur River. In itself the port was not valuable, but it furnished a foothold from which to make certain demands three years later when China was beaten by the combined forces of England and France. By a treaty in 1860, the whole of that region now known as the Maritime Province passed into Russian hands, and Vladivostok became a Russian port. The goal had not yet been attained, however, for ice closes Vladivostok four months of the year, so Russian eyes were still turned southward toward Korea and the Manchurian coast.

The next contact with the Eastern powers was in 1872, when Muravieff, still impelling the Russian foreign policy, made demands on the island of Sakhalin, lying to the north of the Japanese group. A nominal Japanese sovereignty had existed there for two hundred years, but small Russian settlements as well dated from the beginning of the eighteenth century. Muravieff at first thought its possession essential, since it commanded the mouth of the Amur, and therefore, when he was unable to secure its cession from Japan, he resorted to the policy which had been effective on the Amur River — that of sending settlers in numbers. Japan offered to buy the Russian portion, and Russia, recognizing by this time that she had overrated the importance of the island, would probably have made a bargain, but that one of Japan's own statesmen refused to have executed a purchase which was so disadvantageous to Japan. Finally, in

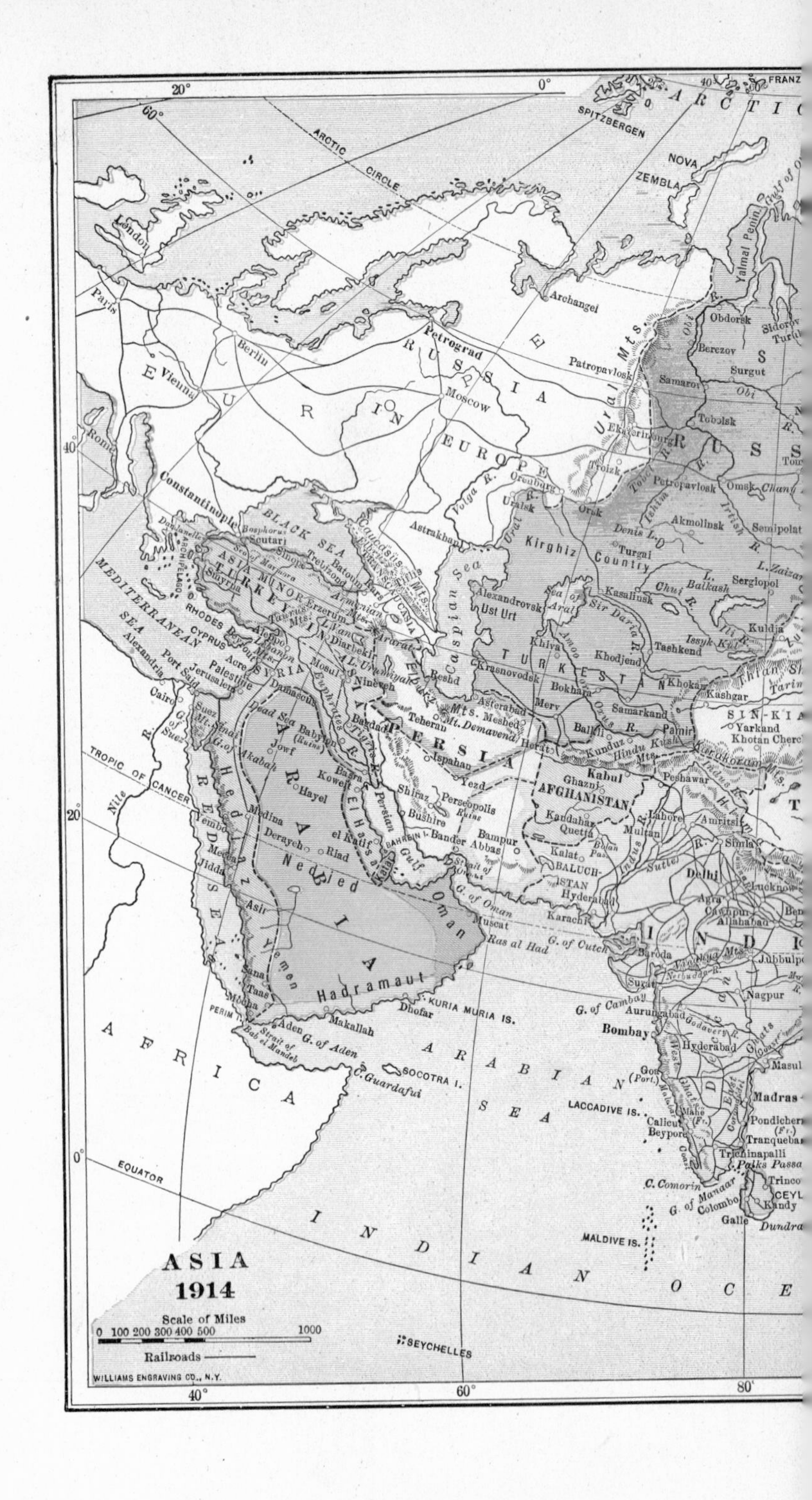
ASIA
1914
Scale of Miles
0 100 200 300 400 500 1000
Railroads
WILLIAMS ENGRAVING CO., N.Y.
ARCTIC CIRCLE
SPITZBERGEN
NOVA ZEMBLA
London
Paris
Berlin
Vienna
Rome
Petrograd
Moscow
Archangel
RUSSIA IN EUROPE
Constantinople
BLACK SEA
MEDITERRANEAN SEA
ASIA MINOR
TURKEY IN ASIA
CYPRUS
RHODES
Smyrna
Trebizond
Erzerum
Aleppo
Damascus
Jerusalem
Palestine
Port Said
Alexandria
Cairo
Suez
Mosul
Nineveh
Bagdad
Babylon (Ruins)
Basra
Koweit
Medina
Mecca
Jidda
RED SEA
ARABIA
Nedjed
Hadramaut
Oman
Muscat
Aden
G. of Aden
Sana
Mocha
Asir
Yemen
Hayel
Riad
Derayeh
Persian Gulf
PERSIA
Teheran
Ispahan
Yezd
Shiraz
Persepolis
Bushire
Bander Abbas
Herat
Meshed
Kabul
AFGHANISTAN
Kandahar
Quetta
BALUCHISTAN
Hyderabad
Karachi
Caspian Sea
Astrakhan
Kirghiz Country
TURKESTAN
Khiva
Bokhara
Merv
Samarkand
Tashkend
Kashgar
Yarkand
Ural Mts.
Orenburg
Ekaterinburg
Obdorsk
Berezov
Tobolsk
Omsk
Petropavlosk
Akmolinsk
Semipolat
Sergiopol
L. Balkash
Kuldja
INDIA
Delhi
Lahore
Amritsir
Multan
Simla
Agra
Cawnpur
Allahabad
Lucknow
Baroda
Surat
Bombay
Nagpur
Jubbulpore
Hyderabad
Goa (Port.)
Calicut
Beypore
Madras
Pondicherry (Fr.)
Tranquebar
Trichinapalli
Colombo
Kandy
Galle
C. Comorin
G. of Manaar
G. of Cambay
G. of Cutch
Ras al Had
G. of Oman
KURIA MURIA IS.
SOCOTRA I.
C. Guardafui
PERIM I.
Strait of Bab el Mandeb
LACCADIVE IS.
MALDIVE IS.
SEYCHELLES
ARABIAN SEA
INDIAN OCEAN
AFRICA
EQUATOR
TROPIC OF CANCER
Nile R.
20°
40°
60°
80°
0°

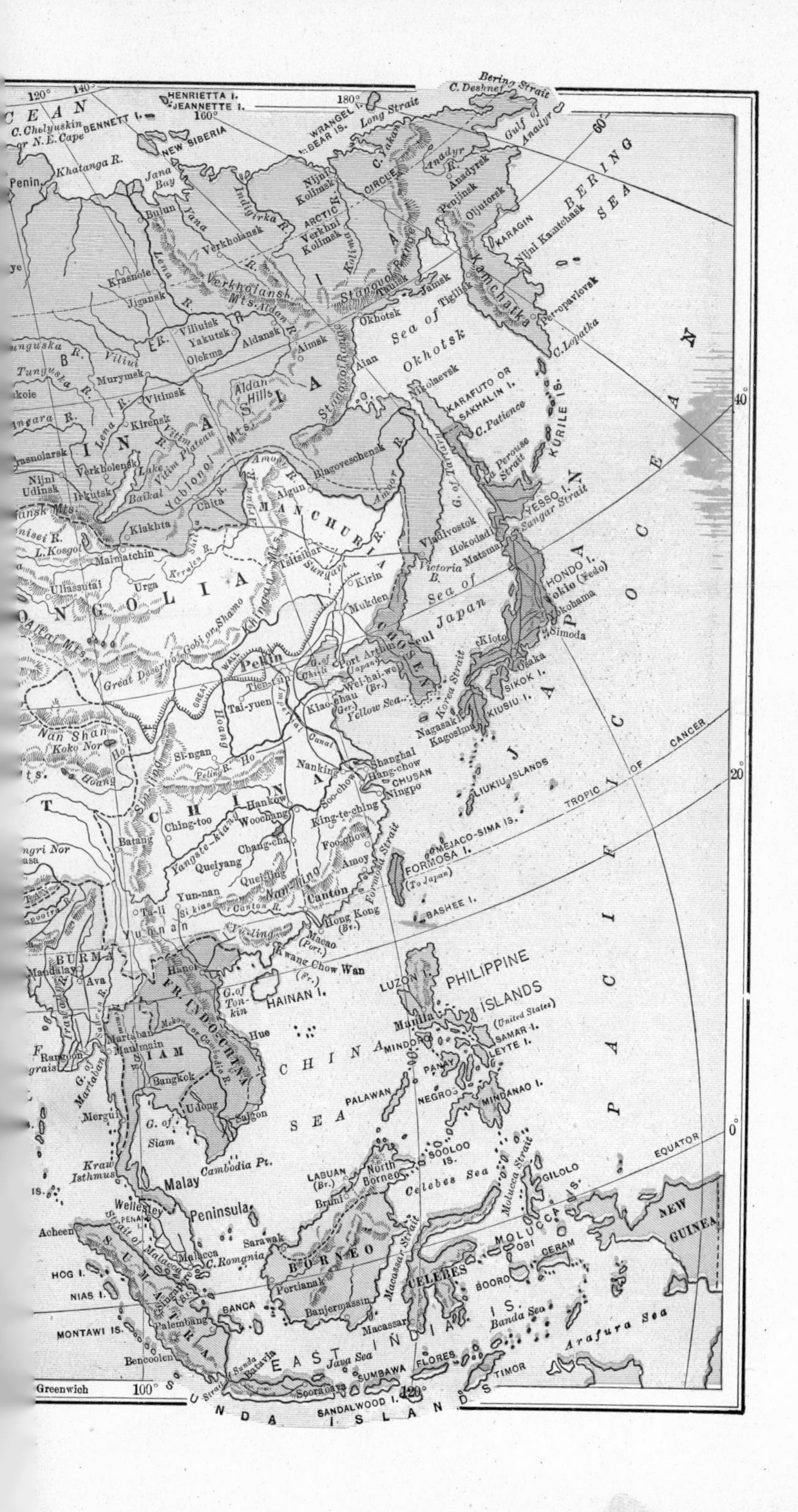

Bering Strait
C. Deshnef
HENRIETTA I.
JEANNETTE I.
BENNETT I.
C. Chelyuskin or N. E. Cape
NEW SIBERIA
WRANGEL I.
BEAR IS.
Long Strait
Gulf of Anadyr
Khatanga R.
Jana Bay
Bulun
Yana
Verkhoiansk
Indigirka R.
Nijni Kolimsk
Verkhni Kolimsk
ARCTIC CIRCLE
Anadyr R.
Anadyrsk
Penjinsk
Oljutorsk
KARAGIN
Nijni Kamtchatsk
BERING SEA
Kamchatka
Petropavlovsk
C. Lopatka
Krasnole
Jigansk
Lena R.
Verkhoiansk Mts.
Aldan R.
Stanovoi Range
Tausk
Jamsk
Okhotsk
Sea of Okhotsk
Viliuisk
Yakutsk
Aldansk
Aimsk
Olekma
Aian
Viliui
Murymsk
Vitimsk
Kirensk
Aldan Hills
Stanovoi Range
Nikolaevsk
KARAFUTO OR SAKHALIN I.
C. Patience
KURILE IS.
La Perouse Strait
Vitim Plateau
Yablonoi Mts.
Lake Baikal
Verkholensk
Irkutsk
Nijni Udinsk
Kiakhta
Chita
Amoor R.
Blagoveschensk
Argun R.
Algun
MANCHURIA
Sungari R.
Vladivostok
Hokodadi
YESSO I.
Sangar Strait
Matsmai
Victoria B.
Sea of Japan
HONDO I.
Tokio (Yedo)
Yokohama
Simoda
Kiakhta
Maimatchin
Kerulen R.
Tsitsihar
Kirin
Mukden
Uliassutai
Urga
MONGOLIA
Great Desert of Gobi or Shamo
CHOSEN
Seul
G. of Chili
Port Arthur (Japan)
Pekin
GREAT WALL
Tien-tsin
Wei-hai-wei (Br.)
Kiao-chau (Ger.)
Yellow Sea
Korea Strait
Kioto
Osaka
SIKOK I.
KIUSIU I.
Nagasaki
Kagosima
Tai-yuen
Hoang Ho
Imperial Canal
Nan Shan
Koko Nor
Si-ngan
Nanking
Shanghai
Hang-chow
CHUSAN
Ningpo
LIUKIU ISLANDS
TROPIC OF CANCER
CHINA
Hankow
Woochang
Ching-too
Soo-chow
King-te-ching
Batang
Yangtse-kiang
Chang-cha
Foo-chow
Amoy
MEJACO-SIMA IS.
FORMOSA I. (To Japan)
Formosa Strait
Queiyang
Yun-nan
Nan-ling
Canton
Canton R.
Hong Kong (Br.)
BASHEE I.
Ta-li
Yunnan
Macao (Port.)
Kwang Chow Wan (Fr.)
BURMA
Mandalay
Ava
Hanoi
G. of Tonkin
HAINAN I.
LUZON I.
PHILIPPINE ISLANDS (United States)
Manila
MINDORO
SAMAR I.
LEYTE I.
FR. INDO-CHINA
Hue
Martaban
Maulmain
Rangoon
SIAM
Bangkok
CHINA SEA
PANAY
NEGROS
PALAWAN
MINDANAO I.
G. of Martaban
Mergui
Udong
Saigon
G. of Siam
SOOLOO IS.
PACIFIC OCEAN
EQUATOR
Krau Isthmus
Cambodia Pt.
Malay Peninsula
LABUAN (Br.)
North Borneo
Bruni
Celebes Sea
Molucca Strait
GILOLO
MOLUCCA IS.
NEW GUINEA
Wellesley
Acheen
Strait of Malacca
Malacca
C. Romania
Sarawak
BORNEO
Macassar Strait
CELEBES
OBI
CERAM
BOORO
HOG I.
NIAS I.
SUMATRA
Singapore
Portianak
Banjermassin
BANCA
Macassar
MONTAWI IS.
Palembang
EAST INDIA IS.
Banda Sea
Arafura Sea
Bencoolen
Sunda Strait
Batavia
Java Sea
SUMBAWA
FLORES
TIMOR
Greenwich
Soorabaya
SANDALWOOD I.
SUNDA ISLANDS

1875, the whole difficulty was solved by a treaty which recognized Russia's possession of Sakhalin and Japan's sovereignty in the Kurile Islands. The settlement was so greatly in Russia's favor that it has been said that Russia purchased one Japanese property and paid for it with another. The unfairness of the treaty was recognized throughout Japan and fostered an anti-Russian feeling which increased with the years.

Once in possession of Vladivostok in the Maritime Province, Russia ceased open aggression in the Far East, but continued her policy of infiltration into Chinese territory. In 1892 was begun the construction of the Trans-Siberian railway. It soon became apparent that to build the railway entirely within Russian territory would be a difficult and costly proceeding. If a course might be followed through Manchuria which would connect Vladivostok with the province of Transbaikalia, there would be a huge saving in distance and expense of construction. Such a plan, however, could be followed only with the consent of China; and for the moment it seemed unlikely that such an agreement would be reached. Never doubting the ultimate success of her plan, Russia began building the railroad from both ends, hoping that circumstances might arise which would enable her to cross Manchuria.

ii. *The Chino-Japanese War and its Results*

The Russian scheme was made possible by Japan. It must not be supposed that Japan was a willing agent, nor, indeed, a conscious one. To further her own ends, she brought about a situation in the Far East from which, without spending a cent, Russia reaped the immediate benefits. The situation was arrived at through the Chino-Japanese War of 1894–1895.

The struggle between the two Oriental powers centered in the question of sovereignty over Korea. China's claim to control dated from the twelfth century; Japan's from the sixteenth. Indeed, Korea at one time or another had recognized both nations as having sovereign powers, and although she had perhaps favored China's claim, she had nevertheless paid a yearly tribute to the Shogun of Japan until the time Japan began adopting the western civilization. With the coming of the western customs, Korea severed all connection with Japan, and even, in 1873, refused to receive a Japanese embassy. Japan replied in accordance with the new methods learned from the European nations, massed an intimidating force of men and ships, and without shedding blood, opened several Korean ports to Japanese trade. In the succeeding years, Japanese interest suffered from insurrections in the peninsula which were relentlessly put down with Chinese assistance. By clever diplomacy Japan emerged from each of these crises with greater and greater privileges, until in 1885 she concluded a convention with the Celestial empire, whereby each power agreed not to send troops into Korea without first notifying the other.

A crisis in 1894 put the treaty to a test. An insurrection having broken out in Seoul, China dispatched troops, having first notified Japan of her intention. The latter power was now determined that the condition in Korea which led to continued disorders was intolerable, and accordingly made proposals to China that the two nations should unite to "guarantee the future peace, order, and good government in Korea." China not only refused these offers, but declined to recognize the right of Japan to make them. In order to protect her own interests, Japan now determined to carry out the reform of the Korean government single-handed. The clash with China was inevitable.

After a few preliminary skirmishes in which the Japanese seized Seoul, the Korean capital, war was formally declared on the 1st of August, 1894. The first decisive event of the war was a Japanese naval victory off the mouth of the

Yalu River against a greatly superior Chinese fleet. This master stroke enabled Japan to send five expeditions against China — into lower and upper Manchuria, the Liao Tung Peninsula, against Port Arthur, and against Wei-hai-wei. The expeditions were everywhere so successful that in April, 1895, China sued for peace. The Treaty of Shimonoseki, which was signed on April 17, 1895, guaranteed the complete independence of Korea, opened several cities and rivers in China to foreign trade, indemnified Japan to the amount of $125,000,000, and ceded to her the Pescadores Islands, Formosa, and the Liao-Tung Peninsula. The way seemed open to commercial and political hegemony in Korea, and a foothold of actual ownership had been gained on the mainland.

Japan, however, was not destined to enjoy her triumph. Here was the happy circumstance for which Russia had been waiting in order to further her own schemes, and almost immediately after the ratification of the Treaty of Shimonoseki, she induced France and Germany to unite with her in "suggesting" to the government at Tokyo that the Japanese possession of any portion of the mainland was undesirable as being a constant menace to the integrity of China and the peace of the Far East. The Japanese, who by this time were sufficiently acquainted with Occidental diplomacy to recognize the veiled threat under the suggestion, declared their willingness to receive a further indemnity of $25,000,000 in lieu of the Liao-Tung territory. They read the signs of the Russian menace, however, and began preparing for the struggle which they foresaw.

Russia now pushed her advantages to the limit. The Russo-Chinese bank, which was organized to further the building of the Trans-Siberian railway, loaned $80,000,000 without security to China, wherewith to pay her war indemnity, and demanded in return the privilege of building the railroad across Manchuria. Vladivostok was connected with Transbaikalia, and a branch road was built southward from Harbin to connect with Port Arthur in the Liao-Tung Peninsula.

All Europe became greatly interested in Chinese affairs. In 1897 Germany took advantage of the murder of two missionaries in the Shantung province to shell and capture the port of Kiao-Chau. The convention which followed gave her a lease of this port and large commercial and financial concession throughout the Shantung province. Great Britain followed suit with a lease of the port and city of Wei-hai-wei. The climax came when Russia, taking advantage of the obligations under which she had placed China by her revision of the treaty of Shimonoseki and the subsequent loan, demanded and received a twenty-five year lease of Port Arthur and the Liao-Tung Peninsula — the very territory which she had protested against Japan's possessing as being inimical to the peace of the Far East! To protect their newly acquired possessions, Great Britain and Germany fortified their new harbors, and Russia began pouring troops into the Manchurian province. It seemed for the moment as if Europe had determined upon a complete dismemberment of China.

iii. *Chinese Affairs*

But a momentary relief was to come from China herself. The Emperor Kwang-Su, who had taken steps to destroy the isolation of the nation and to acquire the advantages of the western civilization, was suddenly halted in his career of progress by an uprising of the conservative element in the Empire. The Empress Dowager, the second wife of the Emperor's father, sympathizing with the conservative party, executed a *coup d'état* which placed her for a second time in the position of ruler of China. The uprising found its expression in the insurrection led by the Society of Harmonious Fists, or "Boxers," one of the many secret organizations of China which had declared the extermination of the "Foreign Devils." Their hatred of everything foreign knew no bounds; they murdered missionaries, tortured and slew Christian converts in great numbers, and finally, in the summer of 1900, laid siege to the foreign legations in Pekin. For weeks the members of the legations withstood the savage attacks of the infuriated Boxers. They were buoyed up in their predicament by news of a relief expedition, which from time to time filtered into the unhappy city. Finally the rumors were verified, and in the middle of August the terrible strain was removed by the entrance into Pekin of a combined relief expedition. Japan, France, Germany, Russia, Great Britain, and the United States had joined forces for the purpose of saving the besieged legations. Pekin once occupied, they proceeded to quell the Boxer disturbances in the neighboring provinces. When quiet was restored, the western nations demanded from China a huge indemnity for the atrocities committed, and signed an agreement for the mutual maintenance of China's integrity, and for the prevention of any further European encroachment upon Chinese territory.

iv. *Russian Relations with China; Japanese Intervention*

The conclusion of the trouble found Russia in full military possession of Manchuria, a position which she might easily have made permanent simply by maintaining the status quo until a complete peace was established in the Far East. Instead, she made the error of proposing to China a convention which if carried out would have made her full owner of Manchuria. Japan, alarmed by this aggressive move on the part of her competitor, persuaded Great Britain and the United States to unite with her in remonstrating against this violation of the convention of 1900. If Japan's occupation of Manchuria in 1895 menaced the Chinese capital and threatened the permanent peace of the Far East, surely Russia's occupation of the same province in 1900 would do no less. The formidable array of nations united to preserve Chinese integrity so convinced Russia of the unwisdom of her demands that she not only recalled them but agreed to withdraw her troops from Manchuria. The evacuation was to take place within eighteen months, one-third of the troops to be removed after each six months.

It appeared from this convention that western aggression at China's expense had been stopped once and for all, and that the Powers were determined to keep open the door of equal rights in the Celestial Empire. The expectation was without foundation, however, for when the time came for the withdrawal of the troops, Russia again proposed an arrangement which would strengthen her hold on Manchuria. She was determined not to give up her hold on that province, and once more she turned covetous eyes on Korea. China's remonstrances passed unheeded. The duty devolved upon Japan, as the power next concerned, of insisting upon Russia's fulfillment of her own agreements.

v. *Outbreak of the Russo-Japanese War*

The Japanese demands were reasonable enough. They recognized Russia's immense commercial interest in Manchuria; in return they asked that Russia recognize the corresponding interest of Japan in Korea. They asked, too, that Russia unite with Japan in maintaining the integrity of China and Korea, and in guaranteeing equal rights within those kingdoms for all nations. In other words, they asked only that Russia should repeat and carry out the promises made at the close of the Boxer outburst. But Russia remained obdurate and would make no satisfactory reply to the Japanese notes. More Russian troops were sent to Manchuria, a fleet was started from Kronstadt on the long trip to Vladivostok, and open aggressions of a minor sort were begun in northern Korea. It was evident to the least astute what Russia was about. She meant to maintain her position, and she hoped that this show of force would enable her to do it without the final resort of war. If she thought to intimidate Japan, she read the Japanese people badly. There had been too many humiliations already — the Sakhalin affair, the treaty of Shimonoseki, the leasing of Liao-Tung, and finally this refusal of Russia to fulfill her own promises. If the Japanese submitted now, their nation was doomed. Without hesitation Japan declared for war and began operations with dramatic suddenness by torpedoing part of the Russian fleet before Port Arthur on the night of the 8th of February, 1904.

In accounting for Japan's determined attitude we must not overlook the undoubted strengthening of national purpose caused by the Anglo-Japanese *Entente* of 1902. The same year that saw Russia's promise to evacuate Manchuria witnessed the signing of the first alliance between a western and an eastern nation. The document set forth that both contracting parties, Great Britain and Japan, explicitly recognized the complete independence of China and Korea; it announced that both nations might take necessary steps to safeguard their interests in the two kingdoms named; it stated that if, in safeguarding those interests, either nation became involved in war, the other would endeavor to keep outside nations neutral, and would enter the war in case the other signatory power faced two or more adversaries; lastly, it stated that Japan "possessed in a peculiar degree, political, commercial, and industrial interest in Korea." At first glance, the agreement seems to be greatly in favor of Japan, since a war between her and Russia was imminent at the time of signing. The explanation probably lies in the fact that the future adversary was Russia, and that in India there still stalked the specter of the "bear that walks like a man." The inequality of terms was corrected when the *Entente* became a defensive and offensive alliance after the close of the Russo-Japanese War.

B. THE RUSSO-JAPANESE WAR

The task before the little empire was a huge one. In some respects, it was not unlike that of 1894 when she defeated China. She had the problem of gaining mastery of the sea, and then advancing against troops in Manchuria, while maintaining her armies from home ports. But in 1894 she was arrayed against an unwieldy empire making war with obsolete weapons, whereas now she was combating a strong nation possessed of huge armies and a modern fleet much stronger than her own. This last feature presented the ultimate question of success or failure. Of the fleets in Eastern waters, Japan's was superior to Russia's, but should it meet with defeat, all hope of landing a force in Manchuria was gone, and the war was lost. Should it be successful and destroy the opposing force, Japan would be able to land and supply sufficient troops in Manchuria to cope with the Russian forces already there. In Russia there were armies large enough to overwhelm the Japanese. In European waters was a fleet immensely superior to that of Japan. But they were both some months away. The Russian armies had to mobilize and travel over 4000 miles of rail; the fleet to make the long trip half around the world. With luck and skill, a decisive blow might be struck before these reinforcements could arrive. Haste was the prime requisite.

i. *Japanese Plan of Operation*

The Japanese plan may be outlined in general terms as follows: the invasion of Korea and its occupation as a base of operations; the separation of the Russian troops in Port Arthur and Dalny from those in the northern part of Manchuria; the capture of Port Arthur by assault if possible; a concentric advance toward some point on the railroad (preferably Liao-yang), there to destroy the

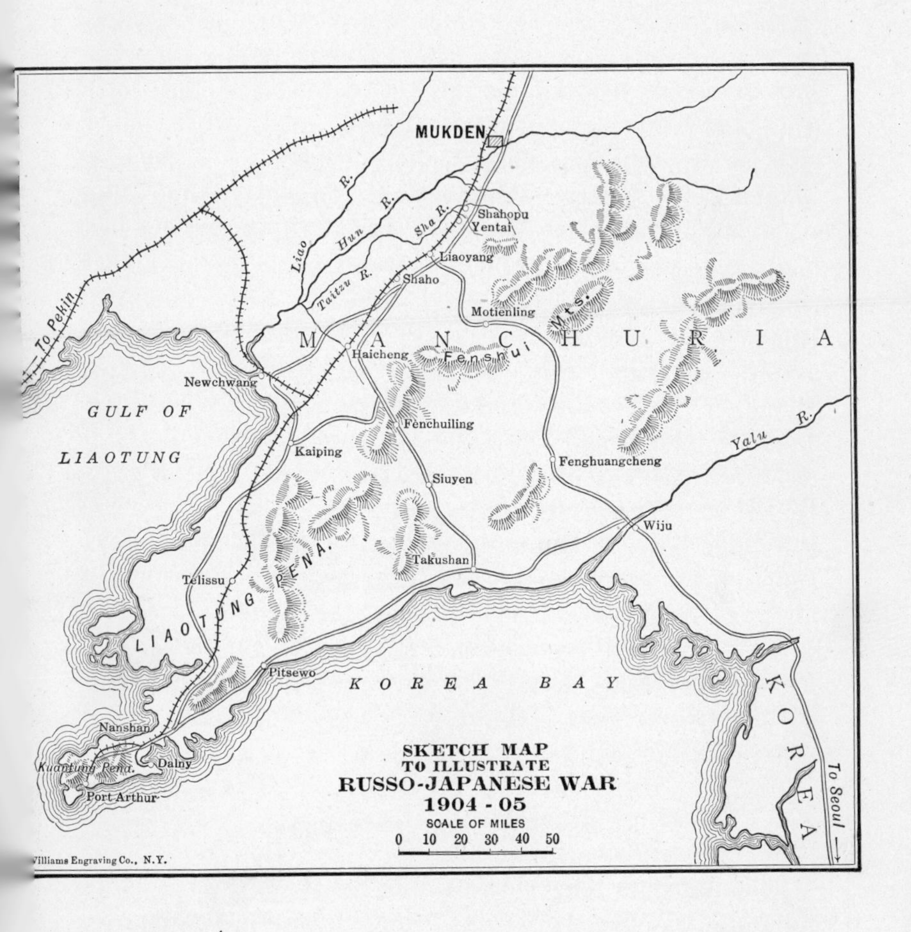
MUKDEN
Liao R.
Hun R.
Sha R.
Taitzu R.
Shahopu
Yentai
Liaoyang
Shaho
Motienling
To Pekin
M A N C H U R I A
Haicheng
Fenshui Mts.
Newchwang
GULF OF
LIAOTUNG
Fenchuiling
Kaiping
Fenghuangcheng
Yalu R.
Siuyen
Wiju
Takushan
Telissu
LIAOTUNG PENA.
Pitsewo
KOREA BAY
KOREA
Nanshan
Kuantung Pena.
Dalny
Port Arthur
To Seoul
SKETCH MAP
TO ILLUSTRATE
RUSSO-JAPANESE WAR
1904 - 05
SCALE OF MILES
0 10 20 30 40 50
Williams Engraving Co., N.Y.

Russian army before help could arrive from Europe. In addition to these, there was the plan to attack the Russian fleet the moment it could be located. At no time did the Japanese even consider an attack on Russian territory — that, of course, was impossible. But she did mean to win such victories in Manchuria as would demonstrate her military superiority and establish beyond question her hegemony in the Far East. In opposition to these, the Russians had but one scheme of defense — delay. Time was essential — time in which to mobilize and ship the European troops, time in which to get the fleet to the China Sea.

ii. *Comparative Armaments*

The army with which Japan hoped to win the war was a modern one, well equipped and well trained. Universal service has existed in the empire since 1871, and many of the officers have been trained in the best European schools. Every physically fit male citizen between the ages of 17 and 40 is liable for service in either the army or navy. Not all those coming of age are chosen for service in the standing army. There are several classes of reserves in which varying amounts of training are given. At the time of the outbreak of war, there were in the active army and first reserve, 380,000 trained men. In the second line were nearly 400,000 men with some training wherewith to replace casualties. The men themselves were as good soldiers as the world has ever seen — intelligent, determined, possessed of a great endurance, and imbued with a wonderful spirit of sacrifice and sense of duty.

The fighting force was divided into thirteen infantry divisions (the Imperial Guard division, and twelve territorial divisions) each having a combatant strength of about 13,000 men. Each division had a reserve brigade, and there were in addition in the first line, two independent cavalry brigades, and two brigades of artillery of eighteen batteries each. Each division, which was a unit complete in itself, consisted in round numbers of 11,400 rifles, 600 sabres, 36 guns, and 750 engineers. The infantry was armed with a modern clip-using rifle; the cavalry carried sabres and carbines of a model similar to the rifle; and the artillery was equipped with an improved breech-loading three-inch fieldpiece, converted to the quick-firing type, but not quite up to date. With each cavalry brigade was a battery of machine guns.

Opposed to Japan's force was the great Russian army of over a million men. The system which the Czar put into effect in 1874 has already been described. In the interval between the War of 1878 and the time under discussion, the system had been adhered to, men had been trained in great numbers, and an excellent military staff had been formed. Not over a tenth of this great force, however, was in Manchuria when the hostilities commenced. The troops already in the Far East were scattered here and there about the province, guarding the railway and the fortresses. When General Kuropatkin took command in the war zone in March of 1904 he organized the troops into the I, II, and III Siberian Corps and a cavalry division. Two rifle divisions remained as fortress troops at Vladivostok and two at Port Arthur. These brought his total forces to 96,000 men. Mobilization of the European troops was begun at once, and the task of shipping them over a single line of railroad was carried out so well that the I, VII, X, XVI, and XVII European Corps, a rifle corps, and five reserve infantry divisions arrived in Manchuria in time to take part in the final great battle of Mukden in March, 1905.

The armament was about the same as that of the Japanese. The infantry arm was a clip-using rifle of modern type; the cavalry, the sabre and rifle; but the artillery was in course of re-armament when war was declared. About one-third was armed with a new quick-firing fieldpiece much superior to the old type, but the excellence of the new gun was more than offset by the unfamiliarity of the men with their weapon. The remainder was armed with a gun of less recent type, but none the less an effective weapon. A number of regiments possessed machine gun companies, but the use of this arm was not general throughout the army.

iii. *Naval Operations*

Not the least important factor in the final success for Japan was the navy. The Russian sea forces greatly outnumbered those of the smaller power, but they were divided into two fleets, one in the Baltic, and one in Asiatic waters. This latter fleet was still further divided into two squadrons which operated from the naval bases of Vladivostok and Port Arthur. Since the Japanese did not wait to gain a mastery of the sea before beginning their land operations, and since the two campaigns were independent of each other, it will be as well to outline briefly at this point the naval engagements of the war. On February 8, 1904, the main Japanese battle fleet under Vice-Admiral Togo surprised the opposing squadron in the harbor at Port Arthur and inflicted losses which temporarily had a paralyzing effect upon the Russians. For a time they remained inactive, until upon the succession to command of Admiral Makároff, they began again to play their proper part in the war. On the night of April 12, Togo was successful in decoying the Russian squadron through a field of mines, using as bait several smaller units of his fleet. As Makároff advanced to the attack, the entire Japanese fleet steamed against him and forced him back through the mine field. One of the floating terrors struck Admiral Makároff's flagship, the *Petropavlovsk*, and sent it to the bottom with every soul on board. This calamity had the effect of keeping the Russians so close to their base at Port Arthur that Togo was able to dispatch a squadron of seven cruisers in search of the Vladivostok fleet.

Disaster fell upon both Russian fleets almost simultaneously. Upon the arrival of a Japanese army before Port Arthur, the squadron at that point put to sea, only to encounter Togo's fleet and be so damaged that it was obliged to put back into port. It was never able to emerge again, and from that day, August 10, 1904, ceased to count as a part of the active naval strength. Four days later, Kaimura located the Vladivostok fleet and defeated it utterly. These two battles established Japan's naval supremacy in the East.

No further efforts were made to control the sea until March, 1905, when the Baltic fleet under Admiral Rozhestvensky set sail for the China Sea. Everything had been staked on the outcome of the voyage, and practically every available ship had been added to the fleet. It was, perhaps, more formidable because of its size than its quality, but still it was a very powerful unit. Admiral Togo wisely waited to receive it in Japanese waters. On the 27th of May, 1905, the two fleets met in the Fushima Straits at the entrance to the Sea of Japan, and here in a battle which lasted all of one afternoon, at intervals through the night, and the following morning, Rozhestvensky's entire fleet was destroyed. Thereafter Japan's position in eastern waters was undisputed.

iv. *Military Operations*

Let us now turn to the operations on land. Simultaneously with Togo's first attack on the Russian squadron at Port Arthur, General Kuroki landed the First Army, composed of the 2d, 12th, and Guard divisions at Chemulpo, and on the following day, February 10, 1904, took possession of Seoul, the Korean capital. This army of 45,000 then started on the laborious march northward. Ice still bound the harbors north of Chemulpo so that the supply of the army was an extremely difficult problem, but little by little they pushed on, and in the early days of April stood face to face with the enemy on the Yalu River. Across from the little town of Wiju at the junction of the Yalu and the Aiho rivers, a Russian force of about 15,000 men and 40 guns under General Zasulich occupied a position of immense strength amongst the rugged hills protected in front by the unfordable river, which was filled at this point with islands. Late in April, Kuroki's forces built bridges across to the islands, and then on the 1st of May began a frontal attack there while the 12th division crossed several miles upstream and bore down on the Russian left flank. But the frontal attack had been sufficient to push back the Russian lines, and in the confused retirement, the retreating regiments encountered the successful 12th division, which insured the victory by a murderous fire on their fleeing enemy. Zasulich now fell back toward Motienling, with Kuroki in full pursuit as far as Fenghuangcheng, at which point he waited for the advance of the other Japanese armies. The Russians had committed a grave error by allowing themselves to become entangled in a battle of such proportions. Zasulich's mission on the Yalu was simply to oppose the advance of Kuroki, and he should have known how impossible it was for his small force to engage successfully the entire First Japanese Army.

The Second Army set sail for the war zone as soon as Kuroki had released the transports. This force, composed of the 1st, 3d, 4th, and 5th divisions under General Oku, waited for the result of the battle of the Yalu, and then, the Port Arthur fleet having been temporarily removed from the sea by the April disaster, landed at Pitsevo on May 5 and started for the Kuan Tung peninsula to attack Port Arthur. At the narrowest portion of the peninsula, Oku discovered the field column of the Port Arthur Army fortified on Nanshan Hill in a position of great strength. The peninsula is not more than two miles wide at this point, and in its center rises a four-hundred-foot hill. Here the Russians had entrenched, constructed entanglements, and mounted field and siege guns. The flanks reached to the sea on both sides, one of which was protected by a gunboat. Twice the Japanese assaulted the position only to be beaten back, but at the third attempt they were able, with the assistance of one of their gunboats, to turn the Russian left and take the hill. The defeated army withdrew in good order into Port Arthur.

A few days later, Dalny was entered by troops of the 1st division without opposition. Meanwhile two more divisions under General Nogi, the 6th and the 11th, had landed at Pitsevo, and had hurried down toward the Kuan Tung Peninsula. The 6th was transferred with the 1st, which latter division joined with the 11th to form the Third Army with General Nogi in command. Nogi was left to invest Port Arthur while Oku turned north to carry out the second part of the plan — the advance on Liao-yang. The siege of Port Arthur, like that of Plevna, belongs properly to a study of fortification and not to a short strategic sketch. It is sufficient to say here that the garrison under General Stössel maintained a splendid defense for seven months. During the last month occurred the assaults on 203 Meter Hill, by which after a frightful loss of life, the Japanese gained the key point of the situation. Within a few days after this victory, General Stössel, on January 2, 1905, surrendered his garrison of 39,000.

The march of General Oku to the north with the Second Army, which occurred in June, 1904, was hurriedly begun in order to prevent the advance of General Stakelberg, who with 35,000 men was marching to the assistance of the Port Arthur troops. Stakelberg's advance was a movement made in direct opposition to the wishes of the Russian Commander-in-chief, but Port Arthur was a place of great political importance, and therefore, as so often happens in war, strategy was sacrificed to politics, with the usual result. General Oku's army encountered the relief expedition near Telissu, and in a brilliant encounter defeated it disastrously. Stakelberg was obliged to abandon his enterprise and fall back to a position near Kaiping. The effect of the maneuver had been to split Kuropatkin's army into smaller parts, which could be more easily disposed of by their opponents. The benefits were all for the enemy.

While the Second Army was advancing against Stakelberg, the 10th division, which formed the nucleus of the Fourth Army, was landed at Takusan. A half division was transferred from the First Army to its commander, General Nodzu, and the combined forces moved on Siuyen preparatory to the advance on Liao-yang.

The three field armies were now ready for the concentration on the railway. Kuroki's army was in the northern part of the Fenshui Mountains, near Motienling; Nodzu's Fourth Army was in the southern part of the same range near Fenshuiling Pass; Oku was advancing along the railway, and by the end of June was close to Kaiping. All three were united under Marshal Oyama as commander-in-chief, who, with his chief-of-staff, General Kodama, sailed from Tokyo to take command on the 6th of July. With his arrival the advance on Liao-yang was begun. The opposing forces were stationed on the rim of a circle whose center was the headquarters at Liao-yang. General Keller who was opposing the advance of General Kuroki retired from his position at Motienling without an action. His withdrawal allowed Kuroki to approach perilously near to the Russian communications to the north, and as a result Kuropatkin ordered the withdrawal upon Liao-yang of General Alexieff, who was opposing Nodzu, and Stakelberg, who was holding Kaiping in front of Oku. This retreat enabled the Second and Fourth Japanese Armies to unite. Still, with all the great need for haste, the Japanese advance was so slow that it was not until the end of August that the Russians occupied their entrenched lines before Liao-yang.

General Kuropatkin had made the most of an excellent

position. The defenses consisted of two lines, an inner and outer — the former, a line of very strong redoubts immediately encircling the village of Liao-yang, the latter a line of trenches extending in a great semicircle from Shoushanpou on the south to Hsiapu on the Taitzu River. To the north of the river were two other detached lines, the one just west of Manjuyama Hill being very important. The trenches themselves, which were constructed with the utmost care, covered the slopes of the hills south of Liao-yang. Reserve trenches, gun emplacements, obstacles, communication lines — everything which could add to the chance of success had been carefully thought out and prepared. The right of the line was protected by the railway embankment, the left rested on Manjuyama Hill. To hold these lines, Kuropatkin had a force of 180,000 men, 560 field guns, and about 35 heavy guns.

Marshal Oyama advanced to the attack with an army inferior in numbers, but with all the confidence which an unbroken string of victories could produce. It numbered about 140,000 men and 524 guns. The Japanese commander having decided upon the offensive, the first operation was a forcing back of the Russians upon their trenches in order that the First and Fourth Armies might establish communications. This part of the plan was carried out in the days of August 25–29, 1904, during which time the fighting to the east and south of Liao-yang gradually forced the Russians to withdraw within their entrenched lines. Three of the Russian corps occupied the trenches south of the Taitzu, one corps held the position north of the river, two cavalry divisions covered the right flank beyond the railway, and a reserve of two corps occupied the town of Liao-yang.

The battle proper commenced on the 30th of August. Six and one-half divisions advanced to the attack of the main lines south of the town, while a division and a half of Kuroki's army crossed the Taitzu without difficulty and

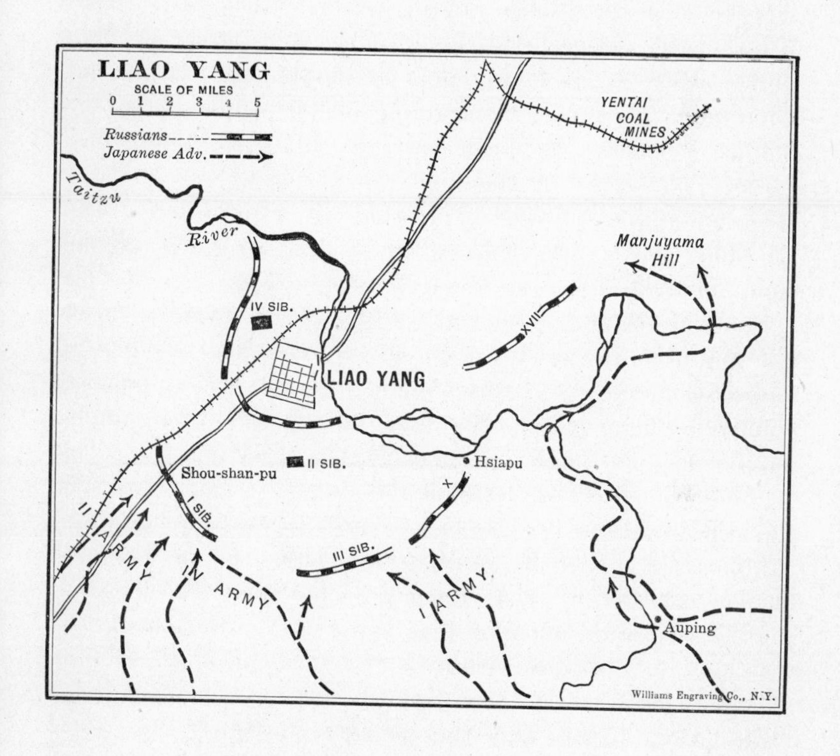
LIAO YANG
SCALE OF MILES
0 1 2 3 4 5
Russians
Japanese Adv.
Taitzu
River
YENTAI
COAL
MINES
Manjuyama
Hill
IV SIB.
XVII
LIAO YANG
II SIB.
Hsiapu
Shou-shan-pu
I SIB.
X
III SIB.
II ARMY
IV ARMY
I ARMY
Auping
Williams Engraving Co., N.Y.

lined up against the Russian left. The attacks to the south on the 30th and 31st of August were repelled without difficulty, and there seemed to be no reason why Kuropatkin could not have caused Oyama serious annoyance by his defensive measures, but that on the night of August 31 disconcerting reports reached the commander from his left. An exaggerated statement of the numbers of the First Army who had crossed the Taitzu caused Kuropatkin to abandon the advanced line of trenches south of the town, and bring in the defenders to the inner line of works. He planned to leave two corps to hold these redoubts and with the remainder of his army attack and destroy the Japanese troops north of the Taitzu. Before he could carry out this plan, however, the 1st Japanese division on September 1 captured the Manjuyama Hill which was the key to the situation north of the river. The Russian commander bent all his efforts to a recapture of this important spot on the following days, but in vain. Moreover, the troops of Stakelberg, whom he had sent against the Japanese extreme right, were so repulsed that the entire position on the Taitzu became untenable. The forces in Liao-yang had resisted all attacks, but notwithstanding their success, Kuropatkin realized that the battle was lost, and consequently in the early morning of September 3 began his retreat upon Mukden. Strong rear guards covered the withdrawal, but there was little pursuit, for the victorious Japanese were as badly exhausted as their foe.

There followed a cessation of hostilities for a month, during which period both armies endeavored to replace their losses. The Russians had fallen back to a position along the Sha River, and here the Japanese were quite content to leave them for a time. Then in the beginning of October, General Kuropatkin began an offensive. He had reorganized his forces into two armies, one of which he sent through the mountains east of Liao-yang against the Japanese right, and the other along the railroad full at the center of his adversary's line. Both advances were checked, the Japanese began a counter-attack, and in the two weeks from October 5 to October 18 they drove the Russians back behind the line of the Sha River with losses of nearly 40,000 men. These engagements are known as the battle of Shaho.

Both armies now entrenched along the Sha River, and operations ceased until January, 1905. The Russians were awaiting reinforcements from Europe, the Japanese were daily expecting the fall of Port Arthur and its consequent strengthening of their forces by the addition of Nogi's army. Two unsuccessful operations marked the opening of hostilities in the new year. General Mischenko, with a large cavalry detachment, made a raid down the Hun Valley with the purpose of destroying the railroad in rear of the Japanese army. The expedition does not seem to have been carried out with vigor, for notwithstanding the size of his command, he was easily repulsed in his efforts to capture points on the railway. The second failure was an attack by General Grippenberg's army with the idea of turning the Japanese left. The battle of Sandepu, which was fought as a result of this offensive movement, took place in a terrible snowstorm on the 26th and 27th of January. General Grippenberg was not checked by the enemy, but in the face of such severe conditions, Kuropatkin decided to abandon the attempt. On the Japanese side, the fall of Port Arthur on January 2 released the army of General Nogi, and it immediately started north to join the command of Marshal Oyama.

Mid-January found the opposing forces occupying a long entrenched line eastward from the Hunho along the Sha River. Kuropatkin had divided his command into three armies, which were disposed as follows: the II Army, under General Kaulbars, occupied the right of the line from Shantan on the Hunho River to Linchunpu on the Sha, with one corps in reserve at Maturan; the III Army,

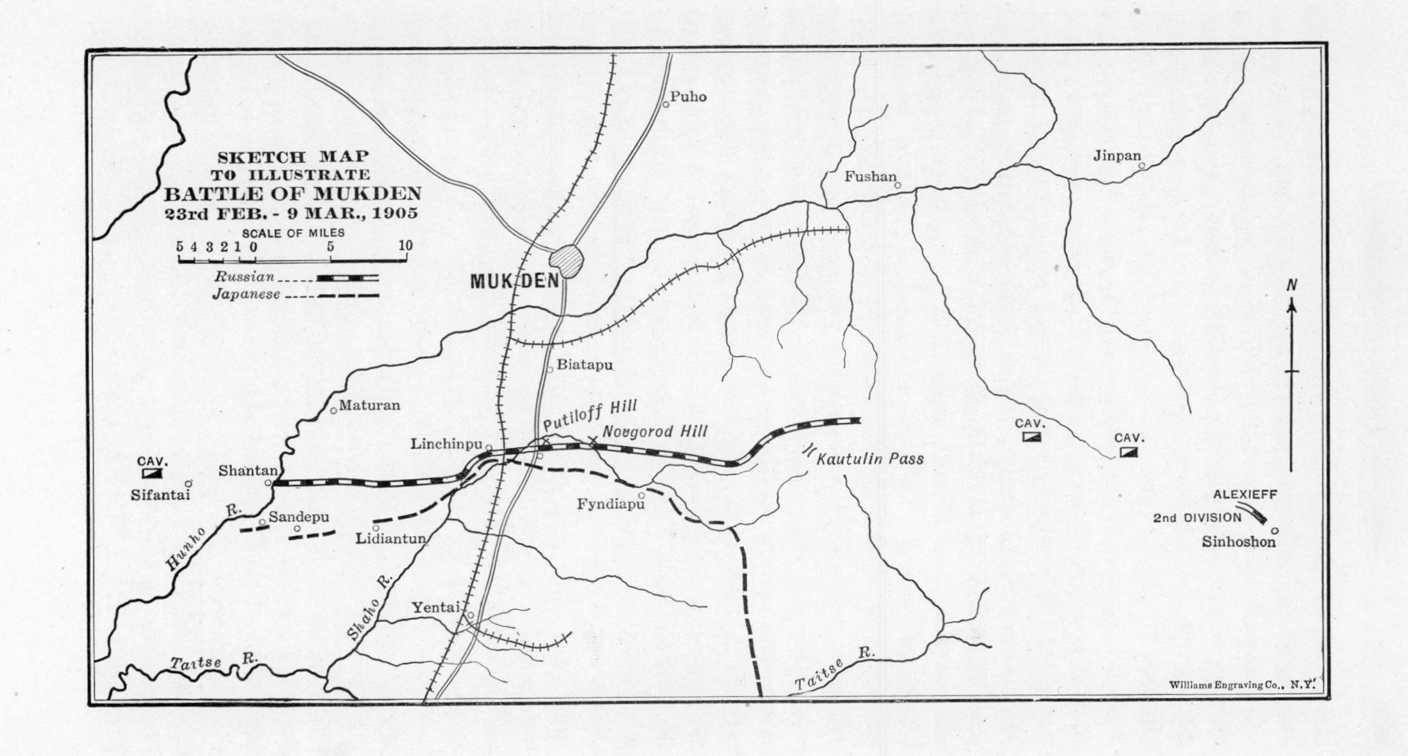
SKETCH MAP
TO ILLUSTRATE
BATTLE OF MUKDEN
23rd FEB. - 9 MAR., 1905
SCALE OF MILES
5 4 3 2 1 0 5 10
Russian
Japanese
MUKDEN
Puho
Fushan
Jinpan
Biatapu
Maturan
Linchinpu
Putiloff Hill
Novgorod Hill
Kautulin Pass
CAV.
CAV.
CAV.
Shantan
Sifantai
Hunho R.
Sandepu
Lidiantun
Fyndiapu
Shaho R.
Yentai
Taitse R.
Taitse R.
N
ALEXIEFF
2nd DIVISION
Sinhoshon
Williams Engraving Co., N.Y.

General Bilderling commanding, continued the line from Linchinpu to Novgorod Hill; and the I Army, commanded by General Linievitch, was widely distributed from Novogorod Hill to Kautulin Pass in the mountains. The right flank was covered by three regiments of cavalry at Sifantai, and on the left the line was extended by minor detachments to the Korean frontier, a hundred miles away. The last detachment of any size was that of General Alexieff who commanded a division at Sinhoshon. A general reserve, the XVI Corps, was at Biatapu. The whole entrenched line was a full fifty miles long.

Facing this line were the Japanese on a front somewhat shorter. Oyama, too, had reorganized his command, had brought up several reserve divisions, and had organized a new army — the Fifth, under General Kawamura. The First Army (General Kuroki, with three divisions) was on the right of the entrenched line from the Taitzu River to Fyndaipu; the Fourth Army (General Nodzu, with three divisions) held the line from Fyndaipu to a point of the line south of Putiloff Hill; and the Second Army (General Oku, with three divisions) extended the line westward to Lidiantun. On the left flank, Hekoutai and Sandepu were strongly enforced. In rear of General Oku was General Nogi's Third Army of four divisions, on the extreme right was General Kawamura with the Fifth Army of four divisions, and a general reserve was held at Yentai. The strength of the adversaries was about 300,000 each.

Oyama's plan seems to have been to feint against the Russian left, and then, when that should be reinforced, drive home his real attack in the shape of an enveloping movement on the Russian right, delivered by the supporting army, of General Nogi. The scheme worked well. Fighting was begun on February 21 by Kawamura's army, which delivered an attack against Alexieff at Sinhoshon. By the 25th, the fighting had spread westward to include Kuroki's army as well, and Kuropatkin, convinced that his left was bearing the brunt of the attack and was in danger of being turned, denuded his right of reserves in order to strengthen his menaced flank. Immediately Oyama began to envelop the Russian right. Nogi's attacks on the west flank began on the 1st of March, and though the Russians resisted desperately, they were slowly forced back, the line pivoting about Putiloff Hill. To the east along the Sha, the Russian line remained unshaken under fierce assaults. But for the error of shifting his reserves to the east, Kuropatkin might have foiled the entire Japanese attack. As soon as he realized that his real danger was from Nogi, he ordered his reserves to return to his right flank, but they did not arrive in position until March 6, and by that time the Japanese reserves were also on the western front to oppose them. In the early days of Nogi's attack, on the 1st and 2d of March, the presence of these troops would have been invaluable and would probably have led to Nogi's repulse, but now their strength was offset by the added Japanese reserves from Yentai.

In desperation, the Russian commander now launched a vicious counter-attack against Nogi, but this collapsed after a brief fight. Nothing was left but to draw in upon Mukden in the hope of holding the line of the Hunho. The withdrawal was accomplished safely on March 7, the Japanese armies to the south following closely. The shortening of the line, however, enabled Nogi to extend his command farther to the north and bend it in toward the Russian line of communications. The impending danger from this source, coupled with news of serious engagements between Linievitch and Kuroki on the east, persuaded Kuropatkin of the inadvisability of holding Mukden longer, and on the night of March 9 he began the retreat toward Tieling. The retreat continued throughout the 10th of March with heavy fighting by the Russian rear guard under General Kaulbars. By nightfall of this day, Nogi's left and Kawamura's right met north of Mukden, but the victorious army was so confused that a serious pursuit of the enemy could be undertaken only after a period of reorganization. Meanwhile the Russians had withdrawn beyond Tieling Pass, at which point the Japanese pursuit was eventually stopped.

Kuropatkin's army suffered heavily by this battle, the losses being estimated at close to 95,000. Apart from the tactical errors the Russian general committed, the battle itself was a serious mistake. Delay was still the trump card of the Russians, and a slow retreat along the railroad would have taken the Japanese farther and farther from their base and at the same time would have allowed Kuropatkin to strengthen his army with troops constantly arriving from Europe. By the end of August, the Russians would have had an army of 600,000 men in Manchuria to which Japan could have opposed not more than 350,000.

The defeat of Rozhestvensky's fleet at Tsu-shima on the 27th of May, 1905, was the culminating disaster of the war. There seems to be no doubt that from a strictly military viewpoint, the certainty of ultimate success lay with Russia. Japan had made her supreme effort, and had staked everything on the outcome. Had Russia still prosecuted the war vigorously, the Japanese must have been driven back to final defeat. But the continued Russian disasters, and political disorders at home, had practically destroyed Russian credit. More, the social unrest in Russia was so menacing that the government felt unable to go on with a foreign war. With revolution imminent, therefore, they accepted readily President Roosevelt's invitation to send ministers to the United States for the purpose of discussing peace.

The plenipotentiaries of the belligerent states met at Portsmouth, New Hampshire, on the 10th of August, 1905, and on the 5th of September had agreed upon terms. The treaty recognized Japan's "paramount political, military, and economic interests in Korea"; provided for the evacuation of Manchuria by both armies; transferred to Japan Russia's lease of the Liao-Tung Peninsula with all privileges attached thereto which had been obtained from China; transferred, also, the Russian railways in lower Manchuria; secured for Japan the lower half of the island of Sakhalin; provided for certain fishing privileges along the Siberian coasts; and reimbursed Japan for the amount of money spent on Russian prisoners over and above that spent by Russia on Japanese prisoners. There was no indemnity. For a time it was thought that the peace negotiations might fail of conclusion because of the question of an indemnity, for it was well known that the people of Japan fully expected to pay the expenses of the war from the Russian treasury. Japan's statesmen, however, knew that it would be futile to demand indemnity from a state whose existence had not been threatened, and therefore, although they knew that they incurred the hostility of their countrymen in so doing, they limited themselves to the demands made by Japan before the outbreak of hostilities.

The little empire has made the most of the advantages gained from the war. Although she was greatly impoverished by the war, she set about enterprises both in Manchuria and Korea. In the latter state particularly, reforms were carrried out, systems of communications established, new industrial enterprises launched, and new methods of agriculture introduced. All these activities were carried on in the face of a smothered antipathy on the part of the Koreans, which finally broke out into open rebellion in 1907, and lasted for over two years. Determined to have order in Korea, Japan put down the insurrection ruthlessly and finally in August, 1910, abolished the kingdom and made Korea an integral part of the Japanese Empire.

CHAPTER IV

THE TRIPLE ENTENTE

THE Russo-Japanese War of 1904 and 1905 had a decided reaction upon the political situation in Europe, especially upon German policies. By weakening the chief military power of Germany's enemies, it gave Germany the opportunity to attempt to nullify the effects of the *Entente Cordiale* between France and Great Britain by a reassertion of her position and influence. Delcassé's remarkable success in his approaches to Italy, thus weakening the bond between that country and the other nations of the Triple Alliance, and in his establishment of the *Entente Cordiale* between France and Great Britain, had filled the German statesmen with alarm. The German leadership in international affairs, which had been the outstanding fact in European policies since 1871, was believed to be seriously threatened by the revival of French initiative and independence. Fully aware of the existence in France of a determined party in favor of measures to recover Alsace and Lorraine, the Germans interpreted every move of the French diplomats as directed toward this end, and believed that such a result was to be thwarted only by the maintenance of unquestioned German hegemony in European affairs.

A. THE MOROCCAN CRISIS

For a demonstration of Germany's position in European affairs, her statesmen chose to raise an issue in Morocco. This country, the richest and most desirable of the remaining unclaimed countries in Africa, had been falling gradually under the influence of France. It had territory of more than 200,000 square miles (slightly larger than France) and a population of only 5,000,000; its climate was temperate, its soil fertile, and its undeveloped resources of enormous value; it was the thoroughfare for the commerce of northern Africa and Sahara; and its government, corrupt and inefficient, was a constant temptation to European powers to intervene. France, having gained control of Algiers to the east and the vast Sahara region to the south, had marked Morocco for her next great colonial extension, and had long kept French agents in the country building and extending French interests. Delcassé had taken a great stride toward the full realization of French ambitions in Morocco by his success in his *Entente Cordiale* with Great Britain, it being recognized in the Anglo-French convention, that "it appertains to France, more particularly as a Power whose dominions are coterminous for a great distance with those of Morocco, to preserve order in that country and to provide assistance for the purpose of all administrative, economic, financial, and military reforms which it may require." In certain secret provisions of this same convention (not made public until 1911) the two countries hinted at "the event of either government finding itself constrained, by the force of circumstances, to modify the policy with respect to Egypt or Morocco" — a direct anticipation of the probability of a French protectorate in the latter country. Furthermore Delcassé treated with Spain in the Moroccan question (October 3, 1904) in a convention which, although openly stating that the two countries were "firmly attached to the integrity of the Moorish Empire under the sovereignty of the Sultan," secretly, as in the Anglo-French Convention, provided for the possible future establishment of French political control over the country. Germany had not been consulted with respect to these treaties, presumably because Delcassé had not believed German interests affected, and the Anglo-French and the Spanish-French conventions had not been directly submitted to the chancellery at Berlin. The German foreign office, however, was well informed by its own agents of what had taken place, probably even to the extent of knowing of the existence and general import of the secret articles in the two conventions. From the German point of view, these confidential and secret negotiations on a colonial matter of great importance, undertaken and carried through by France without taking into account the will or wishes of Germany, presented an opportunity for an effective German protest which might establish Germany's right to a voice henceforth in international affairs in all parts of the world. If her protest were effective, German prestige and authority would be reëstablished.

The government chose a striking time to make its demonstration. On the one hand, the Russian army had just suffered in the operations around Mukden (February 21–March 9, 1905) what seemed to be a decisive defeat at the hands of the Japanese, and the Russian civil population in European Russia was apparently on the verge of open rebellion. On the other hand, France, just beginning to act in conformity with her powers under the Anglo-French and Spanish-French conventions, had loaned 62,500,000 francs to the Moroccan government, and had presented (February, 1905) to that government a program of economic, financial, and military reforms which, if put into effect, would give to France all of the powers of a protectorate over Morocco.

The German intervention was dramatic in the extreme. On the last day of March, 1905, Emperor William II, while cruising in the Mediterranean, suddenly and unexpectedly disembarked at Tangier and spoke to the following effect:

"It is to the Sultan in his position of an independent sovereign that I am paying my visit to-day. I hope that under the sovereignty of the Sultan a free Morocco will remain, open to the peaceful rivalry of all nations, without monopoly or annexation, on the basis of absolute equality. The object of my visit to Tangier is to make it known that I am determined to do all that is in my power to safeguard efficaciously the interests of Germany in Morocco, for I look upon the Sultan as an absolutely independent sovereign."

The attitude and purposes of Germany were at once interpreted in Paris as a direct thrust at the recently acquired initiative and independence of France and at the new alliance with England. Although the German Emperor based his intervention on the commercial interests of his subjects in Morocco, French statesmen were quick to point out the fact that imports of German goods formed the insignificant amount of 9% of the total imports of Morocco, and that no discrimination had been made or threatened against this German commerce. Frenchmen saw a deeper political purpose behind the Emperor's act, an effort to humiliate France and break down the international structure Delcassé had reared during the preceding six years. An interview given out in Paris by Prince Henckel von Donnersmarck, a man of great wealth and of high standing in German official circles, confirmed French opinion:

"If your agreements with England looked only to the maintenance of European peace, we should have sincerely approved them; but unfortunately the opinions of the newspapers which assume to reflect the opinion of the government, certain conversations which had the ear-marks of official declaration, the statements made in Paris by King Edward VII, have all given us to understand that the chief object of the *Entente Cordiale* was the isolation of Germany, preceding and preparing for an approaching attack. At length, in disposing of this matter without consulting us, without informing us of the empire of Morocco where we had interests, you keenly offended the Emperor and the German people.

"Are these the politics of France? Or must we consider them the personal conception of M. Delcassé?

"If you think that your minister of Foreign Affairs has engaged your country in too adventurous a course, acknowledge it by dispensing with his services and especially by giving a new direction to your foreign policy.

"The person of M. Delcassé does not concern us, but his policy constitutes a menace to Germany. You can rest assured that we shall not wait to have it realized. The Emperor does not desire war. His principal wish is to further the development and expansion of German commerce. The German fleet, which he wishes to see numerous and powerful, is only the means for carrying out peaceful purposes. . . .

"Give up the minister whose sole ambition is to disturb the peace of Europe, and adopt frankly with Germany a loyal and open policy, the only one worthy of a great nation like yours, if you wish to preserve the peace of the world." (Tardieu: La France et les alliances. 3e édition. p. 217 ff.)

Germany's next step in this crisis was to enlist the aid of the Sultan of Morocco in a demand for a European conference in the Moroccan question. Again the German diplomats waited until a catastrophe to Russia had emphasized her weakness. On May 27, 1905, the Russian fleet was annihilated in the battle of Tsu-shima. Three days later the Sultan of Morocco, obviously at German dictation, submitted a demand for a conference of the European powers upon the reforms presented by France. Germany took occasion to support officially the Sultan's request, and let it be known informally, but none the less emphatically, that she intended to stand behind the Sultan with all her power.

France was placed in a most difficult position. By her treaties with Italy, Great Britain, and Spain she had acquired special political privileges in her dealings with Morocco, privileges which could lead logically to the establishment of a protectorate. To yield to the Sultan's demand as supported by Germany would mean the loss of all she had gained and would be a national humiliation and disgrace. Her greatest military ally, Russia, however, was powerless to give her the aid that she desired, and careful reports concerning her own military conditions revealed the impossibility of coping successfully with so well-prepared an enemy as Germany. Great Britain's strength was purely naval: her military aid, offered (it has been said) in the shape of 100,000 men to be landed in Schleswig-Holstein, would not be great enough to insure a victory for the Entente. In spite of all these obstacles, Delcassé, desperate at the threatened collapse of his work, urged France to accept the German challenge. M. Rouvier, the prime minister, and his colleagues were reluctantly forced to veto Delcassé's proposals. Delcassé thereupon (June 12, 1905) resigned from the ministry and a few days later Germany was informed that France would recommend the acceptance of the Sultan's request for a conference.

In the first stage of the proceedings, then, German policy had scored a great triumph. She had forced her will on Europe; she had brought about the resignation of a minister in a foreign cabinet, who was supposed to be responsible for policies distasteful to her; she had, it was thought, acquired influence with the Sultan of Morocco by her support; and — perhaps in the eyes of some most important of all — she had by a threat of war tested the strength of the alliance binding France with Russia on the one hand and with Great Britain on the other, and found it weak. Statesmen in Germany looked forward with great confidence to a continuation of the success of her diplomats in the conference.

i. *The Algeciras Conference*

When the representatives of the Powers met in the conference of Algeciras, held in the sleepy little town on the Spanish coast near by the Strait of Gibraltar from January to April, 1906, the international situation had radically changed. Europe had been subjected to an intense strain for the six months preceding and each of the powers had been busy in getting ready for an emergency. France had used the intervening months to prepare herself for possible war; Russia had signed the peace with Japan and, in spite of her weakness, was by no means absolutely helpless; and Great Britain, appreciating more fully the danger to herself from the German policy, had completed her military plans in case of war. Germany was no longer able to count upon the weakness of her enemies for her own success.

The first weeks of the conference were characterized by overbearing and impossible demands on the part of German representatives. Nothing less than the *complete independence* of Morocco and a public recognition of the *absolute sovereignty* of the Sultan would be acceptable to them. They found, however, little support for their demands among the representatives of the other powers. Great Britain, Russia, and Spain supported France as a matter of course, Sir Edward Grey going so far as to make a declaration to the French ambassador:

"If war was forced upon France then on the question of Morocco — a question which had just been made the subject of agreement between this country and France, an agreement extremely popular on both sides — if out of this agreement war was forced on France at this time, in his view public opinion in this country would have rallied to the material support of France."

Italy let it be known that she would not in the Moroccan quarrel sacrifice her understandings with Great Britain and France; and the representatives of the United States, wholly neutral on the issue because the vital interests of their country were in no way involved, voted consistently for the French proposals. Germany and Austria-Hungary stood alone. Under such conditions, the German representatives were forced to moderate their demands.

ii. *The Algeciras Treaty*

The final Act of Algeciras, a document of 123 articles, signed April 7, 1906, was a compromise between the German demands and the French position. Undoubtedly some of the more chauvinistic Germans had hoped for the use of the "mailed fist" to gain a coaling station in Morocco or a port from which German merchants might extend political influences toward the interior; and certainly the German government had hoped for the recognition of the complete independence of Morocco and the full sovereignty of the Sultan: neither of these objects was attained. On the other hand, France earnestly desired recognition of her special political and economic interests in Morocco, with a realization of the possibility of the establishment of a protectorate if conditions demanded: her object likewise was not attained. The compromise embodied in the Final Act accepted the principle of "the sovereignty and independence of his Majesty the Sultan, the integrity of his dominions, and economic liberty without any inequality," but it put the organization and control of the police force into the hands of France (and Spain, for the Riff district under her immediate influence) and gave those nations a more important share in the financial arrangements than other countries had.

The results of the conference were considered unsatisfactory in both the chief countries interested. France, it is true, had gained for all practical purposes the recognition of the powers of her special interests in Morocco. Although she had to give up immediate hope of a monopoly in, or of a protectorate over, Morocco, yet she had been deputed the agent of the powers in carrying out necessary reforms. But the original indignity of having been forced into the conference against her will rankled in the minds of all French statesmen, and the fact that France had been forced to acknowledge thus publicly the principle of the Moroccan independence seemed to postpone indefinitely the coveted protectorate. Public opinion in Germany viewed the Algeciras Act as a diplomatic defeat for the German representatives. Prince von Bülow, the chancellor, attempted to justify his policy in a speech to the Reichstag (April 5,

1906) arguing that the prestige of the German government and the dignity of the German Empire had been vindicated and safeguarded, but a vociferous party throughout the country could discern no material advantages in the settlement and criticized the government unsparingly.

The most important results of the Conference of Algeciras, however, were not the international agreement concerning the policing and financing of Morocco, but the revelation to all the diplomatic world of Germany's real ambitions and methods. The rapidly growing German navy, the lengthening lines of railroads in Turkish Asia Minor, the strong fortifications on Heligoland, the acquisition of Kiau-chau, her energetic development of commercial opportunities in every part of the world, all took on a new character in view of the German action at Tangier and Algeciras. Those statesmen who had hesitated to believe that Germany cherished aggressive plans for world empire, and for a deciding part in world politics, were henceforth convinced, and prepared to shape their policy in accordance with this conviction.

B. GREAT BRITAIN'S NAVAL PREPARATION TO RESIST GERMAN AGGRESSION

The greatest effect of this revelation of German policy was, naturally, produced in Great Britain. Great Britain possessed a world empire whose existence would be menaced by the establishment of a rival empire of similar extent. Great Britain played a part in world politics which was certain to be challenged by like ambitions on the part of Germany. British statesmanship during the next decade was directed toward a careful preparation to meet what was recognized as a "German Peril."

The first and most obvious step for Great Britain to take was to increase the strength and efficiency of her navy. A suspicion existed in the country that the navy had suffered more or less severely from the natural decay and degeneration due to long disuse. Although on paper the ships outnumbered by two to one those of any other European power, it was believed that discipline had been allowed to relax, that the marksmanship of the gunners was inferior, that there was a distinct shortage of sailors, and that a very large number of vessels of obsolete type were carried on the active roster. Furthermore, the disposition of the units of the fleets was intended to guard against France and Russia. The most powerful units were in the Mediterranean Sea; strong fleets were kept in the waters of the Far East to guard against Russia; one fleet was stationed in American waters, though any legitimate reason for such station had long passed; the ships kept on station in the North Sea were mainly of an obsolete or obsolescent type, valuable only for use as training ships. The British fleets, in short, were scattered in force all over the world except in home waters and their efficiency was doubtful.

The imminence of the German peril galvanized the navy into a new activity and efficiency. Sir John Fisher, who had been appointed First Lord of the Admiralty in 1903, took steps to put the British fleets in a state of "instant preparedness for war." He "scrapped" one hundred and seventy-five ships of the old type, using the crews of these "scrapped" ships to complete the complement of the recently built vessels. He introduced new scientific methods of practice to increase the efficiency of the gunnery. He stiffened the discipline of the men and inspired the officers with something of his own energy and capacity. He took advantage of the Anglo-Japanese alliance of 1902 (which assured Japanese coöperation with Great Britain in issues affecting the Far East), and of the Anglo-French *Entente Cordiale*, to make a complete redistribution of the British fleets, whereby the Mediterranean and Far Eastern fleets were greatly weakened, the North Pacific and South Atlantic fleets abolished, and a strong Atlantic fleet with

Gibraltar as its base, and a very powerful home fleet in the English channel and the North Sea, created. These changes were all made and accomplished within three years after Fisher's appointment. During the same period one great and sensational innovation was introduced in the building of the first *Dreadnought*, a vessel of a new class in that its armament consisted entirely of big guns. The *Dreadnought*, begun in 1905 and commissioned late in 1906, with a displacement of 17,900 tons and a speed of 21 knots — two knots faster than the speed of any battleship commissioned before that time — carried ten 12-inch guns. The admiralty committed itself fully to the *Dreadnought* policy by laying down and completing within the next two years two more of these huge vessels.

These naval preparations of Great Britain, combined with the German defeat in the Algeciras Conference, gave German chauvinists just the argument they needed to urge with increased vehemence the necessity of great additions to the navy. The German Navy League throughout the whole year deluged the whole country with newspaper articles and pamphlets, calling for an overwhelming navy to cope with the jealous rivalry of other European powers. Under the stimulus of this propaganda, the Reichstag received favorably the government's naval bill of 1906. The main articles of this bill provided for the substitution of 18 battleships of the largest size for the 18 medium-sized battleships provided in the 1900 bill, for the construction of six of the largest and most powerful type of ships of the cruiser class, and for the enlargement of the Kiel Canal and of certain German harbors and docks to accommodate the new ships. The Reichstag accepted the bill in its entirety, appropriating in excess of two hundred million dollars for the purpose.

The navy enthusiasts were also furnished with new arguments for their propaganda by the innovation introduced by the *Dreadnought* type, or "all big gun" type, of battleship. It was recognized at once that this type of ship, so far superior in speed and armament to previous types, rendered the old ships at once obsolete. The *Dreadnought* type was certain to be the type of the capital ships in the fleets of all countries. Granting this fact, all the superiority of the British fleet might be overcome by equaling Great Britain in the construction of *Dreadnoughts*. Germany and Great Britain could start on even terms in the naval rivalry.

Naval rivalry between the two nations passed into a new phase in 1906 and 1907 just after the enactment of the German Naval Bill. In Great Britain the Liberal party came into power with an overwhelming majority as a result of the elections of January, 1906. The party was pledged to sweeping measures of social reform. The leaders of the party, especially Sir Henry Campbell-Bannerman, the prime minister, realized that the Liberal program, including such projects as old age insurance, sickness insurance, and the like, would entail enormous expense to the government. The problem of how the government should propose to raise the money for these projects was difficult. The huge and constantly increasing cost of naval armaments, due at the time to the rivalry with Germany, could, if diverted to social ends, go far toward meeting the expenses of the liberal program. The liberal and radical press in Great Britain was at this period laying great emphasis upon a statement of the German Chancellor, von Bülow, that Germany had "as little idea of challenging British maritime supremacy as of building a railway to the moon," and was urging the limitation of armaments by mutual consent. In this situation Sir Henry Campbell-Bannerman took the responsibility of inviting the representatives of the German government to discuss the possibilities of a limitation of armament by mutual agreement.

This invitation was not favorably received either in German official or in German popular circles. Prince von

Bülow repudiated the suggestion that the financial burden was weighing heavily upon the German nation, and insisted that German naval plans should not alarm Great Britain. Official Germany, and probably a considerable part of the German nation at large, had no confidence in the sincerity of the British proposals. Many were inclined to construe these proposals as an indication of British weakness, arguing that, when Great Britain saw the possibility of Germany becoming equal to her on the sea by the rivalry in the construction of *Dreadnoughts*, she wished to limit armaments while she was still well ahead in the race. In spite of the unfavorable reception of her proposals in Germany, Great Britain persisted by trying to have the question considered by the representatives of all the nations at the second Hague conference in 1907. Again the German government made its objections evident: the Emperor refused to be represented at the conference if the question of disarmament were to be brought up for discussion. Germany went still further in emphasizing its intention to continue the rivalry in ships: in 1907 it took measures to increase the speed at which the ships provided by the Navy Bill of 1906 were constructed by legislating that three new *Dreadnoughts* a year instead of two should be begun; and in 1908, this annual number was raised to four.

C. GREAT BRITAIN'S DIPLOMATIC PREPARATION TO RESIST GERMAN AGGRESSION

The second important measure that Great Britain took in preparation for meeting the German peril was in the realm of diplomacy. In 1904 Great Britain had composed all her outstanding difficulties with France, her hereditary enemy: her statesmen now approached the even more thorny problem of composing her difficulties with another rival power, Russia.

i. *Anglo-Russian Hostility*

Hostility between Great Britain and Russia, due especially to their conflicting interests in central Asia, and to the Russian desires for the possession of Constantinople, had long been one of the accepted bases of international politics in Europe. In central Asia Great Britain suspected Russia of designs upon Afghanistan which, if carried through successfully, would give Russia a base for a powerful attack upon the rich provinces of Northern India. And again, British statesmen were disturbed at the increase of Russian influence over Persia: Russian trade with Persia doubled between 1890 and 1900, and the Russian financiers secured the privilege of being Persia's only creditors, a privilege which, of course, carried great political influence with it. And still further, Great Britain's aspirations in Thibet conflicted with those of Russia. In 1903 the British government sent Colonel Younghusband on a mission to Thibet, a mission ostensibly commercial, but suspiciously political: this mission drew a vehement protest from Russia, which had long coveted Thibet for herself. Turning from the interests of the two nations in Central Asia to their interests in the Balkan regions and the Dardanelles, we again find Great Britain opposing Russia. Great Britain was the backbone of the alliance which defeated Russia in the Crimean war (1854–1855) and kept her away from the Balkans; and Disraeli, representing the British government in the Congress of Berlin, was the diplomat who forced upon Russia a humiliating revision of the provisions of the Treaty of San Stefano. And in the Far East as recently as 1902 Great Britain had leagued herself with Japan, whose ambitions in Korea had brought her into sharp antagonism to Russia. Thus, in various parts of the world, Central Asia, the Near East, and the Far East, Great Britain's interests had for a long period conflicted with those of Russia.

ii. *Advantages of Anglo-Russian Friendship for Great Britain*

In 1906, however, the German peril to Great Britain was more real and menacing than the Russian peril. The German control which was being developed in Turkish Asia Minor threatened India and the Suez Canal more directly than the Russian ambitions for control of the Dardanelles, and the German navy was growing at the moment faster than the English. Inasmuch as France and Russia were bound in a Dual Alliance, and France and Great Britain in an *Entente Cordiale*, the possibility of removing the differences between Russia and Great Britain, and thus establishing an *Entente* between Great Britain, France, and Russia, was alluring to British statesmen.

iii. *Advantages of Anglo-Russian Friendship for Russia*

Such an *Entente* had undoubted advantages for Russia also. The war with Japan had weakened her, not only in prestige, but in trained troops and naval strength. The losses of the Russian army from wounds and disease had been great. Although in mere man-power Russia's resources continued almost inexhaustible, her supply of trained soldiers had been seriously reduced. Her navy had been practically annihilated at Port Arthur and in the straits of Tsu-shima. The expenses of the war had been enormous, eating up all the accumulated reserves and requiring huge loans.

In addition to these huge losses and expenses, the Russian government was facing insubordination and rebellion, amounting almost to a civil war, at home. The people believed that the Russo-Japanese War had been brought on by persons in the bureaucracy for their own purposes, and that its successful prosecution would in no way react to the advantage of the Russian people as a whole. The calamities of the war offered an opportunity for the liberal element in European Russia to press their demands for political reforms, especially for a representative legislative assembly. They were forced by the autocracy to resort, as they had in the past, to the instigation of disorders on a wide scale in order to compel any favorable action on the part of the government. With the mass of the troops away in the Far East, the government found it difficult to suppress and stifle the evidences of popular discontent as it had so long done in the past. Open discussion abounded; meetings of protest against the government's policy were common; deeds of terrorism were resorted to in order to intimidate the government. Von Plehve, Minister of the Interior, who was held responsible for the iron régime in Russia since 1902, was blown to pieces by a bomb thrown under his carriage in July of 1904. After his death a remarkable manifesto was issued by the central committee of the Revolutionary Socialist party, in which that party assumed responsibility for the assassination and defended the policy of terrorism by stating that "in Russia, where owing to the reign of despotism, no open political discussion is possible, where there is no redress against the impossibility of absolute power throughout the whole bureaucratic organization, we shall be obliged to fight the violence of tyranny with the force of revolutionary right."

For a few months the government hesitated in its policy of suppression. Von Plehve's successor, Prince Mirski, counseled a more liberal attitude, and allowed greater freedom of discussion. Leading men of the Zemstvos (the local governing councils throughout Russia) held a Congress in St. Petersburg without opposition from Mirsky and drew up a petition to present to the Czar containing eleven main requests, including requests for civil equality, inviolability of person, freedom of thought, speech, and press, reform in public instruction, amnesty for political offenders, and a representative assembly with legislative powers. These "eleven points," as they were called, became the rallying cry of the liberal elements in Russia. Upon a Sunday in January, 1905, a host of workingmen, led by a government priest, Father Gapon, marched peaceably to the Winter Palace to present a petition containing requests similar to these "eleven points" to the "little Father." Troops fired upon the unarmed crowds, killing and wounding more than a thousand. "Bloody Sunday" was the government's answer to the universal demand for reform.

In February, 1905, Prince Mirski, who had encountered steady opposition to his leniency from Pobiedonostzeff and the coterie of Grand Dukes, was replaced by Buliguin, and all the old familiar methods of suppression followed. Again the press was muzzled, and the agents of the secret police turned loose to ferret out the liberals. This time, however, the disorders were too widespread to be quelled by the forces at the disposal of the government. The Social Democrats incited strikes and organized demonstrations; in some places the peasants took law into their own hands, terrorized their landlords, and appropriated the lands; whole communes in various parts of Russia rose in revolt; and liberals from all sections deluged the Czar with petitions for reform.

The terrible defeat in the battle of Mukden (March 23, 1905) and the annihilation of the fleet in the Straits of Tsu-shima (May 27–28) disheartened the bureaucrats and encouraged the liberals to present again their demands. A Zemstvo Congress once more convened, this time at Moscow, and sent a deputation with an address to the Czar. In his answer to this deputation the Czar gave the first sign of weakening before the forces of the revolution: he promised the convocation of a Duma. In August, 1905, was published the imperial decree establishing this representative body, the Duma, but giving it merely consultative powers, not legislative, and fixing a very limited franchise.

The promulgation of this decree was the signal for another revolutionary outburst, for its provisions fell far short of the desires of the liberals. Peasants continued to terrorize their landlords, burn their estates, and seize their lands. The workingmen continued their policy of instituting strikes and giant street demonstrations. The culmination of the disorders came with the inauguration in October, 1905, of a general country-wide strike affecting all branches of industry. The railroads, street railways, telegraph offices, post offices, electric light plants — all were paralyzed. Even the professional classes entered to a considerable extent into the strike. The industrial and economic life of the country stopped dead.

The pressure exerted by this universal strike was too great to be resisted. The Czar capitulated. He dismissed Pobiedonostzeff (called by the liberals the "Evil Genius" of Russia), appointed Count Witte premier, and issued the famous manifesto of October 17, 1905, establishing the Duma with legislative powers.

> . . . "We direct our Government to carry out Our inflexible will:
>
> "1. To grant the people the immutable foundations of civil liberty, based on real inviolability of person, freedom of conscience, speech, meetings, and associations;
>
> "2. Without deferring the elections to the State Duma already ordered, to call to the participation in the Duma (as far as it is possible in view of the shortness of the time before assembling of the Duma) those classes of the population now completely deprived of electoral rights, leaving the ultimate development of the principle of electoral right in general to the newly established legislative order.
>
> "3. To establish as an immutable rule that no law can ever come into force without the approval of the State Duma, and that the elected of the people be secured a possibility for real participation in supervising the legality of the acts of authorities appointed by Us."

Although the strike committee was dissatisfied with the provisions of this October decree and attempted to keep the strike in force for another month, the granting of the chief "points" of the liberals brought a quick change for the better in the general situation. Liberals looked to the Duma for their opportunity to advance the demands for further reforms. Groups began to coalesce into political parties, with definite organization and aims. Thus even before the publication of the October decree, one group formed the Constitutional Democratic party — its members have been commonly called "cadets" from the initials of the party name — and just after the decree another group, alarmed by the many disorders and planning to support the government on the basis of that decree, organized under the name of the Octobrist party.

In the meanwhile, the government proceeded in its attempt to create an organization which would partly meet the demands of the liberals, but would still keep its power intact. The Czar had promised his people a Duma, but before the Duma had met, he decreed a Council of Empire, a body to be formed chiefly of appointees from the bureaucracy, with the powers of a kind of upper legislative chamber. All laws must be approved both by the Duma and by the Council of the Empire before their submission to the Czar. Thus the Council of Empire was so constituted as to protect the interests of autocratic power from the people as represented in the Duma.

Elections to the Duma were held in March and April of 1906, and its formal opening by the Czar in person took place May 10. This first Duma contained a large majority of Constitutional Democrats. From its first meeting it showed itself radical and independent, urging upon the government important liberal measures, such as the reformation of the membership and powers of the Council of the Empire, and the responsibility of ministers of the Czar to the legislative body. After two months of stormy and ineffectual existence, the Czar arbitrarily dissolved the Duma (July 22, 1906), stating that "the representatives of the nation, instead of applying themselves to productive legislation, had strayed into spheres beyond their competence, had inquired into the acts of local authorities established by himself, and had commented upon the imperfections of the fundamental laws, which could only be modified by his imperial will." The meeting of the new Duma was set for March, 1907.

iv. *The Anglo-Russian Entente*

Thus, the Russian government, defeated and weakened by the Russo-Japanese War abroad and by the turmoil accompanying the political revolution at home, was willing to lend an ear to British proposals for an understanding. Representatives of the two nations took advantage of their meeting in the Conference of Algeciras to conduct some preliminary discussions on the subject. Count Cassini, the Russian plenipotentiary, had several long and intimate conversations during the tedious weeks of the conference with his British colleague, Sir Arthur Nicholson. After the conference had ended, the attempts of representatives of the two governments to reach an understanding continued. News of the parleys was published. At one time in May of 1906 it was said that a treaty had actually been signed, whereupon Sir Edward Grey, the English foreign minister, took occasion to state in the House of Commons that, although no definite treaty existed, the two governments were discussing amicably the questions at issue between them. In March of 1907 the Russian fleet visited England, and its officers and sailors were cordially received and entertained. In June of the same year it became officially known that the discussion had entered upon the stage of negotiations as to terms, and on the last day of August, 1907, an Anglo-Russian agreement was actually signed at St. Petersburg.

Like the Anglo-French agreement of 1904, the Anglo-Russian accord was no more than a settlement of their outstanding disputes, an allaying of the spirit of suspicion which had so long embittered the relations between the two nations. Its provisions dealt with limitations of political influence and sovereignty in Central Asia, the quarter of the world in which the British and Russian interests had so long conflicted. Persia was divided into three zones, a northern, in which Russia's influence was acknowledged to be paramount, a southern, in which England's was similarly recognized, and a middle zone, for which entire neutrality was stipulated. The control and reform of the finances of unhappy Persia were to be undertaken by the two countries jointly. Afghanistan, which had been one of the most critical issues between the nations, Russia yielded wholly to Great Britain, acknowledging the country to lie within the British sphere of influence, and renouncing the Russian right to send a diplomatic agent to Kabul, the capital. And as concerned Thibet, both nations agreed to respect its territorial integrity and the Chinese sovereignty, and neither to interfere with its internal affairs nor to seek special economic concessions therein.

D. THE TRIPLE ENTENTE

The conclusion of the Anglo-Russian agreement formed the Triple Entente. Great Britain, France, and Russia, although not bound by treaties as definite in their terms as those which united Germany, Austria, and Italy in the Triple Alliance, yet had settled all their reasons for disagreement and were in a position at the first intimation of danger to consolidate their powers in an actual alliance. Great Britain had, in the face of the German danger, entirely abandoned her policy of "splendid isolation." By the most startling and unexpected series of agreements she had fortified her international position against possible attack. In 1902 she had astonished the world by an offensive and defensive treaty with Japan, by which she acquired the aid of the strongest power in the Far East to protect her vast possessions there; in 1904 she composed all of her outstanding difficulties with France; and in 1907 she agreed to an understanding on critical points with Russia. Great Britain, France, Russia — with Japan in the Far East — did not compose an *actual*, but a *potential* alliance.

The significance of these momentous changes in the status of international politics was not lost on Germany and her allies. Although British statesmen were convinced that they were acting in good faith to prepare the ground for defensive measures in case of attack, an aggressive body of German thinkers conceived these measures as offensive in character. These Germans pictured Great Britain as plotting the isolation of Germany in Europe, as drawing an iron ring about her with the evident intention of strangling her. Germans found in their own increasing commerce the motive for what they believed to be British ambitions and policies. The potential entente became an actual entente in their imaginations with the sole purpose of overwhelming Germany. When the news of the discussions between Great Britain and Russia was still diplomatic gossip, the German chancellor, von Bülow, in a notable speech before the Reichstag (November 14, 1906), revealed how the German leaders looked upon the possible alliance:

> "A policy that aims to hem Germany in, to draw around us a circle of the Powers for the purpose of isolating us, would be a very dangerous policy for the peace of Europe."

With the formation of the Triple Entente as described above, Europe became more than ever committed to a policy of rival armaments. Two great groups of powers with clashing interests faced each other, ready at any crisis to mass their forces in a decisive conflict for power. Any quarrel between individual members of the opposing groups might precipitate such a conflict, however sincerely other members might desire peace. We shall see how Europe passed through two periods of intense strain, one in 1908 over the Bosnian incident and another in 1911 over the Moroccan issue, only to succumb at last before a relatively trifling quarrel in the Balkan regions.

CHAPTER V

THE STATES OF EUROPE, 1905–1911. I.

We have in the last few chapters devoted our space to a consideration of the important changes in international politics. We have outlined the growth of mutual hostility between Great Britain and Germany; the departure of Great Britain from her policy of isolation and the formation of the *Entente Cordiale* between Great Britain and France; the Tangier episode, the Algeciras conference, and the resulting added strength to the bond between Great Britain and France; and finally, the removal of the most important elements of misunderstanding and hostility between Great Britain and Russia. With this last agreement, a potential Triple Entente faced the actual Triple Alliance. A real balance of power had been created, with all the possibilities of trouble which friction between any two states might bring. Following the Tangier incident, two crises of the utmost gravity succeeded at three-year intervals, the Young Turk revolution of 1908 with its consequences, and the Agadir episode of 1911. Before we consider these, however, it is well to gain a general idea of the internal conditions in the chief states of Europe during this period. The following two chapters, therefore, will be devoted to an outline of domestic problems and policies in Great Britain, France, Russia, Italy, Austria-Hungary, and Germany.

GREAT BRITAIN

The final years of the Unionist (Conservative) government — that is, the years from 1900 to 1905 — were marked by dissension within the Unionist party and by a steady decline in popularity. Joseph Chamberlain became a convert to tariff reform. He had been in the cabinet from 1895, and for a few years after his conversion remained there, but in 1902 he resigned to place before the country his convictions. In a series of brilliant speeches during the following years he endeavored to convince the electorate of the advantages of departing from free trade principles. He argued, not only for the revenue which would be made available for the proposed measures of social and economic reform, but especially for the possibilities in granting preferential tariffs to the British colonies and thus binding them closer to the mother country. He pleaded with the people to "think imperially." He was able to carry the bulk of his own party with him, and to have fiscal reform made the first plank of the party platform, but the leaders made no clear-cut and definite statement of what they would do. Balfour agreed merely that a general tariff on manufactured goods and a small duty on imported grain were "not in principle objectionable." Chamberlain's speeches resulted in splitting his own party and in gaining extremely few adherents from the Liberals.

An education act, passed in 1902, served to arouse intense hostility on the part of large and important classes of the voters. It provided for the abolition of the familiar school boards, the transfer of their powers to the local governing bodies known as County or Borough Councils, and general local taxation for the support of all schools of whatever denomination. The chief criticism aroused by the bill was directed against the taxation features, in that people were forced to pay for the support both of denominational schools and of Board schools, although they might favor or use but one class. The dissenters and non-conformists were especially enraged, for they regarded the legislation as a definite strengthening of the power of the Church of England over education. For a period after the passage of the law, popular indignation nerved many to defy its provisions. Men refused to pay their taxes. Their property was seized and sold by court order. Over 70,000 summonses were issued. The bill, however, was enforced, and its provisions have not been materially changed since.

The Unionist party, too, lost its hold upon the laboring classes. The growing radicalism of the leaders of the Liberal party presented to the workingmen a more definite appeal than the known conservatism of the Unionists. The members of Trades Unions, especially, who had been trying for years to induce parliament to pass measures of social reform, came to believe that they could never hope for satisfaction under the Unionist government.

The Unionist ministry was not unaware of its loss of popularity. It attempted to cater to certain of the disaffected elements in the parliamentary session of 1905. In particular it put forward three important measures intended to appeal to the workingmen: (1) The Trades Unions and Trades Disputes Bill, (2) the Unemployed Workmen Bill, and (3) the Workmen's Compensation Bill. It was, however, unable to carry with it the majority of its party in the House of Commons. The bills were so mutilated in their committee stages that they were either withdrawn before the final vote or were defeated. Hopeless of successfully continuing the government, the Unionist cabinet resigned in December, 1905. The King at once appointed a Liberal ministry, headed by Sir Henry Campbell-Bannerman, and both parties prepared for the general elections of January and February, 1906, to test their strength throughout the country.

In the campaign the Unionists were on the defensive except in the one feature of tariff reform — and that issue had already alienated a portion of their own party. All the discontent of the people with the conservative policies expressed itself in these elections. The Liberals won the greatest majority that any party had received since the contest over the reform bill of 1832. The new House of Commons showed 378 Liberals, 53 Laborites, and 83 Nationalists, giving the Liberals a total coalition strength of 514; against 131 Conservatives and 25 Labor Unionists, a total of 156.

The task before the Liberals, however, in spite of their huge majority, was by no means simple. Though they might with little opposition control the Lower House, they had no control over the Upper. In the House of Lords, the Conservatives had an overwhelming majority ready to stand firm against any attempts on the part of the Liberals to change the existing local institutions. Over all the particular bills introduced and passed by the Liberals in the Commons, and vetoed, amended, or grudgingly accepted by the Conservatives in the Lords, hung the shadow of an approaching struggle between the two Houses for power. The storm broke in 1909, in the contest precipitated over the Budget in that year, and before it had cleared in 1911, the House of Lords had gone down to defeat, shorn of the powers it had exercised since the beginning of parliamentary government in England.

The period between the general elections of January and February, 1906, and the passage of the epochal Parliament Bill of 1911 may be divided into two parts; the one up to the introduction of the Budget (with its accompanying Finance Bill) in 1909, and the other through the passage of the Parliament Bill of 1911.

The first stage is marked by the initiation of measures of progressive social legislation by the Liberals in the House of Commons. Sir Henry Campbell-Bannerman stated at the opening of the new Parliament in 1906 that underlying every proposal of his government would be a policy of social reconstruction looking toward a greater equalization of wealth and toward the destruction of the monopolies of the land and of liquor. Although we need dwell only upon the bills which were finally enacted into law, we may mention in passing, for the sake of emphasizing the effects of the Conservative majority in the House of Lords upon the Liberal program, a few of the important bills which failed. The House of Lords ruined the Liberal attempts to redress the injustice in the Education Act of 1902, apparently because the Liberal bill might weaken the position of the Anglican Church; the Lords vetoed a Licensing Bill passed by the Liberals in the Commons, because that bill penalized the liquor business which had so long aided the Conservative party and which had important representatives in the Upper House; the Lords destroyed a land valuation proposal because it might lead to "dangerous novelties"; the Lords thwarted a bill against plural voting (*i.e.* the system by which a man who can qualify for the suffrage by his property ownership in two or more constituencies has a vote in each) because they considered it an attack upon vested interests and a danger to one of the fundamental rights of property holders. Each of the above proposals, supported by the Liberals in the House of Commons, unquestionably had the approval of the majority of the people in the country. The successive instances in which the hereditary Lords balked the elected and representative Commons raised popular indignation against the Upper House to a high pitch. These instances must be remembered in the consideration of the historic struggle which took place between the two Houses in 1909–1911.

The Liberals did, however, succeed in passing during this first stage (1906–1909) a few measures in their program of social legislation. On March 26, 1906, the Home Secretary on behalf of the government introduced a Workmen's Compensation Act providing for the compensation of workmen in case of accident. Inasmuch as one element of the Conservative party had in 1905 favored such legislation, this bill had an easy passage through the two Houses and became a law upon the royal approval December 21 of the same year. The general purport of the Act is sufficiently indicated in its first clause:

"If in any employment personal injury by accident arising out of and in the course of the employment is caused to a workman, his employer shall, subject as herein-after mentioned, be liable to pay compensation."

Workmen suffering from what are popularly called "vocational" or "industrial" diseases — that is, diseases contracted because of the particular nature of their duties — were included in the scope of this act.

A second measure introduced in the same year, a bill in connection with Trade Unionism, had a much more difficult time in the House of Lords. The Trade Unions had become by 1906 a great power in England. They were 1200 in number and had a total membership of more than two million. They had by previous legislation received recognition as legal associations, but a recent judicial decision had opened them to suit at law for costs and damages in case any act of their agents caused loss to other persons. The particular object of the Liberals was to reverse the recent decision so far as to allow peaceful "picketing" by the unions. The Conservatives attacked the bill on the ground that it constituted the Trade Unions as a privileged class, exempt from prosecution at law for offenses which would cause the prosecution of other classes. The nature of the bill may be seen from the following extracts:

"An act done in pursuance of an agreement or combination by two or more persons shall, if done in contemplation or furtherance of a trade dispute, not be actionable unless the act, if done without any such agreement or combination, would be actionable.

"It shall be lawful for one or more persons, acting on their own behalf or on behalf of a trade union or of an individual employer or firm in contemplation or furtherance of a trade dispute, to attend at or near a house or place where a person resides or works or carries on business or happens to be, if they so attend merely for the purpose of peacefully obtaining or communicating information, or of peacefully persuading any person to work or abstain from working."

It is probable that the Lords, having already during the

year rejected the Education Bill and the Plural Voting Bill, feared the veto of a third popular bill. After long debate, they reluctantly gave their approval. The bill thereupon received the royal assent and became law December 21, 1906.

A third measure of broader scope and greater importance than the two preceding was introduced and passed in 1908. In that year Sir Henry Campbell-Bannerman died, and Herbert Asquith succeeded him as prime minister, so it was under Mr. Asquith's leadership that the Old Age Pensions Bill was presented to the Commons. This bill, like the Trade Unions Bill, was bitterly opposed by the Lords but was finally passed because the Conservatives, having already defeated the Licensing Bill, feared the political effect upon the fortunes of their party of the rejection of two popular measures in a year. The Old Age Pensions Bill was introduced May 28, 1908, and, after finally passing both Houses, received the royal assent and became law August 1, 1908. The following extracts will show the scope of the Bill:

"The statutory conditions for the receipt of an old age pension of any person are:

"(1) The person must have attained the age of seventy:

"(2) The person must satisfy the pensions authorities that for at least twenty years up to the date of the receipt of any sum on account of a pension he has been a British subject:

"(3) The person must satisfy the pension authorities that his yearly means as calculated under this act do not exceed thirty-one pounds ten shillings."

The schedule of pensions is as follows:

Means of Pensioner	Rate of Pension per Week	
Where the yearly means of the pensioner as calculated under this Act	*s.*	*d.*
Do not exceed £21	5	0
Exceed £21, but do not exceed £23 12*s.* 6*d.*	4	0
Exceed £23 12*s.* 6*d.* but do not exceed £26 5*s.*	3	0
Exceed £26 5*s.* but do not exceed £28 17s. 6*d.*	2	0
Exceed £28 17*s.* 6*d.* but do not exceed £31 10*s.*	1	0
Exceed £31 10*s.*	No pension.	

The post office was used as the agency of distribution of the pension. More than half a million persons drew their first pensions in the opening days of January, 1909, accepting this money as a deserved reward after a lifetime of labor.

A fourth bill bearing upon labor conditions was the Labor Exchanges Bill, introduced May 20, 1909, and passed with little opposition through both Houses, becoming law after the royal assent September 20. The general nature of the provisions of the bill is revealed in the following extracts:

"(1) The Board of Trade may establish and maintain, in such places as they think fit, labor exchanges.

"(2) The Board of Trade may also, by such other means as they think fit, collect and furnish information as to employers requiring work people and work people seeking engagement or employment."

The above were the most important measures of the Liberal program which the Liberals were able to have passed. Three other Bills, the Small Holdings and Allotments Bill (1907), the Housing and Town Planning Bill (1909), and the Development Bill (1909), were attempts at the partial solution of the Housing and Land Problems. In general, these Bills were intended (1) to give opportunities to poor men to acquire with money borrowed from the government small areas of land for cultivation, and (2) to improve living conditions in the more crowded portions of the towns and cities. All three bills were passed, after bitter opposition from the House of Lords. They did not, however, go very far toward a real solution of the problems.

The crisis between the two Houses, and the beginning of the second stage in the history of this period in England, came with the introduction of the Budget with its accompanying Finance Bill in 1909. The program of social legislation to which the Liberals were committed and which in part they had already carried through entailed a large additional expense to the government. The Old Age Insurance Act alone had added at its beginning $40,000,000 a year to the government's outlay, and this expense was certain to grow steadily greater. Provision for Labor Exchanges, Town Planning, and Rural Development, combined with the cost of keeping the naval armament up to the necessary strength in view of the German increase, added further huge financial burdens. One method, of course, would have been the abandonment of the Free Trade principles for a protective tariff, and this method was advocated by a strong element among the Conservatives headed by the redoubtable Joseph Chamberlain. The Liberals, however, were united in their opposition to a protective tariff. It was, therefore, necessary for them, since they were in control of the government, to devise means for raising additional revenue. Their proposed scheme was set forth in the Budget (and Finance Bill) of 1909.

The introduction and defense of this Bill on behalf of the government fell to the lot of the Chancellor of the Exchequer, Mr. David Lloyd George. Lloyd George was a Welshman, small and slight in figure, but alert and audacious in debate, and gifted with spontaneous eloquence. He was the idol of his own people. He has been described as "the uncrowned Prince of Wales." It has been said that "no Welsh leader since the day of Owen Glendower inspired so much enthusiasm among his countrymen." He had sat in the House of Commons among the Liberal opposition to the government during the ten years of Conservative supremacy, 1895 to 1905, and had made his reputation by the brilliancy and force of his arguments. In Sir Henry Campbell-Bannerman's cabinet, Lloyd George became minister at the head of the Board of Trade. In that office he showed prudence, wisdom, and a phenomenal capacity for hard work. He gained the confidence of the English business world. In the reconstruction of the cabinet following Campbell-Bannerman's retirement in 1908, Lloyd George succeeded Asquith as Chancellor of the Exchequer. At the age of twenty-five this Welshman was a lawyer in a small town in North Wales: at the age of forty-five he was Chancellor of the Exchequer and a most prominent figure in the Liberal government.

On April 29, 1909, Lloyd George presented his Budget to the House of Commons. Public expectation had been aroused to the highest pitch, and the chamber was crowded. He dwelt at some length upon the humanitarian nature of the program of the social legislation which the Liberal party was carrying through:

"I come to the consideration of the social problems which are urgently pressing for solution — problems affecting the lives of the people. The solution of all these questions involves finance. What the Government have to ask themselves is this: Can the whole subject of further social reform be postponed until the increasing demand made upon the National Exchequer by the growth of armaments has ceased? Not merely *can* it be postponed, but ought it to be postponed? Is there the slightest hope that if we deferred consideration of the matter, we are likely within a generation to find any more favorable moment for attending to it? And we have to ask ourselves this further question: If we put off dealing with these social sores, are the evils which arise from them not likely to grow and to fester, until finally the loss which the country sustains will be infinitely greater than anything it would have to bear in paying the cost of an immediate remedy. There are hundreds of thousands of men, women, and children in this country now enduring hardships for which the sternest judge would not hold them responsible; hardships entirely due to circumstances over which they have not the slightest command; the fluctuations and changes of trade — even of fashions; ill-health and the premature breakdown or death of the bread-winner. Owing to events of this kind, all of them beyond human control — at least beyond the control of the victims — thousands, and I am not sure I should be wrong if I said millions, are precipitated into a condition of acute distress and poverty. How many people there are of this kind in this wealthy land the figures of old age pensions have thrown a very unpleasant light upon. Is it fair, is it just, is it humane, is it honorable, is it safe to subject such a multitude of our poor fellow-countrymen and countrywomen to continued endurance of these miseries until nations have learnt enough wisdom not to squander their resources on these huge machines for the destruction of human life? I have no doubt as to the answer which will be given to that question by a nation as rich in humanity as it is in store."

At one point, he took occasion to comment upon the German plans for social legislation inaugurated by Bismarck.

"When Bismarck was strengthening the foundations of the new German Empire one of the very first tasks he undertook was the organization of a scheme which insured the German workmen and their families against the worst evils which ensue from these common accidents of life. And a superb scheme it is. It has saved an incalculable amount of human misery to hundreds of thousands and possibly millions of people who never deserved it.

"Wherever I went in Germany, north or south, and whomever I met, whether it was an employer or a workman, a Conservative or a Liberal, a Socialist or a Trade Union Leader — men of all ranks, sections and creeds of one accord joined in lauding the benefits which have been conferred upon Germany by this beneficent policy. Several wanted extensions, but there was not one who wanted to go back. The employers admitted that at first they did not quite like the new burdens cast upon them, but they now fully realize the advantages which even they derive from the expenditure, for it has raised the standard of the workman throughout Germany. By removing that element of anxiety and worry from their lives it has improved their efficiency."

Then he came to the most interesting part of his speech, the presentation of the proposed means for raising money.

"Now what are the principles upon which I intend to proceed in getting . . . taxes? The first principle on which I base my financial proposals is this — that taxation which I suggest should be imposed, while yielding in the present year not more than sufficient to meet this year's requirements, should be of such a character that it will produce enough revenue in the second year to cover the whole of our estimated liabilities for that year. And, moreover, that it will be of such an expansive character as to grow with the growing demand of the social programme which I have sketched without involving the necessity for imposing fresh taxation in addition to what I am asking Parliament to sanction at the present time. The second principle on which I base my proposals is that the taxes should be of such a character as not to inflict any injury on that trade or commerce which constitutes the sources of our wealth.

"My third principle is this, that all classes of the community in this financial emergency ought to be called upon to contribute. I have never been able to accept the theory which I have seen advanced that you ought to draw a hard-and-fast line at definite incomes and say that no person under a certain figure should be expected to contribute a penny toward the burden of the good government of the country. In my judgment all should be called upon to bear their share. No voluntary association, religious or philanthropic or provident, has ever been run on the principle of exempting any section of its membership from subscription. They all contribute, even to the widow's mite. It is considered not merely the duty, but the privilege and pride of all to share in the common burden, and the sacrifice is as widely distributed as is the responsibility and the profit. At the same time, when you come to consider whether the bulk of the taxation is to be raised by direct or indirect means, I must point out at this stage — I shall have a little more to say on this subject later on — that the industrial classes, in my judgment, upon a close examination of their contributions to local and Imperial finance, are paying more in proportion to their incomes than those who are better off. Their proportion to local finances especially is heavier, because, although nominally the rates are not paid by them, as everyone knows, they are really. For that reason the burden at the present moment of new taxation bears much more heavily in proportion to their income on that class than it does upon the wealthier and better-to-do classes."

We cannot give the space here to his own discussion of the new taxes. Briefly summarized, these taxes were as follows: (1) an increase in the income tax; (2) an increase in the inheritance tax (popularly known as "death duties"), (3) increased taxation on such luxuries as tobacco, spirits, motor cars, and gasoline; (4) high license duties on public houses (saloons); and (5) new land taxes, especially directed (*a*) against values of land not due to the enterprise or expenditures of the owner, and (*b*) against land allowed to lie undeveloped. In his peroration he declared his Budget to be a War Budget:

"I am told that no Chancellor of the Exchequer has ever been called on to impose such heavy taxes in a time of peace. This, Mr. Emmott, is a War Budget. It is for raising money to wage implacable warfare against poverty and squalidness. I cannot help hoping and believing that before this generation has passed away we shall have advanced a great step toward that good time when poverty and wretchedness and human degradation which always follow in its camp will be as remote to the people of this country as the wolves which once infested its forests."

Brief thought on the taxes summarized above will reveal that they fall most heavily upon the propertied classes. The license taxes hit the liquor interests; the land taxes touched the proprietors of the huge landed estates so common throughout England; and the income tax and the "death duties" bore upon all the wealthy, from whatever sources their riches might have been derived. The Liberals, especially the more radical element among them, hailed the budget with delight. It was audacious; it was complete; it provided the necessary funds without a protective tariff. The Conservatives, however, both those of the party in the Commons and those in the Lords, inveighed against the Budget as revolutionary, as undermining the essential institutions of the country. A political contest was begun which in bitterness was comparable to that preceding the passage of the famous reform bill of 1832. With courtesy, tact, unfailing good humor, and marvelous skill Lloyd George guided his bill through its various stages in the House of Commons, having it passed finally on November 4 by a vote of 379 to 149, a majority of 230.

In the meanwhile, the Lords had worked themselves into a fury over the Budget (with its accompanying Finance Bill). When in the late summer the passage of the Bill in the House of Commons, practically in the form in which it had come from Lloyd George, was assured, the rumor spread that the Lords intended to reject it. The country could scarcely credit the news. The Lords had never in the memory of man rejected a Finance Bill, and their right to do so was questionable. In a country like Great Britain, which has no written constitution, custom and precedent play a large part in creating rights. Thus by custom and precedent has risen the exclusive right of the Lower House over Finance Bills. Although by no specific law or decision was the House of Lords forbidden to reject a Finance Bill, it had from time immemorial accepted the will of the House of Commons in such legislation. Under these circumstances the declaration of Lord Lansdowne, leader of the Conservative majority in the upper House, on November 16, that he intended to offer the following resolution was recognized as creating a national crisis:

"That this House is not justified in giving its consent to this Bill until it has been submitted to the judgment of the country."

Although by its form this resolution was intended to imply that the Lords did not actually reject the Finance Bill, but merely desired its reference to the people, this form deceived nobody. The Lords were refusing to act in conformance with the tradition of generations. Even among the Lords themselves were members who warned the Upper House solemnly of the gravity of its step. The decisive vote came November 30. Lord Lansdowne's motion was carried by a vote of 350 to 75. The Finance Bill, which had been passed with a majority of 230 by the representatives of the people, was thus defeated with a majority of 275 by the privileged orders in the House of Lords.

Preparations were at once made for new elections. Two days after the rejection by the Lords, the prime minister, Herbert Asquith, rose in the House of Commons and moved:

"That the action of the House of Lords in refusing to pass into law the financial provisions made by this House for the service of the year is a breach of the Constitution and a usurpation of the rights of the Commons."

His motion was enthusiastically carried by a vote of 349

to 134, a majority of 215. Parliament was dissolved and the fight began.

In the contest the Liberals rallied to the issue of the power of the Commons versus the power of the Lords; the Conservatives defended the action of the Upper House on the right of the Lords to exercise the power of forcing a reconsideration of a Finance Bill. All the bitterness of the Liberals over the continued efforts of the Conservatives to thwart their legislation since 1906 was compressed into the campaign. The premier, Asquith, sounded the keynote of his party's policy in a famous speech at the beginning of the campaign, December 10. In a striking passage he said:

"We are suddenly confronted with no less than three constitutional innovations. In the first place, we have the claim of the Upper House not as an archaic legal survival, but as a living and effective right, to control the levying of taxation. In the second place, we have the claim of the same House, a body which cannot itself be dissolved, to compel a dissolution of the popular chamber. And lastly, as a consequence and a corollary of the other two, we have the assertion of its power to make or unmake the executive Government of the Crown.

"We shall demand authority from the electorate to translate ancient usage into an Act of Parliament and to place upon the Statute Book the recognition, explicit and complete, of the settled doctrine of our Constitution that it is beyond the province of the House of Lords to meddle in any way, to any degree or for any purpose, with our national finance.

"So far we are on the defensive. But at the same time and by the same action the House of Lords has not indeed raised but has hurried on a larger issue still. I tell you quite plainly, and I tell my fellow-countrymen outside, that neither I nor any other Liberal Minister, supported by a majority of the House of Commons, is going to submit again to the rebuffs and the humiliations of the last four years. We shall not assume office and we shall not hold office unless we can secure the safeguards which experience shows us to be necessary for the legislative utility and honor of the party of progress.

"Here again what has to be done is to be done by Act of Parliament. The time for unwritten convention has unhappily gone by. We are not proposing the abolition of the House of Lords or the setting up of a single Chamber system, but we do ask, and we are going to ask, the electors to say that the House of Lords shall be confined to the proper functions of a Second Chamber. The absolute veto which it at present possesses must go. The powers which it claims from time to time of, in effect, compelling us to choose between a Dissolution and — so far as legislative projects are concerned — legislative sterility — that power must go also. The people in future, when they elect a new House of Commons, must be able to feel, what they cannot feel now, that they are sending to Westminster men who will have the power not merely of proposing and debating, but of making laws. The will of the people, as deliberately expressed by their elected representatives, must, within the limits of the lifetime of a single Parliament, be made effective."

When the results became known, by the end of January, 1910, it was seen that, although the Conservatives had massed their forces with consummate skill and had won many seats from their opponents, the Liberals had retained, with the aid of the Irish Nationalists, a good working majority. The numbers were as follows in the new House:

Liberals	275
Laborites	40
Nationalists	82
Total coalition	397
Conservatives	273
	124

The Parliament met for the first time February 21, 1910. The Lords accepted the decision of the country at the polls, and with little debate passed on April 28 the Budget and Finance Bill which they had rejected the preceding autumn. Events by this time, however, had passed beyond the mere acceptance or rejection of the Finance Bill. The House of Commons, thoroughly aroused, was proceeding with a bill for the curtailment of the powers of the House of Lords when the death of King Edward VII on May 6, 1910, stopped political strife for the moment. The leaders of the two parties held a series of conferences but were unable to reach an agreement. The Lords proposed certain plans for the reformation and reorganization of their own body, but the Commons was not in a mood to accept a compromise. The Liberal leaders, obtaining guarantees from the new King, George V, to abide by the decision of the voters, preferred to dissolve the Parliament and to have new elections on this new issue. Parliament, therefore, was dissolved November 28, after a session of only ten months, and once more the country was torn by a political struggle.

The fight was again bitter. The Conservatives, seeing that the Irish Nationalists were the support of the Liberals, attacked Home Rule to befog the main issue, and proposed the introduction of a referendum system to satisfy and catch deserters among the Liberal sympathizers. The Liberals on their side canvassed for votes on the direct issue of the supremacy of the Commons over the Lords, the popular House against the privileged House. Early in the new year, 1911, the results showed the following:

Liberals	272
Laborites	42
Nationalists	84
Coalition total	398
Conservatives	272
Coalition majority	126

The Liberals had thus actually gained two seats in an election fought out on the issue of the supremacy of the House of Commons over the House of Lords. The way was entirely clear for vigorous measures to insure their supremacy.

The new Parliament, convened by King George in person, met Monday, February 6, 1911. Two weeks later, February 21, Asquith introduced the Parliament Bill, the same measure which had been prepared and offered in 1910 and which had been the cause of the dissolution and appeal to the country.

The nature of the curb applied to the House of Lords is indicated by the following passages of the Bill (in its final form).

1. Power of House of Lords as to Money Bills

(1) If a Money Bill, having been passed by the House of Commons, and sent up to the House of Lords at least one month before the end of the session, is not passed by the House of Lords without amendment within one month after it is so sent up to that House, the Bill shall, unless the House of Commons direct to the contrary, be presented to His Majesty and become an Act of Parliament on the royal assent being signified, notwithstanding that the House of Lords have not consented to the Bill.

2. Restriction of Powers of House of Lords as to Bills Other than Money Bills

(1) If any Public Bill (other than a Money Bill or a Bill containing any provision to extend the maximum duration of Parliament beyond five years) is passed by the House of Commons in three successive sessions (whether of the same Parliament or not), and, having been sent up to the House of Lords at least one month before the end of the session, is rejected by the House of Lords in each of those sessions, that Bill shall, on its rejection for the third time by the House of Lords, unless the House of Commons direct to the contrary, be presented to His Majesty and become an Act of Parliament on the Royal Assent being signified thereto, notwithstanding that the House of Lords have not consented to the Bill: Provided that this provision shall not take effect unless two years have elapsed between the date of the second reading in the first of those sessions of the Bill in the House of Commons and the date on which it passes the House of Commons in the third of those sessions."

It was recognized, of course, that this Bill would pass the House of Commons and that the real struggle would come in the House of Lords. On the 15th of May the Bill was sent up to the House of Lords by a majority of 121 on its final reading in the Commons. The Liberals had kept their majority intact: they were a united party.

From the middle of May to the middle of July of this eventful year the Parliament Bill was under consideration by the Lords. They added amendment after amendment, until, as every one realized, the original bill had entirely changed its complexion. With these amendments they sent the Bill back to the Commons. The country felt that the crucial and final stage of the constitutional struggle had begun, for all knew that the Commons would not accept the Lords' amendments but no one outside of the government knew what powers the Liberal leaders had for forcing the Bill through Parliament. All depended upon the King. He could, by the creation of a sufficient number of Liberal peers, insure a goverment majority in the Upper House and thus guarantee the passage of the Bill. Would he do this?

The last stages of the fight were marked by scenes of tumult and disorder. In the Lords a group of peers who declared that they were prepared to stand by the Lords' amendments to the last (and who gained the popular nickname of "Die-Hards") rallied around the figure of Lord Willoughby de Broke. In the Commons the Prime Minister was for the first time in parliamentary history insulted and howled down when he attempted to speak. One who witnessed the scene thus describes it:

"It was soon evident that a section of the Tory party had deliberately planned to prevent him being heard. Standing at the Treasury Bench, firm and resolute, the Prime Minister calmly surveyed the turbulent and disorderly Opposition. For a quarter of an hour he endeavored vainly to go on with his speech. Appeal after appeal was made by the Speaker to the Opposition to behave in a manner worthy of the traditions of the House of Commons, and to remember that this was a serious occasion. But the young bloods of the Opposition were not in a mood to listen to any admonitions, even though backed by the high authority of Mr. Lowther. They kept up an indescribable tumult. It was a very unedifying exhibition of manners, and there were ironical cries from the Liberal benches, 'Oh, the British aristocracy!' — an allusion to the fact that several of the noisiest interrupters were sons of peers.

"At length, after he had been on his feet for twenty minutes, Mr. Asquith was able to make himself heard through the din. In loud and resonant tones he reminded the House that in Great Britain there is a majority of nearly sixty in favor of the Parliament Bill, and in the United Kingdom a majority of 120. He claimed that no Bill in our parliamentary history had ever been so clearly and unequivocally a main issue at a general election. The nation not only approved of the principle of the Bill, but also of its machinery. By their amendments the Lords wanted to substitute for the Government plan the alternative plan rejected by the nation.

"At this point the interruptions broke out afresh, and with greater violence than ever, and at 4 : 15, with a despairing gesture, the Prime Minister indicated that he could not go on. Encouraged, however, by a hearty demonstration on the Liberal benches, he made a fresh attempt, but it was to little purpose, and at last he gave up the impossible task, saying, 'I am not going to degrade myself' — (loud Liberal cheers)— 'by addressing arguments to persons who are determined not to listen.' 'A situation has been created,' he added, in a loud voice that could be heard above the din, 'from which there is only one constitutional way of escape. Unless the House of Lords consent to restore this Bill (with reasonable amendments consistent with its principle and purpose) to its original shape, we shall be compelled to invoke the prerogative of the Crown.' "[1]

Asquith was ready with his winning move. He dispatched to Mr. Balfour, the leader of the opposition in the Commons, the following famous letter, which in effect was an announcement that the King had consented to create, if necessary, the number of peers to carry the Bill in the House of Lords.

"10, Downing Street,
"20, July, 1911.

"Dear Mr. Balfour,

"I think it is courteous and right, before any public decisions are announced, to let you know how we regard the political situation.

"When the Parliament Bill in the form which it has now assumed returns to the House of Commons, we shall be compelled to ask the House to disagree with the Lords' amendments.

[1] Quoted in H. Jones: "Liberalism and the House of Lords," pp. 292–293.

"In the circumstances, should the necessity arise, the Government will advise the King to exercise his prerogative to secure the passing into law of the Bill in substantially the same form in which it left the House of Commons, and His Majesty has been pleased to signify that he will consider it his duty to accept and act on that advice.

"Yours sincerely,

"H. H. ASQUITH."

A few days later the leading Lords recognized the hopelessness of the struggle. Lord Lansdowne addressed a letter to his supporters announcing that he had yielded and asking their views.

"Lansdowne House,
"24 July, 1911.

"My Lord,

"The announcement made by the Prime Minister leaves no room for doubt that His Majesty's Government are now empowered to force the passage of the Parliament Bill through the House of Lords by means of a practically unlimited creation of peers. We shall therefore have to decide whether, by desisting from further opposition, we shall render it possible for His Majesty's Government to carry the Bill in the House of Lords as at present constituted; or, whether, by insisting on our amendments, we shall bring about a creation of peers in numbers which will overwhelm the present House and paralyze its action in the future without in any way retarding the passage of the Parliament Bill.

"I have come to the conclusion that the former alternative is preferable in the interests of the House, the Unionist party, and the country. Nor can I bring myself to believe that our supporters will not realize that we are no longer free agents, and that the course that I have indicated involves no responsibility for the Bill, and no complicity with those who are promoting it.

"It is of the utmost importance that I should be made aware of the views of those peers who usually act with us, and I should therefore be grateful if your Lordships would, with the least possible delay, let me know whether you are prepared to support me in the course which I feel it my duty to recommend.

"I have the honor to be, my Lord

"Yours faithfully,

"LANSDOWNE."

The "Die-Hards" stood by their principles and on the final division mustered 117 votes, but the threat of the creation of peerages in unlimited number had been effective, and Lord Morley for the government headed 131 members, giving the Parliament Bill, in the form passed by the House of Commons, a majority of 17 votes in the House of Lords.

We have devoted much space to the Liberal government from 1906 to 1911 because in the events of these years, culminating with the passage of the Parliament Bill, is to be seen the accomplishment of a radical change in the fundamental nature of the English government. The reform of the Upper House, or a limitation of its powers, had been a fruitful theme for Whig and Liberal leaders for many generations past. Gladstone had, perhaps, issued the introduction to the final struggle when, after the defeat of his Irish Home Rule Bill by the Lords, he resigned office in 1894 with a valedictory speech in which he said:

"Sir, I do not wish to use hard words, which are easily employed and as easily retorted — it is a game that two can play at — but without using hard words, without presuming to judge of motives, without desiring or venturing to allege imputations, I have felt it a duty to state what appeared to me to be indisputable facts. The issue which is raised between a deliberative assembly, elected by the votes of more than 6,000,000 people, and a deliberative assembly occupied by many men of virtue, by many men of talent, of course with considerable diversities and varieties, is a controversy which, when once raised, must go forward to an issue."

The natural conservatism of the British people, however, might have postponed the struggle indefinitely had not the House of Lords precipitated matters by rejecting the Budget (and Finance Bill) in 1909. This act forced the hand of the Liberals. Twice the government went to the people to be sure of support for their action, and both times the people gave them a handsome majority. In the final stages, the Lords were themselves convinced that they were fighting a losing fight, but it can hardly be said that they gave in gracefully. The virulence of the personal attacks upon the Liberal leaders has never been surpassed in parliamentary history in Great Britain, not even in the feeling excited over Free Trade and Parliamentary Reform.

And what was the significance of the change effected by the Parliament Bill? Henceforward the Upper House, though its continued existence was to be tolerated, was to be shorn of its power to thwart the will of the House of Commons. Its veto was to operate merely to delay the passage of legislation. The will of the people, as expressed through their representatives in the Commons, was to be assured of supremacy. The passage of the Bill marked the success of a revolution by which democracy in Great Britain took a great stride forward.

CHAPTER VI

THE STATES OF EUROPE, 1905–1911. II.

THE CONTINENTAL STATES

A. *France*

DOMESTIC political issues in France during these years, 1905–1911, revolved about measures of social reform and the various methods proposed by different groups for obtaining such reforms. The avowed aim of each group was the same, namely, the betterment of general social conditions for the masses of the people throughout France: the means for pursuing this aim suggested by the groups devoted to social reform differed radically.

Among the most important of the political groups in numbers and influence during this period was the Socialist. The Socialist movement in France from 1871 to 1905 had had a stormy career, not merely because of government suppression, but also because of internal dissension. And yet, the number of voters who called themselves Socialists had steadily increased. In 1885, the first year the Socialists openly entered the contest for parliamentary representation, they polled only 30,000 votes; in 1889 they polled 120,000; and in 1898, 700,000. In 1905 the two most prominent branches of the party settled their differences and joined in what has been commonly known as the United Socialist party. In the elections of the following year, this party polled nearly 1,000,000 votes and seated 54 of its number in the Chamber of Deputies. The United Socialists are the most compact and the best disciplined of the groups in the Chamber. They constitute to-day the true Socialists in France, holding still to the belief in the necessity of a war of the classes and ultimate revolution to solve the social problems.

Socialistic in nature, but not acknowledged as true Socialists, are two other groups, calling themselves Independent Socialist and Radical Socialist (or Socialist Radical). The Independent Socialists are men who, though accepting socialistic principles in general, refuse to be bound by a strict party organization, or to commit themselves to a definite political program. They polled in excess of 350,000 votes in the elections of 1906, and seated about thirty members in the chamber. The Radical Socialists are the most numerous and important of the groups with socialistic tendencies. They are men who, accepting the socialistic aims, discard the idea of a necessary class war or revolution, and believe that these aims can be reached by a gradual evolution within the state. They form a connecting link between the United Socialists and the Liberal Republicans in the Chamber. They polled over a million and a quarter votes in the 1906 elections, and gained two hundred seats in the Chamber.

The support of the socialistic groups had long been necessary for the continuation of any ministry in power. During the stress of the Dreyfus affair and the subsequent separation of Church and State, the socialistic groups had formed a coalition with the Liberal Republicans to maintain the safety of the government. In 1899 a Socialist, Millerand, was admitted to the cabinet. His acceptance of a place in the ministry created a crisis among the strict Socialists, who asserted that true Socialistic principles prevented any Socialist from taking part in a non-Socialist government. Millerand was, therefore, a few years later read out of his party, and joined the Independent Socialists. During his three years of office (1899–1902), however, his wisdom, tact, and moderation did much to dissipate the distrust of such small property holders as still identified Socialism with seizure of individual property. Briand, another Socialist (who with his acceptance of office automatically lost his standing and became a member of the Independents), entered the ministry during the Church and State issue. And in 1906 as a result of the great vote polled by the several Socialistic groups, Briand again entered the ministry, and his friend and party colleague, Viviani, a well-known lawyer of Paris, accepted a place as head of the newly created Department of Labor and Social Prevision.

Both the United Socialists and the other groups with socialistic principles expected to work for social reform largely through the organizations of workmen into Trade Unions. The methods of the less radical groups — the Independent Socialists and the Radical Socialists — were certain, however, to be slow. A new group, not a political party in the ordinary sense of the word, injected itself into the situation at this time with a program promising more speedy and more complete victory for the workingmen. The Syndicalists, as they became known, interfered seriously with the working out of reform along the lines proposed by the more conservative socialist groups.

Syndicalism has been a relatively recent development. It has been a movement begun and carried on by an energetic group of theorists professing whole-hearted devotion to the welfare of the oppressed laboring classes. Having at the outset socialistic ideals, these writers and organizers revolted from Socialism because, they claimed, in the race for political power in the parliament and ministry the Socialists had thrown aside the truest and most fundamental principles of Socialism. Despising government as it existed, and parliaments, they made no effort to use the electoral machinery to have themselves returned to the legislature. They favored the use of the general strike, with accompanying acts of violence where necessary, by the laboring classes to overthrow the centralized government and to establish a system of communal governments whose sole or chief functions would be to control the economic life of their respective communities for the good of the proletariat. In the last analysis, the syndicalist state would be little more than a collection of federated coöperative trade unions. The syndicalist movement reached its height in France in the years between 1905 and 1908.

The crisis in the syndicalist movement during this period came when the Syndicalists attempted to influence the existing trade unions to demand, and to attempt to gain by strikes and violence, important social reforms. These trade unions had grown from 1000 with 140,000 members in 1890 to 5000 with 850,000 members in 1906. They had been hotbeds of disturbances from their formation, fertile for the sowing of the seeds of revolution. About 2500 of them, containing 300,000 members, were amalgamated into one nation-wide organization, the General Confederation of Labor (Confédération Général du Travail, commonly referred to as the C. G. T.). It was among the C. G. T. members that radical measures spread most rapidly. The Socialists had found in them a ready response in their early years; but now that the main body of Socialists had ceased to have revolutionary aims and sought to ameliorate social conditions by the slow process of reform legislation, the Syndicalists' program proved more attractive. Syndicalists gained great influence over the national council of the C. G. T. and used this influence, in accordance with their policy, to instigate strikes and disorders in the industries of the state. It has been computed that between 1899 and 1907 France endured 855 strikes, involving 215,000 employees.

These strikes and disorders continued during 1908 and 1909, increasing rather than diminishing in number and importance. Every repressive measure adopted by the government caused interpellations in the Chamber of Deputies and long debates on the workmen's right to strike and the justice or injustice of interference on the part of the government. In these debates, the United Socialists, those uncompromising believers in the class war, formed the opposition. A single example will show the gravity of these strikes and of the political disputes arising therefrom. On March 13, 1909, a strike began at Paris in the Postal and Telegraph service, whose men were, of course, state employees. Their special grievance originated in a disapproval of the promotion methods of M. Simyan, the Under-secretary of State for Posts and Telegraphs: their demands were the removal of M. Simyan, freedom from punishment for the strikers, and acknowledgment of the right of state employees as well as the employees of private industrial concerns to form trade unions and to go on strike. Their strike, spreading rapidly to other parts of the country, paralyzed for a time the telegraph and postal service: four days after it began it was estimated that 3,000,000 letters were awaiting delivery in Paris, and for a week the whole of France had no postal system; telegraph service between Paris and London virtually ceased. Conferences between the strike leaders and the government proceeded daily, the government finally being forced to agree not to punish the strikers, but refusing to dismiss M. Simyan until his side of the case had been referred to the Chamber of Deputies. On March 23, the strikers, believing that they had won a victory, ended the strike and returned to work.

At this point the C. G. T. (General Confederation of Labor) entered the dispute. At a great mass meeting organized under its auspices a resolution was passed asserting the unity of the interests of government employees and the proletariat. The postmen, whose expectations of the removal of M. Simyan had been disappointed, were restless and dissatisfied. Hints of the C. G. T. promised a sympathetic strike if the postmen and telegraphers again went out. The dismissal of fifty-three postmen on May 3, 1909, for making revolutionary speeches started the trouble anew. On the 11th of May the postmen declared a country-wide strike, and on the 18th, the C. G. T. gave its assistance by proclaiming a general strike of all its units. These strikes were, however, a failure. The business interests of the country, forewarned by what had happened in the March strike, had taken measures to be prepared, and the government acted energetically. Chambers of Commerce in the towns set up post offices of their own; private automobiles were pressed into service to carry the mails; a government officer was placed in charge of handling and canceling stamps; and soldiers were set to work at sorting letters; popular sympathy, which in the March strike had leaned toward the strikers, was wholly alienated during the May strike. By the end of May the strike was broken.

In the meanwhile, these labor troubles were the subject of constant debate in the Chamber of Deputies. The importance of the issue at stake was fully recognized: either the government must control its employees, or the labor unions would control the government. The government took a firm stand on the principle that it was impossible to allow a strike of the state employees, and the Chamber of Deputies loyally supported it. Both during the March strike and the May strike the Chamber repeatedly voted confidence in the government, and showed itself willing to endorse any measures the government might think it wise to take to enforce its authority.

These labor troubles entered on a new phase in the summer of 1909 when the Clemenceau ministry fell and Aristide Briand, a Socialist, became premier. Briand, it is true, had been outlawed by the extreme Socialists in accordance with a rule they had long before adopted that any Socialist who accepted a position in the government ceased to be a member of the party. He continued to consider himself a Socialist, however, and as a Socialist was elevated to the premiership — the first instance in history of an avowed Socialist being at the head of a great government. Briand had been in former days one of the most outspoken of the advocates of the strike as a means for the workmen to get their rights. In the Socialist Congress at Paris in 1899 he spoke to the following effect:

"The general strike has the seductive advantage that it is nothing but the practice of an intangible right. It is a revolution which arises within the law. The workingman refuses to carry the yoke of misery any farther and begins the revolution in the field of his legal rights." And again, at the same meeting: "If the command to fire is given, if the officers are stubborn enough to try to force the soldiers against their will, then the guns might be fired, but perhaps not in the direction the officers thought."

But experience in the government had sobered him. The strike of state employees was different from the strike of employees in a privately owned industry. It was his duty to maintain the authority of the government in the face of attempts to undermine it. One of the possibilist group, he accepted the form of government as a means by which, without the destruction of existing institutions, the socialist reforms might be gradually introduced. He saw in the efforts of the Syndicalists an attempt only at destruction: it was not inconsistent with his own socialist principles to uphold the government against attacks engineered by the syndicalist intriguers in the C. G. T. and among the state employees.

Elections were held during the two weeks following April 24, 1910, and resulted in the maintenance of a substantial majority of the Radical Socialists. The Radicals and Radical Socialists returned numbered 252, the Independent Socialists 30, and the United Socialists 74; the Republicans 93, the Nationalists 17, the Progressists 60; the Reactionaries of various shades of opinion 71. Briand's position was actually strengthened by these results.

The decisive test of the relations between the government and its employees came with the great railway strike of October, 1910. The C. G. T. had organized a strike on the southern railway lines in the month of May, which had been concluded on terms acceptable to the men. It therefore proceeded to initiate a movement for a general strike on the northern lines. After many futile negotiations, the men's committee set October 11 for the beginning of the strike. Before the end of that day, traffic on the lines of the Northern Railway was completely suspended. In a cabinet meeting the same day, Briand characterized the strike, not as economic in nature, but as political and revolutionary, and announced that the government was prepared to take energetic measures for guarding the line. The following day, October 12, the strike committee called a general strike which at once stopped all work on the northern and western railways. Briand's answer to this act was the startling and unprecedented order, issued on the same day as the general strike decree (October 11, 1910), mobilizing the 30,000 employees of the Northern Railroad for three weeks of military training, such military training to consist in the maintenance of the line in working order and in obedience to their official superiors. Briand's order was a bombshell in the camp of the strikers. They were liable for military duty as loyal French subjects. They were therefore confronted with the alternative of obeying their government or obeying their strike leaders. Disobedience to their government would be followed by military punishment. Briand's measures were effective. Within a few days portions of the line were again in working order. The mobilization order was extended to the other strikers the following day with similar results. On October 18 the men's committee yielded and declared the strike at an end.

The parliament was not in session during the strike, but came together shortly afterwards. Briand was at once forced to defend his course in answer to angry interpellations from the United Socialists. The debate, which began

October 25, was marked by great violence of language and disorder. The United Socialists asserted that the workmen had a legal right to strike, and that the government's act in ordering mobilization had deprived French citizens of their privileges. Briand defended himself on the ground that the government was facing, not an ordinary economic strike, but "an enterprise designed to ruin the country, an anarchistic movement with civil war for its aim, and violence and organized destruction for its method." And in an impassioned moment on October 29 he turned to the group of United Socialists and shouted: "I am going to tell you something that will make you jump. If the government had not found in the law that which enabled it to remain master of the frontiers of France and master of its railways, which are indispensable instruments of the national defense — if, in a word, the government had found it necessary to resort to illegality, it would have done so."

After stormy scenes, and accusations of being a "Dictator," Briand and his entire cabinet resigned November 2, 1910. He was at once recalled by President Fallières, however, and intrusted with the formation of a new ministry. He retained several members of the former cabinet and announced as one of the features of his policy certain changes in the legal status of trade and labor unions. What he intended to propose was, as he outlined it to a cabinet council November 15, 1910, a method of dealing with railroad strikes providing for: (1) a permanent conciliation board, comprising representatives of the employers and of the employees, and a council of arbitration; (2) the prohibition of any strike if arbitration is not accepted or while negotiations are in progress; (3) a measure giving the government authority to requisition railway employees whenever needed; and (4) a measure to secure the railways from damage. He would have had a difficult time in obtaining the passage of legislation to the above effect: his ministry was cut short by his resignation February 27,

1911, when in debates on the subject of church legislation his majority declined to six votes in the Chamber.

No important legislation dealing with the government control of strikes was passed during the succeeding ministries. Briand had successfully coped with the critical situation which confronted him, and had set a precedent for possible action in a future emergency. He had maintained the authority of the government when it was challenged by the Syndicalist methods of the railway unions. Gradually the excitement over the issue died down, as new political questions — the budget, the electoral reform law, old age pensions, and the like — came up for discussion. The United Socialists made repeated efforts to obtain the reinstatement of the strikers who had been dismissed during the great strike, but were uniformly unsuccessful. The ministries kept clear of the dangerous attempt to pass into law the Briand program. Strikes in private industrial concerns continued, and the government was firm in repressing disorders caused by these; but few organizations of state employees ventured again to tempt the government to use its order of mobilization.

B. *Russia*

In Russia during this same period (1905–1911) all political interest centered in the history of the successive Dumas. The First Duma, which had met in May, 1906, was dissolved by the Czar after a short and very stormy session, on July 21, 1906. A group of the irreconcilables in this First Duma assembled, immediately after the dissolution, at Viborg in Finland (in more or less conscious imitation of the Third Estate meeting at the Tennis Court in Versailles, 1789, at the beginning of the French Revolution), and issued a manifesto appealing to the nation not to pay taxes, not to yield recruits for the army, and not to consider itself bound by foreign loans, until the Duma was restored. This Viborg Manifesto created a great sensation among well-informed liberals and aroused the hostility of the government, but it failed to have any marked effect upon the masses of the Russian people. A few isolated army mutinies and Terrorist outrages were the only signs that it had affected any portion of the country. The government, at the time that it dissolved the First Duma, had issued a summons for a second to meet March 5, 1907, and thus had given apparent evidence of its intention to continue the system of representative government. The people at large, although they disapproved of the dissolution of the First Duma, were exhausted by the disorders of the preceding winter, were disappointed at the uncompromising and unconciliatory attitude of the radical element in the First Duma, and were therefore disposed to await the meeting of the Second Duma.

In the meanwhile, between the dissolution of the First Duma and the assembly of the Second, Stolypin (the prime minister) assumed complete control of the situation. His policy was twofold: on the one hand he proposed to suppress ruthlessly all attempts to induce changes in the political system by violence: on the other hand he intended to guarantee civil liberty for such of the population as were peaceably disposed, and to introduce some needed reforms. Naturally, his suppression policy attracted the most attention: revivals of Terrorism were quelled by secret and speedy trial and instant penalty of death; attempts at violence were met by banishment without trial — 35,000 persons suffered this summary punishment. The prisons were filled, and the executions frequent.

The liberal elements carefully organized their forces to win in the elections to the forthcoming Duma. Every obstacle was put in their way by the government through its officials, but the peasants and laborers obeyed their liberal leaders unquestioningly at the polls. The groups in opposition to the government had a large majority in the new Duma.

The Second Duma met for the first time March 5, 1907. The attitude of the government was from the beginning hostile, for the character of the chamber was even more openly democratic than was that of the First Duma. Spies dogged the steps of the Liberal members, and Stolypin addressed the assembly as its master, unwilling to make any concessions to it. The time was taken up in futile proposals and party strife, and no constructive measures of importance were debated and passed. At the beginning of the session, the Duma demanded the repeal of the summary field courts-martial, by which Stolypin on behalf of the government had been trying those persons implicated in acts of Terrorism. A few weeks later an impossible bill for the expropriation of the landlords for the benefit of the peasantry was carried by a two-thirds majority. Stolypin's legislative program, which actually did include radical reforms, was disregarded for measures which the government could not approve. After three months of useless session, the government forced the issue: on June 14 Stolypin demanded a secret session; produced and read an obscurely worded and indefinite accusation of conspiracy against the Czar on the part of the Social Democrats in the assembly; and asked that the Duma consent to the expulsion of these members from its number. The Duma immediately referred the accusations to a special committee for investigation. The Czar, regarding this reference to a committee as a method of sidetracking his demands, did not await the committee report, but published a manifesto June 16 dissolving the Duma, with a statement that its members had not been real representatives of the needs and wishes of the people, and that the Czar would change the manner of election.

Inasmuch as the Czar had expressly declared in his manifesto of October 30, 1905, that the Duma was the legislative body of the empire, he had no legal right without its consent to change the electoral system. His only reasons and excuse for so doing were stated in his manifesto of June 16, 1907:

"He recognized that the composition of the Duma was not satisfactory. . . . Only that power which concedes the first electoral law, the historic power of the Czar, possesses the right to abrogate that law and to replace it by a new law; and as it was God who bestowed upon us our power as autocrat, it is before His altar that we shall answer for the destinies of the Russian state."

He thus based his right to change the electoral law solely on his autocratic power.

The new electoral law reduced the number of representatives in the Duma from 524 to 442, limiting the right of representatives in many districts which had returned liberals to the preceding Duma. Thus Siberia lost 6 out of 21, the Caucasus lost 19 out of 29, Poland lost 22 out of 36, and Central Asia (which was full of Mohammedans) lost its entire representation. Furthermore, by the provisions of the new law many classes were disfranchised altogether, and the method of voting for the remainder was skillfully adapted to insure the election of conservative members. The control over the membership of the Duma was placed in the hands of the wealthy land owners throughout the empire — a class of men naturally favorable to the existing régime.

The dissolution of the Second Duma and the promulgation of the new electoral law, accompanied by a continuation of severe police measures of repression, prostrated temporarily the forces of liberalism. All the past efforts seemed to have been futile, and the autocracy to be reëstablished on an unassailable basis. Thirty-one of the Social Democrats of the last Duma were secretly tried and banished to Siberia; members of the First Duma who signed the Viborg Manifesto were tried and punished with sentences of varying degrees of severity; a new police ordinance provided a penalty of $1500 or three months' imprisonment for any persons publishing or circulating any articles "arousing a hostile attitude toward the government." The government was endeavoring to crush all opposition to its course by the familiar police methods.

And yet the Duma still remained: the Czar did not venture to abolish that institution. And by the development of schools and knowledge of modern business and agricultural methods the general level of intelligence among the masses might be raised, with a corresponding influence upon the political situation. The Liberals, forced to yield to the power of the Czar's police, planned to exert their efforts in developing a healthy and intelligent public interest in political and economic questions, and in organizing a conservative reform group in the forthcoming Duma.

The elections to the Third Duma were held in October, 1907. Carefully hedged about by governmental supervision and regulation, these elections resulted satisfactorily: that is, they returned a large majority of conservatives, willing to support the government. Country gentlemen were in the majority, men who had been identified with the government by service in the army, in local offices, or in the great pervading bureaucracy. These men were not to be considered as reactionaries, that is, as men who desired a return to the old régime of complete autocracy with the effacement of the Duma, but as conservatives, men who were willing to work with the government along the paths of gradual reform.

The Third Duma met November 14, 1907, and remained in session, except for its regular adjournment for holidays, through its full term of five years, until June 21, 1912. Its powers were strictly limited: the prime minister was not responsible to it; although it was permitted to discuss the budget and to vote upon the expenditures, the Czar could at any time overrule its votes by arbitrary decrees promulgated during its adjournment; its strictures upon the government's policies had no marked effect in causing a change. And yet, its very existence as an institution in

Russian political life had a noteworthy influence in stimulating and encouraging freedom of public opinion: public liberties were greater than under the iron régime of Von Plehve; it was able to work in conjunction with Stolypin (until his assassination in September, 1911) to accomplish many reforms and to pass a number of constructive measures of great importance; entire license of debate was allowed in the Duma, even to the extent of criticism of the government or of persons of the imperial family; and Russia did have a parliament, even though the electoral system made that parliament representative of a class rather than of the whole nation. Autocracy and bureaucracy had not regained the whole of the ground they had lost during the civil disturbances of 1905 and 1906: a definite step had been taken toward liberalism, and the Duma was the symbol of the people's rights as contrasted with the Czar's power.

C. *Austria-Hungary*

This period 1905-1911 in the history of the Dual Empire, Austria-Hungary, is a record of a confused struggle between the different races for supremacy in internal politics. The conflict raged both in Austria and in Hungary, at times paralyzing the operation of parliamentary government in both countries. It included the following phases: (*a*) the struggle on the part of a large and influential faction in Hungary for the complete independence of Hungary from Austria; (*b*) the struggle of the non-Magyar elements in Hungary for a political power proportionate to their numerical strength; and (*c*) the struggle of the non-German elements in Austria for a political power proportionate to their strength.

i. The Struggle for Hungarian Independence

It will be remembered that the Ausgleich of 1867 established a Dual Empire consisting of two powers united by the person of their sovereign, by a joint ministry of three departments (Foreign Affairs, War, and Finance), and by mutual tariff and currency arrangements renewable at ten-year intervals. The adjustment of relations between the two powers that composed the empire had caused continual difficulty and irritation from the beginning. In 1867, when the Ausgleich was adopted, a strong group in Hungary had demanded complete independence from Austria except for the person of the sovereign, and adherents of this same policy had gained representation in all the Hungarian parliaments since that time. In the elections of January, 1905, the Independence party became the strongest political group in the parliament. Its special aims were that, in the renewal of the tariff agreement due in 1907, Hungary and Austria should treat with each other just as two foreign, wholly independent powers might treat together; that the charter of the joint Austro-Hungarian bank should not be renewed, the bank's place being taken by a Hungarian bank in Hungary and an Austrian bank in Austria; and that the Hungarian army should be distinct in organization and command from that of Austria.

In the economic treaty the Independents gained for Hungary all that they desired. Austria negotiated with Hungary an international customs treaty and guaranteed that, in future commercial agreements with foreign countries, Hungarian sovereignty and independence should be clearly recognized and Hungarian interests represented. Furthermore, Hungary consented to a reapportionment of the respective contributions of the two countries to the common expenditure, agreeing to pay 36.4% to Austria's 63.6%. Both the economic arrangement and this fiscal arrangement were satisfactory to her as well as to Austria.

To the demands of the Hungarians concerning the army, however, the sovereign offered a resolute resistance. He yielded a few minor concessions, as by allowing Hungarian regiments standards with insignia denoting the sovereignty of Hungary, and by guaranteeing that Hungarian troops should be commanded by Hungarian officers; but he insisted upon the necessity for military unity in the Dual Empire. The Hungarians centered their demands upon the use of the Magyar word of command to the Hungarian troops, but these demands, too, Francis Joseph resisted. The strength of the monarchy rested upon the unity and effectiveness of its military force, and so long as the German-speaking house of Hapsburg was dominant in the empire, German was to be the language of command throughout the army. He was able to base his right to determine the question of discipline and training in the army upon that provision in the Ausgleich, or Compromise, of 1867, which stated that the two powers should act jointly in matters affecting the national defense.

The sovereign and his advisers also objected strongly to the Hungarian proposals to separate the Austro-Hungarian bank into two institutions, one purely Hungarian, and one purely Austrian. Francis Joseph was bound upon principle to resist every effort to disrupt the economic and military unity of his Dual Monarchy. He considered that the maintenance of this single national bank was important in its influence toward unity. The proposal for separation was argued in the Hungarian parliament in 1908 and 1909, and presented to the sovereign and the Austrian parliament for their approval in the summer of the latter year. Francis Joseph pointed out that this question of a separate bank for Hungary was not provided for in the Ausgleich, or Compromise, of 1867, and could not at the present time well be introduced into it; and then he went on to lay emphasis upon the duty of the Hungarian ministry to fulfill its pledges of electoral reform in Hungary, thus implying that the question might be again opened for adjustment before a parliament more truly representative of the various Hungarian interests. His answer was a shrewd political maneuver: it did not actually refuse a request formulated and approved by the Hungarian parliament; and it forced attention of the ministry to electoral reform, which the Magyar element did not sincerely desire because of the fear that such reform would weaken Magyar dominance. The question of the separation of the Austro-Hungarian Bank was thus indefinitely postponed.

ii. Electoral Reform in Hungary

The struggle of the races in Hungary has been during its modern history the most prominent feature of its internal political life. The Magyars, although they are actually a minority in the population of the Kingdom, have tenaciously held the political control against the determined attacks of the Slav elements, composed of Poles, Slovenes, Croats, Rumanians, etc. Slav representatives have consistently adopted dilatory parliamentary tactics, blocking the wheels of government time after time, in the effort to obtain concessions from the Magyars, but without avail. The Magyars have been willing to endure government obstruction to any extent rather than to yield one tittle of their political power.

To understand the attitude of the sovereign, it must be remembered that the Magyar politicians were continually making demands which he, devoted as he was to the essential unity of the two powers he ruled, found it impossible to grant. Examples have been given above: it was the Magyar element which forced the tariff treaties on a new basis; it was the Magyar element which demanded the Magyar word of command to replace German for the Hungarian troops; and it was the Magyar element which sought the separation of the Austro-Hungarian Bank into two institutions. Thus the interests of the sovereign, as he considered them, were often opposed to the wishes of the dominant body in the Hungarian parliament.

After a serious parliamentary crisis forced in 1905 by the

inability of the Hungarian parliament to reconcile its demands with the sovereign's will, more than five months were spent in the search for a ministry who could command a majority to conduct the government. At last, in order to reduce the irreconcilable group in the parliament and to gain support for a ministry, Francis Joseph took the momentous step of permitting it to be known that he would accept electoral reform measures to introduce universal suffrage into Hungary.

The existing system of suffrage in Hungary — one of the most complicated in Europe — was carefully framed by the dominant Magyars to confine the franchise to the privileged classes of their own race so far as possible. As it worked out, the system gave to the Magyars a representation twelve times as great in proportion to their numbers as it gave to the Rumanians, or Slovaks, or Poles. The proposed reform would more than triple the number of electors, and would open the door of politics to the working classes of the population. The sovereign hoped that the readjustment of elements represented in a parliament elected by universal suffrage would result in relatively more attention being paid to economic and social questions, and less proportionately to those racial quarrels which had consumed so much time in the past.

The immediate result of knowledge of the sovereign's attitude was the formation of a ministry and the resumption of the regular form of parliamentary government. The following year, in April, 1906, the Hungarian prime minister, Wekerle, definitely committed the government to measures of electoral reform.

The problem, however, was exceedingly difficult to solve, for the Magyars had no intention of permitting an out-and-out universal suffrage system to be adopted. Such a system would undermine fatally their own political predominance. The years passed, and other issues brought other conflicts, but no serious attempt to pass a reform bill was made. In 1908, it is true, certain proposals were put before the parliament for discussion, but little was accomplished beyond revealing the gulf that lay between the wishes of the Slavs and the will of the Magyars. Successive ministries incorporated electoral reform in their program but were unable to survive crises on other issues long enough to place a well-considered plan before the parliament. Finally, the pressure of the public, whose expectations had been so often disappointed since the first announcement, proved to be too strong to be rejected further. On January 2, 1913, the Hungarian premier introduced the bill.

The provisions of this bill were a terrible disappointment to democratic hopes. The familiar manipulation of the details of the electoral system to insure the continuance of the dominant power aroused intense resentment among the liberals. The total number of electors was doubled, it is true, but by differentiation in age qualification, and by provisions of property qualification, the exercise of the suffrage was kept in the hands of the favored classes. For example: a common laborer, if otherwise qualified, could not vote until he reached the age of 30, but men with an intermediate school education might vote at 24; again, a man without an intermediate school diploma might vote at 24 if he owned eight yoke of oxen, or if he paid a direct tax of 20 kronen (about $4), or if he had for a fixed number of years worked in certain stipulated employments. By such carefully worded provisions as these the ministry had insured the continuance of Magyar political supremacy.

The terms of the bill aroused a tumult in the Chamber. The Social Democrats proved the most violent of the opponents — naturally, since they were largely representative of the interests of those classes who were not enfranchised, and were not to be fully enfranchised by the bill. The meetings of the parliament were stormy. The Social Democrats threatened to organize a general strike as a protest of the laboring classes: the ministry replied that it did not intend to be intimidated by such illegitimate means, and made preparations to suppress the strike by force. These preparations overawed the organizers, and the strike did not materialize. The ministry kept its majority closely in hand and forced the bill through the final stages to passage. It was passed by the Upper House without amendment March 15, 1913, and became law.

iii. Electoral Reform in Austria

The progress of electoral reform in Austria was attended with less difficulty than in Hungary. The Emperor recognized, when he accepted the principle of universal suffrage for Hungary in 1905, that he would be obliged to yield similar reforms to Austria. The Austrian people seized the opportunity to make their wishes known without delay. In November a demonstration organized by the Socialists took place in Vienna in favor of the principle of universal suffrage — for five hours traffic was suspended while a procession of workingmen, ten abreast, marched past the Houses of Parliament. On February 23, 1906, the prime minister, Baron von Gautsch, introduced a series of reform measures.

These measures provided for the franchise for every male Austrian over 24 years old. The new lower chamber was to have 516 members instead of 425 as in the old. The electoral constituencies were arranged so far as was possible on racial bases, so that Germans should vote for Germans, Czechs for Czechs, Slavonians for Slavonians, etc., and the proportion of members from the different races in the chamber was definitely fixed — Germans 233, Czechs 107, Poles 82, Ruthenians 33, Slavonians 24, Italians 19, Serbo-Croatians 13, Rumanians 5. Such a system, arranged according to racial and linguistic differences, seems mechanical, yet it was in accordance with historical traditions and natural agelong distinctions.

The measures, though not enthusiastically received, went through the parliament with astonishingly little opposition. Baron von Gautsch himself fell from power in April, 1906; was succeeded by Prince zu Hohenlohe-Schillingsfürst, who remained in office only six weeks, and was in turn succeeded (June 2, 1906) by Baron von Beck; but through these ministerial changes the policy of the government to pass the electoral reform measures continued firm. The Emperor himself took an active share in bringing about the result, calling the hostile party leaders to the imperial palace and informing them that the reform must be accomplished. Early in December the lower house accepted the measures, and a month later, January 26, 1907, with the approval of the upper chamber, the measures became law.

The new electoral law accentuated rather than lessened the racial bitterness in the parliament. The Czechs of Bohemia proved to be the most troublesome element, demanding the federalization of the empire, an equal official status for the Czechish and German languages in Bohemia, independent Czechish technical schools and universities, and the use of the Czechish language in the Bohemian contingent of the army. When unable to gain these demands, they resorted to the familiar tactics of parliamentary obstruction. Indeed, the Austrian parliament (and the Hungarian parliament as well) is known to be the most disorderly legislative body in Europe. For example: in February, 1909, the Austrian premier, with the hope of reconciling the discordant element, introduced a measure providing for the administrative division of Bohemia into three classes of districts, one class of Czechish districts in which Czechish should be the official language, a second class of German in which German should be the official language, and a third class of mixed in which the two languages should be upon an equal status; at once the Germans in the parliament massed against the Czechs; all parliamentary business was effectually blocked; a free fight ensued at the early closure of the session in which one member had his hand severely bitten and another had his coat torn from his back; and the representatives finally dispersed defiantly singing their racial anthems at each other.

Similar disorderly scenes defeated the attempts of the government to get through parliament sorely needed constructive measures. Financial reforms and military reforms were the chief features of the government's program, but the racial antagonism overshadowed all proposals of whatever nature. Throughout 1910 and 1911 the struggle continued without cessation, marked by recurrent instances of violence. Not until June of 1912 was the government able to have the military reform measures passed, and then only after the personal intervention of the aged Emperor. Broad financial reforms were impossible in the situation: the parliament confined itself to stop-gap measures.

At the close of 1912 the antagonism between the races was still the great unsolved problem confronting the sovereign both in Austria and Hungary. Fears were openly expressed that the heterogeneous mass would fly asunder as soon as the Emperor died — and his death was expected each year. The heir apparent, Francis Ferdinand, had not become popular, so that people feared loyalty to him would not act as a binding force between the different races. The race leaders showed no spirit of compromise or conciliation and, as has been indicated above, did not hesitate to wreck the government policy when their own racial aims were not obtained. Thus the difficulties under which the imperial and royal government labored were overwhelming. Progress was slow, reform handicapped, the finances — especially in provinces like Bohemia, where the racial bitterness was especially extreme — in a badly muddled condition, sections of the army dissatisfied, and the people in a constant turmoil. Government was at a standstill for months at a time, and no improvement was in sight.

D. *Germany*

In the domestic history of Germany, during these years 1905–1911, we find no crisis approaching in seriousness the parliament bill agitation in Great Britain, the revolutionary outbreaks in Russia, or the racial antagonism in Austria-Hungary. The German people were as a whole satisfied with their government, proud of their economic progress and of their own type of civilization (*Kultur*), and willing to accept the burdens of national greatness, such as compulsory military service, heavy taxation for the support of the huge army and navy, and the domination of the military caste. Sharp criticisms there were at times of the national policies, even of the Emperor himself, but such attacks emanated from a relatively small political group. In case of any threat of danger from without, the government could rally an overwhelming majority to its aid. The essential unity of all classes and parties (including even the Social Democrats) in their adherence to their sovereign, their government, and their national ideals was the source of Germany's strength compared with the other states in Europe.

In the elections of 1907 the inherent power of the Emperor and his government was strikingly shown. At the close of 1906 the chancellor, Prince von Bülow, dissolved the Reichstag after a dispute over the action of the government in the German colony in southwest Africa. In the elections immediately ensuing, the government appealed for support on the general policy of "ships, colonies, and empire," that is, on the policy of the expansion of Germany as a foremost world power. In allusions whose meaning was unmistakable, the government orators told the German people that they stood at the turning point of German fortunes: support for the government was a vote for an imperial policy of force and progressiveness in world affairs; support for the opposition was a vote for a restricted German power, the limitation of German influence to the German territory in central Europe. Their imaginations aroused by the visions of world empire, the German voters gave their support to the Emperor and government. Eleven million two hundred and sixty thousand people went to the polls. The Social Democratic party, which had maintained a consistent opposition to the government policies, in its representation in the Reichstag fell from 81 to 43. At midnight on election day, when the results had revealed a sweeping government victory, the Emperor himself came out on the balcony of his palace like a successful candidate for office in a republican country and spoke to the cheering crowds which had gathered:

> "Gentlemen, I thank you for your ovation. To-day all of you have put your hands to the work and have proved the word of the Imperial Chancellor, "Germany can ride if she cares to." I hope this will be true not only to-day but also in the future. If men of all ranks and faiths stand together, we can ride down those who block our path."

The influence of the government's victory was quickly reflected in Germany's foreign relations. In the succeeding chapters the German intervention in the Bosnian crisis in 1908 and the Moroccan situation in 1911 will be described: it should be remembered that the hands of the government's diplomats were strengthened by the victory in these elections of 1907. Had the Social Democrats increased their majority in the Reichstag in those elections, and had the opposition been able to muster enough votes to embarrass the government, it is safe to assume that German diplomacy would have run a very different course during the next five years.

The influence of this victory in the elections was also speedily reflected in domestic conditions. The policy of world empire is an expensive policy. For success it demands according to international methods in the past a strong military and naval force; and the maintenance of such a force requires huge amounts of money. The government was forced to go to the Reichstag year after year with budgets of increasing size and with new suggestions for raising funds. The national debt increased from 4,000,000,000 marks in 1907 to 5,250,000,000 marks in 1911. Each annual budget with its estimated deficits and its proposed new taxes was the occasion for attacks by the opposition upon the government's policy, but with his solid majority in the Reichstag the chancellor consistently carried his measures and the country peacefully accepted the results.

The principal reason why increased taxes and the increased national debt aroused so little strong criticism in the country at large was the continuation of the national prosperity. The population, which was 60,000,000 in 1905, arose to 65,000,000 in 1911. The production of coal and lignite, which had been 173,000,000 tons in 1905, rose to 230,000,000 tons in 1911. The production of pig iron, which had been 10,800,000 tons in 1905, arose to 15,574,000 tons in 1911. The merchant marine, which had contained 3900 vessels with a tonnage of 3,440,000 in 1905, increased to 4700 vessels with approximately the same tonnage (many of the older sailing ships being replaced by steamers). The total import and export business, which had amounted to $3,300,000,000 in 1905, increased to $4,450,000,000 in 1911. These figures speak for themselves: they reveal an unprecedented growth in economic activities, which radiated, of course, through all the branches of industry and thus reached indirectly the smallest hamlet and humblest artisan.

On July 14, 1909, the Imperial Chancellor, Prince von Bülow, resigned after a long and bitter struggle to carry through the annual budget. He was succeeded by Theobald von Bethmann-Hollweg. Von Bethmann-Hollweg was a man fifty-three years old, who had been a successful lawyer and administrator, and had won his way up the various grades of official promotion by his business ability and parliamentary tact. He had been minister of the interior in von Bülow's cabinet, and possessed the full confidence of the Emperor. Inheriting from the previous régime the strong government majority, von Bethmann-Hollweg continued the imperialistic policy.

CHAPTER VII

THE CRISIS OF 1908

In the last two chapters we have outlined the course of internal development in the chief states of Europe during the period from 1905 to 1911. During the same period, the international European situation was twice subjected to severe strain, first in 1908, as a result of certain Turkish complications, and again in 1911, upon the revival of the Moroccan issue. This present chapter will be devoted to the discussion of the revolution of 1908 in Turkey and its far-reaching effects upon the general course of European politics.

A. THE NEAR EASTERN SITUATION

Briefly stated, the following was the political attitude of the great European powers toward the "Eastern Question" in the opening years of the twentieth century: *Great Britain,* which had for a century been the protector of Turkey's position in Europe against the encroachments and ambitions of Russia because of British fears of Russian control of the Dardanelles, had come to a point where her government laid less stress upon this policy because of her general political understandings with France (1904) and Russia (1907) on colonial and territorial issues. *Russia* still held tenaciously to her ideal of gaining ultimately the control of the Dardanelles, and was engaged in constant intrigue in the small adjoining states of the Balkan peninsula to assure her position in this neighborhood. *Austria-Hungary,* whose hold on the Italian peninsula had been shattered by the wars of 1859 and 1866, had definitely turned to the southeast for her hopes of territorial gains, had by the Treaty of Berlin (1878) won the control of the administration and government in the neighboring Turkish provinces of Bosnia and Herzegovina, and was intriguing in the Balkan states to counteract Russian influence there. *Italy* was casting covetous eyes on the disturbed Turkish province of Albania, believing that Italian control of Albania, with its excellent seaport of Avlona, would secure Italy's dominion over the Adriatic Sea. *Germany*, who through the lips of Bismarck once declared that the whole Eastern question was not "worth the bones of a single Pomeranian grenadier," had very recently acquired important railroad and development concessions in Turkish Asia Minor, had invested huge amounts of money in Turkey, and was preparing to invest still more, and had thus become heavily interested in maintaining the existence of Turkey. Each of the *Balkan nations* which had thrown off the Turkish yoke was dissatisfied with its territory and looked forward to increase: *Bulgaria, Serbia, Montenegro,* and *Greece* had conflicting claims in Macedonia and Albania (which were still under Turkish dominion), and were continually intriguing in these districts, each to advance its own ends.

The Great Powers of Europe, recognizing the baffling and serious issues presented by the conflict of interests affecting Turkey and the Balkans, had since the Congress of Berlin (1878) usually acted in concert or agreement in any measures put into operation to relieve critical situations as these arose. Thus, by the Treaty of Berlin, which issued from this Congress, an international commission was provided for drawing up a reform scheme for the European provinces of Turkey. A few years later, 1881, the Turkish government was forced to consent to the establishment of the control of a joint commission of the great powers over Turkish finances. A decade afterwards, the Armenian massacres resulted in another commission of British, French, and Russian officials (1895) to propose and institute reforms in Turkish internal administration. The insurrection of Bulgars in Macedonia in the fall of 1903 resulted in a meeting of the Emperor Francis Joseph of Austria and the Czar Nicholas II of Russia at Mürzteg in 1904, and the adoption of a scheme, the Mürzteg program, by which Austrian and Russian officials were appointed to supervise and control Turkish administration in the disaffected districts, and foreign army officers were designated to reorganize and command the gendarmerie. A year later (1905), the civil officials had obtained so little success that the great powers agreed each to appoint a delegate to a commission which was to have extensive control over Turkish financial matters in Macedonia. In 1908, this commission having met with little success, King Edward VII of Great Britain and Czar Nicholas II of Russia met at Reval and formulated a new program of reforms, known as the Reval program. But the Reval scheme was frustrated by the Turkish revolution which forms the main subject of this chapter.

Thus for thirty years the great powers of Europe, regarding Turkey as a refractory and somewhat irresponsible member of the family of nations, had been attempting to evolve a practicable scheme for her discipline. None of these many schemes had been a success, partly because the Turks themselves in their resentment at outside interference put every obstacle in the way, and partly because the conflicting interests of the nations prevented them from working in close coöperation and harmony. It is not improbable that some of the powers in the Concert secretly desired the unsettled conditions in Turkey to continue in order that they might have a more congenial soil for their intrigues. The Concert of Europe had failed lamentably in its treatment of the Turkish theme.

During this entire period, the Turkish government had shown no sincere desire for reforms. Abdul Hamid, Sultan since 1876, had become an adept in making promises which he had no intention of keeping, and in playing off the ambitions of one great power against those of its rival. His advisers with characteristic oriental fatalism were well content with an administrative inefficiency which offered them opportunities for corruption. Among the people at large, ignorance, race prejudice, and religious fanaticism were counted upon to assure the continuance of the Sultan's autocratic power and to prevent the spread of incendiary liberal ideas. Hence, secure in their authority, the governing classes resisted every movement for reform, whether it was attempted from within or from without the empire.

B. THE TURKISH REVOLUTION

During this generation after 1878, however, a small but very influential group of Turks had been preparing for the overthrow of the old régime in Turkey. These men, many of them officers in the army, had been educated in France or Germany, or in the foreign schools in Turkey itself. They had thus gained a knowledge of the liberal governments existing in western Europe. They were inspired apparently with genuine patriotic indignation at the inefficiency of Turkish administration and the corruption of Turkish officials. They were ashamed of the indignities and humiliations implied in the constant interference of foreign powers in Turkey's internal affairs. This "Young Turkish Party," as the group was called, established a central organization at Paris and published huge quantities of seditious literature which they smuggled into Turkey in the endeavor to enlighten the masses of the people with respect to liberal institutions.

In 1908 the opportunity presented itself for a revolution. The Turkish government was at the moment embarrassed: in Arabia, the Turkish troops were unpaid and mutinous; in Albania the people were irritated to the point of rebellion by new taxes and recent firmans restricting their schools and printing presses. Furthermore, in June of this year King Edward VII and the Czar Nicholas II had formulated their Reval program and were preparing to put it into effect. The prospect of further interference of foreign powers in their internal affairs aroused the Turks to a high pitch of excitement. They believed and feared that the compulsory acceptance of a program of reforms drawn up by the British King and the Russian Czar would place their country in the grip of those powers.

The Young Turks acted with promptness and energy. They transferred their organization from Paris to Salonika; formed a committee of Union and Progress to organize and direct a revolution; and worked with feverish haste during the spring and early summer of 1908 to gain adherents to their cause. They selected the constitution which Abdul Hamid had granted to Turkey in 1876 and had soon after withdrawn as their chief demand of the government. By July their leaders had succeeded in pledging the Albanian chieftains and most of the Turkish army in Europe to this constitution. On the 23d of that month Major Enver Bey, president of the committee of Union and Progress, proclaimed the constitution at Salonika, and the second and third army corps prepared to march against Constantinople if the Sultan did not yield.

The following day, July 24, 1908, the Sultan, impressed with the hopelessness of opposition, yielded wholly to the demands of the Young Turks. He restored the constitution of 1876 and ordered the election of a chamber of deputies. Within a few weeks two other great reforms were instituted by Abdul Hamid: (1) the abolition of the hated spy system; and (2) the abolition of the censorship. A new era seemed to have dawned. Turkey, apparently, had turned into the road of progressive liberalism. Men of all nations and religions in the vast Turkish empire fraternized joyfully at the inception of the new régime. Liberals in foreign countries, especially in Great Britain, foresaw the blessings of free institutions, of equality, toleration, and justice in Turkey, and freely prophesied lasting peace and good will for the new government.

The way of the reformers was, however, beset with difficulties. Once the first enthusiasm had passed and no miracles to remove instantly some of the irritating grievances had been performed, signs of disaffection with the new régime became evident. Revolts broke out in Asia Minor and Albania, serious disturbances occurred in Macedonia, and the massacre of thousands of Christians in Adana and neighboring districts of northern Syria threatened to provoke foreign intervention again. And politically most important of all, in Constantinople itself the Sultan was intriguing against the Young Turks for the overthrow of the constitutional régime and the restoration of his autocratic power.

As the reformers had gained their ends by the army, they now maintained their power by the same means. When the Sultan had made his intentions evident, the Young Turks called upon Shevket Pasha to march with his troops (25,000) against the capital. After a few hours of severe fighting (April 25, 1909) Shevket occupied the city. On April 27 the National Assembly, a body composed of the recently elected Senate and Chamber of Deputies, met in secret session, voted that Abdul Hamid should be deposed, and selected his younger brother Mahommed Reshad Effendi as his successor. On April 28, 1909, Abdul Hamid was taken to live in exile at Salonika. On May 10, Mahommed was formally invested with the sword of Osman as Mahommed V. August 5 the new Sultan formally promulgated the constitution so desired by the Young Turk party. The revolutionists had accomplished the definite end for which they had been working and hopes again ran high that, now Abdul Hamid was removed from baneful activity, Turkey might be regenerated.

The leaders of the new régime in Turkey were, however, handicapped from the beginning in their efforts to solve the perplexing problems of Turkish administration. The necessary political readjustments accompanying a radical revolution demand time, great patience, and unusual sagacity for their successful accomplishment. Unfortunately for those who wished Turkey well, disturbing elements within and without the empire gave the new government no time to test their program of reforms, and laid upon them a diplomatic task beyond their sagacity. The impatient and disaffected element in Macedonia and Albania would give them no rest. Two years after the Young Turks were firmly fixed in power, the Italian-Turkish War broke out (1911). The following year, 1912, the Balkan states leagued to attack Turkey from all sides. In 1913, after the Balkan-Turkish war had ended, the Balkan states fought among themselves, and Turkey was kept in constant turmoil by this war upon her borders. And then in 1914, the great general European war began. In conditions so troubled as these, it is hardly just to blame the new Turk party for accomplishing so little and for reverting to the autocratic methods of the old régime. Their task, immensely difficult under the most favorable circumstances, was made practically impossible by the constant insurrections and wars of the years after 1911. To rally the forces of the empire for defense, arbitrary authority was necessary. The leaders, realizing the impracticability of relying on the inexperienced parliament, were forced by the logic of events to become autocrats. Thus by 1914 the government of Turkey seemed to be the same government as that of the old régime except that it was in different hands.

C. THE BOSNIA-HERZEGOVINA CRISIS

We should not have spent so much space upon the account of this internal revolution in Turkey which seemed to have amounted merely to a change of rulers had it not been that from this revolution came a long chain of consequences which led directly to the outbreak of the general European war in 1914. The first link of this chain was forged with dramatic suddenness by Austria-Hungary when, in the first days of October, 1908, she announced the annexation of the Turkish districts of Bosnia and Herzegovina to the Dual Empire.

It will be remembered that the two Turkish provinces of Bosnia and Herzegovina, along the northeastern Adriatic, had been handed over to the administration of Austria-Hungary by agreement of the powers in the Congress of Berlin (1878). In the thirty years following, a series of wise governors had done excellent constructive administrative work in these provinces. There can be no shadow of doubt that the provinces had been more justly and more satisfactorily governed during this generation than during any of the preceding years under Turkish domination. In accordance with the terms of the Treaty of Berlin, however, Bosnia and Herzegovina were still a part of the Turkish empire and still owed allegiance to the Sultan: Austria-Hungary's rights were merely administrative. No limit had been definitely set on this administration, but it was generally (though tacitly) understood among the great powers that when the final dissolution of "the sick man of Europe" should occur, Austria-Hungary would be recognized as heir to the provinces she had been governing.

One other factor, however, complicated this situation, a factor which later became of overwhelming importance. Little Serbia, a land-locked nation, desired these same provinces in order to give her an outlet to the sea. She looked forward to a greater Serbia which should include, not only large parts of Macedonia (claimed by both Bulgaria and Greece), but all of Bosnia and Herzegovina and portions of Albania. The population in these districts was closely allied to the Serbs in blood, religion, and customs. The Serbs were able to carry on an extensive pan-Serbian propaganda therein, even during the efficient administration of the Austro-Hungarian officials.

Such were the prominent international aspects of this part of the Balkan situation in 1908: — the Austro-Hungarian government had been efficiently administrating the provinces for thirty years, and was confidently looking forward to their incorporation into the empire in the fullness of time; the Serbs were carrying on an active secret propaganda to arouse sentiment for annexation to a greater Serbia; and Turkey had never surrendered her sovereignty, and, not looking forward to her own demise with the same assurance as the other powers, never expected to surrender it.

The revolution of July 24, 1908, changed the situation suddenly. Although all the chancelleries of Europe had been aware of the Young Turk party's activities, none had expected their success. The constitutional Turkey startled the powers. The sick man of Europe seemed rejuvenated. Instead of waiting for the break-up of the empire, the expectant nations might be forced to witness a new and efficient Turkey consolidating its dominions and reasserting its sovereignty and rights of administration over all its territory. Should this possibility become actuality, the new Turkey would certainly at the very beginning demand that Austria-Hungary withdraw her officials from the Turkish provinces of Bosnia and Herzegovina.

In this situation, Austria-Hungary determined to forestall any such demand by Turkey by annexing the provinces outright and at once. Hence, on the 7th of October, 1908, the Emperor Francis Joseph issued a rescript announcing the annexation of Bosnia and Herzegovina to the Hapsburg monarchy. At the same time, Bulgaria declared her full independence of Turkey.

Austria-Hungary's act raised a crisis of the first magnitude in Europe. In 1871 she had been a signatory to the Declaration of London, wherein it was specifically stated that "contracting powers could rid themselves of their treaty engagements only by an understanding with their co-signatories"; in 1878 she had accepted the administration of Bosnia and Herzegovina while at the same time affirming Turkish sovereignty over the provinces; and now in 1908 without conference with the co-signatories of the Treaty of Berlin, she arbitrarily broke the treaty and announced the annexation. Her act, therefore, struck on the one hand at the sacredness of the treaty obligations on which international relations rested, and on the other hand at the existing political situation.

The moral effect of Austria's act was to undermine public confidence in the force of the international obligations which had been carefully and slowly built up since the time of Napoleon by successive treaties. Wise and pacific statesmen had hoped that the foundations of a structure had been laid which might be expanded to insure continued peace in the European family of nations based on the status quo. They had believed that Europe was progressing toward an era in which mutual jealousies and suspicions might be allayed and mutual confidence, resting on inviolable treaty obligations, might take their place. Austria-Hungary's act was a step backward toward the dark ages, toward the period when treaties were observed only when the self-interest of the signatories was involved in observance. It was a step toward the rule of force over the rule of justice and reason. It is impossible to trace here in detail the evil moral effects which this cynical violation of public international engagements had upon European diplomacy as a whole — indeed such effects are so subtle that the task would be hopeless; but it is certain that Austria's act undermined popular confidence in treaties and her ultimate success in thus gaining her desires disheartened statesmen who were striving for progress toward international trust and confidence.

More tangible were the immediate political results. The great powers at once protested against Austria-Hungary's act. The little Balkan powers, Serbia and Montenegro, their hopes for gaining Bosnia and Herzegovina for a greater Serbia thus checked, were aroused to fever heat and prepared for war. Russia, hereditary defender of the Slav nations and constant intriguer against Austrian influence in the Balkan regions, was wholly in sympathy with Serbia's aspirations. Turkey, just beginning her new constitutional régime, was embarrassed by Austria-Hungary's seizure of a part of her territory, and protested vigorously to the powers. Austria-Hungary responded to the threats of Serbia and Montenegro by mobilizing her forces on the frontiers during the autumn. She believed that she would have the moral — and, if need be, the military — support of her ally, Germany, in the step she had taken, and she relied on the weakness of Russia to prevent aggressive action against her. The state of popular excitement in Serbia and Montenegro, however, combined with the sympathies of the masses of the great Slav power, rendered the situation very delicate. No military operations could be undertaken during the severe winter of the Balkan regions, but all Europe dreaded the possibilities of the following spring. It was recognized that actual hostilities between Serbia and Austria-Hungary would inevitably plunge all the greater states of Europe into a conflict.

In this critical situation, the diplomatists welcomed the winter period as an opportunity to avert war. The first thought was to assemble a Congress of the signatories of the Treaty of Berlin (1878) for the discussion and settlement of the question at issue. Sir Edward Grey of Great Britain, answering Turkey's protest, assured the new government in Turkey that Great Britain refused to recognize the breach of the Treaty of Berlin; premier Isvolsky of Russia informed Serbia and Montenegro that Russia would safeguard their interests in a European congress, and declared to Turkey that Russia acquiesced in the view that the annexation was a violation of the Treaty of Berlin. France joined with Great Britain and Russia in the desire for a conference of powers.

In the face of the demands for a Congress, Austria-Hungary took the stand that the issue concerned herself and Turkey alone. Baron von Aehrenthal, the Austro-Hungarian minister of foreign affairs, refused to consider a Congress unless the annexation was to be regarded as a closed incident, *un fait accompli,* and instituted negotiations with Turkey to determine the amount of compensation Austria-Hungary should pay. He refused to discuss compensation for Serbia and Montenegro on the ground that none of their legal or territorial rights had in any way been violated. In the first week of November, 1908, the Serbian Crown Prince and the president of the Montenegrin upper chamber made a hurried visit to St. Petersburg. Upon their return, the Crown Prince issued a statement that he had obtained from the Czar and the Russian people expressions of their sympathy, that he hoped for Russian support in Serbia's struggle, but that, however, Serbia must defend her rights in war whether or not she obtained the assistance of other powers.

The position of Germany in this crisis required the most delicate diplomacy. On the one hand she was determined to maintain her close bonds of alliance with Austria-Hungary; and on the other hand her enormously valuable concessions and investments in Turkey made it necessary for her to retain the friendship of that country. It was a difficult course to steer. Germany used the opportunity with daring and skill to test the strength of the coalition forming against her and to increase her own prestige in European politics. Prince von Bülow, the German imperial chancellor, has interpreted for us the policy of Germany in this crisis:

"In my speeches in the Reichstag I made it quite clear that Germany was resolved to preserve her alliance with Austria at any cost. The German sword had been thrown into the scale of European decision, directly in support of our Austro-Hungarian ally, indirectly for the preservation of European peace, and above all for the sake of German credit and the maintenance of our position in the world.

"It would now be made manifest whether Germany really had been checkmated by the policy of isolation, and whether the Powers that had been drawn into the circle of anti-German policy would find it consistent with their vital interests in Europe to take up a hostile attitude towards the German Empire and its allies." (VON BÜLOW, "Imperial Germany," trans. by M. A. Lewenz, p. 62.)

On October 13, von Bülow notified Sir Edward Grey that, "Germany could not, any more than Austria-Hungary, allow the discussion of the annexation by the conference." At the same time in Turkey, the adroit Baron Marschall von Bieberstein, German ambassador, was in a most friendly and confidential manner smoothing the way for the negotiations between Austria-Hungary and Turkey by persuading the Turkish leaders that their best interests lay in recognizing the annexation, gaining certain desired privileges, and accepting a substantial sum in compensation.

The negotiations between Austria-Hungary and Turkey dragged on through the months of December, 1908, and January and February, 1909. Von Aehrenthal, possibly influenced by suggestions from his German ally, proved conciliatory. Austria-Hungary agreed to an increase of 15 per cent in the Turkish customs duties, to the establishment of Turkish government monopolies in Turkey of cigarette paper and matches, to the religious freedom of Mohammedans in Bosnia and Herzegovina, and, finally, to the payment of an indemnity amounting to twelve and a half million dollars. The protocol containing these (and some less important) provisions was signed February 26, 1909. On April 5, after five hours of debate, it was ratified by the Turkish chamber.

Although the decision by mutual agreement between Austria-Hungary and Turkey concerning the disposition of Bosnia and Herzegovina might seem to have removed the chief disturbing element in the situation, it by no means ended the crisis. Serbia, whose claim for compensation Aehrenthal had consistently refused to admit, was arming for war and was confidently expecting the aid of Russia in her struggle. Great Britain and France, maintaining that under the provisions of the Treaty of Berlin the disposition of Bosnia and Herzegovina had ceased to be a private question between Austria-Hungary and Turkey, were unwilling to recognize the validity of the Austro-Turkish agreement. According to their policy, a greater principle was at stake. They did not wish to take any step which might be interpreted as an acknowledgment that the terms of a general treaty signed by all the great powers might be altered or abrogated by private agreement between two states. And yet, the vital interests of Great Britain and France in the Balkans were so slight that they were not anxious for a war begun over such a question. Russia was in a most difficult position: having committed herself as far as she had in condemning the annexation and in promising aid to Serbia and Montenegro, she could not withdraw without humiliation and disgrace; yet the condition of her army and navy, not recovered from the disastrous war against Japan (1904–1905), and the political unrest amounting almost to a revolution throughout the country, made a conflict with the two powerful and united central powers most dangerous.

The climax to the existing crisis came at the end of March, 1909. Both Serbia and Austria-Hungary had mobilized for hostilities. The treaty of commerce between the two countries was due to expire March 31. The Austro-Hungarian minister to Serbia informed that government that his country could not agree to a new commercial treaty unless Serbia would give assurances that she would return to a peaceful and neighborly attitude. In reply, Serbia addressed a note to the powers (thus attempting to compel their intervention in her favor), stating that she had no intention of provoking a war with Austria-Hungary, that she would continue to fulfill her duties as a neighbor, and that, trusting in the wisdom and justice of the powers, she placed her cause in their hands as a competent tribunal. The Austro-Hungarian government at once declared this answer unsatisfactory and submitted through its minister at Belgrade a set of demands, stating that if these were rejected the Imperial Government would adopt the necessary measures to enforce them.

In the meanwhile Germany was taking steps to guarantee peace. A special messenger with an autograph letter of the German emperor hurried to St. Petersburg and gained an audience with the Czar. What was in the letter, and what was said in the interview, have never been divulged. Possibly the strongest argument against the Russian position was one which, though in the mind both of the German envoy and of the Czar, was not mentioned at the audience — namely, the presence of corps after corps of the German army upon the Polish frontier. The effect of the envoy's message, however, was immediate and conclusive. In the last week of March, the Russian government, without previous notification to Great Britain and France, suddenly announced that it agreed to the Austro-Hungarian-Turkish understanding, and that it recognized the annexation of Bosnia and Herzegovina as *un fait accompli.*

With the withdrawal of the possibility of Russian support, the Serbian opposition collapsed. On the 31st of March, 1909, the Serbian government subscribed to the following document, very important because it formed the basis of Austria-Hungary's ultimatum in July, 1914:

"Serbia recognizes the *fait accompli* regarding Bosnia has not affected her rights, and consequently she will conform to the decisions that the Powers may take in conformity with the Treaty of Berlin. In deference to the advice of the Great Powers, Serbia undertakes to renounce from now onward the attitude of protest and opposition which she has adopted with regard to the annexation since last autumn. She undertakes, moreover, to modify the direction of her policy with regard to Austria-Hungary and to live in future on good, neighborly terms with the latter."

Turkey, Russia, and Serbia having accepted the annexation of Bosnia and Herzegovina, there remained no further reason for Great Britain and France to continue their opposition. On April 8, 1909, the Great Powers finally assented to the abrogation of Article 25 of the Treaty of Berlin, thereby giving official recognition to the annexation.

Thus the crisis of 1908–1909 passed without precipitating a great war, but it left behind the seeds of bitterness and hatred which bore fruit in 1914. Serbia, crushed and disgraced, Russia humiliated, France and Great Britain balked in their efforts to uphold the sanctity of treaty obligations, while Austria-Hungary, aided and abetted by her powerful ally Germany, emerged with increased territory and heightened prestige — such results were certain to create soon an intolerable situation. Outwardly, normal diplomatic relations were soon restored. Austria-Hungary and Serbia signed a new commercial treaty immediately after Serbia's submission of March 31, 1909, and regular intercourse was resumed between Austria-Hungary and Russia in March, 1910. In November of the same year, 1910, the German Emperor entertained the Czar at Potsdam and an important agreement was concluded whereby Germany acknowledged the Russian sphere of influence in northern Persia in return for the withdrawal of Russian opposition to the famous projected Bagdad railroad. These provisions were definitely set forth in a Russo-German convention of August 19, 1911. Thus, superficially, Austria-Hungary, Russia, and Germany were again on excellent terms.

International relations had, however, been profoundly affected and could not easily recover from the shock. The suspicions of the powers of the Entente were directed pointedly to the German machinations in Turkey. That country, which had of old looked to Great Britain for its protector, now fell more and more within the influence of Germany. Von Bieberstein had played throughout the revolution a skillful and difficult part in maintaining German prestige. He it was who, when Abdul Hamid endeavored to regain power by a counter-revolution in 1909, urged the Young Turks to send Shevket Pasha with troops against Constantinople; he it was who with German money financed this short and successful expedition. And after Abdul Hamid had been sent into exile, the leaders of the New Turk party were men who appreciated what German influence had done for them. Von Bieberstein could show that, in spite of the British protestations of friendship for the liberals in Turkey, the British government had given them no assistance. And he could point to the fact that Great Britain, with her vast population of Mohammedan subjects in her dependencies, was the natural enemy of Pan-Islamism, which sought to reëstablish Turkish political influence in Moslem countries. Then, after the revolution was successfully accomplished, von Bieberstein persuaded his friends in the government that their first necessity was to reorganize their military forces, intimating that Germany stood ready to grant all desired assistance. In accordance with this plan, Germany loaned Turkey officers to supervise the remodeling of her army; sold her in August, 1910, two battleships to serve as a nucleus for her navy; and extended her a financial credit of thirty millions of dollars.

The allies, distrustful though they were of German diplomacy in Turkey, took few effectual efforts to check it. They closed their financial markets to Turkish loans, because of the spread of German influence, but that act simply made it easier for German agents to increase their influence. The Entente diplomats did one thing, however, which was destined to have a brief success a few years later: — they attempted to instigate an alliance among the small Balkan states. Apparently the intention was that this alliance should prove a perpetual bar to Austro-Hungarian expansion to the southeast. We shall see in a later chapter how the Balkan league directed its energies, not against Austria-Hungary, but against Turkey.

One general result of the 1908 crisis was more far-reaching than the diplomatic rivalry in Turkey and the Balkans, namely, the moral effect. The shameless cynicism with which one of the great powers had disregarded the obligations of an important international treaty, and the brutal frankness with which the German Emperor boasted in a speech in Vienna a year after the event (1910) of how he had intervened "in shining armor" on behalf of his ally, undermined the mutual confidence on which sympathetic intercourse must be founded. Statesmen harked back to Bismarck's cynicism: — treaties cease to be binding when the private interests of those who lie under them no longer reinforce the text. The cry for disarmament speedily died away. Men who had predicted a millennium of peace and international good will were silenced. In the light of the events of 1908 and 1909 far-sighted leaders began to urge more and more pressing preparation for the great war they saw approaching.

CHAPTER VIII

CONDITIONS IN MOROCCO, 1906–1911

THE success of German diplomacy in the Balkan crisis of 1908 seems to have encouraged the Emperor and his advisers to attempt the settlement of another outstanding issue in a manner satisfactory to them. The Conference of Algeciras, in which the great powers of Europe decided upon the status of Morocco in the first quarter of 1906, had been construed in Germany as a rebuff to the German government's plans and policies. The Entente, standing compactly together, had forced from Germany the concession that France (and Spain) should have the control of the police force in Morocco and should have a privileged position in respect to supplying funds necessary for the development of Moroccan resources. The new police force was inaugurated in November of 1906, and negotiations were begun on financial arrangements. Thus, although the independence of Morocco was formally recognized by the Algeciras Act, France (with Spain) actually had rights in the country which other nations did not have. This situation was thoroughly unsatisfactory to the German statesmen. The German government watched developments in Morocco with keen interest, looking for an opening which would allow them to retrieve their failure in the Algeciras Conference.

During the following years these developments gave good cause for careful attention. Morocco was torn by internal dissensions. A large section of the Arab population bitterly resented the French influence provided by the Algeciras Act of 1906. The Sultan, Abdul Asiz, who was suspected of French sympathies, rapidly lost popularity. Sporadic disturbances and mob violence continued through the latter half of 1906 and the opening months of 1907, resulting in the death of a number of Europeans and the paralysis of the government. These uprisings culminated in the summer of 1907 in an organized rebellion, when Mulai-el-Hafid, the brother of the Sultan, put himself at the head of the disaffected element and rallied around him the most powerful Sheiks in the country. By February of 1908, Mulai-el-Hafid had control of the most important parts of the interior of the country, and had been welcomed into Fez, the capital. In August of the same year he defeated overwhelmingly Abdul Asiz's troops, and a few weeks later asked the powers for recognition as Sultan. The German government ill-advisedly took measures looking toward the recognition of Mulai-el-Hafid, possibly with the hope that Germany might thus obtain a favored position with the new sovereign, but most of the powers awaited the leadership of France. The French diplomats negotiated with Mulai-el-Hafid during the following months, demanding that he should guarantee the safety of the monarch he was deposing, and that he should assume all of the debts, pay all the just claims, and recognize the validity and authority of all the treaty engagements, of the preceding government.

Just at this time an incident, relatively trivial in itself, tended to accentuate the ill-feeling between France and Germany, and to embarrass the French diplomats in their attempts to adjust the Moroccan situation. In September (1908) a handful of deserters from the Foreign Legion took refuge with the German consul at Casablanca. A few of these were German subjects. The consul gave a safe-conduct to all the refugees and undertook to embark them on board a German steamer bound for Europe. The French authorities interfered and forcibly took the refugees from the hands of the consul. The German government, of course, at once vigorously protested against this infringement upon the immunity under international custom of their representative. The French statesmen stood their ground, asserting that the German consul had forfeited his privileges by granting safe-conduct to the non-German refugees in the party. The situation was fraught with serious possibilities, for France was determined to maintain what she considered her rights and Germany seemed disposed to resent emphatically what she believed to be an insult to her national dignity and prestige.

The internal situation in Morocco was pressing for a decision, however, and France held off the conference with Germany on the Casablanca affair until her diplomats could carry through the negotiations with Mulai-el-Hafid. The rebel leader was in a delicate situation: he had headed a rebellion inspired by mistrust and hatred of the French, and now he was being forced to treat with the French and being asked to subscribe to the very treaties (especially the Algeciras Act) which his followers did not wish to observe. At the same time, his hold upon the tumultuous elements in the country he had captured was precarious and could be maintained only by the liberal use of money for the organization of government, and by foreign aid. His funds were running low, and he realized that France was actually the only Power authorized by the general consent of Europe to give him the necessary money and armed police assistance. At last he grudgingly gave his written consent to the French terms (December 5, 1908) and in return the powers, December 17, officially recognized him as Sultan of Morocco. The deposed Sultan, Abdul Asiz, gave up his power gracefully, accepted a pension of $35,000 a year, and retired to a villa at Tangier to spend the remainder of his life.

Now that the internal problem in Morocco was disposed of, France turned to Germany to settle the issue involved in the Casablanca affair. Both countries, apparently, were willing to use the incident to reopen between themselves the whole question of the status of Morocco. Their representatives met in conference at the end of 1908 and the beginning of 1909. The Algeciras Act had to be the basis of discussion, of course, but it is noteworthy that the representatives of the other signatories to that Act were not invited to attend. The discussion proceeded between the diplomats of Germany and France alone. By the final agreement, signed at Berlin February 9, 1909, the German government conceded "the special political interests of France" in Morocco, and expressed itself "resolved not to impede those interests"; the French government announced itself "firmly attached to the maintenance and integrity of the Sheerefian empire," and "resolved to safeguard the principle of economic equality," and consequently not to obstruct German commercial and industrial interests in that country; and both governments agreed not to "pursue or encourage any measure of a nature to create in their favor or in that of any Power an economic privilege," and "to associate their nationals in affairs for which the latter may obtain a concession."

This agreement of February is important in view of ensuing events. It was an agreement between two powers on matters fundamentally affecting the conditions established by the Algeciras Act of 1906 without the consent of the other signatories to that Act. It created an involved and delicate situation in itself, for it allowed one group of powers to regard the Algeciras Act as determining the status of Morocco and another group to refer to the Berlin agreement. Furthermore, the wording of the agreement itself was one which could (and did) lead to misunderstanding. In spite of the reaffirmation of the independence of Morocco, France understood that Germany, by recognizing "the special political interests" of France, was actually consenting to the extension of French political control over the country. The German statesmen, however, were disposed to lay special stress on the economic provisions of the treaty, particularly on the final clause providing for the association of their nationals in affairs for which these nationals might obtain a concession. Germany showed her interest in this aspect of the situation by her proposal (June 2, 1909) that in the future all concessions in Morocco should be reserved to certain French and German groups of financiers and captains of industry who enjoyed the confidence of their respective governments, third parties being admitted only at the expense of the French group. Apparently, German statesmen were trying to establish a joint economic monopoly of Morocco with France, possibly with an ulterior political purpose of weakening the Anglo-French *Entente* by thus associating France with Germany. Although France, in reply to this proposal, insisted that British and Spanish interests should be admitted to concessions, her ministers did agree that all enterprises should be reserved for groups officially recognized by the respective governments.

In accordance with its understanding of its powers under the Algeciras Act and the Berlin agreement, the French government now proceeded to press upon the new Sultan its scheme for internal reforms in Morocco. The French emissary, M. Regnault, was met, however, by a persistent opposition on the part of Mulai-el-Hafid. The Sultan himself had no fondness for France or for Europeans in general, and had gained his throne by heading an anti-foreign revolution. Thus, although he needed French money for the reorganization of his government and for the stimulation of commercial and economic interests, and although he needed French armed assistance to maintain order in the more distant parts of the country, he stubbornly refused the French demands. On his part he insisted upon the withdrawal of French troops from the country before he would enter into any further arrangement with France. Negotiations dragged slowly along. On August 14, 1909, the French submitted to the Sultan a definite plan providing for the withdrawal of French forces from certain specified districts, for the settlement of the frontier questions at issue, for the establishment of a frontier police, and for the liquidation of the Moroccan debt and the payment of French claims. Again the Sultan evaded acceptance, and prolonged negotiations. Finally the French sent through their emissary an ultimatum (February 19, 1909) giving Mulai-el-Hafid forty-eight hours in which to accept the "Franco-Moroccan Accord." Thus brought to bay, the Sultan yielded, and his representatives on March 4, 1910, signed the formal treaty incorporating the French demands. At the end of the year, December 23, Mulai-el-Hafid similarly yielded to Spanish demands affecting the Moroccan territory within the Spanish sphere of influence.

These treaties, which in effect secured the actual control of Morocco to France (and Spain, in the small part of the country over which it had influence), aroused burning resentment throughout Morocco. The Arab leaders who had supported Mulai-el-Hafid for the Sultanate did not appreciate the difficulties of his situation and felt that they had been betrayed. January 14, 1911, a French Lieutenant, Marchand, with a squad of men was massacred. A few weeks later several of the tribes banded together in open rebellion. A pretender to the throne, a younger brother of the Sultan, put himself at the head of the rebel forces, attacked and drove back Mulai-el-Hafid's troops, and besieged the capital, Fez. The French at once sent out a relieving column which successfully dispersed the rebel forces, entered Fez, and began the pacification of the country.

In the meanwhile, Germany had been observing closely the progress of events and had been trying under the provisions of the Berlin agreement to advance her economic opportunities in Morocco. Two enterprises had been undertaken, but neither had succeeded. The Moroccan Mines

Company (Union des Mines Marocaines), proposed to develop the rich mineral resources of the country, but the German government was unable to decide between the conflicting claims of two rival German groups. A second enterprise, the Moroccan Public Works Corporation (Société Marocaine des Travaux Publics), failed because the French government refused to guarantee the Moroccan loans which would be necessary to finance its operations. A third enterprise, proposed by France in 1910, consisted in the construction of strategic military railways in two of the disaffected provinces of Morocco. Necessarily these railroads would have to be built, run, and controlled wholly by France. When this project was made known to Germany, the German diplomats consented but demanded that Germany be given economic concessions elsewhere. While negotiations on this issue were proceeding, Sir Edward Grey intervened early in 1911 to protest against any joint German and French economic monopoly of Morocco, and to insist upon equality of opportunity for British concerns. The intervention of Great Britain quickly brought matters to a focus.

France now reaped the fruits of her mistake in making the Berlin agreement without conference with other signatories of the Algeciras Act. Sir Edward Grey based his protest upon the Algeciras Act, which guaranteed freedom of economic opportunity to all nations. But France had entered into the subsequent agreement with Germany (the Berlin agreement) whereby in reality Germany and France were to have exceptional privileges in Morocco. Her act in laying before Germany the question of the construction of the proposed military strategic railways and in entertaining the idea of economic compensation elsewhere to Germany, seemed a sufficient indication that she looked upon Germany as occupying a favored position under the Berlin agreement as compared with the other countries. For France, grave political principles were at stake: to defy

Great Britain involved a rupture of the friendship which had been cemented between the two countries in 1904 and which was the strength of the Triple Entente; on the other hand, strong intimations of German ill-will if France yielded to Great Britain were conveyed to the French government.

While France was in this quandary, the revolutionists in Morocco besieged Fez, as stated above, and a French relieving force started into the interior. There were two possible ways of regarding this French expedition: first, as a genuine attempt to protect French residents and settle the disturbances, the French forces to withdraw at once after their task was completed; and second, as an act of military occupation intended to destroy definitely Moroccan independence. In support of the first view, it was known that the French consul in Fez had described conditions as dangerous and had appealed for aid: in support of the second, it was recalled that during the similar revolution which Mulai-el-Hafid conducted against Abdul Asiz the French forces had abstained wholly from any interference.

Germany adopted the second view, and gave ample warning of her position to the French government. When the French columns were preparing to march toward Fez, the French minister at Berlin was warned, "If you go to Fez, you will not depart. It raises the whole question of Morocco." And again a week later, he was told, "If the Algeciras Act goes by the board, we shall reserve our liberty of action." From the first of April the German press began to dwell with increasing emphasis upon the actions of the French in Morocco, claiming that Morocco was about to be divided up and that Germany was in danger of being cheated out of her joint share.

When the German government saw that France persisted in her expedition to Fez, it acted with characteristic determination and decision. At noon on July 1, 1911, the German ambassadors presented to their respective powers the following note:

"Some German firms established in the south of Morocco, notably at Agadir and in the vicinity, have been alarmed by a certain ferment which has shown itself among the local tribes, due it seems to the recent occurrences in other parts of the country. These firms have applied to the imperial government for protection for the lives of their employees and their property. At their request the imperial government has decided to send a war-ship to the port of Agadir, to lend help and assistance, in case of need, to its subjects and employees, as well as to protect the important German interests in the territory in question. As soon as the state of affairs in Morocco has resumed its former quiet aspect the ship charged with this protective mission will leave the port of Agadir."

Granting that Morocco was a free and independent country and that German interests were endangered by the unrest in the country, no one could legitimately criticize Germany's act in sending the warship *Panther* to the harbor of Agadir. The French, however, knowing that the German government had recognized the special political interests of France in Morocco, and knowing further that no German citizens were at Agadir and that the German commercial interests were insignificant and were safe, were disposed to interpret the appearance of the *Panther* as signifying the intervention of the German government in an effort to gain a permanent foothold in the rich African territory. Their suspicions were supported by the disclosures in a trial for libel in Germany some time after the crisis had passed, in which the following unrefuted testimony was offered:

"Herr von Kinderlen-Waechter stated: 'The Pan-German demand for Morocco is absolutely justified. You can rely upon it that the government will stick to Morocco. M. Cambon is wriggling before me like a worm. The German Government is in a splendid position. You can rely upon me, and you will be very pleased with our Morocco policy. I am as good a Pan-German as you are.'

"On 1 July Herr Class called at the German foreign office and, failing to find Herr von Kinderlen-Waechter, was received by Herr Zimmerman, the under-secretary. Herr Zimmerman told him: 'You come at a historic hour. To-day the *Panther* appears before Agadir and at this very moment (12 o'clock midday). The foreign cabinets are being informed of its mission. The German Government has sent two *agents provocateurs* to Agadir, and these have done their duty very well. German firms have been induced to make complaints and to call upon the government in Berlin for protection. It is the government's intention to seize the district, and it will not give it up again. The German people absolutely require a settlement colony. Please prevent, wherever in the press you have influence, the raising of claims for compensation elsewhere. Possibly France will offer us the Congo. However, the German Government does not want compensation elsewhere, but a part of Morocco.'"

The French government, then, interpreting Germany's warship as a threat of force in the Morocco issue, at once sounded Great Britain to learn how far that country would be willing to go in its opposition to German demands. Although Great Britain was at the moment in the throes of the great political struggle culminating in the Parliament Bill of 1911, her representatives made it evident to France that she would stand firmly by her *Entente*. In a ringing speech at a banquet at the Mansion House July 21, 1911, Mr. David Lloyd George for the ministry made Great Britain's position clear:

"But, I am also bound to say this — that I believe it is essential in the highest interests, not merely of this country but of the world, that Britain should at all hazards maintain her place and her prestige amongst the Great Powers of the world. Her potent influence has been many a time in the past, and may yet be in the future, invaluable to the cause of human liberty. It has more than once in the past redeemed Continental nations, who are sometimes too apt to forget that service, from overwhelming disaster and even from international extinction. I would make great sacrifices to preserve peace. I conceive that nothing would justify a disturbance of international good will except questions of the gravest national moment. But if a situation were to be forced upon us in which peace could only be preserved by the surrender of the great and beneficent position Britain has won by centuries of heroism and achievement — by allowing Britain to be treated, where her interests are vitally affected, as if she were of no account in the cabinet of nations — then I say emphatically that peace at that price would be a humiliation intolerable for a great country like ours to endure. National honor is no party question. The security of our great international trade is no party question; the peace of the world is much more likely to be secured if all nations realize fairly what the conditions of peace must be. And it is because I have the conviction that nations are beginning to understand each other better, to appreciate one another's point of view more thoroughly, to be more ready to discuss calmly and dispassionately their differences, that I feel assured that nothing will happen between now and next year which will render it difficult for the chancellor of the exchequer in this place to respond to the toast proposed — of the continued prosperity of the public peace."

A few days later (July 27) Mr. Asquith, the prime minister, referred in the House of Commons to the negotiations then in progress between France and Germany:

"Conversations are proceeding between France and Germany; we are not a party to these conversations; the subject-matter of them may not affect British interests. On that point, until we know the ultimate result, we cannot express a final opinion. But it is our desire that those conversations should issue in a settlement honorable and satisfactory to both parties and of which His Majesty's Government can cordially say that it in no way prejudices British interests. We believe that to be possible. We earnestly and sincerely desire to see it accomplished. The question of Morocco itself bristles with difficulties, but outside Morocco, in other parts of West Africa, we should not think of attempting to interfere with territorial arrangements considered reasonable by those who are more directly interested. Any statements that we have interfered to prejudice negotiations between France and Germany are mischievous inventions without the faintest foundation in fact. But we have thought it right from the beginning to make quite clear that, failing such a settlement as I have indicated, we must become an active party in the discussion of the situation. That would be our right as a signatory of the treaty of Algeciras; it might be our obligation under the terms of our agreement of 1904 with France; it might be our duty in defense of British interests directly affected by further developments."

A few days later Mr. Asquith again made the British position clear by reiterating in the House of Commons his statement that if the "conversations" then proceeding between France and Germany should fail, it would be the duty of the British government to take an active part in the discussions. On both these occasions in the House of Commons, Balfour, speaking for the opposition Conservative party, pledged united support for the government if it felt obliged to intervene.

The Moroccan issue had thus again, as after the Tangiers incident, become a sharply marked issue between the chief powers of the Triple Entente and the chief powers of the Triple Alliance. The resulting European tension was extreme. For months it seemed as though the great general European war would break out.

M. de Selves, the French Foreign Secretary, later (in a speech to the Chamber of Deputies December 14, 1911) declared that Germany had refused a second European conference like that of Algeciras for the settlement of the Moroccan question, and had insisted upon negotiations between the two governments interested. He asserted that, after some preliminary exorbitant and unacceptable demands, the negotiations had been conducted on a reasonable basis; and he denied that Germany had shown any desire to incite war and said, on the contrary, that her attitude had been conciliatory.

So far as we can now judge from the evidence available, Germany seems to have been willing from the outset of the actual negotiations, after the government had tested the spirit of France, to permit the establishment of a French protectorate in Morocco, but to have set herself to limit the boundaries of the French protectorate, to gain for Germany special economic privileges which would accomplish the Franco-German monopoly which Germany had hoped would result from the Berlin agreement of 1909, and to acquire from France territorial compensations elsewhere in

Africa in return for definitely acknowledging the French protectorate in Morocco. The French government, however, would not listen to a suggestion of the limitation of their protectorate, or to a suggestion of any special privileges which would put Germany in a more favorable economic position than other nations (Great Britain, for example), but showed a willingness from the beginning to entertain the idea of territorial compensation elsewhere.

Various considerations influenced Germany to recede from her extreme demands. Of great importance, of course, was the declaration of Lloyd George in his great Mansion House speech, which, though couched in most general terms, was understood everywhere as a direct reference to the existing crisis. This declaration, coupled with the definite statements of Asquith and Balfour in the House of Commons, revealed to the German statesmen that a resort to force would involve them in a war, not only with France, but with Great Britain (and probably with Russia) as well. A second consideration which caused them to hesitate in pressing their demands to the point of war was the financial situation. In times of peace, money had ignored to a considerable extent the political boundaries of Europe. The enormous increase in manufacturing and commercial industries in Germany had demanded huge amounts of capital, amounts much greater than the German government or the German bankers were able to supply. German business, therefore, had gone to French bankers for loans to finance their operations. As the prospect of war loomed nearer and nearer in July and August of 1911, the French bankers began to "call" their loans in Germany. The result was immediate and calamitous. The German business firms found extreme difficulty in raising the money to pay these loans at short notice; the tightening of the money market sharply restricted all economic operations in Germany; the prices of securities on the Berlin Bourse rapidly fell; and all Germany was threatened by a great financial panic. A third consideration which restrained the government in pressing its demands was the difficulty of arousing great and general enthusiasm throughout the German people for a war on the Moroccan issue. A small and vociferous group was willing to go to extremes to uphold what it deemed to be the prestige and interest of the Empire, but the mass of the people cared little about Morocco. The Socialists, especially, were outspoken in their denunciation of the prospects of a war to be waged solely for the Pan-German idea at the will of the militaristic class.

The negotiations dragged on through the summer. Rumors of war and of great military preparations were rife. At one time in the middle of August France was aroused by a report that the German general staff was engaged in framing the details of a plan to land troops in Morocco; at another time it was said that the plan for Anglo-French military coöperation had been decided upon; it is certain that great quantities of coal were shipped across England for the use of the navy, and it was reported that all ships were cleared for action; and the German government is known at one stage to have given its preliminary notice to officers and men in the reserves. In spite of the difficulties afforded by these rumors and suspicions, the representatives of the two countries managed to reach a peaceful agreement, which was incorporated in two conventions, the Moroccan Convention and the Congo Convention, both signed November 4, 1911.

The Moroccan Convention was considered to be supplementary to the Berlin agreement of 1909. In it, Germany declared that she had no interests in Morocco other than economic and that she would not interfere with France in her conduct of the necessary military, financial, or administrative reforms. Although the word "protectorate" was not actually used in the convention in deference to the old Algeciras Treaty, to the Sultan of Morocco, and to the chauvinistic group in Germany, the German minister in an official letter to the French foreign minister made the German position clear: "I have the honor to inform your Excellency, that in the event of the French government deeming it necessary to assume the Protectorate of Morocco, the Imperial Government would place no obstacle in the way." France, on her part, guaranteed freedom and equality of treatment of foreign trade and commerce, thus pledging herself to observe in letter and spirit the principle of the "open door."

The Congo Convention provided for a rearrangement of territory in the Congo regions, whereby Germany gained in what was known as the *Cameroons* a territory in excess of 100,000 square miles. The term "compensation" was nowhere used to describe this "rearrangement," but the people in France and Germany understood the principle. The German government had been paid in the equatorial region of the Congo for submitting to the establishment of a French protectorate over Morocco.

The above settlement of the Morocco issue satisfied neither of the chief nations most interested. The French people, and their allies the British, refused to believe that Germany had ever possessed any rights in Morocco for which she should have received "compensation." France had gained, it is true, one of her most cherished colonial ambitions, but at a price. The government was severely attacked in the chamber for its willingness to give up to Germany any part of its African colonial possessions in return for the recognition of the protectorate over Morocco. The character, situation, and possibilities of the Cameroons region surrendered were described and their importance exaggerated. As prominent a man as M. Hanotaux, formerly minister of Foreign Affairs, said: "The French Congo has its loins shattered and its throat tightly gripped; it will perish by paralysis or strangulation. We possessed an empire: they have left us corridors." The government's chief defense was that the Conventions once and for all ended the Moroccan question, took it out of foreign politics where it had long been a bone of contention.

Herr von Bethmann-Hollweg had an even more unfavorable reception when he endeavored to explain the German diplomacy and its results in a speech in the Reichstag November 11, 1911. The mass of people had not wanted a portion of Morocco enough to fight for it, and yet they felt that the *coup d'Agadir* had been a failure, that Germany had been put in a position of playing for a certain stake and losing, that German dignity and prestige had suffered a humiliating setback. Germany had appeared in "shining armor," had "rattled the saber," had imperiled the peace of Europe, and in return had been forced to give up all claim to a political interest in rich Morocco and to accept a morsel of land in equatorial Africa. Herr von Bethmann-Hollweg's speech was greeted with jeers and derisive laughter. The outline of his argument was:

"The assertion that the warship *Panther* was sent to Agadir with the object of acquiring territory in Morocco is incorrect.

"In the negotiations the leading idea was that it was impossible for the Moors to establish or maintain order, and that the intervention of a foreign power was necessary. France was the only possible and acceptable power for the greater part of the country.

"Parts of Morocco, as southern Morocco, were not really desirable country for Germany, because the establishment and maintenance of order therein, and the necessary provisions for defense, would cost far more than the country was worth.

"And most important of all: Morocco had been a continual source of trouble, not only in German relations with France, but also in the relations with England. The French expedition to Fez led to acute trouble and made an operation necessary. Germany and France had performed the operation."

In one other parliament was the Moroccan diplomacy discussed — namely the House of Commons. Although Great Britain had not been an actual party to the "conversations" between Germany and France, the British support of France had gained for the French their victory. Great

Britain, therefore, had exerted a real influence over the proceedings. In a notable speech to the Commons (November 27, 1911), Sir Edward Grey, the minister of Foreign Affairs, explained the British connection with the Moroccan issue. He went into the conversations he had had with the German minister, he defended the British course throughout the crisis, and in a notable passage disclaimed any idea of restricting legitimate German expansion:

> "If there are to be big territorial changes in Africa, brought about, of course, by the good will of and negotiation with other Powers, then we are not an ambitious competing party; and being not an ambitious competing party ourselves, if Germany has friendly arrangements to negotiate with other foreign countries with regard to Africa, we are not anxious to stand in her way any more than in theirs."

The resentment of Germans against Great Britain for her decisive influence against Germany in the Moroccan issue blazed forth in speeches, newspaper and magazine articles, pamphlets, and books for months after the extent of the German diplomatic defeat became realized. Herr von Heydebrandt sounded the keynote in a notorious anti-British speech in the Reichstag:

> "Like a flash in the night all this had shown the German people where the enemy is. We know now, when we wish to expand in the world, when we wish to have our place in the sun, who it is that lays claim to world-wide domination. . . . We shall secure peace, not by concessions, but with the German sword."

General von Bernhardi at this time published his famous book "Germany and the Next War." Treitschke's lectures, bitterly anti-British in tone, were read and taken to heart. The German people were led to believe all the theory of Great Britain's malevolence toward Germany, to feel the encircling ring being drawn around their own country by British diplomacy.

The extent to which the mutual ill-feeling in Germany and Great Britain progressed brought within a year a strong reaction. Thinking men realized that, if the world were not to see some insignificant dispute magnified into a cause for a most terrible war, they must forward measures at once to better the feeling between the two countries. The German Emperor took the lead in the effort to promote better relations by requesting in February, 1912, that Lord Haldane, then Lord High Chancellor of Great Britain, visit Berlin to discuss Anglo-German relations. At Berlin Herr von Bethmann-Hollweg submitted for Lord Haldane's consideration the draft of a treaty of friendship, by the provisions of which the two Powers were to pledge themselves each of them not "to make or prepare to make any unprovoked attack upon the other, or join in any combination or design against the other for the purpose of aggression," and were to promise, in the event either Power became "entangled in war with one or more Powers" to observe "toward the Power so entangled benevolent neutrality." The discussion did not get very far, for Lord Haldane on Great Britain's behalf objected to any pledge of unconditional neutrality and began to put pointed questions concerning Germany's policy in continually strengthening her fleet. Further negotiations, which were removed to London, and carried on by Sir Edward Grey, all hinged on the wording of the clause requiring neutrality of either power in the event of the other becoming "entangled" in war. Germany insisted upon the declaration of a policy of neutrality: Great Britain would not commit herself further than the proposition:

> "England declares that she will neither make nor join in any provoked attack upon Germany. Aggression upon Germany forms no part of any treaty, understanding, or combination to which England is now a party, nor will she become a party to anything which has such an object."

The German government was unwilling to accept anything short of a promise of neutrality, so that, in the autumn of 1912, negotiations were discontinued. A real advance seemed to have been made, however, toward more cordial relations between the two countries. Under the influence of a determined band of peacemakers, newspapers and magazines took on a more friendly tone; the Liberal party in Great Britain, and leaders of the Socialist party in Germany, forwarded efforts for a better mutual understanding; and travel between the two countries increased. By the end of 1912 much of the animosity aroused by Agadir and its aftermath seemed to have been allayed.

PART IV

THE CONFLICT OF ALLIANCES

CHAPTER I

THE NEAR EASTERN PROBLEM, 1911–1913

A. THE TURCO-ITALIAN WAR, 1911–1912

EVEN before the Moroccan negotiations had been carried through to a successful conclusion, the attention of Europe was drawn back to the Turkish problem, not again to be released therefrom until all the nations became embroiled in The Great War.

September 26, 1911, the Italian government dispatched to the Porte an ultimatum reciting the many grievances of Italy on account of the disorder and neglect in which Turkey had left Tripoli and Cyrenaica (Barca), characterizing the policy of the Porte as inimical to the safety of Italian subjects and to legitimate interests, and demanding within twenty-four hours a satisfactory guaranty of substantial reforms and full protection of foreigners. The direct threat was made that in the event of an unsatisfactory reply Italian forces would at once proceed to the military occupation of the two provinces. The Turkish answer, submitted within the stipulated period, was conciliatory, offering protection to Italian subjects and interests and reasonable economic and commercial concessions, and asking what guaranty was desired by Italy. The Italian government, however, was not disposed to accept any answer which Turkey might submit. It therefore declared the Turkish reply was unsatisfactory and recognized a state of war as existing from the 29th of September.

The first acts of the war which followed showed how fully Italy had prepared for her act. On the 29th, the very day a state of war was declared, an Italian squadron sank three Turkish torpedo boats off the coast of Epirus. On October 3 a squadron appeared off the city of Tripoli and bombarded the fortifications, effecting a landing of seamen and marines on the 5th. On October 8 Derna was bombarded and reduced, and on the 18th a landing was forced at Benghazi. By the end of October the Italian government had secured all the coastal points of importance and had landed expeditionary forces of between thirty and forty thousand fully trained and well-equipped troops in the larger towns. Having complete control of the sea, Italy was in a position to prevent Turkey from sending any reinforcements to her attacked colonies. The success of her *coup* seemed certain. On November 5 the government formally proclaimed the annexation of Tripoli and the neighboring district of Cyrenaica (Barca).

Italy's ultimatum and her prompt and decisive war measures seem to have taken diplomatic Europe by surprise. Yet Italy had made her intentions toward Tripoli evident during all the preceding decade. As early as December, 1900, when France had sought Italy's consent for French penetration in Morocco, the Italian government had stipulated that in return for her approval France should give Italy a free hand in developing her interests in Tripoli. This arrangement with France was renewed in a protocol signed in November, 1902. Giolitti, one of the most prominent men in Italian political life, premier from November, 1903, to March, 1905, again from May, 1906, to December, 1909, and appointed once more in March of 1911, had consistently proclaimed the acquisition of Tripoli as one of the cardinal points of Italian policy. And the government had been attempting to further peaceful penetration and economic control during all these years by such devices as the establishment of branches of the Italian banks, subsidized steamship lines, and the encouragement of sound and cordial business relations between Italian concerns and the Arab traders. All Italy's efforts, however, were looked upon with natural suspicion by the Turkish government, and every possible obstacle was put in her way. The Turkish press contained frequent bitter attacks upon Italy; sporadic uprisings endangered the lives and property of Italian subjects; and business concessions were without reason refused or limited. Especially after the Young Turk revolution in 1908 did the Turkish officials hinder and thwart the consummation of the Italian policies. Hence, when Giolitti acceded to the premiership in March of 1911, he had little difficulty in obtaining the support of the leading parties in parliament to the direct attack upon Turkey for the seizure of the African territory.

The time was opportune. The Young Turk government, hardly yet secure in power, was embarrassed at home by insurrections and disturbances in Macedonia and Albania and had taken no steps to reinforce the Turkish troops in Tripoli. Turkish finances had not yet been straightened out and put on a sound basis. The Turkish army and navy reorganization, begun under German advisers, had not yet been completed. Furthermore, at this period Italy was bound by friendly engagements with members of both of the great alliances in Europe. She was on the one hand the third member of the Triple Alliance (Germany, Austria-Hungary, Italy), and had, as indicated above, entered into reciprocal agreements with France, one of the most powerful units of the Triple Entente, with respect to the very enterprise which she was undertaking. And members of both these alliances had recently engaged in enterprises which might give a reasonable justification for Italy's act. Austria-Hungary had seized Bosnia and Herzegovina in 1908, and Germany had supported her, so Italy could refer the other members of the Triple Alliance to that act as a precedent for her own: France was obtaining Morocco, after having guaranteed Italy a free hand in Tripoli as a reward for Italian approval, so that Italy could be sure of no opposition from the French government in attempting to gain her ends. Giolitti and his colleagues felt that Turkish internal troubles and Italy's relation to the great powers in the opposing alliances secured them a free hand in carrying through their policy.

Italy's act in precipitating the war, however, was unpopular both among the people and among the chancelleries of Europe. An attack upon Turkey which deprived her of one of her outlying possessions might so weaken the precarious hold of the Young Turks upon the government that the country would fall to pieces in civil war; and the dissolution of Turkey, so long expected, was feared as the probable beginning of a terrible European war among the nations anxious to annex the pieces. The Italian government did what it could to provide against such a contingency by proclaiming at the outset that it would confine military and naval operations to Tripoli and Cyrenaica and their coasts, and by sending special messages to the restless Balkan states that Italy wished to maintain the integrity of Turkey and did not intend either to wage a general war against Turkey or to invade Turkish territory in Europe or Asia Minor. In spite of these assurances, diplomats made sincere efforts to patch up an agreement between the two countries for fear of complications. Germany and Austria-Hungary were especially urgent in requesting their ally, Italy, to permit the dispute to be submitted to mediation. Germany's position was peculiarly difficult, for, as in 1908, she desired on the one hand to maintain the friendship of Turkey where she had so many important interests, and on the other she was bound with Italy in the Triple Alliance. Italy, however, refused all offers of mediation until her terms (which included recognition of the annexation of the two provinces) were met; and Turkey refused these offers of mediation until Italian troops were withdrawn from the provinces.

In the meanwhile the war dragged on without important

or decisive action. The Italians held all the coastal towns securely, but found it impossible to advance any considerable distance into the interior. The fanatical Arab tribesmen, organized and led by trained Turkish officers and thoroughly familiar with desert fighting, were a formidable opposition when the Italian forces drew away from their sea bases. The war threatened to come to an *impasse*, Italy being unable to advance and carry out the military occupation of the country, and Turkey, secure against direct attack on account of her European position, losing few men and incurring little expense, being willing to let the war continue indefinitely on these terms. In this situation, Italy felt compelled to violate her pledge given at the beginning of the war to confine operations to Tripoli and Cyrenaica. She initiated an attack upon European Turkey and Syria in order to gain a decision. At the end of February Beirut was bombarded; in March a blockade of the Syrian coast was established; in April (April 16–19) a naval demonstration was made at the mouth of the Dardanelles, which resulted in Turkey's closing the straits, to the great embarrassment of neutral shipping; and in late April and May, Rhodes and several islands in the Ægean Sea (the Sporades) were captured.

It was not the military and naval operations of Italy which at last brought Turkey to terms, however, but the threat of an attack from a newly formed league of the Balkan states. In the face of such threat, accompanied by an intimation that unless peace were made Italy would throw troops into European Turkey to aid the Balkan states when war was declared, informal discussions began in Switzerland early in June, 1912, between Turkish and Italian representatives. Turkey's obstinate failure to recognize the inevitable kept these discussions from progressing rapidly. Nothing important was accomplished during July, August, and September. In October, however, the Balkan states were on the point of declaring war, and

Turkey suddenly became more conciliatory. On October 13 the states of the Balkan league dispatched their ultimatum to Turkey, and the Turkish representatives in Switzerland hurried the Italian negotiations to a conclusion. The preliminaries of the peace were signed October 15, and the final treaty, known as the Treaty of Lausanne, three days later.

The terms of the Treaty of Peace included the usual stipulations for the cessation of hostilities and resumption of relations between the two contestants, provided for the withdrawal of Italian forces from the Ægean islands "immediately after the evacuation of Tripoli and Cyrenaica by the Ottoman officers, troops, and civil functionaries," and bound Italy to pay 2,000,000 lire ($400,000) annually from the Tripolitan revenues into the Administration of the Public Debt of Turkey. The spiritual authority of the Sultan was not to be disturbed, but it was understood that this implied no political authority whatever. Neither country paid an indemnity. Italy had thus gained from the war all that she had attempted, and her government looked forward to the development of Tripoli in time into a most prosperous and valuable colony.

Italy's little adventure would not seem to a casual observer to have had any important influence upon international affairs in Europe, and yet, indirectly, the results of her success had some part in determining the action of the Balkan states and in deciding Italy's choice at the outbreak of the Great War.

Italy had made a direct attack upon Turkey and had gained her objects without bringing on the dreaded European war. The Balkan states had waited long for the death and dissolution of the "sick man of Europe," expecting great territorial profits from the wreck. The Italian example seemed to show them that, without involving other nations, they might themselves hasten the coveted end to their own profit.

Italy's annexation of Tripoli and her expectations of developing that country into an important colony had an indirect effect upon her relations with the two coalitions of Powers in Europe. The Triple Entente had complete naval control on the Mediterranean Sea. Consequently, Italy's communications with her new colony were at the mercy of the British and French fleets. Possibly the British government realized the effect the ownership of Tripoli might have upon Italian policy, for at the beginning of the Turco-Italian war it sent Lord Kitchener to Egypt to prevent Turkey from sending reinforcements through Egypt to Tripoli. Italy was thus bound by gratitude and by expediency to Great Britain and France.

B. THE FIRST BALKAN WAR

While the Turco-Italian war was in progress, conditions in European Turkey became very threatening. The league of Balkan states, that league whose beginning had been fostered by nations of the Entente for the purpose of checking German and Austrian influence in Turkey and the Balkan regions, planned to fall in force upon the Ottoman empire. The European chancelleries were more perturbed over the possibilities of such a war than they were over the Turco-Italian struggle, for they realized the difficulties of keeping the greater powers out of the conflict. The vital interests of Russia and Austria-Hungary were almost certain to be involved, with consequences which all Europe feared.

The revolution of 1908 had awakened high hopes among all the subject peoples of Turkey. Begun and carried through for professed liberal ends, it had been supported loyally by Albanians and Macedonians in the belief that its success would insure the principles of liberty and equality throughout the empire. In the first days Bulgar, Serb, and Greek fraternized joyfully with the Turk, all looking forward to the regeneration of the country: in the days when Abdul Hamid attempted to regain his power, these peoples still supported the Young Turks. But as the new government became firmly established and showed its hand, these parties were gradually alienated. It was too soon evident that the Young Turks were less interested in internal reforms than in maintaining Turkey's international position; that they were planning to persist in the policy of centralization and assimilation which had been the source of such continual bitter feeling during the old régime. The political privileges which had been promised by the Young Turks were withheld or, where temporarily put in force, soon suppressed; districts in Macedonia which were predominantly Christian in character were systematically colonized with Mohammedans in the effort to counterbalance Christian political influence; public meetings and the formation of constitutional clubs were forbidden; forcible disarmament of Christian communities was undertaken. These policies, and the sporadic massacres of innocent and unoffending people, such as the massacre of Istib in December, 1911, of Senitza in July of 1912, of Kotchana in August of 1912, and of Berani in September, 1912, awakened the people to the fact that the Young Turks were as devoted to the policies of Pan-Islamism as were Abdul Hamid and his advisers.

Their wrongs incited the people in Macedonia and Albania to rebel, and the sympathies of Greeks, Bulgars, Serbs, and Montenegrins with those of their own blood and religion in these disaffected districts led them to lay aside for the time being their own bitter rivalries and to make common cause against the Turk. A wider political motive inspired the governments to encourage the sympathies and passions of their subjects. The Young Turk revolution of 1908 had caused a marked change in the political hopes of these governments. A continuance of the old inefficient Turkish régime would have made it practically certain that ultimately Bulgaria, Serbia, and Greece would have the opportunity to profit by the inevitable dissolution of the Moslem empire, but the Young Turk government made them fear, as it had made Austria in the case of Bosnia and Herzegovina, that Turkey would never give up her subject European territories. Bulgaria was willing to fight for Macedonia, Serbia for the Sanjak of Novibazar and possible access to the Adriatic, Greece for Crete, and Montenegro for Scutari, now that Turkey seemed to be more determined than before to retain these possessions.

In the negotiations that proceeded between these Balkan states, M. Venizelos, the prime minister of Greece, emerged as the most influential figure. He had the advantage of representing a power whose coöperation was absolutely necessary to the other Balkan states because it was the only one of their number that had a navy. The Balkan states sorely needed this navy to offset the naval power of the Turks. Venizelos realized his advantageous position. To him is attributed the skill and diplomacy which welded Greece, Bulgaria, Serbia, and Montenegro into an alliance. By February of 1912 a definite understanding had been reached, and the league awaited a propitious moment for attack.

An element which helped materially to determine the time of their attack was the progress of the rebellion in Albania against Turkish rule. During 1910 and 1911 these rebels had required a Turkish army of between 60,000 and 70,000 for their suppression. In May of 1912 the Albanian chieftains in conference drew up and presented to the government and to the great powers a list of reforms for which they were fighting, including principally the precise determination of the boundaries of Albania, the recognition of the flag of Albania, the appointment of a governor-general from an old ruling family of Albania, the appointment of Albanian officials instead of Turks, the adoption of Albanian as the official language, and lastly, the guarantee of the great powers to the institution of these reforms. They supplemented these demands in August by a program of reforms submitted to the Turkish government including a special judicial system, the increase in the number of schools, progress in road building and railroad construction, and a general amnesty. The Young Turks seem to have realized the impossibility of coping successfully with continual insurrection in Albania and announced themselves willing to accept practically all the reforms demanded. A commission was dispatched to inquire into the Albanian grievances. In a remarkably short time the Albanians and Turks reached an agreement. On August 20 it was announced that in a conference at Prishtina the Albanian chiefs had accepted the government's terms and were returning quietly to their homes.

The success of the Italians in gaining their ends by war upon Turkey, and the success of the Albanians in gaining their longed-for reforms by continued insurrection were an example and an inspiration to the people in the Balkan states. The successive massacres upon their borders had inflamed their peoples to a point where they believed they were to engage in a kind of sacred war to save their kindred in blood and religion. All through the summer of 1912 they were preparing themselves for the struggle.

In the meanwhile, the diplomats of the great powers were putting forth all their efforts to prevent war. Count Berchtold of Austria-Hungary, who had succeeded von Aehrenthal in February of 1912, was the leading figure in these efforts. Since Germany and Austria-Hungary had become interested financially and commercially in Turkey, and since at the propitious moment Austria-Hungary hoped to expand to the southeast by absorbing outlying Turkish provinces, it was to Austro-Hungarian interest to maintain the status quo. A successful war by the Balkan league might, on the one hand, serve to discredit Austria-Hungary and Germany in Turkey — for the Turks would blame these powers for allowing Turkish defeat — and would certainly, on the other hand, increase the strength of the barrier against ultimate Austro-Hungarian expansion.

Animated by these motives, Count Berchtold undertook to maintain the peace on the basis of existing conditions. By April, Austria-Hungary and Russia had agreed, as stated by the Russian foreign minister Sazonoff in a speech to the Duma, on the following principles: the maintenance of the status quo in the Balkans, the independence and peaceful development of the Balkan states, and the support of the new régime in Turkey. As the situation grew more and more threatening, Count Berchtold endeavored to revive the defunct concert of Powers by obtaining general consent of the European chancelleries to a policy which would secure peace and the maintenance of the status quo in the Balkans. To meet the existing crisis he proposed a court of arbitration consisting of three representatives of the Powers and two of Turkey to decide the issue between Turkey and the states of the Balkan league; and further, the immediate initiation of a policy of "progressive decentralization" in Macedonia and Albania. He succeeded in gaining the provisional agreement of the Powers dependent upon a fuller explanation of the meaning of "progressive decentralization." His diplomacy, however, had aroused the suspicions of Russia, and much comment was made on the fact that it was to Russia's interest to strengthen the Balkan states, which were mainly Slav peoples, at the expense of Turkey, whereas it appeared to be Berchtold's policy to keep the Balkan states overawed by a powerful Turkey.

Events were moving too rapidly in the late summer for a full discussion of a plan of "progressive decentralization" in Macedonia and Albania: it was recognized that unless radical measures were at once taken, war would be upon them. September 8 Count Berchtold had a long conference with von Bethmann-Hollweg; later in the same month M. Sazonoff (Russia) talked with Sir Edward Grey

(Great Britain) and with M. Poincaré (France). Agreement was reached that Russia and Austria-Hungary should be deputed jointly to act for the powers in the Balkan capitals, and that all the powers should act collectively at Constantinople.

In accordance with this agreement the Austro-Hungarian and Russian ministers handed the following joint note to the Balkan states October 8, 1912:

"The Russian and Austro-Hungarian Governments declare to the Balkan states:

"1. That the Powers condemn energetically every measure capable of leading to a rupture of peace;

"2. That, supporting themselves on Article 23 of the Treaty of Berlin, they will take in hand, in the interest of the populations, the realization of the reforms in the administration of European Turkey, on the understanding that these reforms will not diminish the sovereignty of His Imperial Majesty the Sultan and the territorial integrity of the Ottomon Empire; this declaration reserves, also, the liberty of the Powers for the collective and ulterior study of the reforms;

"3. That if, in spite of this note, war does break out between the Balkan States and the Ottoman Empire, they will not admit, at the end of the conflict, any modification in the territorial status quo in European Turkey.

"The Powers will make collectively to the Sublime Porte the steps which the preceding declaration makes necessary."

This declaration was ineffective, for it was not supported by the use of force, and it was presented too late. The effectual way of stopping the war would have been for the Powers to unite naval and military forces in a joint demonstration against the Balkan states, but the opposing interests of Russia and Austria-Hungary would not permit such a demonstration. Austria-Hungary and Germany would have approved, undoubtedly, but Russia, the hereditary and natural defender of the Slav peoples, would never risk the loss of her prestige in the Balkans by threatening those peoples when they were attempting to rescue other Slavs from Turkish bondage. And for reasons of higher international policy, Great Britain and France would, of course, follow Russia's lead in Balkan affairs. So the mutual jealousies and suspicions, and the rival ambitions of the great powers, prevented any effective steps toward stopping the war.

And the declaration which was submitted was too late. September 30 Bulgaria, Serbia, Montenegro, and Greece ordered the mobilization of their troops. Turkey at once responded with a similar order. October 8 Montenegro formally declared war:

"In conformity with the authorization of King Nicholas, I have the honour of informing you that I leave Constantinople to-day. The Government of Montenegro breaks off all relations with the Ottoman Empire, leaving to the fortunes of arms of the Montenegrins the recognition of their rights scorned through centuries of their brothers of the Ottoman Empire.

"I leave Constantinople.

"The royal government will give to the Ottoman representative at Cettinje his passports.

"PLAMENATZ.

"October 8, 1912."

The following day this little nation began operations by bombarding the Turks out of their fortified positions on the Podgoritza heights. On October 13 Bulgaria, Serbia, and Greece dispatched a joint note to Turkey demanding the establishment of Macedonian autonomy under European governors. The Porte at once withdrew its representatives from the Balkan capitals and, on October 16, announced the fact to the Powers. Two days later Turkey declared war on Bulgaria and Serbia; and on that evening (October 18) Greece declared war on Turkey.

There was much uncertainty in Europe with respect to the chances of success of the Balkan states. It was expected that Turkey could mobilize close to half a million men; it was known that for three years past famous German officers had been laboring with the reorganization and training of the Turkish army; it was realized that German guns, German equipment, and German efficiency in drill might have accomplished the miraculous in Turkey; and it was pointed out that the Turkish forces had the undoubted military advantage of operating on interior lines, thus being able to shift troops at will, without effective opposition from the enemy, from point to point of the line of defense. In contrast to the Turkish, the military resources of the Balkan allies were somewhat belittled. It was recognized that these allies could put more men in the field at the beginning, the early estimates being Bulgaria 350,000, Serbia 150,000, Greece 100,000, and Montenegro 50,000, but the efficiency of the military training, morale, and equipment of these troops was seriously doubted.

The plans of the Balkan allies had been laid with great care during the months of preparation preceding the outbreak of the war. Little Montenegro was assigned the task of a drive southward against Scutari; Serbia, of the overthrow of the Turkish forces in Macedonia and thereafter the seizure of the Adriatic port of Durazzo; Greece, of gaining and retaining control of the water communications between Asia Minor and European Turkey to prevent the transportation of troops, and of an attack by land directly against Salonika; and Bulgaria, much the largest and most powerful of the allies, of a straight push against the bulk of the Turkish forces in Thrace with the attempt to threaten Constantinople. The plans thus contemplated a coördinated attack from four different directions, thus not permitting the Turks to relieve pressure at one point by the withdrawal of troops from other quiet fronts. At the same time, each nation of the alliance was assigned a task, not only valuable against Turkey, but in accordance with its ambitions for territorial expansion. Montenegro had long wished for the possession of Scutari; Serbia looked forward to the annexation of the greater part of Macedonia and to an outlet to the Adriatic sea; Greece had for generations cherished hopes of gaining Salonika; and Bulgaria desired the increase of her territory by the annexation of Thrace. Thus national interests were strongly enlisted for the accomplishment of each nation's share in the general plan.

The operations proceeded with astonishing success. Turkish forces were paralyzed by the breakdown of the supply system. The armies of the allies gained their respective objectives with unexpected speed. By October 26 the Montenegrins had begun the investment of Scutari. By the end of October the Serbians had cleared the Sanjak of Novibazar of Turks and defeated the enemy in the great battle of Kumanovo (October 22–25). November 18 they captured Monastir, and November 28 they entered Durazzo in triumph. The Greeks forced the retreat of the demoralized Turks to Salonika, and captured that port after a two-days' investment, November 8. The Bulgarians with great bravery and heavy losses defeated the Turks in two great pitched battles, Kirk Kilisse, October 22–24, and Lule Burgas, October 29–31, and drove them behind the Tchataldja lines, the last remaining defensive lines in front of Constantinople.

At this crisis the Turkish government requested the great powers to mediate, but was rebuffed by a reply stating that no terms unacceptable to *all* the belligerents would be forced upon them. Turkey thereupon opened direct negotiations with the Bulgarians to procure an armistice for the discussion of terms of peace. This armistice, agreed to by all the belligerents except Greece, was signed December 3. Greece continued hostilities alone against Turkey, but without important results.

While the military situation remained stationary, the peace conference met in London, December 16, 1912. The place of meeting emphasized the international character of the issues to be settled. The representatives of the Turks and of the Balkan allies were not to be allowed to discuss and determine among themselves the terms of peace, but all the chancelleries of Europe were interested spectators and at times prime movers in the negotiations. At the end of November Sir Edward Grey had proposed that representatives of the great powers should meet to confer upon the Balkan question — again an attempt to revive the Concert of Powers — and these representatives were actually in session in London in December. Thus two conferences were being held at the same time on the same issues — the one a conference of the great powers, and the other a peace conference between the representatives of Turkey and of the Balkan allies.

The most difficult and thorny of the many issues raised by the war among the European powers was the question of the disposition of Albania. Serbia had seized Durazzo and resolutely refused to surrender it. Austria-Hungary, who looked upon Albania as within her sphere of influence, advocated autonomy for the entire district and considered it incompatible with her vital interests to have one of its chief ports held by a hostile state, especially by one legitimately suspected of being supported diplomatically by Austria-Hungary's traditional enemy, Russia. The possession of Durazzo, with the narrow corridor from southern Serbia to the coast, would bar Austria-Hungary definitely from possible expansion to the southeast. When Serbia continued to insist upon her right to Durazzo, Austria-Hungary began, in November, 1912, the mobilization of her troops. This threat of war led to declarations by the great powers indicating a general alignment according to the great alliances: in November, von Bethmann-Hollweg announced that if other members of the Triple Alliance were attacked by a third power while they were maintaining their interests, Germany would support them; in the same month the British prime minister, Mr. Herbert Asquith, stated that public opinion in Great Britain was unanimously opposed to a policy which would rob the victors of their spoils; early in December the French premier declared that France would stand by her allies and her friendships; and Russia's position in favor of Serbia was well understood. It was, therefore, the Albanian question which occupied most of the attention of the representatives of the great powers when they met in conference in London.

Their decision was announced December 20, 1912, in time to be known by the representatives sitting in the peace conference. Austria-Hungary, supported by Germany, won her point. The powers recommended the acceptance of the principle of Albanian autonomy, accompanied by a guarantee to Serbia of commercial access to the Adriatic Sea. The danger of a general European war was for the time being averted by the sacrifice to a large extent of Serbia's territorial ambitions, and an important part of the reward which she had been led to expect as a result of the war.

In the meanwhile the peace conference came to a halt. Delayed in its deliberations in the beginning by the natural unwillingness of the Turkish representatives to admit the Greek so long as Greece had not acknowledged the armistice, it soon came to a full stop over the proposed terms. The Balkan allies demanded an indemnity and the surrender of all of Turkey in Europe except a small strip around Constantinople: Turkey, considering these terms too humiliating, asked for the retention of the province of Adrianople, and of her sovereignty over Macedonia and Albania, which were to be given autonomy, and the payment by the allies of a proportion of the Turkish debt corresponding to the share of the lost territory. On January 6, 1913, the representatives of the Balkan allies suspended the discussions. The representatives of the great powers thereupon intervened in the hope of preventing a resumption of hostilities. On January 16 they presented a joint note to the Turkish government advising it to yield on the cession of Adrianople and to leave the other questions at issue to the powers for adjudication.

There was a chance that this advice would be accepted, for a committee of notables, assembled at Constantinople, agreed to it January 22, but the situation was suddenly changed by a *coup d'état* in Constantinople January 23 by which a "no surrender" group of Young Turks overthrew the ministry and installed members of their own faction. The new government stiffened the opposition of the Turkish representatives to the terms of the Balkan allies and the first peace conference shortly afterwards came to a close without accomplishing anything.

Hostilities were resumed February 3, 1913. The Bulgarians, though unable to force the Tchataldja lines, defeated all aggressive movements of the Turks, and the situation on this front did not materially change. The Greeks resolutely pushed the siege of Janina, and received its surrender March 6. The Bulgarians and Serbians carried the defenses of Adrianople and compelled its surrender March 26. The Montenegrins, in spite of the intervention of allied diplomacy, continued the siege of Scutari through all of March.

In the meanwhile the representatives of the powers exerted every effort to promote peace. The danger of involving all Europe in the war was very grave, especially as a result of little Montenegro's attack upon Scutari, which Austria-Hungary regarded as an integral part of the autonomous Albania. On March 1, 1913, the great powers proposed mediation. After a month of preliminary discussions, both the Turkish representatives and the representatives of the Balkan states (with the exception of Montenegro, which persisted in its siege of Scutari) agreed to mediation on the following general terms: (1) the boundary of the Turkish territory should be a direct line between Enos on the Ægean Sea and Midia on the Black Sea; (2) the status of the Ægean islands should be left to the decision of the powers; (3) the question of indemnity, and of the assumption by the allies of a proportion of the Turkish public debt should be settled by a financial commission to sit at a later date in Paris; and (4) the boundaries of Albania should be determined by the powers. On April 19 an armistice in accordance with the above provisions was signed at Bulair by all the belligerents except Montenegro.

Montenegro's obstinacy in refusing to retire from the siege of Scutari not only delayed final peace negotiations, but was responsible for another European crisis similar in nature and effect to that created by Serbia's capture of Durazzo the previous autumn. On the 1st of April, 1913, the powers had notified the King of Montenegro that he must raise the siege of Scutari and allow that city to be incorporated into Albania. Upon his refusal, the warships of the great powers blockaded Antivari, the Montenegrin seaport. The Montenegrins still persisted in their siege of Scutari and captured it April 22. Two days later Austria-Hungary demanded that immediate measures be taken to put Albania in possession of Scutari. At once Russia was on the alert. Although she had been a party to the agreement of the powers determining the boundaries of Albania, public opinion in Russia would not countenance the use of force against the small Slav nation. Meetings of protest were held at various points and great indignation against Austria-Hungary was expressed. Austria-Hungary proceeded with the mobilization of her troops and announced on May 1 that if Montenegro did not agree to withdraw, she would take individual action against that state. Italy, who had ambitions of her own in Albania, was unwilling to give Austria-Hungary free individual action in Albanian affairs, and announced that she would support her ally of the Triple Alliance. The situation, at the moment very serious, was cleared on May 5 by the act of King Nicholas of Montenegro in yielding to the pressure put upon him and in putting Scutari into the hands of the powers. On May 14, sailors from the international fleet which had blockaded Antivari occupied the city in the name of Albania.

The Albanian crisis ended, the second peace conference met in London May 2, 1913. The representatives received a stern warning from Sir Edward Grey that protracted deliberations such as made the first peace conference ineffectual would not be tolerated by the great powers. They thereupon came to a quick decision, embodying in a treaty (signed May 30, 1913) the provisions agreed upon in the preliminary armistice at Bulair the preceding month. All the issues were accordingly referred to the powers for final judgment.

C. THE SECOND BALKAN WAR

Even before the signing of the Treaty of Peace rumors were abroad that the Balkan allies were at odds and would shortly be involved in another war. The Balkan alliance had in the first place been a league of small nations, each with its long tradition of racial grievances and hatreds. Greek hated Serb, Serb hated Bulgar, and Bulgar hated Greek, and the inherited hatred of one people for another was scarcely less than the common hatred each felt against the Turk. It was next to miraculous that the alliance held together for the eight months' war against Turkey: it was altogether natural that once this common link was dissolved, the various nations should fly at each other's throats — such was the normal condition of affairs in the Balkan regions.

Certain results of the war that had just ended bred special disaffection at this time. Although the allies had succeeded beyond their wildest expectations, their hopes of increase of territory had grown in proportion to this success. Each state was now prepared to claim many times the amount which would have abundantly satisfied it at the beginning of the war. Each state, with its revised demands, had an irritating special grievance. By the terms of the secret treaty of alliance (1912) under which Bulgaria and Serbia had leagued against the Turk, Serbia had sur-

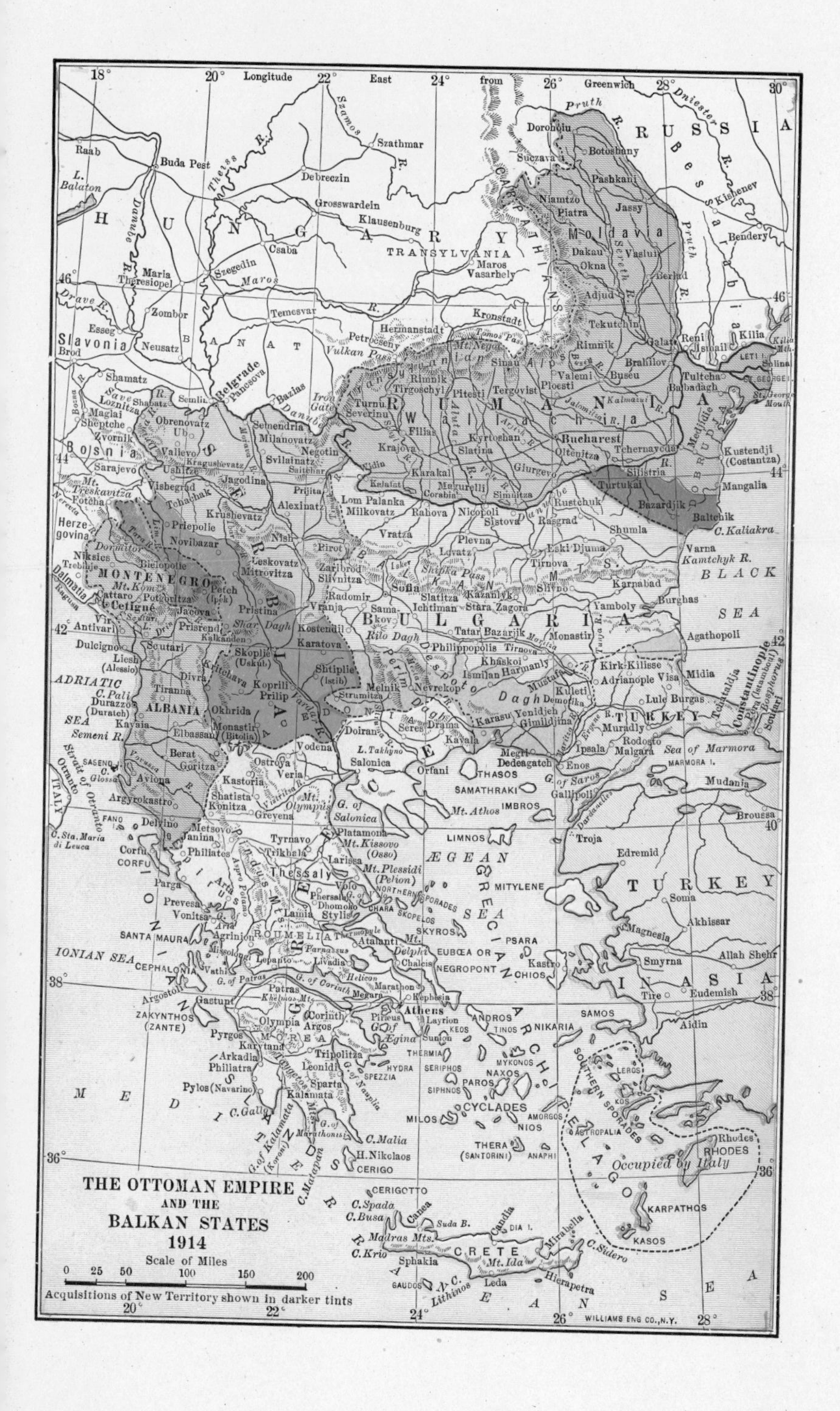

THE OTTOMAN EMPIRE AND THE BALKAN STATES 1914

Scale of Miles: 0, 25, 50, 100, 150, 200

Acquisitions of New Territory shown in darker tints

rendered all claim to valuable territory in Macedonia in return for the assurances of Durazzo and a large part of Albania. Unfortunately for her assurances, the great powers had stepped in and prevented Serbia from having Durazzo or any part of Albania. Serbia thereupon demanded as a matter of equity "that the new conditions which had arisen and which had entirely altered the situation should be given consideration and that Bulgaria should not expect the preliminary engagements to be carried out." Bulgaria retaliated by calling attention to the fact that she had borne the brunt of the fighting, and that the new conditions in no way invalidated the old agreement. Bulgaria itself had a distinct grievance in that Serbia had captured and was occupying Monastir, a town which Bulgaria had strongly desired for itself.

Greece, too, as well as Serbia, had a burning complaint against Bulgaria. Although she had no written engagements guaranteeing her territorial increase, she had looked with covetous eyes on southern Albania, which was lost to her by the intervention of the powers. She envied Bulgaria, who would secure three-fifths of the territory wrested from Turkey and leave two-fifths to be divided among the three allies. Montenegro lost Scutari, Serbia lost Durazzo and northern Albania, and Greece lost southern Albania, but Bulgaria gained and held actually more than she had expected to get when she entered the war. Bulgaria showed no disposition to treat with Greece in a conciliatory manner. M. Daneff, Bulgarian minister, minimized the achievements of the Greek troops during the war, pointed out that Greece had gained Crete and would probably get some of the Ægean islands in addition to a slice of the mainland, and asserted that she had actually been overpaid for her efforts. As in the case of Serbia, Greece had one city, Salonika, which Bulgaria desired: possibly the hope that in the event of war she might win Salonika led Bulgaria to repulse the Greek negotiations.

Fighting between Bulgars and Serbs and Bulgars and Greeks, wherever the troops were in contact, broke out before the treaty was signed. The conflicts degenerated into barbarism, fights for extermination, with inhuman and inconceivable brutality. Each side committed atrocities in disregard of all principles of international law. Conditions grew rapidly worse after the treaty was signed. On June 10 the Serbian government demanded a categorical answer to Serbia's request for a revision of the 1912 secret treaty. A week later M. Daneff refused Serbia's request. June 22 the Serbian minister withdrew from Sofia and the Bulgarians, without the formality of a declaration of war, on June 29 put their troops in motion against the Greek and Serbian lines. War was officially declared July 5, Montenegro joining Serbia and Greece against Bulgaria.

A new and decisive factor entered the situation at this point. Rumania had remained neutral at the beginning of the First Balkan War, perhaps under the influence of Russia and out of sympathy with the general purposes of the allies, but when it became evident that each of the allies intended to profit greatly by increase of territory, the Rumanian government demanded as a price of continued neutrality the cession of the city of Silistria and of a small strip of the Black Sea coast to strengthen her southern boundaries. In February, 1913, when relations between the two countries were severely strained, the issue between them was referred at the Czar of Russia's suggestion to a conference of foreign ambassadors at St. Petersburg. In May this conference agreed that Bulgaria should cede to Rumania the town of Silistria with the land three kilometres around, but forbade either country to build fortifications in the neighborhood and awarded Rumania nothing of the seaboard. The Rumanian government and the Rumanian people were dissatisfied with the decision of this conference and, when the Second Balkan War was on the point of breaking out, warned Bulgaria that she would not continue neutral unless Bulgaria would agree to a further territorial compensation. When M. Daneff hesitated to take measures so unpopular in his own country, Rumania prepared to throw in her lot with Greece, Serbia, and Montenegro. On July 10, Rumania, who had completed her mobilization, declared war and attacked Bulgaria from the north.

Bulgaria now reaped the fruits of her unconciliatory policy. The odds against her were too great. On all sides her troops were defeated and forced back: the Rumanians captured Turtukai and Baltchik and sent on a column to threaten Sofia; the Greeks, though stubbornly contested, fought their way up the Struma river toward the Bulgarian boundary; the Serbians repulsed the Bulgarians in Macedonia and prepared to descend through the Osogovska Pass upon the Bulgarian town of Kustendill; and, to complete Bulgarian humiliation, the Turks, taking advantage of the Bulgarian difficulties, recaptured Adrianople and pressed forward close to the former Turkish boundary in Macedonia.

On July 21 King Ferdinand asked for mediation. A week later (July 29, 1913) delegates from the various Balkan states assembled in Bucharest, the capital of Rumania, and at once agreed upon an armistice. On August 10, without extended deliberations, the Treaty of Bucharest was signed. Rumania gained the territory she desired, namely, an extension of her southeastern frontier to a line from Turtukai on the Danube River to Baltchik on the Black Sea. Greece acquired Salonika, Doiran, Demirhassa, Seres, Drama, and Kavala. Serbia took Kotchana, Istib, and Radovishta. And Montenegro, for the assistance she rendered Serbia, was awarded a slice of the Sanjak of Novibazar, including the towns of Plevlye, Bielopolie, Ipek, and Jacova.

Bulgaria was now under the necessity of determining her

southern boundary by arrangement with Turkey. While the Bulgarians had been involved in the war with the other Balkan states, Turkish troops had been pushed forward from the Enos-Midia line, had occupied the territory around Adrianople, and had consolidated their power therein. Bulgaria had expected the great powers to force Turkey to observe the provisions of the Treaty of London, and the representatives of these powers did actually present (August 7, 1913) a joint demand to the Porte to this effect, but as the days went by and the powers took no steps to enforce their demand, Bulgaria realized that she must bargain directly with Turkey. September 3, therefore, two Bulgarian ambassadors went to Constantinople to negotiate a new treaty. Turkey was in a favorable position. Her government relied upon the weakness of Bulgaria and the non-interference of the powers. By the provisions of the Treaty of Constantinople, signed September 29, 1913, the Turco-Bulgarian boundary followed the course of the Maritza River from its mouth to a point near Mandra, thence due north to Mustapha Pasha, thence easterly to the Black Sea. Turkey thus more than doubled the territory left to her by the Treaty of London (May, 1913) ending the First Balkan War.

In the meanwhile the representatives of the great powers were considering the problems set for them by the provisions of the Treaty of London of May 30, 1913. The most important of these problems were those connected with the boundaries and government of Albania, and those connected with the disposition of the Ægean islands.

The clash of interests was especially dangerous in the settlement of the Albanian question. Austria-Hungary and Italy had been instrumental in causing the formation of this new principality, neither of them, however, with a sincere desire to see it develop into a powerful and self-reliant state. Each of these countries cherished hopes of ultimately acquiring large parts of Albania for itself. The final boundaries determined by the conference of ambassadors were considered too narrow by both countries, for, looking at their own interests, they realized that the narrower the boundaries, the less territory there would be for division. Serbia entertained a bitter resentment at her exclusion from Durazzo and was very hostile, not only toward Austria-Hungary, who had been responsible for this exclusion, but also toward the newly created Albania. Montenegro felt that she had been cheated out of Scutari, and also felt intense bitterness against Austria-Hungary and Albania. Greece, the neighbor on the south, had confidently expected to gain a large part of the territory of the southern part of Albania: her disappointment naturally embittered her against the new principality. With Austria-Hungary and Italy supporting its existence only for selfish ends, and with every one of its immediate neighbors intensely hostile, Albania entered the family of nations under distinctly bad auspices.

Late in July the conference of the ambassadors agreed that Albania should be governed by a prince, to be nominated six months thence. Its government until the prince should accept the throne was to be managed by an international commission composed of appointed representatives of Great Britain, France, Italy, Russia, Germany, and Austria-Hungary.

It can be easily appreciated that the government of such an unruly population as the Albanian tribesmen under the conditions was not an inviting prospect. The man selected for the task was Prince William Frederick Henry of Wied, a German Protestant prince related to the Queen of Rumania. Early in 1914 this prince made the round of the capitals of Europe, possibly in the endeavor to negotiate a loan for his new country, possibly to gain the good will of the powers. February 23, 1914, he formally accepted the crown, and March 7 he landed in Durazzo, which had been selected as his capital. With the announcement of his title, William I of Albania, and his ministry, appointed March 17, 1914, the career of Albania as an independent principality began.

The disposition of the Ægean islands was the other problem which brought to the front the clash of international interests in the Balkan regions. The population of these islands was preponderatingly Greek in race and political sympathies. Greece had conquered and put military forces upon all the islands except those held by Italy, and now insisted that she be allowed to retain them. Turkey on the other hand demanded their return as essential to the defense of Asia Minor and the Dardanelles. After long deliberation the conference of the powers dispatched notes to Greece and Turkey (February 13 and 14, 1914) stating its decision to be that Greece should retain all the islands of which she had actual military possession except Tenedos, Imbros, and Castelosizo, which were to be returned to Turkey. Greece accepted the decision gracefully, though disappointed that Italy should be allowed to retain the twelve Sporades, but Turkish resentment was exceedingly intense.

Thus, the years from 1911 to 1913 were epochal in the history of the Near Eastern Question. Italy had taken a distant Turkish province by a direct attack upon Turkey; the Balkan states had buried their differences for a few months and taken from Turkey all her European provinces except the land for a few miles around Constantinople; they had partitioned Macedonia and Thrace among themselves after much quarreling; the great powers had intervened to create a new principality, Albania, along the Adriatic sea. These were momentous changes, exceeding in importance any single previous stage of Turkey's retreat from her once vast territory in Europe. With a few years of peace to allow the separate states to put in effect the necessary political readjustments and to forget (at least, partially) the bitter animosities aroused by the wars, there seemed some reason to hope that the most difficult element in the Near Eastern Question — namely, the relation of Mohammedan Turkey to its Christian dependencies in Europe — had been forever removed from international politics. But these few years of peace were not to be: the very animosities developed by these wars were to set the spark of the greatest war of history.

CHAPTER II

THE EVE OF THE GREAT WAR

A. UNREST IN THE BALKANS

Although the Balkan wars had been ended and treaties signed without involving Europe in a general war, they had added greatly to the accumulation of bitter feeling between nations. This feeling was especially notable, naturally, in the Balkan regions.

i. *Greece*

Greece, by gaining much of her most cherished territorial ambitions, including the island of Crete, many islands in the Ægean, all of Thessaly, and large and important parts of Macedonia and Thrace, had more than doubled her territory, but these additions had brought new and troublesome problems. The Greeks in the Sporades, which since the Turco-Italian war were held by Italy, clamored for union with Greece, and naturally had the sympathy of the Greek nation; and the tribe of Epirotes in the lower Albanian country, included in the principality to suit the interests of Italy, likewise protested violently against being deprived of Greek citizenship. Greece was thus brought into opposition to the territorial ambitions of Italy. Her government was unable to do more than protest against the Italian occupation of the Sporades, but since it still had Greek troops in occupation of lower Albania as a result of the Balkan wars, it had some hopes of forcing the powers to yield up this district to the enlarged Greece. In January and February of 1914 the prime minister, Venizelos, made the round of the chief European capitals — Rome, Paris, London, Berlin, Vienna, St. Petersburg, and Bucharest — in the endeavor to gain a hearing for the Greek cause. Though not entirely successful, he did obtain by negotiation a slight extension ("rectification," as it was euphemistically called) of the Greek boundaries in the Albanian region, and the guarantee that the government of the new principality would protect the rights of its Greek subjects in respect to their language, religion, and their unwillingness to be governed by Mohammedans.

In her relations with her former ally, Bulgaria, Greece had a more critical time. As a result of the Second Balkan War, Greece had annexed the maritime parts of Macedonia, including the ports of Salonika and Kavala, which had a large admixture of Bulgarian inhabitants and had been regarded as essential for Bulgarian commercial development. Bulgaria cherished keen resentment against Greece for these annexations; the Bulgarian inhabitants in the districts, hating the Greeks and fearing oppression, emigrated by the thousand; and the rumor spread in the spring of 1914 that Bulgaria intended to join Turkey in an attack upon Greece to win back the coveted provinces.

And still further, Greek relations with Turkey during the spring and summer of 1914 were strained nearly to the breaking point. Turkey resented the decision of the powers to give to Greece the islands in the Ægean, which, although predominantly Greek in population, had considerable Turkish Mohammedan communities. These Turkish communities found their position under the Greek government very unsatisfactory and emigrated by thousands to Turkish Asia Minor. Similarly, the many Greeks who had settled in Asia Minor now found their position unsafe with the renewal of the traditional hatreds between the races and thousands of them emigrated to Greece. In some cases the Turks pouring into Asia Minor forcibly ousted the Greeks from their communities, and robbed them of their possessions. Thus through the fall of 1913, the two tides of emigrants crossed each other, Turks fleeing from the new Greece into Asia Minor, and Greeks fleeing from Asia Minor to Greece. And strong recriminations passed between the two governments. War seemed imminent. Turkey purchased in January, 1914, two Dreadnoughts which were being constructed in the English naval yards, one from Brazil and the second from Chile: Greece retaliated in July by buying the *Idaho* and the *Mississippi* from the United States. Other nations now intervened in the effort to stop the conflict: Serbia warned Turkey that in case of war she would not remain friendly with Turkey; Russia and Rumania notified the Porte that they would consider it a serious blow to commerce if in the event of war Turkey should close the Dardanelles; and Bulgaria, which had been rumored to be leaguing with Turkey, decided to remain neutral, thus effectually preventing any military operations between Greece and Turkey. Both nations adopted a more conciliatory tone, agreeing finally that M. Venizelos and the Grand Vizier of Turkey (Talaat Bey) should meet at Brussels at the end of July, 1914, to discuss the provisions of a better mutual understanding. When that time arrived, however, Europe was in the throes of the great international crisis and the meeting was indefinitely postponed. Soon after, of course, the dispute was swallowed up in the main current of European events.

ii. *Bulgaria*

In the northern Balkans, Bulgaria had been defeated in the Second Balkan War and humiliated by being deprived of much of the territory she had gained from Turkey in the First Balkan War. Her ambition to have the unquestioned hegemony among the Balkan states had been shattered by Rumania, and her territorial extension to Kavala and Salonika in the Ægean Sea, and to Monastir in Macedonia had been stopped by Greece and Serbia. Weakened as she was after the conclusion of the two wars, she was in no position to enforce her claims. She nursed her grievances against Serbia, Rumania, and Greece, however, and awaited a favorable opportunity for revenge.

iii. *Serbia*

Serbia had gained much territory during the Second Balkan War, but had been disappointed in her dearest ambition — access to the Adriatic Sea at Durazzo. Her blame for this disappointment was focused against Austria-Hungary. Patriotic Serbs, remembering how Austria-Hungary had annexed the provinces of Bosnia and Herzegovina in 1908, were inflamed by Austria-Hungary's intervention to force Serbia out of Durazzo. They considered they had sufficient evidence of a fundamental Austro-Hungarian policy directed against Serbia with the object of preventing her from access to the sea. They believed that a land-locked country had little opportunity to expand industrially and commercially; they had visions of Serbian strangulation at the hands of Austria-Hungary; their dreams of a greater Serbia, which should revive the glories of the ancient Serb Kingdom and should include all people of Serbian language, blood, and traditions, were never to be fulfilled so long as Austria-Hungary was permitted to rest secure in her possession of Bosnia and Herzegovina and in her policy of keeping Serbia from the Albanian coast. Serbian animosity, unable to measure itself in an armed conflict with the Dual Empire, found its outlet in secret intrigue. Serbian agents infested the Austro-Hungarian provinces inhabited by people of Serbian race, especially Bosnia and Herzegovina, and endeavored to foment insurrection. And the Serbian government took advantage of every small issue that rose to magnify the quarrel with the hope of enlisting ultimately the armed assistance of the great Slav power, Russia. An example of the Serbian machinations was given in the autumn of 1913. Raiding parties of unruly Albanians pushed across the border and captured the town of Dibra September 22, 1913, which had fallen to Serbia's share as a result of the First Balkan War. Serbia instantly put a large army in motion against the marauders, recovered all the territory, and captured the leader of the raiders. Then she pushed her army across the boundary line and took Albanian territory west of the river Drin. Austria-Hungary at once presented an ultimatum demanding the prompt withdrawal of these troops. Serbia had brought on the issue knowingly and willfully, but she was forced to withdraw when Russia showed no sign of coming to her aid. On October 20, 1913, she agreed to the Austro-Hungarian demands and shortly afterwards withdrew her troops to her own side of the border. An incident of this kind contributed its part, of course, to keeping alive the intense hatred between the two nations.

Thus in the Balkan regions the expulsion of Turkey by the war of 1912–1913 had by no means solved the Near Eastern Question. That part of the "Question" relating to the treatment by the Porte of its subject Christian peoples had been removed, of course, but it had been replaced by the problem of keeping the peace among the Christian nations which had absorbed the former Turkish territory, and the problem of adjusting the relations between these small nations and those of the great powers who had vital interests in that section of Europe.

iv. *Effect of Balkan Unrest upon Austria-Hungary and Russia*

The radiations of the Balkan troubles extended beyond the Balkan regions to the inner councils of members of the two great alliances. The continual irritation of Serbia's anti-Austrian policy was the subject of secret discussions among the members of the Triple Alliance. Austria-Hungary in the late summer of 1913, even before the Serbian seizure of Albanian territory beyond the river Drin, planned to chastise Serbia, and notified her allies, Germany and Italy, of her intention. As related by the Italian premier, Giolitti, at a later date:

"On the 9th of August, 1913, I, being then absent from Rome, received from my colleague, San Giuliano, the following telegram: 'Austria has communicated to us and to Germany her intention to act against Serbia, and defines such action as defensive, hoping to apply the *casus foederis* of the Triple Alliance, which I consider inapplicable. I intend to join forces with Germany to prevent any such action by Austria, but it will be necessary to say clearly that we do not consider such eventual action as defensive, and therefore do not believe that the *casus foederis* exists. Please telegraph to Rome if you approve.'

"I replied that: 'If Austria intervenes against Serbia, it is evident that the *casus foederis* does not arise. It is an action that she undertakes on her own account since there is no question of defense, as no one thinks of attacking her. It is necessary to make a declaration in this sense to Austria in the most formal way, and it is to be wished that German action may dissuade Austria from her most perilous adventure.'"

Austria-Hungary was dissuaded from her "perilous adventure" at this time by the united protests of her allies, Germany and Italy. The incident is most interesting, however, as showing the importance ascribed by Austria-Hungary to the Serbian propaganda and as indicating the German influence exerted at that time to prevent Austria-Hungary from taking measures which might draw all the powers into a great war.

The Balkan troubles had little effect on two members of the Triple Entente, Great Britain and France, for these nations were removed from the immediate vicinity of the Balkans and their vital interests were not involved. The third member of the Entente, Russia, occupied a different position. Russia was the great Slav power. The peoples of the Balkans, with the exception of the Greeks and the Turks, were chiefly of the Slav race. Russia had been largely responsible for their original freedom from the Turk; the sympathies of the thinking Russian people were with the small Slav nations as against Austria-Hungary and Turkey; and the Russian government persisted in its hope of gaining control of its back door to the sea, the Dardanelles. All these facts united to make Russia the defender and upholder of the rights of the Slav states in the Balkans. Hence, in the First Balkan War, public opinion in Russia was unitedly on the side of the Balkan allies; and in the territorial negotiations that followed, Russia wanted to see all chance for Austro-Hungarian expansion to the southeast definitely checked. Russia therefore favored Serbia in her aspirations for Durazzo, Bulgaria in her demands for Adrianople, and Montenegro in her retention of Scutari. Wild enthusiasm in Russia greeted the fall of Adrianople. At St. Petersburg a thanksgiving service was held in the church of the Resurrection and the Bulgarian national anthem was sung in the streets. Similar enthusiasm was manifested for little Montenegro's attempt to gain Scutari: a huge procession one Sunday marched into the famous Nevsky Prospekt with banners inscribed with the words, "Scutari to Montenegro"; and when Scutari finally surrendered, a great popular demonstration was held, April 24.

Naturally, the drift of public opinion and the anti-Austrian policy of the government were well known throughout Austria-Hungary. Relations were strained between the two countries in the winter of 1912–1913. In February of 1913 the tension was so great that war seemed probable. Prince Hohenlohe was at this crisis dispatched from Austria-Hungary with an autograph letter of the Emperor Francis Joseph to the Czar, and undoubtedly his assurances in the audience he had with the Czar influenced the Russian government toward a more conciliatory attitude. After the terms of the Treaty of London (May 30, 1913), which left the whole Balkan question to the decision of the Concert of Powers, became known, the excitement died down. The diplomats in Europe breathed more freely and congratulated themselves on their success in preventing the threatened conflict.

B. DOMESTIC PROBLEMS IN EUROPEAN STATES

While the problems created by the Balkan struggles had occupied the attention of those responsible for the foreign relations in the various governments, the industrial, economic, and political life within the separate states not directly affected by the wars proceeded in its regular course.

i. *Great Britain — Irish Home Rule*

In Great Britain all attention in domestic politics was focused upon the question of Home Rule for Ireland. The power of the House of Lords, which defeated Gladstone's Home Rule Bill of 1886 and 1893, had been definitely curtailed by the Parliament Bill of 1911. The Parliament Bill of 1911 had been passed by a coalition of Liberals and Irish Nationalists, and as soon as it was a law the Irish Nationalists expected their Liberal associates to repay their assistance by introducing and forcing through Parliament a Home Rule Bill.

Even before the Parliament Bill became a law, the Liberal leaders began to plan a Home Rule Bill which should carry out their pledges to their Irish supporters. Keen speculation was indulged in by outsiders respecting the nature of the proposed legislation. Questions were asked in Parliament, but the party leaders kept their counsel. Mr. Birrell, the able chief secretary to the Lord-Lieutenant of Ireland, answered questions in a general way, carefully avoiding concrete or specific facts, and Mr. Redmond, leader of the Irish Nationalists, stated that he could not discuss the measure in detail but that it would be entirely satisfactory to the Nationalists in Ireland.

The difficulties of the Irish question had long been before the people, but now that it was evident the government had the power to force a Home Rule Bill through parliament, the peculiarly thorny nature of the problem became accentuated.

The root of the trouble lay in the fact that Ireland was divided into two parts, the one part different from and hostile to the other part. To realize this difference we must go back in history for a moment to the time of James I of England, who reigned from 1603 to 1625. In overcoming one of the many rebellions in the unhappy island, the English government undertook the experiment of colonizing a part of the conquered territory with Scotch and English, who would supposedly be more tractable than the natives. In pursuance of this policy, about 1610, Scotch and English were poured into the province of Ulster, comprising the northern and northeastern counties of Ireland, where they were given ample lands and privileges. In Ulster they thrived, and eighty years later these Orangemen, as they were called because they adhered to the cause of William of Orange against the deposed King James, overwhelmed the Irish of the rest of the island in the famous and bloody battle of the Boyne. The differences between the Orangemen of Ulster province and the people of the rest of Ireland, thus founded upon oppression, hatred, and bloodshed in the seventeenth century, have never been reconciled in the succeeding centuries. The people of Ulster have continued to thrive during the interval. They have created great industries and manufactories, they have taken to commerce and business, they have become wealthy, whereas the rest of Ireland, dependent upon agriculture under an obsolete and unjust land system, has been impoverished. They have been fat and prosperous, while the rest of Ireland has been decimated by famine. They have maintained all their racial

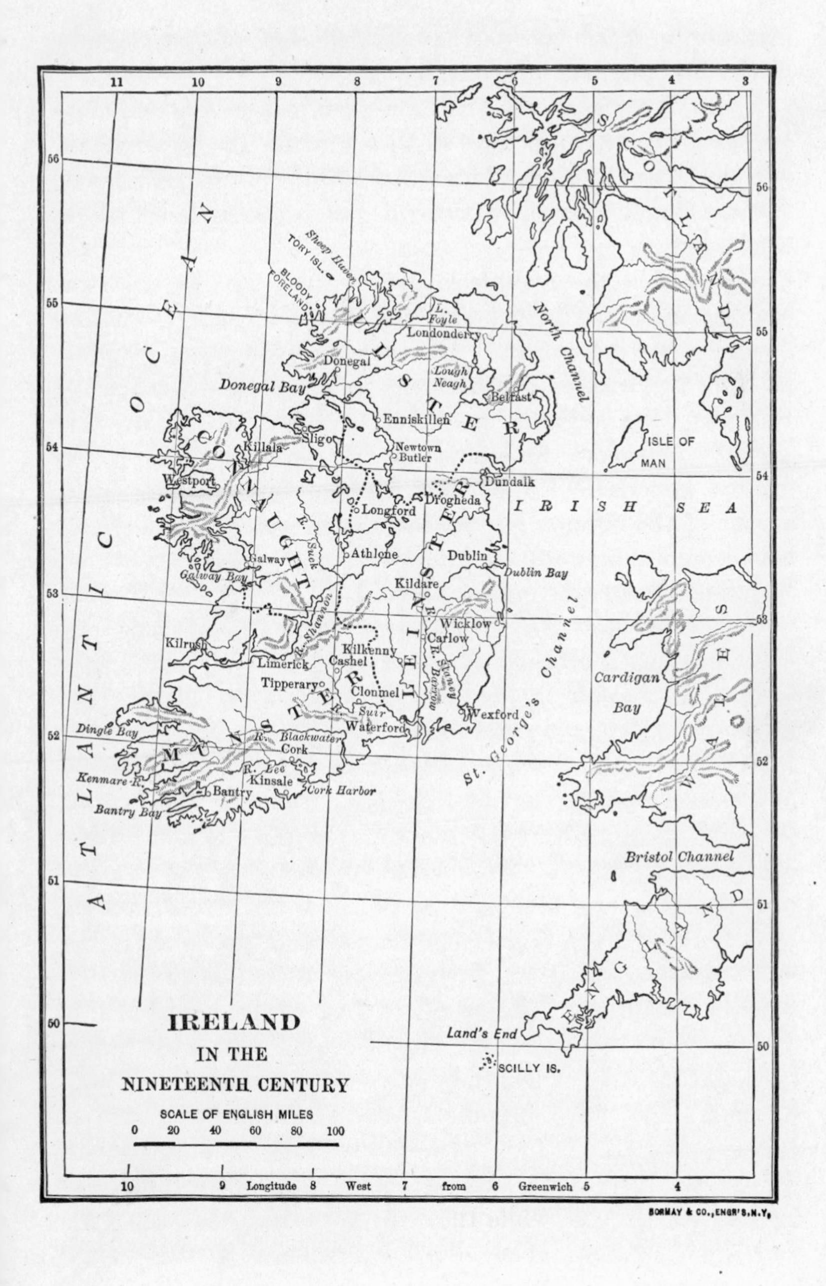

BORMAY & CO., ENGR'S. N.Y.

characteristics of their ancestors while the Irish are as Celtic to-day as they were three centuries ago. The Ulsterites have clung to their Protestant religion while all the rest of Ireland was suffering martyrdom for its adherence to Catholicism. Thus from an economic point of view, from a racial point of view, and from a religious point of view the differences between Ulster province and the rest of Ireland have seemed irreconcilable.

As the possibility of a Home Rule Bill became evident, the Ulsterites became very much inflamed. Any scheme for Home Rule for all Ireland would create a parliament in which the Catholics outside of Ulster province would have a majority. Any scheme for Home Rule would give to that Irish Parliament the control of Irish taxation and Irish finances. As the Ulsterites were by far the most prosperous people in Ireland, it was certain that the taxation to fill the Irish treasury would fall heaviest upon them, and yet the expenditure of the money received from such taxation would be under the control of an Irish parliament in which Ulsterites would be in a hopeless minority. There would be, therefore, in the opinion of the Ulsterites, a continual drain of money from Ulster to be expended throughout the rest of Ireland, a tax on the Protestants of English blood and traditions to benefit the Catholics of Celtic blood and traditions.

Under the stress of arguments such as this one indicated, the Ulsterites began to take what they deemed to be protective measures even before the law was introduced into Parliament. September of 1911, in a remarkable meeting, the Ulsterites solemnly pledged themselves not to recognize a Home Rule government, and chose a commissioner to draw up a plan for a provisional government for Ulster, to go into operation if a Home Rule Law were passed. Thus, before a Home Rule Law was introduced, even, into Parliament, the threats of a revolution were heard from Ulster.

The prime minister, Mr. Asquith, introduced the "Government of Ireland Bill," as the Home Rule measure was officially called, in the House of Commons April 11, 1912. Its chief features were: (1) Autonomy for Ireland in all purely Irish matters; (2) an Irish parliament of two houses; (3) representation for Ireland in the English parliament; (4) the Irish executive to be the King represented by the Lord-Lieutenant, and the cabinet to be chosen from the Irish parliament; and (5) financial questions between England and Ireland to be under the control of a joint exchequer board consisting of two members appointed by the English parliament, two by the Irish parliament, and a president appointed by the King. Certain subjects were specifically stated to be outside the jurisdiction of the Irish parliament, as questions of peace, war, naval or military affairs, foreign affairs, currency, foreign commerce arrangements, religious legislation, marriage or divorce laws, and the like.

The first reading passed the Commons by 360 to 266 on April 16. The second reading on May 9 by a vote of 372 to 271. The third reading, after the most bitter debates, on January 16, 1913, by a vote of 367 to 257.

Just two weeks later, January 30, 1913, the Home Rule Bill was unceremoniously rejected by the House of Lords by a vote of 326 to 69. This rejection was, of course, expected by the Liberals. The prime minister took the necessary steps to put the machinery of the Parliament Bill of 1911 in motion for the passage of the Bill.

Near the beginning of the next session of parliament, he introduced the same bill. On May 7, 1913, it passed its first reading. In the debates preceding the vote on the second reading, the passions again rose very high. Sir Edward Carson, who was emerging as the leader of the Ulsterites, on the floor of the House of Commons stated that "the whole force of this whole Conservative and Unionist party" would support Ulster in armed resistance.

Thus revolution was a word openly bandied about in the councils of the national representative body, a previously unheard-of situation. The Irish Nationalists found an able leader in Mr. Redmond, who maintained steadfastly the principle that Home Rule must include all of Ireland.

"Ireland to-day," said Mr. Redmond in a great speech defining the nationalist position, "is full of hope and expectation. Beware how you dash that hope to the ground. Rebellion is threatened. Rebellion is justified in high quarters. The rebellion of a portion of the population of four counties, because they disapprove of the act of the imperial parliament before any wrong has been done, and before any oppression has been attempted, would be a crime and a calamity. Rebellion by over three-fourths of a people of a country distracted, tortured and betrayed, deprived of the rights of freemen, and condemned to a barren policy of coercion, would be too horrible a thing to contemplate; and it is because this is so that I rejoice with all my heart to believe and to know that the future of this bill is safe, and that the future of Ireland is assured."

The bill continued to have Liberal support. On June 10th it passed its second reading, and on July 17 its third, with a majority of about one hundred. Again the House of Lords refused by the enormous majority of 302–64 to give consideration to the bill.

The comparatively easy passage of the bill, and the assurance of its passage for the third time and its enactment into law under the provisions of the Parliament bill, aroused the Ulsterites to a frenzy. Sir Edward Carson took measures to prove that his threats of civil war were not idle. Fifty thousand "Ulster volunteers" were enlisted and drilled; a commander-in-chief appointed; arms and ammunition smuggled across the Irish Sea. All through the summer and autumn of 1913 the drilling and military preparations went on. The example of the Ulsterites inspired the Irish Nationalists to arm on a similar scale. Ireland began to assume the aspect of an armed camp divided against itself.

Meanwhile the debates went on. The new parliament, the one in which Home Rule was to pass for the third time, was to meet February 10, 1914. The leaders of the Home Rule Party and of the Ulsterites could reach no compromise. Civil war seemed inevitable. The bill was immediately introduced, passed its first reading, and on March 9 was introduced for its second reading.

On March 14, 1914, the government, foreseeing the inevitable clash, ordered movements of troops to guard government property and military supplies in the disaffected area of Ulster province. Brigadier General Gough and 57 officers of the Third Cavalry Brigade announced that they preferred to accept dismissal from the service rather than be ordered north with the probability of acting against the Ulsterites. This mutiny of the army officers had an astounding effect throughout the country. It was, of course, inconceivable that the government could allow a group of army officers to defeat its will or dictate the use of the military arm. A Special Order on Discipline was published, declaring that in the future the army would be expected to give unconditional obedience to all lawful commands, without asking or receiving information in advance as to what services would be required.

The government had asserted its authority over the army and now pressed on for the passage of the bill. The second reading, introduced on March 9, was finally passed April 6 by 356 to 276, a majority of eighty. Scenes of great disorder took place in the House. On one occasion, May 21, when the third reading was under discussion, the opposition joined in a continued unanimous chant of "Adjourn," "Adjourn," until proceedings could not be carried on. Nothing, however, stopped the government from its intention of passing the bill. On May 25 the third reading was carried by 351 to 274, a majority of 77, and the bill was sent up to the Lords for their action.

The crisis was now actually at hand, that crisis to which

the country had been looking forward for over two years. The Home Rule Bill had gone through the various stages in precisely the manner laid down in the Parliament Bill of 1911, and was on the point of becoming law under the provisions of that Bill. The volunteers in Ulster had increased to 100,000, drilling with steady determination; the Nationalists in Ireland were recruiting their ranks rapidly and smuggling huge numbers of guns and huge quantities of ammunition for their use. Civil war might break out at any moment.

Face to face with civil war, the government on June 23 introduced the Home Rule Amending Bill, containing provisions intended to constitute the last measure of compromise which the government would yield. This Amending Bill provided that if within three months after the passage of the Amending Act, not less than one-tenth of the Parliamentary electors in any county in Ulster should so petition, a poll would be taken on the question of temporary exclusion from the operation of the Home Rule Bill. If in such a poll, the majority favored exclusion, the Home Rule Bill should not operate in that area for six years. When this Amending Bill was submitted to the House of Lords, that House so amended it that the government would not accept it. Thus the government's attempt at compromise failed.

Inspired by the gravity of the situation, the King summoned representatives of the interests at stake to conference at Buckingham palace. Asquith and Lloyd George for the government, and Redmond and Dillon for the Irish Nationalists were to confer with Lord Lansdowne and Bonar Law of the Unionists and Sir Edward Carson and Captain Craig of the Ulsterites. The King in a carefully worded but vigorous speech urged them to agree upon a compromise which should avert civil war. These men held four meetings July 21, 22, 23, 24 and were unable to agree either in principle or in detail upon the possibility of defining an area which should be excluded from the operation of the Home Rule Bill.

Upon the break-up of this conference, the last hope of a peaceful settlement seemed gone. Civil war was inevitable, apparently, only to be delayed until the bills were actually set forth on the statute book. Then, in the temporary lull between the final attempts at compromise and conference, came the European crisis caused by Austria's ultimatum to Serbia, and all thoughts were turned away from the Irish question to the larger issues involved in the threatened European conflict. Early in August, Great Britain entered the war. By mutual consent the bill was enacted and put upon the statute books September 18, but the operation of the law was suspended until after the war.

ii. *France*

In France during the same years (1911 to 1914), outside of the routine parliamentary debates on finance bills and the government policy toward labor organizations, and extended discussion of the Moroccan issue, two measures of great importance were considered. The first of these was a bill providing for the introduction of a system of proportional representation in the legislature, and the second a bill for an extension of the period of military service.

Agitation for a change in the electoral system had been carried on a decade past, especially by a well-organized party called the *Action Libérale* ("Liberal Action" party), formed in 1901. A measure of reform had been advocated by every French ministry beginning with that of Clemenceau (1906–1909). A majority of the members in each branch of the legislature favored a reform. Under these circumstances, it might be supposed that an electoral reform bill would have an excellent chance of easy passage, but unfortunately the members who desired the reform were unable to agree upon a satisfactory system.

Under the existing conditions, France was divided into local areas known as *Départements, Arrondissements, Cantons,* and *Communes,* the *Départements* being the largest area, and the *Communes* (corresponding roughly to our town) being the smallest. Members of the French Senate in the national legislature represented the *Départements,* and were chosen by an "electoral college" consisting of the deputies of the *Département,* the members of the general council of the *Département,* the members of the councils of the *Arrondissements* in the *Département,* and delegates elected by the councils of the *Communes* in the *Départements.* The members of the Chamber of Deputies were elected by direct vote of the people of the *Arrondissements,* each *Arrondissement* returning one deputy except in cases where its population exceeded 100,000, when it was divided into single-member constituencies, one for each 100,000 or fraction thereof. The Senators were elected for nine years, one-third retiring each three years: the deputies were elected for four years, and all elections were held at the same time.

The criticism of the above-outlined system was directed, not against the Senatorial elections — for the upper chamber had gained the respect and admiration of all France by the quality of its membership since the beginning of the Third Republic — but against the method of choosing the Deputies. The advocates of reform agreed that the *Arrondissement* was too small to be a satisfactory electoral unit, and that the local interests in such a restricted constituency were liable to outweigh nation-wide issues in the effect upon the election of deputies for the national legislature.

In 1906 a special committee of the Chamber of Deputies (*Commission du Suffrage Universel*) was appointed to consider the various proposals submitted for electoral reform. Its report of March, 1907, accompanying a suggested Act, favored a system known as the *Scrutin de liste.* The general principles of the *Scrutin de liste* were that deputies should be elected by direct vote of the people in the *Départements*, one member for each 75,000 inhabitants or fraction thereof; that each voter in a *Département* should have as many votes as there were members to be elected; that the voter was free to distribute his votes as he wished (either cumulating them on one candidate or dividing them among various candidates); and that each party group should submit its candidates to the voters on a list (hence the name, *Scrutin de liste*).

Unexpected change of ministers prevented this Act from having its due consideration in the Chamber, but the agitation continued. In November of 1909 the Chamber of Deputies passed a general resolution favoring the principles of the *Scrutin de liste* and proportional representation. In the spring elections of 1910 the question of electoral reform was one of the chief issues, and in June of that year M. Briand introduced a comprehensive measure; but again the ministry fell before a vote was secured. In 1911 the new prime minister (M. Monis) made electoral reforms along the plan proposed by the committee one of the cardinal features of his policy as outlined in his speech before the Chamber March 6, but the Monis cabinet fell June 30, before it had time to accomplish anything. In January, 1912, the strong Poincaré ministry included electoral reform among its most important policies, and shortly afterwards introduced its bill on this subject.

The Poincaré bill differed from that proposed by the special committee of the Chamber and also from the general resolution passed by the Deputies in 1909 in favor of proportional representation. It contained a plan based on the *Scrutin de liste* and providing for minority (*not proportional*) representation. Although the bill encountered serious opposition in the Chamber, the government support secured its passage July 12, 1912, by a vote of 339 to 217. In the Senate it was at once referred to a committee which, reporting in November, 1912, approved the *Scrutin de liste* system, but strongly condemned the minority representation features of the bill.

On January 17, 1913, M. Poincaré was elected President of the Republic to succeed M. Fallières, whose term had expired, and the defense of the bill in its passage through the upper house fell to the lot of M. Briand, head of the ministry. The hostile attitude of the Senatorial committee affected the opinions of the upper chamber. On March 18 M. Briand made a two-hour impassioned appeal for the passage of the bill, but without avail. He was defeated on an amendment and at once resigned. Electoral reform was defeated, at least for the time being.

The succeeding ministry, headed by M. Barthou, at once presented a new reform bill slightly changed from the Poincaré bill in the attempt to find a compromise between the position of the Chamber and that of the Senate. This bill passed the Lower House in the winter of 1913–1914, but was promptly rejected by the Senate, which, on March 10, 1914, reaffirmed its adherence to the *Scrutin de liste* without provision for the representation of minorities. The outbreak of the great war a few months later prevented further attempts to pass a measure for electoral reform.

Thus, up to the present time, although the general desire for a change in the electoral system exists, no reform bill has passed. The two legislative houses, both approving the *Scrutin de liste* method, are at variance on the question of the introduction of clauses providing for the representation of minorities. Undoubtedly, after the war has finished and the nation returns to its normal condition, the question of electoral reform will be one of the first important issues to be met by the government.

Outside of business and routine affairs, the second measure of prime importance considered by the French legislature was the increase of the military establishment. The recurrent crises in international European politics were so many warnings of the necessity of complete preparedness. France had abandoned in 1905, after the *Entente* with England, the system of requiring three years of service, and since that year had kept her recruits with the colors for only two years before they passed to the reserves. The activity of her traditional enemy to the east, Germany, in threatening her in the Agadir crisis of 1911, and the German legislation of May, 1912, increasing the German standing army, combined to arouse Frenchmen to a high pitch of patriotic zeal. On March 4, 1913, the Superior Council of War issued a statement declaring that for the increase of the effective army it was necessary to exact three years of service from all Frenchmen without exemption. March 6 the Minister of War introduced a three-year-service bill in the Chamber of Deputies. March 7 the Municipal Council of Paris recorded its approval of the measure. And May 9 the Army Committee of the Chamber of Deputies accepted it.

Only two groups in the Chamber, the Radicals led by M. Caillaux, and the Unified Socialists led by M. Jaurés, opposed the enactment of this legislation, but their opposition was exceedingly bitter. They could not, it is true, command a majority, but they were able by the introduction of amendments and substitute proposals to delay action on the bill. On June 26 the prime minister, M. Barthou, made an impassioned appeal to the Chamber not to allow politics to interfere with the fulfillment of a "national duty." Some further delay ensued, but the weight of the government majority was too strong to be resisted. At midnight on July 19, the bill was passed by the Chamber of Deputies by a vote of 376 to 199.

The Senate took speedy action. The committee reported favorably on the bill, the Senate began its consideration July 31, and voted the whole of the bill by 254 to 37 on August 7, 1913.

The principal provisions of the bill were as follows: (1) Service to be required of all physically qualified Frenchmen for three years in the active army, eleven years in the reserve, seven years in the territorial army, and seven in the territorial reserve; (2) one franc and twenty-five centimes, plus fifty centimes for each child, to be allowed each day for the support of the families of soldiers; (3) recruits ordinarily to begin their service at the age of twenty; (4) no exemptions to be permitted (except of those physically disqualified), but students and apprentices to be allowed to postpone their service, and physicians, pharmacists, and veterinary surgeons to be permitted to elect to spend two years out of the three of active service in their professional capacities rather than as common soldiers; (5) students in the schools for officers, like the École Polytechnique and St. Cyr, to be required to spend two months as a soldier in actual military maneuvers after the first year of study, and a similar period as a non-commissioned officer after the second year, and to agree that after graduation they will perform two years of service as sub-lieutenants in the reserve or eight years in the service of the state; and (6) the new law not to apply to the classes of 1910, 1911, and 1912 (called in October, 1913).

The effect of the law was to increase the numbers in the effective army by 170,000 and to make possible an extensive reorganization, bringing the peace strength to 673,000. The increase in annual expenditure was estimated at 170,000,000 francs. The bill was exceedingly unpopular among masses of French people. While it was under consideration in the Legislature, popular demonstrations against it were held in many cities, the crowds uniting in shouts of "à bas l'armée," and calling for the downfall of the ministry. Before the necessary reorganization had been completed and the full benefits of the increase had become apparent in the military establishment, the Great War broke out, and all criticism of the military was, of course, instantly stifled. The Radicals and Unified Socialists rallied loyally to the support of the government with the other parties, and France presented a united front to the invader.

iii. *Germany*

In Germany the chief internal issues, outside of the regular financial measures, were concerned during these years with Alsace-Lorraine, the increase in the German army, and the continued opposition of the Socialist party to the government.

Since its seizure in 1870, the imperial province of Alsace-Lorraine had proved a source of constant embarrassment to the German government. In the western part the inhabitants, strongly French in sympathy, thwarted every effort of Germany to placate them. A group of irreconcilables, at the risk of being denounced for treason, advocated from time to time such schemes as the friendly surrender of the provinces to France, or the taking of a referendum among the people to determine the popular desire with respect to German or French sovereignty. The German government met this agitation with a stern hand. The provinces were constituted as imperial provinces; their representatives did not have in the Reichstag the rights of other units of the German empire; their local government, instead of being determined by themselves, as in other units, was dictated by the Emperor and his counsellors; and, in order to remove the sources of trouble, the German government attempted to "Germanize" the people by colonization, by edicts making German the only official language, and by similar measures.

In the summer of 1910 the Emperor caused an announcement of a change of policy to be made. His ministers informed the Reichstag that the government contemplated the grant of a constitution to the provinces. Shortly afterwards the government's bill was introduced into the Bundesrath and, after comparatively short debate, passed. By this bill, as passed in the Bundesrath, the provinces were given self-government, but they were still not allowed the status of other units of the empire, for their governor was to be appointed by the Emperor, and they were not given any representation in the Bundesrath.

The bill did not have so easy a passage in the Reichstag. Introduced January 28, 1911, it met immediate opposition from the liberal elements in the Chamber. They demanded for the provinces the same status as that possessed by other units of the empire. After long debate, the government accepted an amendment granting the provinces three votes in the Bundesrath. With this change the measure gained the support of enough of the Liberals to insure its passage.

Autonomy for Alsace-Lorraine did not by any means settle the problem. Disturbances and seditious propaganda were continued. So troubled was the situation that a year later the emperor personally threatened to take back the liberties he had granted and to annex the provinces to Prussia. An unpleasant incident in 1913, known as the Zabern affair, intensified the bitter feeling of the inhabitants. A lieutenant of the 99th Infantry, stationed in the quiet little Alsatian town of Zabern, gained the hatred of the people on one occasion, remarking that he would gladly give ten marks to any German soldier who would run his bayonet through a certain Alsatian blackguard, and on another occasion, by striking with the flat of his sword a lame shoemaker who had laughed at him in the street. Great demonstrations were held in Metz and Strassburg to emphasize popular Alsatian sympathy with the people of Zabern; the Social Democrats held anti-militarist meetings; and members of the Reichstag put embarrassing questions to the ministers. The lieutenant was court-martialed, but, after two trials, was allowed to escape unpunished. The government plea was that the military authorities had to be upheld, but the general impression left by the affair was bad throughout all Germany. In Alsace, of course, the Zabern affair intensified the sullen hatred with which the French element regarded their German masters. Alsace and Lorraine continued to be conquered provinces, unreconciled, kept in subjection only by military force, up to the time the great war broke out.

Since the reorganization of the German army following the Franco-Prussian war, German military policy has been regularly revised every five years. Thus, the Army Bill of April 1, 1905, fixed the strength and establishments to be attained March 31, 1910, the increase to be divided into successive increments added annually through the five-year period. By the above-mentioned bill, the peace strength of the German army was fixed for March 31, 1910, at 615,000 men of all ranks. The quinquennial period having ended in 1910, the country expected a new Army Bill to provide for the forthcoming period.

This new bill, under consideration early in 1911 (February), possessed no startling features. It provided that at the end of March, 1916, the total force should be raised from 615,000 to 625,000. The bill passed without serious opposition March 7, 1911, and became law April 1.

Before this law had any appreciable effect upon the military establishment, however, the rebuff of Germany in the Moroccan negotiations (the Agadir crisis) led the War Office to advocate an immediate further increase in the army. Many in Germany believed that the German defeat in Morocco was due to the lack of a sufficient military strength to overawe France. In the early months of 1912, therefore, the government proposed a new Army Bill which would result in an increase of the effectives by approximately 30,000 men. The Reichstag discussed the measure in April, and, promptly and loyally supporting the government in a measure said to be for necessary defense, passed the measure in May. The German bill provided for the formation of two new army corps to protect the Franco-German frontier. It increased the total number in the German army in times of peace to approximately 655,000. The reorganization measures were hastened and on October 1, 1912, the two new corps were formally constituted.

The expansion did not end here. The Balkan wars, the Austro-Russian crisis, the general tenseness of the European situation in 1912–1913 inspired the War Office to seek still further increases. At the beginning of 1913 an Army Bill, with supplementary Finance Bills, was introduced into the Bundesrath and rushed through its various stages until its final passage March 28. It went to the Reichstag at once. Although the expense of the increase was huge, the threat of England's naval armament, the Austro-Hungarian diplomacy leading apparently directly toward a general European war, the revival of the French desire for revenge and for the "lost provinces," and the bonds which the Triple Entente was welding over Italy, were a sufficient justification for the cost in the eyes of the patriotic Germans. After the preliminary committee stages, the bill, with little opposition or discussion, was passed June 30. By its provisions, which went into effect October 1, the total number of effectives was to be raised to, and maintained at, 870,000. It was the passage of this bill in the Bundesrath which stirred the French to their legislation for military increase in the same year. In May of 1914 von Falkenhayn, the German Minister of War, stated that the reorganization provided for by the 1913 bill was completed, and that the German army was in splendid condition.

A notable feature of the internal political life of Germany during this period was the astonishing gain of the Social Democrats (the party name of the Socialists) in the elections of 1912. This party polled 3,250,000 votes in the elections of 1907 and obtained 43 seats out of the 397 in the Reichstag; in 1912 it polled 4,250,000 votes and obtained 110 seats in the Reichstag. Since the total number of those who voted in the 1912 elections was but 12,200,000, the Socialists had the proud record of having polled more than one-third of the entire vote cast. The Social Democratic party became the most important party in the Reichstag.

The significance of these elections was considered by political thinkers. The Social Democratic party had grown from 102,000 to 4,250,000 in forty years, yet the enrolled Socialists in Germany numbered only 970,000 (including 108,000 women). It was obvious, therefore, that the Social Democratic party ticket had received the support of many voters who were not out-and-out Socialists. The reason for such support was that the Social Democratic party, maintaining a policy of consistent and continual opposition to the government, drew to its standards at elections all men of various degrees and opinions who had any kind of grievance against the government.

> "It has been distinctly the party of discontent and protest. Every discontented and disappointed man is liable at any time to express his dissatisfaction with society in general by voting the Social Democratic ticket. Has the young medical student failed of an appointment, has the citizen soldier been given a verbal castigation by the officer during his drill with the reserve, has a postal clerk been docked in his pay, has the grocer's wife had a snub from the factory owner's, — each sufferer can give vent to his private grievance against society by voting for the Social Democrat and thus making trouble for the powers that be. None of these persons has the slightest sympathy with the ultimate socialist program, and none of them would think of overthrowing the present state of society, except in a moment of ill humor. This habit of 'voting to the left' has attacked large classes of democratically inclined persons of the lower middle class following such a period of reaction as that which ended with the election of the *Reichstag* of 1912." (Fife: "German Empire between Two Wars." pp. 195–196.)

After the elections, however, the government had to confront a condition, not a theory; had to conduct the affairs of state in the face of a strong, united, critical, and outspoken opposition party of Social Democrats. The government, the regular conservative representation upon whom it had rested for support so long having been weakened, had to seek votes among portions of the liberal groups in the legislature. Such votes were to be had only by liberal concessions. The government therefore prepared to yield such concessions as were necessary from time to time to gain liberal support, but looked forward to an implacable political war against the Social Democrats. The Social Democrats retaliated with force. Every incident which might discredit the government was seized upon as an excuse for an attack. Their leaders opposed the military increase and made charges of bribery and corruption against the great German munitions makers, the Krupps; they made a national issue of the Zabern incident; instituted a Red Week (March 8–14, 1914) during which they held many great mass meetings and carried on an active propaganda for Socialism; and at the final sitting of the Reichstag, when the President proposed the usual *Hoch auf den Kaiser*, the Social Democrat members sat silent and sullen to show their Republican sympathies. The government on its side declared open war upon the Social Democrats. In January of 1914, the Secretary of State, von Delbrück, announced that the government would discontinue its program of social legislation; a few weeks later the Chancellor, von Bethmann-Hollweg, stated openly that it was the intention of the government to fight against the menace of Socialism. A few months later, however, the outbreak of the Great War stifled the minor internal political dissensions. The Socialists rallied to the support of the government, and in deeper patriotism sloughed off the superficial internationalism they were so fond of professing.

C. GENERAL INTERNATIONAL SITUATION IN EUROPE

i. *Increase of Armament*

When we turn from a consideration of the internal problems of a few of the leading states back to the general international situation, the outstanding feature remains the opposition between the two great Alliances, the Triple Alliance and the Triple Entente. On every question which had arisen out of the Balkan wars, the alignment of nations had followed these alliances. The significance of the recurring crises was not lost upon the diplomats. We have seen how Germany strengthened her army, and how France at once passed the three-year-service bill to meet Germany's increase. Two other continental nations added to their armaments at this same time, Austria-Hungary and Russia. By reorganization measures in 1912 and 1913, Austria-Hungary raised her peace strength from 460,000 effectives to 560,000, and provided for an increase in artillery from 1900 guns to 3000 guns. At the same time the Russian government put into effect a revised recruiting law, by which the effectives would be radically increased, and planned with the aid of capital borrowed from France to construct an elaborate scheme of strategic railroads to facilitate rapid mobilization on the German border. The Russian peace strength in Europe and the Caucasus was estimated at 950,000; the strategic railways, when completed, would theoretically allow mobilization on the German border to proceed as rapidly as German troops could mobilize on the Russian border.

All of these war preparations, of course, added just so much tinder to the inflammable masses in Europe. The year 1913, and the spring of 1914, were marked by outbursts of intense bitterness between Germany and France, and Germany and Russia. The French press took occasion to magnify slight incidents into occasions for strong diatribes against German brutality. In both the French and German parliaments orators referred openly to the enemy across the Vosges. The suppression by Germany of a pro-French newspaper in Alsace, and the notorious Zabern case awakened patriotic resentment throughout France. The accidental landing of a German military biplane inside the French frontier, and the transgression upon French territory of a German dirigible increased the French passions. French newspapers declaimed in the most fiery style against their traditional enemy and by open and covert references fanned the spirit of revenge. In eastern Europe the military measures of Russia aroused the German press to a frenzy in the spring of 1914. A series of newspaper articles outlining the state of preparedness which would result in 1916 or 1917 if the Russian plans were perfected created something akin to a panic in Germany. The militant periodicals gave free rein to their anti-Slav feelings and aroused great excitement. Much stress was laid upon the personal visits of the German Emperor to Francis Joseph of Austria-Hungary, and to Francis Ferdinand, the heir-apparent, and to Victor Emmanuel of Italy. Von Jagow, the German minister of foreign affairs, during the budget discussion in May, 1914, spoke of the dangerous agitation in the press and emphasized the solidarity of the Triple Alliance. Russian journals, of course, answered the German propaganda in kind; and the Russian government allowed a paper in St. Petersburg to declare in June, 1914, that "France and Russia did not desire war, but Russia is prepared and hopes that France will likewise be prepared."

ii. *German Diplomacy*

The German government was, of course, fully cognizant of the danger of the ill-feeling engendered between the Germans and the French in one direction and the Germans and the Russians in another. To offset this to some extent, overtures were offered in 1913 and the spring of 1914 to Great Britain. An attempt was made to pave the way for an amicable understanding on two of the chief issues which had caused bitterness during the past decade, the colonial issue and the naval issue.

Germany's incursion into the colonial field had not been attended with marked success. A large part of her African territories, which constituted her chief overseas territory, was under the equator and unfit for white men to inhabit. The expense of administration had been very large with no corresponding return in income. The governors, too often unaccustomed to native ways, had more than once by their autocratic methods and tactlessness involved the imperial authorities in trouble. And the German pursuit of colonies had been an important factor in awakening the suspicion and hostility of other members of the European family of nations. And yet a considerable portion of the thinking German people, conscious of their strength and ability, ardently desired to play as important a part in the world's politics as their neighbors. German dignity and prestige demanded that, so long as England and France possessed great colonial empires, Germany should straightway acquire such an empire. These Germans were bitterly piqued at English and French success in expanding their colonial territory in all quarters of the globe during the very years in which Germany was striving in vain to acquire desirable colonies. The failure in Morocco was the most recent instance of German effort along these lines, and the acquiescence of the government in the final decision which yielded up Morocco to French protection called forth intense criticism.

One desirable region for colonial expansion remained, however, in which German enterprise had already gained a foothold. Asia Minor and Mesopotamia had been in ancient times one of the richest parts of the known world:

there was no reason why under proper development they might not be restored to their former fertility and productiveness. The natural resources were there: German energy and brains were anxious for the opportunity to cultivate them.

In a previous chapter we mentioned briefly the initial steps by which German enterprise penetrated Turkish Asia Minor and Mesopotamia. The construction of the so-called Bagdad railroad was expected to gain for Germany economic and political control of Turkey, and the completed road might possibly, by its extensions toward Central Asia or toward the Persian Gulf, become the great carrier of the products of the East to the people of western Europe. The mining, commercial, and industrial concessions along the lines, which were granted at the same time with the railroad concessions, gave marvelous opportunities to the Germans for their genius in development. Between 1899 and 1911 the German interests in Turkish Asia Minor and Mesopotamia rose to the position of first importance.

Great Britain had looked with suspicion and hostility from the beginning upon the growth of German influence over Turkey, and especially upon the project of the Bagdad railroad. Her objections were political, economic, and financial. She feared that German control of Asia Minor and Mesopotamia would give Germany and Turkey a base from which in case of war they could seize the Suez Canal and attack Egypt. She feared, secondly, that the extension of the railroad to the Persian Gulf and to central Asia would tap the rich eastern field and deprive British ships of their large carrying profits. And she feared, lastly, that under the financial arrangements by which the road was built, arrangements which required Turkey to guarantee a certain sum on each kilometer of the line, the Turkish treasury would be so depleted that it could not meet its normal obligations, of which British investors held a large amount.

Moved by these fears, British diplomatists took what steps they could to thwart the German plans. The best harbor at the northern part of the Persian Gulf was Koweit, the principal town of a small district ruled by the Sheik of Koweit, a subject of the Turk. Great Britain had long cultivated friendly relations with this Sheik, and in 1899 induced him to hand over his little district secretly to the protection of Great Britain. Strengthened by this protection, the Sheik was able to resist all Turkish (and German?) efforts to gain control of his harbor. In 1913 by a treaty with Turkey, Great Britain openly acquired the protectorate which she had actually possessed for fourteen years. The British, established at Koweit, were in a position to prevent Germany from access to the Persian gulf.

To guard against the extension of the German line to central Asia it was necessary to block the way by obtaining control of Persia. In 1907 the British and Russian governments agreed to the division of Persia into three parts, the northern to be under the influence of Russia, the southern under that of Great Britain, and only the middle part to be left to the unhappy Shah. Since the British sphere of influence was the district through which any extension of the Bagdad railroad must naturally go, the government had effectually checked the German plans in this district as well as towards the Persian Gulf.

In her opposition to the financial arrangements between German financiers and Turkey for the building of the road, Great Britain had less success. It was not practicable for the British government to dictate to the Porte the terms upon which Turkey should allow internal commercial developments to be carried on; so Great Britain confined itself to a disapproval of the concession and a general complaint that British interests had not been sufficiently recognized.

In the meanwhile the construction of the railroad proceeded. Although delayed by the Young Turk revolution of 1908, the adroit diplomacy of Marshal von Bieberstein maintained German influence with the new régime, so that the German concessions were renewed and work continued. In the late autumn of 1910 the Czar of Russia visited the Emperor of Germany at Potsdam, and the Bagdad railroad, which had been opposed by Russian commercial interests, was one of the chief of the questions discussed. From this meeting resulted an agreement, signed August 19, 1911, by which Russia withdrew its opposition to the completion of the Bagdad railroad and agreed to link up the German line, when finished, to the Persian lines in the Russian sphere of influence; and Germany in return recognized Russia's predominant interests in northern Persia and pledged herself not to seek concessions therein. A year later Germany began negotiations with Great Britain by which it was hoped to gain British approval of the road and, possibly, an outlet to the Persian Gulf at Koweit. The use of Koweit as a harbor for a German railroad the British government resolutely refused. It was conciliatory, however, in the negotiations, and a preliminary agreement was reached (in May, 1913) by which the German rights to economic and financial control of the railroad as far as Bagdad were recognized, and tentative plans made for the extension southward to Bassona under international control with both German and British members on the governing board. England reserved for herself the right to control the railroad from Bassora to a point on the Persian Gulf (Bassora to Koweit, 85 miles). Negotiations for a triangular convention on the above basis between Great Britain, Germany, and Turkey were proceeding satisfactorily at the time the European crisis arose in 1914.

German diplomacy had thus removed one of the chief causes of disagreement between Great Britain and Germany, and had smoothed the way for a mutual understanding on colonial issues in general. In the same years the

German government suddenly changed its attitude on the subject of increase in naval armaments, and welcomed a discussion of that same project of limitation which it had rejected so contemptuously a few years before.

It will be remembered that Germany's answer to Great Britain's plea for limitation of armaments in 1908 was a new naval program increasing the annual quota of Dreadnoughts to four. Thus between the years 1906 and 1908 Germany had actually authorized the construction of nine of these capital ships whereas Great Britain had authorized but eight. The refusal of the German government to discuss limitation, and prophecies of the relative big-ship naval strength within a half dozen years, combined with sensational articles in the press and the excitement produced by the Turkish revolution with its possibilities in the reopening of the whole Eastern question, created what may be called a naval panic in Great Britain in the spring of 1909. Conservative newspapers made a rallying cry of "we want eight and we won't wait." The opposition in parliament demanded a two-power standard, that is, two capital British ships for one of any enemy. The sensational press had continual references to Great Britain's danger, and a reduction of the government's vote in some of the bye-elections showed that the people at large were becoming uneasy and anxious. The liberal government thereupon yielded and authorized a radical increase in its building policy. Great Britain and Germany were openly competing for supremacy in the number of Dreadnoughts constructed. All hopes of any end to this competition seemed dashed by von Bethmann-Hollweg's speech in the Reichstag after three years of such rivalry March 30, 1911:

"I consider any control of armaments as absolutely impracticable, and every attempt in that direction would lead to nothing but continual mutual distrust and perpetual friction. Who would be content to weaken his means of defense without the absolute certainty that his neighbor was not secretly exceeding the proportion allowed to him in the disarmament agreement? No, gentlemen, anyone who seriously considers the question of increased disarmament must inevitably come to the conclusion that it is insoluble so long as men are men and states are states."

But Germany found, once the British were aroused to the peril, that any hope of equaling Great Britain's naval force was vain. Lord Haldane expressed the British position: "Whatever efforts Germany may make, she must reckon upon our making efforts which will be still greater, because sea power is our life, and in sea power we intend to remain superior." British resources were equal, and more than equal, to the strain of the increased program, whereas the size of the German naval budget was calling forth strong criticisms from the opposition in the Reichstag.

Finally, in February, 1913, the German Admiral von Tirpitz stated that the ratio of 16 to 10 for the construction of battleships was acceptable to Germany. Mr. Churchill, who was head of the British admiralty, at once welcomed the change in Germany's attitude, and invited von Tirpitz to proclaim a "naval holiday." Later in the same year, when nothing came of the "naval holiday" suggestion, Churchill proposed (October 18, 1913) that Great Britain and Germany should agree to postpone for twelve months the laying down of the new ships in the 1914 program, provided that other powers would agree to do the same. Again, nothing followed from the proposal. Early in 1914, however, the British and German governments agreed to mutual discussions on naval matters. Such was the situation when the war broke out.

Although no agreement or convention on the limitation of armaments resulted, and the statements and speeches mentioned above may therefore seem utterly futile for our record, it is a fact that Great Britain and Germany seemed in the summer of 1914 to be on the verge of an agreement which would have done much to allay the ill-feeling which had grown up between the two countries. The question of the Bagdad railway and the development of Turkish Asia Minor was settled, and the door had been opened for serious negotiations for mutual limitation of armaments. The English people had come to accept the idea of a German navy, and the German people had learned to appreciate the reasons why Great Britain believed that the British navy must be supreme. What the course of events would have been had not the assassin's bullet killed the heir apparent to the Austrian throne, it is difficult to say. It is possible that the German diplomats, taking a leaf from Great Britain's recent international history, were planning for a general Entente with Great Britain based on the removal of the causes for disagreement; it is possible that the German government, foreseeing a continental war, was cultivating friendly relations with Great Britain in order to keep the British neutral; it is possible that these attempts at conciliation were but the first steps in an attempt on the part of Germany to remove the chief grievances between each of her more important enemies and herself.

Whatever Germany's ulterior motives, the negotiations were suddenly halted by the outbreak of the great European War.

CHAPTER III

THE OUTBREAK OF THE GREAT WAR

A. THE MURDERS AT SERAJEVO

JUNE 28, 1914, the Archduke Francis Ferdinand and his wife, the Duchess of Hohenberg, were assassinated in the Bosnian capital of Serajevo. The circumstances of the deed, as related in the Austro-Hungarian version, were as follows:

"The Archduke Francis Ferdinand and his wife, the Duchess of Hohenberg, were going to the City Hall to attend the official reception, when a bomb was thrown at them. It fell in the arms of the archduke, who with a simple movement threw it aside. This bomb exploded after the passage of the carriage. Count Boor-Waldeck and his aide-de-camp lieutenant-colonel Mirizzi, who were in an automobile following, were slightly injured, and several persons in the crowd pressing near the carriages were severely injured. The author of this attempt is a certain Kaprinovic, printer, native of Trebinge. He was immediately arrested.

"After the official reception at the City Hall, the archduke was returning to the government house when a second attempt was made with a Browning revolver. The archduke was struck in the face and the duchess in the abdomen. The archduke and the duchess were at once carried to the government house where they died. The author of the second attempt is a student of the 8th class in the lycée, a certain Princip, born at Grahovo. He was immediately arrested. The two assassins have been kept from the fury of the mob who wished to lynch them. The author of the attempt, Gravilo Princip, aged 19 years, born at Grahovo in the district of Livro (Bosnia), has stated to the police that he had studied for several years at Belgrade and that he had maintained for a long time the intention of killing a high personage to show his devotion to the nationalist cause.

"He waited until the prince passed on the quai General-Appel before making the attempt. Princip stated that the carriage of the archduke, returning from the city hall, slowed up at the corner of the street Francis Joseph. He, Princip, hesitated a second because the duchess was in the carriage. Then quickly fired two shots. He denies having accomplices.

"The printer Medeljko Kaprinovic, age twenty years, author of the first attempt, has stated to the police that he received the bomb from the hands of an anarchist in Belgrade whose name he does not know. He also declares that he had no accomplice. His attitude during the questioning of the police was cynical.

"Scarcely had the news of the attempt spread than mourning banners were hung at all the houses of the city. Grief is general throughout all classes of society. Order and calm reign everywhere in the district."

The inquiry set on foot at once by the Austro-Hungarian police developed the following facts: that both assassins were members of the notorious *Narodna Odbrana*, a Serbian secret society organized for the special purpose of carrying on pro-Serb revolutionary propaganda in the Austrian provinces of Bosnia and Herzegovina; that the two assassins were instigated by higher officials in the secret society, notably one Milan Ciganovich of the Serbian state railways, and by one Major Voija Tankositch of the Serbian army; and that Major Tankositch had secured from government arsenals the bombs and pistols used by the conspirators, had instructed these men in their use, and had arranged for the assassins' secret crossing of the Serbo-Bosnian frontier. The introduction of Ciganovich and Tankositch into the case, men who were connected with the Serbian government service, caused the Austro-Hungarian government to charge that the infamous *Narodna Odbrana* was "entirely dominated by the Belgrade foreign office," and that its anti-Austrian policy represented the ambitions of the Serbian government.

There is no reason to doubt the material truth of the Austro-Hungarian charges. The Serbian government undoubtedly desired the disintegration of the Austro-Hungarian empire that Serbia might annex the portions that were Serb in race, language, and traditions; many Serbian officials were surely members of the *Narodna Odbrana,* and were familiar with its aims and its methods; the Serbian people were the most ignorant, unprincipled, and savage of the Balkan people (except the Albanians) and their history had shown them willing to resort to intrigue and assassination to accomplish their ends. Austria-Hungary, of course, cannot be wholly freed from blame for the conditions which resulted in the tragedy, for her own intrigues in the Balkans (as outlined in previous chapters) were primarily responsible for the Serbian animosity; but in the first days after the assassination the sympathy of the great powers went out to the aged Francis Joseph. The introductory narrative of events in the British Blue Book states: "No crime has ever aroused deeper or more general horror throughout Europe; none has ever been less justified. Sympathy for Austria was universal. Both the government and the public opinion of Europe were ready to support her in any measures, however severe, which she might think it necessary to take for the punishment of the murderer and his accomplices."

The diplomacy of Austria-Hungary during the three weeks following the archduke's assassination is still shrouded in absolute mystery. Not until the archives are thrown open to the study of historians shall we know fully the various steps which that government took during this period. One slight glimpse is given us of Austria-Hungary's determination during this period to hold Serbia responsible for the outrage and to take revenge upon that little nation. In the German White Book we find the following passage:

"It was clear to Austria that it was not compatible with the dignity and the spirit of self-preservation of the monarchy to view idly any longer this agitation across the border. The imperial and royal government apprised Germany of this conception and asked for our opinion. With all our heart we were able to agree with our ally's estimate of the situation, and assure him that any action considered necessary to end the movement in Serbia directed against the conservation of the monarchy would meet with our approval. . . . We permitted Austria a completely free hand in her action toward Serbia, but have not participated in her preparations."

From this evidence, supplied by the German government, we are justified in deducing that within a short time after the tragedy the Austro-Hungarian government determined to take aggressive action against Serbia. She had wished to do this in 1913, as we have seen, but had been restrained by her allies Germany and Italy: her case in July of 1914 was much stronger, and she received the full approval of her most powerful ally in any measures she might take. All of her intentions and preparations, however, were kept a profound secret (except, apparently, for the notification to Germany indicated in the passage quoted above) and the chancelleries of Europe were led to expect nothing further than the regular punishment of the conspirators after due process of law. So completely deluded were the various diplomats that many of the most important of them proceeded to take their annual summer vacations: Sir Edward Goschen, the British ambassador to Berlin, absented himself from the German capital; the Russian ambassador to Berlin likewise turned over his office to a chargé d'affaires and went on a leave; President Poincaré and Premier Viviani of France made an official visit to the Czar at St. Petersburg; the Russian ambassador to Vienna left that city on the 20th of July for a fortnight's rest; and the German Emperor was cruising along the shores of Norway. Only the press of Austria-Hungary and Serbia reflected the shadow of the coming war. The newspapers in these two countries were filled with the most inflammatory recriminations.

B. THE AUSTRO-HUNGARIAN ULTIMATUM

Austria-Hungary's note to Serbia was presented July 23, and, since its contents were not revealed to the other chancelleries of Europe until it was actually delivered (unless possibly to Germany a few hours before) the seriousness of the situation was not realized until that date. The note was as follows:

"On the 31st of March, 1909, the Serbian Minister in Vienna, on the instructions of the Serbian government, made the following declaration to the Imperial and Royal Government:

"'Serbia recognizes that the *fait accompli* regarding Bosnia has not affected her rights, and consequently she will conform to the decisions that the Powers may take in conformity with Article 25 of the Treaty of Berlin. In deference to the advice of the Great Powers, Serbia undertakes to renounce from now onwards the attitude of protest and opposition which she has adopted with regard to the annexation since last autumn. She undertakes, moreover, to modify the direction of her policy with regard to Austria-Hungary and to live in future on good neighborly terms with the latter.'

"The history of recent years, and in particular the painful events of the 28th June last, have shown the existence of a subversive movement with the object of detaching a part of the territories of Austria-Hungary from the Monarchy. The movement which had its birth under the eye of the Serbian Government has gone so far as to make itself manifest on both sides of the Serbian frontier in the shape of acts of terrorism and a series of outrages and murders.

"Far from carrying out the formal undertakings contained in the declaration of the 31st March, 1909, the Royal Serbian Government has done nothing to repress these movements. It has permitted the criminal machinations of various societies and associations directed against the Monarchy, and has tolerated unrestrained language on the part of the press, the glorification of the perpetrators of outrages, and the participation of officers and functionaries in subversive agitation. It has permitted an unwholesome propaganda in public instruction, in short, it has permitted all manifestations of a nature to incite the Serbian population to hatred of the Monarchy and contempt of its institutions.

"This culpable tolerance of the Royal Serbian Government had not ceased at the moment when the events of the 28th June last proved its fatal consequences to the whole world.

"It results from the depositions and confessions of the criminal perpetrators of the outrage of the 28th June that the Serajevo assassinations were planned in Belgrade; that the arms and explosives with which the murderers were provided had been given to them by Serbian officers and functionaries belonging to the Narodna Odbrana; and finally that the passage into Bosnia of the criminals and their arms was organized and effected by the chiefs of the Serbian frontier service.

"The above-mentioned results of the magisterial investigation do not permit the Austro-Hungarian Government to pursue any longer the attitude of expectant forbearance which they have maintained for years in the face of the machinations hatched in Belgrade, and thence propagated in the territories of the Monarchy. The results, on the contrary, impose on them the duty of putting an end to the intrigues which form a perpetual menace to the tranquillity of the Monarchy.

"To achieve this end the Imperial and Royal Government see themselves compelled to demand from the Royal Serbian Government a formal assurance that they condemn this dangerous propaganda against the Monarchy; in other words, the whole series of tendencies, the ultimate aim of which is to detach from the Monarchy territories belonging to it, and that they undertake to suppress by every means this criminal and terrorist propaganda.

"In order to give a formal character to this undertaking the Royal Serbian Government shall publish on the front page of their Official Journal of the 13/26 July the following declaration:

"'The Royal Government of Serbia condemn the propaganda directed against Austria-Hungary — *i.e.* the general tendency of which the final aim is to detach from the Austro-Hungarian Monarchy territories belonging to it, and they sincerely deplore the fatal consequences of these criminal proceedings.

"'The Royal Government regret that Serbian officers and functionaries participated in the above-mentioned propaganda and thus compromised the good neighborly relations to which the Royal Government were solemnly pledged by their declaration of March 31, 1909.

"'The Royal Government, who disapprove and repudiate all idea of interfering or attempting to interfere with the destinies of the inhabitants of any part whatsoever of Austria-Hungary, consider it their duty formally to warn officers and functionaries and the whole population of the kingdom, that henceforward they will proceed with the utmost rigor against persons who may be guilty of such machinations, which they will use all their efforts to anticipate and suppress.'

" This declaration shall simultaneously be communicated to the Royal Army as an order of the day by His Majesty the King and shall be published in the Official Bulletin of the Army.

" The Royal Serbian Government further undertake:

" 1. To suppress any publication which incites to hatred and contempt of the Austro-Hungarian Monarchy and the general tendency of which is directed against its territorial integrity;

" 2. To dissolve immediately the society styled 'Narodna Odbrana,' to confiscate all its means of propaganda, and to proceed in the same manner against other societies and their branches in Serbia which engage in propaganda against the Austro-Hungarian Monarchy. The Royal Government shall take the necessary measures to prevent the societies dissolved from continuing their activities under another name and form;

" 3. To eliminate without delay from public instruction in Serbia, both as regards the teaching body and also as regards the methods of instruction, everything that serves, or might serve, to foment the propaganda against Austria-Hungary;

" 4. To remove from the military service, and from the administration in general, all officers and functionaries guilty of propaganda against the Austro-Hungarian Monarchy whose names and deeds the Austro-Hungarian Government reserve to themselves the right of communicating to the Royal Government;

" 5. To accept the collaboration in Serbia of representatives of the Austro-Hungarian Government for the suppression of the subversive movement directed against the territorial integrity of the Monarchy;

" 6. To take judicial proceedings against accessories to the plot of the 28th June who are on Serbian territory; delegates of the Austro-Hungarian Government will take part in the investigation relating thereto;

" 7. To proceed without delay to the arrest of Major Voija Tankositch and of the individual named Milan Ciganovitch, a Serbian State employee, who have been compromised by the results of the magisterial inquiry at Serajevo;

" 8. To prevent by effective measures the coöperation of the Serbian authorities in the illicit traffic in arms and explosives across the frontier, to dismiss and punish severely the officials of the frontier service at Schabatz and Loznica guilty of having assisted the perpetrators of the Serajevo crime by facilitating their passage across the frontier;

" 9. To furnish the Imperial and Royal Government with explanations regarding the unjustifiable utterances of high Serbian officials, both in Serbia and abroad, who, notwithstanding their official position, have not hesitated since the crime of 28th June to express themselves in interviews in terms of hostility to the Austro-Hungarian Government; and, finally,

"10. To notify the Imperial and Royal Government without delay of the execution of the measures comprised under the preceding heads.

"The Austro-Hungarian Government expect the reply of the Royal Government by 6 o'clock on Saturday evening the 25th July."

The communication of the contents of this note to the ministries of other powers awakened them at once to the gravity of the Austro-Hungarian ultimatum. The absent ambassadors sped back to their posts; the telegraphs began to hum with long messages between the different governments and their representatives; the German Kaiser cut short his Norwegian holiday and returned posthaste to Berlin. For there were provisions in the Austro-Hungarian ultimatum which no self-respecting independent state could possibly accept. The European diplomatic world realized, apparently, for the first time, that Austria-Hungary actually desired a war with Serbia. The dangers to European peace involved in a war between Austria-Hungary and Serbia were well recognized — behind Serbia loomed Russia, allied with Russia was France, against France stood Germany, and should Russia and France become actually engaged against Austria-Hungary and Germany there was no prophecy of what other nations would be drawn in. Austria-Hungary was consciously firing a train which led directly to the powder magazine of Europe.

i. *Austro-Hungarian and German Motives*

We must stop for a moment at this point to speculate upon the motives which underlay Austria-Hungary's ultimatum and Germany's support of her ally. Such speculation begins with the feeling caused by the Serajevo outrage, rapidly widens to the Austro-Hungarian relation toward the difficult Balkan problem, and leads us finally to the Austro-Hungarian and German view of the general European situation.

The Archduke Francis Ferdinand of Austria was a man of powerful physique and excellent mind. Although a man of few words, he had made it known that he favored a new and kindlier treatment of the subject peoples, especially of the Slavs, in the Austro-Hungarian empire. He passed, indeed, as a federalist, a believer in the establishment of a government of federated peoples in Austria-Hungary, in which each of the most important races should have local autonomy and representation in an imperial legislature. He was a forward-looking man, well equipped and well trained for the extremely difficult task of ruling the Austro-Hungarian dominions, a man upon whom the aged and beloved Francis Joseph depended for advice and assistance, and to whom the more liberal elements in the empire looked confidently for needed reforms. His assassination, therefore, not only struck down a prop of the existing government, but was a blow to the hopes of those who expected the increase of liberal institutions. To the personal grief of the emperor and the court circle was added the sincere sorrow of the liberals throughout all the country.

Yet the bitter anger aroused by the murder of the Archduke heir apparent would not alone have induced the Austro-Hungarian government to incur all the risks of forcing a war against Serbia. The Balkan situation resulting from the Balkan wars did not at all conform to the Austro-Hungarian plans, and the Serajevo tragedy furnished the best possible excuse for an attempt at a forcible readjustment. In the first of the Balkan wars the opinion of the imperial government favored Turkey, and Turkey lost; in the second war that opinion favored Bulgaria, and Bulgaria lost: the Austro-Hungarian government had in both cases "backed the wrong horse," as the phrase goes. In both the wars Russian public opinion and government opinion had been with the victors. The Treaty of Bucharest had enlarged Serbia and Rumania at the expense of Bulgaria, and had further pleased Russia and embittered Austria-Hungary. Thus the years 1912–1913 had seen an overwhelming increase of Russian prestige and influence in the Balkan regions, and a corresponding diminution of Austrian. We have already noted that in the fall of 1913 Austria-Hungary was ready and anxious to take measures to regain by a war against Serbia the advantages she had lost, and was restrained only by the united persuasion of her allies Italy and Germany: she now had, as a result of the assassination of the Archduke, a full warrant from her most powerful military ally to go to any lengths against Serbia. Hence she prepared by a single and bold stroke to punish Serbia and regain her influence in those regions in which, according to her policies, her interests were vital.

Her chances of success appeared excellent. Serbia had not recovered from the effects of the Balkan wars: her army was weakened; her stock of munitions and military equipment was temporarily exhausted; her finances were involved. Her government had not had the time to organize the new territory she had acquired by the Treaty of Bucharest; her forces were embarrassed by continual frontier difficulties on the borders of Albania. She was in no position to offer effective resistance. Although Austro-Hungarian statesmen unquestionably recognized the possibility of involving Russia in the conflict, they hoped that this result might be avoided. They knew that internal conditions in Russia were much disturbed — indeed, Russian economic life in the centers of industry was at the moment partially paralyzed by great strikes — and believed that the Slav power was in no position to enforce her protests by war. And again, already promised German support, they counted on the power of the united central Germanic powers overawing Russia, as had been the case in the

Bosnia-Herzegovina crisis of 1908. And they were tempted to believe that, even if Russia accepted the challenge of war, France and Great Britain would not rally to her assistance on a matter so far removed from their own vital interests as the Balkan issue. Some conclusions such as the above must have been reached by the Austro-Hungarian statesmen in their consideration of the political situation before they forwarded the fateful ultimatum of July 23, 1914.

The Emperor of Germany and his advisers likewise must have weighed carefully the European conditions before they were willing to guarantee to Austria "a completely free hand in her action toward Serbia." In addition to the facts presented above, which were of course taken into account by the German counsellors, certain other influences operated to render them willing at this time to accept the risk of war. Probably the chief of these was the general decline of German prestige in European international politics. We have referred already to the fact that the German leaders believed that Germany's very existence, located as she was between hostile powers, depended upon her being the leading power in Europe, upon her being able to cast the deciding vote in all questions of continental European politics. With peculiar short-sightedness, the Germans as a whole could not apparently appreciate why other states on the continent would not understand Germany's right to be the dominant power, and even took steps, as by alliances and treaties, to protect themselves against such domination. The Germans were so confident of their own political theory, and so proud of their own degree and kind of civilization, that they expected, seemingly, that the other states of Europe would cheerfully accept their superior power and influence in European councils. From 1870 to 1900 Germany had been successful in her politics: from 1900 to 1914 her prestige had steadily waned. The formation of the Triple Entente had seemed to her a deliberate attempt to encircle her with hostile nations;

the weaning of Italy away from the Triple Alliance was a shrewd and malicious effort to weaken her military power; the seizure of Morocco, the partition of Persia, and the thwarting of plans for the Bagdad railroad were all — in the German mind — parts of a deep and general European plan to choke Germany, to limit her influence, and to discredit her in the council of the powers. The need of a bold and determined stroke to restore her lost prestige was pressing. The present crisis was admirably suited for the purpose. It was a stroke in which her chief ally, Austria-Hungary, was vitally interested; and success in it would be the sharpest kind of a rebuff to Russia, the chief military bulwark of the hostile Entente.

Furthermore, the chances of success were promising from the German point of view. The central powers, thus unified in their policy, might even gain their end without a general war, just as they had in 1908. But if a general war were to come, the present moment was most favorable. The Russian strategic railroads were not completed, as they would be within two or three years; and Russian internal conditions, as mentioned before, were troubled. The effects of the new French three-year-service law were not yet felt in the French army; French political life was disturbed by the political revelations of a certain Caillaux trial; and the French minister of war had just acknowledged to the Chamber the unpreparedness of the French army. And across the English channel, the outbreak of civil war in Ireland was momentarily expected. The military assistance which Great Britain could offer at the beginning of a war was known to be negligible. In contrast to these conditions in the Entente countries, Germany and Austria-Hungary were united and ready. Austria-Hungary had already mobilized eight army corps on the Serbian frontier, and Germany, by the aid of her scientific system of strategic railroads, could mobilize either on the Russian or the French frontier with greater speed than her adversaries. The factors which make for success certainly favored Germany and Austria-Hungary.

And what did they count upon as the result of their success? For Austria-Hungary it would mean the humiliation of Serbia, the end of Serbian propaganda in Austro-Hungarian provinces, and the reinstatement of Austria-Hungary as the most influential nation in the affairs of the western Balkans. For Germany it would mean the resumption of her former proud status of political dictator on the continent of Europe, the humiliation of the threatening enemy to the east, Russia, and possibly a weakening of the bonds of the Triple Entente. To the statesmen of the central powers the advantages of success warranted the risk, and Austria-Hungary was committed to the fatal ultimatum.

ii. *The Serbian Reply*

This ultimatum was delivered July 23: an answer was demanded by six o'clock of July 25. The diplomats of the Powers were, therefore, given but a brief two days in which to work. They reached the conclusion at once that Serbia could not accept the demands as a whole, so they bent all their efforts toward preventing the actual outbreak of hostilities between the two countries. Their first step was to request Austria-Hungary to extend the time of the ultimatum in order to give all the nations an opportunity to study the nature of the evidence in the case. Russia made the strongest protest against the time limit, and Great Britain, France, and Italy seconded her efforts both at Vienna and through Berlin. Austria-Hungary, however, refused the request. The diplomats then turned their attention to Serbia and endeavored to influence the government of that state to make as conciliatory a reply as possible to the Austro-Hungarian note. Serbia's position was difficult: To accept Austria-Hungary's terms *in toto* would probably result in a popular revolution; to reject them would result in a war for which she was in no way prepared. Her government attempted a different course and threw itself upon the mercy of Russia: "We are ready to accept the Austro-Hungarian conditions which are compatible with the situation of an independent state," telegraphed the Serbian Prince Regent to the Russian Czar, "as well as those the acceptance of which may be advised by your Majesty." Russia thus practically dictated Serbia's reply to the Austro-Hungarian ultimatum.

This reply, which was handed to the Austro-Hungarian minister at Belgrade just two minutes before the time limit, was as follows:

"The Royal Serbian Government have received the communication of the Imperial and Royal Government of the 10th instant, and are convinced that their reply will remove any misunderstanding which may threaten to impair the good neighborly relations between the Austro-Hungarian Monarchy and the Kingdom of Serbia.

"Conscious of the fact that the protests, which were made both from the tribune of the National Skupchtina and in the declarations and actions of the responsible representatives of the State, — protests which were cut short by the declarations made by the Serbian government on the 18th (31st) March, 1909, — have not been renewed on any occasion as regards the great neighboring Monarchy, and that no attempt has been made since that time, either by the successive Royal Governments or by their organs, to change the political and legal state of affairs created in Bosnia and Herzegovina, the Royal Government call attention to the fact that in this connection the Imperial and Royal Government have made no representation except one concerning a school book, and that on that occasion the Imperial and Royal Government received an entirely satisfactory explanation. Serbia has several times given proofs of her pacific and moderate policy during the Balkan crisis, and it is thanks to Serbia and the sacrifice that she has made in the exclusive interests of European peace that that peace has been preserved. The Royal Government cannot be held responsible for manifestations of a private character, such as articles in the press and the peaceable work of societies — manifestations which take place in nearly all countries in the ordinary course of events, and which, as a general rule, escape official control. The Royal Government are all the less responsible, in view of the fact that at the time of the solution of a series of questions which arose between Serbia and Austria-Hungary they gave proof of a great readiness to oblige, and thus succeeded in settling the majority of these questions to the advantage of the two neighboring countries.

"For these reasons the Royal Government have been pained and surprised at the statements, according to which members of the Kingdom of Serbia are supposed to have participated in the preparations for the crime committed at Serajevo; the Royal Government expected to be invited to collaborate in an investigation of all that concerns this crime, and they were ready, in order to prove the entire correctness of their attitude, to take measures against any persons concerning whom representations were made to them. Falling in, therefore, with the desire of the Imperial and Royal Government, they are prepared to hand over for trial any Serbian subject, without regard to his situation or rank, of whose complicity in the crime of Serajevo proofs are forthcoming, and more especially they undertake to be caused to be published on the first page of the Journal official, on the date of the 13th (26th) July, the following declaration:

"'The Royal Government of Serbia condemn all propaganda which may be directed against Austria-Hungary, that is to say, all such tendencies as aim at ultimately detaching from the Austro-Hungarian Monarchy territories which form part thereof, and they sincerely deplore the baneful consequences of these criminal movements. The Royal Government regret that, according to the communication from the Imperial and Royal Government, certain Serbian officers and officials should have taken part in the above-mentioned propaganda, and thus compromised the good neighborly relations to which the Royal Serbian Government was solemnly engaged by the declaration of the 31st March, 1909, which declaration disapproves and repudiates all idea or attempt at interference with the destiny of the inhabitants of any part whatsoever of Austria-Hungary, and they consider it their duty to warn the officers, officials, and the entire population of the kingdom that henceforth they will take the most rigorous steps against all such persons as are guilty of such acts, to prevent and to repress which they will use their utmost endeavor.'

"This declaration will be brought to the knowledge of the Royal Army in an order of the day, in the name of His Majesty the King, by His Royal Highness the Crown Prince Alexander, and will be published in the next official army bulletin.

"The Royal Government further undertake:

"1. To introduce at the first regular convocation of the Skuptchina a provision into the press law providing for the most severe punishment of incitement to hatred or contempt of the Austro-Hungarian Monarchy, and for taking action against any publication the general tendency of which is directed against the territorial integrity of Austria-Hungary. The Government engage at the approaching revision of the Constitution to cause an amendment to be introduced into article 22 of the Constitution of such a nature that such publication may be confiscated, a proceeding at present impossible under the categorical terms of article 22 of the Constitution.

"2. The Government possess no proof, nor does the Imperial and Royal Government furnish them with any, that the 'Narodna Odbrana' and other similar societies have committed up to the present any criminal act of this nature through the proceedings of any of their members. Nevertheless the Royal Government will accept the demand of the Imperial and Royal Government, and will dissolve the 'Narodna Odbrana' Society and every other society which may be directing its efforts against Austria-Hungary.

"3. The Royal Serbian Government undertake to remove without delay from public educational establishments in Serbia all that serves or could serve to foment propaganda against Austria-Hungary, whenever the Imperial and Royal Government furnish them with facts and proofs of this propaganda.

"4. The Royal Government also agree to remove from military service all such persons as the judicial inquiry may have proved to be guilty of acts directed against the integrity of the territory of the Austro-Hungarian Monarchy, and they expect the Imperial and Royal Government to communicate to them at a later date the names and the acts of these officers and officials for the purposes of the proceedings which are to be taken against them.

"5. The Royal Government must confess that they do not clearly grasp the meaning or the scope of the demand made by the Imperial and Royal Government that Serbia shall undertake to accept the collaboration of the organs of the Imperial and Royal Government upon their territory, but they declare that they will admit such collaboration as agrees with the principle of international law, with criminal procedure, and with good neighborly relations.

"6. It goes without saying that the Royal Government consider it their duty to open an inquiry against all such persons as are, or eventually may be, implicated in the plot of the 15th (28th) June, and who happen to be within the territory of the kingdom. As regards the participation in this inquiry of Austro-Hungarian agents or authorities appointed for this purpose by the Imperial and Royal Government, the Royal Government cannot accept such an arrangement, as it would be a violation of the Constitution and of the law of criminal procedure; nevertheless, in concrete cases communications as to the result of the investigation in question might be given to the Austro-Hungarian agents.

"7. The Royal Government proceeded, on the very evening of the delivery of the note, to arrest Commandant Voija Tankositch. As regards Milan Ciganovitch, who is a subject of the Austro-Hungarian Monarchy and who up to the 15th (28th) June was employed (on probation) by the directorate of railways, it has not yet been possible to arrest him.

"The Austro-Hungarian Government are requested to be so good as to supply as soon as possible, in the customary form, the presumptive evidence of guilt, as well as the eventual proofs of guilt which have been collected up to the present, at the inquiry at Serajevo for the purposes of the later inquiry.

"8. The Serbian Government will reinforce and extend the measures which have been taken for the illicit traffic of arms and explosives across the frontier. It goes without saying that they will immediately order an inquiry and will severely punish the frontier officials on the Schabatz-Loznitza line, who have failed in their duty and allowed the authors of the crime of Serajevo to pass.

"9. The Royal Government will gladly give explanations of the remarks made by their officials, whether in Serbia or abroad, in interviews after the crime, which, according to the statement of the Imperial and Royal Government, were hostile toward the Monarchy, as soon as the Imperial and Royal Government have communicated to them the passages in question in these remarks, and as soon as they have shown that the remarks were actually made by the said officials, although the Royal Government will itself take steps to collect evidence and proofs.

"10. The Royal Government will inform the Imperial and Royal Government of the execution of the measures comprised under the above heads, in so far as this has not already been done by the present note, as soon as each measure has been ordered and carried out.

"If the Imperial and Royal Government are not satisfied with this reply, the Serbian Government, considering that it is not to the common interest to precipitate the solution of this question, are ready, as always, to accept a pacific understanding, either by referring this question to the decision of the International Tribunal of The Hague, or to the great powers which took part in the drawing up of the declaration made by the Serbian Government on the 18th (31st) March, 1909.

"Belgrade, July 12th (25th), 1914."

The Austro-Hungarian minister at Belgrade received the above note at 5:58 P.M., on June 25: he formally withdrew from Serbia on the 6:30 train the same evening. Acting, of course, under instructions from Vienna, he had at once severed diplomatic relations with Serbia as soon as a glance at the note showed that Serbia had not yielded absolutely and unqualifiedly to Austro-Hungarian demands. His withdrawal from Belgrade did not actually imply a declaration of war but was the usual preliminary step toward such. Serbia mobilized her troops and moved her government from the exposed border city of Belgrade to the interior town of Nish.

The publication of the Serbian reply produced a most favorable impression of Serbia's correct diplomatic attitude in the chancelleries of the great powers. With the exception of Germany and Austria-Hungary, all the states agreed that Serbia had gone as far as any independent and self-respecting state could go in accepting the Austro-Hungarian demands. The general impression of the Entente powers was that the Serbian reply should at least be treated as a basis for discussion and pause, and that if Austria-Hungary took offensive measures in the face of the conciliatory attitude of the little state, these indicated that she was determined to crush Serbia at all costs. Again strong representations were made to Austria-Hungary, both directly and through her German ally, to withhold action.

To the efforts to persuade her to accept the Serbian note as a basis for discussion, the Austro-Hungarian government replied by the statement that past incidents had shown the impossibility of crediting Serbia's pledges, and by the assertion that the hostile measures they were going to take had no aggressive tendency. Especially did the government endeavor to reassure Russia: Count von Berchtold, the Austro-Hungarian Minister of Foreign Affairs, informed the Russian representative at Vienna that the Dual monarchy entertained no thought of conquest of Serbia and would not claim Serbian territory, but was impelled by circumstances to check effectually Serbian intrigues. After three days of delay, Austria-Hungary delivered (July 28, 1914) to the Powers the following formal declaration of war against Serbia:

"In order to bring to an end the subversive intrigues originating from Belgrade and aimed at the territorial integrity of the Austro-Hungarian Monarchy, the Imperial and Royal Government delivered to the Royal Serbian Government a note in which a series of demands were formulated, for the acceptance of which a delay of forty-eight hours was allowed the Royal Government.

"The Royal Serbian Government not having answered this note in a satisfactory manner, the Imperial and Royal Government are obliged themselves to see to the safeguarding of their rights and interests, and for this purpose to have recourse to force of arms."

The Austro-Hungarian refusal to delay action and enter upon a general European discussion after the receipt of the Serbian note put the Dual empire definitely in the wrong. Before this refusal, great sympathy for her cause was felt in the European chancelleries. Undoubtedly they would have united in an agreement which would have guaranteed Serbia's correct attitude toward Austria-Hungary in the future, and which would have punished her for her laxity in permitting anti-Austrian propaganda to be fostered in her soil. But the Austro-Hungarian stubbornness in ignoring the greater issues involved, in disregarding the pleas of the other powers in Europe, and in persisting upon a course which led to a general European war, completely alienated the other powers.

In the meanwhile, the diplomats of the Entente, even before the declaration of war, had begun their efforts to prevent a general conflagration. They realized that the focus of their efforts must be upon the foreign office in Wilhelmstrasse, Berlin. Everything depended upon Germany's attitude. On July 26 Sir Edward Grey suggested the familiar expedient of an European Congress, and, already assured of Russian approval, telegraphed the French, Italian, and German governments requesting them to instruct their ambassadors in London to meet with him "in conference immediately for the purpose of discovering an issue which would prevent complications." The French and Italian governments at once accepted this proposal: von Jagow, the head of the German foreign office, with some quibbling over phraseology, rejected the proposal, adding, however (to the French ambassador, M. Cambon) "that he was ready to join England and France in a common effort, but that it was necessary to find a form for this intervention which he could accept, and that the Cabinets must come to an understanding on this point." When further efforts were made to move the German government, von Jagow refused to advise his ally (Austria-Hungary) to desist from her measures, and insisted that the diplomatic efforts should be directed toward a localization of the conflict.

With the declaration of war July 28, the crisis entered a new and more serious phase. As Austria-Hungary began to mobilize her troops, Russia responded by a mobilization in the provinces adjacent to the Austrian frontier. Diplomatic efforts, though continued during these trying hours, became of less importance than military measures. The Russian mobilization deeply stirred Germany. Although Russia officially informed Germany that its mobilization was in the southern districts alone, German consular reports to Berlin indicated that the preliminary steps were being taken for mobilization along the German frontier districts as well. On July 29 the German military attaché in

St. Petersburg reported to his government a conversation in which the chief of the General Staff of the Russian army assured him that no mobilization had been begun on the German border, but he commented that in view of the abundant and positive information which reached him about the calling out of reserves, he considered the conversation as an attempt to mislead the German government. Thus the issue had now become, not a question of diplomatic negotiation as to the justice of Austria-Hungary's demands upon, and action against, Serbia, but a question of the extent of military preparations on the part of Russia.

The menace of a general war was now, July 30, immediate. The diplomats frantically hurried messages over the wires in an endeavor to find a basis for successful negotiation. The Russian mobilization was, however, extended, with the natural result of bringing on the German mobilization. On July 31 the German chancellor dispatched the following telegram to the German ambassador at St. Petersburg:

"In spite of negotiations still pending and although we have up to this hour made no preparations for mobilization, Russia has mobilized her entire army and navy, hence also against us. On account of these Russian measures, we have been forced, for the safety of the country, to proclaim the threatening state of war, which does not yet imply mobilization. Mobilization, however, is bound to follow if Russia does not stop every measure of war against us and against Austria-Hungary within twelve hours, and notifies us definitely to that effect. Please to communicate this at once to M. Sazonoff and wire hour of communication."

This message was delivered to M. Sazonoff, the Russian foreign minister, at midnight on July 31. At the same time the German chancellor telegraphed to France asking the French government to state "whether it intends to remain neutral in a Russo-German war. Reply must be made in eighteen hours. Wire at once hour of inquiry. Utmost speed necessary."

At 12:52 P.M., the next day, August 1, 1914, von Bethmann-Hollweg, not having had an answer to his ultimatum of the night before, dispatched the following telegram to the German ambassador at St. Petersburg:

"In case the Russian Government gives no satisfactory answer to our demand, Your Excellency will please transmit at 5 o'clock this afternoon (Central European time) the following statement:

"The Imperial Government has endeavored from the beginning of the crisis to bring it to a peaceful solution. In accordance with a wish expressed to him by His Majesty the Emperor of Russia, His Majesty the Emperor of Germany, in coöperation with England, took upon himself the rôle of mediator between the Cabinets of Vienna and St. Petersburg; but Russia, without awaiting the outcome, proceeded to mobilize her entire land and naval forces.

"As a consequence of this threatening measure, occasioned by no military preparation on the part of Germany, the German Empire found itself confronted by a serious and imminent peril. If the Imperial Government had failed to meet this peril, it would have jeopardized the safety and even the existence of Germany. Consequently, the German Government was obliged to address the Government of the Emperor of all the Russias and insist upon the cessation of all these military measures. Russia not having thought it should reply to this demand, and having manifested by this attitude that her acts were directed against Germany, I have the honor by order of my Government to make known to Your Excellency the following communication:

"His Majesty the Emperor, my august sovereign, in the name of the Empire, takes up the defiance and considers himself in a state of war against Russia.

"I urgently ask you to wire the hour, according to Russian time, of arrival of these instructions, and of their carrying out.

"Kindly ask for your passports and hand over the protection of German interests to the American embassy."

On the same day the German ambassador in Paris telegraphed von Bethmann-Hollweg:

"Upon my repeated definite inquiry whether France would remain neutral in the event of a Russo-German war, The Prime Minister declared that France would do that which her interests dictated."

At 7:10 P.M., August 1, the German ambassador at St. Petersburg, in accordance with his instructions, presented the German declaration of war against Russia. Two days later, August 3, 1914, the German ambassador to France alleged several acts of French hostility on German soil, demanded his passports, and stated that: "The German empire considered itself in a state of war against France in consequence of the acts of this latter Power."

Thus was the issue carried to the point of war. The Central Powers had taken advantage of the Serajevo tragedy to attempt an attack upon Serbia which would have humiliated Russia, reëstablished Austro-Hungarian prestige throughout the Balkans, and placed Germany again indisputably in a predominant position in European international politics. They had incurred consciously the risk of involving Europe in war. Undoubtedly they had hoped that, when faced with the reality of war, Russia would yield as she had yielded in 1909 after the Bosnia-Herzegovina crisis, but after it became evident that she would not yield, the Central Powers made no determined and sincere effort to find a peaceful way out of the situation. They accepted the prospect of war, confident in their military strength.

CHAPTER IV

THE EXPANSION OF THE FIELD OF CONFLICT

THE evening of August 3, 1914, saw the nations of the original Dual Alliance in arms against those of the original Dual Entente — Germany and Austria-Hungary, allied since 1879, against France and Russia, allied since 1891. Could the war have been confined to these four great powers, it would still have been one of the greatest and most important wars in history: it was quickly recognized, however, even in those days when the action of the minute so absorbed all thought that men hardly found time to consider the future, that the friendships, alliances, and ententes in the world system would inevitably bring in other great states. The most immediate interest, of course centered in the action of Great Britain on the side of the Entente, and of Italy on that of the Alliance.

A. GREAT BRITAIN

The decision of Great Britain might have been delayed for a considerable period had not the military plans of the German staff provided for an attack upon France through Belgium. The neutrality of Belgium was guaranteed by the Treaty of April 19, 1839, which had been signed by Prussia and recognized as valid by Germany. Great Britain had long considered it a point of vital interest to maintain this neutrality of Belgium, for it was dangerous to her security to have established across the English channel a strong and possibly hostile nation ready to launch a force against English coasts at a moment's notice. It will be remembered that at the beginning of the Franco-German war of 1870, Great Britain exacted from both of the belligerents pledges to respect Belgian neutrality. In the present war, as soon as hostilities were inevitable, the British government proceeded to try to obtain knowledge of the attitude of the belligerents on this same question. On July 31 Sir Edward Grey informed the Belgian government that he had "asked the French and German governments separately if they were each of them ready to respect Belgian neutrality provided that no other Power violated it." The following day France officially pledged herself to respect Belgian neutrality: Germany was silent. On the evening of August 2, to the astonishment of the world, the German government, after alleging French violation of Belgian neutrality, delivered to the Belgian government an ultimatum demanding that German forces be permitted to cross Belgian territory. The Belgian government immediately refused the German demand and notified the other powers of Europe of her action. The following day the German ambassador handed to the Belgian minister an official statement that the German government "find themselves compelled to take — if necessary by force of arms — those measures of defense already foreshadowed as indispensable in view of the menace of France." On the same day German troops entered Belgian territory. Great Britain's response was immediate: August 4, Sir Edward Grey sent the following ultimatum to the British minister at Berlin:

"(Telegraphic) Foreign Office, August 4, 1914.

"We hear that Germany has addressed note to Belgian Minister for Foreign Affairs stating that German Government will be compelled to carry out, if necessary, by force of arms, the measures considered indispensable.

"We are also informed that Belgian territory has been violated at Gemmenich.

"In these circumstances, and in view of the fact that Germany declined to give the same assurances respecting Belgium as France gave last week in reply to our request made simultaneously at Berlin and Paris, we must repeat that request, and ask that a satisfactory reply to it and to my telegram of this morning be received here by 12 o'clock to-night. If not, you are instructed to ask for your passports, and to say that His Majesty's Government feel bound to take all steps in their power to uphold the neutrality of Belgium and the observance of a treaty to which Germany is as much a party as ourselves."

So important was Great Britain's entrance into the war that we yield to the temptation to quote in full the British Ambassador's report to Sir Edward Grey of what happened when he presented the British ultimatum to the German government:

"London, August 8, 1914.

"Sir:

"In accordance with the instructions contained in your telegram of the 4th instant I called upon the Secretary of State that afternoon and enquired, in the name of His Majesty's Government, whether the Imperial Government would refrain from violating Belgian neutrality. Herr von Jagow at once replied that he was sorry to say that his answer must be 'No,' as, in consequence of the German troops having crossed the frontier that morning, Belgian neutrality had been already violated. Herr von Jagow again went into the reasons why the Imperial Government had been obliged to take this step, namely, that they had to advance into France by the quickest and easiest way, so as to be able to get well ahead with their operations and endeavour to strike some decisive blow as early as possible. It was a matter of life and death for them, as if they had gone by the more southern route they could not have hoped, in view of the paucity of roads and the strength of the fortresses, to have got through without formidable opposition entailing great loss of time. This loss of time would have meant time gained by the Russians for bringing up their troops to the German frontier. Rapidity of action was the great German asset, while that of Russia was an inexhaustible supply of troops. I pointed out to Herr von Jagow that this fait accompli of the violation of the Belgian frontier rendered, as he would readily understand, the situation exceedingly grave, and I asked him whether there was not still time to draw back and avoid possible consequences both he and I would deplore. He replied that, for the reasons he had given me, it was now impossible for them to draw back.

"During the afternoon I received your further telegram of the same date, and, in compliance with the instructions therein contained, I again proceeded to the Imperial Foreign Office and informed the Secretary of State that unless the Imperial Government could give assurance by 12 o'clock that night that they would proceed no further with their violation of the Belgian frontier and stop their advance, I had been instructed to demand my passports and inform the Imperial Government that His Majesty's Government would have to take all steps in their power to uphold the neutrality of Belgium and the observance of a treaty to which Germany was as much a party as themselves.

"Herr von Jagow replied that to his great regret he could give no other answer than that which he had given me earlier in the day, namely, that the safety of the Empire rendered it absolutely necessary that the Imperial troops should advance through Belgium. I gave his Excellency a written summary of your telegram and, pointing out that you had mentioned 12 o'clock as the time when His Majesty's Government would expect an answer, asked him whether, in view of the terrible consequences which would necessarily ensue, it were not possible even at the last moment that this answer should be reconsidered. He replied that if the time given were even twenty-four hours or more, his answer must be the same. I said that in that case I should have to demand my passports. This interview took place at about 7 o'clock. In a short conversation which ensued Herr von Jagow expressed his poignant regret at the crumbling of his entire policy and that of the Chancellor, which had been to make friends with Great Britain, and then, through Great Britain, to get closer to France. I said that this sudden end to my work in Berlin was to me also a matter of deep regret and disappointment, but that he must understand that under the circumstances and in view of our engagements, His Majesty's Government could not possibly have acted otherwise than they had done.

"I then said that I should like to go and see the Chancellor, as it might be, perhaps, the last time I should have an opportunity of seeing him. He begged me to do so. I found the Chancellor very agitated. His Excellency at once began a harangue, which lasted about twenty minutes. He said that the step taken by

His Majesty's Government was terrible to a degree; just for a word — 'neutrality,' a word which in war time had so often been disregarded — just for a scrap of paper Great Britain was going to make war on a kindred nation who desired nothing better than to be friends with her. All his efforts in that direction had been rendered useless by this last terrible step, and the policy to which, as I knew, he had devoted himself since his accession to office had tumbled down like a house of cards. What we had done was unthinkable; it was like striking a man from behind while he was fighting for his life against two assailants. He held Great Britain responsible for all the terrible events that might happen. I protested strongly against that statement, and said that, in the same way as he and Herr von Jagow wished me to understand that for strategical reasons it was a matter of life and death to Germany to advance through Belgium and violate the latter's neutrality, so I would wish him to understand that it was, so to speak, a matter of 'life and death' for the honor of Great Britain that she should keep her solemn engagement to do her utmost to defend Belgium's neutrality if attacked. That solemn compact simply had to be kept, or what confidence could anyone have in engagements given by Great Britain in the future? The Chancellor said, 'But at what price will that compact have to be kept. Has the British Government thought of that?' I hinted to his Excellency as plainly as I could that fear of consequences could hardly be regarded as an excuse for breaking solemn engagements, but his Excellency was so excited, so evidently overcome by the news of our action, and so little disposed to hear reason that I refrained from adding fuel to the flame by further argument. As I was leaving he said that the blow of Great Britain joining Germany's enemies was all the greater that almost up to the last moment he and his Government had been working with us and supporting our efforts to maintain peace between Russia and Austria. I said that this was part of the tragedy which saw the two nations fall apart just at the moment when the relations between them had been more friendly and cordial than they had been for years. Unfortunately, notwithstanding our efforts to maintain peace between Russia and Austria, the war had spread and had brought us face to face with a situation which if we held to our engagements, we could not possibly avoid, and which unfortunately entailed our separation from our late fellow workers. He would readily understand that no one regretted this more than I.

"After this somewhat painful interview I returned to the embassy and drew up a telegraphic report of what had passed. This telegram was handed in at the Central Telegraph Office a little before 9 P.M. It was accepted by that office, but apparently never dispatched.

"At about 9:30 P.M. Herr von Zimmerman, the Under-Secretary of State, came to see me. After expressing his deep regret that the very friendly official and personal relations between us were about to cease, he asked me casually whether a demand for passports was equivalent to a declaration of war. I said that such an authority on international law as he was known to be must know as well or better than I what was usual in such cases. I added that there were many cases where diplomatic relations had been broken off, and, nevertheless, war had not ensued; but that in this case he would have seen from my instructions, of which I had given Herr von Jagow a written summary, that His Majesty's Government expected an answer to a definite question by 12 o'clock that night and that in default of a satisfactory answer they would be forced to take such steps as their engagements required. Herr Zimmerman said that that was, in fact, a declaration of war, as the Imperial Government could not possibly give the assurance required either that night or any other night.

"In the meantime, after Herr Zimmerman left me, a flying sheet, issued by the *Berliner Tageblatt*, was circulated stating that Great Britain had declared war against Germany. The immediate result of this news was the assemblage of an exceedingly excited and unruly mob before His Majesty's Embassy. The small force of police which had been sent to guard the embassy was soon overpowered, and the attitude of the mob became most threatening. We took no notice of this demonstration as long as it was confined to noise, but when the crash of glass and the landing of cobble stones into the drawing-room, where we were all sitting, warned us that the situation was getting unpleasant, I telephoned to the Foreign Office an account of what was happening. Herr von Jagow at once informed the Chief of Police, and an adequate force of mounted police, sent with great promptness, very soon cleared the street. From that moment on we were well guarded, and no more direct unpleasantness occurred.

"After order had been restored Herr von Jagow came to see me and expressed his most heartfelt regrets at what had occurred. He said that the behavior of his countrymen had made him feel more ashamed than he had words to express. It was an indelible stain on the reputation of Berlin. He said that the flying sheet circulated in the streets had not been authorized by the Government; in fact, the Chancellor had asked him by telephone whether he thought that such a statement should be issued, and he had replied, 'Certainly not, until the morning.' It was in consequence of his decision to that effect that only a small force of police had been sent to the neighborhood of the embassy, as he had thought that the presence of a large force would inevitably attract attention and perhaps lead to disturbances. It was the 'pestilential "Tageblatt,"' which had somehow got hold of the news, that had upset his calculations. He had heard rumors that the mob had been excited to violence by gestures made and missiles thrown from the embassy, but he felt sure that that was not true (I was able soon to assure him that the report had no foundation whatever), and even if it was, it was no excuse for the disgraceful scenes which had taken place. He feared that I would take home with me a sorry impression of Berlin manners in moments of excitement. In fact, no apology could have been more full and complete.

"On the following morning, the 5th of August, the Emperor sent one of his Majesty's aides-de-camp to me with the following message:

"'The Emperor has charged me to express to your Excellency his regret for the occurrence of last night, but to tell you at the same time that you will gather from these occurrences an idea of the feelings of his people respecting the action of Great Britain in joining with other nations against her old allies of Waterloo. His Majesty also begs that you will tell the King that he has been proud of the titles of British Field-Marshal and British Admiral, but that in consequence of what has occurred he must now at once divest himself of those titles.'

"I would add that the above message lost none of its acerbity by the manner of its delivery.

"On the other hand, I should like to state that I received all through this trying time nothing but courtesy at the hands of Herr von Jagow and the officials of the Imperial Foreign Office. At about 11 o'clock on the same morning Count Wedel handed me my passports — which I had earlier in the day demanded in writing — and told me that he had been instructed to confer with me as to the route which I should follow for my return to England. He said that he had understood that I preferred the route via the Hook of Holland to that via Copenhagen; they had therefore arranged that I should go by the former route, only I should have to wait until the following morning. I agreed to this, and he said that I might be quite assured that there would be no repetition of the disgraceful scenes of the preceding night as full precautions would be taken. He added that they were doing all in their power to have a restaurant car attached to the train, but it was rather a difficult matter. He also brought me a charming letter from Herr von Jagow couched in the most friendly terms. The day was passed in packing up such articles as time allowed.

"The night passed quietly without any incident. In the morning a strong force of police was posted along the usual route to the Lehrter Station, while the embassy was smuggled away in taxi-cabs to the station by side streets. We there suffered no molestation whatever, and avoided the treatment meted out by the crowd to my Russian and French colleagues. Count Wedel met us at the station to say good-bye on behalf of Herr von Jagow and to see that all the arrangements ordered for our comfort had been properly carried out. A retired Colonel of the Guards accompanied the train to the Dutch frontier and was exceedingly kind in his efforts to prevent the great crowds which thronged the platforms at every station where we stopped from insulting us; but beyond the yelling of patriotic songs and a few jeers and insulting gestures we had really nothing to complain of during our tedious journey to the Dutch frontier.

"Before closing this long account of our last days in Berlin I should like to place on record and bring to your notice the quite admirable behavior of my staff under the most trying circumstances possible. One and all, they worked night and day with scarcely any rest, and I cannot praise too highly the cheerful zeal with which counsellor, naval and military attachés, secretaries, and the two young attachés buckled to their work and kept their nerve with often a yelling mob outside, and inside hundreds of British subjects clamouring for advice and assistance. I was proud to have such a staff to work with, and feel most grateful to them all for the valuable assistance and support, often exposing them to considerable personal risk, which they so readily and cheerfully gave me.

"I should also like to mention the great assistance rendered to us all by my American colleague, Mr. Gerard, and his staff. Undeterred by the hooting and hisses with which he was often greeted by the mob on entering and leaving the embassy, his Excellency came repeatedly to see me to ask how he could help us and to make arrangements for the safety of stranded English subjects. He extricated many of these from extremely difficult situations at some personal risk to himself, and his calmness and savoir-faire and his firmness in dealing with the Imperial authorities gave full assurance that the protection of British subjects and interests could not have been left in more efficient and able hands.

"I have, etc.,

"W. E. GOSCHEN."

In accordance with the terms of her ultimatum, Great Britain declared war upon Germany as of 11 A.M., August 5.

We may insert a few words at this point concerning Germany's motives for the infringement upon Belgian neutrality. These motives, so far as we can judge from the knowledge we have, were almost exclusively military. Germany's situation exposed her to attack upon two sides, from Russia on the east and from France on the west. It was an accepted fact, however, that Russian mobilization would be relatively slow and inefficient, whereas the French mobilization would be as rapid as that of Germany. To insure certain prospects of success according to the German plan, therefore, it was essential to crush France first and then allow sufficient time and free great forces to withstand the Russian hordes in the east. A direct attack against France across the Franco-German border, however, would encounter the enormously strong line of fortifications especially prepared by the French for their defense, and would be marching the German army directly against the line of mobilization of the French forces. Such an attack would be costly in time and in men, and would not be certain of success. An attack through Belgium, on the contrary, would encounter only the weak Belgian army, would have the element of surprise, and (where made with great rapidity) would catch the mobilizing French armies upon an exposed flank. The French mobilization, elaborately planned for the line from Toul to Belfort, could not be changed at a moment's notice, but had to be carried out in accordance with a hard and fast daily program. The German staff counted confidently on the speed and surprise of the German attack, and the resulting disorganization and confusion in the French armies, to insure a complete success in this campaign and leave them free to turn against Russia.

In the face of this probability of quick success, the Germans ignored the moral issue involved in the infringement of Belgian neutrality. Their leaders, realizing that treaties had often been disregarded in the past, that no nation could hold up a record of consistent adherence to the highest standards of international honor where its vital interests were at stake, went on the principle that necessity knows no law. Their statesmen acknowledged the wrong: von Bethmann-Hollweg in his famous speech in the Reichstag August 5, 1914, said:

> "We have been forced into a state of self-defense, and the necessity of self-defense knows no other law. Our troops have occupied Luxemburg, and have perhaps already been obliged to enter Belgian territory. This is against the rules of international law. . . . We were obliged to disregard the protest of the Luxemburg and Belgian government. For the wrong we have done thereby we shall try to atone, as soon as our military end is obtained."

The German act in overrunning this relatively defenseless country stirred the conscience of the whole civilized world. It drove England into instant hostilities, and gave her a moral issue of telling effect in enlisting the sympathy of neutrals. It gave the war from its beginning a broader and higher nature than that of merely one of the many European conflicts on issues of European politics: the forceful subjugation of Belgium in the minds of many, especially among the neutrals, stamped the German diplomacy, policy, and military strategy as of a peculiarly barbarous and immoral character. The moral handicap incurred by this first act of the war more than outweighed any temporary military advantage they might gain. Though German apologists have tried to prove their country's act justified on other grounds, especially by bringing forward their evidence that France and England contemplated the violation of Belgian neutrality in operations against Germany under certain contingencies, they have been unable to obliterate the anti-German feeling incited at the beginning. The world at large has never accepted any justification for German ruthlessness in Belgium.

Two other nations now quickly joined hostilities, little Montenegro, because of her blood kinship with Serbia, and Japan, because of her treaty obligations with Great Britain. Montenegro had cast its fortunes uniformly with Serbia in the Balkan politics of recent years. On August 7, 1914, it followed the popular demands and the interests of its leaders by declaring war upon Austria-Hungary.

The British-Japanese alliance was originally formed in 1905 and revised and reaffirmed in 1911. Originally entered into by Great Britain for the purpose of relieving her of part of the burden of safeguarding her far eastern possessions against attack, and by Japan for the purpose of securing her from possible Russian revenge for defeats in the Russo-Japanese war, it provided for guarantees of the maintenance of general peace in eastern Asia and India, for the preservation of the independence and territorial integrity of China, and of the principle of equal opportunities for the commerce and industry of all nations in that country, for the security of the territorial rights and special interests of the two powers in Eastern Asia and India, and further — of special importance — for the assistance of each nation to the other in case one is involved in war by reason of unprovoked attack or aggressive action to defend its territorial rights or special interests. In accordance with this last-mentioned provision, Japan decided that Germany was the aggressor and declared war against her August 23, 1914.

One nation, Portugal, was directly influenced by Great Britain's participation to enter the war, although she did not take the step for a year and a half. The alliance between Portugal and England dated from the Napoleonic period. In 1898 treaties were made public under the conditions of which each party agreed not to give assistance to a Power attacking the other, or to offer asylum to the enemies of the other. Early in 1916 the British government apparently desired the direct participation of Portugal in the war, possibly that Portuguese troops in Africa might assist in conquering the German colonies. Portugal, on her part, was willing to enter the war, not only because of her long-sustained friendship with Great Britain, but because of her expectation of increasing her colonial domain by her conquests. Consequently, Portugal formally declared war upon Germany March 9, 1916.

B. ITALY

The attitude of Italy, the third member of the Triple Alliance, was complicated by the conflict of her aims with those of Austria-Hungary, and by her peculiarly defenseless position in the Mediterranean. When Italy became united and free, by the wars of 1859 and 1866, and by the seizure of Rome in 1870, she had to be content with less territory to the north and east than she desired. The districts of Trent and Trieste, including the important harbor of Trieste, were predominantly Italian in population and sentiment, but Italy was forced to leave them in the hands of Austria-Hungary. "*Italia Irredenta,*" as these territories were called in Italian circles, formed an issue in the politics of the peninsula: patriots looked forward to the time when they would be united with Italy. Yet it was recognized that Austria-Hungary would never yield these lands except by force. The city of Trieste, especially, was valuable to Austria-Hungary as her only great seaport.

The Albanian country also presented a conflict of interests. Austria-Hungary considered the eastern coast of the Adriatic as directly within her sphere of political influence and undoubtedly looked forward to its annexation in due time. Italian statesmen, however, had conceived the idea of establishing their control over an important part of southern Albania, including the fine harbor of Avlona. The advantage of the possession of Avlona for Italy would be that it would insure her the complete control of the Adriatic Sea. She could stretch her navy from her own shore to the Albanian port and absolutely prevent the entrance or egress of hostile ships.

In addition to this conflict of interests between Italy and one of her colleagues in the Triple Alliance, her geographical position prevented her from casting in her lot with the Central Powers and exposing herself to the attack of England and France. The Italian peninsula juts out into the Mediterranean Sea. The coast line is very long and exposed. The fleets of France and Great Britain, either one far more powerful than the Italian navy, had from the opening of hostilities complete control of the Mediterranean. If Italy cast in her lot with the Central Powers, the immediate result would be the paralysis of her commerce, the loss of Tripoli for which she had spent blood and treasure so recently, and possibly invasion from France. Self-preservation dictated neutrality at least.

During the negotiations which ensued preliminary to the outbreak of war, Italian statesmen bent every effort toward the maintenance of peace. When in spite of their efforts and the efforts of other governments, war became imminent, Italy took the stand that, inasmuch as the action taken by Austria-Hungary was aggressive, the bonds of the Triple Alliance did not hold her. The following communication sent by the French ambassador to Rome to the French government explains Italy's decision:

"Rome, August 1, 1914.

"I went to see the Marquis di San Giuliano this morning at half-past eight, in order to get precise information from him as to the attitude of Italy in view of the provocative acts of Germany and the results which they may have.

"The Minister for Foreign Affairs answered that he had seen the German Ambassador yesterday evening. Herr von Flotow had said to him that Germany had requested the Russian Government to suspend mobilization, and the French Government to inform them of their intentions; Germany had given France a time limit of eighteen hours and Russia a time limit of twelve hours.

"Herr von Flotow as a result of this communication asked what were the intentions of the Italian Government.

"The Marquis de San Giuliano answered that as the war undertaken by Austria was aggressive and did not fall within the purely defensive character of the Triple Alliance, particularly in view of the consequences which might result from it according to the declaration of the German Ambassador, Italy could not take part in the war.

"Barrère."

As the war developed, immense pressure was brought by the Entente powers to persuade Italy to join them. What arguments they used and what inducements they offered are, of course, not definitely known, but it is probable that the promise of Italia Irredenta was given. Popular opinion in Italy reinforced the efforts of the Entente allies. The government finally yielded, and, after negotiations with Austria-Hungary in the endeavor to persuade her to give up peaceably the territory in question, Italy declared war on Austria-Hungary May 23, 1915.

The tiny republic of San Marino naturally cast her lot with Italy and declared war a few days later.

In the Balkans, the outbreak of the Great War dimmed every other interest. Each of the nations felt that the continuance of the war for any considerable length of time was certain to involve it, and that the results of the war were all-important upon their future fortunes. Great speculation attached to the attitude of Turkey. The German element had builded well, however, and soon gained control of the situation. Turkey "bought" the German warships *Goeben* and *Breslau*, which, after committing depredations in the Mediterranean in September and October of 1914, had fled to Constantinople pursued to the Dardanelles by the allies. Such a purchase in time of war was a questionable proceeding. Still keeping the German crews on board, the Turkish government (under control of the German element) sent the warships forth upon a raiding expedition into the Black Sea. On November 2 they bombarded the defenses of Odessa, and sank a number of Russian ships in the harbor. Russia at once declared a state of war with Turkey, and Great Britain and France followed suit by a declaration of war against the Porte (Great Britain, November 5, France, November 6, 1914). On November 25 the Porte proclaimed a Jehad, or Holy War, against the Entente Powers.

In the northern Balkans, conflicting influences struggled to gain predominance in Bulgaria and Rumania. The Entente Powers were badly handicapped in Bulgaria from the beginning by the fact that they (especially Russia) had sympathized with Serbia and Rumania in their attack upon Bulgaria in the Second Balkan War, and had accepted without protest the iniquitous treaty of Bucharest. The Central Powers, on the other hand, had the advantage of having sympathized with Bulgaria in this same war, and Austria-Hungary had protested against the treaty which ended it. Furthermore, the animosity between the Bulgars and the Serbs was acute, actually more intense than that between the Bulgars and the Turks. The fact that the Serbs were on the Entente side, therefore, was in itself a motive for Bulgarian adhesion to the Central Powers. After long delay, the Bulgarian government took its final decision by a declaration of war againt Serbia, October 14, 1915.

In Rumania, the diplomats of the Entente allies were more successful. Rumania, like Italy, coveted a part of the Austro-Hungarian dominions. The rich and populous district of Transylvania, bordering on Rumania, was inhabited by people of Rumanian race, speech, and traditions. We cannot know at present by what treaty engagements the Entente allies induced Rumania to cast in her lot with them, but it is reasonable to suppose that they offered in the event of their success the whole of Transylvania to the Balkan state. The negotiations lasted for many months, Rumania apparently waiting until she felt sure of the success of the allied cause and of active assistance from Russia. Finally, on August 27, 1916, Rumania declared war against Austria-Hungary.

Thus at the close of 1916, the alignment of powers was as follows:

Great Britain		Germany
France		Austria-Hungary
Russia	vs.	Turkey
Italy		Bulgaria
San Marino		
Belgium		
Portugal		
Serbia		
Montenegro		
Rumania		
Japan		

The progress of the war up to this time, December 31, 1916, had been, so far as the fighting in Europe was concerned, almost uninterruptedly favorable to the central powers. Their armies had overrun Belgium and the immensely rich northern districts of France; they had conquered Serbia and Montenegro and a large part of Rumania; they had pushed forward through Warsaw to the boundaries of Poland; they had held the Dardanelles against attack by land and sea; they had barred the Italians from

Trent and Trieste; and they had captured the first British expedition sent against Bagdad at Kut-el-Amara. Their only losses were in their colonial territories, a small portion of southern Alsace, and the eastern portion of Galicia.

And yet the military situation did not represent accurately the chances of ultimate victory. The resources of the allied powers were so much greater than those of the central powers that the element of time was constantly favorable to the former. Great Britain awoke to a realization that in the success of the allied cause was her salvation as a great nation. The British navy, which had swept German commerce from the seas in the first few weeks of the conflict, was now set to the task of blockading every ingress to Germany in the endeavor to starve the most powerful of the central powers into submission. The British government, which had adopted conscription during the year, prepared to send millions of trained soldiers to the firing line in France. The British treasury was open to all the enemies of Germany. Supported by British ships, men, and money in limitless measure, the allied powers discounted the existing military situation and looked forward confidently to final success.

The German government, though naturally inclined to emphasize their military successes, were not blind to the fact that Great Britain's resources, applied continuously over a long period, would mean German defeat. They realized that Great Britain had become the bulwark of the allied coalition, that their other enemies would quickly be forced to an ignominious peace could Great Britain's assistance be removed.

Inspired by this knowledge, and using certain questionable acts in the British blockade as a pretext, the German government in the early spring of 1917 declared a submarine blockade of the British isles. They intended to sink all ships going to or coming from Great Britain, whether these ships were British or foreign. Their expectation was that the interruption of supplies of food and munitions would in a short time force Great Britain to submit.

The execution of this submarine warfare quickly brought the United States into the war. After brief negotiations and a final warning, the United States declared war against Germany as of date April 6, 1917. The United States government at once took measures to put her great potential strength into condition to be of real assistance to the allies in the struggle.

Within the next few months, Liberia, Cuba, China, and Siam broke off relations with Germany. Although the military strength of these nations was negligible, the moral effect of their declarations against German methods was considerable. More and more Germany was seen to occupy in the eyes of the world at large the position of an outlaw among nations — a position gained by her disregard of all the dictates of humanity in her methods of waging war.

The Great War has now entered upon its fourth year, with its ever-increasing waste of life and treasure. It requires no gift of prophecy to state that it will be considered in the future as the death throes of an old era and the birth throes of a new. One definite stage of history will have ended with the conclusion of peace. A new stage will begin, one whose character will be largely determined by the wisdom and justice of the diplomats who assemble in the congress at the termination of The Great War.

LIST OF REFERENCE BOOKS

[Excellent bibliographies for a short general history are readily accessible in Hazen's "Europe since 1815" and Hayes' "Political and Social History of Modern Europe." The following list contains only a few of the more important and illuminating reference books.]

GENERAL HISTORIES

(Arranged Alphabetically)

ANDREWS, C. M. Contemporary Europe, Asia, and Africa, 1871–1901 (Vol. XX in History of all Nations).

ANDREWS, C. M. The Historical Development of Modern Europe from the Congress of Vienna to the Present Time (1898). 2 vols.

BROWNING, O. A History of the Modern World.

CAMBRIDGE MODERN HISTORY. Vols. XI, XII.

FYFFE, C. A. A History of Modern Europe, 1792–1878.

GOOCH, G. P. History of Our Time, 1885–1911.

HAWKESWORTH, C. E. M. The Last Century in Europe, 1814–1910.

HAYES, C. J. H. A Political and Social History of Modern Europe, Vol. II.

HAZEN, C. D. Europe since 1815.

HERTSLET, SIR E. The Map of Europe by Treaty, Vols. II and III.

MARRIOTT, J. A. R. The Remaking of Modern Europe, 1789–1878.

MURDOCK, H. The Reconstruction of Europe.

PHILLIPS, W. A. Modern Europe, 1815–1899.

ROBINSON (J. H.) and BEARD (C. A.). The Development of Modern Europe.

ROSE, J. H. The Development of the European Nations, 1870–1900.

SCHWILL, F. A Political History of Modern Europe from the Reformation to the Present Day (1911).

SEIGNOBOS, C. A Political History of Europe since 1814.

INTERNATIONAL ISSUES

ALBIN, P. La guerre allemande: d'Agadir à Serajevo, 1911–1914.

ALBIN, P. Les grands traités politiques, 1815–1912.

DEBIDOUR, A. Histoire diplomatique de l'Europe, 1814–1878, Vol. II.

DICKINSON, G. L. The European Anarchy.

FULLERTON, W. M. Problems of Power: a Study of International Politics from Sadowa to Kirk-Kilissé.

GIBBONS, H. A. The New Map of Europe, 1911–1914: the Story of the Recent European Diplomatic Crises and Wars and of Europe's Present Catastrophe.

HOBSON, J. A. Imperialism: a Study.

LIPPMANN, W. The Status of Diplomacy.

MAHAN, A. T. Armament and Arbitration, or, the Place of Force in the International Relations of States.

REINSCH, P. S. World Politics at the End of the Nineteenth Century.

SEYMOUR, C. The Diplomatic Background of the War, 1870–1914.

BARCLAY, SIR T. Thirty Years: Anglo-French Reminiscences, 1876–1906.

CRAMB, J. A. The Origins and Destiny of Imperial Britain and Nineteenth-century Europe.

JOHNSTON, SIR H. Commonsense in Foreign Policy.

LÉMONON, E. L'Europe et la politique brittanique, 1882–1911.

PERRIS, G. H. Our Foreign Policy and Sir Edward Gray's Failure.

CRAMB, J. A. Germany and England.

SAROLEA, C. The Anglo-German Problem.

SCHMITT, B. E. England and Germany.

MAURICE, J. F. The Franco-German War. Translated from Pflugk-Hartung's Krieg und Sieg.

MOLTKE, H. VON. Franco-German War of 1870–1871. Translated by C. Bell and H. W. Fisher.

PINON, R. France et Allemagne, 1870–1913.

TARDIEU, A. France and the Alliances: the Struggle for the Balance of Power.

SOREL, A. Histoire diplomatique de la guerre franco-allemande.

BERNHARDI, F. VON. Germany and the Next War. Translated by A. H. Powles.

FRIED, A. H. The German Emperor and the Peace of the World.

FROBENIUS, H. The German Empire's Hour of Destiny.

MACH, E. VON. Germany's Point of View.

MACH, E. VON. What Germany Wants.

REVENTLOW, E. ZU. Deutschlands auswärtige Politik, 1888–1913.

ROHRBACH. Germany's Isolation.

TREITSCHKE, H. VON. Germany, France, Russia, and Islam.

USHER, R. G. Pan-Germanism.

CHÉRADAME, A. L'Europe et la question d'Autriche au seuil du XXe siècle.

DRIAULT, É. La question d'orient depuis ses origines jusqu'à nos jours.
DUGGAN, S. P. H. The Eastern Question: a Study in Diplomacy.
HOLLAND, T. E. The European Concert in the Eastern Question: a Collection of Treaties and Other Public Acts.
VILLARI, L., editor. The Balkan Question (1905).
SETON-WATSON, R. W. (pseudonym, Scotus-Viator). The Balkans, Italy, and the Adriatic.
TARDIEU, A. La conférence d'Algésiras.
DIERCKS, G. Die Marokkofrage und die Konferenz von Algeciras.
TARDIEU, A. La conférence d'Algésiras: histoire diplomatique de la crise marocaine.
TARDIEU, A. Le mystère d'Agadir.
BARCLAY, SIR T. The Turco-Italian War and Its Problems.
ASAKAWA, K. The Russo-Japanese Conflict, Its Causes and Issues.
BRINKLEY, F., and KIKUCHI. A History of the Japanese People from the Earliest Times to the End of the Meiji Era (1915).
BROWNE, E. G. The Persian Revolution of 1905–1909.
DOUGLAS, SIR R. K. Europe and the Far East.
DRIAULT, É. La question d'extrême orient.
ALLEN, G. H., WHITEHEAD, H. C., and CHADWICK, F. E. The Great War.
BUCHAN, T. Nelson's History of the War.
BULLARD, A. The Diplomacy of the Great War.
COLLECTED DIPLOMATIC DOCUMENTS RELATING TO THE OUTBREAK OF THE EUROPEAN WAR. Published by Harrison & Sons, London.
FISHER, H. A. L. The War, Its Causes and Its Issues.
GUERRE DE 1914: documents officielles, textes législatifs et réglementaires.
HEADLAM, J. W. History of Twelve Days, July 24–August 4, 1914.
HELMOLT, H. F. Die geheime Vorgeschichte des Weltkrieges.
LONDON TIMES. History of the War.
MANCHESTER GUARDIAN. History of the War.
PRICE, M. P. The Diplomatic History of the War.
ROSE, J. H. The Origins of the War (1914).
SIMONDS, F. H. The Great War.
STOWELL, E. C. The Diplomacy of the War of 1914.

GOVERNMENT

DAWSON, W. H. Municipal Life and Government in Germany.
DODD, W. F. Modern Constitutions.
DRIAULT, É. Les problèmes politiques et sociaux à la fin du XIXe siècle.
JAMES, H. G. Principles of Prussian Administration.

KRÜGER, FRITZ-K. Government and Politics of the German Empire.
LESTRADE, C. DE. Les monarchies de l'empire allemand, organisation constitutionelle et administrative.
LOWELL, A. L. Government and Parties in Continental Europe. 2 vols.
LOWELL, A. L. The Governments of France, Italy, and Germany.
LOWELL, A. L. The Government of England.
OGG, F. A. The Governments of Europe.

SOCIAL AND ECONOMIC PROBLEMS

ASHLEY, P. Modern Tariff History: Germany — United States — France.
BROOKS, J. G. Compulsory Insurance in Germany.
DAWSON, W. H. Bismarck and State Socialism.
DAWSON, W. H. Protection in Germany, a History of German Fiscal Policy during the XIX Century.
DAWSON, W. H. Social Insurance in Germany, 1883–1911.
HARLEY, J. H. Syndicalism.
HELFFERICH, K. Germany's Economic Progress and National Wealth, 1888–1913.
HOWARD, E. D. The Cause and Extent of the Recent Industrial Progress of Germany.
LOUIS, P. Le syndicalisme européen.
OGG, F. A. Economic Development of Modern Europe.
OGG, F. A. Social Progress in Contemporary Europe.
ORTH, S. P. Socialism and Democracy in Europe.
SNOWDEN, P. Socialism and Syndicalism.
STATISTICS FOR GREAT BRITAIN, GERMANY, AND FRANCE, 1867–1909. (U. S. Senate Document No. 578, Washington, D. C., 1910.)

COLONIAL PROBLEMS

ASHMEAD-BARTLETT, E. The Passing of the Shereefian Empire.
GIBBONS, H. A. The New Map of Africa, 1900–1916: a History of European Colonial Expansion and Colonial Diplomacy.
HARRIS, N. D. Intervention and Colonization in Africa.
HERTSLET, SIR E. The Map of Africa by Treaty. 3 vols.
JOHNSTON, SIR H. M. A History of the Colonization of Africa by Alien Races.
KELTIE, J. S. The Partition of Africa.
LEWIN, E. The Germans and Africa, Their Aims on the Dark Continent and How They Acquired Their African Colonies.
BARING, E. (Earl of Cromer). Modern Egypt. 2 vols.
DOYLE, SIR A. C. The War in South Africa, Its Cause and Conduct.

GRESWELL, W. P. Growth and Administration of the British Colonies, 1837–1897.
HOBSON, J. A. War in South Africa, Its Causes and Effects.
WEIGALL, A. E. P. B. A History of Events in Egypt from 1798 to 1914.
WOODWARD, W. H. A Short History of the Expansion of the British Empire, 1500–1911.
ZIMMERMAN, A. Geschichte der deutschen Kolonialpolitik.
SKRINE, F. H. The Expansion of Russia.
WRIGHT, G. F. Asiatic Russia. 2 vols.
REINSCH, P. S. Colonial Government.

GREAT BRITAIN

BRIGHT, J. F. History of England, Vols. IV and V.
GRETTON, R. H. A Modern History of the English People, 1880–1910.
INNES, A. D. A History of England and the British Empire. (Vol. IV. 1802–1914.)
LOW, S., and SANDERS, L. C. Political History of England, 1837–1901.
MCCARTHY, J. A History of Our Own Times, 1837–1901.
MARRIOTT, J. A. R. England since Waterloo.
MAXWELL, SIR H. A Century of Empire. Vol. III, 1867–1900.
OMAN, C. M. England in the Nineteenth Century.
PAUL, H. W. A History of Modern England. 5 vols.
WALPOLE, SIR S. History of Twenty-five Years, 1856–1880. 4 vols.
MONYPENNY, W. F. (and BUCKLE, G. E.). The Life of Benjamin Disraeli, Earl of Beaconsfield. 4 vols. now published.
MORLEY, (VISCOUNT) J. The Life of William Ewart Gladstone.
HAYES, C. British Social Politics.
JONES, H. Liberalism and the House of Lords.
SEYMOUR, C. Electoral Reform in England and Wales.
MORRIS, W. O'C. Ireland, 1798–1898.
SMITH, G. Irish History and the Irish Question.
O'CONNOR, T. P. Parnell Movement, with a Sketch of Irish Parties from 1843.
PLUNKETT, SIR H. Ireland in the New Century.

FRANCE

BERRY, W. G. France since Waterloo.
HANOTAUX, G. Contemporary France. 4 vols., 1870–1882. Translated by J. C. Tarver.
VIZETELLY, E. A. Republican France, 1870–1912.
JERROLD, B. The Life of Napoleon III. 4 vols.
LEPELLETIER, E. Histoire de la commune de 1871. 2 vols.

LISSAGARAY, P. O. History of the Commune of 1871. Translated by E. M. Aveling.

SIMON, J. The Government of M. Thiers from 8 February, 1871, to 24 May, 1873. 2 vols.

VIZETELLY, E. A. My Days of Adventure 1870–1871.

WASHBURNE, E. B. Franco-German War and Insurrection of the Commune.

WASHBURNE, E. B. Recollections of a Minister to France 1869–1877. 2 vols.

DEBIDOUR, A. L'Église catholique et L'État sous la troisième république, 1870–1906. 2 vols.

GALTON, A. Church and State in France, 1300–1907.

SABATIER, P. Disestablishment in France.

RUSSIA

ALEXINSKY, G. Modern Russia. Translated by B. Miall.

KORNILOV, A. Modern Russian History. 2 vols.

BARING, M. The Russian People.

DRAGE, G. Russian Affairs.

RAMBAUD, A. Histoire de la Russie depuis les origines jusqu'à nos jours. Completed to 1913 by É. Haumant.

SNODGRASS, J. H., et al. (Publ. by U. S. Gov't.) Russia, a Handbook on Commercial and Industrial Conditions.

VINOGRADOFF, P. The Russian Problem.

WALLACE, SIR D. M. Russia.

WIENER, L. An Interpretation of the Russian People.

HIMMELSTJERNA, H. G. S. VON. Russia under Alexander III and in the Preceding Period. Translated by J. Morrison.

LOWE, C. Alexander III.

POBÊDONOSTSEV, K. P. Reflections of a Russian Statesman. Translated by R. C. Long.

HARPER, S. N. The New Electoral Law for the Russian Duma.

PARES, B. Russia and Reform.

PERRIS, G. H. Russia in Revolution.

KOVALEVSKY, M. Russian Political Institutions.

KROPOTKIN, (PRINCE) P. Memoirs of a Revolutionist.

ZILLIACUS, K. The Russian Revolutionary Movement.

ITALY

GODKIN, G. S. Life of Victor Emmanuel II, First King of Italy. 2 vols.

KING, B. A History of Italian Unity, 1814–1871.

KING, B., and OKEY, T. Italy To-day.

LÉMONON, E. L'Italie économique et sociale, 1861–1912.
THAYER, W. R. Italica.
UNDERWOOD, F. M. United Italy.

GERMANY

BARKER, J. E. Modern Germany.
BÜLOW, B. VON. Imperial Germany. Translated by M. A. Lewenz.
DAWSON, W. H. The Evolution of Modern Germany.
HENDERSON, E. F. A Short History of Germany.
HOWARD, B. E. The German Empire.
HURD, A., and CASTLE, H. German Sea-Power, its Rise, Progress, and Economic Basis.
LAMPRECHT, K. Deutsche Geschichte der jüngsten Vergangenheit und Gegenwart.
LICHTENBERGER, H. Germany and Its Evolution in Modern Times. Translated by A. M. Ludovici.
MALLESON, G. B. The Refounding of the German Empire, 1848–1914.
MARRIOTT, J. A. R., and ROBERTSON, C. G. The Evolution of Prussia: the Making of an Empire.
PRIEST, G. M. Germany since 1740.
SCHEVILL, F. The Making of Modern Germany.
BLUM, H. Das deutsche Reich zur Zeit Bismarcks.
BUSCH, M. Bismarck in the Franco-German War, 1870–1871. 2 vols.
BUSCH, M. Bismarck — Some Secret Pages of His History.
BISMARCK, O. VON. Reflections and Reminiscences. Translated by A. J. Butler.
BISMARCK'S LETTERS. Translated by F. Maxse.
BISMARCK'S LETTERS TO HIS WIFE FROM THE SEAT OF WAR, 1870–1871. Translated by A. Harder.
BISMARCK'S SPEECHES AND LETTERS. Selections edited by H. Schoenfeld.
DENIS, E. La fondation de l'empire allemand.
HEADLAM, J. W. Bismarck and the Foundation of the German Empire.
HOHENLOHE-SCHILLINGSFÜRST, PRINCE VON. Memoirs of. Translated by G. W. Chrystal. 2 vols.
KALKSCHMIDT, E. Otto von Bismarck, Setzen wir Deutschland in den Sattel, Reden aus der grossen Zeit.
KOHL, H., editor. Die politischen Reden des Fürsten Bismarck.
LOWE, C. Prince Bismarck: an Historical Biography.
MARCKS, E. Kaiser Wilhelm I.
MATTER, P. Bismarck et son temps. 3 vols.
SMITH, M. Bismarck and German Unity.

SYBEL, H. VON. The Founding of the German Empire by William I. Translated by M. L. Perrin and G. Bradford. 7 vols.
FIFE, R. H. The German Empire between Two Wars: a Study of the Political and Social Development of the Nation between 1871 and 1914.
SCHIERBRAND, W. VON., Translator and editor. The Kaiser's Speeches, Forming a Character Portrait of Emperor William II.
TOWER, C. Germany of To-day.
VEBLEN, T. B. Imperial Germany and the Industrial Revolution.

AUSTRIA-HUNGARY

BERTHA, A. DE. La Hongrie moderne, 1849–1901.
DRAGE, G. Austria-Hungary.
EISEMMANN. Le compromis Austro-hongrois de 1867; étude sur le dualisme.
KNACHTBULL-HUGESSEN, C. M. The Political Evolution of the Hungarian Nation.
LEGER, L. History of Austria-Hungary. Publ. 1889.
MAHAFFY, R. P. Francis Joseph I, His Life and Times.
SETON-WATSON, R. W. (pseudonym, Scotus-Viator). Corruption and Reform in Hungary.
SETON-WATSON, R. W. (pseudonym, Scotus-Viator). Racial Problems in Hungary.
SETON-WATSON, R. W. (pseudonym, Scotus-Viator). The Southern Slav Question and the Hapsburg Monarchy.
SOSNOSKY, T. VON. Die Balkanpolitik Oesterreich-Ungarns seit 1866. 2 vols.
STEED, H. W. The Hapsburg Monarchy.

TURKEY AND THE BALKANS

BAKER, B. G. The Passing of the Turkish Empire in Europe.
JORGA, N. Geschichte des osmanischen Reiches, Vol. V.
LANE-POOLE, S. The Story of Turkey.
MILLER, W. The Ottoman Empire, 1801–1913.
PEARS, SIR E. Forty Years in Constantinople.
PINON, R. L'Europe et la jeune Turquie.
CHÉRADAME, A. Douze ans (1900–1912) de propagande en faveur des peuples balkaniques.
FORBES, N., TOYNBER, A. J., MITRANY, D., HOGARTH, D. G. The Balkans; a History of Bulgaria, Serbia, Greece, Rumania, Turkey.
MILLER, W. The Balkans: Roumania, Bulgaria, Servia, and Montenegro.
MURRAY, W. S. The Making of the Balkan States.

NEWBIGIN, M. I. Geographical Aspects of Balkan Problems in Their Relation to the Great European War.
SLOANE, W. M. The Balkans: a Laboratory of History.
FORD, C. S. The Balkan Wars.
SCHURMAN, J. G. The Balkan Wars, 1912–1913.

ANNUALS

AMERICAN YEAR BOOK. An annual, beginning in 1910.
ANNUAIRE HISTORIQUE UNIVERSEL. A French annual, 1818–1861, continued as L'année politique, 1874–1905, and as La vie politique dans les deux mondes, 1906–.
ANNUAL REGISTER. An annual synopsis of political events, beginning publication in 1758.
DAS STAATSARCHIV: Sammlung der offiziellen Aktenstücke zur Geschichte der Gegenwart. A German annual beginning 1861.
EUROPÄISCHER GESCHICHTSKALENDER. A German annual beginning with 1861.
INTERNATIONAL YEAR BOOK. An annual, 1899–1902; continued as the New International Year Book, 1907.
JAHRBUCH DER ZEIT- UND KULTURGESCHICHTE. A German annual beginning in 1908.
STATESMAN'S YEAR BOOK. Published annually beginning 1864.
WHITAKER'S ALMANAC. Published annually since 1868.

MILITARY CAMPAIGNS

I. *The Campaign in Denmark, 1864*

CROUSSE, F. Invasion du Danemark en 1864.
SYBEL, H. VON. The Founding of the German Empire.

II. *The Austro-Prussian War*

HOZIER, H. M. The Seven Weeks' War.
GLÜNECKE, G. J. R. The Campaign in Bohemia.
MALCOLM, N. Bohemia, 1866.
FAY, C. A. Étude sur la guerre d'Allemande de 1866.
OUVRY, H. A. The Prussian Campaign of 1866.
MOLTKE, H. VON. Histoire de la campagne de 1866.

III. *The Franco-German War*

MOLTKE, H. VON. The Franco-German War.
PRATT, S. C. The Franco-German War: Saarbrück to Paris.
FIEBEGER, G. J. First Epoch of the Franco-Prussian War.

IV. *The Russo-Turkish War*

Greene, F. V. Report on the Russian Army and Its Campaigns in Turkey in 1877 and 1878.
Trotha, T. von. Tactical Studies from the Battles around Plevna.
Maurice, F. The Russo-Turkish War.

V. *The Russo-Japanese War*

Ross, C. The Russo-Japanese War.
Sedgwick, F. R. The Russo-Japanese War.
Hamilton, Ian. A Staff-Officer's Scrap Book.
Rowan-Robinson, H. The Campaign of Liao-Yang.
German General Staff. Official Account of the Russo-Japanese War.
War Department, U. S. Army. Epitome of the Russo-Japanese War.

INDEX

A

B

D

E

H

I

J

N

Z

Printed in the United States of America.

THE following pages contain advertisements of books by the same author or on kindred subjects.